Andrew Jenson

Church Chronology

A Record of Important Events Pertaining to the History of the Church of Jesus Christ

of Latter-day Saints

Andrew Jenson

Church Chronology
A Record of Important Events Pertaining to the History of the Church of Jesus Christ of Latter-day Saints

ISBN/EAN: 9783337162153

Printed in Europe, USA, Canada, Australia, Japan

Cover: Foto ©Lupo / pixelio.de

More available books at **www.hansebooks.com**

Church Chronology.

A Record of Important Events

Pertaining to the History of the Church of Jesus Christ of Latter-day Saints.

COMPILED BY ANDREW JENSON,

ASSISTANT CHURCH HISTORIAN.

SECOND EDITION, REVISED AND ENLARGED.

PRINTED AT THE DESERET NEWS,
SALT LAKE CITY, UTAH.
1899.

PREFACE

TO THE FIRST EDITION.

In offering to the public this work of reference, the author has the satisfaction of knowing that he has been conscientious in its preparation. It embodies years of patient labor—a labor of love, rather than a labor with prospects of pecuniary gain—and if it shall prove acceptable and satisfactory to the people, in whose interest it has been compiled, his object will be fully attained. In regard to dates and incidents the work will be found reliable, although not perfect. As the sources of information have necessarily in some instances been confined to current literature, and foreign affairs have been frequently dealt with, there may be a few technical errors. The author will be thankful to any readers, who may discover such mistakes, if they will direct his attention to them, that they may not appear in any further editions that may be published.

ANDREW JENSON.

PREFACE

TO THE SECOND EDITION.

This edition of Church Chronology, consisting of 25,000 copies, is a thorough revision of the first edition, with many new features added, and the chronological thread brought down to the close of 1898. Before printing, the copy was carefully read to a committee appointed by Historian Franklin D. Richards, consisting of Assistant Historians John Jaques and Charles W. Penrose and Elder A. Milton Musser. Great pains have been taken to make the work accurate and in all respects reliable as a work of reference, and as such it is respectfully presented to the public at large, and particularly to those who desire correct information in regard to the Latter-day Saints and their most remarkable history.

THE PUBLISHER.

INTRODUCTORY.

The Church of Jesus Christ of Latter-day Saints was organized with six members, April 6, 1830, at a meeting held at Fayette, Seneca Co., N. Y. Since that time is has continually grown, and its members have steadily increased until the greater portion of Utah and parts of Idaho, Arizona, Nevada, Wyoming, Colorado and New Mexico are peopled with Latter-day Saints. There are also colonies of Saints in Old Mexico and Canada, besides branches and conferences in nearly every State in the Union and in Great Britain, Denmark, Sweden, Norway, Germany, Switzerland, Holland, Belgium, Turkey, New Zealand, Australia, Tasmania, Hawaii, Samoa, Society Islands, Tuamotu Islands, and other countries. The Church in her gathered condition consists at the present time of forty organized Stakes of Zion, of which twenty-five are in Utah, or mostly so, seven in Idaho, four in Arizona, one in Colorado, one in Wyoming, one in Old Mexico, and one in Canada. The Saints in Nevada and New Mexico belong to Stakes, the headquarters of which are located in Utah.

The general authorities of the Church consists of, 1, The First Presidency; 2, The Council of Twelve Apostles; 3, Presiding Patriarch; 4, The First Council of Seventies; 5, The Presiding Bishopric; 6, Church Historians.

THE FIRST PRESIDENCY.

Joseph Smith the Prophet, "who was called of God and ordained an Apostle of Jesus Christ,to be the first Elder of this Church" (Doc. and Cov., 20:2), was the first President of the Church of Jesus Christ of Latter-day Saints. For nearly three years after its organization he acted without Counselors, but close by his side and associated with him in nearly all his administrations, stood Oliver Cowdery, "who was also called of God, an Apostle of Jesus Christ, to be the second Elder of this Church,and ordained under his (Joseph's)|hand." (Doc. and Cov.,20:3.)

March, 18, 1833, agreeable to a revelation given March 8, 1833, the Prophet Joseph ordained Sidney Rigdon to be his first and Frederick G. Williams to be his second Counselor. Prior to this, at a conference held at Amherst, Lorain Co., Ohio, Jan. 25, 1832, Joseph the Prophet had been acknowledged as President of the High Priesthood. A similar action was taken at a general council, held April 26, 1832, at Independence, Jackson Co., Mo.

At an important conference held at Far West, Caldwell Co., Mo., Nov. 7, 1837, Frederick G. Williams was rejected as a Counselor to Pres. Smith, charges having previously been made against him at a conference held at Kirtland, Ohio, Sept. 3, 1837. On the same occasion Hyrum Smith was appointed his successor by unanimous vote. Hyrum Smith filled his position with honor and ability, until some time after the demise of his father, Joseph Smith, sen., who died at Nauvoo, Ill., Sept. 14, 1840.

DIAGRAM OF THE FIRST PRESIDENCY

OF THE CHURCH OF JESUS CHRIST OF LATTER-DAY SAINTS.

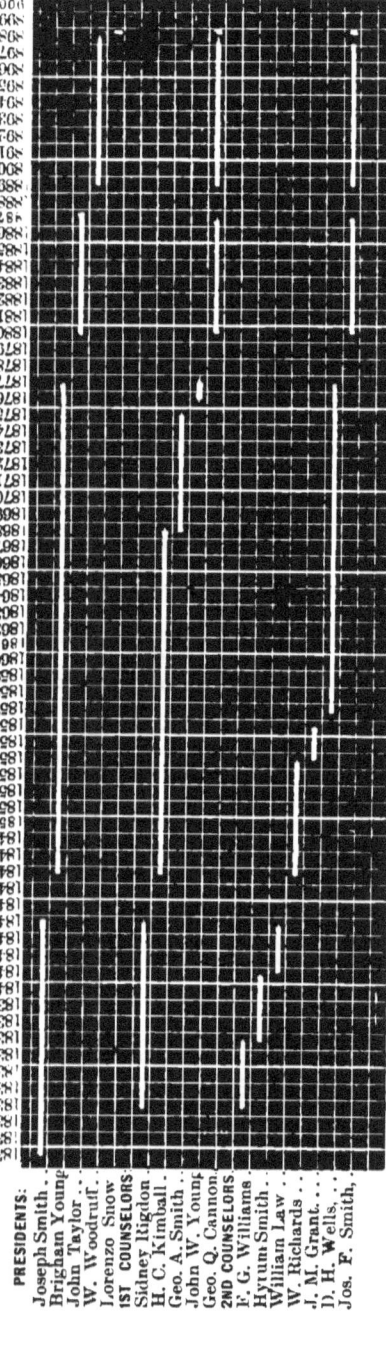

PRESIDENTS:
Joseph Smith..
Brigham Young
John Taylor...
W. Woodruff..
Lorenzo Snow
1ST COUNSELORS
Sidney Rigdon
H. C. Kimball.
Geo. A. Smith.
John W. Young
Geo. Q. Cannon
2ND COUNSELORS
F. G. Williams
Hyrum Smith
William Law .
W. Richards ..
J. M. Grant....
D. H. Wells..
Jos. F. Smith,

In a revelation given through Joseph the Prophet at Nauvoo, Jan. 19, 1841, Hyrum Smith was called to take the office of Patriarch to the Church, as his father's successor. In the same revelation William Law was called to succeed Hyrum Smith as second Counselor to Pres. Joseph Smith. William Law occupied this position until April 18, 1844, when he, together with others, who like himself had apostatized, were excommunicated from the Church..

Joseph the Prophet was martyred at Carthage, Ill., June 27, 1844, when the responsibility of presiding over the Church fell upon the Twelve Apostles. They constituted the presiding Council of the Church till Dec. 5, 1847, when an important council meeting was held at the house of Apostle Orson Hyde. On this occasion Brigham Young was unanimously elected President of the Church, with authority to choose his Counselors, which he did by naming Heber C. Kimball for his first and Willard Richards for his second Counselor. The following Apostles attended this council meeting: Brigham Young, Heber C. Kimball, Orson Hyde, Willard Richards, Wilford Woodruff, Geo. A. Smith, Amasa M. Lyman and Ezra T. Benson. These transactions on the part of the Twelve were ratified by the Church at a conference held in the Log Tabernacle, at Council Bluffs, Iowa, Dec. 27, 1847, and at the general conference held in G. S. L. Valley, Oct. 8, 1848.

Counselor Willard Richards died of dropsy in G. S. L. City, March 11, 1854. At the general conference, held April 6, 1854, Jedediah M. Grant was called to fill the vacancy thus created.

Counselor Jedediah M. Grant died Dec. 1, 1856, and Daniel H. Wells succeeded him as second Counselor to Pres. Brigham Young, being ordained and set apart to that position, Jan. 4, 1857. Daniel H. Wells acted in that capacity till the death of Pres. Young.

Counselor Heber C. Kimball died June 22, 1868, in Salt Lake City. The vacancy occasioned thereby was filled by the appointment of George A. Smith to the position of first Counselor in the First Presidency. He served in that capacity until his death, which occurred in Salt Lake City, Sept. 1, 1875. John W. Young succeeded him as first Counselor, being sustained as such by the general conference held Oct. 8, 1876.

Pres. Brigham Young died in Salt Lake City, Aug. 29, 1877, after which the Twelve Apostles again presided over the Church, continuing to do so for three years, or until the general conference held in Salt Lake City in October, 1880, when the First Presidency was organized, for the third time, by the appointment of John Taylor as President, with Geo. Q. Cannon as his first and Joseph F. Smith as his second Counselor.

Pres. John Taylor died at Kaysville, Davis Co., Utah, July 25, 1887, after which the Twelve Apostles presided over the Church till the general conference, held in Salt Lake City, in April 1889, on which occasion a First Presidency was again organized, consisting of Wilford Woodruff, President; Geo. Q. Cannon, first Counselor; and Joseph F. Smith, second Counselor.

Pres. Wilford Woodruff died in San Francisco, Cal., Sept. 2, 1898. At an important council meeting of the Apostles, held in Salt Lake City, Sept. 13, 1898, the First Presidency was once more organized, as follows: Lorenzo Snow, President; Geo. Q. Cannon, first Counselor; Joseph F. Smith, second Counselor.

By the foregoing it will be seen that five Apostles, namely, Joseph Smith, Brigham Young, John Taylor, Wilford Woodruff and Lorenzo

Snow, have filled the exalted position of President of the Church; five (Sidney Rigdon, Heber C. Kimball, Geo. A. Smith, John W. Young and Geo. Q. Cannon) have acted as first Counselors; and seven (Frederick G. Williams, Hyrum Smith, William Law, Willard Richards, Jedediah M. Grant, Daniel H. Wells and Joseph F. Smith) as second Counselors in the First Presidency, since the first organization of the Council in 1833.

COUNCIL OF TWELVE APOSTLES.

In a revelation, given through Joseph the Prophet, in June 1829, at Fayette, Seneca Co., N. Y., the Lord made known that Twelve Apostles should be called in this dispensation. (Doc and Cov., Sec. 18.) Nearly six years later, on Feb. 14, 1835, at a special meeting, held at Kirtland, Ohio, Joseph the Prophet, in accordance with that revelation, blessed Oliver Cowdery, David Whitmer and Martin Harris, the Three Witnesses to the Book of Mormon, to select twelve men who should constitute the Council of Twelve Apostles. They were chosen by the Three Witnesses in the following order:- Lyman E. Johnson, Brigham Young, Heber C. Kinball, Orson Hyde, David W. Patten, Luke S. Johnson, Wm. E. McLellin, John F. Boynton, Orson Pratt, William Smith, Thos. B. Marsh and Parley P. Pratt./ Most of these brethren the previous year (1834) had proved their faithfulness and integrity to the Church as members of Zion's Camp, which journeyed from Kirtland, Ohio, to Missouri and back, subject to much suffering and many privations. They were ordained to the Apostleship by Joseph Smith, Oliver Cowdery, David Whitmer and Martin Harris as follows: Lyman E. Johnson, Brigham Young and Heber C. Kimball on Feb. 14, 1835; Orson Hyde, David W. Patten, Luke S. Johnson, Wm. E. McLellin, John F. Boynton and William Smith on the following day, Feb. 15th; Parley P. Pratt on Feb. 21st; and Thomas B. Marsh and Orson Pratt, who had been absent on missions, in April, 1835. At a grand council, held at Kirtland, Ohio, May 2, 1835, at which the First Presidency was in attendance, the Twelve were arranged according to their age, after which they stood as follows, commencing with the eldest: Thomas B. Marsh, David W. Patten, Brigham Young, Heber C. Kimball, Orson Hyde, William E. McLellin Parley P. Pratt, Luke S. Johnson, William Smith, Orson Pratt, John F. Boynton and Lyman E. Johnson.

In 1837 and 1838 four of the Twelve apostatized, namely, John F. Boynton, disfellowshipped Sept. 3, 1837, at Kirtland, Ohio; Lyman E. Johnson and Luke S. Johnson, excommunicated April 13, 1838, at Far West, Missouri; and Wm. E. McLellin, excommunicated May 11, 1838, at Far West.

July 8, 1838, John Taylor, John E. Page, Wilford Woodruff and Willard Richards were called by revelation to fill the places of those who had fallen. Elders Page and Taylor were ordained Dec. 19, 1838; Wilford Woodruff April 26, 1839, at Far West, Missouri; and Willard Richards April 14, 1840, at Preston, England.

In the meantime other vacancies occurred. David W. Patten was killed in the Crooked River battle, in Missouri, Oct. 25, 1838, and Thos. B. Marsh was excommunicated for apostasy, March 17, 1839, at Quincy, Ill. To fill the two vacancies occasioned thereby, George A. Smith (ordained April 26, 1839, at Far West, Mo.) and Lyman Wight (ordained April 8, 1841, at Nauvoo, Ill.), were chosen.

William Smith was rejected as an Apostle, at the general conference held at Nauvoo, in October, 1845, and finally excommunicated from the Church, Oct. 12, 1846. John E. Page was disfellowshipped, Jan. 9, 1846, at a council meeting held at Nauvoo, Ill. Amasa M. Lyman, who had been ordained an Apostle, Aug. 20, 1842, at Nauvoo, and Ezra T. Benson, ordained July 16, 1846, at Council Bluffs, Iowa, were chosen to fill the vacancies.

The reorganization of the First Presidency in December, 1847, with three of the Apostles (Brigham Young, Heber C. Kimball and Willard Richards), and the excommunication of Lyman Wright for apostacy, Feb. 12, 1849, made four vacancies in the Council of the Twelve. These were filled Feb. 12, 1849, at an important council meeting held in the "Old Fort," G. S. L. City, when Elders Charles C. Rich, Lorenzo Snow, Erastus Snow and Franklin D. Richards were ordained Apostles.

The next vacancy occurred May 13, 1857, when Parley P. Pratt was assassinated near Van Buren, Arkansas. George Q. Cannon was chosen to fill the vacancy, being ordained an Apostle Aug. 20 1860, in G. S. L. City, Utah.

In October, 1867, Amasa M. Lyman was dropped from the Council of the Twelve; and Joseph F. Smith, who had previously been ordained to the Apostleship, was chosen to fill the vacancy, Oct 6, 1867, at a general conference.

Geo. A. Smith was chosen as first Counselor to Pres. Brigham Young, after the demise of Heber C. Kimball in 1868. Elder Brigham Young, jun., who previously had been ordained an Apostle, was chosen to fill the vacancy, being sustained as a member of the Council of the Twelve at the general conference held Oct. 9, 1868.

Elder Ezra T. Benson died Sept. 3, 1869, at Ogden, Utah. Albert Carrington was chosen to fill the vacancy, and was ordained an Apostle, July 3, 1870, in Salt Lake City.

Orson Hyde, who had acted as president of the Twelve Apostles, from the reorganization of the First Presidency in 1847, to October, 1875, died Nov. 28, 1878, at Spring City, Sanpete Co., Utah. At the annual conference, held April 7, 1879, Elder Moses Thatcher was chosen to fill the vacancy.

After the death of Pres. Brigham Young, in 1877, the Twelve Apostles presided over the Church nearly three years. Daniel H. Wells and John W. Young, who had acted as Pres. Brigham Young's Counselors, were sustained by the Church as Counselors to the Twelve.

Another reorganization of the First Presidency took place, Oct. 10, 1880, at the general conference held in Salt Lake City, three of the Apostles (John Taylor, Geo. Q. Cannon and Joseph F. Smith) being chosen to constitute said Presidency. This caused three vacancies in the Council of the Twelve, two of which were filled Oct. 27, 1880, by the ordination of Francis M. Lyman and John Henry Smith to the Apostleship.

Orson Pratt, the last surviving member of the first Council of Twelve Apostles, died in Salt Lake City, Utah, Oct. 3, 1881. The vacancy occasioned by his demise, and the vacancy left since October, 1880, was filled by the calling of George Teasdale and Heber J. Grant to the Apostleship. These brethren were called by direct revelation, through Pres. John Taylor, and were ordained in Salt Lake City, Oct. 16, 1882.

Charles C. Rich died at Paris, Bear Lake Co., Idaho, Nov. 17,

DIAGRAM OF THE COUNCIL OF TWELVE APOSTLES.

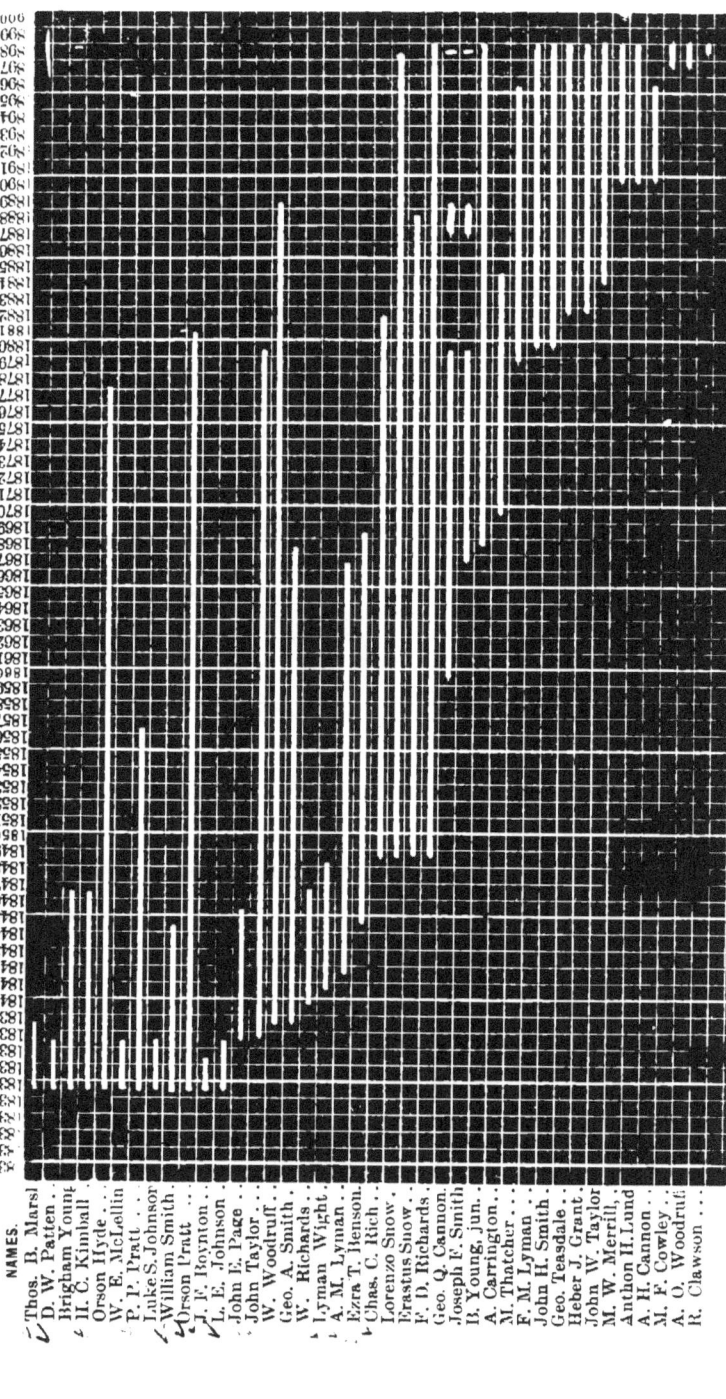

NAMES.

Thos. B. Marsh
D. W. Patten
Brigham Young
H. C. Kimball
Orson Hyde
W. E. McLellin
P. P. Pratt
Luke S. Johnson
William Smith
Orson Pratt
J. F. Boynton
L. E. Johnson
John E. Page
John Taylor
W. Woodruff
Geo. A. Smith
W. Richards
Lyman Wight
A. M. Lyman
Ezra T. Benson
Chas. C. Rich
Lorenzo Snow
Erastus Snow
F. D. Richards
Geo. Q. Cannon
Joseph F. Smith
B. Young, jun.
A. Carrington
M. Thatcher
F. M. Lyman
John H. Smith
Geo. Teasdale
Heber J. Grant
John W. Taylor
M. W. Merrill
Anthon H. Lund
A. H. Cannon
M. F. Cowley
A. O. Woodruff
R. Clawson

1883, and the vacancy caused thereby, in the Council, was filled by the ordination of John W. Taylor to the Apostleship, Oct 16, 1883.

After the death of Pres. John Taylor, July 25, 1887, the Twelve Apostles acted as presiding Council of the Church for about one year and nine months, during which time Geo. Q. Cannon and Joseph F. Smith occupied their former positions as members of the Council of Twelve Apostles.

At the general conference, held in April, 1889, the First Presidency was reorganized, with Wilford Woodruff as President. The vacancy in the Council of the Apostles caused thereby, as well as that occasioned by the excommunication of Albert Carrington, in November, 1885, and a third vacancy caused by the demise of Erastus Snow, May 27, 1888, were filled at the general conference, held in October, 1889, by the calling of Marriner W. Merrill, Anthon H. Lund and Abraham H. Cannon to the Apostleship.

Abraham H. Cannon died in Salt Lake City, July 19, 1896, and Moses Thatcher was dropped from his position as one of the Twelve Apostles, Nov. 19, 1896. The two vacancies thus occasioned were filled at the general conference held in Salt Lake City, in October, 1897, when Matthias F. Cowley and Abraham Owen Woodruff were sustained as members of the Council of Twelve Apostles.

After the death of Pres. Wilford Woodruff, Sept. 2, 1898, the Twelve Apostles once more became the presiding Council of the Church, and Geo. Q. Cannon and Joseph F. Smith were returned to their former positions among the Twelve Apostles. But the Apostles only retained the presidency a few days. Sept. 13, 1898, the First Pesidency was organized the fifth time since the organization of the Church, Lorenzo Snow, Geo. Q. Cannon and Joseph F. Smith being the three Apostles chosen to form the new Presidency. This caused a vacancy in the Council of the Apostles, which was filled at the general conference, held in Salt Lake City, Oct. 9, 1898, when Rudger Clawson was sustained as one of the Twelve Apostles.

The Council of Twelve Apostles now stands as follows: Franklin D. Richards, president, Brigham Young, Francis M. Lyman, John Henry Smith, Geo. Teasdale, Heber J. Grant, John W. Taylor, Marriner W. Merrill, Anthon H. Lund, Matthias F. Cowley, Abraham Owen Woodruff and Rudger Clawson.

PRESIDING PATRIARCHS:

Joseph Smith, sen., father of the Prophet Joseph Smith, was the first Patriarch in the Church. He was ordained to that high and holy calling, Dec. 18, 1833, at Kirtland, Ohio, under the hands of the Prophet Joseph. Oliver Cowdery, Sidney Rigdon and Frederick G. Williams. Father Smith continued as Patriarch until his death, which occurred at Nauvoo, Ill., Sept. 14, 1840. In an important revelation, given through the Prophet Joseph, Jan. 19, 1841, Hyrum Smith, Father Smith's eldest living son, who then acted as second Counselor in the First Presidency, was called to succeed his father as Patriarch. He "received" the office, Jan. 24, 1841, and kept it until his martyrdom in Carthage Jail, Ill., June 27, 1844. His brother William Smith, who was also a member of the Council of Twelve Apostles, succeeded him by virtue of his birthright, or age, but he apostatized. At the general conference, held in October 1845, he was rejected as an Apostle and as a Patriarch. He was finally excommunicated from the Church, Oct. 12, 1845.

After the rejection of William Smith, the Patriarchal office, according to the hereditary order belonged to Asahel Smith (a brother of Joseph Smith, sen.), who had been ordained a Patriarch at Nauvoo in 1844; but his health being poor, he is not known to have magnified his office as a Patriarch. Soon afterwards (July 20, 1848) he died at Iowaville, Wapello Co., Iowa.

John Smith, another brother of the late Joseph Smith, sen., who had previously been ordained a Patriarch at Nauvoo, was ordained presiding Patriarch in the Church, Jan. 1, 1849, at G. S. L. City, under the hands of Brigham Young and Heber C. Kimball. He had been sustained as a "Patriarch in the Church" as early as the general conference, held at Winter. Quarters, April 6, 1847.

Uncle John Smith, as he was familiarly called, died May 23, 1854, in G. S. L City. John Smith, eldest son of the martyred Hyrum Smith, to whom the Patriarchal Priesthood descended direct from his father, was chosen as his successor. At the time of his father's death he was too young to receive the office. He was ordained presiding Patriarch, Feb. 18, 1855, in G.S.L.City, by Pres. Brigham Young, and is the present incumbent of the office of Presiding Patriarch.

FIRST COUNCIL OF SEVENTIES.

The organization of the first quorum of Seventy was commenced at Kirtland, Ohio, Feb. 28, 1835. Nearly all the first members consisted of men who had distinguished themselves for their faithfulness as members of Zion's Camp. When the quorum was fully organized the following were chosen to act as its seven presidents; Hazen Aldrich, Joseph Young, Levi W. Hancock, Leonard Rich, Zebedee Coltrin, Lyman Sherman and Sylvester Smith.

Questions arose among some of the brethren in regard to the corresponding grades of the Seventies and High Priests, and it was ascertained that five or six of the seven presidents had previously been ordained High Priests. The Prophet Joseph Smith, in a meeting held in the Kirtland Temple, April 6, 1837, counseled these brethren, namely, Hazen Aldrich, Leonard Rich, Zebedee Coltrin, Lyman Sherman and Sylvester Smith, to join the High Priests' quorum, which five of them did, and the following named Elders were chosen to fill the vacancies thus created in the First Council of the Seventies: John Gould, in place of Hazen Aldrich; James Foster, in place of Leonard Rich; Daniel S. Miles, in place of Zebedee Coltrin; Josiah Butterfield, in place of Lyman Sherman; Salmon Gee, in place of Levi W. Hancock, and John Gaylord, in place of Sylvester Smith.

In the summer of 1837 it was ascertained that Levi W. Hancock, who was in Missouri at the time of the April meeting, was not a High Priest, and he was therefore received back into his former position as one of the First Seven Presidents of Seventies, at an important meeting held at Kirtland, Ohio, Sept 3, 1837. John Gould, one of the newly appointed presidents, was asked by the Prophet Joseph to join the High Priests, which he did. After these changes the First Council of Seventies stood as follows: Joseph Young, Levi W. Hancock, James Foster, Daniel S. Miles, Josiah Butterfield, Salmon Gee, and John Gaylord.

Jan. 13, 1838, John Gaylord, together with many others, was excommunicated from the Church by the High Council at Kirtland, Ohio, for rising up in rebellion against the Church authorities. Elder Henry Harriman was called and ordained Feb. 6, 1838, to fill the vacancy in the First Council of Seventies.

In a meeting of the Seventies, held at Kirtland, Ohio, March 6, 1838, the council withdrew their fellowship from Salmon Gee for neglect of duty and other causes. Elder Zera Pulsipher was chosen and ordained to fill the vacancy the same day. The foregoing information about the Seventies is obtained from the original record of Seventies kept at Kirtland, Ohio.

After these two changes the council stood unchanged until the Church had removed to Nauvoo, Ill. It appears that James Foster, instead of gathering with the Saints, settled at Jacksonville, Morgan Co., Ill., and had no direct communication with his brethren. Prior to the October conference, 1844, he was dropped from his position by the council of the Seventies. In the following spring (1845), Albert P. Rockwood was called to fill the vacancy caused by the removal of Foster.

Josiah Butterfield retained his standing as one of the seven Presidents until a misunderstanding arose between the Prophet Joseph and him, and he was finally cut off from the Church, Oct. 7, 1844, at the general conference held at Nauvoo, for neglect of duty, etc. The vacancy was filled the same day by the appointment of Jedediah M. Grant as one of the council of the Seventies, but he was not ordained until some time afterwards.

Elder Daniel S. Miles died a faithful man in the early part of 1845, in Hancock County, Ill., and the vacancy occasioned by his death was filled by Elder Benjamin L. Clapp, in April, 1845. Elder Albert P. Rockwood, Benjamin L. Clapp and Jedediah M. Grant were ordained to the positions to which they had been elected Dec. 2, 1845.

After the demise of Willard Richards in 1854, Elder Jedediah M. Grant was selected by President Brigham Young to fill the office of second Counselor in the First Presidency, thus leaving another vacancy in the council of Seventies. Elder Horace S. Eldrege was called, at the October conference, 1854, to fill that vacancy, and was ordained about the same time in G. S. L. City.

Elder Benjamin L. Clapp, after living some years in G. S. L. City, removed his family to Ephraim, Sanpete Co., where he had some difficulty with Bishop Warren S. Snow. After investigation before the Council of Seventies, he was dropped from his position in the council, and finally excommunicated from the Church, at the general conference, held in G. S. L. City, April 7, 1859. Elder Jacob Gates was called to fill the vacancy, at the April Conference, 1860, but, being absent on a mission to Europe, he was not ordained until October, 1862, some time after his return home.

Elder Zera Pulsipher transcended the bounds of the Priesthood in the ordinance of sealing, for which he was cited to appear before the First Presidency of the Church, April 12, 1862. It was there voted, that he be rebaptized, reconfirmed and ordained to the office of a High Priest, or go into the ranks of the Seventies. Subsequently he was ordained a Patriarch. Elder John Van Cott was called to fill the vacancy in the council of the Seventies, at the October conference, 1862.

Albert P. Rockwood died in Sugar House Ward, Salt Lake Co., Nov. 26, 1879, and at the April conference, 1880. Elder Wm. W. Tay-

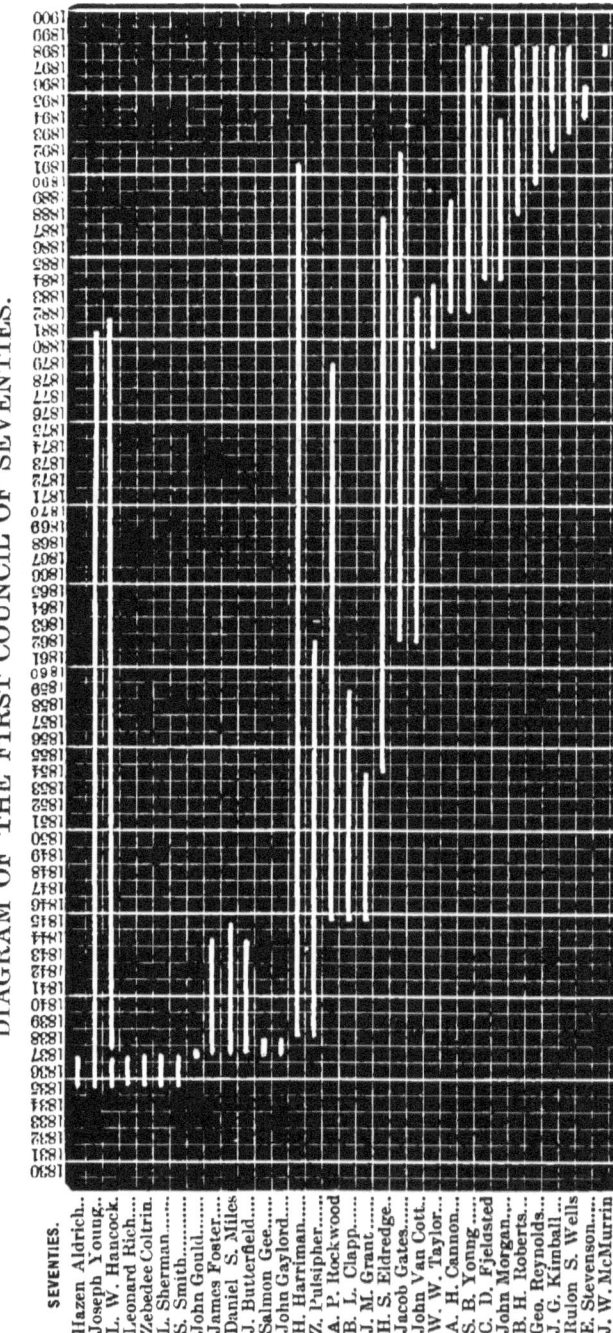

DIAGRAM OF THE FIRST COUNCIL OF SEVENTIES.

or was called to fill the vacancy and soon afterwards ordained one of the First Seven Presidents of Seventies.

The vacancies caused by the death of Pres. Joseph Young, July 16, 1881, and of Levi W. Hancok, June 10, 1882, were filled by the ordination of Abraham H. Cannon as one of the First Seven Presidents, Oct. 9, 1882, and Seymour B. Young as another, Oct. 16, 1882.

Elder John Van Cott died Feb. 18, 1883. Christian Daniel Fjeldsted was called to fill the vacancy. He was ordained, April 28, 1884, after his return from a mission to Scandinavia.

The demise of Elder Wm. W. Taylor, Aug. 1, 1884, caused another vacancy, which was filled Oct. 7, 1884, by the ordination of John Morgan as one of the First Seven Presidents.

Horace S. Eldredge died in Salt Lake City, Sept. 6, 1888, and the vacancy caused thereby was filled by the calling of Brigham H. Roberts to act as one of the council, at the October conference, 1888.

Abraham H. Cannon having been ordained an Apostle in October, 1889, George Reynolds was sustained as one of the First Seven Presidents of Seventies, at the April conference, 1890.

Elder Henry Herriman died at Huntington, Emery Co., Utah, May 17, 1891. Elder Jacob Gates died at Provo, Utah Co., April 14, 1892. The vacancies caused by the demise of those two veteran presidents were filled by the selection of Jonathan G. Kimball and Rulon S. Wells as members of the First Council of Seventies. The former was sustained at the general conference, held in October, 1892, and the latter at the general conference, held in April, 1893.

Elder John Morgan died at Preston, Idaho, Aug. 14, 1894. At the following October conference, Edward Stevenson was chosen to fill the consequent vacancy in the council.

Elder Edward Stevenson died in Salt Lake City, Jan. 27, 1897; and at the general conference of the Church, held in Salt Lake City, in October, 1897, Joseph W. McMurrin was chosen to fill the vacancy. He was ordained by Apostle Anthon H. Lund in Liverpool, England, Jan. 21, 1898.

The council now stands as follows: Seymour B. Young, Christian D. Fjeldsted, Brigham H. Roberts, George Reynolds, Jonathan G. Kimball, Rulon S. Wells and Joseph W. McMurrin.

PRESIDING BISHOPRIC.

Edward Partridge, the first Bishop of the Church, was called to that position Feb. 4, 1831, by revelation. (Doc. and Cov., Sec. 41.) Later, when other Bishops were ordained, he became known as the first or presiding Bishop. June 6, 1831, at solemn meeting, held at Kirtland, Ohio, Isaac Morley and John Corrill were ordained and set apart as counselors to Bishop Partridge.

In a letter written by the First Presidency at Kirtland, Ohio, to Wm. W. Phelps and others, in Missouri, under date of June 25, 1833, the following occurs: "Let Brother Isaac Morley be ordained second Bishop in Zion, and let brother John Corrill be ordained third. Let Brother Edward Partridge choose, as counselors in their place, Brother Parley P. Pratt and Brother Titus Billings, ordaining Brother Billings to the High Priesthood."

Owing to the persecutions which befell the Saints in Missouri, these

DIAGRAM OF THE PRESIDING BISHOPRIC.

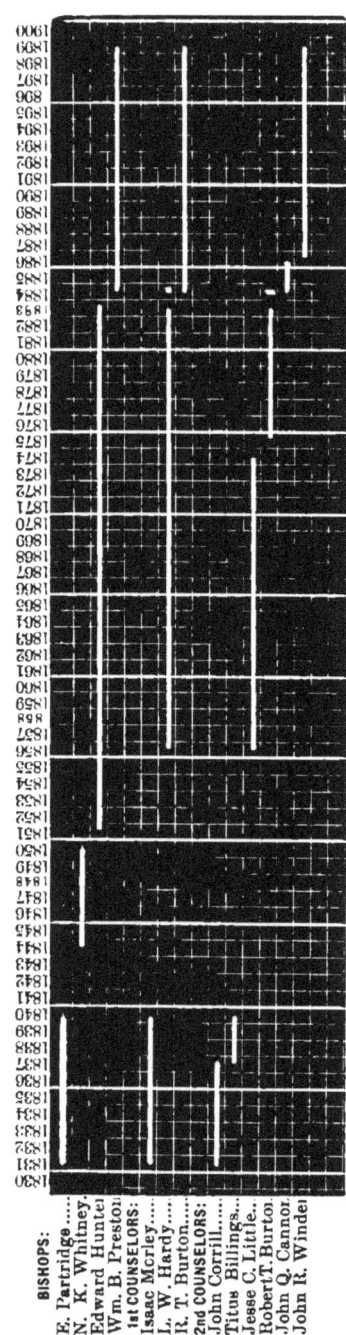

BISHOPS:
E. Partridge.....
N. K. Whitney.
Edward Hunter
Wm. B. Preston
1st COUNSELORS:
Isaac Mcrley.....
L. W. Hardy.....
R. T. Burton.....
2nd COUNSELORS:
John Corrill.....
Titus Billings....
Jesse C. Little...
Robert T. Burton.
John Q. Cannon.
John R. Winder

appointments were not made; but at a meeting, held at Far West, Mo., Aug. 1, 1837, Titus Billings was elected Bishop's counselor, in place of John Correll; and at a conference held at the same place, Nov. 7, 1837, Edward Partridge "was nominated to still act as Bishop;" after which he nominated Isaac Morley and Titus Billings for his counselors, and they "were unanimously chosen."

These three constituted the head Bishopric of the Church during the life time of Bishop Partridge.

Bishop Edward Partridge filled his responsible position faithfully, in the midst of the most severe persecutions, until his death, which occurred at Nauvoo, Ill., May 27, 1840.

In a revelation given through Joseph the Prophet, Jan. 19, 1841, George Miller was called to the position of Bishop, in place of Edward Partridge, deceased. (Doc. and Cov., 124. 21.) In the same revelation, Sec. 141, the Lord says: "I give unto you, Vinson Knight, Samuel H. Smith and Shadrach Roundy, if he will receive it, to preside over the Bishopric."

From the documents at our command at present, we are unable to learn whether or not the above named brethren officiated in the callings whereunto they were called; but at the general conference, held in October, 1844, at Nauvoo, Ill., Newel K. Whitney (who had been called by revelation to act as Bishop at Kirtland, Ohio, Dec. 4, 1831) was sustained as "first Bishop," and George Miller as "second Bishop" in the Church. From that time till his death Newel K. Whitney was recognized, and after April, 1847, sustained by the voice of the general conference, as presiding Bishop of the Church. He had no regularly appointed Counselors; but recognized Brigham Young and Heber C. Kimball as his chief counselors and advisers.

Bishop Newel K. Whitney died in G. S. L. City, Sept. 23, 1850. At the general conference of the Church, held in April, 1851, Edward Hunter, who had been ordained a Bishop in Nauvoo in 1844, was sustained as presiding Bishop. It appears, however, that he was not ordained and set apart to that position till a year later. Like his predecessor, he received immediate advice from Presidents Brigham Young and Heber C. Kimball, and chose no other counselors until October, 1856, when, at the general conference, held in G. S. L. City, Leonard W. Hardy was sustained as first and Jesse C. Little as second counselor to Bishop Edward Hunter.

Counselor Jesse C. Little resigned his position as counselor. At the general conference held in Salt Lake City, in October, 1874, Robert T. Burton was sustained as second counselor to Bishop Hunter. He was ordained and set apart to this position, Sept. 2, 1875, after his return from a mission to England.

Bishop Edward Hunter died in Salt Lake City, Oct 16, 1883. At the general conference, held in April 1884, Wm. B. Preston, who had previously presided over the Cache Stake of Zion, was sustained as presiding Bishop, with Leonard W. Hardy as his first and Robert T. Burton as his second counselor.

Counselor Leonard W. Hardy died in Salt Lake City, July 31, 1884. At the general conference, held in October, 1884, Robert T. Burton was sustained as first and John Q. Cannon as second counselor to Bishop Wm. B. Preston.

Counselor John Q. Cannon, because of transgression was released

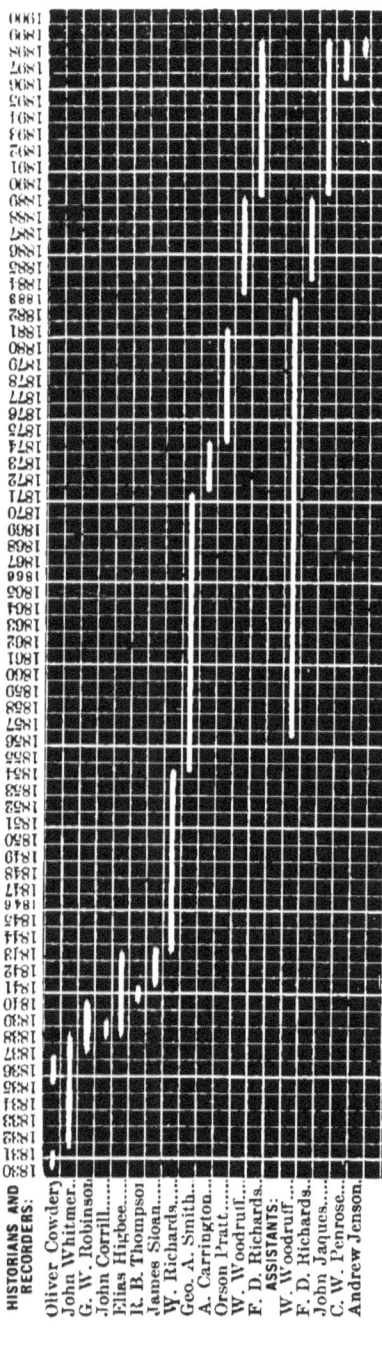

DIAGRAM OF CHURCH HISTORIANS AND ASSISTANTS.

from his position. At the general conference, held at Provo, Utah, Co., in April, 1886, John R. Winder was sustained as second counselor in the Presiding Bishopric.

Thus Wm. B. Preston, Robert T. Burton and John R. Winder constitute at the present time the presiding Bishopric of the Church.

CHURCH HISTORIANS AND RECORDERS.

The office of Church Recorder was provided for by direct revelation, given April 6, 1830, immediately after the organization of the Church. In that revelation the Lord says, "Behold, there shall be a record kept among you," etc. (Doc. and Cov., 21:1.) Oliver Cowdery, who had acted as a scribe for the Prophet Joseph, while translating the Book of Mormon, received the appointment as the first Church Recorder.

March 8, 1831, John Whitmer, one of the Eight Witnesses to the Book of Mormon, was called by revelation to the position of Church Historian. "Behold, it is expedient in me", said the Lord, "that my servant John (Whitmer) should write and keep a regular history," and "it shall be appointed unto him to keep the Church record and history continually, for Oliver Cowdery I have appointed to another office." (Doc. and Cov., Sec. 47.) John Whitmer removed to Missouri in the winter of 1831-32, and he was consequently unable to attend to his duties as Historian and Recorder at the headquarters of the Church, which were still at Kirtland. Hence, at a meeting of the Presidency of the Church and the High Council, held at Kirtland, Ohio, Sept. 14, 1835, Oliver Cowdery was again appointed "Recorder for the Church."

At a conference of the authorities of the Church and of the Saints, held in the Kirtland Temple, Sept. 17, 1837, Geo. W. Robinson was elected General Church Recorder, in place of Oliver Cowdery, who had removed to Missouri.

At a general conference, held at Far West, Mo., April 6, 1838, John Corrill and Elias Higbee were appointed Church Historians, "to write and keep the Church history;" and Geo. W. Robinson was sustained as General Church Recorder and clerk to the First Presidency.

John Corrill apostatized during the Missouri persecutions, and was excommunicated from the Church, at a conference, held at Quincy, Ill., March 17, 1839.

Elias Higbee was selected to accompany the Prophet Joseph to Washington, D.C., as a delegate from the Church to the Federal Government, and later was chosen as a member of the committee appointed to superintend the building of the Nauvoo Temple. Owing to these additional responsibilities, he was unable to devote much of his time to the writing of Church history. He finally died, at Nauvoo, June 8, 1843.

At the general conference of the Church, held at Nauvoo, Ill., Oct. 3, 1840, Robert B. Thompson was appointed General Church Clerk, in place of George W. Robinson, who intended to remove to Iowa.

Elder Thompson entered upon the duties of his office faithfully, but took suddenly sick and died, at Nauvoo, Aug. 27, 1841.

Oct. 2, 1841, at a general conference, held in the Grove, at Nauvoo, Ill., James Sloan was elected General Church Clerk, in place of Robert B. Thompson, deceased.

At a special meeting, held at Nauvoo, July 30, 1843, Elder Willard Richards was appointed General Church Recorder, succeeding James Sloan, who had left Nauvoo on a mission to Ireland.

• Elder Richards returned from his mission to England in August, 1841. Dec. 13, 1841, he was appointed by Joseph Smith to act as Recorder for the Temple, and also as private secretary and general clerk to the Prophet. He entered immediately upon the duties of his office, and continued the labors connected therewith till June 28, 1842, when he committed the business of the office to Wm. Clayton, and left Nauvoo, July 1, 1842, on a visit to the New England States. From this visit he returned Oct. 20, 1842. Dec. 21, 1842, the Prophet Joseph again appointed him private secretary and historian, while Wm. Clayton was retained as Temple Recorder and clerk of the Prophet's temporal business.

At the general conference of the Church, held at Nauvoo, in October, 1845, President Brigham Young remarked that "about three years ago, Elder Willard Richards was appointed by Pres. Joseph Smith as historian for the Church and General Church Recorder." The Saints had previously acted on his appointment as recorder, but not as historian. He therefore moved that the Church receive the appointment of Brother Joseph, and that we continue and sustain Elder Richards as Historian for the Church and General Church Recorder." The motion was carried unanimously. Since that time the double office of Church Historian and General Church Recorder has been vested in the same person.

Willard Richards filled the office faithfully until his death, which occurred in G. S. L. City, March 11, 1854. At the general conference, held in G. S. L. City, in April, 1854, Geo. A. Smith was chosen and sustained as Church Historian and General Church Recorder.

As the Church grew and increased in numerical strength and importance, the labors of the Church Historian increased proportionately, and it became necessary to appoint assistants to the Church Historian. Accordingly, Apostle Wilford Woodruff was sustained as assistant Church Historian, at the general conference, held in Salt Lake City, in October, 1856. Elder Woodruff was the first Elder sustained in that capacity by a general conference of the Church.

Apostle Geo. A. Smith, having been chosen as First Counselor to Pres. Brigham Young, was released from his position as Church Historian. At the general conference, held in April, 1871, Apostle Albert Carrington was sustained in that position, with Wilford Woodruff as his assistant.

Apostle Orson Pratt succeeded Albert Carrington as Church Historian and General Church Recorder, being sustained as such at the general conference, held in Salt Lake City, May 9, 1874. With Wilford Woodruff as his assistant, he filled the position till his death, which occurred in Salt Lake City, Oct. 3, 1881.

At the semi-annual conference, held in October, 1883, Apostle Wilford Woodruff was sustained as Church Historian and General Church Recorder, and at the next general conference, held in April, 1884, Franklin D. Richards was sustained as Assistant Church Historian.

At the general conference, April 7, 1889, Wilford Woodruff was chosen and sustained as President of the Church, and Franklin D. Richards was appointed his successor as Church Historian and General Church Recorder. At the next general conference, held in October, 1889, Elder John Jaques was sustained as assistant Church Historian. Elder Charles W. Penrose was sustained in a similar capacity at the general conference, held in April, 1896; and Elder Andrew Jenson at the general conference, held in April, 1898.

THE HOLY PRIESTHOOD.

The Church, which was established on the earth by Jesus Christ and his Apostles anciently, ceased in course of time to exist, through the martyrdom of many of its chief representatives and the final "falling away" of the remnant of its members, as predicted by the Apostles Paul (2 Thess. 2·3), and Peter (2 Pet. 2:1), and others.

In the present century the gospel of Christ, with its ancient powers and Priesthood, has been restored to earth anew, through the administration of heavenly messengers. Early in the spring of 1820, God the Father and his Son Jesus Christ appeared to Joseph Smith and revealed the true spiritual condition of the world. About three years later the angel Moroni appeared to him and subsequently visited him periodically for several years, imparting important instructions. On Sept. 22, 1827, he gave into the hands of Joseph Smith the plates on which was inscribed history of the early inhabitations of America.

While Joseph Smith and Oliver Cowdery were engaged in translating the Book of Mormon, from the plates, at Harmony, Susquehanna Co., Pa., they went into the woods to enquire of the Lord respecting baptism for the remission of sins. While thus employed, on the 15th of May, 1829, a messenger from heaven descended in a cloud of light. Having laid his hands upon them, he ordained them, saying: "Upon you, my fellow servants, in the name of Messiah, I confer the Priesthood of Aaron, which holds the keys of the ministering of angels, and of the gospel of repentance and of baptism by immersion for the remission of sins; and this shall never be taken again from the earth, until the sons of Levi do offer again an offering unto the Lord in righteousness."

The heavenly messenger told Joseph Smith and Oliver Cowdery that the "Aaronic Priesthood had not the power of laying on of hands for the gift of the Holy Ghost," but that this should be conferred on them later. He then commanded them "to go and be baptized," and directed that Joseph Smith should baptize Oliver Cowdery, after which he should baptize Joseph.

The messenger told them "that his name was John, the same that is called John the Baptist in the New Testament, and that he acted under the direction of Peter, James and John, who held the keys of the Priesthood of Melchisedek," which Priesthood he said should in due time be conferred on them (Joseph and Oliver).

In accordance with the commandment aforesaid, Joseph Smith baptized Oliver Cowdery, who then baptized Joseph. Joseph Smith then laid his hands upon the head of Oliver Cowdery and ordained him to the Aaronic Priesthood. Finally Oliver laid his hands on Joseph and ordained him to the same Priesthood.

Soon after these important events, Joseph Smith and Oliver Cowdery "became very anxious" to receive the Melchisedek Priesthood, which John the Baptist had promised them, if they continued faithful. They had for some time made this matter a subject of humble prayer, and at length they met "in the chamber of Mr. Whitmer's house," at Fayette, Seneca Co., N. Y., one day in June, 1829. They engaged in solemn and fervent prayer, when the word of the Lord came to them in the chamber commanding that Joseph Smith "should ordain Oliver Cowdery to be an Elder in the Church of Jesus Christ," and that Oliver should ordain Joseph to the same office. After that, they were to ordain others, as it should be made known unto them from time to time. However, they were commanded to defer these ordinations until "such times as it should be practicable to have their brethren, who had been and who should be baptized, assemble together."

This commandment was complied with, April 6, 1830, the day on which the Church was organized. On that occasion Joseph Smith laid his hands upon Oliver Cowdery and ordained him an Elder in the Church, after which Oliver ordained Joseph to the office of an Elder. Next, they administered the Sacrament, and then laid their hands on each individual member of the Church present, that they might receive the Holy Ghost and be confirmed members of the Church.

The exact date of the ordination of Joseph Smith and Oliver Cowdery to the Melchisedek Priesthood by Peter, James and John is not stated, but it is generally believed to have taken place in June or July, 1829. In proof of the ordination we have the word of the Lord Jesus Christ, in a revelation, given to Joseph Smith at Fayette, N. Y., in September, 1830, as follows: "Listen to the voice of Jesus Christ, your Lord, your God, and your Redeemer, whose word is quick and powerful. * * * The hour cometh that I will drink of the fruit of the vine with you on the earth, and with Moroni, whom I have sent unto you to reveal the Book of Mormon, containing the fulness of my everlasting gospel. * * * And also John, the son of Zacharias. * * which John I have sent unto you, my servants, Joseph Smith, jun., and Oliver Cowdery, to ordain you unto this first Priesthood, which you have

received, that you might be called and ordained even as Aaron. * * * And also with Peter, and James, and John, whom I have sent unto you, by whom I have ordained you and confirmed you to be Apostles and especial witnesses of my name, and bear the keys of your ministry, and of the same things which I revealed unto them." (Doc. and Cov., 27:1, 5, 7, 8, 12.)

In a revelation on Church Government, given through Joseph Smith, the Prophet, in April, 1830, at Fayette, the following passage occurs: "Commandment were given to Joseph Smith, jun., who was called of God and ordained an Apostle of Jesus Christ, to be the first Elder of this Church; and to Oliver Cowdery, who was also called of God, an Apostle of Jesus Christ, to be the second Elder of this Church, and ordained under his (Joseph's) hand." (Doc. and Cov., 20:2, 3.)

In the light of the foregoing it is plain that none among the children of men at the present time possess the holy Priesthood, with divine authority to administer in the ordinances of the gospel, except those who have received their ordinations through the laying on of hands by men whose commissions rest upon the divine calling of Joseph the Prophet. This being the case, it is desirable that every Apostle, Prophet, Patriarch, High Priest, Seventy, Elder, Bishop, Priest, Teacher and Deacon in the Church should be able to trace the Priesthood they hold back to the Prophet Joseph.

For the benefit of the brethren who are endeavouring to make proper records of these things, we publish the subjoined biographical notes, which contain the ordinations of nearly all the Elders who have been sustained and who at the present time are being sustained as the general authorities of the Church. The lack of space in this little work of reference prevents us from including other officers.

ALDRICH, Hazen; ordained a Seventy Feb. 28, 1835, under the hands of Joseph Smith and others.

BENSON, Ezra Taft; born Feb. 22, 1811; baptized July 19, 1840, at Quincy, Ill.; ordained a High Priest Oct. 25, 1840, by Hyrum Smith; ordained an Apostle July 16, 1846, by Pres. Brigham Young; died Sept. 3, 1869.

BILLINGS, Titus; born March 25, 1793, at Greenfield, Franklin Co., Mass.; baptized at Kirtland, Ohio, in November, 1830, by Parley P. Pratt; ordained a High Priest and counselor to Bishop Edward Partridge, Aug. 1, 1837, under the hands of Edward Partridge and Isaac Morley; died Feb. 6, 1866, at Provo, Utah.

BOYNTON, John Farnham; born Sept. 20, 1811; baptized in September, 1832, by Joseph the Prophet; ordained an Elder in 1832, by Sidney Rigdon; ordained an Apostle Feb. 15, 1835, under the hands of Oliver Cowdery, David Whitmer and Martin Harris; died Oct. 20, 1890.

BURTON, Robert Taylor; born Oct. 25, 1821, in Amersburgh, Ontario, Canada; ordained a High Priest and Bishop and set apart as second counselor to Bishop Edward Hunter, Sept. 2, 1875, by Edward Hunter, assisted by Brigham Young and Daniel H. Wells.

BUTTERFIELD, Josiah; ordained and set apart as one of the First Council of Seventies, April 6, 1837, under the hands of Sidney Rigdon and Hyrum Smith.

CANNON, Abraham Hoagland; born March 12, 1859; baptized March 12, 1867, by his father Geo. Q. Cannon; ordained an Elder July 7, 1875, by Geo. Q. Cannon; ordained a Seventy by   ; ordained an Apostle Oct. 7, 1889, by Joseph F. Smith, assisted by Wilford Woodruff and George Q. Cannon and nearly all the Apostles; died July 19, 1896.

CANNON, George Quayle; born Jan. 11, 1827; baptized in June, 1840, by John Taylor; ordained an Elder at Nauvoo, by John Taylor; ordained a Seventy Feb. 9, 1845, by Arza Adams; ordained an Apostle Aug. 26, 1860, by Pres. Brigham, assisted by his Counselors and ten of the Apostles.

CANNON, John Q.; born April 19, 1857, at San Francisco, Cal.; baptized April 19, 1865, by his father, George Q. Cannon; ordained an Elder by Geo. Q Cannon; ordained a Seventy Aug. 8, 1881, by Joseph F. Smith; ordained a High Priest and set apart as second counselor to Bishop Wm. B. Preston in October, 1884, by Pres. John Taylor.

CARRINGTON, Albert; born Jan. 8, 1813; baptized in July, 1841, by Wm. O. Clark; ordained an Apostle July 3, 1870, by Pres. Brigham Young; died Sept. 19, 1889, in Salt Lake City, Utah.

CLAPP, Benjamin L.; born Aug. 19, 1814, in Alabama; ordained and set apart as one of the presidents of the 8th quorum of Seventy, Oct. 20, 1844, under the hands of Joseph Young and Levi W. Hancock; set apart as one of the First Council of Seventies Dec. 2, 1845, under the hands of Apostles Brigham Young, Heber

C. Kimball, Orson Hyde, Parley P. Pratt and George A. Smith; died in California about 1860.

CLAWSON, Rudger; born March 12, 1857, in Salt Lake City, Utah; baptized when about eight years old; ordained a Seventy March 7, 1875, by Hiram B. Clawson, who was ordained a Seventy Feb. 2, 1845, by Joseph Young; ordained a High Priest Feb. 12, 1888, by Lorenzo Snow; ordained an Apostle Oct. 10, 1898, by Lorenzo Snow, assisted by his Counselors and all the Apostles.

CORRELL, John; ordained a High Priest and set apart as second counselor to Bishop Edward Partridge, June 6, 1831, under the hands of Edward Partridge and others.

COLTRIN, Zebedee; ordained a Seventy Feb. 28, 1835, under the hands of Joseph Smith and others; died July 21, 1887, at Spanish Fork, Utah Co., Utah.

COWDERY, Oliver; born in 1805; ordained to the Aaronic Priesthood in connection with Joseph Smith, May 15, 1829, by John the Baptist; baptized and reordained by Joseph Smith the same day; later in 1829, together with Joseph Smith, ordained to the Melchisedek Priesthood by Peter, James and John; confirmed a member of the Church and reordained an Elder, April 6, 1830, by Joseph Smith; together with David Whitmer and Martin Harris, he was "blessed by the laying on of the hands of the Presidency" (Joseph Smith, Sidney Rigdon and Fred. G. Williams) to select twelve Elders to constitute the Council of Twelve Apostles, Feb. 14, 1835; died March 3, 1850.

COWLEY, Matthias Foss; born Aug. 25, 1858, in Salt Lake City, Utah, baptized in 1866 by Samuel Turnbow; ordained an Elder Dec. 28, 1874, by Oluf F. Due; ordained a Seventy Oct. 11, 1880, by Joseph Young; ordained a High Priest Oct. 25, 1884, by Francis M. Lyman; ordained an Apostle Oct. 7, 1897, by Geo. Q. Cannon.

ELDREDGE, Horace S.; born Feb. 26, 1816, at Brutus, Cayuga Co., N. Y.; baptized June 4, 1836, by Libbeus T. Coon; ordained a Seventy Oct. 13, 1844, by Joseph Young; chosen one of the First Seven Presidents of Seventies in 1854; died Sept. 6, 1888, in Salt Lake City.

FJELDSTED Christian Daniel; born Feb. 20, 1829, in Sundbyvester, Amager, Copenhagen Amt, Denmark; baptized Feb. 20, 1852, by Chr. Samuel Hansen; confirmed by Ole U. C. Mønster; ordained an Elder July 25, 1853, by Peter O. Hansen, who was ordained a Seventy Nov. 17, 1844, by Joseph Young; ordained a Seventy Feb. 5, 1859, by Wm. H. Walker, who was ordained a Seventy Nov. 24, 1844, under the hands of Harrison Burgess, who was ordained a Seventy Feb. 28, 1835, by Sidney Rigdon; set apart as one of the First Council of Seventies, April 28, 1884, by Wilford Woodruff.

FOSTER, James; ordained and set apart as one of the First Seven Presidents of Seventies April 6, 1837, under the hands of Sidney Rigdon and Hyrum Smith.

GATES, Jacob; born March 9, 1811, at

LITTLE, Jesse Carter; born Sept. 26, 1815, at Belfast, Maine; ordained a High Priest April 17, 1845, by Parley P. Pratt; ordained a Bishop and set apart as second counselor to Bishop Edward Hunter, in 1856; died Dec. 26, 1893.

LUND, Anthon Henrik; born May 15, 1844; baptized May 15, 1856, by Jacob Julander; ordained an Elder a few years later; ordained a Seventy March 23, 1864, by Peter Madsen Peel, who was ordained a Seventy Nov. 21, 1862, by John Tidwell; ordained an Apostle Oct. 7, 1889, by Geo. Q. Cannon.

LYMAN, Amasa Mason; born March 30, 1813; baptized April 27, 1832, by Lyman E. Johnson; confirmed the following day by Orson Pratt; ordained an Elder Aug. 23, 1832, by Joseph Smith; ordained a High Priest Dec. 11, 1833, by Lyman E. Johnson, assisted by Orson Pratt; ordained an Apostle Aug. 20, 1842, by Brigham Young, assisted by Heber C. Kimball and Geo. A. Smith; died Feb. 4, 1877.

LYMAN, Francis Marion; born Jan. 12, 1840, at Good Hope, McDonough Co., Ill.; baptized in the Elkhorn river, Neb., and confirmed July 1, 1848, by Amasa M. Lyman; ordained an Elder in 1856, at San Bernardino, Cal., by Amasa M. Lyman; ordained a Seventy Jan. 7, 1860, at Farmington, Davis Co., Utah, by John S. Gleason, who was ordained a Seventy Oct. 30, 1843, by Pres. Brigham Young; ordained a High Priest March 13, 1869, at Fillmore, Millard Co., Utah, by Thomas Callister, who was ordained a High Priest and Bishop Sept. 17, 1855, in G. S. L. City, Utah, by Edward Hunter; ordained one of the Twelve Apostles Oct. 27, 1880, in Salt Lake City, Utah, by John Taylor, assisted by his Counselors and nearly all the Apostles.

MARSH, Thomas Baldwin; born Nov. 1, 1799; baptized in September 1830, by David Whitmer; ordained a High Priest June 6, 1831, by Lyman Wight; ordained an Apostle April 26, 1835, under the hands of Oliver Cowdery, David Whitmer and Martin Harris; died about 1866, at Ogden, Utah.

McLELLIN, William E.; born 1806, baptized, confirmed and ordained an Elder in 1831, under the hands of Samuel H. Smith and Reynolds Cahoon; ordained an Apostle Feb. 15, 1835, under the hands of Oliver Cowdery, David Whitmer and Martin Harris; died April 24, 1883.

McMURRIN, Joseph William; born Sept. 5, 1858, at Tooele, Tooele Co., Utah; baptized in 1866, by Henry W. Lawrence; ordained a Seventy April 21, 1884, by Royal Barney, who was ordained a Seventy in 1835, under the hands of Joseph Smith and Sidney Rigdon; set apart as one of the First Council of Seventies Jan. 21, 1898, by Apostle Anthon H. Lund, in Liverpool, England.

MERRILL, Marriner Wood; born Sept. 25, 1832; baptized April 6, 1852, by John Skerry; ordained an Apostle Oct. 7, 1889, by Wilford Woodruff, assisted by his Counselors and most of the Apostles.

MILES, Daniel S.; ordained a Seventy April 6, 1837, by Hazen Aldrich; set apart as one of the First Seven Presidents of Seventies April 6, 1837, under the hands of Sidney Rigdon and Hyrum Smith.

MORGAN, John; born Aug. 8, 1842, near Greensburgh, Decatur Co., Ind.; baptized Nov. 26, 1867, in Salt Lake City, Utah, by Robert Campbell; ordained an Elder Oct. 23, 1868, by Wm. H. Folsom, who was ordained a High Priest Oct. 7, 1862, by Pres. Brigham Young; ordained a Seventy Oct. 8, 1875, by Joseph Young; died Aug. 14, 1894.

MORLEY, Isaac; born March 11, 1786, in Montague, Hampshire Co., Mass.; baptized in November, 1830, at Kirtland, Ohio, by Parley F. Pratt; ordained a High Priest June 6, 1831, by Lyman Wight, and on the same day set apart as a counselor to Bishop Edward Partridge; ordained a Patriarch at Far West, Mo., Nov. 7, 1837, under the hands of Joseph Smith, Sidney Rigdon and Hyrum Smith; died June 24, 1865.

PAGE, John E.; baptized Aug. 18, 1833, by Emer Harris; ordained an Elder in September, 1833, by Nelson Higgins; ordained an Apostle Dec. 19, 1838, under the hands of Brigham Young and Heber C. Kimball; died near Sycamore, DeKalb Co., Ill., in the fall of 1867.

PARTRIDGE, Edward; born Aug. 27, 1793; baptized Dec. 11, 1830, by Joseph the Prophet; ordained an Elder Dec. 5, 1830, by Sidney Rigdon; called by revelation to be the first Bishop of the Church, and ordained and set apart to that position Feb. 4, 1831, by Sidney Rigdon; ordained a High Priest June 6, 1831, by Lyman Wight; died May 27, 1840.

PATTEN, David W.; born 1800; baptized June 15, 1832, by John Patten; ordained an Elder June 17, 1832, by Elisha H. Groves; ordained an Apostle Feb. 15, 1835, under the hands of Oliver Cowdery, David Whitmer and Martin Harris; died Oct. 25, 1838.

PENROSE, Charles William; born Feb. 4, 1832, in London, England, baptized May 14, 1850, by John Hyde, sen.; ordained an Elder Jan. 6, 1851, by Geo. B. Wallace; ordained a Seventy Oct. 27, 1861, by Truman Leonard; later ordained a High Priest.

PRATT, Orson; born Sept. 19, 1811; baptized Sept. 19, 1830, by Parley P. Pratt; ordained an Elder Dec. 1, 1830, by Joseph Smith; ordained a High Priest Feb. 2, 1832, by Sidney Rigdon; ordained an Apostle April 26, 1835, under the hands of David Whitmer and Oliver Cowdery; died Oct. 3, 1881.

PRATT, Parley Parker; born April 12, 1807; baptized, confirmed and ordained an Elder by Oliver Cowdery, in September, 1830; ordained a High Priest June 6, 1831, by Joseph Smith; ordained an Apostle Feb. 21, 1835, by Joseph Smith; died May 13, 1857.

PRESTON, William Bowker; born Nov. 24, 1830, at Halifax, Franklin Co., Va.; baptized in February, 1857, by Henry G. Boyle; ordained an Elder by Geo. Q. Cannon; ordained a High Priest and Bishop Nov. 14, 1859, by Orson Hyde; set apart as Presiding Bishop of the Church in 1884, by Pres. John Taylor.

PULSIPHER,Zera; born June 24,1789, in Rockingham, Windham Co., Vt.; baptized and ordained to the ministry in 1832; ordained and set apart as one of the First Seven Presidents of Seventies March 6, 1838, under the hands of James Foster and Joseph Young; died Jan. 1, 1872.

REYNOLDS, George; born Jan. 1, 1842, in London, England; baptized May 4, 1856; ordained a Seventy March 18, 1866, by Israel Barlow, who was ordained a Seventy in 1835, by Sidney Rigdon; set apart as one of the First Seven Presidents of Seventies, April 10, 1890, by Lorenzo Snow.

RICH, Charles Coulson; born Aug. 21, 1809; baptized April 1, 1832, by Geo. M. Hinkle, ordained an Elder May 16, 1832, under the hands of Zebedee Coltrin and Solomon Wixom; ordained a High Priest in April 1836, under the hands of Hyrum Smith and Uncle John Smith; ordained an Apostle Feb. 12, 1849, by Pres. Brigham Young; died Nov. 17, 1883.

RICH, Leonard; ordained a Seventy Feb. 28. 1835, under the hands of Joseph Smith and others.

RICHARDS, Franklin Dewey; born April 2, 1821; baptized June 3, 1838, by Phinehas Richards, at Richmond, Berkshire Co., Mass.; confirmed June 10, 1838, by Gibson Smith; ordained a Seventy April 9, 1840, at Nauvoo, Ill., by Joseph Young; ordained a High Priest May 17, 1844, at Nauvoo, Ill., by Brigham Young; ordained an Apostle Feb. 12, 1849, in the "Old Fort," G. S. L. City, by Heber C. Kimball.

RICHARDS, Willard; born June 24, 1804; baptized Dec. 31, 1836, by Brigham Young; ordained an Elder March 6, 1837, by Alma Beeman; ordained a High Priest April 1, 1838, under the hands of Heber C. Kimball and others; ordained an Apostle April 14, 1840, by Brigham Young; died March 11, 1854.

RIGDON, Sidney; born Feb. 19, 1793; baptized, confirmed and ordained an Elder late in 1830, under the hands of OliverCowdery,Parley P. Pratt, Peter Whitmer, jun., and Ziba Peterson. Subsequently he was ordained a High Priest by Joseph the Prophet, and on March 18, 1833, he was ordained and set apart as first Counselor in the First Presidency by Joseph Smith; died July 14, 1876.

ROBERTS, Brigham Henry; bornMarch 13, 1857, in Warrington, Lancashire, England; baptized in 1867, by Seth Dustin; ordained a Seventy March 8, 1877, by Nathan T. Porter, who was ordained a Seventy Oct. 6, 1844, by Joseph Young; set apart as one of the First Council of Seventies in October, 1889, by Lorenzo Snow.

ROCKWOOD, Albert P.; born June 5, 1805, in Holliston, Middlesex Co., Mass.; baptized in 1833; ordained a Seventy Jan. 5, 1839, under the hands of Joseph Young, Zera Pulsipher, Henry Harriman and Levi W. Hancock; set apart as one of the First Council of Seventies Dec. 2, 1845, under the hands of Apostles Brigham Young, Heber C. Kimball, Orson Hyde, Parley P. Pratt and Geo. A. Smith; died Nov. 26, 1879.

SHERMAN, Lyman; ordained a Seventy Feb. 28, 1835, at Kirtland, Ohio, under the hands of Joseph Smith and others.

SLOAN, James; born at Donaghmore, Tyrone Co., Ireland; ordained a High Priest Feb. 18, 1838, under the hands of Joseph Smith, sen.

SMITH, Asahel, son of Asahel Smith and Mary Duty; born May 21,1773,atWindham, Rockingham Co , N. H.; baptized June 29, 1835, at Stockholm, Lawrence Co., N. Y., by Lyman E. Johnson; ordained a High Priest in 1836, by Don Carlos Smith; ordained a Patriarch Oct.7,1844, atNauvoo, Ill., under the hands of the Twelve Apostles.

SMITH, George Albert; born June 26, 1817; baptized Sept. 10, 1832, by Joseph H. Wakefield; ordained a Seventy March 1, 1835, by Sidney Rigdon; ordained an Apostle April 26, 1839, by HeberC.Kimball;died Sept. 1, 1875.

SMITH, Hyrum; born Feb. 9, 1800; baptized by Joseph Smith in Seneca lake, N. Y., in June 1829; ordained a High Priest June 6, 1831, by Joseph Smith; chosen as second Counselor in the First Presidency Nov. 7, 1837; ordained a Patriarch Jan. 28, 1841, under the hands of Joseph the Prophet and others; died June 27, 1844.

SMITH,John,familiarly known as Uncle John Smith; born July 16, 1781, in Derryfield,Rockingham Co., N.H.; baptized, confirmed and ordained an Elder Jan. 9, 1832, by his brother JosephSmith, sen.; ordained a High Priest June 6, 1833, by Sidney Rigdon; ordained a Patriarch Jan. 10, 1844, by Joseph Smith; ordained Presiding Patriarch Jan. 1, 1849, under the hands of Brigham Young and Heber C. Kimball; died May 23, 1854.

SMITH, John, eldest son of Hyrum Smith; born Sept. 22, 1832, at Kirtland, O.; baptized in 1841, by John Taylor; ordained Presiding Patriarch in the Church Feb.18, 1855, by Pres. Brigham Young.

SMITH, John Henry; born Sept. 18, 1848; baptized Sept. 18, 1856, by Geo. A. Smith; ordained an Elder Jan. 16, 1864, by Samuel L. Sprague; ordained a High Priest and Bishop Nov. 22, 1875, by Pres. Brigham Young; ordained an Apostle Oct. 27, 1880, by Wilford Woodruff.

SMITH, Joseph, the Prophet; born Dec. 23, 1805; ordained to the Aaronic Priesthood May 15, 1829, by John the Baptist; baptized and re-ordained the same day by Oliver Cowdery; later, perhaps in June or July, 1829, he and Oliver Cowdery were ordained to the Melchisedek Priesthood by Peter, James and John, three of the ancient Apostles, who held the keys of that Priesthood; confirmed a member of the Church and ordained the first Elder in the Church April 6, 1830, by Oliver Cowdery; died June 27, 1844.

SMITH, Joseph, sen.; born July 12, 1771; baptized April 6, 1830; ordained a High Priest June 6, 1831, by Lyman Wight; ordained a Patriarch Dec. 18, 1833, under the hands of Joseph Smith, Oliver Cowdery, Sidney Rigdon and Frederick G. Williams; died Sept. 14. 1840.

SMITH, Joseph Fielding; born Nov. 13, 1838; baptized in 1850 or 1851 by Heber C.

Kimball; ordained an Elder in May, 1854, by Geo. A. Smith; ordained a Seventy March 20, 1858, by George Meyer, who was ordained a Seventy July 13, 1845, by Jesse P. Harmon, who was ordained a Seventy Oct. 8, 1844, by Brigham Young; ordained a High Priest Oct. 16, 1859; ordained an Apostle July 1, 1866, by Pres. Brigham Young, and set apart as one of the Twelve Apostles Oct. 8, 1867, by Pres. Brigham Young, assisted by all the members of the Council of Twelve Apostles.

SMITH, Sylvester; ordained a Seventy Feb. 28, 1835, at Kirtland, Ohio, under the hands of Joseph Smith and others.

SMITH, William; born March 13, 1811; ordained a High Priest June 6, 1833, by Sidney Rigdon; ordained an Apostle Feb. 15, 1835, under the hands of Oliver Cowdery, David Whitmer and Martin Harris; died Nov. 13, 1893.

SNOW, Erastus; born Nov. 9, 1818; baptized Feb. 3, 1833; ordained an Elder Aug. 16, 1835, by Luke S. Johnson; ordained a High Priest in October, 1839; ordained an Apostle Feb. 12, 1849, by President Brigham Young; died May 27, 1888.

SNOW, Lorenzo; born April 3, 1814; baptized June, 1836, by John F. Boynton; confirmed by Hyrum Smith; ordained an Elder in the winter of 1836-37 by Alva Beeman; ordained a Seventy July 17, 1840, by Joseph Young; ordained a High Priest July 18, 1840, by Don Carlos Smith; ordained an Apostle Feb. 12, 1849, by Heber C. Kimball.

STEVENSON, Edward; born May 1, 1820, at Gibraltar, Spain; baptized in 1834 by Japhet Fosdick; ordained a Seventy May 1, 1845, under the hands of Joseph Young and others; set apart as one of the First Council of Seventies, Oct. 9, 1894, by Apostle Brigham Young; died Jan. 27, 1897.

TAYLOR, John; born Nov. 1, 1808; baptized, confirmed and ordained an Elder in 1836, by Parley P. Pratt; ordained an Apostle Dec. 19, 1838, under the hands of Brigham Young and Heber C. Kimball; died July 25, 1887.

TAYLOR, John Whittaker; born May 18, 1858, at Provo, Utah Co., Utah; ordained an Elder March 13, 1876, by Wm. J. Smith; ordained an Apostle April 9, 1884, by John Taylor, assisted by his Counselors and most of the Apostles.

TAYLOR, William W.; born Sept. 11, 1853, in Salt Lake City, Utah; baptized by his father, John Taylor; ordained a Seventy Oct. 11, 1875, by Orson Pratt, and chosen as one of the First Council of Seventies in 1880; died Aug. 1, 1884.

TEASDALE, George; born Dec. 8, 1831, in London, England; baptized Aug. 8, 1852, by Robert Till; ordained an Elder April 30, 1854, by John Tuddenham; ordained a Seventy Oct. 18, 1875, by Joseph Young; ordained a High Priest July 9, 1877, by Pres. Brigham Young; ordained an Apostle Oct. 16, 1882, by John Taylor.

THATCHER. Moses; born Feb. 2, 1842, in Sangamon County, Ill.; baptized and confirmed Dec. 25, 1856, by Henry G. Boyle; ordained an Elder March 23, 1857, by Henry G. Boyle; ordained a Seventy by Brigham

Young; ordained a High Priest and set apart to preside over the Cache Stake of Zion in 1877, by Pres. Brigham Young; ordained an Apostle April 9, 1879, by John Taylor.

THOMPSON, Robert Blashel; born Oct. 1, 1811, in Great Driffield, Yorkshire, England; baptized and confirmed in May, 1836, in Canada, by Parley P. Pratt; ordained an Elder July 22, 1836, by John Taylor; died Aug. 27, 1841.

VAN COTT, John; born Sept. 7, 1814, at Canaan, Columbia Co. N. Y.; baptized in September, 1845, by Parley P. Pratt; ordained a Seventy Feb. 25, 1847, by Joseph Young; died Feb. 18, 1883.

WELLS, Daniel Hanmer; born Oct. 27, 1814; baptized Aug. 9, 1846, by Almon W. Babbitt, at Nauvoo, Ill.; ordained an Apostle and set apart as second Counselor in the First Presidency Jan. 4, 1857, by President Brigham Young; died March 24, 1891.

WELLS, Rulon Seymour; born July 7, 1854, in Salt Lake City, Utah; baptized about 1862, by Daniel H. Wells; confirmed by John V. Long; ordained an Elder Aug. 15, 1866, by Wm. J. Smith; ordained a Seventy Oct. 22, 1875, by Pres. Brigham Young; set apart as one of the First Seven Presidents of Seventies April 5, 1893, by George Q. Cannon.

WHITMER, David; born Jan. 7, 1805; baptized in June 1829, by Joseph Smith; confirmed April 6, 1830; ordained an Elder soon afterwards, and subsequently ordained a High Priest; set apart in 1834 by Joseph Smith to preside over the Saints in Missouri; "blessed by the laying on of hands of the Presidency" (Joseph Smith, Sidney Rigdon and Frederick G. Williams), in connection with Oliver Cowdery and Martin Harris, Feb. 14, 1835, to choose the Twelve Apostles, in accordance with revelation (Doc. and Cov., 18:37); died Jan. 25, 1888.

WHITMER, John; born Aug. 27, 1802; baptized and ordained an Elder at an early day; ordained a High Priest June 6, 1831, at Kirtland, Ohio, by Lyman Wight; died July 11, 1878.

WHITNEY, Newel K.; born Feb. 5, 1795; baptized late in 1830; called by revelation Dec. 4, 1831, to the office of a Bishop; died Sept. 23, 1853.

WIGHT, Lyman; born May 9, 1796; baptized in 1830, by Oliver Cowdery; ordained a High Priest June 6, 1831, by Joseph the Prophet; ordained an Apostle April 8, 1841, by Joseph Smith; died March 31, 1858.

WILLIAMS, Frederick Granger; born Oct. 28, 1787, in Sheffield, Hartford Co., Conn.; baptized, confirmed and ordained an Elder in November 1830, under the hands of Oliver Cowdery, Parley P. Pratt, Peter Whitmer, jun., and Ziba Peterson; called by revelation to "be a High Priest" and a Counselor to Joseph the Prophet in March, 1832; ordained and set apart by Joseph Smith as his second Counselor March 18, 1833; died Oct. 25, 1842, at Quincy, Ill.

WINDER, John Rex; born Dec. 11, 1820, in Biddenden, County of Kent, England;

baptized Sept. 20, 1818; ordained a Seventy iu 1854; ordained a High Priest March 4. 1872, by Edward Hunter; ordained a Bishop and set apart as second counselor to Bishop Wm. B. Preston in 1886, by Franklin D. Richards, assisted by George Q. Cannon.

WOODRUFF, Abraham Owen; born Nov. 23, 1872, near Salt Lake City, Utah; baptized May 3, 1881, by Henry Fowler; ordained an Elder Jan. 8, 1894, by Samuel H. Harrow; ordained a Seventy June 19, 1894, by Wilford Woodruff; ordained an Apostle Oct. 7, 1897, by Wilford Woodruff.

WOODRUFF, Wilford;bornMarch 1,1807; baptized by Zera Pulsipher Dec. 31, 1833; ordained an Elder by Warren Parrish in 1835; ordained a Seventy May 31, 1836, under the hands of David W. Patten and Warren Parrish, ordained an Apostle April 26, 1839, by Brigham Young; died Sept. 2, 1898.

YOUNG, Brigham, born June 1, 1801; baptized, confirmed and ordained an Elder April 14, 1832, by Eleazer Miller; ordained an Apostle Feb, 14, 1835, under the hands of Oliver Cowdery, David Whitmer and Martin Harris; died Aug. 29, 1877.

YOUNG, Brigham, jun.; born Dec. 18, 1836; baptized in 1845, by his father, ordained an Apostle Nov. 22, 1855, by Brigham Young, and admitted into the Council of Twelve Apostles Oct. 9, 1868, being set apart by Brigham Young.

YOUNG, John W.; born Oct. 1, 1844; ordained an Apostle Nov. 22, 1855, by Pres. Brigham Young, but has never been admitted into theCouncil of TwelveApostles.

YOUNG, Joseph; born April 7, 1797, in Hopkinton,Middlesex Co.,Mass.; baptized April 6, 1832, by Daniel Bowen; ordained an Elder in 1832, by Ezra Landen; ordained a Seventy Feb. 28, 1835, under the hands terwards chosen as one of the seven Presidents of Seventy; died July 16, 1881.

YOUNG, Seymour Bicknell; born Oct. 3, 1837, at Kirtland, Ohio; baptized in 1848, at Carterville, Ohio, by Ezekiel Lee; ordained an Elder in the Endowment House, Salt Lake City, Utah, April 15, 1856, by Samuel L. Sprague; ordained a Seventy Feb. 18, 1857, by Edmund Ellsworth, who was ordained a Seventy March 8, 1843, by Joseph Young.

CHURCH CHRONOLOGY.

1805-1820.

During the two first decades of the Nineteenth Century a number of men who were destined to take a most active part in the ushering in of the new gospel dispensation were born. Chief among these was the Prophet Joseph Smith, to whom the Father and the Son appeared in a glorious vision and revealed the apostate condition of the religious world.

1805.

December. *Mon. 23.*—Joseph Smith, the Prophet, was born in Sharon, Windsor Co., Vt.

Among the prominent men, older than the Prophet, who became intimately associated with him in establishing the great Latter-day work, were the following: Joseph Smith, sen., born July 12, 1771, in Topsfield, Essex Co., Mass.; Martin Harris, born May 18, 1783, in Easttown, Saratoga Co., N. Y.; Sidney Rigdon, born Feb. 19, 1793, in St. Clair, Allegheny Co., Pa.; Edward Hunter, born June 22, 1793, in Newtown, Delaware Co., Pa.; Edward Partridge, born Aug. 27, 1793, in Pittsfield, Berkshire Co., Mass.; Newel K. Whitney, born Feb. 5, 1795, in Marlborough, Windham Co., Vt.; Lyman Wight, born May 9, 1796, in Fairfield, Herkimer Co., N. Y.; John E. Page, born Feb. 25, 1799, in Trenton, Oneida Co., N. Y.; Thomas B. Marsh, born Nov. 1, 1799, in Acton, Middlesex Co., Mass.; Hyrum Smith, born Feb. 9, 1800, in Tunbridge, Orange Co., Vt.; David W. Patten, born about 1800, in the State of New York; Brigham Young, born June 1, 1801, in Whitingham, Windham Co., Vt.; Heber Chase Kimball, born June 14, 1801, at Sheldon, Franklin Co., Vt.; Willard Richards, born June 24, 1804, at Hopkinton, Middlesex Co., Mass.; David Whitmer, born Jan. 7, 1805, near Harrisburg, Dauphin Co., Pa.; Orson Hyde, born Jan. 28, 1805, in Oxford, New Haven Co., Conn.; Oliver Cowdery, born in October, 1805, in Wells, Rutland Co., Vt.

1806.

Wm. E. McLellin was born this year in Tennessee.

1807.

March. *Sun. 1.*—Wilford Woodruff was born in Farmington, Hartford Co., Conn.

April. *Sun. 12.*—Parley Parker Pratt was born in Burlington, Otsego Co., N. Y.

November. *Tues. 3.*—Luke S. Johnson was born in Pomfret, Windsor Co., Vt.

1808.

November. *Tues. 1.*—John Taylor was born in Milnthorpe, Westmoreland, England.

1809.

August. *Mon. 21.*—Charles Coulson Rich was born in Campbell County, Mass.

1811.

February. *Fri. 22.*—Ezra Taft Benson was born in Mendon, Worcester Co., Mass.

March. *Wed 13.*—Wm. Smith was born in Royalton, Windsor Co., Vt.

September. *Thurs. 19.*—Orson Pratt was born in Hartford, Washington Co., N. Y.

Fri. 20.—John F. Boynton was born in Bradford, Essex Co., Mass.

October. *Thurs. 24.*—Lyman Eugene Johnson was born in Pomfret, Windsor Co., Vt.

1813.

January. *Fri. 8.*—Albert Carrington was born in Royalton, Windsor Co., Vt.

March. *Tues. 30.*—Amasa M. Lyman was born in Lyman, Grafton Co., N. H.

1814.

April. *Sun. 3.*—Lorenzo Snow was born in Mantua, Portage Co., O.

October. *Thurs. 27.*—Daniel Hanmer Wells was born in Trenton, Oneida Co., N. Y.

1815.

Joseph Smith, sen., removed with his family from Vermont to Palmyra, Wayne Co., N. Y.

1816.

February. *Wed. 21.*—Jedediah Morgan Grant was born in Windsor, Broome Co. N. Y.

1817.

June. *Thurs. 26.*—George Albert Smith was born in Potsdam, St. Lawrence Co., N. Y.

1818.

November. *Mon. 9.*—Erastus Snow was born in St Johnsbury, Caledonia Co., Vt.

1820.

The Baptists, Methodists and Presbyterians held protracted revival meetings in and about Palmyra, N. Y., which resulted in great contention among the preachers and members of the different sects who sought to influence the new converts to join their respective churches. Joseph Smith, jun., (then about fourteen years old), being unable to decide which of all the sects was right, and being deeply impressed with the promise in James 1, 5: "If any of you lack wisdom, let him ask of God that giveth to all men liberally, and upbraideth not; and it shall be given him," retired to a grove near his father's house, early in the spring of the year, where he sought the Lord in earnest prayer. While thus engaged, he beheld two glorious beings wrapped in a brilliant light, standing above him in the air. One of them spoke to him, calling him by name, and said (pointing to the other), "This is my beloved Son, hear Him." Joseph then asked the personages, standing above him in the light, which of the sects was right and which he should join. He was answered that he must join none of them, for they were all wrong. The person speaking said further that all their creeds were an abomination in his sight and that "those professors were all corrupt." "They draw near to me with their lips, but their hearts are far from me; they teach for doctrine the commandments of men, having a form of godliness; but they deny the power thereof."

1821-1828.

These eight years may be termed the preparatory period preceeding the restoration of the Priesthood and the organization of the Church of Christ on the earth. The angel Moroni appeared to the Prophet Joseph Smith, jun., several times and finally delivered to him the plates of the Book of Mormon. The translation of the sacred records was begun, and Joseph commenced to receive revelations.

1821.

April. *Mon. 2.*—Franklin Dewey Richards was born in Richmond, Berkshire Co., Mass.

1823.

September. *Sun. 21.*—Joseph Smith, jun., while engaged in earnest prayer in his father's house in Manchester, near Palmyra, N. Y., saw the room in which he had retired for the night filled with light surpassing that of noonday, in the midst of which stood a person dressed in white, whose countenance was as lightning, and yet full of innocence and goodness. This was the angel Moroni (sometimes erroneously called Nephi), who informed Joseph that God had a work for him (Joseph) to do, and that his "name should be had for good and evil among all nations." The angel quoted many passages of Scripture, and told Joseph that the native inhabitants of America were a remnant of Israel who had anciently enjoyed the ministry of inspired men, that records engraved on plates of gold, containing their

history and also the fulness of the everlasting Gospel had been preserved and were buried in a neighboring hill. While conversing with the angel, a vision was opened to Joseph's view, so that he could see the place where the plates were deposited, and he was told by the angel that he should obtain them at some future day, if he was faithful. After imparting many instructions, the angel disappeared, but returned twice during the night, and repeated what he had said on his first visit; he also gave further instructions. *Mon. 22.*—Joseph Smith, jun., again visited by the angel Moroni and received further instructions. He related what he had seen and heard to his father, who believed his words, and advised him to do as he had been instructed. He then went to the hill (Cumorah) that he had seen in his vision the previous night, and soon found the spot where the plates containing the ancient records were buried in a stone box. He lifted the lid of the box and beheld "the plates, the Urim and Thummim and breastplate, as stated by the angel." While attempting to "take them out," the angel informed him "that the time for bringing them forth had not yet arrived, neither would, until four years from that time."

1824.

September. *Wed. 22.*—Joseph Smith, jun., again visited the hill Cumorah, according to previous commandment, and there received further instructions from the angel. On the same day of the two following years he made similar visits to the hill, receiving instructions from the angel each time.

1827.

January. *Thurs. 11.*—George Quayle Cannon was born in Liverpool, Lancashire, England.

Thurs. 18.—Joseph Smith, jun., married Emma Hale, a daughter of Isaac Hale, while in the employ of Josiah Stoal, in Chenango County, N. Y.

September. *Sat. 22.*—The angel Moroni delivered to Joseph Smith, jun., the ancient records, or the plates of the Book of Mormon; also the Urim and Thummim, with which to translate them, and the breastplate.

When it became known that Joseph Smith, jun., had obtained the plates, severe persecutions arose against him and his father's family, and every effort was made to rob him of the sacred treasure.

December.—Owing to persecutions Joseph Smith, jun., removed from Manchester, N. Y., to Harmony, Susquehanna Co., Pa., but there also persecution awaited him. During this and the following month he translated some of the characters of the plates.

1828.

February.—Martin Harris visited Joseph Smith, jun., at Harmony, Pa., and took some of the characters, which had been transcribed, and the translation of them, to New York City, where he showed them to Professor Charles Anthon and Doctor Mitchell.

April.—Martin Harris returned from New York City and commenced to write for

Joseph Smith, jun., who continued to translate from the plates until June 14th.

June.—Martin Harris lost the manuscript which he had obtained contrary to the will of the Lord. It consisted of 116 written pages translated from the plates by Joseph Smith, jun., and has never since been recovered.

July.—Joseph Smith, jun., having returned to Harmony, Pa., from a visit to his father's family in Manchester, N. Y., enquired of the Lord through the Urim and Thummim and received the first revelation published in the Book of Doctrine and Covenants. (Doc. and Cov., Sec. 3.)

1829.

During this year the translation of the Book of Mormon was completed by Joseph Smith, jun., who was assisted by Oliver Cowdery as scribe; the plates were shown to the Three Witnesses and the Eight Witnesses; the Aaronic Priesthood was restored to the earth by John the Baptist, and, later, the Melchisedec Priesthood by Peter, James and John; Joseph Smith, jun., and Oliver Cowdery also commenced to preach and baptize.

February.—Joseph Smith, jun., was visited by his father Joseph Smith, sen., at Harmony, Pa., and received a revelation addressed to him. (Doc. and Cov., Sec. 4.)

March.—The revelation known as Section 5 of the Doctrine and Covenants was given at Harmony.

April. Sun. 5.—Joseph Smith, jun., and Oliver Cowdery met for the first time.

Tues. 7.—Joseph Smith, jun., resumed the translation of the Book of Mormon, assisted by Oliver Cowdery as scribe, at Harmony.

Later in April, Oliver Cowdery was called by revelation to assist Joseph Smith, jun., in his labors and stand by him in his difficulties. Oliver was also promised the gift of translating like Joseph, if he desired it. (Doc. and Cov., Sec. 6.)

The Lord revealed to Joseph Smith, jun., that John, the beloved Disciple, was given power over death, that he might live and bring souls to Christ and to prophesy before nations, kindreds, tongues and people until the coming of Christ in his glory. (Doc. and Cov., Sec. 7.)

Oliver Cowdery was instructed by revelation through Joseph Smith, jun., to exercise great faith, that he might know the mysteries of God, translate and receive knowledge from ancient records. (Doc. and Cov., Sec. 8.)

As Oliver Cowdery did not translate, according to his former desire, he was commanded to write for Joseph Smith, jun., until the translation of the Book of Mormon was finished. (Doc. and Cov., Sec. 9.)

May.—A revelation concerning the alteration of the forepart of the Book of Mormon was given to Joseph Smith, jun., at Harmony. (Doc. and Cov., Sec. 10.)

— Joseph Smith, jun., was visited by Joseph Knight, sen., from Broome Co., N. Y., who brought him provisions. Mr.

Knight being anxious to know his duty in relation to the work of God, Joseph Smith, jun., enquired of the Lord and received a revelation. (Doc. and Cov., Sec. 12.)

Fri. 15.—While Joseph Smith, jun., and Oliver Cowdery were engaged in prayer in the woods, near Harmony, John the Baptist descended as a messenger from heaven in a cloud of light and ordained them to the Priesthood of Aaron and commanded them to baptize and ordain each other. This they did the same day. Immediately after being baptized, the Holy Ghost fell upon them in great measure and both prophesied. (See Doc. and Cov., Sec. 13, and History of Joseph Smith.)

Mon. 25.—Samuel Harrison Smith, who had come to visit his brother Joseph at Harmony, was baptized by Oliver Cowdery.

A few days later Hyrum Smith visited Harmony to make enquiries about the work of God, and received through his brother Joseph a revelation, calling him to assist in the work. (Doc. and Cov., Sec. 11.)

June.—Joseph Smith, jun., removed from Harmony, Pa., to the home of Peter Whitmer, sen., at Fayette, Seneca Co., N. Y., where he resided while finishing the translation of the Book of Mormon. The Whitmer family was very kind to Joseph, and John Whitmer rendered efficient aid as a scribe.

— David Whitmer, John Whitmer and Peter Whitmer, jun., being very desirous to know their respective duties, besought Joseph Smith, jun., to "enquire of the Lord concerning them." He did so through the Urim and Thummim, and received the revelations known as Sections 14, 15 and 16 of the Doctrine and Covenants.

— Hyrum Smith, David Whitmer and Peter Whitmer, jun., were baptized in Seneca lake, near Fayette.

— As Joseph Smith, jun., progressed with the work of translation, he ascertained that three special witnesses "were to be provided by the Lord" to see the plates and bear record of the same. (Ether. 5: 2-4.)

Oliver Cowdery, David Whitmer and Martin Harris, being very desirous to "be these three special witnesses," received the promise by revelation through Joseph Smith, jun., that they should "have a view of the plates, and also of the breastplate, the sword of Laban, the Urim and Thummim and the miraculous directors." (Doc. and Cov., Sec. 17.)

— A few days later an angel showed the plates of the Book of Mormon to the Three Witnesses.

— Soon afterwards the plates were shown by Joseph Smith, jun., to Christian Whitmer, Jacob Whitmer, Peter Whitmer, jun., John Whitmer, Hiram Page, Joseph Smith, sen., Hyrum Smith and Samuel H. Smith, who subsequently gave their testimony as the Eight Witnesses to the Book of Mormon.

—A revelation was given to Joseph Smith, jun., Oliver Cowdery and David Whitmer, "making known the calling of Twelve Apostles in these last days," and containing "instructions relative to building up the Church of Christ, according to the fulness of the gospel." (Doc. and Cov., Sec. 18.)

— Joseph Smith, jun., and Oliver Cowdery being desirous to obtain the Melchisedec Priesthood which had been promised them by John the Baptist, engaged in "solemn and fervent prayer," at Fayette, when "the word of the Lord came," commanding them to ordain each other. But they were to wait for this ordination till the others who had been baptized assembled together.

1830.

In the beginning of this year the Book of Mormon was printed and published in the English language. This first edition of the book, consisting of 5,000 copies, was printed by Egbert Grandin, at Palmyra, N. Y. Soon afterwards the Church was organized; the first conferences were held, the first missionaries sent out to preach the fulness of the gospel, and several revelations given for the government of the Church; a large branch was established at Kirtland, Ohio, etc.

March. Martin Harris was commanded by revelation through Joseph Smith, jun., at Manchester, N.Y., to repent of his sins. (Doc. and Cov., Sec. 19.)

April. An important revelation on Priesthood and Church government in general was given through Joseph Smith, jun. (Doc. and Cov., Sec. 20.)

Tues. 6. The Church (afterwards named by revelation the Church of Jesus Christ of Latter-day Saints) was organized according to the laws of the State of New York, in the house of Peter Whitmer, sen., at Fayette, Seneca Co., N. Y., with six members, namely, Joseph Smith, jun., Oliver Cowdery, Hyrum Smith, Peter Whitmer, jun., Samuel H. Smith and David Whitmer. Joseph Smith, jun., and Oliver Cowdery ordained each other Elders—the first Elders in the Church—according to commandment from God. They then laid hands on all the baptized members present, "that they might receive the gift of the Holy Ghost and be confirmed members of the Church." The Holy Ghost was poured out upon them "to a very great degree." Some prophesied and "all praised the Lord and rejoiced exceedingly."

The Church was commanded by revelation to keep a record, and Joseph Smith, jun., was named by the Lord a Seer, a Revelator, a Prophet, an Apostle of Jesus Christ, etc. (Doc. and Cov., Sec. 20.)

Soon after the organization of the Church the Prophet's parents (Joseph Smith, sen., and Lucy Smith), Martin Harris and A. Rockwell were baptized.

Some persons who had been baptized in the sectarian denominations desired to join the Church without further baptism, but the Lord,by revelation through the Prophet Joseph, instructed them to enter in at the gate, as He had commanded, and not seek to counsel God. (Doc. and Cov., Sec. 22.)

Oliver Cowdery, Hyrum Smith, Samuel H. Smith and Joseph Knight being anxious to know their respective duties in relation

to the work of God, Joseph the Prophet inquired of the Lord and received a revelation. (Doc. and Cov., Sec. 23.)

Sun. 11.—Oliver Cowdery preached the first public discourse delivered by any of the Elders in this dispensation. The meeting was held in the house of Peter Whitmer, sen., at Fayette. Hiram Page, Catherine Page, Christian Whitmer, Annie Whitmer, Jacob Whitmer and Elizabeth Whitmer were baptized by Oliver Cowdery, in Seneca lake.

Sun. 18.—Peter Whitmer, sen., Mary Whitmer, Wm. Jolly, Elizabeth Jolly, Vincent Jolly, Ziba Peterson and Elizabeth Anne Whitmer were baptized by Oliver Cowdery in Seneca lake.

Late in April the Prophet Joseph visited Joseph Knight, at Colesville, Broome Co., N. Y., where, under the Prophet's administration, the first miracle was wrought in this dispensation, viz: casting out devils.

May.— Newel Knight visited Joseph Smith, jun., at Fayette and was baptized by David Whitmer.

June.—The Church held its first conference, at Fayette. Several of the brethren were ordained to the Priesthood; the Holy Spirit was poured out in a miraculous manner; many of the Saints prophesied and Newel Knight and others had heavenly visions.

—Later in June David Whitmer baptized Wm. Smith, Don Carlos Smith, Catherine Smith and six others in Seneca lake.

—Joseph Smith, jun., returned with his family to his own home at Harmony, Pa.

—Joseph Smith, jun., Oliver Cowdery, John Whitmer and David Whitmer visited Colesville, N. Y., where they held meeting, notwithstanding the mob, and baptized thirteen persons, among whom were Emma Smith and Joseph Knight. Joseph Smith, jun., was arrested, charged with setting the country in an uproar by his preaching, tried and acquitted in South Bainbridge, Chenango Co., N. Y. Immediately afterwards he was again arrested, tried and acquitted at Colesville.

—Joseph Smith, jun. and Oliver Cowdery again visited Colesville, but were driven away by a mob.

—An important revelation (Words of Moses) was given to Joseph Smith, jun. (Pearl of Great Price, page 1.)

—Joseph Smith, jun. and Oliver Cowdery again visited Colesville and confirmed the newly baptized members.

July.—Joseph Smith, jun., was commanded by revelation to devote all his time to the interest of the Church, but in temporal labors he should "not have strength." (Doc. and Cov., Sec. 24.)

— Emma Smith, the Prophet's wife, was called by the Lord to expound scriptures, exhort the Church, and make a selection of sacred hymns for the use of the Saints. (Doc. and Cov., Sec. 25.)

— The Lord commanded that "all things" in the Church should "be done by common consent." (Doc. and Cov., Sec. 26.)

— Oliver Cowdery returned to Fayette where he and the Whitmer family became disaffected because of a paragraph in one of the revelations (Doc. and Cov., 20: 37); but Joseph the Prophet paid them a visit and set matters right.

August.—Newel Knight and wife visited Joseph Smith, jun., at Harmony, Pa., which gave occasion for the appearance of a heavenly messenger and a revelation on the Sacrament. (Doc. and Cov., Sec. 27, and History of Joseph Smith.)

— Joseph Smith, jun., and others visited the branch of the Church at Colesville, N. Y., where they barely escaped mob violence.

— Joseph the Prophet removed with his family to Fayette, N. Y., on account of the persecutions prevailing against them at Harmony. At Fayette, Hiram Page had obtained possession of a stone by means of which he received false revelations.

September.—In a revelation, given through Joseph the Prophet to Oliver Cowdery, the Lord said that "those things" which Hiram Page had written from the stone were not of God, and that none could receive commandments and revelations for the Church except Joseph Smith, jun. (Doc. and Cov., Sec. 28.)

— In a revelation given through Joseph the Prophet in the presence of six Elders at Fayette, N. Y., the Lord spoke of the gathering of the Saints, the end of the world, the reward of the righteous, the punishment of the wicked, etc. (Doc. and Cov., Sec. 29.)

— The second conference of the Church, which was continued three days, was held at Fayette, N. Y. After considerable discussion, Hiram Page and the whole Church renounced the stone and all things connected therewith," after which the power of God was made manifest. David Whitmer, Peter Whitmer, jun., and Thos. B. Marsh were called by revelation to preach the gospel. (Doc. and Cov., Sec. 30 and 31.)

October.—Oliver Cowdery, Parley P. Pratt, Peter Whitmer, jun., and Ziba Peterson were called by revelation to preach the gospel to the Lamanites. (Doc. and Cov., Sec. 32.)

— Oliver Cowdery, Parley P. Pratt, Peter Whitmer, jun., and Ziba Peterson started westward as the first missionaries to the Lamanites. On their journey they established a large branch of the Church at Kirtland, Geauga Co., O. Among those baptized by Parley P. Pratt was Sidney Rigdon.

— A revelation calling Ezra Thayre and Northrop Sweet to the ministry was given through Joseph Smith, jun., at Fayette. (Doc. and Cov., Sec. 33.)

November.—*Thurs. 4.*—Orson Pratt, then nineteen years old, was called to the ministry by revelation through Joseph Smith, jun. Brother Pratt was visiting the Prophet at Fayette. (Doc. and Cov., Sec. 34.)

Wed. 24.—William B. Preston was born in Franklin County, Va.

December.—Sidney Rigdon and Edward Partridge, from Ohio, visited Joseph Smith, jun., at Fayette, N. Y. Sidney Rigdon was called by revelation to assist Joseph in his labors,and both he and Edward Partridge were commanded to preach the gospel. (Doc. and Cov., Sec. 35 and 36.)

— The prophecy of Enoch was revealed to Joseph the Prophet. (See Pearl of Great Price.)

— The Saints in the State of New York

were commanded by revelation to gather to Ohio. (Doc. and Cov., Sec. 37.)

Sat. 11.—Edward Partridge was baptized by Joseph Smith, jun., in the Seneca river.

1831.

The first Elders arrived in Jackson County,Mo., and the Saints from the State of New York and other places commenced to build up Kirtland, O., where the Prophet Joseph also located with his family. Jackson County, Mo., was named by the Lord a land of Zion where the New Jerusalem should be built, and where the Saints were to gather. The land was dedicated for that purpose, a Temple site selected and dedicated, and the building of a settlement commenced. The Elders also began to preach the gospel with great zeal.

January. *Sun. 2.*—The third conference of the Church was held at Fayette, Seneca Co., N. Y., and a revelation given through Joseph Smith, jun., in which the Lord promised the Saints a land of inheritance. (Doc. and Cov., Sec. 38.)

Wed. 5.—James Coville, a Baptist minister, who had come to visit Joseph at Fayette,was commanded by revelation through Joseph the Prophet to receive the fulness of the gospel. (Doc. and Cov., Sec. 39.)

As James Coville rejected the word of the Lord and returned to his former doctrines and people, the Lord gave a revelation explaining why he did so. (Doc. and Cov., Sec. 40.)

In the latter part of this month, Joseph Smith, jun. and wife, in company with Sidney Rigdon and Edward Partridge, left Fayette, N. Y., for Kirtland, Geauga Co., O., where they arrived about the first of February.

—Oliver Cowdery and fellow - missionaries arrived in Jackson County, Missouri, where they commenced their mission among the Lamanites on its western border.

February. *Fri. 4.*—Edward Partridge was called by revelation to leave his merchandise and be ordained the first Bishop of the Church. (Doc. and Cov., Sec. 41.) This was the first revelation given through Joseph the Prophet at Kirtland, O.

Wed. 9.—In the presence of twelve Elders, the Lord gave through Joseph Smith, jun., an important revelation on Church government and how transgressors should be dealt with. The Elders were commanded to go out two and two to preach the gospel. (Doc. and Cov., Sec. 42.)

Mon. 14.—Oliver Cowdery, Parley P. Pratt, Ziba Peterson, Peter Whitmer, jun., and Frederick G. Williams (who had joined the mission at Kirtland, O.) held a council at Independence, Mo., and decided that Parley P. Pratt should return to the East to report their labors to the heads of the Church.

A woman, who pretended to receive commandments, laws and other "curious matters," visited Joseph Smith, jun., who inquired of the Lord and received a revelation in which God said that none but Joseph would be appointed to receive revelations and commandments, as long as he lived and remained faithful. (Doc. and Cov., Sec. 43.)

A revelation instructing the Elders who had gone on missions to assemble at Kirtland in June following was given to Joseph Smith, jun., and Sidney Rigdon, at Kirtland. (Doc. and Cov., Sec. 44.)

March. *Mon. 7.*—An important revelation concerning the salvation of man and the calamities of the last days was given through Joseph Smith, jun., at Kirtland. The Saints were also commanded to gather means wherewith to purchase a land of inheritance on which to build a New Jerusalem. (Doc. and Cov., Sec. 45.)

Tues. 8.—A revelation was given through Joseph Smith, jun., at Kirtland, relative to the gifts of the Holy Ghost, and John Whitmer was called by revelation to be Church Historian. (Doc. and Cov., Sec. 46 and 47.)

Later in March, the Saints were commanded by revelation to save their money to purchase land for an inheritance; and Sidney Rigdon, Parley P. Pratt and Lemon Copley were called by revelation to preach the gospel to the Quakers. (Doc. and Cov., Sec. 48 and 49.)

April.—Joseph Smith, jun., continued to translate the Scriptures.

May.—As a number of Elders did not understand the different spirits which manifested themselves at the time, Joseph Smith, jun., inquired of the Lord and received a revelation. (Doc. and Cov., Sec. 50.)

—The Saints from the State of New York and other places commenced to gather to Kirtland, O., and vicinity; and Edward Partridge was appointed by revelation through Joseph Smith, jun., to locate them for a short time at Thompson, Geauga Co., O., agreeable to the principles of the United Order. (Doc. and Cov., Sec. 51.)

June. *Mon. 6.*—The fourth conference of the Church was held, at Kirtland, O., on which occasion several brethren were called by revelation to the office of High Priests. This was the first occasion in which this office in the Priesthood was fully revealed and conferred upon any of the Elders in this dispensation.

Tues. 7.—Joseph Smith and about thirty other Elders were called by revelation to go to Missouri and preach the gospel by the way. (Doc. and Cov., Sec. 52.)

Later in June, a revelation was given through Joseph Smith, jun., at Kirtland, to Algernon Sidney Gilbert. (Doc. and Cov., Sec. 53.)

The Saints in Thompson, O., were commanded by revelation to remove to Missouri. (Doc. and Cov., Sec. 54.)

The Elders, in obedience to revelation, began to take their departure for the western country two and two.

About the middle of the month, Wm. W. Phelps arrived at Kirtland with his family. He was commanded by revelation to receive the fulness of the gospel, and then to assist in writing and printing for the Church, and also accom-

pany the Prophet Joseph and Sidney Rigdon to Missouri. (Doc. and Cov., Sec. 55.)

Thomas B. Marsh and others were commanded by revelation through the Prophet Joseph to go to Missouri. (Doc. and Cov., Sec. 56.)

Sun. 19.—Joseph Smith, jun., Sidney Rigdon, Martin Harris, Edward Partridge, Wm. W. Phelps, Joseph Coe and A. S. Gilbert and wife left Kirtland, O., for Missouri.

July.—About the middle of this month Joseph Smith, jun., and his companions arrived at Independence, Jackson Co., Mo. The first Sabbath after their arrival Wm. W. Phelps preached to a western audience, over the boundary line of the United States. The following week the Colesville branch arrived. The Lord revealed the location of the New Jerusalem and the spot upon which the Temple was to be built. (Doc. and Cov., Sec. 57.)

August. *Mon. 1.*—A revelation, directing the Saints how to locate in the land of Zion, was given in Jackson County. (Doc. and Cov., Sec. 58.)

Tues. 2.—The Saints commenced erecting houses in Jackson County, the first log being laid in Kaw Township, twelve miles southwest of Independence. The log was carried and placed in position by twelve men, in honor of the twelve tribes of Israel. On that occasion the land of Zion was consecrated and dedicated by Elder Rigdon for the gathering of the Saints.

Wed. 3.—The spot for the Temple, a short distance west of Independence, was dedicated in the presence of eight brethren, among whom were Joseph Smith, jun., Sidney Rigdon, Edward Partridge, Wm. W. Phelps, Oliver Cowdery, Martin Harris and Joseph Coe.

Thurs. 4.—The fifth conference of the Church, and the first in the land of Zion, was held at the house of brother Joshua Lewis, in Kaw Township, Jackson Co., Mo.

Sun. 7.—Polly Knight, wife of Joseph Knight, sen., died in Jackson County, Mo. This was the first death among the Saints in that land. On the same day Joseph the Prophet received a revelation about the Sabbath. (Doc. and Cov., Sec. 59.)

Mon. 8.—A revelation, directing some of the brethren to return to the East, was given through Joseph Smith, jun., in Jackson County. (Doc. and Cov., Sec. 60.)

Tues. 9.—Joseph the Prophet, in company with ten Elders, left Independence, Mo., in sixteen canoes, on their return to Kirtland, O.

Thurs. 11.—The returning Elders reached McIlwair's Bend (of the Missouri river) where Wm. W. Phelps "saw in open vision, by daylight, the Destroyer in his most horrible power ride upon the face of the water; others heard the noise, but saw not the vision."

Fri. 12.—A revelation was given through Joseph Smith, jun. at McIlwair's Bend, about the cursing of the waters in the last days. (Doc. and Cov., Sec. 61.)

Sat. 13.—Joseph Smith, jun., and company met several of the Elders on their way to the land of Zion. A revelation was given to them through Joseph.Smith, jun., on the bank of the Missouri river. (Doc. and Cov., Sec. 62.)

Sat. 27.—Joseph Smith, jun., Sidney Rigdon and Oliver Cowdery arrived at Kirtland, O., from their visit to Missouri.

Late in August, the Saints were commanded by revelation, through Joseph the Prophet, to purchase lands in Jackson County, Mo., and the future persecutions of the Church were foreshadowed. (Doc. and Cov., Sec. 63.)

September. *Sun. 11.*—The Saints were commanded by revelation through Joseph Smith, jun., to forgive one another; and the Lord, in speaking of the present time, said it was a day of sacrifice and a day of tithing for His people. (Doc. and Cov., Sec. 64.)

Mon. 12.—Joseph Smith, jun., removed with his family from Kirtland to Hiram, Portage Co., O., about thirty miles from Kirtland, where he continued the translation of the Bible.

Ezra Booth, formerly a Methodist minister, came out as an apostate.

A conference was held in Hiram, at which Wm. W. Phelps was instructed to purchase a press and type, at Cincinnati, O., for the purpose of establishing and publishing a monthly paper at Independence, Jackson Co., Mo., to be called the *Evening and Morning Star.*

October.—Early in this month the revelation on prayer was given. (Doc. and Cov., Sec. 65.)

Tues. 11.—A conference was held at Father John Johnson's house, in Hiram, at which the Elders were instructed about the ancient manner of holding meetings.

Tues. 25.—An important conference was held at Orange, Cuyahoga Co., O. Wm. E. McLellin and Samuel H. Smith were called by revelation through Joseph the Prophet to preach the gospel. (Doc. and Cov., Sec. 66.)

November. *Tues. 1.*—At a special conference held at Hiram, Oliver Cowdery was appointed to go to Independence, Jackson Co., Mo., with the revelations which Joseph the Prophet had received up to that time and get them printed. The revelation known as the Preface to the Doctrine and Covenants was given. (Doc. and Cov., Sec. 1.)

Some of the brethren having criticised the language used in some of the revelations, given through Joseph the Prophet, the Lord gave the wisest among the Elders permission to write a revelation like the least of those the Prophet had received, on certain conditions. (See Doc. and Cov., Sec. 67.)

Wm. E. McLellin, as the " wisest man in his own estimation," failed in his attempt to write a revelation. (See History of Joseph Smith.)

Thurs. 3.—The revelation called the Appendix was given through Joseph Smith, jun. (Doc. and Cov., Sec. 133.)

In a revelation given through Joseph Smith, jun., at Hiram, to Orson Hyde, Luke S. Johnson, Lyman E. Johnson and Wm. E. McLellin, the Lord explained the nature and authority of the Aaronic Priesthood, the duties of parents towards their children, etc. (Doc. and Cov., Sec. 68.)

John Whitmer was called by revelation to accompany Oliver Cowdery to Missouri, and to travel among the different branches of the Church in order to obtain informa-

tion in his capacity as Church Historian. (Doc. and Cov., Sec. 69.)

Joseph Smith jun., Martin Harris, Oliver Cowdery, John Whitmer, Sidney Rigdon and Wm. W. Phelps were appointed by revelation ' to be stewards over the revelations and commandments " which had been given. (Doc. and Cov., Sec. 70.)

Oliver Cowdery and John Whitmer started for Missouri with the revelations, after which Joseph the Prophet, assisted by Sidney Rigdon as scribe, resumed the translation of the Scriptures.

December. *Thurs. 1.*—Joseph Smith, jun., and Sidney Rigdon were called by revelation to go out and preach the gospel. (Doc. and Cov., Sec. 71.)

Sat. 3.—Joseph Smith, jun., and Sidney Rigdon went to Kirtland in obedience to revelation.

Sun. 4.—Joseph Smith, jun., and a number of other Elders and members of the Church assembled at Kirtland to learn their duties. Newel K. Whitney was called by revelation to act as Bishop in Kirtland, and the duties of that calling were made known. (Doc. and Cov., Sec. 72.)

Thurs. 8.—Geo. Teasdale was born in London, England.

1832.

Joseph the Prophet visited Missouri a second time. The *Evening and Morning Star*, the first organ of the Church, was commenced at Independence, Jackson Co., Mo., and many important revelations for the government of the Church and the instructions of the Saints were given.

January.—Joseph Smith, jun., preached in Shalersville, Ravenna and other places in Portage County, Ohio.

Tues. 10.—The Elders were commanded by revelation to continue their preaching till the next conference. (Doc. and Cov., Sec. 73.)

Later in the month, a revelation, explaining 1 Cor. 7:14, was given to Joseph Smith, jun., at Hiram. (Doc. and Cov., Sec. 74.)

Wed. 25.—A conference was held at Amherst, Loraine Co., O., at which a number of Elders were called by revelation on special missions and to preach the gospel in different parts of the country. (Doc. and Cov., Sec. 75.)

February. *Thurs. 16.*—The revelation known as the "Vision" was given at Hiram, in which the beautiful doctrine of the three glories was explained. In this vision Joseph Smith, jun., and Sidney Rigdon "beheld the glory of the Son on the right hand of the Father," and "saw the holy angels and they who are sanctified before His throne." And after the many testimonies which had been given of the Son, they, last of all, gave this testimony, that he lived, for they "saw him, even at the right hand of God," and "heard the voice bearing record that he is the Only Begotten of the Father." (Doc. and Cov , Sec. 76.)

March.—A key to John's Revelation was given to Joseph Smith, jun., at Hiram. (Doc. and Cov., Sec. 77.)

— The order of the Lord in relation to

the poor was revealed. (Doc. and Cov., Sec. 78.)

— Jared Carter, Stephen Burnett and Eden Smith were called by revelation to preach the gospel, and Frederick G. Williams to be a Counselor to Joseph Smith, jun. (Doc. and Cov., Sec. 79, 80 and 81.)

Sun. 25.—Joseph Smith, jun., and Sidney Rigdon were mobbed and nearly killed at Hiram.

April. *Sun. 1.*—Joseph Smith, jun., left Hiram, O., to make a second journey to Missouri, accompanied by Newel K. Whitney, Peter Whitmer, jun., and Jesse Gause to fulfil a revelation. (See Doc. and Cov., Sec. 78: 9.)

Sat. 14.—Brigham Young was baptized by Eleazer Miller at Mendon, Monroe Co., N. Y.

Tues. 24.—Joseph Smith, jun., and company arrived at Independence, Jackson Co., Mo.

Thurs. 26.—At a general council, held in Jackson County, Mo., Joseph Smith, jun., was acknowledged the president of the High Priesthood.

A revelation "showing the order given to Enoch and the Church in his day" was given. (Doc. and Cov., Sec. 82.)

Mon. 30.—A revelation concerning the rights of women and children in the Church was given through Joseph Smith, jun., at Independence, Mo. (Doc. and Cov., Sec. 83.)

May. *Tues. 1.*—At a council, held at Independence, it was decided to print 3,000 copies of the "Book of Commandments."

Sun 6.—Joseph Smith, jun., Sidney Rigdon and Newel K. Whitney left Independence, Mo., for Ohio. On the journey Bro. Whitney broke his leg and was miraculously healed. Joseph was poisoned by his enemies, but was restored in an instant.

June.—Joseph Smith, jun., arrived at Kirtland, O., and recommenced the translation of the Scriptures; thus he spent most of the summer.

— The first number of the *Evening and Morning Star* was issued at Independence, Mo. *The Upper Missouri Advertizer*, a newspaper, was commenced about the same time in connection with the *Star*.

September. *Sat. 22 and Sun. 23.*—An important revelation on Priesthood was given through Joseph Smith, jun., at Kirtland, O., as the Elders began to return from their missions to the Eastern States. (Doc. and Cov., Sec. 84.)

Tues. 25.—Marriner Wood Merrill was born in Sackville, County of Westmoreland, New Brunswick.

November. *Tues. 6.*—Joseph Smith returned home from a rapid journey to Albany, New York and Boston. On the day of his return his son Joseph was born.

Tues. 27. Joseph Smith, jun., wrote an encouraging letter and revelation to the Saints in Jackson County, Mo. (Doc. and Cov., Sec. 85.)

December. *Thurs. 6.*—A revelation, explaining the parable of the wheat and tares, was given through Joseph Smith, jun., at Kirtland. (Doc. and Cov., Sec. 86.)

Tues. 25.—Joseph Smith, jun., prophesied about the civil war between the North and the South which commenced about twenty-eight years afterwards. (Doc. and Cov., Sec. 87.)

Thurs. 27.—The revelation known as the

"Olive Leaf" was given through Joseph Smith, jun., at Kirtland, O. It contains grand and glorious principles and tells of important future events. The Saints were commanded to build a House of the Lord at Kirtland and to open a school for the benefit of the Elders to be known as the School of the Prophets. (Doc. and Cov., Sec. 88.)

Joseph Smith, jun., spent the winter of 1832-33 translating the Scriptures, attending the School of the Prophets and sitting in conferences.

1833.

During this year the First Presidency of the Church was organized and the translation of the Bible finished by the Prophet Joseph; the corner stones of the Kirtland Temple were laid, and the Saints driven by a mob from their homes in Jackson County, Mo. The Church printing office having been destroyed by the mob in Missouri, a new press and type were secured, and the publication of the *Evening and Morning Star* was recommenced at Kirtland, O.

January. *Tues. 22.*—Joseph Smith, jun., Sidney Rigdon, Frederick G. Williams, Newel K. Whitney, Hyrum Smith, Zebedee Coltrin, Joseph Smith, sen., Samuel H. Smith, John Murdock, Lyman E. Johnson, Orson Hyde, Ezra Thayer, Levi W. Hancock and William Smith assembled in conference at Kirtland, O. On this occasion the Prophet Joseph, Zebedee Coltrin and Wm. Smith spoke in tongues, "after which the Lord poured out his spirit in a miraculous manner, until all the Elders and several members, both male and female, spoke in tongues." Praises were sung to God and the Lamb, and speaking and praying in tongues occupied the conference until a late hour at night. (See History of Joseph Smith.)

Wed. 23.—The conference was continued at Kirtland. "After much speaking, singing, praying and praising God, all in tongues," the brethren "proceeded to the washing of feet, as commanded of the Lord," according to the practice recorded in John 13: 4-15. (See History of Joseph Smith.)

February. *Sat. 2.*—Joseph Smith, jun., completed the translation of the New Testament.

Wed. 27.—The revelation known as the "Word of Wisdom," was given through Joseph Smith, jun., at Kirtland. (Doc. and Cov., Sec. 89.)

March. *Fri. 8.*—A revelation concerning the keys of the kingdom and the oracles of God was given to Joseph Smith, jun., at Kirtland. (Doc. and Cov., Sec. 90.)

Sat. 9.—Joseph Smith, jun., was commanded by revelation not to translate the Apocrypha. (Doc. and Cov., Sec. 91.)

Fri. 15.—A revelation concerning Frederick G. Williams was given through Joseph Smith, jun., at Kirtland. (Doc. and Cov., Sec. 92.)

Mon. 18.—Sidney Rigdon and Frederick

G. Williams were appointed and set apart by President Joseph Smith to be his Counselors in the Presidency of the Church, according to the revelation given March 8th. On the same occasion "many of the brethren saw a heavenly vision of the Savior and concourses of angels." (See History of Joseph Smith.)

Sat. 23.—A committee was appointed to purchase lands for the Saints at Kirtland.

Tues. 26.—An important council was held by the High Priests in Jackson County, Mo., in which some misunderstanding in regard to the presiding authorities in that land was amicably settled.

April.—In this month the first mob gathered at Independence, Jackson Co., Mo., to consult upon a plan for the removal or immediate destruction of the Church in that county.

Sat. 6.—About eighty official and some unofficial members of the Church met at the ferry on Big Blue river, near the western boundary of Jackson County, Mo., and, for the first time, celebrated the birthday of the Church.

May. *Sat. 4.*—Hyrum Smith, Jared Carter and Reynolds Cahoon were appointed a committee to obtain subscriptions for building a house for the Priesthood at Kirtland.

Mon. 6.—A revelation on the pre-existence of man was given through Joseph Smith, jun., at Kirtland, and on the same date the Saints were commanded by revelation to build a House to the Lord at Kirtland. (Doc. and Cov., Sec. 93 and 94.)

June. *Sat. 1.*—The Lord gave further instructions to Joseph the Prophet about the Temple to be built at Kirtland. (Doc. and Cov., Sec. 95.)

Tues. 4.—A revelation, showing the order of the Kirtland Stake of Zion, was given to Joseph Smith, jun. (Doc. and Cov., Sec. 96.)

Thurs. 6.—A conference of High Priests held at Kirtland, O., instructed the committee for building the House of the Lord to proceed at once in obtaining material for its construction.

Sun. 23.—Doctor P. Hurlburt, afterwards connected with the spurious Spaulding story, was excommunicated from the Church for adultery.

Tues. 25.—An explanation of the plat of the city of Zion was sent to the brethren in Jackson County, Mo. (See History of Joseph Smith.)

July.—By this time about twelve hundred Saints, including children, had gathered to Jackson County, Mo.

Tues. 2.—Joseph the Prophet finished the translation of the Bible.

Sat. 20.—The printing office belonging to the Saints at Independence, Jackson County, Mo., was destroyed by a mob, who also tarred and feathered Bishop Edward Partridge and a Brother Allen.

—Orson Pratt preached in Patten, Canada. This is supposed to be the first discourse preached by a Latter-day Saint Elder in The Dominion.

Tues. 23.—The Saints at Independence, Mo., made a treaty with the mob and consented to leave Jackson County. Oliver Cowdery was dispatched as a special messenger to Kirtland, O., to consult with the First Presidency.

—The corner stones of the Lord's House at Kirtland, O., were laid.

August. *Fri. 2.*—In a revelation given through Joseph Smith, jun., at Kirtland, the Lord commanded that a house be built to Him in the land of Zion by the tithing of His people. (Doc. and Cov., Sec. 97.)

Tues. 6.—The Saints were commanded by revelation to observe the constitutional laws of the land, to forgive their enemies and cultivate a spirit of charity toward all men. Their rights of self-defense were also made clear. (Doc. and Cov., Sec. 98.)

A few days later John Murdock was called to the ministry by revelation. (Doc. and Cov., Sec. 99.)

September. Wed. 11.—It was decided in council to establish a printing press at Kirtland, and publish a paper to be called the *Latter-day Saints' Messenger and Advocate;* also that the *Evening and Morning Star,* formerly published in Jackson County, Mo., should be published at Kirtland.

—Bishop Edward Partridge was acknowledged as the head of the Church in Zion, and ten High Priests were appointed to watch over the ten branches of the Church there.

October.—Orson Hyde and John Gould arrived in Jackson County, Mo., as messengers from Kirtland; and the Church in Zion dispatched Wm. W. Phelps and Orson Hyde to Governor Daniel Dunklin at Jefferson City, with a petition from the Saints.

Sat. 5.—Joseph Smith, jun., in company with Elders Sidney Rigdon and Freeman Nickerson, left Kirtland on a visit to Canada.

Tues. 8.—Wm. W. Phelps and Orson Hyde presented to Governor Daniel Dunklin, of Missouri, the petition from the Saints in Jackson County.

Sat. 12.—In a revelation given at Perrysburg, N. Y., Joseph Smith, jun., and Sidney Rigdon were commanded to continue their missionary labors in the East. (Doc. and Cov., Sec. 100.)

Sat. 19.—In answer to the petition from the Saints in Jackson County, Gov. Dunklin, of Missouri wrote a letter to the leading men of the Church in that county, promising to enforce the laws.

Sat. 26.—Joseph Smith, jun., preached and baptized twelve persons at Mount Pleasant, Upper Canada.

Thurs. 31.—A mob attacked a branch of the Church, west of the Big Blue, in Jackson County, Mo., destroyed ten houses, and beat several of the brethren in a most brutal manner.

November. *Fri. 1.*—The Saints at Independence were attacked by a mob, and Gilbert & Whitney's store was partly destroyed, besides many private dwellings.

Sat. 2.—The mob attacked the Saints on the Big Blue, Jackson County, and beat David Bennett severely.

Mon. 4.—A skirmish took place between a company of Saints and a mob, several miles west of the Big Blue, in Jackson County. Andrew Barber, one of the Saints, was mortally wounded, two of the mob were killed, and several others wounded on both sides.

—Joseph Smith, jun., returned to Kirtland, O., from his mission to Canada.

Tues. 5.—Col. Thos. Pitcher, commanding the mob militia, in Jackson County, demanded that the Saints should give up their arms, which order was reluctantly complied with. During the following night and the next day the mob drove the Saints from their homes at the point of the bayonet. The exiles were thereby exposed to the most severe sufferings from cold and hunger.

Thurs. 7.—On this and the following day the exiled Saints were busy crossing the Missouri river from Jackson to Clay County, Mo., where the inhabitants received them with some degree of kindness. Others of the Saints found temporary shelter in Ray, Van Buren, Lafayette and other counties.

Wed. 13.—A grand meteoric shower or "falling of the stars" was witnessed throughout the land, which cheered the Saints and alarmed their enemies.

December.—Persecution raged against the Saints who had fled to Van Buren County, Mo.

—Oliver Cowdery and Bishop Newel K. Whitney arrived at Kirtland, O., with a new printing press.

Fri. 6.—The Saints in Clay County, Mo., sent another petition to Gov. Dunklin, praying for redress.

Mon. 16.—Joseph Smith, jun., received a revelation at Kirtland, O., in which the Lord said that he had allowed afflictions to come upon the Saints in Missouri because of their transgressions, but that he in His own due time would permit the pure in heart to return to their inheritances. This was illustrated by a parable. (Doc. and Cov., Sec. 101.)

Wed. 18.—The printing office at Kirtland, O., was dedicated and the publication of the *Evening and Morning Star* recommenced with Oliver Cowdery as editor.

—Joseph Smith, sen., was ordained Patriarch to the whole Church.

Thurs. 19.—Wm. Pratt and David W. Patten left Kirtland, O., for Missouri, bearing a message from the First Presidency to the exiled Saints.

Mon. 23.—Four aged families, living near Independence, Mo., whose penury and infirmities, incident to old age, forbade a speedy removal, were driven from their houses by a mob.

Fri. 27.—The printing press and materials, taken from the Saints at Independence, Mo., were disposed of by the mob to Davis & Kelley, who removed them to Clay County, and there commenced the publication of the *Missouri Enquirer.*

Tues. 31.—Wilford Woodruff was baptized at Richland, N. Y., by Zera Pulsipher.

1834.

The first High Council of the Church was organized at Kirtland, O. Zion's Camp made its famous march to Missouri, and a High Council was organized in Clay County, Mo., where most of the Saints, who had been expelled from Jackson County, had located.

January. *Wed. 1.*—A conference of the scattered Saints in Clay County, Mo., resolved to send Lyman Wight and Parley P. Pratt as special messengers to the First Presidency at Kirtland, O.

February. *Mon. 17.*—The first High Council of the Church was organized at Kirtland. The members were Joseph Smith, sen., John Smith, Joseph Coe, John Johnson, Martin Harris, John S. Carter, Jared Carter, Oliver Cowdery, Samuel H. Smith, Orson Hyde, Sylvester Smith and Luke S. Johnson. Joseph Smith, jun., Sidney Rigdon and Frederick G. Williams were acknowledged as presidents by the voice of the council. (Doc. and Cov., Sec. 102.)

Wed. 19.—The first case brought before the High Council was tried at Kirtland.

Thurs. 20.—Lyman Leonard, who had returned from Van Buren County, Mo., and Joseph Summer and Barnet Cole were severely beaten with clubs by a mob in Jackson County, Mo.

Mon. 24.—A revelation concerning the redemption of Zion was given through Joseph Smith, jun., at Kirtland, O. (Doc. and Cov., Sec. 103.)

Wed. 26.—Joseph Smith, jun., commenced to obtain volunteers for the redemption of Zion, in obedience to the revelation given on the 24th.

March. *Fri. 28.*—Joseph Smith, jun., returned to Kirtland from his trip to the State of New York, whither he went to get volunteers for the expedition to Missouri.

April. *Wed. 9.*—Dr. P. Hurlburt, the apostate, who had threatened the life of Joseph the Prophet, was put under $300 bonds in Chardon, Ohio.

Thurs. 10.—The United Order at Kirtland was dissolved.

—The Saints, who had been expelled from Jackson County, Mo., wrote a petition to the President of the United States, asking for redress.

Wed. 23.—A revelation was given through Joseph Smith, jun., concerning the order of Enoch. (Doc. & Cov., Sec. 104.)

Thurs. 24.—On this and the following six days the mob burned about one hundred and fifty houses belonging to the Saints in Jackson County, Mo.

May. *Thurs. 1.*—Over twenty men with four baggage wagons left Kirtland, O., for Missouri and traveled to New Portage, about fifty miles distant, where they waited for the rest of the company from Kirtland.

Sat. 3.—At a conference of Elders, held at Kirtland, the Church was first named "The Church of Jesus Christ of Latter-day Saints."

Mon. 5.—Joseph Smith, jun., left Kirtland with the remainder of the company, which was being organized for the relief of the suffering Saints in Missouri.

Wed. 7.—The Prophet's company of volunteers, known in the history of the Church as Zion's Camp, was partly organized, consisting of over one hundred and fifty men with twenty baggage wagons.

Thurs. 8.—The organization of Zion's Camp was completed, and it traveled twelve miles.

June. *Wed. 4.*—On this and the following day Zion's Camp crossed the Mississippi river into Missouri. Sylvester Smith rebelled against the order of the company.

Sun.8.—Zion's Camp was strengthened by a company of volunteers led by Hyrum Smith and Lyman Wight. It then numbered two hundred and five men and twenty-five baggage wagons.

Mon. 16.—A large meeting of the citizens of Clay County, Mo., held at the Liberty court house, failed to adjust the difficulties between the Saints and the Jackson County people. From the meeting Samuel C. Owens, James Campbell and about thirteen other mob-leaders started for Jackson County to raise a mob, in which, however, they failed, as Mr. Campbell and six others were drowned in attempting to cross the Missouri River.

Thurs. 19.—Notwithstanding the threats of enemies, Zion's Camp passed through Richmond, Mo., and camped at night between two branches of Fishing river. A mob, numbering over three hundred men, who had arranged to concentrate that night to attack them, were prevented from crossing the river by a terrible storm.

Sun. 22.—An important revelation was given to Joseph Smith, jun., on Fishing river, in which the Lord told his Saints that the time for the redemption of Zion had not yet come. (Doc. &. Cov., Sec. 105.)

Mon. 23.—Zion's Camp arrived at a point near Liberty, Clay County, Mo.

Tues. 24.—The cholera, which during several preceding days had attacked some of the brethren, broke out in its most terrible form in Zion's Camp. It continued its ravages about four days; sixty-eight of the Saints were attacked and thirteen died, among whom was A. Sidney Gilbert, a prominent man in the Church; he expired on the 26th.

July, Tues. 1.—In company with a few friends, Joseph Smith, jun., visited Jackson County, Mo., secretly.

Thurs. 3.—The High Priests of Zion assembled in Clay County, Mo., and organized a High Council with David Whitmer as president and Wm. W. Phelps and John Whitmer as counselors. The members of the council were: Christian Whitmer, Newel Knight, Lyman Wight, Calvin Bebee, Wm. E. McLellin, Solomon Hancock, Thos. B. Marsh, Simeon Carter, Parley P. Pratt, Orson Pratt, John Murdock and Levi Jackman.

Wed. 9.—Joseph Smith, jun., started on his return journey to Kirtland, where he arrived in the latter part of the month.

October—The first number of the *Latter-day Saints' Messenger and Advocate* was published at Kirtland, O., taking the place of the *Evening and Morning Star*, suspended.

Thurs. 16.—Joseph Smith, jun., and other Elders left Kirtland to visit the Saints in Michigan, from which trip they returned in the latter part of the month.

November. Tues. 25.—Warren A. Cowdery was called by revelation to preside over the Saints at Freedom, N. Y., and the regions round about. (Doc. and Cov., Sec. 106.)

Sat. 29.—Joseph Smith, jun., and Oliver Cowdery covenanted with the Lord to pay their tithing.

1835.

The Council of Twelve Apostles and the First Quorum of Seventy were organized at Kirtland, O. The Book of Doctrine and Covenants was accepted by the Church, and Joseph Smith, jun., obtained some Egyptian rolls of papyrus containing the writings of Abraham, etc.

February.—The *Northern Times*, a weekly newspaper supporting democracy, was commenced by the Saints at Kirtland, O.

Sat. 14.—At a special meeting held in Kirtland twelve Apostles were chosen by the Three Witnesses to the Book of Mormon according to revelation (Doc. and Cov., Sec. 18: 37), namely: Thos. B. Marsh, David W. Patten, Brigham Young, Heber C. Kimball, Orson Hyde, Wm. E. McLellin, Parley P. Pratt, Luke S. Johnson, Wm. Smith, Orson Pratt, John F. Boynton and Lyman E. Johnson. Brigham Young and Heber C. Kimball were ordained and blessed the same day.

Sun. 15.—Orson Hyde, David W. Patten, Luke S. Johnson, Wm. E. McLellin, John F. Boynton and Wm. Smith were ordained Apostles.

Sat. 21.—Parley P. Pratt was ordained to the Apostleship. Thos. B. Marsh and Orson Pratt, who were absent on missions, were not ordained until their return in April.

Sat. 28.—The organization of the First Quorum of Seventy was commenced at Kirtland.

March. Sat. 28.—An important revelation concerning the order of the Priesthood was given to Joseph Smith, jun., at Kirtland. (Doc. and Cov., Sec. 107.)

May. Sat. 2.—Elders Brigham Young, John P. Greene and Amos Orton were appointed to preach the gospel to the Lamanites.

Mon. 4.—The Twelve left Kirtland on their first mission as Apostles.

July. Fri. 3.—Michael H. Chandler arrived at Kirtland to exhibit four Egyptian mummies and some rolls of papyrus, covered with hieroglyphic figures and devices. They were afterwards purchased by some of the Saints, and Joseph the Prophet translated some of the characters on the rolls. One was found to contain the writings of Abraham, subsequently published in the Pearl of Great Price; another the writings of Joseph in Egypt.

August. Mon. 17.—At a general assembly of the Church, held at Kirtland, the Book of Doctrine and Covenants was approved, and thus became a law of faith and practice to the Church.

September. Mon. 14.— Oliver Cowdery was appointed to act as Church Recorder, and Emma Smith to make a selection of sacred hymns, according to revelation. (Doc and Cov., 25: 11.)

October. Sun. 25.—The Twelve returned to Kirtland from their mission to the East.

Thurs. 29. — Joseph Smith, jun., was abused by his brother William in a council meeting, held at Kirtland.

November, *Fri. 27.*—Christian Whitmer, one of the Eight Witnesses to the Book of Mormon, died in Clay County, Missouri.

December. *Wed. 16.*—Wm. Smith became enraged in a debating school, held at Kirtland, and used violence upon the person of his brother Joseph Smith, jun., and, others.

Sat. 26.—Joseph Smith, jun., with other Elders, commenced studying the Hebrew language, having previously commenced reading Greek. Mr. Seixas, a competent professor of languages, was subsequently employed as teacher.

—A revelation, concerning Lyman Sherman, was given through Joseph Smith, jun., at Kirtland. (Doc. and Cov. Sec. 108.)

1836.

The Kirtland Temple was dedicated, and the Savior, Moses, Elias and Elijah the Prophet appeared to the Elders in that building and committed the keys of their respective dispensations to the Prophet Joseph Smith. The Saints who had resided temporarily in Clay County, Mo., removed to another location on Shoal Creek, which was organized into Caldwell County.

January. *Fri. 1.*—Wm. Smith received forgiveness of his brother Joseph, and a general family reconciliation took place in the house of the latter, at Kirtland.

Wed. 6.—At a council meeting, held at Kirtland, the High Council of Zion (Missouri) was reorganized.

Thurs. 7.—A sumptuous feast, to which the lame, the halt and the blind were invited, was held in Bishop Newel K. Whitney's house, at Kirtland.

Sat. 16.—In a council of the Twelve Apostles, held at Kirtland, President Joseph Smith said: "The Twelve are not subject to any other than the First Presidency. * * * Where I am not, there is no First Presidency over the Twelve." (See History of Joseph Smith.)

Sun. 17.—Joseph the Prophet organized the several councils of the Priesthood at Kirtland, on which occasion the Lord poured out His Spirit in a great measure upon the brethren, who confessed their faults to each other; the congregation was overwhelmed in tears and the spirit of tongues came upon them "like the rushing of a mighty wind." (See History of Joseph Smith.)

Thurs. 21. — The Presidency of the Church, and the councils of Kirtland and Zion, met in the evening in the Lord's House, at Kirtland, and attended to the ordinance of anointing with oil and blessing each other. The visions of heaven were opened, angels administered to them, and the house was filled with the glory of God. Joseph the Prophet "beheld the celestial kingdom of God and the glory thereof," the "transcendent beauty of the gate through which the heirs of that kingdom will enter, the throne of God whereon was seated the Father and Son," and the beautiful streets of the kingdom. He also

saw Fathers Adam and Abraham. On seeing his brother Alvin, who died before the Church was organized, the Prophet marvelled, but the voice of the Lord told him that all who had died without a knowledge of the gospel, who would have received it if they had been permitted to tarry, should be heirs of the celestial kingdom of God. (See History of Joseph Smith.)

Fri. 22.—The Twelve Apostles, the presidency of the Seventy and others were blessed and anointed in the Lord's House, at Kirtland.

Thurs. 28. — The leading authorities of the Church administered in the Lord's House at Kirtland, on which occasion angels again appeared to the brethren, and other great manifestations of the power of God were witnessed. (See History of Joseph Smith.)

February. *Sun. 7.*—The organization of the second quorum of Seventy was commenced at Kirtland.

Mon. 22.—The sisters at Kirtland met in the Lord's House to commence their work of making the vail for that building.

March. *Sun. 27.*—The Lord's House, at Kirtland, afterwards known as the Kirtland Temple, was dedicated. It is a rock building, 80 feet long and 60 feet wide the walls are 50 feet and the tower 110 feet high. (For dedicatory prayer, see Doc. and Cov., Sec. 109.)

Tues. 29.—On this and the following day the ordinance of the washing of feet was attended to in the Kirtland Temple.

April. *Sun. 3.*—Joseph Smith, jun., and Oliver Cowdery saw and heard the Savior in the Kirtland Temple. Moses also appeared before them and committed unto them " the keys of the gathering of Israel from the four parts of the earth, and the leading of the Ten Tribes from the land of the north." Then Elias appeared and committed the dispensation of the gospel of Abraham, and finally Elijah the Prophet " stood before them " and committed to them the keys of turning " the hearts of the fathers to the children, and the children to the fathers." (See History of Joseph Smith and Doc. and Cov., Sec. 110.)

Mon 4.—The Elders began to spread abroad from Kirtland into all parts of the land, preaching the gospel.

May. *Tues. 17.*—Mary Smith, aged 93 years old, and grandmother of Joseph the Prophet, arrived at Kirtland from the East.

June.—Warren Parrish and other Elders were mobbed and arrested in Tennessee for preaching the gospel, and subsequently compelled to leave the country.

Wed. 29.—A large meeting of citizens held at Liberty, Clay Co., Mo., passed resolutions to expel the Saints from Clay County.

July. *Fri. 1.*—In a large meeting of Elders, held in Clay County, Mo., it was agreed that the Saints should leave the county, agreeably to the request of the older settlers.

Mon. 25.—Joseph Smith, jun., left Kirtland for a trip to the Eastern States.

August.—Joseph Smith, jun., arrived at Salem, Mass., where he, on August 6th, received a revelation, in which the Lord said He had many people in that city. (Doc. and Cov., Sec. 111.)

September.—Joseph Smith returned to Kirtland from his trip to the East.

—The Saints in Missouri began to remove from Clay County to their newly selected location on Shoal Creek (later known as Far West), in the territory attached to Ray County. That part of the State of Missouri was at that time almost uninhabited, but in the following December it was organized under the name of Caldwell County.

Thurs. 22.—Peter Whitmer, jun., one of the Eight Witnesses to the Book of Mormon, died near Liberty, Clay County, Mo.

November. *Wed. 2.*—Preparations were made for organizing a banking institution at Kirtland, O., to be called the "Kirtland Safety Society."

December. *Sun. 18.*—Brigham Young, jun., was born at Kirtland.

Sat. 31.—Dr. Willard Richards was baptized at Kirtland, by Brigham Young.

1837.

Far West, Caldwell Co. Mo., was surveyed, and the first foreign mission of the Church called and sent to England, where a successful opening was made. A great apostacy took place in the Church, both in Kirtland, O., and in Missouri.

April. *Thur. 6.*—An important Priesthood meeting was held in the Kirtland Temple, in which new presidents were ordained to preside over the Seventies, as some of the former presidents were High Priests.

April. *Fri. 7.*—The city plat of Far West, Caldwell County, Mo., having been surveyed, the sale of town lots was left to Wm. W. Phelps, John Whitmer and Edward Partridge. Jacob Whitmer, Elisha H. Groves and Geo. M. Hinkle were appointed a building committee for the erection of a house of the Lord at Far West.

May—A spirit of apostacy and speculation, affecting every quorum of the Church, more or less, became very prevalent at Kirtland.

June.—Early in this month Apostles Heber C. Kimball and Orson Hyde were set apart by the First Presidency of the Church to go on a mission to England. This was the first foreign mission of the Church. A few days later Willard Richards was called to accompany them.

Tues. 13.—Apostles Heber C. Kimball and Orson Hyde and Elders Willard Richards and Joseph Fielding left Kirtland, O., on their missions to England.

July. *Sat. 1.*—Apostles Heber C. Kimball and Orson Hyde and Elders Willard Richards and Joseph Fielding, accompanied by three brethren from Canada, namely, John Goodson, Isaac Russell and John Snider, sailed from New York on the ship *Garrick*. They arrived in Liverpool, England, on the 20th.

July. *Mon. 3.*—Ground was broken at Far West, Mo., for the foundation of a Temple, which, however, was not built, on account of persecutions.

Sun. 23.—A revelation concerning the Twelve Apostles was given through Joseph

the Prophet, at Kirtland. (Doc. & Cov. Sec. 112.)

—The gospel was first preached by Latter-day Saint Elders in England, in the church of the Rev. James Fielding, at Preston.

Thur. 27.—Joseph, the Prophet, was persecuted with a vexatious lawsuit at Painesville, Ohio.

Sun. 30.—Nine persons were baptized in the river Ribble, at Preston, England, as the first converts to the fulness of the gospel in England. Geo. D. Watt was the first person baptized.

August.—In the latter part of this month Joseph Smith, jun., returned to Kirtland, O, from a mission to Canada, on which he had started July 27th.

September. *Sun. 3.*—At a conference, held at Kirtland, Oliver Cowdery, Joseph Smith, sen., Hyrum Smith and John Smith were appointed assistant counselors to the First Presidency. Luke S. Johnson, Lyman E. Johnson and John F. Boynton, three of the Twelve Apostles, were disfellowshipped.

Sun. 10.—Luke S. Johnson, Lyman E. Johnson and John F. Boynton made confessions and were received back into fellowship.

Sun. 17.—Geo. W. Robinson was elected General Church Recorder, in place of Oliver Cowdery, who had removed to Missouri.

Wed. 27.—Joseph Smith, jun., and Sidney Rigdon left Kirtland, O., to establish other places of gathering for the Saints, and to visit with the Saints in Missouri, where they arrived in the latter part of October.

About this time the "Voice of Warning" was published in New York City by Parley P. Pratt.

October.—The first number of the *Elders' Journal*, edited by Joseph Smith, jun., and published at Kirtland, O., bears date of this month. It was published instead of the *Messenger and Advocate*, which had been discontinued.

Fri. 13. — Jerusha F. Smith, Hyrum Smith's wife, died at Kirtland.

November. *Tues. 7.* — An important conference was held at Far West, Mo., Joseph Smith, jun., having arrived from Kirtland. Frederick G. Williams was rejected as a counselor to Pres. Joseph Smith, and Hyrum Smith appointed in his stead. David Whitmer, John Whitmer and Wm. W. Phelps were sustained as the presidency at Far West, and a High Council was organized consisting of John Murdock, Solomon Hancock, Elias Higbee, Calvin Bebee, John M. Hinkle, Thos. Grover, Simeon Carter, Lyman Wight, Newel Knight, Geo. M. Hinkle, Levi Jackman and Elisha H. Groves.

Fri. 10.—At a general meeting held at Far West it was voted that the town of Far West "be enlarged so as to contain two square miles."

December. — The printing office at Kirtland was destroyed by fire, and the publication of the *Elders' Journal* ceased.

—Joseph Smith, jun. arrived at Kirtland O., from Missouri. During his absence a number of prominent men, including Warren Parrish, John F. Boynton, Luke S. Johnson and Joseph Coe, had united together for the overthrow of the Church at Kirtland.

Fri. 22.—Apostle Brigham Young left Kirtland on account of the fury of the mob, who threatened to kill him because he would proclaim publicly and privately that he knew by the Holy Ghost that Joseph Smith, jun., was a Prophet of the Most High God.

Mon. 25.—The first general conference by Latter-day Saints in England was held in the "Cock Pit," at Preston. The Church in England numbered already about one thousand members. At this conference the Word of Wisdom was first publicly taught in England.

Apostacy, persecution, confusion and mobocracy reigned in Kirtland, O., at the close of the year.

1838.

Joseph Smith, jun., and most of the faithful Saints left Kirtland, O., on account of apostasy and persecution, and removed to Missouri. Adam-ondi-Ahman, in Daviess County, Mo., was surveyed, and organized into a Stake of Zion; the revelation on tithing was given; persecutions were renewed against the Saints in Missouri, and DeWitt, Adam-ondi-Ahman and Far West were taken and sacked by the mob; nearly a score of Saints were massacred at Haun's Mill, Joseph the Prophet and other Elders imprisoned, and all the Saints ordered out of Missouri, under pain of death by the exterminating order of Gov. Lilburn W. Boggs.

January. *Fri. 12.*—Joseph Smith, jun., and Sidney Rigdon left Kirtland, O., on horseback to escape mob violence. They traveled toward Missouri.

February. *Mon. 5.*—In a general assembly of Saints at Far West, Mo., David Whitmer, John Whitmer and Wm. W. Phelps were rejected as the presidency of the Church in Missouri, because of transgression.

Sat. 10.—Thomas B. Marsh and David W. Patten were appointed presidents *pro tem.* of the Church in Missouri, until the arrival of Joseph Smith, jun., or Sidney Rigdon from Kirtland.

March.—Answers to certain questions on Scripture, principally the 11th chapter of Isaiah, were given by revelation through Joseph Smith, jun. (Doc. and Cov., Sec. 113.)

Sat. 10.—Wm. W. Phelps and John Whitmer were excommunicated from the Church by the High Council at Far West, Mo. Some time afterwards Wm. W. Phelps was received back into the Church by baptism.

Wed. 14.—Joseph the Prophet arrived at Far West, Mo., with his family, accompanied by Apostle Brigham Young and others.

April. *Fri. 6.*—The Saints in Missouri met at Far West to celebrate the anniversary of the organization of the Church and

transact business. John Corrill and Elias Higbee were appointed historians and Geo. W. Robinson General Church Recorder and clerk to the First Presidency. Thomas B. Marsh was sustained as president *pro tem.* in Missouri, with Brigham Young and David W. Patten as assistant presidents.

Sat. 7.—On this and the following day, the Church held its first quarterly conference at Far West.

John Whitmer refused to give up the records of the Church in his possession to the newly appointed Church clerk and recorder.

Thurs. 12.—Oliver Cowdery was excommunicated from the Church by the High Council, at Far West, Mo. The following day David Whitmer and Lyman E. Johnson were cut off.

Tues. 17.—Apostle David W. Patten was called by revelation through Joseph the Prophet, at Far West, Mo., to "make a disposition of his merchandise," and prepare for a mission. (Doc. and Cov., Sec. 114.)

Fri. 20.—Apostles Heber C. Kimball and Orson Hyde sailed from Liverpool, England, for America on the ship *Garrick*. They arrived in New York May 12th, and at Kirtland, O., May 22nd.

Thurs. 26.—A revelation was given through Joseph Smith, jun., at Far West, Mo., concerning the building up of that place and the Lord's House. (Doc. and Cov., Sec. 115.)

May. *Fri. 11.*—Wm. E. McLellin was excommunicated from the Church, at Far West.

Sat. 19.—Joseph Smith, jun., Sidney Rigdon and others visited a place on the north side of Grand river (about twenty-five miles north of Far West) called by the Saints Spring Hill, which by revelation was named Adam-ondi-Ahman, because "it is the place where Adam shall come to visit his people or the Ancient of Days shall sit, as spoken of by the Prophet Daniel." (Dan. 7: 9—14; Doc. and Cov., Sec. 116.)

June. *Thurs. 28.*—A Stake of Zion called Adam-ondi-Ahman was organized in Daviess County, Mo., with John Smith as president and Reynolds Cahoon and Lyman Wight as his counselors. A High Council was also organized with John Lemon, Daniel Stanton, Mayhew Hillman, Daniel Carter, Isaac Perry, Henry Harrison Sagers, Allanson Brown, Thomas Gordon, Lorenzo D. Barnes, George A. Smith, Harvey Olmstead and Ezra Thayer as members.

July.—The third number of the *Elders' Journal* was published at Far West, Mo. The first two numbers had been published at Kirtland, O.

Wed. 4.—The corner stones of the House of the Lord, at Far West, Mo., were laid, agreeable to a commandment of the Lord, given April 26th, 1838.

Fri. 6.—Five hundred and fifteen Saints left Kirtland, O., for Missouri, under the direction of the Seventies.

Sun. 8.—Wm. Marks, Newel K. Whitney and Oliver Granger were commanded by revelation to leave Kirtland, O., and remove to Missouri. (Doc. and Cov.,Sec. 117.)

—John Taylor, John E. Page, Wilford

Woodruff and Willard Richards were called by revelation to the Apostleship, "to fill the places of those who had fallen." (Doc. and Cov., Sec. 118.)

—In answer to the question, "O Lord, show unto thy servants how much thou requirest of the properties of the people for a tithing," the Lord gave a revelation on tithing. (Doc. and Cov., Sec. 119.)

Wed. 18.—A revelation making known the disposition of property tithing was given through Joseph the Prophet, at Far West. (Doc. & Cov., Sec. 120.)

August.—During this month the Saints at De Witt, Carroll Co., Mo., were threatened by a mob.

Mon. 6.—The Missourians opposed the voting of the Saints at Gallatin, Daviess County, and a skirmish occurred, in which about twelve brethren gained a victory over about one hundred and fifty mobbers. Some of the brethren took their families into the hazel brush and guarded them during the night, through fear of the mob.

Wed. 8.—Joseph Smith, jun., and others called on Adam Black, a justice of the peace in Daviess County, Mo., and had a friendly conversation with him about the trouble in Gallatin.

Thurs.30.—Gov.Lilburn W.Boggs,of Missouri, ordered out a part of the State militia to quell the civil disturbances in Caldwell, Daviess and Carroll Counties. The whole upper Missouri was in an uproar and state of confusion about the "Mormons."

September. *Mon 3.*—A great number of mobbers had collected in Daviess County, Mo., with headquarters at Millport.

Tues 4.—Joseph Smith, jun., and Sidney Rigdon commenced to study law, under the instructions of Generals David R. Atchison and Alexander W. Doniphan.

Fri. 7.—Joseph Smith, jun., and Lyman Wight appeared before Judge Austin A. King, in Daviess County, they and others having been falsely accused of threatening Adam Black's life on their visit to his house, Aug. 8th.

Sun. 9.—Captain William Allred, of Far West, frustrated the plans of the mob, by arresting three men who were bringing guns and ammunition from Richmond, Ray Co., Mo., to the mobbers in Daviess County.

October. *Mon. 1.*—As the militia, under Generals Atchison, Doniphan and Parks had succeeded in restoring temporary peace in Daviess County, the mobbers went to De Witt, Carroll Co., and attacked the Saints there.

Thurs. 4.—The Kirtland Camp arrived at its destination, Adam-ondi-Ahman.

Sat. 6.—Joseph the Prophet arrived at De Witt, Carroll Co.,Mo., whither he went to assist the brethren who were trying to defend themselves against an overwhelming mob force.

Thurs. 11.—After several days' bombardment, the mob succeeded in driving the Saints from De Witt. During the siege some of them had perished from starvation, and their sufferings had been very great.

Fri. 12.—The exiles from De Witt arrived at Far West.

Mon. 15.—The brethren at Far West organized for self-defense.

The mobbers renewed their depredations in Daviess County, by burning the houses of the Saints, driving off their stock, etc. Col. Lyman Wight, agreeable to an order from General Parks, organized a company in self-defense. This frightened the mobbers, who fled from the neighborhood, after burning some of their own houses, of which they wickely accused the Saints.

Tues. 23.—The Saints were fleeing from the smaller settlements into Far West for safety, the mobs increasing in numbers all around. The most wicked lies were circulated about the Saints, and their movements in self-defense were by the State authorities construed into treason.

Thurs. 25.—A battle was fought between a mob and about seventy-five brethren on Crooked river, Ray County, Mo., in which Gideon Carter was killed and eleven others wounded, among these were Apostle David W. Patten and Patterson O'Banion who died soon afterwards.

Sat. 27.—Apostle David W. Patten was buried at Far West.

—Gov. Lilburn W. Boggs issued his famous exterminating order, which gave the Saints the choice between banishment from Missouri and death.

About this time Sampson Avard, an apostate, secretly organized a company called Danites. The Church used all proper means to expose and counteract his schemes.

Tues. 30.—A mob under the leadership of Col. Wm. O. Jennings attacked a little settlement of Saints at Haun's Mill, Caldwell Co., Mo., and killed and mortally wounded Thomas McBride, Levi N. Merrick, Elias Benner, Josiah Fuller, Benjamin Lewis, Alexander Campbell, Warren Smith, Geo. S. Richards, Wm. Napier, Austin Hammer, Simon Cox, Hiram Abbott, John York, John Lee, John Byers, Sardius Smith and Charles Merrick. Others were severely wounded, but recovered. Among these were Alma L. Smith, who was healed in a most miraculous manner, through prayers and faith.

—The mob-militia, about two thousand strong, under command of Samuel D. Lucas, arrived near Far West, and the citizens prepared for their own defense.

Wed. 31.—Joseph Smith, jun., Sidney Rigdon, Parley P. Pratt, Lyman Wight and Geo. W. Robinson were betrayed by Col. George M. Hinkle and made prisoners in the camp of the mob-militia.

November. *Thurs. 1.*—Hyrum Smith and Amasa M. Lyman were brought as prisoners into camp. A court martial was held, and the prisoners were sentenced to be shot the following morning; they were, however, saved through the interference of General Doniphan.

On demand of General Samuel D. Lucas the citizens of Far West were forced to give up their arms, after which the mob-militia pillaged the town, ravished women, and committed other acts of barbarity.

Fri. 2.—Joseph Smith, jun., and fellow-prisoners were taken to Far West under a strong guard and permitted to see their families, from whom they then were rudely torn and started under a strong guard, commanded by Generals Samuel D. Lucas and Robert Wilson, for Independence, Jackson Co., where they arrived on the 4th.

Sun. 4.—Gen. John B. Clark arrived at Far West with about two thousand troops, and the following day he made most of the brethren prisoners.

Tues. 6.—John B. Clark delivered an insulting speech to the brethren at Far West, in which he advised the Saints to scatter abroad and never again organize with Bishops, presidents, etc. Of the leaders of the Church, who had been imprisoned, he said their fate was fixed, their die cast, and their doom sealed, and that they would never be seen by their friends again.

The brethren were compelled to sign deeds of trust for paying the expense of the mob. About sixty men were retained as prisoners, and the remainder of the Saints ordered to leave the State, according to the exterminating order of Gov. Boggs.

Thurs. 8.—Gen. Wilson placed guards around Adam-ondi-Ahman, took all the men prisoners and put them under guard. A court of inquiry was organized, with Adam Black on the bench, which resulted in the acquittal of the prisoners.

Fri. 9.—Joseph Smith, jun., and fellow-prisoners arrived at Richmond, Ray County, Mo., where they were put in chains and much abused by their guards. On one occasion the Prophet Joseph rebuked the wicked guard with the power of God, and stopped the foul conversation with which the prisoners were being tantalized.

Sat. 10.—Gen. Wilson ordered every family to be out of Adam-ondi-Ahman in ten days, with permission to go to Caldwell County and tarry till spring, then to leave the State under pain of extermination.

Tues. 13.—Joseph Fielding Smith was born at Far West, Mo.

—A mock trial, which lasted sixteen days, was commenced at Richmond, and nearly sixty of the brethren were brought before Judge Austin A. King, charged with treason, murder, burglary, arson, robbery and larceny. Up to that date about thirty of the brethren had been killed and many wounded since the hostilities commenced the previous August.

Sat. 24.—Twenty-three of the Far West prisoners were discharged at Richmond, Mo., as nothing could be found against them.

Wed. 28.—The remaining prisoners in Richmond were released, or admitted to bail, except Joseph Smith, jun., Lyman Wight, Caleb Baldwin, Hyrum Smith, Alex. McRae and Sidney Rigdon, who were sent to jail in Liberty, Clay Co., to stand their trial for treason and murder, of which they were falsely accused; and Parley P. Pratt, Morris Phelps, Luman Gibbs, Darwin Chase and Norman Shearer were confined in the Richmond jail to stand their trial on a similar charge.

December. Wed. 19.—John Taylor and John E. Page were ordained Apostles, at Far West, Mo.

—A petition from the Saints in Caldwell County was presented to the Missouri legislature, causing much warm debate, but the petition was finally laid on the table, which meant that the legislature would do nothing for the suffering Saints.

Thurs. 27.—Anson Call was brutally whipped by a mob, near Elk Horn, Ray Co., Mo.

1839.

The Saints who were banished from Missouri escaped to Illinois; Joseph the Prophet and the other imprisoned brethren made their escape. After being kindly treated by the citizens of Quincy, Commerce, Hancock Co., Ill., was selected as a new gathering place for the Saints; the building of a city was commenced and a Stake of Zion organized. Most of the Apostles started on a mission to Great Britain.

January. Tues. 29.—The Elders met at Far West to complete measures for the removal of the poor from Missouri, and pledged themselves to assist each other until all were removed.

February. Thurs. 14.—Brigham Young, President of the Twelve, left Far West, Mo., for Illinois, on account of persecution.

Sat. 23.—Many of the fugitive Saints having arrived at Quincy, Adams Co., Ill., the citizens of that place met to adopt measures for their relief.

About this time Sidney Rigdon was released from prison in Liberty jail, Mo., on bail.

March. Sun. 17.—Thomas B. Marsh, formerly President of the Twelve, Wm. W. Phelps, Frederick G. Williams, George M. Hinkle and others were excommunicated from the Church at a conference held at Quincy, Ill.

Wed. 20.—Joseph Smith, jun., who was still imprisoned in Liberty jail, Mo., wrote an excellent epistle "to the Saints at Quincy, Ill., and scattered abroad," in which was embodied a most fervent prayer in behalf of the suffering Saints, and words of prophecy. (See Doc. and Cov., Sec. 121, and History of Joseph Smith.)

A few days later the Prophet Joseph continued his epistle and wrote among other beautiful gems that which constitutes Sections 122 and 123 of the Doctrine and Covenants.

April. Fri. 5.—A company of about fifty men in Daviess County, Mo., swore that they would never eat or drink until they had murdered Joseph the Prophet.

Sat. 6.—Joseph Smith, jun., and fellow-prisoners were started from Liberty jail, to Gallatin, Daviess County, Mo., where they arrived on the 8th, and were again subjected to a mock trial before a drunken court and jury.

Thurs. 11.—Ten mobbers made an unsuccessful attempt to kill Stephen Markham in Daviess County, Mo., because he had testified truthfully in the case of the prisoners.

Sun. 14.—The committee for the removal of the Saints from Missouri moved 36 families into Tenney's Grove, about twenty-five miles from Far West.

Mon. 15.—Joseph Smith, jun., and fellow-prisoners, started from Daviess towards Boone County, Mo., under a change of venue.

Tues. 16.—The guard being drunk, Joseph Smith, jun., and fellow-prisoners made their escape. After a severe journey they arrived at Quincy, Ill., on the 22nd.

Sat. 20.—The last of the Saints left Far West. Thus a whole community, numbering about fifteen thousand souls, were expelled from their homes on account of their religion.

Wed. 24.—Parley P. Pratt and fellow-prisoners were brought before the grand jury of Ray County, at Richmond. Darwin Chase and Norman Shearer were dismissed after having been imprisoned for six months.

Thurs.25.—Joseph Smith, jun., and others visited Iowa for the purpose of finding a location for the Church. Commerce, Hancock Co., Ill., was finally selected as a gathering place for the Saints.

Fri. 26.—Early in the morning a conference was held on the Temple site at Far West, Mo., in fulfilment of the revelation given July 8, 1838. Among those present were Apostles Brigham Young, Heber C. Kimball, Orson Pratt, John E. Page and John Taylor, who ordained Wilford Woodruff and George A. Smith Apostles, "to fill the places of those who had fallen." Alpheus Cutler, the master-workman of the Temple, then commenced laying its foundation, in accordance with revelation, by rolling up a large stone near the south-east corner. Isaac Russell, John Goodson, Luman Gibbs and twenty-eight others were excommunicated from the Church.

May. Wed. 1.—The first purchase of land for the Church at Commerce, Ill., was made by Joseph Smith, jun., and others of the committee. The purchase consisted of two farms bought respectively of Hugh White and Isaac Galland.

Fri. 3.—Six of the Apostles met Joseph the Prophet near Quincy, Ill., for the first time after his liberation from prison.

Sat. 4.—A two days' conference was commenced on the Presbyterian camp ground, near Quincy, Ill. The doings of the Twelve at Far West on April 26th were sanctioned. Elder Oliver Granger was appointed to go to Kirtland, O., to preside, and the Saints in the Eastern States were advised to gather to Kirtland and settle that place as a Stake of Zion. On the 5th it was decided to send Sidney Rigdon as a delegate to Washington, D. C., to lay the grievances of the Saints before the General Government.

Mon. 6.—At a conference, held at Quincy, Ill., Wm. Marks was appointed to preside at Commerce, and John P. Greene over the Saints in New York. A number of Seventies and High Priests were called to accompany the Apostles on their missions to Europe.

Thurs. 9. — Joseph Smith, jun., left Quincy with his family, and arrived the following day at Commerce.

Wed. 22. — Parley P. Pratt, Morris Phelps, Luman Gibbs and King Follett, having obtained a change of venue, left Richmond, Mo., handcuffed, for Columbia, Boone County, where they arrived on the 26th and were thrown into a filthy dungeon.

June.—The first house erected by the Saints in Commerce was raised by Theodore Turley.

Mon. 24. — The Church purchased the town of Nashville, in Lee County, Iowa Territory, and twenty thousand acres of land adjoining it. About the same time another tract of land lying west of Montrose, Iowa, opposite Nauvoo, was purchased.

July.—Much sickness prevailed among the Saints at Commerce, which at that time was a very unhealthful place, but many of them were miraculously healed by the power of God.

Tues. 2. — Joseph the Prophet advised that a town be built on the Iowa purchase, to be called Zarahemla.

Thurs. 4. — After more than seven months' imprisonment without conviction, Parley P. Pratt and Morris Phelps escaped from the Columbia jail, Boone County, Mo. They arrived in Quincy, Ill., after days of dreadful suffering from hunger and fatigue. King Follett, who also tried to escape, was retaken.

Mon. 22.—Elijah Fordham, Henry G. Sherwood, Benjamin Brown, Joseph B. Noble and many others, at Commerce, Ill., and Montrose, Iowa, were miraculously healed under the powerful administrations of the Prophet Joseph, assisted by other Elders.

August. Thurs. 8.—Apostles John Taylor and Wilford Woodruff left Commerce, Ill., on a mission to England.

Thurs. 29.—Apostles Parley P. Pratt and Orson Pratt and Elder Hiram Clark departed from Commerce on a mission to England.

September. Wed. 18.—Apostles Brigham Young and Heber C. Kimball started from Commerce on a mission to England, leaving their families sick and poverty-stricken.

Sat. 21.—Apostle Geo. A. Smith and Elders Reuben Hedlock and Theodore Turley left Commerce for England on a mission

October. Sat. 5.—At a general conference, held at Commerce, William Marks was appointed president of that Stake, Edward Partridge, Bishop of the upper Ward, and Vinson Knight, Bishop of the lower Ward. Geo. W. Harris, Samuel Bent, Henry G. Sherwood, David Fullmer, Alpheus Cutler, Wm. Huntington, Thomas Grover, Newel Knight, Chas. C. Rich, David Dort, Seymour Brunson and Lewis D. Wilson were chosen members of the High Council. John Smith was appointed to preside over the Saints on the other side of the Mississippi river, in Iowa Territory, with Alanson Ripley as Bishop. Asahel Smith, John M. Burk, Abraham O. Smoot, Richard Howard, Willard Snow, Erastus Snow, David Pettigrew, Elijah Fordham, Edward Fisher, Elias Smith, John Patten and Stephen Chase were chosen as members of the High Council.

Thurs. 17.—Apostle Heber C. Kimball was poisoned at Terre Haute, Indiana, but his life was saved by the administration of Apostle Brigham Young.

Sat. 19.—The High Council appointed for the Church in Iowa met for the first time, at Nashville, Iowa. Reynolds Cahoon and Lyman Wight were appointed counselors to John Smith.

Tues. 29.—Joseph Smith, jun., accompanied by Sidney Rigdon, Elias Higbee and O. Porter Rockwell left Commerce for Washington, D. C., to lay the grievances of the Saints before the President and Congress of the United States.

In the latter part of this month King Follett, the last of the Missouri prisoners, was tried and set free.

November.—The first number of the *Times and Seasons* was published at Commerce, Ill.

Sun. 3.—James Mulholland, Joseph Smith's clerk, died at Commerce.

Wed. 27.—Brigham Young rebuked the wind and waves on Lake Erie, and he was obeyed.

Thurs. 28.—Joseph Smith, jun., arrived at Washington, D. C.

December. *Thurs. 19.*—Apostles Wilford Woodruff and John Taylor and Elder Theodore Turley sailed from New York for England; they arrived at Liverpool Jan. 11, 1840.

Sat. 21.—Joseph Smith, jun., arrived at Philadelphia, Pa., (from Washington), where he remained until the 30th, preaching the gospel.

1840

Joseph the Prophet and other Elders visited Washington, D. C., to seek redress for the Saints from the Federal Government, but were unsuccessful. Commerce, Ill., was incorporated as the City of Nauvoo, and Stakes of Zion were organized in different parts of Illinois. The Apostles performed a great missionary work in England, whence also the first missionary was sent to Australia.

January. *Sun. 12.*—Francis Marion Lyman was born at Macomb, McDonough Co., Ill.

March.—Multitudes were baptized into the Church in the United States and England. Apostle Wilford Woodruff built up large branches in Herefordshire, England.

Wed. 4.—Joseph Smith, jun., arrived in Commerce, Ill., from Washington, D. C., after a fruitless endeavor to obtain redress for the wrongs suffered by the Saints in Missouri. He had presented to Congress claims against Missouri from 491 individuals for about $1,381,000. President Martin Van Buren, in answer to Joseph's appeal, said, "Your cause is just, but I can do nothing for you." The Committee on the Judiciary, to whom was referred the memorial of the Saints, reported adversely to the prayer of the petitioners.

Mon. 9.—Brigham Young, Heber C. Kimball, Parley P. Pratt, George A. Smith and Reuben Hedlock sailed from New York on the ship *Patrick Henry* for Liverpool, where they arrived April 6th.

April. *Mon. 6.*—A general conference of the Church was commenced at Nauvoo, Ill. It continued three days, On the first day Apostle Orson Hyde was called on a mission to Jerusalem and on the 8th Apostle John E. Page was appointed to accompany him. The conference also adopted a series

of resolutions, expressive of sorrow and disappointment at the action of the Committee of the Judiciary at Washington, D. C.

Tues. 14.—At a council of the Apostles held at Preston, England, Willard Richards was ordained one of the Twelve Apostles.

Wed. 15.—Apostle Orson Hyde left Commerce, Ill., on his mission to Jerusalem.

—At a conference held at Preston, England, where 34 branches and 1,686 members were represented, it was decided to publish a monthly periodical in the interest of the Church in England.

Tues. 21.—The Postmaster General at Washington, D. C., changed the name of the postoffice at Commerce, Hancock Co., Ill., to Nauvoo, and appointed George W. Robinson postmaster.

May. *Sat. 9.*—Elder Theodore Turley, who had been imprisoned in Stafford jail, England, at the instigation of a Methodist preacher, was released.

Wed. 27.—Bishop Edward Partridge died at Nauvoo, 46 years old. He lost his life in consequence of the Missouri persecutions.

—The first number of *The Latter-day Saints' Millennial Star* was published at Manchester, England; Apostle Parley P. Pratt, editor.

June. By this time the Saints had erected about two hundred and fifty houses in Nauvoo.

Sat. 6.—Forty-one Saints sailed from Liverpool, England, on the ship *Britannia*, for the United States, being the first Saints that gathered from a foreign land. John Moon was leader of the company.

Sun. 14.—The Bran Green and Gadfield Elm conference was organized by Apostle Wilford Woodruff in Worcestershire, England, consisting of twelve branches. This was the first conference organized in the British mission.

Sun. 21.—At a meeting held on Stanley Hill, Herefordshire, England, the Froome's Hill conference was organized by Apostle Wilford Woodruff, consisting of twenty branches.

July.—The first British edition of the Latter-day Saints' Hymn Book was published in England.

Tues. 7.—James Allred, Noah Rogers, Alanson Brown and Benjamin Boyce were kidnapped from Hancock County, Ill., by Missourians, and taken to Tully, Lewis Co., Mo., where they were imprisoned, whipped and ill-treated until nearly dead. Brown and Allred escaped a few days afterwards.

Sat. 11.—Apostle Geo. A. Smith ordained and set apart Wm. Barratt at Burslem, Staffordshire, England, for a mission to South Australia. He was the first missionary to that country.

Mon. 20.—John Moon's company of British emigrants arrived at New York.

Mon. 27.—Apostle John Taylor sailed from Liverpool for Ireland to open the door of the gospel in that country.

August.—Elder Wm. Donaldson, of the British army, sailed from England for the East Indies. He was the first member of the Church to visit that country.

Fri. 21.—Noah Rogers and Benjamin Boyce escaped from their unlawful imprisonment in Missouri, during which they had been put in irons and suffered much.

Mon. 31.—Apostle Heber C. Kimball baptized Henry Conner, a watchmaker, in London, England, as the first fruit of preaching the fulness of the gospel in that city.

September.—Apostle John Taylor and others first preached the gospel on the Isle of Man.

Mon. 8.—The ship *North America* sailed from Liverpool, England, with about two hundred Saints, under the presidency of Theodore Turley, bound for Nauvoo, Ill.

Sun. 14.—Joseph Smith, sen., Patriarch to the Church, died at Nauvoo.

Mon. 15.—Gov. Lilburn W. Boggs, of Missouri, made a demand on Gov. Thos. Carlin, of Illinois, for Joseph Smith, jun., Sidney Rigdon, Lyman Wight, Parley P. Pratt, Caleb Baldwin and Alanson Brown as fugitives from justice.

October. *Fri. 3.*—At a conference held at Nauvoo, Robert B. Thompson was appointed General Church Clerk, instead of Geo. W. Robinson. Almon W. Babbitt was appointed to preside over the Church at Kirtland, O., and a committee was appointed to organize new Stakes for the gathering of the Saints.

Wed. 22.—A Stake was organized by the committee at Lima, Hancock Co., Ill., with Isaac Morley as president and John Murdock and Walter Cox as his counselors.

Sat. 25.—A Stake was organized at Quincy, Adams Co., Ill., with Daniel Stanton, Stephen Jones and Ezra T. Benson as the presidency.

Mon. 27.—A Stake called Mount Hope was organized at the steam mills, Columbus, Adams Co., Ill., with the following brethren as the presidency: Abel Lamb, Sherman Gilbert and John Smith.

November. *Sat. 1.*—The committee organized a Stake called Geneva, in Morgan Co., Ill., with Wm. Bosley, Howard S. Smith and Samuel Fowler as the presidency.

December. *Wed. 16.*—The charter for the incorporation of Nauvoo, granted by the State legislature, was signed by Governor Thomas Carlin, but not to take effect until the first of February following.

1841.

During this year Nauvoo, Ill., began its career as an incorporated city; the Nauvoo Legion was organized, and the corner stones of the Nauvoo Temple were laid. The Twelve Apostles returned from their missions to England, and baptism for the dead was commenced in the Church.

January.—The first number of the *Gospel Reflector*, a semi-monthly periodical published in the interest of the Church, was issued in Philadelphia, Pa.; Benjamin Winchester, editor.

—The first British edition of the Book of Mormon was published in Manchester, England.

Tues. 19.—The Saints were commanded by revelation to build a Temple at Nauvoo, Ill., and also a " boarding house " for the

accommodation of strangers, which subsequently became known as the Nauvoo House. The general authorities of the Church and other officers were named in the revelation, which also contains important explanations on the order of the Priesthood. (Doc. and Cov., Sec. 124.)

Sun. 24.—Hyrum Smith succeeded his father, Joseph Smith, sen., as Patriarch to the Church, and Wm. Law was appointed a Counselor in the First Presidency, succeeding Hyrum Smith, in that capacity, according to revelation.

Sat. 30.—At a meeting held at Nauvoo, Ill., Joseph Smith was elected sole Trustee for the Church, to hold the office during life, his "successors to be the First Presidency" of the Church.

February. *Mon. 1.*—The first election took place for members of the city council of Nauvoo. John C. Bennett was elected mayor; Wm. Marks, Samuel H. Smith, Daniel H. Wells and Newel K. Whitney, aldermen; Joseph Smith, Hyrum Smith, Sidney Rigdon, Charles C. Rich, John F. Barnett, Wilson Law, Don Carlos Smith, John P. Greene and Vinson Knight, councilors.

Wed. 3.—The city council of Nauvoo elected Henry G. Sherwood, marshal; James Sloan, recorder; Robert B. Thompsen, treasurer; James Robinson, assessor; Austin Cowles, supervisor of streets.

Thurs. 4.—The Nauvoo Legion, originally consisting of six companies, was organized with Joseph Smith as lieutenant-general.

Sun. 7.—The ship *Sheffield* sailed from Liverpool, England with 235 Saints, under the leadership of Hiram Clark.

Sat. 13.—Apostle Orson Hyde sailed from New York for Liverpool, on his mission to Jerusalem.

Sun. 14.—The London (England) conference was organized with Lorenzo Snow as president.

Tues. 16.—The ship *Echo* sailed from Liverpool, England, with 109 Saints, under the direction of Daniel Browitt.

March.—The Saints were commanded by revelation to build a city in Iowa Territory, opposite Nauvoo, to be called Zarahemla. (Doc. and Cov.. Sec. 125.)

Mon. 1.—The city council divided the city of Nauvoo into four wards. An ordinance was passed, giving free toleration and equal privileges in the city to all religious sects and denominations.

Wed. 10.—Governor Thos. Carlin, of Illinois, commissioned Joseph Smith lieutenant-general of the Nauvoo Legion.

Wed. 17.—The ship *Uleste* sailed from Liverpool, England, with 54 Saints, under the direction of Thomas Smith and Wm. Moss, bound for America.

Mon. 29.—Charles C. Rich and Austin Cowles were chosen counselors to Wm. Marks, president of the Nauvoo Stake of Zion.

April. *Tues. 6.*—A general conference of the Church was commenced at Nauvoo, and the corner stones of the Nauvoo Temple were laid. The conference was continued till the 11th.

Thurs. 8.—Lyman Wight was chosen one of the Twelve Apostles, in place of David W. Patten, martyred in Missouri.

Wed. 21.—Apostles Brigham Young, Heber C. Kimball, Orson Pratt, Wilford Woodruff, John Taylor, Geo. A. Smith and Willard Richards sailed from Liverpool, England, on the ship *Rochester*, accompanied by 130 Saints. They arrived at New York May 20th.

May. *Sat. 22.*—At a conference held at Kirtland, O., Almon W. Babbitt was chosen president of the Kirtland Stake, with Lester Brooks and Zebedee Coltrin as counselors.

Mon. 24.—The First Presidency at Nauvoo called upon all scattered Saints to gather to Hancock County, Ill., and Lee County, Ia. All neighboring Stakes outside of these two counties were discontinued.

June. *Sat. 5.*—Joseph Smith was arrested on a requisition from the State of Missouri. He was tried on the 9th and liberated on the 10th on a writ of *habeas corpus*, at Monmouth, Warren Co., Ill.

Tues. 22.—Theodore Curtis, who had been under arrest in Gloucester, England, five days for preaching the gospel, was acquitted.

July. *Thurs. 1.*—Apostles Brigham Young, Heber C. Kimball and John Taylor arrived at Nauvoo from their missions to England.

Fri. 9.—By revelation, through Joseph the Prophet, Apostle Brigham Young was commanded to send the "word" abroad, and to take special care of his family. (Doc. and Cov., Sec. 126.)

Tues. 13.—Apostle Geo. A. Smith returned to Nauvoo from his mission to England.

Sun. 25.—Wm. Yokum lost his leg by amputation, as the result of a wound received in the massacre at Haun's Mill, Mo.

August. *Sat. 7.*—Don Carlos Smith, the youngest brother of the Prophet, died at Nauvoo.

Thurs. 12.—Joseph Smith preached to about one hundred Sac and Fox Indians (among whom were the chiefs Keokuk, Kiskuhosh and Appenoose), who had come to visit him at Nauvoo.

Mon. 16.—Apostle Willard Richards arrived at Nauvoo from his mission to England.

Wed. 25.—Oliver Granger died at Kirtland, O.

Fri. 27.—Robert B. Thompson, Joseph Smith's scribe, died at Nauvoo.

September. *Tues. 21.*—The ship *Tyrean* sailed from Liverpool for New Orleans with 204 Saints, under the direction of Joseph Fielding, bound for Nauvoo.

Wed. 22.—A company of brethren left Nauvoo for the Pineries, Wisconsin, about five hundred miles north, to procure lumber for the Nauvoo Temple.

October. *Sat. 2.*—An important general conference was commenced in the Grove at Nauvoo. It was continued till the 4th. Joseph Smith declared, as the will of the Lord, that the Church should not hold another general conference until the Saints could meet in the Temple. James Sloan was elected Church clerk, instead of Robert B. Thompson deceased.

Wed. 6.—Apostle Wilford Woodruff ar-

rived at Nauvoo from his mission to England.

Thurs. 7.—In a council of the Twelve, a number of brethren were called on missions, among whom were Joseph Ball to South America and Henry Harrison Sagers to Jamaica, West Indies.

Sun. 24.—Apostle Orson Hyde, who had arrived at Jerusalem, ascended the Mount of Olives and dedicated the land of Palestine by prayer for the gathering of the Jews.

November. *Mon. 8.*—The temporary baptismal font in the Nauvoo Temple was dedicated.

—The ship *Chaos* sailed from Liverpool with 170 Saints, under the direction of Peter Melling, bound for Nauvoo.

Sun. 21.—Baptisms for the dead were commenced in the font in the basement of the Nauvoo Temple.

Wed. 24.—The *Tyrean* company of British Saints arrived at Warsaw, intending to settle Warren, a new town site, one mile south of Warsaw, which had been selected for a settlement of the Saints, but they soon afterwards removed to Nauvoo, because of oppression on the part of anti-Mormons.

December. *Sat. 4.*—The Stake organization at Ramus, Hancock County, Ill., was discontinued.

Mon. 13.—Apostle Willard Richards was appointed Joseph Smith's private secretary and general clerk for the Church.

Wed. 22.—John Snider was called by revelation on a special mission to Europe, bearing a message from the Twelve.

1842.

A large number of Saints from Great Britain arrived at Nauvoo, Ill. John C. Bennett, who turned traitor against the Church, sought the Prophet Joseph's life. Joseph Smith was arrested on a false charge, tried and acquitted; and when the officers planned to arrest him again, he hid himself and from his places of seclusion wrote important communications to the Saints.

January. *Thurs. 6.*—A conference was held at Zarahemla, Ia., opposite Nauvoo, when a Stake of Zion, previously organized there, was discontinued, and a branch organized in its stead, with John Smith as president.

Wed. 12.—The ship *Tremont* sailed from Liverpool with 143 Saints bound for Nauvoo *via* New Orleans.

February. *Wed. 2.*—Moses Thatcher was born in Sangamon County, Ill.

Thurs. 3.—Apostle Wilford Woodruff took the superintendency of the printing office and Apostle John Taylor the editorial department of the *Times and Seasons*, at Nauvoo.

Sat. 5.—The ship *Hope* sailed from Liverpool for New Orleans with 270 Saints.

Sun. 20.—The ship *John Cumming* sailed from Liverpool with about two hundred Saints.

March.—The *Millennial Star* office in

England was moved from Manchester (No. 47 Oxford Street) to the Church emigration office in Liverpool (No. 36 Chapel Street).

Sat. 12.—The ship *Hanover* sailed from Liverpool with about two hundred Saints, under the direction of Amos Fielding.

Thus. 15.—Joseph Smith took charge of the editorial department of the *Times and Seasons.*

Thurs. 17.—The organization of the Female Relief Society of Nauvoo was commenced. It was completed on the 24th, with Emma Smith as president; Mrs. Elizabeth Ann Whitney and Mrs. Sarah M. Cleveland, counselors; Miss Elvira Cowles, treasurer; and Eliza R. Snow, secretary.

Sun. 20.—Joseph Smith baptized eighty persons for the dead in the Mississippi river, after which he confirmed about fifty.

Sat. 26.—John Snider left Nauvoo on his special mission to England.

Sun. 27.—Joseph Smith baptized 107 persons for the dead in the Mississippi river.

April. *Wed. 6.*—A special conference of the Church wes held at Nauvoo; it was continued till the 8th, and during its sessions 275 brethren were ordained Elders.

Wed. 13.—About two hundred Saints arrived at Nauvoo from Great Britain.

Sat. 16.—The *Wasp*, a miscellaneous weekly newspaper, was first published at Nauvoo; Wm. Smith, editor.

Fri. 29.—Joseph Smith wrote: "A conspiracy against the peace of my household was made manifest, and it gave me some trouble to counteract the design of certain base individuals and restore peace. The Lord makes manifest to me many things, which it is not wisdom for me to make public, until others can witness the proof of them."

May. *Wed. 4.*—Joseph Smith gave James Adams, Hyrum Smith, Newel K. Whitney, George Miller, Brigham Young, Heber C. Kimball and Willard Richards instructions about holy endowments.

Fri. 6. — Ex - Governor Lilburn W. Boggs, of Missouri, was shot, but not killed, at Independence, Mo.

Sat. 7.—The Nauvoo Legion, now numbering 26 companies, or 2,000 men, was reviewed and it fought a sham battle, in which John C. Bennett conspired against the Prophet's life, but failed to carry out his design.

Thurs. 19.—John C. Bennett having resigned the mayorship of Nauvoo, Joseph Smith was elected by the city council to fill the vacancy.

Tues. 24.—Chauncey L. Higbee was excommunicated from the Church by the High Council of Nauvoo, for unchaste and unvirtuous conduct.

Wed. 25.—The authorities of the Church had at this time withdrawn their fellowship from John C. Bennett, who soon afterwards left Nauvoo.

June. Wed. 1.—At a general conference held in Manchester, England, 8,265 officers and members of the Church were represented.

July. *Sun. 3.*—Joseph Smith spoke to eight thousand people at Nauvoo.

August.—Apostle Orson Hyde published a pamphlet of 120 pages in the German language, in Germany, entitled "A Cry in the Wilderness," etc., setting forth the rise, progress and doctrines of the Church.

Sat. 6.—Joseph Smith prophesied that the Saints would be driven to the Rocky Mountains, where they should become a mighty people.

Mon. 8.—Joseph Smith was arrested by a deputy sheriff at Nauvoo, by requisition from Gov. Thos. Reynolds, of Missouri, falsely accused of being accessory to the shooting of ex-Governor Boggs. O. Porter Rockwell was also arrested as principal. A writ of *habeas corpus* was issued by the municipal court of Nauvoo, by which the prisoners were released for the time being.

Wed. 10.—The deputy sheriff returned to Nauvoo to re-arrest Joseph Smith and O. Porter Rockwell, but they could not be found. To escape imprisonment the Prophet had to keep concealed for some time. His first retreat was the house of his uncle John Smith, at Zarahemla, Ia.

Thurs. 11.—Joseph Smith concealed himself in the house of Edward Sayer, in Nauvoo.

Thurs. 18.—Rumors being afloat that the Prophet's hiding place was discovered, he changed his quarters from the house of Edward Sayer to that of Carlos Granger, who lived in the northeast part of Nauvoo. Great excitement prevailed among the people around Nauvoo on account of John C. Bennett's lies.

Fri. 19.—Joseph Smith returned to his own house.

Sat. 20.—Amasa M. Lyman was ordained one of the Twelve Apostles.

Sun. 21.—Sidney Rigdon testified in public meeting, at Nauvoo, that his daughter, Eliza, had been raised from the dead by the power of God.

Mon. 29.—After not showing himself in public for three weeks, Joseph Smith spoke to an assembly of Saints at Nauvoo; 380 Elders volunteered to take missions to the various States of the Union for the purpose of refuting John C. Bennett's lies.

September. *Thurs. 1.*—Joseph Smith wrote an address to the Saints at Nauvoo concerning baptism for the dead. (Doc. and Cov., Sec. 127.)

Sat. 3.—Another effort was made to arrest Joseph Smith without legal process. His house was searched, but he eluded pursuit, and afterwards kept himself hid for some time in the house of Edward Hunter.

Tues. 6.—Joseph Smith wrote another important address to the Saints in relation to baptism for the dead, and the necessity of keeping records. (Doc. and Cov., Sec. 128.)

Sat. 10.—Joseph Smith returned home undiscovered.

Sat. 17.—The ship *Sidney* sailed from Liverpool with 180 Saints; it arrived at New Orleans Nov. 11th.

Sun. 25.—The ship *Medford* sailed from Liverpool with 214 Saints, under the presidency of Apostle Orson Hyde; it arrived at New Orleans Nov. 13th.

Thurs 29.—The ship *Henry* sailed from Liverpool for New Orleans, with 157

Saints, under the direction of John Snider.

October. *Sun. 2.*—Reports reached Joseph Smith that Gov. Thos. Reynolds, of Missouri, had offered a reward for the arrest of himself and O. Porter Rockwell.

Fri. 7.—Joseph Smith again left home to elude the pursuit of his enemies, leaving his wife Emma sick. He returned on the 20th.

Thurs. 13. - Some of the brethren arrived at Nauvoo from the Pineries, Wisconsin, with 90,000 feet of lumber and 24,000 cubic feet of timber for the Temple and Nauvoo House.

Thurs. 20.—Thomas Ward succeeded Apostle Parley P. Pratt as president of the British Mission, with Lorenzo Snow and Hiram Clark as counselors.

Sat. 29.—The ship *Emerald* sailed from Liverpool with 250 Saints, under the leadership of Apostle Parley P. Pratt. Because of ice in the Mississippi river the company was detained during the winter in St. Louis, Alton, Chester and other places, and did not arrive in Nauvoo until April 12, 1843.

November. *Tues. 13.*—Apostle John Taylor succeeded Joseph Smith as editor of the *Times and Seasons.*

Thurs. 17.—Alpheus Harmon was frozen to death on the prairie, between Nauvoo and Carthage, Ill., as he was returning home from a mission.

December. *Sun. 4.*—The city of Nauvoo was divided into ten Bishop's wards.

Wed. 7.—Apostle Orson Hyde returned to Nauvoo from his mission to Jerusalem.

Tues. 20.—Lorenzo D. Barnes died at Bradford, England. His was the first death of an Elder on a foreign mission.

Wed. 21.—Apostle Willard Richards, who had been in the East several months, was appointed Church Historian, etc.

Mon. 26.—Joseph Smith was arrested the third time on a requisition from the State of Missouri.

Tues. 27.—Joseph Smith, accompanied by several brethren, left Nauvoo for Springfield, Ill., where they arrived on the 30th.

1843.

During this and the preceding year Joseph the Prophet preached many powerful sermons and uttered a number of important prophecies. While on a visit to Dixon, Ill., he had a narrow escape from being kidnapped under legal pretense and taken to Missouri. The revelation on celestial marriage was given and the first missionaries sent to the Society Islands.

January. *Mon. 2.*—Joseph Smith prophesied that he should not go to Missouri dead or alive.

Wed. 4.—Joseph Smith was on trial before Judge Pope, of Springfield, on the accusation of being an accessory to the shooting of ex-Governor Boggs of Missouri.

Thurs. 5.—Joseph Smith was proven innocent and acquitted.

Tues. 10.—Joseph Smith and company

arrived at Nauvoo from the rip to Springfield.

Mon. 16.—The ship *Swanton* sailed from Liverpool with 212 Saints for New Orleans, led by Lorenzo Snow. The emigrants arrived at Nauvoo April 12th.

Tues. 17.—The Saints being overjoyed because of Joseph Smith's release, meetings of prayer and thanksgiving were held at Nauvoo.

February. *Tues. 7.*—Apostle Parley P. Pratt arrived at Nauvoo from his mission to England.

Thurs. 9.—Joseph Smith received by revelation three grand keys, by which bad angels, or spirits, may be known. (Doc. and Cov., Sec. 129.)

March.—A "Young Gentlemen's and Ladies' Relief Society" was organized at Nauvoo, with Wm. Cutler as president.

—Joseph Smith studied the German language.

Fri. 3.—The Illinois legislature passed a bill for repealing the Nauvoo city charter, which, however, was not approved.

Sat. 4.—O. Porter Rockwell was taken prisoner in St. Louis by the Missourians.

Wed. 8.—The ship *Yorkshire* sailed from Liverpool, England, with 82 Saints on board, led by Thomas Bullock; the emigrants arrived at Nauvoo, May 31st, *via* New Orleans.

Wed. 15.—Joseph Smith prophesied that O. Porter Rockwell would get away honorably from the Missourians.

Tues. 21.—The ship *Claiborne* sailed from Liverpool with 106 Saints.

April. *Sun. 2.*—"Important Items of Instruction" were given by Joseph Smith, at Nauvoo, who also prophesied "that the commencement of the difficulties which will cause much bloodshed previous to the coming of the Son of Man, will be in South Carolina." (Doc. and Cov., Sec. 130.)

Thurs. 6.—At a conference held in the Temple, at Kirtland, O., it was decided that all the Saints residing at that place should remove to Nauvoo, Ill.

—An important conference, which continued its sessions till the 8th, was commenced on the floor of the Temple, at Nauvoo, Ill. Joseph Smith prophesied that Christ would not come until he (Joseph) was eighty-five years of age.

Mon. 10.—About one hundred and fifteen Elders were called on missions to different States, at a special conference held at Nauvoo.

Thurs. 13.—Joseph Smith preached to the British Saints, who had arrived at Nauvoo the day previous.

Sun. 23.—Six brass plates and a skeleton were found by Mr. R. Wiley and others, near Kinderhook, Pike Co., Ill.

May. *Wed. 3.*—The first number of the *Nauvoo Neighbor*, a newspaper, was issued at Nauvoo, instead of the *Wasp*, suspended.

Tues. 16.—On this and the following day Joseph Smith made some important remarks about the celestial glory, at Ramus, Ill. (Doc. and Cov., Sec. 131.)

Thurs. 18.—Returning to Nauvoo from his visit to Ramus, Joseph Smith dined with Judge Stephen A. Douglas, at Carthage, Hancock Co., Ill. During the conversation which took place Joseph prophesied that Judge Douglas would aspire to the Presidency of the United States, and added that if he ever turned his hand against the Latter-day Saints, he should feel the hand of the Almighty upon him, etc.

Tues. 23.—Addison Pratt, Noah Rogers, Benjamin F. Grouard and Knowlton F. Hanks were set apart for a mission to the Pacific Islands.

Fri. 26.—Joseph Smith gave endowments, and also instructions on the Priesthood and the new and everlasting covenant, to Hyrum Smith, Brigham Young, Heber C. Kimball and others, at Nauvoo.

June. *Thurs. 1.*—Addison Pratt, Benjamin F. Grouard, Knowlton F. Hanks and Noah Rogers left Nauvoo on their missions to the Pacific Islands.

Thurs. 8.—Elias Higbee died in Nauvoo.

Sun. 11.—A conference was held at Lima, Ill., and the branch at that place reorganized, with Isaac Morley as president, and Gardiner Snow, Bishop.

Tues. 13.—Joseph Smith left Nauvoo with his wife Emma to visit her sister, living near Dixon, Lee County, Ill.

Fri. 23.—Joseph Smith was arrested and brutally treated by Joseph H. Reynolds, sheriff of Jackson Co., Mo., and Constable Harmon T. Wilson, of Carthage, Ill., without legal process, and only through interference of friends at Dixon saved from being kidnapped and taken to Missouri.

Sat. 24.—The corner stones of the Masonic Temple at Nauvoo were laid.

—Joseph Smith secured a writ of *habeas corpus* and started towards Ottawa to have his case examined by Judge John D. Caton, but, arriving at Pawpaw Grove, the company learned that Judge Caton was not at home, and, therefore, returned to Dixon the following day.

Sun. 25.—News of Joseph Smith being kidnapped reached Nauvoo, and 175 men immediately started on horseback to his rescue.

Mon. 26.—Joseph Smith started under guard towards Quincy, Ill.

Tues. 27.—The company traveling with Joseph Smith was met by the brethren from Nauvoo, when it was decided that instead of going to Quincy to have the writ of *habeas corpus* examined, the prisoner and escort should proceed to Nauvoo.

Fri. 30.—Joseph Smith and company arrived at Nauvoo, nearly the whole city turning out to meet him. In the afternoon he addressed the people, giving the history of his arrest. While he was speaking Officers Reynolds and Wilson started for Carthage and tried to raise a mob; afterwards they petitioned Gov. Thos. Ford for militia to take Joseph out of Nauvoo by force.

July. *Sat. 1.*—Joseph Smith was tried before the municipal court of Nauvoo on a writ of *habeas corpus* and acquitted.

Sun. 2.—Joseph Smith had a pleasant interview with several Pottawattamie chiefs who had come to visit him, and a very good impression was made upon the Indians.

—The steamboat *Maid of Iowa* returned to Nauvoo, after a very adventurous trip in search of Joseph. The brethren who had participated in that river expedition,

numbering about eighty, were blessed by the Prophet.

Mon. 3.—A number of Elders were called to visit the various counties of Illinois, to preach the gospel and disabuse the public mind with regard to Joseph Smith's arrest.

—Charles C. Rich and a company of twenty-five men, who had been out searching for the Prophet, returned to Nauvoo, having traveled about five hundred miles on horseback in seven days.

Tues. 4.—Nauvoo was visited by about one thousand gentlemen and ladies from St. Louis, Quincy and Burlington.

Fri. 7.—Mr. M. Braman arrived at Nauvoo as a messenger from the governor, to learn the particulars of Joseph Smith's late arrest.

Sat. 8.—Bishop George Miller arrived at Nauvoo from the Pineries with 157,000 feet of lumber and 70,000 shingles for the Temple.

Wed. 12.—The revelation on celestial marriage was written in the presence of Hyrum Smith and Wm. Clayton. (Doc. and Cov., Sec. 132.)

August. *Fri. 11.*—General James Adams, of Springfield, died at Nauvoo.

Thurs. 31.—Joseph Smith moved into the Nauvoo Mansion.

September. *Tues. 5.*—The ship *Metoka* sailed from Liverpool with 280 Saints, bound for Nauvoo.

Wed. 6.—At an anti-Mormon meeting, held at Carthage, Hancock Co., Ill., resolutions were adopted against Joseph Smith and the Saints in Nauvoo.

Fri. 15.—Joseph Smith opened the Nauvoo Mansion as a hotel.

Sat. 30.—Reuben Hedlock and other missionaries from Nauvoo arrived at Liverpool, England.

October. *Tues. 3.*—Joseph Smith gave a dinner party in the Nauvoo Mansion to about two hundred Saints.

Fri. 6.—A special conference of the Church, which continued its sessions on the 8th, was commenced at Nauvoo, Ill. Serious complaints were made against Sidney Rigdon.

Sun. 8.—At a meeting of the special conference at Nauvoo, Sidney Rigdon was sustained as a Counselor to Joseph Smith, although the Prophet said, "I have thrown him off my shoulders, and you have again put him on me; you may carry him, but I will not."

Mon. 9.—Addison Pratt, Noah Rogers, Benjamin F. Grouard and Knowlton F. Hanks sailed from New Bedford, Mass., on board the ship *Timoleon*, for the Pacific Islands.

Fri. 20.—John P. Greene returned to Nauvoo, from a mission to the State of New York, with about one hundred emigrants.

Sat. 21.—The ship *Champion* sailed from Liverpool with 91 Saints, bound for Nauvoo.

Sun. 22.—Apostles Brigham Young, Heber C. Kimball and George A. Smith returned to Nauvoo from a mission to the Eastern States.

November. *Fri. 3.*—Knowlton F. Hanks, one of the missionaries to the Pacific Islands, died. He was the first

Latter-day Saint Elder who died and was buried at sea.

Mon. 6.—Erastus Snow returned to Nauvoo with a company of immigrants from Massachusetts.

Sun. 19.—Philander Avery was kidnapped from the neighborhood of Warsaw and carried forcibly across the Mississippi river to Missouri.

December. Sat, 2.—Apostles Orson Hyde, Parley P. Pratt, Wilford Woodruff and George A. Smith and Elder Orson Spencer received their endowments at Nauvoo, Ill.; 35 persons were present.

—Daniel Avery was kidnapped from Bear Creek, Hancock Co., Ill., by a company of Missourians, and imprisoned in Monticello jail, Lewis Co., Mo., where his son Philander was already confined.

Thurs. 7.—The German brethren met at the Assembly Room at Nauvoo, chose Bishop Daniel Garn as their presiding Elder, and organized to have preaching done in their own language.

Mon. 18.—John Ellioth, a schoolmaster, was arrested and brought to Nauvoo, where he was tried and found guilty of having kidnapped Daniel Avery and son.

Tues. 19.—The Nauvoo Legion paraded near the Temple, was inspected by the officers and instructed to prepare for meeting the mob, which was gathering in the neighborhood.

Thurs. 21.—The city council of Nauvoo signed a petition to Congress, praying for redress for the Missouri persecutions.

Fri. 22.—David Holman's house, near Ramus, Hancock Co., Ill., was burned by the mob.

Mon. 25.—O. Porter Rockwell arrived in Nauvoo from nearly a year's imprisonment in Missouri without conviction, during which time he was subjected to very cruel treatment.

—Daniel Avery was liberated from his imprisonment in Missouri, his son having previously escaped.

Fri. 29.—Forty policemen were sworn into office in the city of Nauvoo.

1844.

Joseph the Prophet became a candidate for the Presidency of the United States. Mobs gathered around Nauvoo, and during the ensuing troubles Joseph and his brother Hyrum were martyred in Carthage jail. The Twelve Apostles returned from their missions to the Eastern States and were accepted by the Saints as the presiding Council of the Church. A great number of Seventies were ordained.

January. Tues. 2.—Jonathan Pugmire, sen., and Thos. Cartwright, who had been imprisoned in Chester, England, about six weeks, for the accidental drowning of Mrs. Cartwright during an attempt to baptize her, Nov. 23, 1843, were acquitted.

Wed. 3.—A special session of the city council was held at Nauvoo because of Wm. Law's intimation that his life was in danger.

Fri. 5.—Wm. Marks, president of the

Nauvoo Stake of Zion, being alarmed on account of a fire being kindled near his house, made statements before the city council; his fears were unfounded.

Tues. 9.—Elder Horace S. Eldredge, a county constable, was prevented by mob force from performing an official duty at Carthage.

Wed. 10..—John Smith, uncle to Joseph Smith, the Prophet, was ordained a Patriarch.

Tues. 16.—Francis M. Higbee was tried before the municipal court of Nauvoo for slandering Joseph Smith.

Tues. 23.—The ship *Fanny* sailed from Liverpool, England, with 210 Saints under the direction of Wm. Kay, bound for Nauvoo. It arrived at New Orleans, March 7th.

Mon. 29.—At a political meeting, held at Nauvoo, Joseph Smith was nominated a candidate for the Presidency of the United States. Soon afterwards a large number of Elders were sent to the various States of the Union to electioneer for him.

February. Tues. 6.—The ship *Isaac Allerton* sailed from Liverpool with 60 Saints, bound for Nauvoo.

Wed. 7.—Joseph Smith completed his address to the people of the United States, entitled: "Views of the Powers and Policy of the Government of the United States."

Sun. 11.—The ship *Swanton* sailed from Liverpool with 81 Saints, bound for Nauvoo, where they arrived April 18th.

Sat. 17.—The anti-Mormons held a convention at Carthage, Ill., the object being to devise ways and means for expelling the Saints from the State.

Tues. 20.—Joseph Smith instructed the Twelve Apostles to send a delegation to California and Oregon, to search for a good location, to which the Saints could remove after the completion of the Temple.

Wed. 21.—A meeting of the Apostles was held at Nauvoo for the purpose of selecting "a company to explore Oregon and California and select a site for a new city for the Saints." Jonathan Dunham, Phinehas H. Young, David D. Yearsley and David Fullmer volunteered to go; and Alphonso Young, James Emmett, Geo. D. Watt and Daniel Spencer were requested to go.

Fri. 23.—Another meeting was held at Nauvoo, in favor of the California and Oregon expedition. Several of the brethren volunteered to go; among whom were Samuel Bent, John A. Kelting, Samuel Rolfe, Daniel Avery and Samuel W. Richards.

Sun. 25.—Joseph Smith prophesied that in five years the Saints would be out of the power of their old enemies, whether apostates or of the world.

Thurs. 29.—Moses Smith and Rufus Beach volunteered to join the Oregon exploring expedition.

March. Mon. 4.—It was decided in council at Nauvoo to cease work on the Nauvoo House until the Temple was completed.

Tues. 5.—The ship *Glasgow* sailed from Liverpool with 150 Saints, led by Hiram Clark, bound for Nauvoo, where they arrived April 26th.

Mon. 11.—Joseph Smith and the leading

authorities of the Church held another council at Nauvoo about the Saints moving to the mountains.

Sun. 24.—Joseph Smith spoke in public meeting against Chauncey L. Higbee, Robert D. Foster, Wm. and Wilson Law and others, as conspirators against his life.

Tues. 26.—Joseph Smith petitioned Congress to protect the citizens of the United States, emigrating west; this he did in view of the Saints going to the mountains in the near future.

April. *Fri. 5.*—The Masonic Temple, which had been erected at Nauvoo, was dedicated. About five hundred and fifty members of the Masonic fraternity from various parts of the world were present.

Sat. 6.—A conference, which lasted five days, commenced at Nauvoo. The Prophet spoke to 20,000 Saints on the 7th, and on the 8th declared the whole of North and South America to be the land of Zion.

Sat. 13.—Under the leadership of Wm. Kay, 210 British Saints arrived at Nauvoo.

Thurs. 18.—Wm. and Wilson Law, Robert D. Foster and other apostates, formerly prominent in the Church, were excommunicated.

Fri. 26.—Augustine Spencer, Robert D. Foster, Charles Foster and Chauncey L. Higbee were arrested and fined, in Nauvoo, for assault and resisting the officers.

May. *Wed. 1.*—Elders Addison Pratt, Noah Rogers and Benjamin F. Grouard landed on the island of Tubuai (one of the Austral group), as the first missionaries of the Church to the islands of the Pacific.

Mon. 6.—Joseph Smith was arrested at Nauvoo on complaint of Francis M. Higbee, but took out a writ of *habeas corpus*, and was tried on the 8th before the municipal court of Nauvoo, which resulted in Joseph's acquittal, and Higbee was sentenced to pay the cost of suit.

Tues. 14.—Elders Noah Rogers and Benjamin F.Grouard landed at Papeete, Tahiti, Society Islands, as the first Latter-day Saint missionaries to that group.

Wed. 15.—Anthon H. Lund was born at Aalborg, Denmark.

Fri. 17.—A State convention was held at Nauvoo, Ill., in which Joseph Smith was nominated as a candidate for the Presidency, and Sidney Rigdon for the Vice Presidency of the United States.

Sat. 18.—The first number of *The Prophet*, a weekly paper devoted to the interests of the Church, was issued in New York City, by a society of Saints.

Tues. 21.—Apostles Brigham Young, Heber C. Kimball and Lyman Wight, and about a hundred other Elders,left Nauvoo, Ill., on political missions to the East. Apostles Wilford Woodruff and Geo. A. Smith and others had left on the 9th.

Thurs. 23.—Joseph Smith had a talk with a number of Sac and Fox Indians at Nauvoo.

Sat. 25.—Joseph Smith learned that the grand jury at Carthage had found two indictments against him, one of them for polygamy.

Mon. 27.—Joseph Smith, accompanied by a number of friends, went to Carthage to have the indictments against him investigated by the circuit court, but, the

prosecution not being ready, the case was continued until next term.

June. *Fri. 7.*—The first and only number of the Nauvoo *Expositor* was published, edited by Sylvester Emmons.

Mon. 10.—The paper and printing material of the Nauvoo *Expositor* were destroyed, according to the proclamation of the city council, declaring it a nuisance.

Wed. 12.—Joseph Smith was arrested on a charge of destroying the *Expositor*, tried before the municipal court of Nauvoo and acquitted. The following day the other members of the city council were tried before the same court, on a similar charge, and honorably acquitted.

Fri. 14.—Joseph Smith communicated the facts connected with the removal of the *Expositor's* printing materials, by letter, to Gov. Thos. Ford.

Sun. 16.—In a public meeting, held at Nauvoo, a number of delegates were called to visit the different precincts in Hancock County, Ill., to lay a truthful statement of the troubles in Nauvoo before the people. Joseph Smith, as mayor of the city, also stated the facts in a proclamation.

—Addison Pratt baptized Ambrose Alexander, a white man, on the island of Tubuai, as the first convert to "Mormonism" on the Pacific Isles.

Mon. 17.—Joseph Smith and a number of others were arrested, on complaint of W. G. Ware, for riot in destroying the *Expositor*, tried before Justice Daniel H. Wells, and, after a long and close examination, acquitted.

—Mobs began to gather in the surrounding country, threatening to drive the Saints from Nauvoo.

Tues. 18.—The Nauvoo Legion was ordered out and the city declared under martial law, by the proclamation of the mayor, Joseph Smith. The Prophet delivered his last public address. An extra of the *Warsaw Signal* was read, in which all the "old citizens" were called upon to assist the mob in driving away the Saints.

Wed. 19.—Mobs were gathering at different points to attack Nauvoo.

Thurs. 20.—General Joseph Smith, with other officers of the Legion, examined the approaches to Nauvoo as a preparatory measure for defense. The Prophet also sent for the Twelve Apostles, who were on missions, to come home immediately.

Sat. 22.—Late in the evening Joseph and Hyrum Smith and Willard Richards left Nauvoo and crossed the Mississippi river, with the intention to flee to the West, and thus escape from their enemies.

Sun. 23.—Through the solicitation of Emma Smith, and several supposed friends, Joseph Smith and his companions returned to Nauvoo.

Mon. 24.—Joseph and Hyrum Smith, accompanied by seventeen friends, started for Carthage, to submit to another trial, under pledge of protection from Gov. Thos. Ford. On the way they received a demand from the governor to surrender the State arms in possession of the Nauvoo Legion; Joseph returned and complied with the request, and then proceeded to Carthage.

Tues. 25.—Joseph Smith and his brethren surrendered themselves to a constable at

Carthage and submitted to a trial, after which they were, contrary to law, remanded to prison.

Wed. 26.—Gov. Thos. Ford had a long interview with the prisoners in Carthage jail. He renewed his promises of protection and said, if he went to Nauvoo, he would take them with him.

Thurs. 27.—Gov. Thos. Ford went to Nauvoo, leaving the prisoners in jail to be guarded by their most bitter enemies, the "Carthage Greys." About 5:20 p. m. an armed mob with blackened faces surrounded and entered the jail, and murdered Joseph and Hyrum Smith in cold blood; Apostle John Taylor was severely wounded, while Apostle Willard Richards only received a slight wound on his ear.

Fri. 28.—Apostle Willard Richards and Samuel H. Smith conveyed the bodies of the martyrs to Nauvoo, where they were met by the officers of the Nauvoo Legion, and a very large number of citizens.

Sat. 29.—About ten thousand persons visited and viewed the remains of the martyred Prophet and Patriarch at Nauvoo. The funeral took place in the evening.

July. *Tues. 2.*—Apostle John Taylor was brought home to Nauvoo from Carthage.

Mon. 8.—Apostle Parley P. Pratt arrived at Nauvoo; he was the first of the absent Twelve to return.

Sun. 21.—Addison Pratt baptized four white men and four natives on the island of Tubuai. These natives, whose names were Nabota and his wife Telii, Pauma and Hamoe, were the first of the Polynesian race to embrace the fulness of the gospel.

Thurs. 25.—Erastus Snow and many other Elders arrived at Nauvoo. All seemed weighed down with gloom.

Sun. 28.—Apostle Geo. A. Smith and a party of brethren arrived at Nauvoo.
—A branch of the Church, consisting of eleven members, was organized by Addison Pratt on the island of Tubuai (Society Islands mission). This was the first branch of the Church on the Pacific Islands.

Tues. 30.—Samuel H. Smith, brother of the Prophet, died at Nauvoo, as a martyr to persecution.

Wed. 31.—Apostle Amasa M. Lyman arrived at Nauvoo.

August. *Fri. 2.*—A political meeting of the citizens of Hancock County, Ill., was held near the Temple at Nauvoo. Great excitement prevailed throughout the county. The mob party was determined to elect officers who would screen the murderers of Joseph and Hyrum Smith and exterminate the "Mormons."

Sat. 3.—Sidney Rigdon arrived at Nauvoo from Pittsburgh, Pa.

Sun. 4.—Sidney Rigdon preached to the Saints at Nauvoo, declaring that a guardian should be appointed to build up the Church to Joseph, intimating that he was the man who should lead the Saints.

Tues. 6. — Apostles Brigham Young, Heber C. Kimball, Lyman Wight, Orson Hyde, Orson Pratt and Wilford Woodruff arrived at Nauvoo.

Wed. 7.—The Twelve met in council with Elder Taylor, at his house at Nauvoo; they found him recovering from his wounds. In the afternoon, the Twelve, the High Council and High Priests held a meeting in the Seventies' Hall, where Sidney Rigdon's claim to lead the Church was considered.

Thurs. 8.—A special meeting of the Church was held at Nauvoo, in which Elder Rigdon harangued the Saints about choosing a guardian, etc. In the afternoon meeting the Twelve Apostles, through their President, Brigham Young, asserted their right to lead the Church, which claim was recognized by the unanimous vote of the people.

Mon. 12.—At a council of the Twelve Apostles, Amasa M. Lyman was admitted into their quorum, having been previously ordained to the Apostleship. Elder Wilford Woodruff was appointed to go to England to preside over the British mission.

Thurs. 15.—The Twelve issued an epistle to the Saints in all the world, giving such instructions and words of counsel to the Church as were necessary after the martyrdom of the Prophet.

Wed. 28.—Wilford Woodruff, Dan Jones and Hiram Clark, with their families, left Nauvoo for England.

Sat. 31.—Brigham Young was elected lieutenant-general of the Nauvoo Legion, and Charles C. Rich, major-general.

September. *Sun. 8.*—At a meeting of the High Council of Nauvoo, Sidney Rigdon was excommunicated from the Church.

Thurs. 19.—The ship *Norfolk* sailed from Liverpool with 143 Saints, bound for Nauvoo.

Tues. 24.—Seventy presidents to preside over the Seventies, and fifty High Priests to preside in different sections of the country, were ordained.

Fri. 27.—Gov. Thos. Ford visited Nauvoo with about five hundred troops and three pieces of artillery, ostensibly for the purpose of bringing the murderers of Joseph and Hyrum Smith to justice.

Sat. 28.—About this time several persons in Hancock County were indicted for the murder of Joseph and Hyrum Smith, among whom was Jacob C. Davis.

October. *Mon. 7.* — At the general conference held in Nauvoo Wm. Marks was rejected as president of the Stake and John Smith appointed in his stead.

Tues. 8.—A reorganization of the Seventies took place in the general conference at Nauvoo. At the close eleven quorums were filled and properly organized, and about forty Elders organized as a part of the 12th quorum. The senior presidents of these twelve quorums were Joseph Young (1st), Edson Barney (2nd), Elias Hutchins (3rd), Jacob Gates (4th), Henry Jacobs (5th), Israel Barlow (6th), Randolph Alexander (7th), John Pack (8th), Philip Ettleman (9th), Albert P. Rockwood (10th), Jesse P. Harmon (11th), and Hyrum Dayton (12th).

About the same time the 16th quorum of Seventy was organized, with Dana Jacobs as senior president.

November. *Sat. 23.*—Edward Hunter was ordained a Bishop and set apart to take care of the 5th Ward in Nauvoo.

December. *Sun. 1.*—Apostle Parley P. Pratt was appointed to go to the city of

New York to regulate and counsel the emigration from Europe and preside over all the eastern branches of the Church.

Sun. 22.—The 13th,14th and 15th quorums of Seventy were organized in Nauvoo,with Charles Bird, Jonathan Dunham and John Lytle as senior presidents.

1845.

Work on the Nauvoo Temple was prosecuted with much vigor; mobs attacked the outlying settlements in Hancock County, Ill., burned a number of houses, and caused much suffering among the Saints.

January.—During this month the legislature of Illinois repealed the city charter of Nauvoo.

Fri. 3.—Apostle Wilford Woodruff and accompanying missionaries arrived at Liverpool, England. Wilford Woodruff succeeded Reuben Hedlock as president of the British mission.

Sun. 12.—The 17th quorum of Seventy was organized at Nauvoo, with Daniel M. Kepsher as senior president.

Fri. 17.—The ship *Palmyra* sailed from Liverpool, England, with a company of Saints, under the direction of Amos Fielding, bound for Nauvoo.

Sun. 26.—The 18th quorum of Seventy was organized in Nauvoo, with John W. Bell as senior president.

February. *Sun. 9.*—The 19th quorum of Seventy was organized at Nauvoo, with Samuel Moore as senior president.

March. *Sun. 2.*—The 21st quorum of Seventy was partly organized at Nauvoo, with Erastus H. Derby as senior president.

Tues. 18.—The 20th quorum of Seventy was organized at Morley's Settlement, Hancock Co., Ill., with Hiram Blackman, of Bear Creek branch, as senior president.

April. *Sun. 6.*—The Twelve Apostles issued "A proclamation to all the kings of the world, to the President of the United States of America, to the governors of the several States, and to the rulers and people of all nations."

—The general conference of the Church was commenced at Nauvoo, Ill. It was continued till the 9th and attended by about twenty-five thousand people. In honor of the Prophet Joseph it was decided by vote to change the name of Nauvoo to "City of Joseph."

Mon. 7.—At a conference held in Manchester, England, Dan. Jones, who had lately arrived from America, was appointed president of the Wrexham conference (Wales), consisting of himself and wife. One year later there were seven hundred members of the Church in Wales, largely through his instrumentality.

Tues. 8.—At a conference held in Manchester, England, the so-called Joint Stock Company was organized, with Thomas Ward as president.

Wed. 9.—The 22nd, 23rd, 24th, 25th and 26th quorums of Seventy were organized at Nauvoo, with David Clough (22nd), Benjamin Sweatt (23rd), Lewis Eger (24th), Thomas Spiers (25th), and Benjamin Jones (26th) as senior presidents.

Sat. 12.—A U. S. deputy marshal of Illinois arrived at Nauvoo, with writs for Brigham Young and others, but failed to arrest them.

Wed. 16.—As the city charter of Nauvoo had been repealed, a small part of the city was incorporated as the town of Nauvoo.

Thurs. 24.—In a general council held at Nauvoo, it was decided to send a written appeal in behalf of the Saints to the President of the United States, and to the governor of every State in the Union, except the State of Missouri. This resolution was subsequently acted upon, but without any response, except from the governor of Arkansas, who replied in a respectful and sympathetic letter.

May. *Mon 19.*—Some of the citizens of Nauvoo went to Carthage, to attend the trial of the murderers of Joseph and Hyrum Smith.

Sat. 24.—President Brigham Young and others who had been secreted for some time, to avoid arrest and persecution by their enemies, appeared at Nauvoo and took part in the laying of the cap stone of the Temple, in the presence of a large number of Saints.

Fri. 30.—The murderers of Joseph and Hyrum Smith were acquitted by the jury at Carthage, although every one who witnessed the trial was satisfied of their guilt.

June.—At the close of its fifth volume the *Millennial Star* (England) was changed from a monthly to a semi-monthly periodical.

Sun. 8.—The organization of the 27th quorum of Seventy was commenced in Nauvoo.

Tues. 10.—The 27th quorum of Seventy was organized at Nauvoo, with Rufus Beach as senior president.

Mon. 23.—A constable came to Nauvoo with writs for the arrest of Apostles Brigham Young and John Taylor, and others, but he did not succeed in finding them.

Thurs. 26.—The first stone was laid for a new baptismal font in the Nauvoo Temple.

Fri. 27.—This being the first anniversary of the martyrdom of Joseph and Hyrum Smith, the day was spent in prayer and fasting by the Saints in Great Britain.

July. *Thurs. 3.*—Noah Rogers sailed from Tahiti, Society Islands, per ship *Three Brothers*, on his return to Nauvoo, Ill., where he arrived Dec. 29, 1845. He was the first Latter-day Saint Elder who circumnavigated the globe as a missionary.

Sat. 5.—The first number of the New York *Messenger* was published by Samuel Brannan in New York City, as a continuation of the *Prophet*, suspended.

Sun. 27.—The 28th and 29th quorums of Seventy were organized in Nauvoo, with John Gaylord and Angustus A. Farnham as senior presidents.

August. *Sat. 9.*—Twenty-eight persons were killed by an explosion in a colliery at Cromstoek, near Aberdare, South Wales. Several of the Saints employed in the colliery escaped, having been warned by vision of the catastrophe.

Sat. 23.—The dome of the Nauvoo Temple was raised.

Sun. 31.—The 30th quorum of Seventy was organized in Nauvoo, with Sahiel Savage as senior president.

September.—One hundred and thirty-five teams were sent from Nauvoo to bring in the families and grain from the surrounding country.

—The few Saints who still remained at Kirtland, O., were persecuted by their enemies, who took possession of the Temple.

—The ship *Oregon* sailed from Liverpool, England, with a company of Saints bound for Nauvoo, Ill.

Wed. 10.—A mob attacked the house of Edmund Durfee, in Morley's Settlement, Hancock Co., Ill., turned the people out of doors, set fire to the buildings and threatened instant death to men, women and children. The mob then burned all the other houses, barns and shops in the settlement and turned the inhabitants into the open air. Also a farming settlement called Green Plains, inhabited by about eighty members of the Church, was burned by the mob.

Mon. 15.—The mob drove Jacob Backenstos, sheriff of Hancock County, from his home at Carthage.

Tues. 16.—The mob made an effort to kill the sheriff. In his defense O. Porter, Rockwell killed Frank A. Worrell, one of the leaders of the mob, who was an officer of the guard at Carthage jail when Joseph and Hyrum Smith were killed.

Thurs. 18.—Sheriff Backenstos, with a *posse* consisting of some seven hundred men, surrounded Carthage, Ill., to make arrests, but the house-burners had fled. He also issued a proclamation to the mobbers to disperse, which, however, was not obeyed, as they went to Missouri and other places, preparing for new depredations.

Wed. 24.—As the persecutions in Hancock County continued to rage, the Saints commenced to leave their possessions in the smaller settlements and flee to Nauvoo for protection. The authorities of the Church made a proposition to the mob to have the Saints leave the State of Illinois the following spring.

Tues. 30.—General John J. Hardin arrived at Nauvoo with four hundred troops, pretending to hunt for criminals, but undoubtedly had other motives for his diligent search of the Temple and other public buildings.

October. *Wed. 1.*—The Apostles at Nauvoo had an important consultation with General John J. Hardin, Senator Stephen A. Douglas, W. B. Warren and J. A. McDougal, commssioners from a convention held in Carthage, about the removal of the Saints.

Sun. 5.—The Nauvoo Temple was so far completed that a meeting, attended by five thousand people, was held in it.

Mon. 6.—The first general conference of the Saints for three years was commenced in the Temple, the Prophet Joseph having ordered that they should not hold another general conference until they could meet in that house. The conference continued for three days. Wm. Smith was dropped as an Apostle and Patriarch.

Sun. 12.—Wm. Smith was excommunicated from the Church at Nauvoo.

Sat. 25.—Major Warren came into Nauvoo with a body of troops and threatened to put the place under martial law. After he had left, the authorities of the Church sent E. A. Bedell and Bishop Geo. Miller with a communication to Gov. Thomas Ford. They informed him of Major Warren's threats and implored him to dismiss the troops under his command, as the Saints had more to fear from them than from the mob at large. The governor did not grant their request.

Sun. 26.—The 31st quorum of Seventy was partly organized at Nauvoo, with Edmund M. Webb as senior president.

November.—Edmund Durfee was killed by the mob in Green Plains, Hancock Co., Ill. About the same time Joshua A. Smith was poisoned at Carthage.

Sun. 30.—The attic story of the Nauvoo Temple was dedicated.

December. *Mon. 15.*—After laboring nearly one year and eight months on Tubuai, Elder Addison Pratt left that island to join Elder Benjamin F. Grouard, who had commenced a most successful missionary work on Anaa, one of the Tuamotu Islands.

Sun. 21.—The 32nd quorum of Seventy was organized at Nauvoo, with Geo. Mayer as senior president.

Tues. 23.—The famous "Bogus Brigham" arrest was made, as the officers taking Elder Wm. Miller to Carthage, believing that they had captured Apostle Brigham Young.

Sat. 27.—A U. S. deputy marshal visited Nauvoo, again searching for the Twelve and others, but failed to make any arrest.

During this month many of the Saints received their blessings and endowments in the Nauvoo Temple.

1846.

Early in the year the Saints commenced to leave Nauvoo, fleeing from the mob, which later drove the remnants out and took forcible possession of the city. The Nauvoo Temple was dedicated, and many of the Saints received their endowments before going into the wilderness. While traveling through Iowa, the exiled Saints were called upon to raise five hundred men to participate in the war with Mexico. Winter Quarters as established on the Missouri river.

January.—The 33rd quorum of Seventy was organized with Albern Allen as senior president.

Tues. 13.—At a council held in the Nauvoo Temple, to take into consideration the means of organizing for the removal of the Saints, 140 horses and 70 wagons were reported ready for immediate service.

Fri. 16.—The ship *Liverpool* sailed from Liverpool, England, with 45 Saints, under the direction of Hiram Clark, bound for Nauvoo *via* New Orleans.

Thurs. 22.—Apostle Wilford Woodruff sailed from Liverpool to return to America, because of the contemplated removal of the Church to the mountains. Reuben Hedlock, with Thomas Ward and John Banks as counselors, succeeded him in the presidency of the British Mission.

Sat. 24.—A general meeting of the official members of the Church was held in the Nauvoo Temple, for the purpose of arranging the affairs of the Church, prior to its removal from Nauvoo.

Fri. 30.—The vane was placed on the Nauvoo Temple.

February. *Wed. 4.* — The Saints at Nauvoo commenced crossing the Mississippi river for the purpose of moving west. Charles Shumway was the first to cross the river.

—The ship *Brooklyn* sailed from New York with 235 Saints on board. They were well supplied with implements of husbandry, and necessary tools for establishing a new settlement. They also took with them a printing press and materials, which afterwards were used in publishing the first newspaper issued in California.

Thurs. 5.—The 34th quorum of Seventy was organized at Nauvoo, with David W. Rogers as one of the presidents.

About the same time the 35th quorum of Seventy was organized.

Mon. 9—A fire, which broke out in the Nauvoo Temple, was put out before it did much damage.

—John E. Page was disfellowshipped.

Tues. 10.—Joseph Young was appointed to preside over the Saints who remained at Nauvoo.

Sun. 15.—Apostles Brigham Young and Willard Richards, with their families, and Apostle Geo. A. Smith crossed the Mississippi river for the West. They traveled nine miles, and camped on Sugar Creek, where Pres. Young spent the following day organizing the camps of the Saints.

Tues. 17.—Apostle Heber C. Kimball arrived in the camp on Sugar Creek. Willard Richards was appointed camp historian and Wm. Clayton clerk.

Wed. 18.—President Young and a few others returned to Nauvoo, but rejoined the camp the following day.

Wed. 25.—Bishop George Miller and company were the first to leave the camp ground on Sugar Creek to travel westward.

Sat. 28.—A petition to the governor of Iowa, in which the Saints asked for protection while passing through the Territory, was approved by the Twelve. At this time the camp consisted of four hundred wagons, very heavily loaded. The teams were too weak for rapid journeying. Most of the families had provisions for several months, while some were quite destitute.

March.—During the month the camps of the Saints in Iowa traveled about one hundred miles. The roads were almost impassable most of the way, and the Saints suffered much from cold and exposure, the weather being very windy and stormy.

Sun. 1.—The camps of the Saints made a general move from Sugar Creek and traveled five miles in a north-westerly direction.

Fri. 27.—At a council held at Apostle Parley P. Pratt's camp, near the east fork of Shoal Creek, the camps of the Saints

were more perfectly organized. Brigham Young was elected president over all the "Camps of Israel."

April.—The Saints in England suffered spiritually and financially on account of the Joint Stock Company business, which was urged upon them by speculating Elders.

Fri. 24.—The advance portion of the camps arrived at a place on the east fork of Grand river, 145 miles from Nauvoo, which the Saints called Garden Grove, where a temporary settlement was commenced for the benefit of the companies which should follow after.

Thurs. 30.—The Nauvoo Temple was dedicated privately, Elder Joseph Young offering the dedicatory prayer.

May. *Fri. 1.*—The Nauvoo Temple was publicly dedicated by Apostle Orson Hyde.

Sun. 10.—About three thousand Saints met in the Temple at Nauvoo. Apostle Wilford Woodruff preached.

Mon. 11.—Part of the camps continued the journey from Garden Grove, and on the 18th arrived at the middle fork of Grand river, on the land of the Pottawattamie Indians, where another temporary settlement was established, called Mount Pisgah. This was 172 miles from Nauvoo.

Thurs. 21.—A general council of the camps at Mount Pisgah had under consideration the subject of sending an exploring company to the Rocky Mountains that year. The subsequent call for the Mormon Battalion, however, made this impossible.

Sun. 31.—Elder Noah Rogers, recently returned from a mission to the Society Islands, died at Mount Pisgah, Iowa. His remains were the first interred in the burying ground at that place.

—A three days' conference convened in Manchester, England, in which the business of the Joint Stock Company was the main topic.

June.—Amos Fielding, who returned to Nauvoo this month, counted 902 west-bound wagons in three days. By this some idea may be formed of the number of teams on the road at that time.

Mon. 1.—Elder Jesse C. Little wrote an appeal to James K. Polk, President of the United States, in behalf of the Saints. He afterwards called on the President, Vice-President and several members of the cabinet.

—A conference of the Church was organized on the Isle of Man, with Samuel J. Lees as president.

Tues. 2.—Pres. Brigham Young left Mount Pisgah and continued the journey westward.

Fri. 12.—Elder Jesse C. Little left Philadelphia for the West, accompanied by Col. Thos. L. Kane, who had decided to visit the camps of the Saints.

Sun. 14.—Pres. Brigham Young, Heber C. Kimball, Geo. Miller and Parley P. Pratt arrived on the banks of the Missouri river, with their respective companies. Here a ferry boat was built soon afterwards, when some of the Saints commenced to cross the river.

Tues. 16.—The advance camps of the exiled Saints moved back to the bluffs across Mosquito Creek, and encamped near good water, about nine miles from the trading post. There they remained till the ferry boat was built.

Mon. 22.—At this date about five hundred wagons had arrived on the Missouri river; nine of the Apostles were already there.

Thurs. 25.—The ship *Brooklyn* arrived at Honolulu, Hawaii, on its way to California.

Fri. 26.—Capt. James Allen, of the U. S. army, arrived at Mount Pisgah and had an interview with Apostle Wilford Woodruff and Pres. Wm. Huntington and council. He was the bearer of a circular to the "Mormons," making a requisition on the camps of the Saints for four or five companies of men, to serve as volunteers in the war with Mexico. Capt. Allen was advised to visit the authorities of the Church at Council Bluffs.

Sat. 27.—John E. Page was excommunicated from the Church.

Tues. 30.—Capt. Allen arrived at Council Bluffs, and on the following day he met with the authorities of the Church, showing his authority for raising five hundred volunteers from the camps of the Saints. The same day Pres. Young and Capt. Allen addressed the brethren who had assembled, and the general council voted unanimously to comply with the requisition from the government.

July.—The first number of *Prophwyd y Jubili* (The Prophet of Jubilee) was published by Dan Jones, in Wales, as the Church organ in that country.

—The Saints having continued to arrive from the East, there were now fourteen companies encamped on the bluffs near the Missouri river.

Fri. 3.—Pres. Brigham Young and others started for Mount Pisgah, where they arrived on the 6th, after having met eight hundred wagons and carriages.

Tues. 7.—Pres. Brigham Young, Heber C. Kimball and Jesse C. Little addressed a meeting of the brethren at Mount Pisgah on the subject of raising a battalion to march to California. Sixty-six volunteered. Geo. W. Langley was sent to Garden Grove with a letter to the presiding brethren there upon the same subject. A similar communication was sent to Nauvoo.

Thurs. 9.—Pres. Brigham Young and others left Mount Pisgah for Council Bluffs, where they arrived on the 12th.

Sat. 11. — John Hill, Achibald N. Hill, Caleb W. Lyons, James W. Huntsman, Gardiner Curtis, John Richards, Elisha Mallory and J. W. Phillips were severely whipped by mobocrats, while harvesting wheat twelve miles from Nauvoo.

Mon. 13.—In obedience to a call of the authorities of the camps of the Saints the men met at head-quarters on Mosquito Creek. Col. Thos. L. Kane, who had arrived in camp, and Capt. Allen were present. Pres. Young, Capt. Allen and others addressed the people in regard to furnishing the battalion. Four companies were raised on that day and the day following. The fifth company was organized a few days later.

At this time severe persecutions were again raging against the few remaining Saints at Nauvoo, and also against the

"new citizens" who had bought the property of the members of the Church, who had already left the city for the west.

Thurs. 16.—At a council of the Twelve held at Council Bluffs, Ia., Ezra T. Benson was ordained an Apostle, and took the place of John E. Page, who had apostatized. Apostles Orson Hyde, Parley P. Pratt and John Taylor were appointed to go to England to set the Church in order there; Reuben Hedlock and Thomas Ward, who at that time presided over the British mission, were disfellowshipped for disregard of counsel.

—Four companies of the volunteers were brought together in a hollow square and mustered into service by their respective captains. They were interestingly addressed by several of the Apostles. A few days later (July 20th) they commenced their march towards Fort Leavenworth.

Fri. 17.—A number of men were selected to take care of the families of the volunteers.

Tues. 21.—A High Council was selected to preside in all temporal and spiritual matters at Council Bluffs.

Wed. 22.—The fifth and last company of the Mormon Battalion left the camps of the Saints and started for Fort Leavenworth.

Thurs. 23.—Samuel Boley, a member of the Mormon Battalion, died on the road to Fort Leavenworth.

Wed. 29.—The Mormon Battalion passed through St. Joseph, Mo.

—The ship *Brooklyn*, with the Saints from the State of New York, arrived at Yerba Buena (now San Francisco), Cal.

August. *Sat. 1.* — The Mormon Battalion, now numbering 549 souls, including officers, privates and servants, arrived at Fort Leavenworth.

Fri. 7.—At a council of the Apostles it was decided that the brethren on the west side of the Missouri river should settle together. A municipal High Council, consisting of Alpheus Cutler, Winslow Farr, Ezra Chase, Jedediah M. Grant, Albert P. Rockwood, Benjamin L. Clapp, Samuel Russell, Andrew Cahoou, Cornelius P. Lott, Daniel Russell, Elnathan Eldredge and Thomas Grover, was appointed to superintend the affairs of the Church there.

—A small company of Saints from Mississippi, under the direction of John Brown, arrived at Pueblo, on the Arkansas river, where it wintered, waiting till the following spring for the advance companies of the "Mormon" emigration.

Sun. 9.—The first meeting was held at Cutler's Park, where the exiled Saints at that time intended to spend the winter. The municipal High Council was accepted by the people and the place named Cutler's Park, in honor of Alpheus Cutler. This place, which now became the temporary headquarters of the camps, is three miles from the spot where Winter Quarters afterwards was built.

Thurs. 13.—Three companies of the Mormon Battalion began to move west from Ft. Leavenworth, after having received their arms, camp equipage, etc. On the 14th the other two companies took up the line of march.

—About this time the mobbers in Hancock County, Ill., concluded to drive the few remaining "Mormon" families from Nauvoo.

Sun. 23.—Col. James Allen, commander of the Mormon Battalion, died at Ft. Leavenworth. The command then devolved on Capt. Jefferson Hunt, as the ranking officer, but notwithstanding this, Lieut. A. J. Smith shortly after assumed the command.

September. *Tues. 8.*—Col. Thos. L. Kane left the camps of the Saints for the East.

Thurs. 10.—The few remaining Saints at Nauvoo, of whom only about one hundred and twenty-five were able to bear arms, were attacked by an armed mob, about eighteen hundred strong, who with five pieces of artillery bombarded the city for several days. The brethren organized for self-defense and stopped the mobbers about two miles from the city.

Fri. 11.—The mobbers were prevented from entering Nauvoo by the gallantry of the "Spartan Band," who fired on the enemy with cannons made of steamboat shafts.

—A site for building winter quarters for the Saints was selected on the west bank of the Missouri river. Teams began to return to Nauvoo after the poor.

—The Mormon Battalion reached the Arkansas river.

Sat. 12.—The battle of Nauvoo took place. Wm. Anderson, his son Augustus and Isaac Norris were killed, and others of the defenders were wounded. The mob force, which again was driven back, also sustained considerable loss.

Wed. 16.—The enemy was driven back from Nauvoo the fourth time. Through the negotiations of one hundred citizens of Quincy, a treaty was completed, by which the Saints should be allowed to move away in peace.

—Some of the families accompanying the Mormon Battalion left the main body on the Arkansas river, in care of Capt. Higgins, for Pueblo. About this time Alva Phelps, a member of the Battalion, died.

Thurs. 17.—The mob entered Nauvoo, and, notwithstanding the treaty, immediately drove out the Saints, and treated some of the brethren in a most brutal manner.

Sun. 20.—Norman Sharp, a member of the Mormon Battalion, accidentally shot himself in the arm and died a few days later, from the effect of the wound.

Tues. 22.—A partial reorganization of the Nauvoo Legion took place at Cutler's Park.

Wed. 23.—The Saints began to move to the new location for Winter Quarters.

Thurs. 24.—A conference was held at Putuahara, Anaa, at which 852 members of the Church in the Society Islands mission were represented.

Sun. 27.—The first public meeting at Winter Quarters was held. By this time most of the Saints had removed from Cutler's Park to Winter Quarters.

October.—Apostle Orson Hyde succeeded Reuben Hedlock as president of the British Mission, and the Joint Stock Company was dissolved.

—Martin Harris and others, followers of the apostate James J. Strang, preached among the Saints in England, but could get no influence.

Fri. 2.—The Mormon Battalion reached Red river.

Sat. 3.—The Battalion was divided in two divisions, of which the first, containing the strongest and most able-bodied men, arrived at Santa Fe, N. M., on the 9th, and the second, containing the sick and the women, on the 12th.

—Apostles Orson Hyde and John Taylor arrived at Liverpool, England, and immediately issued a circular to the British Saints, advising them to "patronize the Joint Stock Company *no more for the present.*"

Wed. 7.—The teams which were sent back to help the poor away from Nauvoo, arrived at the Mississippi river, opposite Nauvoo.

Fri. 9.—The camp of the poor was organized and started for the West. Flocks of quails visited the camp and were easily caught. This was a providential supply of food for the suffering exiles.

Tues. 13.—Capt. P. St. George Cooke assumed command of the Mormon Battalion at Santa Fe, by order of General Kearney.

Wed. 14.—Apostle Parley P. Pratt and Elders Franklin D. Richards, Samuel W. Richards and Moses Martin arrived at Liverpool, England, from the camps of the Saints in the wilderness.

Sat. 17.—On this and the following day a general conference was held in Manchester, England, under the presidency of Apostles Hyde, Pratt and Taylor. Dan Jones reported one thousand Saints in Wales, and a conference was organized in Ireland, with Paul Jones as president.

Sun. 18.—The sick detachment of the Mormon Battalion, consisting of about ninety men, left Santa Fe for Pueblo, under command of Capt. James Brown.

Mon. 19.—The Battalion left Santa Fe for California. On the journey it suffered much from excessive marches, fatigue and short rations.

Tues. 27.—Milton Smith, a member of the Battalion, died on his way with the sick detachment to Pueblo.

November.—A memorial to the Queen of England "for the relief, by emigration, of a portion of her poor subjects," was circulated for signatures among the British Saints.

Tues. 3.—James Hampton, a member of the Mormon Battalion, died.

Wed. 4.—Milton Kelly, a member of the Battalion, died at Pueblo.

Tues. 10.—A detachment of fifty-five sick men of the Battalion, under the command of Lieutenant W. W. Willis, was separated from the main body and started back to Pueblo. Two days later John Green died.

Tues. 17.—Capt. Brown's sick detachment of the Battalion arrived at Pueblo.

Sat. 21.—John D. Lee and Howard Egan arrived at Winter Quarters, as messengers from the camps of the Mormon Battalion beyond Santa Fe.

—Joseph Wm. Richards, a member of the Mormon Battalion, died at Pueblo.

Fri. 27.—Capt. O. M. Allen with the remainder of the sick camp from Nauvoo, arrived at the east bank of the Missouri river.

Sat. 28.—Elijah Freeman and Richard Carter, members of the Battalion (Lout. Willis' detachment), died, and were buried by their comrades four miles south of Secora, on the Rio Grande.

—The main body of the Battalion reached the summit of the Rocky Mountains.

December. — Winter Quarters, afterwards known as Florence, Nebraska, consisted at this time of 538 log houses and 83 sod houses, inhabited by 3,483 souls, of whom 334 were sick and 75 were widows. There were 814 wagons, 145 horses, 29 mules, 388 yoke of oxen and 463 cows. The place was divided in 22 Wards, each presided over by a Bishop. The Ward on the east side of the river contained 210 souls.

—The Saints on the banks of the Missouri river made great exertions to provide themselves with shelter and food for the winter. Notwithstanding this, there was much privation and suffering among them.

—The presidency of the Church in England published a balance sheet of the Joint Stock Company, showing that the Saints had been swindled and their means squandered by officers of the company.

Fri. 11.—The Mormon Battalion had an extraordinary encounter with wild buffalos on the San Pedro river.

Fri. 18.—The Battalion left Tucson. During the remainder of the month it suffered almost beyond human endurance from overmarching, and want of food and water.

Sun. 20.—Capt. Willis' detachment of the Battalion joined the detachments of Captains Brown and Higgins at Pueblo.

Tues. 22.—The Battalion arrived at the Pima village, and encamped the following day by a village of Maricopa Indians.

1847.

The Mormon Battalion arrived in California, and the company of Pioneers, under the leadership of Pres. Brigham Young, crossed the plains and mountains to the valley of the Great Salt Lake, where they founded Great Salt Lake City. After the return to the Missouri river the First Presidency of the Church was reorganized. About two thousand souls and nearly six hundred wagons arrived in G. S. L. Valley in the fall.

January.—The committee who had been appointed to settle up the Joint Stock Company business in England were able to pay one shilling and three pence on the pound of capital stock paid in.

Fri. 8.—The Mormon Battalion reached the mouth of the Gila river. Two days later (10th) it crossed the Colorado.

Thurs. 14.—A revelation was given through Pres. Brigham Young, at Winter Quarters, showing the will of the Lord concerning the camps of Israel (Doc. and Cov., Sec. 136); in accordance with which the Twelve Apostles proceeded to organize the camps by appointing captains of hundreds and fifties. The captains were directed to organize their respective companies.

Tues. 19.—John Perkins, a member of the Mormon Battalion, died at Pueblo.

—Apostles Parley P. Pratt and John Taylor and a small company of Saints sailed from Liverpool, England, bound for New Orleans, but were on account of storms obliged to return to Liverpool, after nine days of rough sailing.

Sat. 23.—Orson Spencer arrived at Liverpool, England, to preside over the British Mission as successor to Apostle Orson Hyde. Elder Franklin D. Richards had had temporary charge of the mission.

Wed. 27.—The Mormon Battalion arrived at San Luis Rey, a deserted Catholic mission, and from a neighboring bluff first saw the Pacific Ocean.

Fri. 29.—The Battalion arrived at a point near San Diego, Cal.

February. *Mon. 1.*—The Battalion was ordered back to San Luis Rey, where it rested a short time.

—Apostles Parley P. Pratt and John Taylor again sailed from Liverpool, bound for New Orleans, where they landed March 10th.

Mon. 15.—John H. Tippetts and Thomas Woolsey arrived at Winter Quarters, as messengers from the Battalion boys at Pueblo, after extreme sufferings on the journey.

Tues. 23.—Apostle Orson Hyde sailed from Liverpool, England, returning to America. He arrived at New York April 6th, and at the camps of the Saints, on the Missouri river, May 12th.

Sun. 28.—Arnold Stevens, a corporal in the Mormon Battalion, died at Pueblo.

March.—At this time Winter Quarters contained 41 blocks, 820 lots, 700 houses, 22 wards, etc.

Thurs. 4.—Thomas Ward, formerly president of the British mission, died in England.

Mon. 15.—Company *B* of the Mormon Battalion was ordered from San Luis Rey to garrison San Diego.

Fri. 19.—Most of the Mormon Battalion, except company *B*, (which was stationed as a garrison at San Diego), left San Luis Rey for Pueblo de los Angeles, where it arrived on the 23rd.

Sun. 28.—After nearly three years missionary labors in the Society Islands mission, Elder Addison Pratt sailed from Papeete, Tahiti, per ship *Providence*, on his return to America, leaving Benjamin F. Grouard in charge of the mission.

Mon. 29.—A number of the Pioneers at Winter Quarters reported themselves ready to start for the mountains.

—About that time David Smith, of the Mormon Battalion, died at San Luis Rey.

April. *Mon. 5.*—Apostle Heber C Kimball moved out four miles from Winter Quarters, with six teams, and formed a nucleus to which the company of Pioneers could gather.

Thurs. 8.—Apostle Parley P. Pratt returned to Winter Quarters from his mission to England.

Sat. 10.—M. S. Blanchard, of the Mormon Battalion, died at Pueblo.

Sun. 11.—Company *C* of the Mormon Battalion was ordered to the Cajon Pass, about forty-five miles east of Los Angeles.

Wed. 14.—Pres. Brigham Young and his brethren of the Twelve left Winter Quarters for the Rocky Mountains. They joined the Pioneer camp near the ·Elkhorn river.

Thurs. 16.—The Pioneer company was organized. It consisted of 73 wagons, 143 men, 3 women and 2 children—148 souls.

Sat. 24.—The Mormon Battalion was ordered to erect a fort on a hill near Los Angeles.

Tues. 27.—Mrs. Hunter, wife of Captain Jesse D. Hunter, of the Battalion, died at San Diego, Cal.

May. *Tues. 11.*—Albert Dunham, of the Battalion, died at San Diego, from an ulcer on the brain.

Thurs. 13.—Gen. Stephen F. Kearney left Los Angeles for Ft. Leavenworth, accompanied by about fifteen brethren of the Battalion. The general and four of the men went by water and the rest by land to Monterey.

Mon. 24.—The sick detachments of the Battalion which had wintered at Pueblo, took up the line of march for California.

Mon. 31.—Gen. Stephen F. Kearney's detachment of theBattalion leftMonterey and traveled by way of the Sacramento Valley, over the Sierra Nevadas, *via* Ft. Hall, Soda Springs, and the Platte River, where it met several companies of Saints, going west, and arrived at Ft. Leavenworth in August.

June. *Tues. 1.*—The Pioneers arrived at Ft. Laramie. A company of Saints, numbering seventeen persons, who had left the State of Mississippi the previous year, joined the Pioneers at that place. It was a part of the company who had wintered at Pueblo; the remainder of it came on with Capt. Brown's detachment of the Battalion.

Thurs. 3.—The Pioneers crossed the North Fork of the Platte river at Ft. Laramie, having traveled on the left bank of the Platte, from the Elkhorn to that point.

Fri. 11.—Amasa M. Lyman, who had been sent back from the Pioneer camp, and other Elders, met the sick detachment of the Mormon Battalion on Pole Creek.

Mon. 14.—The Pioneers recrossed the Platte river from its south to north side, 124 miles west of Ft. Laramie.

—The first company of emigrating Saints was organized at Elkhorn river for journeying west, and on the 19th about five hundred and seventy-five wagons from Winter Quarters had crossed the "Horn."

Wed. 16.—Capt. Brown's detachment of the Mormon Battalion reached Ft. Laramie, and continued the following day westward, intending, if possible, to overtake the Pioneers, who had passed twelve days before.

Sun. 20.—Thomas Smith was arrested and imprisoned at Covington, Warwickshire, England, for having cast out evil spirits. After examination, he and Richard Currell, the subject of administration, were dismissed, there being no cause of action.

Sun. 27.—The Pioneers crossed the

South Pass of the Rocky Mountains. On the following day they met Capt. James Bridger who considered it imprudent to bring a large population into the Great Basin, until it could be ascertained that grain could be raised there. So sanguine was he that it could not be done, that he said he would give one thousand dollars for the first ear of corn produced there.

Tues. 29.—Henry W. Bigler and others of the Mormon Battalion, stationed at San Diego, cleared the first yard for moulding brick in California.

Wed. 30.—Samuel Brannan, on his way from California, met the Pioneers at Green river, with news from the Saints who went out in the ship *Brooklyn* the year previous.

July. *Sun. 4.*—Thirteen men of Capt. Brown's detachment of the Mormon Battalion, overtook the Pioneers on Green river.

Wed. 7.—The Pioneers· arrived at Fort Bridger.

Tues. 13.—The Pioneers were encamped at the head of Echo Canyon; Apostle Orson Pratt was appointed to take 23 wagons and 42 men and precede the main company of Pioneers into Great Salt Lake Valley.

Thurs .15.—Company *B* of the Mormon Battalion joined the main body at Los Angeles.

Fri. 16.—The Battalion was honorably discharged at Los Angeles.

Tues. 20.—Eighty-one of the members of the Battalion re-enlisted for six months at Los Angeles. Four days later they were ordered to San Diego, where they arrived on Aug. 2nd, and were stationed as a provost guard to protect the citizens from Indian raids, etc.Those who did not re-enlist, organized into companies for traveling, and a few days later took up the line of march towards the East.

Wed. 21.—The advance company of the Pioneers camped in Emigration Canyon. went into the valley, and a circuit of about twelve miles was made before they got back to camp at 9 p. m.

Thurs. 22.—The advance company of Pioneers entered Great Salt Lake Valley and camped on Canyon Creek.

Fri. 23.—The advance company moved about three miles and camped on what was subsequently known as the 8th Ward Square of Salt Lake City. Apostle Orson Pratt called the camp together, dedicated the land to the Lord, invoked his blessings on the seeds about to be planted, and on the labors of the Saints in the valley. The camp was organized for work. The first successful plowing was done by Wm. Carter. A company commenced the work of getting out water for irrigation. Pres. Brigham Young, who was sick, and those with him, encamped at the foot of the Little Mountain.

Sat. 24.—Pres. Young entered Great Salt Lake Valley and joined the main body of Pioneers at 2 p. m. Not a member of the company had died on the journey.

Sun. 25.—Religious services were held for the first time in Great Salt Lake Valley. Geo. A. Smith preached the first public discourse and the Sacrament was administered there for the first time.

Mon. 26.—Pres. Young and others ascended what is now known as Ensign Peak, north of Salt Lake City, and named it.

Tues. 27.—Some Ute Indians visited the Pioneer camp. The Twelve and a few others started west from the Pioneer camp on an exploring expedition. Crossing the stream which forms the outlet of Utah lake, they named it the Jordan river, and then proceeded to Black Rock, eighteen miles further, where the company took a bath in the lake.

Wed. 28.—The exploring party returned to camp, a council was held and the Temple Block located.

Thurs. 29.—The detachment of the Mormon Battalion, which had wintered at Pueblo, on the Arkansas river, under Capt. James Brown, arrived in G. S. L. Valley, accompanied by the Saints from Mississippi. This increased the number in camp to about four hundred souls.

August. *Mon. 2.*—The survey of a city was commenced in G. S. L. Valley.

Wed. 4.—Twenty-seven of the re-enlisted Battalion boys were ordered to San Luis Rey, Cal., to protect the mission property.

Fri. 6.—The Apostles in G. S. L. Valley renewed their covenants by baptism, and the rest of the company soon after followed their example.

Mon. 9.—Catharine C. Steele, wife of John Steele, of the Battalion, gave birth to a female child who was named Young Elizabeth Steele. She was the first white child born in the Valley.

Tues. 10.—The building of the "Old Fort" was commenced by the Pioneers in G. S. L. Valley on what is now known as the Pioneer Square, Sixth Ward, Salt Lake City.

Wed. 11.—Milton H. Therlkill, three years old, was accidentally drowned near the Pioneer camp. This was the first death among white people in G. S. L. Valley.

Wed. 18.—Nearly half of the Pioneers left G. S. L. Valley with ox teams, on their return to Winter Quarters for their families.

Fri. 20.—The returning Battalion boys arrived on the Sacramento river. On the 24th they reached a settlement of white people, and received the first news of the Saints settling in G. S. L. Valley.

Sat. 21.—Albert Carrington, John Brown and Wm. W. Rust ascended to the summit of the Twin Peaks, the highest mountain near G. S. L. Valley.

Sun. 22.—At a special conference held in G. S. L. Valley, the city, which had been commenced by the Pioneers, was named Great Salt Lake City; the river Jordan and the mountain streams on the east side of the Valley were also named.

Thurs. 26.—The second company of returning Pioneers left G. S. L. Valley for Winter Quarters to forward the emigration, where they arrived Oct. 31st. On their trip they met several companies of Saints who followed in the track of the Pioneers. Between six and seven hundred wagons, with about two thousand souls, arrived in the Valley that fall. When the Pioneers left for Winter Quarters, the colonists in the Valley had laid off a fort, built

27 log houses, plowed and planted 84 acres with corn, potatoes, beans, buckwheat, turnips, etc.

September.—The members of the Mormon Battalion who had returned to California from the Truckee river were employed by Capt. John A. Sutter, digging mill-races and erecting mills, near the place where Sacramento City now stands.

Fri. 3.—The returning Battalion boys, having crossed the Sierra Nevada Mountains, reached the place where the unfortunate Hastings company had perished the previous winter. A number of human bodies were yet lying unburied on top of the ground. Henry P. Hoyt died. A few days later the soldiers were met by Samuel Brannan, James Brown and others, on the Truckee river. Brannan brought word from Pres. Brigham Young for those who had no means of subsistence to remain in California and work during the winter, and come to the Valley in the spring. About half of the company then returned to California.

Wed. 8.—Sergeant Lafayette N. Frost, of the re-enlisted Mormon Battalion company, died at San Diego.

Mon. 20.—Harriet P. Young, wife of Lorenzo D. Young, gave birth to a male child, which was subsequently named Lorenzo Dow. He died March 22, 1848. This was the first white male child born in G. S. L. Valley.

October. *Sun. 3.*—The Saints in G. S. L. Valley were organized into a Stake of Zion with John Smith as president and Charles C. Rich and John Young as counselors. Selections for a High Council were also made. Charles C. Rich was elected chief military commander in the Valley.

Sat. 16.—Those of the discharged Battalion boys who did not return to California arrived in G. S. L. City.

Mon. 18.—Thirty-two of the Battalion boys, who were anxious to meet their families at Winter Quarters, left G. S. L. City for that place, where they arrived Dec. 18th, after a hard journey.

November.—Capt. James Brown returned to G. S. L. Valley from a visit to California, bringing about $5,000 in gold.

Fri. 5.—Neal Donald, one of the Battalion boys who had re-enlisted, died at San Diego.

December.—Apostle Parley P. Pratt and others visited the Utah lake, where they launched a boat.

Sun. 5.—At a council of the Apostles held in the house of Apostle Orson Hyde, (attended by Brigham Young, Heber C. Kimball, Orson Hyde, Willard Richards, Wilford Woodruff, Geo. A. Smith, Amasa M. Lyman and Ezra T Benson), Brigham Young was unanimously elected President of the Church, with authority to nominate his Counselors, which he did by naming Heber C. Kimball as his first and Willard Richards as his second Counselor.

Mon. 6.—John Smith, the Prophet's uncle, was chosen by the Council of the Apostles, as Patriarch to the whole Church.

Sat. 11.—Philemon C. Merrill, with fifteen others of the Mormon Battalion, arrived at Winter Quarters; they left G. S. L. City Oct. 8th.

Thurs. 23.—The Twelve issued an important epistle from Winter Quarters to all the Saints, announcing, among other things, that emigration could be recommenced.

Fri. 24.—A general conference of the Church was commenced in a log Tabernacle erected by the Saints on the east side of the Missouri river (on the present site of Council Bluffs). It lasted four days. On the last day (Dec. 27th) Brigham Young was unanimously sustained as President of the Church, with Heber C. Kimball as his first and Willard Richards as second Counselor. John Smith was sustained as presiding Patriarch to the Church.

1848.

Gold was discovered in California by members of the Mormon Battalion. Winter Quarters was vacated and most of the Saints who had spent the winter there removed to Great Salt Lake Valley. About one thousand wagons arrived in the Valley during the year, with immigrating Saints. Ogden was founded by Capt. James Brown and others. Many extraordinary and miraculous cases of healing strengthened the faith of the Saints in the British Isles.

January. *Mon. 24.*—Gold was discovered in Sutter's mill race, which had been dug by the Mormon Battalion boys. This discovery soon put the whole country in a fever of excitement.

February.—Nathaniel Thos. Brown, one of Pres. Brigham Young's Pioneer corps, was shot and killed at Council Bluffs, Ia.

Wed. 2.—By the treaty of Guadalupe Hidalgo, Mexico, Upper California, including what is now Utah, was ceded to the United States.

Sun. 20.—The ship *Carnatic* sailed from Liverpool, England, with 120 Saints, bound for G. S. L. Valley, under the direction of Franklin D. Richards. It arrived at New Orleans about April 19th, whence the company proceeded up the Mississippi and Missouri rivers to Winter Quarters, and thence commenced the journey across the plains.

March.—About this time Davis County was settled by Perrigrine Sessions, who located the settlement subsequently called Bountiful.

Mon. 6.—The G. S. L. City fort contained 423 houses and 1,671 souls. The adjoining farming field consisted of 5,133 acres of land, of which 875 acres were sown with winter wheat.

Thurs. 9.—The ship *Sailor Prince* sailed from Liverpool, England, with 80 Saints, under the direction of Moses Martin.

Tues. 14.—The re-enlisted company of the Mormon Battalion was disbanded at San Diego, and on the 25th twenty-five men, with Henry G. Boyle as captain, started for G. S. L. Valley, where they arrived June 5th.

April. *Thurs. 6.*—At a conference held in the log Tabernacle (Miller's Hollow), on the east side of the Missouri river, the settlement at that place was called Kanesville, in honor of Col. Thomas L. Kane.

Thurs. 20.—Elder Mephibosheth Sirrine died of consumption on the steamer *Niagara*, near the mouth of the Ohio river, on his way to St. Louis, Mo.

May.—A company of Saints from Great Britain arrived at Winter Quarters.

Tues. 9.—Twenty-two wagons—the first of the season—left Winter Quarters for the Valley and traveled twenty-seven miles to the Elkhorn river.

Thurs. 11.—Apostle Orson Pratt left Winter Quarters on a mission to England.

Fri. 26.—Pres. Brigham Young left Winter Quarters for the second time for G. S. L. Valley.

Wed. 31.—At Elkhorn river, Pres. Young commenced to organize the emigrating Saints into companies of hundreds, fifties and tens.

June.—In the commencement of this month Pres. Young broke camp at the Elkhorn and started for G. S. L. Valley, with a company consisting of 1,229 souls and 397 wagons. He was followed by Heber C. Kimball's company of 662 souls and 226 wagons, and Willard Richard's company, consisting of 526 souls and 169 wagons. The last wagons left Winter Quarters July 3rd, leaving that place almost destitute of inhabitants.

—Myriads of big crickets came down from the mountains into G. S. L. Valley, and began to sweep away fields of grain and corn. The grain, however, was mostly saved by the arrival of immense flocks of sea gulls, which devoured the crickets.

Tues. 6.—Capt. James Brown entered into negotiations with Miles M. Goodyear, an Indian trader, located on the present site of Ogden City, for the purchase of all the lands, claims and improvements, owned by Goodyear, by virtue of a Spanish grant. Brown paid $3,000 for the improvements, and soon after located himself on the Weber.

Sat. 24.—Captain Daniel Browett, Daniel Allen and Henderson Cox, three of the Battalion boys, left Sutter's Fort, Cal., on an exploring trip across the Sierra Nevada Mountains. A few days later they were killed and their bodies terribly mutilated by Indians.

July. *Sun. 2.*—About thirty-seven of the Battalion boys, who had spent the winter and spring in the Sacramento Valley, Cal., commenced their eastward journey from Pleasant Valley, fifty miles from Sutter's Fort, with 16 wagons, bringing with them two cannons. After a dangerous and adventurous journey they arrived in G. S. L. City, Oct. 1st.

Sat. 22.—Patriarch Asahel Smith died at Iowaville, Wapello Co., Iowa.

Wed. 26.—Apostle Orson Pratt and family arrived in England from Winter Quarters.

August.—Apostle Orson Pratt succeeded Orson Spencer as president of the British mission.

Wed. 9.—The G. S. L. City fort contained 450 buildings and 1,800 inhabitants. There were three saw mills and one temporary flouring mill running, and others in course of construction.

Thurs. 10.—The Saints in G. S. L. City had a feast to celebrate the first harvest gathered in the Great Basin.

Sun. 13.—At a general conference, held in Manchester, England, on this and the following day, 28 conferences and 350 branches, with a total of 17,902 members were represented in the British mission. Wm. Howell was called to go to France to open up a missionary field in that country.

September. *Thurs. 7.*—The ship *Erin's Queen* sailed from Liverpool, England, with 232 Saints, under the direction of Simeon Carter, bound for St. Louis, where the emigrants arrived Nov. 6th. Most of them remained there during the winter.

Mon. 18.—John Henry Smith was born at Carbunca, near Kanesville, Ia.

Wed. 20.—Pres. Brigham Young arrived in G. S. L. Valley with the advance portion of his company. Pres. Kimball's division arrived a few days later, and the other companies all reached the Valley in good season.

Sat. 23.—Reuben Brinkworth, who had been deaf and dumb for five years, was restored to his speech and hearing under the administration of the Elders, at Newport, Monmouthshire, England.

Sun. 24.—The ship *Sailor Prince* sailed from Liverpool, England, with 311 Saints on board, under the direction of L. D. Butler, bound for G. S. L. Valley.

Thurs. 28.—Addison Pratt arrived in G. S. L. City from a five years' mission to the Society Islands, where about twelve hundred persons had been baptized.

October. *Sun. 1.*—At a public meeting held in G. S. L. City, it was voted to build a council house by tithing labor, and Daniel H. Wells was appointed superintendent of its erection.

Sun. 8.—At a general conference held in the G. S. L. City fort, Brigham Young was unanimously sustained as President of the Church, with Heber C. Kimball and Willard Richards as his Counselors.

Mon. 9.—The Nauvoo Temple was burned through the work of an incendiary.

Tues. 10.—Apostle Willard Richard's company arrived in G. S. L. City, having been met by teams from the Valley.

Thurs. 19.—Apostle Amasa M. Lyman's company arrived in G. S. L. City.

Sat. 21.—Oliver Cowdery bore his testimony to the truth of the Book of Mormon, in a conference held at Kanesville, Ia.

November.—The High Council at Kanesville voted to receive Oliver Cowdery back into the Church by baptism, according to his own humble request. Soon afterwards he was baptized, and he made preparation to take a mission to England.

December. *Sun. 3.*—At a meeting, held in the G. S. L. City fort, fellowship was withdrawn from Apostle Lyman Wight and Bishop Geo. Miller.

1849.

During this year Utah Valley was settled by John S. Higbee and others, Tooele Valley by John Rowberry and several others,

and Sanpete Valley by Isaac Morley and company. G. S. L Valley was surveyed by Capt. Howard Stansbury and Lieutenant John W. Gunnison, according to order from the government. About five hundred wagons and fourteen hundred immigrating Saints arrived in the Valley, besides a number of California emigrants who, during their sojourn among the Saints, were converted to "Mormonism" and remained in the Valley. The five companies of Saints which crossed the plains from the Missouri river to the Valley this season were led by Elders Orson Spencer, Allen Taylor, Silas Richards, Geo. A. Smith and Ezra T. Benson. Capt. Dan Jones, with quite a number of Welsh Saints, were included in Geo. A. Smith's company. Elder Wm. Howell commenced to preach the gospel in France. In consequence of the scanty harvest of 1848, breadstuff and other provisions became very scarce in G. S. L. Valley, and many of the people were compelled to eat raw hides and to dig sego and thistle roots, for months, upon which to subsist. Those persons who had, imparted measurably to those who had not, so that extreme suffering from hunger was avoided.

January.—The first number of *Udgorn Seion* (Zion's Trumpet), was issued in the interest of the Church in Wales, as a continuation of *Prophwyd y Jubili*.

Mon. 1.—John Smith, uncle of the Prophet Joseph, was ordained Patriarch to the whole Church.

—The first $1 bill of "Valley Currency" was signed by Brigham Young, Heber C. Kimball and Thos. Bullock.

Fri. 19.—Marcus B. Thorpe, one of Pres. Brigham Young's Pioneers, was murdered in California.

Mon. 22. — Pres. Brigham Young and Thos. Bullock were engaged in setting type for the 50-cent bills of the Valley paper currency. This was the first type setting in G. S. L. Valley.

Mon. 29.—The ship *Zetland* sailed from Liverpool, England, with 358 Saints, bound for G. S. L. Valley, under the presidency of Orson Spencer. It arrived at New Orleans April 2nd, and the emigrants arrived at Kanesville, Iowa, May 17th, having suffered much from cholera while passing up the Missouri river.

February.—The Stake of Zion in G. S. L. Valley was reorganized with Daniel Spencer as president and David Fullmer and Willard Snow counselors. A High Council was also organized, of which the members were: Isaac Morley, Titus Billings, Eleazer Miller, John Vance, Levi Jackman, Ira Eldredge, Elisha H. Groves, Wm. W. Major and Edwin D. Woolley.

Mon. 5.—This was a very cold day in G.

S. L. City, the thermometer showed 33 degrees F. below zero.

Tues. 6.—The ship *Ashland* sailed from Liverpool, England, with 187 Saints, under the direction of John Johnson, bound for G. S. L. Valley.

Wed. 7.—The first number of the *Frontier Guardian*, a semi-monthly four-page newspaper, was published by Apostle Orson Hyde, at Kanesville, Iowa.

—The ship *Henry Ware* sailed from Liverpool, England, with 225 Saints on board, bound for G. S. L. Valley, under the direction of Robert Martin.

Mon. 12. — Charles C. Rich, Lorenzo Snow, Erastus Snow and Franklin D. Richards were ordained Apostles, to fill the vacancies in the Council of Twelve Apostles caused by the reorganization of the First Presidency and the rejection of Lyman Wight.

Wed. 14.—G. S. L. City was divided into nineteen ecclesistical Wards of nine blocks each.

Fri. 16. — The First Presidency and the Apostles, in council assembled, divided the country lying south of G. S. L. City into four Bishop's Wards, namely, Canyon Creek (afterwards Sugar House), Mill Creek, Holladay (afterwards Big Cottonwood) and South Cottonwood.

Thurs. 22.—At a council meeting held in G. S. L. City, the following Bishops were ordained and set apart to preside in the City Wards: David Fairbanks, 1st Ward; John Lowry, 2nd Ward; Christopher Williams, 3rd Ward; Wm. Hickenlooper, 6th Ward; Wm. G. Perkins, 7th Ward; Addison Everett, 8th Ward; Seth Taft, 9th Ward; David Pettigrew, 10th Ward; Benjamin Covey, 12th Ward; Edward Hunter, 13th Ward; John Murdock, 14th Ward; Abraham O. Smoot, 15th Ward; Isaac Higbee, 16th Ward; Joseph L. Heywood, 17th Ward and James Hendricks, 19th Ward.

Sun. 25.—The ship *Buena Vista* sailed from Liverpool, England, with 249 Welsh Saints, under the direction of Dan Jones.

Mon. 26.—Work was commenced on the Council House, G. S. L. City.

March.—Provo, Utah Valley, was settled by John S. Higbee and some thirty others. On March 18th a branch of the Church was organized with John S. Higbee as president. During the year the settlers had some trouble with the Indians.

—A post office was established in G. S.L. City, with Joseph L. Heywood as postmaster.

—The Icarians arrived at Nauvoo, Ill., and bought the ruins of the Temple, with a view to refit it for school purposes.

Mon. 5.—The ship *Hartley* sailed from Liverpool, England, with 220 Saints bound for G. S. L. Valley, under the direction of W. Hulme. It arrived at New Orleans April 28th.

Thurs. 8.—A convention, which was held for three days, convened in G. S. L. City. Before its adjournment a State constitution for the proposed State of Deseret was adopted. Almon W. Babbitt was soon after sent as delegate to Congress, with a petition asking for admission into the Union.

Mon. 12.—An election took place for officers of the provisional government of the State of Deseret. Brigham Young was chosen governor; Willard Richards, secretary; Newel K. Whitney, treasurer; Heber C. Kimball, chief judge; John Taylor and Newel K. Whitney, associate judges; Daniel H. Wells, attorney general; Horace S. Eldredge, marshal; Albert Carrington, assessor and collector of taxes; Joseph L. Heywood, surveyor of highways. Magistrates were also appointed for the several Wards.

—The ship *Emblem* sailed from Liverpool, England, with about one hundred Saints, under the direction of Robert Deans, bound for G. S. L. Valley.

Thurs. 15.—John Van Cott sold a peck of potatoes for $5 in G. S. L. City, which was considered cheap.

Sun. 25.—The first public meeting was held on the Temple Block, G. S. L. City.

Wed. 28.—The Nauvoo Legion was partly reorganized; Daniel H. Wells was appointed major-general. The first company organized was under the command of Capt. George D. Grant, and those who belonged to it were styled "minute men."

April.—The settlers in Utah Valley built a fort near the present site of Provo City.

Sun. 8.—The Fourth Ward, G. S. L. City, was organized with Benjamin Brown as Bishop.

Mon. 9.—The First Presidency issued the "First General Epistle" to the whole Church from G. S. L. Valley. By this time the people in the G. S. L. City fort had commenced to move out to their city lots.

May. *Sat. 5.*—Elder Elijah Malin, of Winter Quarters, died of cholera, in St. Louis, Mo., returning from a mission to Pennsylvania.

June. *Mon. 11.*—Caleb Baldwin, one of the brethren who had been imprisoned with the Prophet Joseph in Liberty jail, Mo., died in G. S. L. City.

Sat. 16.—Parties from the east *en route* for the California gold mines began to arrive in the Valley, and during the summer they traveled through by thousands. They brought all kinds of merchandise, wagons, tools and farming implements, etc., which were sold to the Saints below original cost, in exchange for provisions.

July.—Elder William Howell visited France and began to preach the gospel; he baptized the first person on July 30th, at Havre, and during the remainder of the year he baptized a few more. Among the number was a Baptist preacher about sixty years old.

Mon. 2.—The General Assembly of the Provisional State of Deseret met for the first time in G. S. L. City.

Sat. 21.—The first endowment in G. S. L. Valley was given to Addison Pratt on Ensign Peak.

Tues. 24.—The first celebration to commemorate the entrance of the Pioneers into G. S. L. Valley was held in G. S. L. City.

August. *Fri. 24.*—Wm. W. Phelps ascended to the top of Mount Nebo, south of Utah Valley, to make scientific observations.

Tues. 28.—Captain Howard Stansbury and party of surveyors arrived in G. S. L.

Valley, accompanied by Lieutenant John W. Gunnison.

September. *Sat. 1.*—Wm. Dayton was accidentally killed and Geo. W. Bean crippled for life, by the premature discharge of a cannon at Fort Utah (Provo), Utah.

Sun. 2.—The ship *James Pennell* sailed from Liverpool, England, with 236 Saints, under the direction of Thomas H. Clark, bound for G. S. L. Valley. It arrived at New Orleans Oct. 22nd.

Wed. 5.—The ship *Berlin* sailed from Liverpool with 253 Saints, under James G. Brown's direction, bound for G. S. L. Valley; it arrived at New Orleans Oct. 22nd. Twenty-six died on the voyage, of cholera.

Sun. 23.—Orson Spencer arrived in G. S. L. Valley, with his company of British Saints.

October. *Wed. 3.*—Three companies of emigrating Saints were exposed to the fury of a tremendous snow storm near the South Pass. Sixty head of cattle perished.

Sat. 6.—The Deseret Dramatic Association was organized in G. S. L. City.

—On this and the following day a general conference of the Church was held in G. S. L. City, at which the Perpetual Emigration Fund was commenced. John Taylor, Curtis E. Bolton and John Pack were called on missions to France; Erastus Snow and Peter O. Hansen to Denmark; Lorenzo Snow and Joseph Toronto to Italy; Franklin D. Richards, Joseph W. Johnson, Joseph W. Young, Job Smith, Haden W. Church, Geo. B. Wallace and John S. Higbee to Great Britain; Charles C. Rich and Francis M. Pomeroy to Lower California; Addison Pratt, James S. Brown and Hiram H. Blackwell to the Society Islands, and John E. Forsgren to Sweden. A "Carrying Company," for carrying goods from the Missouri river to the Valley and also to run a wagon passenger train, was organized. It was voted to lay off a city in Capt. James Brown's neighborhood (Ogden), and another one in Utah Valley (Provo); also to make a settlement in Sanpete Valley (Manti). For the latter Isaac Morley, Charles Shumway and Seth Taft were appointed a presidency.

Fri. 12.—The First Presidency issued the "Second General Epistle" from G. S. L. Valley, to the Saints in all the world.

Fri. 19.—The missionaries' camp was organized for traveling, Shadrach Roundy being appointed president. The company consisted of 35 men, with 12 wagons, 1 carriage, and 42 horses and mules. Among the Elders were Apostles Lorenzo Snow, Erastus Snow and Franklin D. Richards, Bishop Edward Hunter and other prominent men. It was the first company of missionaries sent from the Rocky Mountains.

November. *Sat. 10.*—The ship *Zetland* sailed from Liverpool, England, with 250 Saints, under the direction of S. H. Hawkins. It arrived at New Orleans Dec. 24th.

Mon. 12.—The missionaries traveling east were attacked by about two hundred Cheyenne warriors, on the Platte river, but escaped unhurt.

Mon. 19.—Sanpete Valley was settled by

a company, under the guidance of Isaac Morley, Seth Taft and Charles Shumway. They located near the present site of Manti.

Fri. 23.—An exploring company, consisting of about fifty men, was organized at Capt. John Brown's house, on Big Cottonwood, with Apostle Parley P. Pratt as president; it started the next day to explore what is now southern Utah.

December.—The general assembly of the Provisional State of Deseret met for the second time and held adjourned meetings at intervals through the winter. Among the important business done was the creating of Great Salt Lake, Weber, Utah, Sanpete, Juab and Tooele counties, appointing a supreme court, chartering a State University, etc.

—The first Sunday school in Utah was opened by Elder Richard Ballantyne, in the 14th Ward, G. S. L. City.

Sat. 1.—Nineteen men on foot arrived in G. S. L. City from the East in a very destitute condition, having left their wagons in the snow on Echo creek, forty miles back.

Fri. 7.—After an adventurous journey, during which an overruling Providence was clearly made manifest in behalf of the Elders, the missionaries arrived at Old Ft. Kearney, on the Missouri river.

Mon. 24.—A terrific wind swept over G. S. L. Valley from the south.

Before the end of the year, the Saints who had settled on the Little Cottonwood creek, south of G. S. L. City, were organized into a Ward, named Little Cottonwood, with Silas Richards as Bishop.

1850.

In Utah Valley, where a number of new settlements were founded during the year, the Saints had trouble with the Indians. The first mission of the Church were opened in France, Italy and Denmark by Apostles John Taylor, Lorenzo Snow and Erastus Snow respectively, assisted by other Elders. Later in the year the first Latter-day Saint Elders also arrived in Switzerland and in Hawaii (Sandwich Islands) and commenced missionary labors. The Territory of Utah was created by act of Congress.

January.—The British Mission contained about twenty eight thousand Saints, having increased more than ten thousand during the last sixteen mouths.

—Apostle Parley P. Pratt's company explored the southern country as far south as the mouth of the Santa Clara river, beyond the Rim of the Basin.

Thurs. 10.—The ship *Argo* sailed from Liverpool, England, with 402 Saints, under the direction of Jeter Clinton. It arrived at New Orleans March 8th.

Mon. 21.—Apostle Parley P. Pratt's company on its return from the South went into winter camp on Chalk Creek (near the present site of Fillmore), unable to travel further with wagons through the deep snow. Twenty-four of the men with the best horses and mules pushed on to G. S. L. City, and the remainder followed in March.

February. *Thurs. 7.*—A company of about one hundred minute men, under command of Capt. Geo. D. Grant, left G. S. L. City for Utah County, to protect the settlers there against the depredations of the Indians (Utes).

Fri. 8.—On this and the following day a battle was fought between the "minute men" and about seventy Indian warriors under Big Elk, close to Utah Fort (now Provo), in which several were killed and wounded on both sides. The Indians subsequently retreated to the mountains.

Mon. 11.—General Daniel H. Wells, who had arrived in Utah Valley with more men, pursued the Indians and overtook them near Table Rock. Five warriors were killed and the rest taken prisoners. The next day, when the Indians tried to overpower the guard, another battle ensued in which several natives were killed. The squaws and children were subsequently taken to G. S. L. City, and a number of the children adopted by citizens.

Mon. 18.—The ship *Josiah Bradley* sailed from Liverpool, England, with 263 Saints under the direction of Thomas Day. It arrived at New Orleans April 18th.

Fri. 22.—A light shock of earthquake was felt in G. S. L. Valley.

March. *Sat. 2.*—The ship *Hartley* sailed from Liverpool, England, with 109 Saints, under David Cook's direction. It arrived at New Orleans May 2nd.

Sun. 3.—Oliver Cowdery died in the faith, at Richmond, Ray Co., Mo., of consumption.

Tues. 5.—A branch of the Church was organized at Ogden with Lorin Farr as president.

Tues. 26.—Col. Thos. L. Kane delivered his famous lecture on the "Mormons" before the Historical Society of Pennsylvania, at Philadelphia.

April. *Sat. 6.*—The 20th annual conference of the Church was commenced in G. S. L. City; it was continued until the 8th; a number of missionaries were called to Great Britain, the Society Islands, the United States, etc.

—Elder Wm. Howell organized a branch of the Church with six members at Boulogne-sur-mer, France. This was the first branch of the Church raised up in that country.

Fri. 12.—The First Presidency issued the "Third General Epistle" to all the Saints.

May. *Fri. 24.*—Addison Pratt arrived at Papeete, Tahiti, on his second mission to the Society Islands, accompanied by Elder James S. Brown.

Mon. 27.—The walls of the Nauvoo Temple were blown down by a hurricane.

June.—The water was higher in G. S. L. Valley than ever before since the Pioneers arrived. A number of bridges were washed away and other damage done. Emigrants en route to California passed through G. S. L. City almost daily.

Sat. 8.—The first mail of the season from the States arrived in G. S. L. Valley.

Fri. 14.—Apostle Erastus Snow and Elders John E. Forsgren and Geo. P. Dykes landed in Copenhagen, Denmark, as the first missionaries to Scandinavia, except Elder Peter O. Hansen, who had arrived there a few weeks before.

Sat. 15.—The first number of the *Deseret News* was published in G. S. L. City; Willard Richards, editor.

Tues. 18.—Apostle John Taylor and Elder Curtis E. Bolton, accompanied by Wm. Howell, arrived at Boulogne, France. John Pack arrived a few days later. Soon afterwards they all proceeded to Paris.

Tues. 25.—Apostle Lorenzo Snow and Elders Joseph Toronto and Thos. B. H. Stenhouse arrived at Genoa, Italy, as the first Latter-day Saint missionaries to that country.

July.—Under the new management of Apostle Orson Pratt, the *Millennial Star* had increased its circulation from about three thousand seven hundred to over twenty two thousand.

Mon. 1—Elder Thos. B. H. Stenhouse and Joseph Toronto left Genoa, Italy, according to appointment by Apostle Lorenzo Snow, to visit the Protestant valleys of Piedmont.

Thurs. 4.—Parley's Canyon, Utah, was opened for travel under the name of the "Golden Pass"; Parley P. Pratt, proprietor. The toll was 75 cts. for each conveyance drawn by two animals, and 10 cents for each additional draught, pack or saddle animal, etc. The Newark Rangers of Kendall County, Ill., was the first company to follow Apostle Pratt through the pass, which opened a new road through the mountains from the Weber river to G. S. L. Valley.

—The general assembly of the State of Deseret held a joint session and passed an ordinance taxing the sale of liquor at the rate of 50 per cent. ad valorem.

Fri. 19.—Elder John E. Forsgren baptized his brother Peter A. Forsgren, near Gefle, Sweden. This was the first baptism in Sweden by divine authority in this dispensation.

Tues. 23.—Apostle Lorenzo Snow left Genoa, Italy, and traveled *via* Turin to La Tour, in the valley of Luzerne, Piedmont.

Wed. 24.—Pioneer day was celebrated in grand style in G. S. L. City; the brass band occupied a carriage built for the occasion, 9 feet wide and 29 feet long, drawn by 14 horses. Willard Richards delivered the oration.

Wed. 31.—Pres. Brigham Young and Heber C. Kimball left G. S. L. City on their first visit to Sanpete Valley; they returned Aug. 12th.

August.—Lehi, Utah Valley, was first settled; about the same time the two neighboring towns of American Fork and Pleasant Grove were settled.

Mon. 5.—Pres. Brigham Young pointed out the site for a Temple on the hill where the Manti Temple, Sanpete Co., Utah, now stands.

Mon. 12.—The first baptisms in Denmark, by divine authority in this dispensation, took place in Copenhagen, Apostle Erastus Snow baptizing fifteen persons in Øresund. The first man baptized was Ole

U. C. Mønster and the first woman Anna Beckstrøm.

Thurs. 15.—Apostle Orson Hyde arrived in G. S. L. City from Kanesville, Iowa, and reported eight hundred wagons with "Mormon" emigrants organized for crossing the plains.

Sun. 25.—The Sacrament was administered for the first time in Denmark by divine authority in this dispensation, at a meeting held in Copenhagen.

Wed. 28.—Capt. Howard Stansbury and suite, having completed their surveys, left G. S. L. City, on their return to Washington, D. C.

—Presidents Brigham Young and Heber C. Kimball, Apostle Orson Hyde, Bishop Newel K. Whitney, Daniel H. Wells and others left G. S. L. City for the purpose of locating a city on the Weber (Ogden). They returned on the 31st, having located the corner stake and given a plan for the city of Ogden.

September. *Sun. 1.*—A small branch of the Church was organized in Dublin, Ireland, by Elder Edward Sutherland.

Wed. 4.—The ship *North Atlantic* sailed from Liverpool, England, with 357 Saints, under the presidency of David Sudworth and Hamilton G. Park. It arrived at New Orleans Nov. 1st.

Fri. 6.—The semi-annual conference of the Church was commenced in G. S. L. City; it continued until the 8th. Willard Snow, Edward Hunter and Daniel Spencer were chosen as a committee to transact the business of the Perpetual Emigrating Fund Company. Isaac Morley was authorized to select one hundred men, with or without families, to settle Sanpete Valley.

Mon. 9.—The act of Congress providing for the organization of the Territory of Utah was approved. The original size of the Territory was about 225,000 square miles, being bounded on the north by Oregon, east by the summit of the Rocky Mountains, south by the 37th parallel of north latitude, and west by California.

Thurs. 12.—Capt. Johnson's second fifty of emigrants arrived in G. S. L. City.

Sat. 14.—An ordinance incorporating the Perpetual Emigrating Fund Company was passed by the general assembly of the State of Deseret.

Sun. 15.—At a public meeting (resolved into a special conference of the Church), held in the Bowery, Salt Lake City, Brigham Young was chosen president of the Perpetual Emigrating Fund Company, with Heber C. Kimball, Willard Richards, Newel K. Whitney, Orson Hyde, George A. Smith, Ezra T. Benson, Jedediah M. Grant, Daniel H. Wells, Willard Snow, Edward Hunter, Daniel Spencer, Thomas Bullock, John Brown, William Crosby, Amasa M. Lyman, Charles C. Rich, Lorenzo Young and Parley P. Pratt as assistants.

—The first branch of the Church in Scandinavia was organized in Copenhagen, Denmark, with fifty members.

Wed 18.—Jabez Woodard joined Lorenzo Snow and fellow-missionaries in Italy.

Thurs. 19.—Apostle Lorenzo Snow and Elders Joseph Toronto, Thos. B. H. Stenhouse and Jabez Woodard ascended a high

mountain, which they named Mount Brigham, near La Tour, Valley of Luzerne, Piedmont, Italy, and organized themselves into the first branch of the Church in that country.

Fri. 20.—Pres. Brigham Young was appointed governor of Utah Territory: Benjamin D. Harris, of Vermont, secretary; Joseph Buffington, of Pennsylvania, chief justice; Perry C. Brocchus, of Alabama, and Zerubbabel Snow, of Ohio, associate justices; Seth M. Blair, of Utah, U. S. attorney, and Joseph L. Heywood, of Utah, U. S. marshal.

Mon. 23.—Newel K. Whitney, presiding Bishop of the Church, died in G. S. L. City.

Fri. 27.—The First Presidency issued the "Fourth General Epistle," from G. S. L. Valley, to all the Saints.

Sun.29.—Amasa M. Lyman arrived in G.S. L. City from California, accompanied by a number of brethren who returned from an unsuccessful trip to the California gold mines. A similar company arrived in November.

October.—Springville, Utah Co., was settled by Aaron Johnson and others.

Tues. 1.—Apostle Orson Hyde left G. S. L. City for Kanesville, Iowa.

Wed. 2.—The ship *James Pennell* sailed from Liverpool, England, with 254 Saints under the direction of Christopher Layton. It arrived at New Orleans Nov. 22, 1850.

Sat. 5.—The general assembly of Deseret met and passed a bill, providing for the organization of Davis County.

Thurs. 10.—Elder Geo. P. Dykes arrived as a missionary in Aalborg, Jutland, Denmark, where he commenced to baptize Oct. 27th. A month later (Nov. 25th) he organized a branch of the Church at Aalborg, which was the second branch in Scandinavia.

Sun. 13.—Bishop Edward Hunter arrived in G. S. L. City with the first company of P. E. Fund emigrants from the United States.

Mon. 14.—Apostle Wilford Woodruff and family arrived in G. S. L. City with a company of emigrants.

Tues. 15.—The mail bringing the first information to the Valley of the organization of the Territory of Utah, arrived in G. S. L. City.

Thurs. 17.—The ship *Joseph Badger* sailed from Liverpool, England, with 227 Saints on board, under the direction of John Morris; it arrived at New Orleans Nov. 22nd.

Sun. 20.—James Pace and others with their families arrived on Peteetneet Creek, Utah Valley, and settled what is now Payson.

Sat. 26.—At an adjourned meeting of the Seventies, held in the Bowery, G. S. L. City, it was resolved to build a hall, to be called "The Seventies' Hall of Science"; $5,200 worth of shares were subscribed for at once, each share being $25.

Sun. 27.—Apostle Lorenzo Snow baptized a man at La Tour, Valley of Luzerne, Piedmont, Italy, as the first fruit of preaching the fulness of the gospel in that land. Soon afterwards a number of others were baptized in the same locality.

Mon. 28.—Elder Joseph A. Stratton died in G. S. L. City.

November. *Sun. 3.*—Thomas Ford, ex-governor of Illinois, died at Peoria, Ill.

Tues. 12.—Apostle Charles C. Rich, O. Porter Rockwell and about fifty other brethren arrived in G. S. L. City from California.

Mon. 18.—Apostle Orson Hyde arrived at Kanesville, Iowa, from his visit to G. S. L. Valley.

Sun. 24.—Apostle Lorenzo Snow ordained Jabez Woodard a High Priest and called him to preside over the Church in Italy. He also ordained Thos. B. H. Stenhouse a High Priest and appointed him to open up the gospel door in Switzerland. This was done on "Mount Brigham," Piedmont, Italy.

Wed. 27.—The Warm Springs bath-house, north of G. S. L. City, was opened with a festival attended by the First Presidency, a number of the Apostles and other leading men; Heber C. Kimball offered the dedicatory prayer.

December.—Thirty families, including 118 men, left G. S. L. City with 101 wagons and six hundred head of stock, under the direction of Apostle Geo. A. Smith, for the Little Salt Lake Valley, to locate a settlement there.

—Elder Thos. B. H. Stenhouse commenced to preach the gospel in Geneva, the first Latter-day Saint missionary in Switzerland.

Mon. 2.—The general assembly of Deseret opened its third session in G. S. L. City. After sitting four days the house adjourned till the first Monday in January, 1851.

—The first meeting in the Council House, G. S. L. City, was held.

Sat. 7.—A branch of the Church was organized by Apostle John Taylor and colaborers in Paris, France.

Thurs. 12.—Hiram Clark, Thos. Whittle, Henry W. Bigler, Thos. Morris, John Dixon, Wm. Farrer, James Hawkins, Hiram H. Blackwell, James Keeler and Geo. Q. Cannon arrived at Honolulu as the first Latter-day Saint missionaries to Hawaii (Sandwich Islands).

Fri. 20.—A branch of the Church was organized by Apostle Geo. A. Smith at Payson, Utah Co., with James Pace as president.

1851.

Great Salt Lake City, Utah, was incorporated and the first officers elected. The newly appointed officers for the Territory of Utah entered upon the duties of their offices. The first Territorial legislature convened in G. S. L. City and passed important laws. In the spring of the year school houses were built in most of the Wards in G. S. L. City, and also in the country Wards. A railroad (with wooden rails) was built from G. S. L. City to Red Butte canyon, to bring rocks to the Temple Block. Cedar City, Iron Co., North Wil-

low Creek (now Willard City), Box Elder Co., and Nephi, Juab Co., were settled this year. North Ogden, Weber Co., was settled by Solomon, Jonathan and Samuel Campbell, John Riddle and others; Santaquin, Utah Co., by Benjamin F. Johnson and others, and Carson County (now in the State of Nevada) by Col. John Reese. A settlement of the Saints (San Bernardino) was founded in Southern California. Missions were opened in New South Wales, (Australia), and in India.

January.—City charters were granted to Ogden, Provo, Manti and Parowan, by the general assembly of the State of Deseret.

—*Udgorn Seion* (Zion's Trumpet), the organ of the Church in Wales, was changed from a monthly to a semi-monthly periodical.

Wed. 1.—Apostle Franklin D. Richards succeeded Apostle Orson Pratt as president of the British Mission.

—The first native Elder in the Scandinavian mission (Christian Christiansen) was ordained by Apostle Erastus Snow, at Copenhagen, Denmark.

Fri. 3.—The first criminal trial by jury took place in the Provisional State of Deseret, in G. S. L. City.

Mon. 6.—The general assembly of the State of Deseret met in G. S. L. City; daily meetings were held until the 17th, when it adjourned until the first Tuesday in February. Much important business was transacted.

Wed. 8.—The ship *Ellen* sailed from Liverpool, England, with 466 Saints, under the direction of James W. Cummings; it arrived at New Orleans, March 14th.

Thurs. 9.—The bill incorporating G. S. L. City was passed by the general assembly of Deseret, and the following officers were appointed by the governor and assembly: Jedediah M. Grant, mayor; Nathaniel H. Felt, Wm. Snow, Jesse P. Harmon and Nathaniel V. Jones, aldermen; Vincent Shurtliff, Benjamin L. Clapp, Zera Pulsipher, Wm. G. Perkins, Lewis Robison, Harrison Burgess, Jeter Clinton, John L. Dunyon, and Samuel W. Richards, councilors.

Sat. 11.—The G. S. L. City council assembled in the Representatives Hall, and the officers elect took their oath of office from Thomas Bullock, clerk of the county court; when the council proceeded to complete the city organization by electing Robert Campbell, recorder; Thomas Rhodes, treasurer; and Elam Luddington, marshal. The city was divided into four municipal wards.

Mon. 13.—Apostle Geo. A. Smith and company of settlers arrived on Centre Creek, Little Salt Lake Valley, Utah, where they located a town site, which later was named Parowan. They commenced their settlement by building a fort.

Sat. 18.—On this and the following day the Seventies held a special conference in the Bowery, G. S. L. City; a number of vacancies were filled and other important business was transacted.

Mon. 20.—Presidents Brigham Young and Heber C. Kimball, Apostle Amasa M. Lyman, Elder Jedediah M. Grant and others left G. S. L. City to visit the settlements in Davis and Weber Counties. In the evening they preached in the house of Perrigrine Sessions,and organized a branch of the Church; John Stoker was ordained Bishop. The place at that time was known as Sessions settlement.

Tues. 21.—Pres. Brigham Young and party held meeting with the people of North Cottonwood (Farmington), in the school house, and appointed Gideon Brownell presiding Elder of that branch.

Wed. 22.—The ship *George W. Bourne* sailed from Liverpool, England, with 281 Saints, under the direction of William Gibson; it arrived at New Orleans March 20th.

Sun. 26.—Pres. Brigham Young and party held meetings with the Saints in the south fort, Ogden, when Lorin Farr was chosen president of the Weber Stake,with Charles R. Dana and David B. Dille as counselors. A High Council was also organized. Isaac Clark was ordained Bishop of the South Ward, with James Browning and James Brown as counselors; and Erastus Bingham Bishop of the North Ward, with Charles Hubbart and Stephen Perry as counselors.

Mon. 27.—Pres. Brigham Young and party held a meeting with the Saints who had settled on Kay's creek,(now Kaysville, Davis Co.,) and appointed William Kay Bishop of that Ward.

—Official news of the organization of the Territory of Utah first reached G. S. L. City.

Tues. 28.—Pres. Brigham Young and party returned to G. S. L. City from their visit to the settlements in Weber and Davis Counties.

Wed. 29.—Elder James Henry Flanigan, a good and faithful American missionary, died of small-pox at Birmingham, England.

February. *Sun. 2.*—The ship *Ellen Maria* sailed from Liverpool, England, with 378 Saints on board, under George D. Watt's direction. Apostle Orson Pratt and family also returned with that company. The ship arrived at New Orleans April 6th.

Mon. 3.—Brigham Young took the oath of office as governor of the Territory of Utah.

Tues. 4.—The general assembly of Deseret again met in G. S. L. City and was in session on that and the following day; also on the 10th and on the 24th; it finally adjourned to the fourth Saturday in March.

Sun. 9.—The settlers who had located on Centre Creek (Parowan), Iron Co., Utah, were organized into a branch of the Church, under the presidency of Apostle George A. Smith.

Mon. 17.—Robert Dickson opened a school in the 14th Ward, G. S. L. City, with 18 scholars, teaching phonography.

March.—G. S. L. City, Box Elder Co., was settled by William Davis, James Brooks and Thomas Pierce.

Tues. 4.—The ship *Olympus* sailed from Liverpool, England, with 245 Saints, bound for Utah, under the direction of Wm.

Howell. Some fifty non-Mormon passengers were converted and baptized on the voyage to New Orleans, where the company arrived about April 27th.

Mon. 17.—Presidents Brigham Young and Heber C. Kimball and others left G.S. L. City on a visit to Utah County.

—Elder Wm. Burton, of G. S. L. City, died at Edinburgh, Scotland, where he labored as a missionary.

Wed. 19.—A Stake of Zion was organized by Pres. Brigham Young at Provo, Utah Co., with Isaac Higbee as president, and John Blackburn and Thos. Willis as counselors.

Thurs. 20.—A branch of the Church was organized by Pres. Brigham Young, at Springville, Utah Co., Utah, with Asahel Perry as president and Aaron Johnson as Bishop.

Sun. 23.—Benjamin Cross was ordained a High Priest and set apart to act as the first Bishop of Payson.

Mon. 24.—A company of settlers for Southern California was organized for traveling, at Payson, Utah Co., and commenced the journey the same day, under the presidency of Apostles Amasa M. Lyman and Charles C. Rich, accompanied by Apostle Parley P. Pratt and a party of missionaries going to different countries to preach the gospel.

Wed. 26.—Pres. Brigham Young and party returned to G. S. L. City from their visit to Utah County.

Fri. 28.—The general assembly of Deseret met and passed a number of resolutions expressive of their good feelings toward the government for creating the Territory of Utah.

April.—Pres. Brigham Young dictated the plan for a tabernacle to be erected on the southwest corner of the Temple Block, G. S. L. City.

—The Eighteenth Ward, G. S. L. City, was organized with Lorenzo D. Young as Bishop.

—The schooner *Ravaai*, which had been built by the Elders and Saints on Tubuai, Society Islands mission, for missionary purposes, was finished and launched.

Sat. 5.—The general assembly of the Provisional State of Deseret was dissolved. Among a number of other acts passed during the session of 1850-51 was one providing for the organization of Iron County.

Sun. 6.—The 21st annual conference of the Church convened in G. S. L. City, but after the opening exercises it was adjourned to the 7th, on account of the heavy rains.

Mon. 7.—At the general conference held in G. S. L. City it was voted to build a Temple. Edward Hunter was appointed successor to the late Newel K. Whitney as presiding Bishop of the whole Church. At this time there were about thirty thousand inhabitants in Utah, of which nearly five thousand were in G. S. L. City. The First Presidency issued the "Fifth General Epistle" to the Saints in all the world.

Tues. 22.—Presidents Brigham Young and Heber C. Kimball and many other prominent men left G. S. L. City to visit the Saints in the southern settlements and explore the Sevier Valley.

Wed. 30.—Pres. Brigham Young organized a High Council at Manti, Sanpete Co.. Utah.

May.—The Book of Mormon in the Danish language, translated by Peter O. Hansen, was published by Erastus Snow in Copenhagen, Denmark; it was the first edition of the book printed in a foreign language.

—The first number of the *Etoile du Deseret* (Star of Deseret), a monthly periodical published in the interest of the Church, was issued by Apostle John Taylor, in Paris, France.

Wed. 7.—The first wagons of the season direct from Fort Laramie arrived in G. S. L. City,laden with provisions.

Sat. 10.—Pres. Brigham Young and party arrived at Parowan, Iron Co., where they remained until the 16th.

Mon. 12.—The first job of blacksmithing with Utah stone coal was done by Mr. Bringhurst at Parowan, Iron Co., in the presence of Gov. Brigham Young and party.

Tues. 13.—The foundation of the Seventies' Hall of Science in G. S. L. City was completed.

Wed. 21.—Work was commenced on the "Old Tabernacle," in G. S. L. City.

Sat. 24.—Pres. Brigham Young and party returned to G. S. L. City from their visit to the southern settlements.

Sun. 25.—The Saints who had settled at American Fork, Utah Co., Utah, were organized into a Ward; Leonard E. Harrington, Bishop.

June.—Apostles Amasa M. Lyman and Charles C. Rich, with about five hundred souls from Utah, arrived at San Bernardino, Cal., for the purpose of making a settlement.

—Elder Joseph Richards, member of the British army, arrived at Calcutta, India, having been authorized by the presidency of the British mission to introduce the gospel in that country.

Tues. 3.—The Channel Islands' mission was transferred from the British to the French mission, at a special conference, held in London, England.

Sat. 7.—Judge Lemuel G. Brandenbury arrived in G. S. L. City.

Tues. 10.—The Indians stole about sixty head of stock near Black Rock, Salt Lake Co.

Sat. 21.—The Saints' assembly hall at Aalborg, Denmark, was demolished by a mob, which also ill-treated some of the brethren.

Sun. 22.—Elder Geo. Q. Cannon commenced to baptize natives in the district of Kula, on the island of Maui, Hawaii. This was the commencement of a great missionary work on that island; a few natives had previously been baptized on the island of Hawaii, and one or more at Honolulu.

—Elder Joseph Richards baptized James Patrick Meik, Mary Ann Meik, Matthew McCune and Maurice White, at Calcutta, India, as the first converts to the fulness of the gospel in Asia in this dispensation. These four, together with Elder Richards, were organized into a branch of the Church, called the Wanderers' branch.

July. Tues. 1.—Gov. Brigham Young issued a proclamation appointing the first Monday in the following August for electing members to the first Territorial legislature, according to the organic act.

Fri. 4.—The citizens of G. S. L. City celebrated the day by an excursion to Black Rock, in the Great Salt Lake.

Fri. 11. — Apostle Parley P. Pratt and company of missionaries arrived at San Francisco, Cal.

—Apostle Orson Hyde and traveling companions, en route for G. S. L. Valley, were attacked by about three hundred Pawnee Indians, near Loupe Fork, and robbed of several thousand dollars' worth of property.

Sun. 13.—The Eleventh Ward, G. S. L. City, was organized with John Lytle as Bishop.

Sat. 19.—Four of the newly appointed Federal officers for Utah, namely, Judge Zerubbabel Snow, Secretary Benjamin D. Harris and Indian Agents Stephen B. Rose and Henry R. Day arrived in G. S. L. City, accompanied by Dr. John M. Bernhisel and Almon W. Babbitt.

Mon. 21.—Gov. Brigham Young, by proclamation, divided the Territory of Utah' into three Indian agencies, and assigned the sub-agents, Rose and Day, their respective districts.

Thurs. 24.—Pioneer day was celebrated in excellent style in G. S. L. City and the different settlements of the Saints in Utah.

August.—The first kiln of earthen ware was burned at the Deseret Pottery, located near the head of Emigration or Third South Streets.

Mon. 4.—The first election for delegate to Congress and members of the Territorial legislature took place in Utah. Dr. John M. Bernhisel was elected Utah's first delegate to Congress.

Wed. 6.—The first branch of the Church in the Hawaiian Islands was organized by Elder Geo. Q. Cannon,in the Kula district, on the island of Maui.

Fri. 8.—Gov. Brigham Young, by proclamation, divided the Territory of Utah into three judicial districts. Hon. Lemuel G. Brandenbury was assigned to the first, Hon. Zerubbabel Snow to the second and Hon. Perry E. Brocchus to the third judicial district.

Sat. 16.—The first general conference in the Scandinavian mission convened in Copenhagen, Denmark, Erastus Snow presiding. It was continued three days.

Sun. 17.—Apostle Orson Hyde, Albert Carrington and others arrived in G. S. L. City from Kanesville, Ia., accompanied by Perry E. Brocchus, one of the newly appointed judges for Utah; they brought with them a brass cannon.

September.—Juab County was settled by Joseph L. Heywood and others, who located on Salt Creek (now Nephi).

—Chief Justice Brandenbury, Associate Judge Perry E. Brocchus and Secretary Benjamin D. Harris deserted their official posts in Utah and went to the States, taking with them the $24,000 which had been appropriated by Congress for the legislature.

—The *Athrawiaeth a Chyfammodau*

(Doctrine and Covenants) was published in the Welsh language, in Wales.

Sun. 7.—The general conference of the Church convened in the Bowery, G. S. L. City; it was continued four days. During the conference Judge Perry E. Brocchus, who with the other Federal officers had been invited to the stand, spoke insultingly to the large assembly.

Thurs. 11.—Elder Hans F. Petersen arrived at Riisør, as the first Latter-day Saint missionary to Norway.

Sun. 21.—The First Presidency issued an epistle to the Saints in Iowa, counseling them to come to the Valley.

Mon. 22.—The first legislature of Utah Territory convened in G. S. L. City and organized by electing Heber C. Kimball president of the Council, and Wm. W. Phelps speaker of the House.

—The First Presidency issued the "Sixth General Epistle" to the whole Church.

—Amasa M. Lyman and party purchased the Ranche of San Bernardino, containing about one hundred thousand acres of land. The location was about one hundred miles from San Diego, seventy miles from the seaport of San Pedro and fifty miles from Pueblo de los Angeles.

October. The first number of *Skandinaviens Stjerne*, a monthly (now semi-monthly) periodical, was published by Apostle Erastus Snow, in Copenhagen, Denmark.

Wed. 1.—John Hartley, who had met with a railroad accident, was miraculously healed under the administration of Elders, at Accrington, England.

Sat. 4.—A joint resolution, passed by the Utah legislature, legalizing the laws of the provisional government of the State of Deseret, was approved by the governor.

Sun. 5.—Elder Maurice White baptized Anna, a daughter of a high caste Brahmin, at Calcutta, India, as the first native convert to "Mormonism" in the East India mission.

Tues. 21—Gov. Brigham Young, Heber C. Kimball, Geo. A. Smith and others left G. S. L. City on a tour to the South, for the purpose of locating the Territorial seat of government. They reached Chalk creek, Pauvan Valley, Oct. 28th.

Fri. 24.—The last company of the immigrating Saints for the season arrived in G. S. L. City.

—Elders Hans Peter Jensen and Hans Larsen received very cruel treatment from a mob on Bornholm, Denmark, for preaching the gospel.

Wed. 29.—Fillmore, Millard Co., Utah, which had just been settled by Anson Call and thirty families, was selected for the capital of the Territory.

—Elder James S. Brown was arrested by order of the French officials at Anaa, Society Islands mission, and the next day placed on board a French man-of-war.

Thurs. 30.—John Murdock and Charles W. Wandell, arrived at Sydney, as Latter-day Saint missionaries to Australia, and commenced to preach the gospel.

November.—The first number of *Zions Panier* (Zion's Banner), a monthly 16-page periodical, was published at Hamburg, Germany, by Apostle John Taylor.

Sun. 2.—The first meeting by Latter-day Saint Elders in New South Wales, Australia, was held by Elders John Murdock and Charles W. Wandell at Sydney.

Fri. 7.—Pres. Brigham Young and party returned to G. S. L. City from Fillmore, having come by way of Sanpete Valley.

Sat. 8.—Apostle Parley P. Pratt and Rufus Allen arrived as missionaries in Valparaiso, Chili, South America, after 64 days' rough sailing from San Francisco.

Tues. 11.—The "University of the State of Deseret" was opened in G. S, L. City.

Sat. 15.—The *Deseret News*, which had been suspended for lack of paper since Aug. 19th, commenced its second volume.

Wed. 26.—Elder Hans F. Petersen baptized Peter Adamsen and John Olsen in Riisør, as the first fruits of preaching the gospel in Norway.

December.—Three families commenced a settlement on Clover Creek (Mona), eight miles north of Nephi, Juab Co.

—The San Bernardino settlers had erected about one hundred dwellings and built a stockade fort for defense against the Indians.

—A number of Saints were cruelly treated by a mob in Brøndbyøster, Sjælland, Denmark.

Mon. 1.—The British mission consisted of 44 conferences and 679 branches, with 32,894 members. This is the greatest number of Saints ever reported in that mission.

Tues. 2.—A number of fishermen at Arnager, Bornholm, Denmark, armed themselves and defended two "Mormon" missionaries against mob violence.

Wed. 3.—The first baptism by divine authority in New South Wales, Australia, took place in Sydney.

Sun. 7.—Peter Adamsen and John Olsen were confirmed members of the Church by Elder Hans F. Petersen, at Riisør. This was the first confirmation by Latter-day Saints in Norway. The Sacrament was also administered for the first time by divine authority in that country.

Sun. 21.—A branch of the Church was organized at Spanish Fork, Utah Co., (recently settled), with Stephen Markham as president and Wm. Pace, as Bishop.

Thurs. 25.—Elder Wm. Willes arrived at Calcutta, India, as a Latter-day Saint missionary from England, sent by Apostle Lorenzo Snow to preach the gospel in India.

1852.

In the spring of this year John D. Lee located a ranch on Ash Creek (near the present Harmony, Washington Co.), and Cedar Valley was settled by Allen Weeks, Alfred Bell and others. Early in the year post offices were established at American Fork, Springville and Payson, Utah Co., Salt Creek (Nephi), Juab Co., and Fillmore, Millard Co. About twenty companies of emigrating Saints arrived in the Valley which included most of the Saints who had been located temporarily in and about Kanesville (Council Bluffs), Iowa. During this year the Book of Mormon was published in the Welsh, French, German and Italian languages. The missionaries sent to labor in Norway were imprisoned at Frederikstad. In Hawaii and Australia the Elders met with considerable success, but the attempt to open a mission in Chili, South America, proved a failure. The Elders were banished from the Society Islands mission. Missionaries were called to India, China, Siam, Cape of Good Hope, Prussia, Gibraltar, the West Indies and other countries.

January. *Sun. 4.*—The first branch of the Church in New South Wales, Australia, was organized at Sydney, with twelve members.

Sat. 10.—The ship *Kennebec* sailed from Liverpool, England, with 333 Saints, under the direction of John S. Higbee. It arrived at New Orleans March 11th.

Mon. 19.—The Saints who had settled on the river Jordan, south of G. S. L. City, were organized into a Ward with John Robinson as Bishop.

Tues. 20.—Elder Knud H. Bruun was fearfully whipped and nearly killed by a mob at Falkersløv, on Falster, Denmark.

Tues. 27.—Elder Geo. Q. Cannon commenced the translation of the Book of Mormon in the Hawaiian language, at Wailuku, Maui.

Sat. 31.—Nine Saints sailed from Copenhagen, Denmark, for America, being the first "Mormon" emigrants from Scandinavia.

February. — The Territorial Library was opened in the Council House, G. S. L. City, with Wm. C. Staines, as librarian. Congress had appropriated $5,000 towards the purchase of books, which were selected by Delegate Bernhisel.

Tues. 3.—Legislative acts, providing for the organization of the counties of Great Salt Lake, Weber, Utah, Sanpete, Juab, Tooele, Iron, Davis (previously created by acts of the general assembly of Deseret), Millard, Washington, Green River and Deseret Counties were approved.

Thurs. 5.—The Utah legislature adjourned, but met again on the 16th.

Sat. 7.—Gov. Brigham Young approved an act, recently passed by the Utah legislature, appointing probate judges in the counties in Utah; to wit., Isaac Clark, Weber Co.; Joseph Holbrook, Davis Co.; Elias Smith, G. S. L. Co.; Preston Thomas, Utah Co.; Alfred Lee, Tooele Co.; Geo. W. Bradley, Juab Co.; Geo. Peacock, Sanpete Co.; Anson Call, Millard Co.; Chapman Duncan, Iron Co.

Tues. 10.—A branch of the Church was organized at Mountainville (Alpine), Utah Co., Utah; Charles S. Peterson, president.

—The ship *Ellen Maria* sailed from Liverpool, England, with 369 Saints, under the direction of Isaac C. Haight. It arrived in New Orleans April 6th.

Sat. 14. — The legislative assembly of Utah Territory memorialized Congress for the construction of a great national central railroad from the Missouri river to the Pacific coast. The memorial was approved on the 3rd of March following. At the same session, the legislature petitioned Congress for the establishment of a telegraph line across the continent.

Thurs. 26.—Lorenzo Snow and Jabez Woodard arrived as the first missionaries of the Church on the island of Malta, and commenced preaching. A branch of the Church, consisting of 26 members, was organized there on the 28th of June following.

March.—A site for a city at San Bernardino was surveyed by the Saints in California.

Tues. 2.—After an unsuccessful attempt to open a mission in South America, Apostle Parley P. Pratt and Rufus Allen sailed from Valparaiso, Chili, for San Francisco, Cal., where they arrived May 21st.

Thurs. 4.—After establishing a mission in Scandinavia, Erastus Snow sailed from Copenhagen, Denmark, to return home, accompanied by 19 emigrating Saints.

Sat. 6.—The ship *Rockaway* sailed from Liverpool, England, with 30 Saints and machinery purchased by Apostle John Taylor for the manufacture of sugar in Utah. It arrived at New Orleans after seven weeks' passage.

—Apostle John Taylor, accompanied by about twenty Saints, sailed from Liverpool for Boston, on his return home.

Thurs. 11.—The ship *Italy* sailed from Liverpool, England, with 28 Scandinavian Saints—the first from the Scandinavian mission—under the direction of Ole U. C. Mønster. The company arrived at New Orleans May 10th and in G. S. L. City Oct. 16th, crossing the plains in Eli B. Kelsey's company.

Mon. 15.—G. S. L. County was organized with Elias Smith as county and probate judge.

April.—The *Millennial Star*, the Church organ in Great Britain, was changed from a semi-monthly to a weekly periodical.

Tues. 6.—The building subsequently known as the Old Tabernacle, which had been erected and just completed on the southwest corner of the Temple Block, in G. S. L. City, was dedicated. This structure, built of adobe, was 126 feet long, 64 feet wide and arched without a pillar. It was capable of seating about twenty-five hundred people. The ground is now occupied by the Assembly Hall.

—The first general conference of the Church in the Hawaiian mission was commenced in the valley of Iao, near Wailuku, Maui.

Fri. 9.—A number of emigrating Saints lost their lives by the explosion of the steamboat *Saluda*, at Lexington, Missouri. There were about one hundred and ten Saints on board when the calamity occurred.

Sun. 18.—The First Presidency issued its "Seventh General Epistle" to the whole Church.

Thurs. 22.—Pres. Brigham Young, accompanied by Heber C. Kimball, Orson Pratt, Wilford Woodruff, Geo. A. Smith and others, left G. S. L. City on an exploring trip. After visiting all the southern settlements and several Indian tribes, the party returned on May 21st.

Thurs. 29.—The Deseret Iron Company was organized at Liverpool, England, and Erastus Snow and Franklin D. Richards were appointed general agents and managers of the same.

May. *Wed. 5.*—Sixty-nine men were killed by an accident in a coal pit, at Cymback, near Merthyr Tydfil, Wales; among them were nineteen brethren.

Sat. 8.—Apostles Erastus Snow and Franklin D. Richards sailed from Liverpool on the steamship *Africa*, homeward bound.

—Samuel W. Richards succeeded Franklin D. Richards as president of the British mission. Previous to this the mission was divided into pastorates, presided over mostly by American Elders,while the native brethren generally had charge of the conferences. Each pastorate embraced a number of conferences.

Sat. 15.—Wm. Willes reported 189 members of the Church in Calcutta and vicinity, India, of whom 170 were "Ryots," who previously professed Christianity.

Sun. 16.—The Elders laboring on the Society Islands being forbidden by the French authorities to continue their missionary labors, Elder Addison Pratt and Benjamin F. Grouard with their families sailed from Papeete, Tahiti, per ship *Calao* bound for America. The other missionaries followed soon afterwards.

Mon. 31.—Elders John F. F. Dorius, A. Andersen and others were subjected to wicked mob violence, near Skive, Jutland, Denmark.

June, *Sun. 27.*—Elder Hugh Findlay arrived at Poonah, India, from Bombay,as the first Latter-day Saint missionary to that part of the country.

July.—A townsite called Palmyra was surveyed on the Spanish Fork river, Utah Co., on which the first house was built in the following August. This settlement was afterwards united with and absorbed in Spanish Fork.

—The first branch of the Church in Norway was organized with eighteen members by Hans Peter Jensen, at Risør. A few days later another branch was organized at Frederikstad. The third branch was established at Brevig, where a hall was rented for holding meetings. Brevig was made the headquarters of the Norwegian mission for some time.

Sat. 17.—A special conference was held at Provo, at which Apostle Geo. A. Smith was appointed to preside over the Saints in Utah County. He chose Isaac Higbee and Dominicus Carter for his counselors.

Tues. 27.—The thermometer stood 127 degrees F. in the sun, in G. S. L. City.

Sat. 31.—Elder Christoffer O. Folkman was brutally whipped and nearly killed by a mob at Tinstad, Bornholm, Denmark, where he labored as a missionary.

August.—Provo, Utah Co., was divided into five Bishop's Wards, with Jonathan O. Duke as Bishop of the First, James Bird of the Second, Elias H. Blackburn of the Third, Wm. M. Wall of the Fourth and Wm. Faucett of the Fifth Ward.

—Elder Michael Johnson, who was sent to Sweden to continue the work commenced there by John E. Forsgren two years previously, was arrested and brought as a prisoner to Stockholm, after which he was sent in chains six hundred miles to Malmø, together with two thieves.

Sun. 1.—A small branch of the Church was organized in Hamburg, Germany, by Elder Daniel Garn.

Thurs. 12.—Hiram Page, one of the Eight Witnesses to the Book of Mormon, died near Excelsior Springs, Ray Co., Mo.

Tues. 17.—Elder Matthew McCune, a member of the British army, arrived at Rangoon, Burmah, authorized by the American Elders laboring in India to preach the gospel in that empire.

Fri. 20.—Apostles John Taylor, Erastus Snow and Franklin D. Richards, accompanied by other Elders, arrived in G. S. L. City from their foreign missions.

Sat. 28.—A special two days' conference was commenced in G. S. L. City; 106 Elders were called to go on missions, namely 6 to the United States, 4 to Nova Scotia and the British N. A. Provinces, 2 to British Gulana (South America), 4 to the West Indies, 39 to Great Britian, 1 to France, 4 to Germany. 3 to Prussia, 2 to Gibraltar, 1 to Denmark, 2 to Norway, 9 to Calcutta and Hindostan, 4 to China, 3 to Siam, 3 to Cape of Good Hope, Africa, 10 to Australia and 9 to the Hawaiian Islands.

Sun. 29.—The revelation on celestial marriage was first made public. It was read in the conference held in G. S. L. City, and Apostle Orson Pratt delivered the first public discourse on that principle.

Mon. 30.—Apostle Lorenzo Snow returned to G. S. L. City from his foreign mission.

Tues. 31.—The Utah "run away judges" were superseded by the appointment of Lazarus H. Reed, as chief justice, and Leonidas Shaver, as associate justice. Ben. G. Ferris had previously been commissioned as secretary.

September.—Over seventy Elders left G. S. L. City for Europe and the United States, Apostle Orson Pratt being among the number.

—Elders John A. Ahmanson and Jeppe G. Folkman were imprisoned four days at Brevig, Norway, for preaching the gospel.

Fri. 3.—The first company of P. E. Fund emigrants arrived at G. S. L. City from Europe with 31 wagons; Abraham O. Smoot, captain. It was met by the First Presidency, Capt. Wm. Pitt's band and many leading citizens. This company brought the remains of Elder Lorenzo D. Barnes and Wm. Burton, who died while on missions in Great Britain.

Sun. 12.—A branch of the Church, consisting of twelve members, was organized in the city of Poonah, British India, by Elder Hugh Findlay.

Tues. 21.—Apostle Orson Hyde arrived in G. S. L. City, with his family from Iowa. Nearly all the Saints had left Kanesville for the Valley.

—Mary Fielding Smith, widow of Hyrum Smith, died in G. S. L. County.

October. *Wed. 6.*—The general semi-annual conference of the Church was commenced in G. S. L. City; it was continued till the 10th. A number of home missionaries were called to preach in the various settlements of the Saints in Utah.

Wed. 13.—The First Presidency issued the "Eighth General Epistle" to the whole Church.

Thurs. 14.—Elders Jeppe G. Folkman and Niels Hansen were arrested at Ingolsrud, Norway, for preaching the gospel. John F. F. Dorius, Christian Knudsen, Christian Larsen and Svend Larsen were arrested the following day, and Peter Beckstrøm on the 16th, on similar charges. Christian Larsen, Svend Larsen, Dorius and Beckstrøm were imprisoned at Frederikstad, while Ole Olsen (who had been arrested two weeks previously), Christian Knudsen, Jeppe G. Folkman, and Niels Hansen were confined at Elverbø].

Mon. 18.—Apostle Parley P. Pratt arrived in G. S. L. City from his mission to South America.

Sun. 24.—A number of missionaries left G. S. L. City for India and the Pacific Islands.

November.—A number of native Saints in the Society Islands mission were imprisoned and sentenced to hard labor in the mountains for holding meetings.

Wed. 10.—Elders Wm. Willes and Joseph Richards left Calcutta, on a trip to the interior of India.

Thurs. 11.—Apostles Erastus Snow and Franklin D. Richards left G. S. L. City for Iron County where they surveyed a tract of land for the "Deseret Iron Company." They returned to the city Dec. 12th.

Fri. 12.—Elder John A. Ahmanson was brought as a prisoner to Frederikstad, Norway. Thus all the missionaries in that country were in jail.

December. *Sun. 5.*—Peter Beckstrøm, one of the imprisoned brethren in Norway, was liberated on bail.

Mon. 13.—The second session of the Utah legislature convened at G. S. L. City, and was organized by the election of Willard Richards for president of the Council and Jed. M. Grant for speaker of the House.

1853.

This year the Indians under Chief Walker waged war against the citizens of Utah, of whom a number were killed. The "Spanish wall" was built in part around G. S. L. City, as a means of protection against the Indians. Summit County, Utah, was settled by Samuel Snyder, who built saw-mills in Parley's Park; a settlement of Saints (Fort Supply) was commenced on Green river. New missions were opened up on the Island of Malta (in the Mediterranean), at Gibraltar (Spain), and in the Cape Colony, Africa. The missionaries and Saints in Sweden were subjected to cruel and barberous persecution. Some were whipped, others imprisoned and a number compelled to go into exile.

January. *Sat. 1.*—The Social Hall, on First East Street, G. S. L. City, was dedicated; it was erected the year previous.

Wed. 12.—Elder Daniel Garn was arrested in Hamburg, Germany, for preaching the gospel. Soon afterwards he was ordered out of the city.

Sun. 16.—The ship *Forest Monarch* sailed from Liverpool, England, with 297 Scandinavian Saints, under John E. Forsgren's direction. The company arrived at New Orleans March 12th; at Keokuk, Iowa, in the beginning of April; and most of the emigrants reached G. S. L. City, Sept. 30th. This was the first large company of Saints who emigrated to Utah from Scandinavia.

Mon. 17.—The Deseret Iron Company was chartered by the Utah legislature.

—The ship *Ellen Maria* sailed from Liverpool, England, with 332 Saints, under the direction of Moses Clawson. It arrived at New Orleans March 6th, where Elder John Brown acted as Church emigration agent that season. The emigrants continued up the Mississippi river to Keokuk, Iowa, which had been selected as the outfitting place for the Saints crossing the plains in 1853.

Wed. 19.—The first theatrical play in the Social Hall was presented.

Fri. 21.—The Utah legislature closed its second regular session.

Sun. 23.—The ship *Golconda* sailed from Liverpool, England, with 321 Saints, under the direction of Jacob Gates; it arrived at New Orleans, March 26th.

Tues. 25—Elders Orson Spencer and Jacob Houtz, arrived as missionaries in Berlin, Prussia. They were banished Feb. 2nd following.

Sat. 29.—The missionaries, bound for Hindostan and Siam, sailed from San Francisco, Cal., per sailing ship *Monsoon.* John M. Horner, a wealthy member of the Church in California, contributed nearly $6,000 toward defraying the expenses of these missionaries, and of those going to China, Australia and Hawaii.

Mon. 31.—Elder Christian Larsen, one of the imprisoned missionaries in Frederikstad, Norway, was liberated.

February. *Sat. 5.*—The ship *Jersey* sailed from Liverpool, England, with 314 Saints, under the direction of Geo. Halliday; it arrived at New Orleans, March 21st.

Mon. 14.—The Temple Block, in G. S. L. City, was consecrated, and the ground broken for the foundation of the Temple.

Tues. 15.—The *Elvira Owen* sailed from Liverpool, England, with 345 Saints, under the direction of Joseph W. Young. It arrived at New Orleans March 31st.

Mon. 28.—The ship *International* sailed from Liverpool, England, with 425 Saints, under the direction of Christopher Arthur. It arrived at New Orleans April 23rd.

March. *Mon. 7.*—Edward Stevenson and Nathan T. Porter arrived at Gibraltar, as the first Latter-day Saint missionaries to Spain.

Wed. 16.—After being confined in prison for several months, Svend Larsen was liberated from the Frederikstad jail, and ordered to preach "Mormonism" no more in Norway.

Mon. 28.—The ship *Falcon* sailed from Liverpool, England, with 324 Saints, under Cor. Bagnall's direction. It arrived at New Orleans May 18th.

Wed. 30.—Augustus Farnham and nine other American Elders arrived at Sydney, New South Wales, as Latter-day Saint missionaries to Australia.

April. *Sun. 3.*—The Saints who had settled in Cedar Valley, Utah, were organized into a Ward; Allen Weeks, Bishop.

Tues. 5.—Elder Jacob F. Secrist was imprisoned at Wissen an der Sieg, Prussia, whither he had gone from Hamburg, on a visit. The following day he was liberated and ordered out of the country.

Wed. 6.—The corner stones of the Temple in G. S. L. City were laid under the direction of the First Presidency of the Church.

—A small company of Saints, in charge of Elder Charles W. Wandell, and bound for America, sailed from Sydney, Australia, per ship *Envelope*.

—The ship *Camillus* sailed from Liverpool, England, with 228 Saints, under the direction of Curtis E. Bolton. It arrived at New Orleans in the latter part of May.

Mon. 11.—The Fifth ward, G. S. L. City, was organized with Thos. W. Winter as Bishop.

Wed. 13.—The First Presidency issued the "Ninth General Epistle" to all the Saints.

Mon. 18.—Elders Jesse Haven, Leonard I. Smith and Wm. Walker arrived as the first Latter-day Saint missionaries at the Cape of Good Hope. In about four months they baptized thirty-nine persons.

Sun. 24.—The first branch of the Church in Sweden was organized by Anders W. Winberg at Skurup, in Skaane, called the Sjønabæck branch.

Tues. 26.—Elders Nathaniel V. Jones, Amos Milton Musser, Richard Ballantyne, Robert Skelton, Robert Owen, Wm. F. Carter, Wm. Fotheringham, Truman Leonard, Samuel A. Woolley, Chauncey W. West, Elam Luddington, Levi Savage and Benjamin F. Dewey arrived at Calcutta as missionaries from Utah to Hindostan and Siam, after 86 days' voyage from San Francisco, Cal.

Wed. 27.—Elders Hosea Stout, James Lewis and Chapman Duncan arrived as the first Latter-day Saint missionaries to China. Soon afterwards they commenced to preach the gospel, but meeting with no success, they returned to California.

Fri. 29.—At a conference of American Elders held at Calcutta, Hindostan, Nathaniel V. Jones was sustained as president of the East India mission; Richard Ballantyne, Robert Skelton and Robert Owens were appointed to labor in Madras; Wm. F. Carter and Wm. Fotheringham in Dinaghpore; Truman Leonard and Samuel A. Woolley in Chinsurah, and Nathaniel V. Jones and A. Milton Musser in Calcutta.

—Rodney Badger, one of the Pioneers of 1847, was accidentally drowned in the Weber river, Utah.

May. *Thurs. 5.*—Elder John F. F. Dorius and fellow prisoners, in Norway, were finally liberated, after nearly seven months' imprisonment for the gospel's sake.

Mon. 23.—A branch of the Church was organized at Cape Town, Africa.

June.—High water did much damage in G. S. L. City. City Creek cut a deep channel through the Seventeenth Ward.

Wed. 1.—The Utah legislature convened in the Social Hall, G. S. L. City, and after three days' sitting adjourned. This was a special session.

Sun. 5.—Chief Justice Lazarus H. Reed arrived at G. S. L. City, and next day took the oath of office.

Sun. 12.—The first emigrant train of the season arrived in G. S. L. City.

Sun. 19.—A branch of the Church was organized on Westmanøen, Iceland, with six members.

Sat. 25.—Elders Wm. F. Carter and Wm. Fotheringham returned to Calcutta, India, from an unsuccessful missionary trip to Dinaghpore, Chunar and Mirzapore.

July. *Mon. 18.*—Alexander Keel was killed by Indians under the chief Walker, near Payson, Utah Co. This was the commencement of another Indian war.

Tues. 19.—The guard at Pleasant Creek, Sanpete Co., was fired upon by Indians who also, during the following night, stole some cattle at Manti, drove away horses at Nephi (Juab Co.), and wounded Wm. Jolley, at Springville (Utah Co.).

Sat. 23.—Peter W. Connover's company of militia, sent out from Provo to protect the weaker settlements, had an engagement with the Indians, near the Pleasant Creek settlement (Mount Pleasant), Sanpete Co., in which six Indians were killed.

Sun. 24.—John Berry and Clark Roberts were fired upon and wounded by Indians at Summit Creek (Santaquin), while bringing an express through. The inhabitants had deserted the place and moved to Payson.

—Elders Richard Ballantyne and Robert Skelton arrived at Madras, India, to introduce the gospel.

Tues. 26.—The guard at Nephi, Juab Co., was fired upon by Indians and David Udall wounded in the leg.

August. *Mon. 1.*—John M. Bernhisel was re-elected delegate to Congress from Utah.

Wed. 10.—The Indians fired upon a company of ten men on Clover Creek (Mona), Juab Valley, wounding Isaac Duffin and killing two horses.

Sat. 13.—The first number of *Zion's Watchman*, a monthly eight-page octavo periodical, published in the interest of the Church in Australia, was issued at Sydney by Augustus Farnham.

Wed. 17.—John Dixon, a Utah Pioneer of 1847, and John Quayle were killed and John Hoagland was wounded by Indians, near Parley's Park, Utah.

Fri. 19.—Gov. Brigham Young issued a proclamation, ordering the Territorial militia to be kept in readiness for marching against Indians, who were killing people and stealing stock in various parts of the Territory.

Sun. 21.—Elder Willard Snow died on board the steamer *Transit*, on the German Ocean, during his return voyage from Copenhagen, Denmark, to England. He was buried at sea.

Tues. 23.—At a Bishop's meeting, held in

the Council House, G. S. L. City, it was decided to build a wall around the city.

Wed. 24.—Elders Samuel A. Woolley and Wm. Fotheringham left Calcutta in a government bullock train on a missionary trip to the interior of India.

Sat. 27.—John Hyde, an American Elder, died at Sydney, Australia, where he labored as a missionary.

Mon. 29.—Resolutions were adopted by the city council, in compliance with expressed request of the inhabitants, to build a Spanish wall around G. S. L. City.

September. *Sat. 3.*—A terrible flood caused considerable damage to property in Iron County, Utah.

Wed. 7.—Joseph Chatterly, a member of the High Council, in the Parowan Stake of Zion, died in Cedar City, Iron Co., Utah, from the effects of a wound.

Fri. 9.—Daniel A. Miller's ox-train of emigrants, consisting of the last Saints from Pottawattamie County, Iowa, arrived in G. S. L. City. The company consisted of 282 souls, 70 wagons, 27 horses, 470 head of cattle and 153 sheep, and had left camp at Winter Quarters June 9th, 1853.

Tues. 13.—Wm. Hatton was killed by Indians, while standing guard at Fillmore, Utah.

October. *Sat. 1.*—James Nelson, Wm. Luke, Wm. Reed and. Thos. Clark were killed by Indians at the Uintah Springs, Sanpete Valley.

Sun. 2.—At a skirmish between the whites and Indians, at Nephi, Juab Co., Utah, eight Indians were killed, and one squaw and two boys taken prisoners.

Tues. 4.—John E. Warner and Wm. Mills were killed by Indians, a few hundred yards above the grist mill, at Manti, Sanpete Co., Utah.

Thurs. 6.—The general conference of the Church was commenced in G. S. L. City. It continued four days. Apostles Geo. A. Smith and Erastus Snow were called to gather fifty families to strengthen the settlements of Iron County, Wilford Woodruff and Ezra T. Benson fifty families to strengthen the settlements in Tooele, Lyman Stevens and Reuben W. Allred fifty families for each of the settlements in Sanpete, Lorenzo Snow fifty families to go to Box Elder, Joseph L. Heywood fifty families to Nephi, Juab Co., and Orson Hyde to raise a company to make a permanent settlement on Green river, near Fort Bridger.

—According to the Bishops' reports read at conference, the number of souls in the various settlements in the Territory was as follows: Great Salt Lake City: 1st Ward, 260; 2nd Ward, 149; 3rd Ward, 170; 4th Ward, 183; 5th Ward, 69; 6th Ward, 206; 7th Ward, 384; 8th Ward, 236; 9th Ward, 289; 10th Ward, 219; 11th Ward, 180; 12th Ward, 345; 13th Ward, 454; 14th Ward, 662; 15th Ward, 501; 16th Ward, 444; 17th Ward, 406; 18th Ward, 241; 19th Ward, 572. Great Salt Lake County: Butterfield Settlement, 71; West Jordan, 361; Mill Creek, 668; Big Cottonwood, 161; South Cottonwood, 517; Little Cottonwood, 273; Willow Creek, 222. Utah County: Dry Creek, 458; American Fork, 212; Pleasant Grove, 290; Provo: 1st

Ward, 423; 2nd Ward, 264; 3rd Ward, 248; 4th Ward, 424; Mountainville no report; Springville, 799; Palmyra,404; Payson and Summit, 427; Cedar Valley, 115. Juab County: Salt Creek, 229. Sanpete County: Manti, 647; Pleasant Creek, 118. Millard County: Fillmore, 304. Iron County: Parowan, 392; Cedar, 455. Tooele County: Grantsville, 215; Tooele, no report. Davis County: North Kanyon, 574; Centreville, 194; North Cottonwood, 413; Kays Ward, 417. Weber County: East Weber, 233; Ogden: 1st Ward. 449; 2nd Ward, 683; 3rd Ward, 200; Willow Creek, 163. Box Elder, 204.

Thurs. 13.—The First Presidency issued the "Tenth General Epistle" to all the Saints.

Fri. 14.—About thirty Indians attacked a few men, who were securing their crops at Summit Creek (Santaquin), Utah Co., killed and scalped F. F. Tindrel, and drove off a number of head of stock.

Sun. 16.—The main company of the season's P. E. Fund emigrants arrived in G. S. L. City.

Wed. 26.—Capt. John W. Gunnison, of the U. S. Topographical Engineer Corps, and seven other men, were killed by Indians, near the swamps of the Sevier river, in revenge for the killing of an Indian and the wounding of two others, alleged to have been perpetrated by a company of emigrants bound for California.

November. *Tues. 1.*—The first number of the *Journal of Discourses*, a semi-monthly 16-page octavo paper, was published in Liverpool, England.

Wed. 2.—Thirty-nine men, equipped with farming implements, seeds and other things necessary for establishing a new settlement, left G. S. L. City for Green River County. They arrived at Fort Bridger Nov. 12th.

Previous to this Pres. Brigham Young purchased of James Bridger a Mexican grant for 30 square miles of land and some cabins, afterwards known as Ft. Bridger. This was the first property owned by the Saints in Green River County.

Sun. 6.—Chase's sawmill, in Sanpete County, was burned by Indians.

Wed. 9.—The Indians burned six houses at Summit Creek (Santaquin), Utah Co.

Sun. 13.—The mail train was attacked by Indians six miles from Laramie, and three men were killed. C. A. Kinkead, of G. S. L. City, was robbed of $10,500.

Tues. 15.—Another company of settlers left G. S. L. City for Green River County. They, together with the preceding company, located on Smith's Fork and called their town Fort Supply. The whole colony consisted of 53 men from Great Salt Lake and Utah Counties; John Nebeker and Isaac Bullock were among the number.

December. *Thurs. 1.*—Elder Wm. Willes returned to Calcutta, India, from a missionary trip into the interior, after being absent nearly one year.

Mon. 12.—The Utah legislature (third annual session) convened in G. S. L. City and organized by electing Willard Richards president of the Council, and Jedediah M. Grant speaker of the House.

Wed. 28.—Hiram Clark, once a prominent

missionary, committed suicide at San Bernardino, Cal.

Thurs. 29.—Elders A. Milton Musser and Truman Leonard, after laboring in Calcutta and Chinsurah, India, about nine months, sailed from Calcutta for Bombay, where they arrived Feb. 9, 1854.

The so-called Spanish wall built in part around G. S. L. City this year was twelve feet high, six feet thick at the base, tapering to two feet six inches six feet from the ground, and preserving that thickness to the top. It was six miles in length.

1854.

This year the crops in Utah were partly destroyed by grasshoppers; the so-called Walker war was terminated and the Deseret alphabet was formulated. Hundreds of emigrating Saints from Europe died from cholera while sailing up the Mississippi and Missouri rivers and crossing the plains. A Stake of Zion was organized at St. Louis, Mo., and a mission opened up in New Zealand.

January. — The *Deseret News* was changed from a semi-monthly to a weekly paper.

Tues. 3.—The ship *Jesse Munn* sailed from Liverpool, England, with 300 Scandinavian and 33 German Saints, under the direction of Christian Larsen. It arrived at New Orleans Feb. 10th, and the emigrants continued up the rivers to Kansas City, Mo., which this year was selected as the outfitting place for the Saints crossing the plains.

Fri. 6.—Allred's Settlement (Spring City), Sanpete Co., which had been deserted by its inhabitants the previous summer, because of Indian troubles, was burned to the ground.

Thurs. 12.—The 37th quorum of Seventy was organized in G. S. L. City, with Cyrus H. Wheelock, John Lyon, Jesse W. Crosby, Jonathan Midgley, David J. Ross, George Halliday and Claudius V. Spencer as presidents.

Some time previous the 36th quorum had been organized, with Jesse W. Fox as one of the presidents.

Wed. 18.—Elders Samuel A Woolley and Wm. Fotheringham arrived, as missionaries, at Agra, Hindostan.

Fri. 20.—The legislative assembly of Utah adjourned. Among the acts passed and approved were those providing for the organization of Summit, Green River and Carson Counties, and defining the boundaries of Davis County.

Sun. 22. — The ship *Benjamin Adams* sailed from Liverpool, England, with 378 Scandinavian and 6 British Saints, under the direction of Hans Peter Olsen. The company arrived at New Orleans, March 22nd, and at Kansas City in the beginning of April.

Mon. 23.—A branch of the Church was organized by Edward Stevenson, at Gibraltar, Spain, with 10 members.

Tues. 31.—Bishop Isaac Clark died at Ogden.

—A mass meeting was held in G. S. L. City for the purpose of taking steps towards memorializing Congress to construct a national railroad from the Missouri river, *via* the South Pass and G. S. L. City, to the Pacific.

February. *Sat. 4.*—The ship *Golconda* sailed from Liverpool, England, with 464 Saints, under the direction of Dorr P. Curtis; it arrived at New Orleans March 18th.

Sun.5.—At a Seventies' quarterly conference held in G. S. L. City, the 38th and 39th quorums of Seventy were organized with Benjamin F. Cummings and Daniel McIntosh as senior presidents.

Tues. 7.—John C. Fremont, with a company of nine whites and twelve Delaware Indians, arrived at Parowan, Iron Co., in a state of starvation. One man had fallen dead from his horse near the settlement, and others were nearly dead. Animals and provisions were supplied by the Saints, and, after resting until the 20th, Fremont and company continued their journey to California.

Tues. 14.—Clarissa Smith, Patriarch John Smith's wife, died in G. S. L. City.

Wed. 22.—The ship *Windermere* sailed from Liverpool, England, with 484 Saints, under Daniel Garn's direction; it arrived at New Orleans April 23rd. Many died on board from the small pox.

—Elders A. Milton Musser and Truman Leonard sailed from Bombay, India, for Kurrachee, Scinde, which place they reached Feb. 26th. Kurrachee is about 900 miles northwest of Bombay.

March.—Elias Smith succeeded the late Willard Richards as postmaster of Great Salt Lake City.

—Ephraim, Sanpete Co.,was first settled.

—The first number of the *Latter-day Saints' Millennial Star and Monthly Visitor*, an eight-page periodical (octavo size), was published at Madras, Hindostan; Elder Richard Ballantyne editor and publisher.

Sun. 5.—The ship *Old England* sailed from Liverpool, England, with 45 Saints, under the direction of John O. Angus. It arrived at the mouth of the Mississippi river April 24th.

Mon. 6.—Elders Samuel A. Woolley and Wm. Fotheringham returned to Calcutta from an unsuccessful mission to the interior, on which they visited Benares, Belaspore, Marat, Delhi, Kurnaul, Agra, Cawnpore, Allahabad, etc.

Sat. 11.—Dr. Willard Richards, second Counselor to Pres. Brigham Young, and editor of the *Deseret News*, died in G. S. L. City, of dropsy.

Sun 12.—The ship *John M. Wood* sailed from Liverpool, with 393 Saints, including 58 from Switzerland and Italy, under the direction of Robert L. Campbell. It arrived at New Orleans May 2nd.

Wed. 22.—The ship *Julia Ann* sailed from Sydney, Australia, with about seventy Saints, bound for Utah, under the direction of Wm. Hyde. The company landed at San Pedro, Cal., June 12th.

Fri. 24.—Geo. E. Ashburner, captain of the police, peremptorily ordered Elders A. Milton Musser and Truman Leonard out of the cantonment of Camp Kurrachee,

India, and admonished them not to return.

Wed. 29.—Under the administration of Elders John S. Fulmer and David B. Dille, Halsden Marsden, 18 years old, who was born deaf and dumb, was miraculously healed from his deafness, at Rochdale, England.

April.—A number of Elders were called on a mission to the Indians in southern Utah. This more directly resulted in opening up that part of Utah south of the Great Basin to settlement.

Tues. 4.—The ship *Germanicus* sailed from Liverpool, England, with 220 Saints, under the direction of Richard Cook. The company arrived at New Orleans June 12th.

Thurs. 6.—The 24th annual conference of the Church was commenced in G. S. L. City; it was continued till the 9th. On the 7th, Jedediah M. Grant was chosen second Counselor to Pres. Brigham Young, in place of Willard Richards deceased. Bro. Grant was set apart on the 9th. Geo. A. Smith was sustained as Church Historian. A number of missionaries were called to Great Britain, the United States, Canada and the Pacific Islands.

Sat. 8.—The ship *Marshfield* sailed from Liverpool, with 366 Saints, including about forty from the French mission, under the direction of Wm. Taylor. The company arrived at New Orleans May 29th.

Mon. 10.—The First Presidency issued its "Eleventh General Epistle" to the whole Church.

Sun. 23.—The Sugar House Ward, G. S. L. Co., Utah, was organized with Abraham O. Smoot as Bishop.

Mon. 24.—Twenty-nine Saints sailed from England on the ship *Clara Wheeler*, bound for Utah.

May. *Thur 4.*—Pres. Brigham Young left G. S. L. City, accompanied by many leading men, on a tour through the southern settlements, from which he returned on the 30th.

Fri 5.—Apostle Parley P. Pratt left G. S. L. City on his second mission to California. He arrived at San Bernardino June 9th, and in San Francisco July 2nd.

Mon. 8.—A branch of the Church, consisting of 19 members, was organized in Piedmont, Italy, where considerable persecution had raged.

Tues. 23.—Patriarch John Smith died in G. S. L. City, and on June 28th John Smith, son of Hyrum Smith, was chosen Patriarch to the Church in place of the deceased.

Late in May, (after a "talk" with Pres. Brigham Young), the Indian chief Walker, surrounded by his braves, and Kanosh, chief of the Pauvan Indians, entered into a formal treaty of peace at Chicken Creek, Juab Co. This ended the Ute war, during which 19 white persons and many Indians had been killed, a number of the smaller settlements had been broken up, and their inhabitants moved to the larger towns.

June.—Apostle Franklin D. Richards succeeded Samuel W. Richards as president of the British mission. His letter of appointment authorized him "to preside over all the conferences and all the affairs of the Church in the British Islands and adjacent countries." This was the beginning of what has since been called the

European mission, which embraces all the missions in Europe, and at one time also the Church organizations in Africa, Australia, India, etc.

Fri. 2.—The first company of emigrants of the season, bound for California, passed through G. S. L. City, having left Council Bluffs April 12th.

Fri. 16.—The workmen began at the south-east corner to lay the foundation of the Temple, in G. S. L. City.

July.—The grasshoppers made their appearance in the fields of some of the settlements in Utah and did much damage.

Sat. 8.—Apostle Erastus Snow, accompanied by other Elders, left G.S.L.City for the East, to take charge of the Church in St. Louis and the Western States.

Thurs. 13.—The Jordan river bridge, west of G. S. L. City, was crossed by teams and herds for the first time.

Thurs. 20.—Elder Gudmund Gudmundsen left Iceland, where he had labored upwards of three years preaching the gospel, and had baptized nine persons. He returned to Denmark.

Tues. 25.—Elder Richard Ballantyne sailed from Madras, India, bound for London, where he arrived Dec. 6, 1854.

August.—The native Saints in the Hawaiian mission commenced to gather to the island of Lanai, which had been selected as a gathering place for them, and the building of a city was commenced in the valley or basin known as Palawai.

Wed. 2.—Pres. Brigham Young advised the presidency of the British mission to ship the emigrating Saints from Europe to a more northern port than New Orleans, as the latter place was very unhealthful.

Tues. 8.—Wm. and Warren Weeks, sons of Bishop Allen Weeks, were killed by Goshute Indians, in Cedar Valley.

Sat. 12.—Peter Whitmer, sen., died in Richmond, Ray Co., Mo. He was born April 14, 1773.

Sun. 13.—Elders Geo. C. Riser and Jens C. Nielsen, who labored as missionaries in Hamburg, Germany, were arrested and imprisoned for preaching the gospel and baptizing a few persons.

Tues. 15.—The wall around the Temple Block, in G. S. L. City, was completed.

Tues. 22.—Elder Truman Leonard left Kurrachee, India, with a Masonic friend for Kotree, about one hundred miles inland.

Thurs. 24.—John F. Kinney, of Iowa, succeeded Lazarus H. Reed as chief justice of Utah.

Tues. 29.—Geo. Mills, one of the Utah Pioneers of 1847, died in G. S. L. City.

Thurs. 31.—Col. E. J. Steptoe, who had been appointed governor of Utah, arrived in G. S. L. City with about one hundred and seventy-five soldiers.

September. *Tues. 5.*—After 23 days' imprisonment, Elders Geo. C. Riser and Jens C. Nielser, through the influence of Mr. Bromberg, the American consul, were liberated from prison, in Hamburg, on conditions that they should leave the country forthwith.

Fri. 29.—Capt. James Brown's company of immigrating Saints (with 42 wagons) arrived in G. S. L. City.

Sat. 30.—Capt. Darwin Richardson's

company of immigrating Saints (40 wagons) arrived in G. S. L. City.

October. *Sun. 1.*—Daniel Garn's company of immigrating Saints, including the Germans, arrived in G. S. L. City.

Mon. 2.—Elder Wm. W. Major, of G. S. L. City, died in London, England, where he labored as a missionary.

Thurs. 5.—Elder Hans Peter Olsen's company of immigrating Saints, including the Scandinavians, arrived in G. S. L. City. Many had died from cholera while crossing the plains.

Sun. 8.—A printing press and the necessary material for printing the Book of Mormon in the Hawaiian language arrived at Honolulu, Hawaii, but subsequently it was shipped to San Francisco, Cal., and the printing done there.

Tues. 24.—Wm. A. Empey's company of immigrating Saints (with 43 wagons) arrived in G. S. L. City.

Fri. 27.—Augustus Farnham, president of the Australasian Mission, and Wm. Cooke arrived at Auckland, as the first missionaries to New Zealand.

Sat. 28.—Robert L. Campbell's company of immigrating Saints, the last of the season, arrived in G. S. L. City.

November. *Sat. 4.*—Apostle Erastus Snow organized a Stake of Zion in St. Louis, Mo., with Milo Andrus as president and Charles Edwards and George Gardiner as counselors. A High Council was also organized, consisting of James H. Hart, Andrew Sproule, John Evans, Wm. Morrison, James S. Cantwell, Wm. Lowe, Samuel J. Lees, Edward Cook, James S. Brooks, William Gore, John Clegg and Charles Chard.

Sat. 11.—Professor Orson Pratt discovered "a new and easy method of solution of the cubic and biquadratic equations."

Wed. 22.—The first number of the *St. Louis Luminary* was published by Erastus Snow, in St. Louis, Mo.

Monday. 27.—The ship *Clara Wheeler* sailed from Liverpool, England, with 422 Saints, under the direction of Henry E. Phelps. The company arrived at New Orleans Jan. 11, 1855, and at St. Louis Jan. 22nd.

Tues. 28.—Apostle Charles C. Rich arrived in G. S. L. City from San Bernardino, and Geo. Q. Cannon and others from the Sandwich Islands.

December. *Mon. 11.*—The Utah legislature (4th annual session) convened in the Council House, in G. S. L. City, and organized by electing Heber C. Kimball president of the Council, and Jedediah M. Grant speaker of the House.

Sun. 24.—Patriarch William Draper died at Draperville, Salt Lake Co.

Mon. 25.—The Seventies' Council Hall, in G. S. L. City, was dedicated. It way 53x25 feet, and had cost $3,500.

Sat. 30.—A petition praying for the reappointment of Brigham Young to the governorship of Utah, and signed by Col. Steptoe and the leading officials and business men of G. S. L. City, was sent to Washington, D. C.

Sun. 31.—The European mission, consisted of 67 conferences, 788 branches and

32,627 members. Of these 29,441 were in Great Britain, 2,447 in Scandinavia, 299 in Switzerland and Italy, 326 in the French mission, 56 in the German mission, 40 on the island of Malta and 18 at Gibraltar.

1855.

This year walls were built around some of the settlements in Utah as a 'means of protection against the Indians. The county court house, the "Lion House" and other notable public and private buildings were erected in G. S. L. City. The mails arrived very irregularly from the States. In the spring of this year Morgan County, Utah, was settled by Jedediah M. Grant, Thomas Thurston and others. During the summer grasshoppers did serious damage to crops, destroying nearly everything green in many parts of Utah. The loss and suffering was aggravated by drought, the combined evils causing a great failure in crops. In trying to establish a settlement (now Moab) near the Elk Mountains (now La Salle Mountains), Utah, troubles arose with the Indians and several of the brethren were killed. A settlement of the Saints was established on Salmon river, Oregon (now in Idaho). The Book of Mormon was published in the Hawaiian language by Geo. Q. Cannon in San Francisco, Cal.

January. *Mon. 1.*—A grand party was given by the Utah legislature as a compliment to Judge John F. Kinney and other Federal officials in the Territory, and also Lt.-Col. Steptoe with the officers of his command.

Sat. 6.—The ship *Rockaway* sailed from Liverpool, England, with 24 Saints, under the direction of Samuel Glasgow. The company arrived at New Orleans, Feb. 28th, and at St. Louis about the 16th of March.

Sun. 7.—The ship *James Nesmith* sailed from Liverpool, with 440 Scandinavian and 1 British Saints, under the direction of Peter O. Hansen. It arrived at New Orleans, Feb. 23rd, and the company continued up the rivers to Ft. Leavenworth; afterwards to Mormon Grove.

Tues. 9.—Thirteen Saints, under the presidency of Thomas Jackson, sailed from Liverpool on the ship *Neva*, bound for Utah. The company arrived at New Orleans, Feb. 22nd.

Thurs. 11.—After making a number of futile attempts to reach the English speaking people of Camp Kurrachee, Elder A. Milton Musser entered into a contract with David Sair Mohammed to build a meeting house, 26x20 feet, on the main thoroughfare between Camp Kurrachee, and the landing near the cantonment. The house was soon built and dedicated, after which regular meetings were held in it till September, 1855.

Fri. 12.—Archibald Bowman was accidentally killed while quarring rock for the Temple, at the quarry, near G. S. L. City.

Wed. 17.—The ship *Charles Buck* sailed from Liverpool, England, with 403 Saints, under the direction of Richard Ballantyne. The company arrived at New Orleans about March 14th, and at St. Louis March 27th.

Fri. 19.—The Utah legislature adjourned after the usual session of forty days.

Mon. 29.—Walker, chief of the Ute Indians, died at Meadow Creek, Millard Co. His brother Arrapeen succeeded him as chief.

February.—The 40th quorum of Seventy was organized at Farmington, Davis Co., Utah, with Ezra T. Clark, John S. Gleason, James Harrison, Hyrum Judd, Daniel Rawson, Lot Smith and Sanford Porter as presidents. Most of the members were ordained March 4, 1855.

Sat. 3. — Geo. C. Riser, Jacob F. Secrist and a small company of Saints (16 souls) sailed from Liverpool, England, on the ship *Isaac Jeans*, bound for Utah. They landed in Philadelphia, March 5th.

Mon. 5.—Dr. Garland Hurt, of Kentucky, Indian Agent for Utah, arrived at G. S. L. City.

Tues. 6.—A grand festival, lasting two days, was commenced in G. S. L. City, in honor of the Mormon Battalion.

Sat. 17.—The first number of the *Mormon*, a weekly paper, published in the interest of the Church, was issued in the city of New York, by Apostle John Taylor.

Sun. 18.—John Smith was ordained to his calling as Patriarch to the whole Church.

Tues. 27.—The name of Sessions' Settlement, Davis Co., Utah, was changed to Bountiful.

—The ship *Siddons* sailed from Liverpool, England, with 430 Saints, under the direction of John S. Fullmer. It arrived at Philadelphia April 20th, from which place the company went by rail to Pittsburg, Pa., thence on steamboats down the Ohio river to St. Louis and up the Missouri river to Atchison, Kan.

March.—Mormon Grove, near Atchison, Kan., was selected as an outfitting place for the Saints crossing the plains this year. Eight companies, with 337 wagons, commenced the journey for G. S. L. Valley from that place in 1855.

Mon. 5.—Elders Nathaniel V. Jones and William Fotheringham sailed from Calcutta, India, homeward bound, *via* China and San Francisco, Cal., after laboring zealously, together with their co-laborers, to introduce the fulness of the gospel to the inhabitants of India. Elder Robert Skelton was left in charge of the mission.

Thurs. 15.—Elder Hugh Findlay, accompanied by a few emigrating Saints, sailed from Bombay, India, homeward bound, *via* China.

Tues. 27.—Lazarus H. Reed, late chief justice of Utah, and a friend to her people, died at his home at Bath, N. Y.

Sat. 31.—The ship *Juventa* sailed from Liverpool, England, with 573 Saints, under the direction of Wm. Glover. It arrived at Philadelphia May 5th. From

there the company went by rail to Pittsburgh, and further on steamboats down the Ohio river to St. Louis, Mo.

April.—The First Presidency issued the "Twelfth General Epistle" to the whole Church.

Sun. 1.—The *Millennial Star* and Church Emigration office in Liverpool, England, was removed from 15 Wilton Street to 36 (now 42) Islington, where it has been ever since.

Fri. 6.—The 25th annual conference of the Church was held in G. S. L. City; it was continued for three days; 154 Elders were called on foreign missions.

Tues. 17.—The ship *Chimborazo* sailed from Liverpool, England, with 431 Saints, including 70 from the Channel Islands, under the direction of Edward Stevenson. The company arrived at Philadelphia May 21st.

Sun. 22.—The ship *Samuel Curling* sailed from Liverpool with 581 Saints, under Israel Barlow's direction; it arrived at New York May 27th. The emigrants continued by rail to Pittsburgh, thence by steamboat on the rivers, *via* St. Louis, Mo., to Atchison, Kan.

Thurs. 26.—The ship *Wm. Stetson* sailed from Liverpool, with 293 Saints, under Aaron Smithurst's direction. It arrived at New York May 27th.

Fri. 27.—Seventy-two Saints from Adelaide (South Australia) and Victoria, sailed from Melbourne, on board the brig *Tarquenia*, bound for Utah, *via* San Pedro, Cal., under the direction of Burr Frost. Arriving at Honolulu, Sandwich Islands, the vessel was condemned as unsafe and the emigrants landed. Shortly afterwards some of them engaged another passage to San Pedro, Cal.

May.—The first number of *Der Darsteller der Heiligen der letzten Tage*, a monthly 16-page octavo periodical, was published by Daniel Tyler at Geneva, Switzerland, in the German language, in the interest of the Church.

Sat. 5.—The Endowment House, in G. S. L. City, was dedicated.

Tues. 8.—Pres. Brigham Young and others left G. S. L. City on a trip to the southern settlements. He returned on the 27th.

Thurs. 10.—Charles C. Rich, Geo, Q. Cannon, Joseph Bull and Matthew F. Wilkie left G. S. L. City on a mission to California.

Fri. 11.—A treaty of peace was concluded with the Ute Indians.

Sun. 13.—Albert Gregory, who was returning west from a mission to the States, died at Atchison, Kan.

Wed. 16.—Apostle Orson Hyde and company left G. S. L. City for Carson Valley, where they arrived June 17th.

Sun. 20.—The camp of the missionaries, called to settle on the Salmon river, Oregon (now Idaho), was organized by Thomas S. Smith on the bank of Bear river, with Francillo Durfee as captain.

Mon. 21.—A company of about forty men, under the presidency of Alfred N. Billings, left Manti, Sanpete Co., for a valley near the Elk Mountains (La Salle Mountains), where they arrived June 15th and commenced a settlement on the left bank of Grand river, where Moab now stands.

Tues. 29.—A small company of Saints emigrating to Utah sailed from Calcutta, India, per ship *Frank Johnson.*

June. Wed. 13. — Andrew L. Lamoreaux, returning missionary from Europe, died at St. Louis, Mo.

Fri. 15.—Fort Limhi (Idaho) was located by Thomas S. Smith and his company of settlers, on the Salmon river, and on the 18th they moved to the site.

Mon. 18. — Pres. Brigham Young and others left G. S. L. City on a visit to the northern settlements, from which they returned on the 25th.

Fri. 29.—Judge Leonidas Shaver died in G. S. L. City.

July. Sun. 1.—The manufacture of molasses from beets at the sugar factory, in the Sugar House Ward, G. S. L. Co., was commenced.

Mon. 2.—Jacob F. Secrist, captain of the second company of the season's emigration, and returning missionary, died on Ketchum's Creek, west of Ft. Kearney.

Wed 18.—Elder John Perry died at Mormon Grove, Kansas, on his return from a mission to England.

Mon. 23.—The massive foundation of the Temple in G. S. L. City was finished.

Tues. 24.—Wm. Nixon was killed at Provo, Utah Co., by the bursting of a cannon.

Fri. 27. — David H. Burr, surveyor-general for Utah, arrived in G. S. L. City.

Sun. 29.—The ship *Cynosure* sailed from Liverpool, England, with 159 Saints, under the direction of George Seager. It arrived at New York Sept. 5th.

August. Thurs. 2.—Thomas Tanner, foreman of the Public Works' blacksmith shop in G. S. L. City, and a Utah Pioneer of 1847, died from the effects of a fall, which occurred on July 31st.

Mon. 6.—John M. Bernhisel was elected the third time as delegate to Congress from Utah.

Fri. 10.—Jane Amanda Stevens Lewis, wife of Philip B. Lewis, died near San Bernardino, Cal., on her return from a mission to the Hawaiian Islands.

Sat. 18.—Apostle Parley P. Pratt returned to G. S. L. City, after a fifteen months' mission to California, accompanied by a few immigrants.

September. Sat. 1.—Erastus Snow and Chas. H. Bassett arrived in G. S. L. City from their mission to the States.

Sun.—The Ute and Shoshone Indians met in front of the *Deseret News* office, G. S. L. City, and entered into a treaty of peace.

—David Lewis, a survivor of the Haun's Mill massacre, died at Parowan, Iron Co.

Mon. 3.—Capt. John Hindley's company of immigrating Saints, the first of the season, arrived in G. S. L. City. It consisted of 46 wagons and about two hundred souls.

Fri. 7.—The second company of immigrating Saints of the season, consisting of 58 wagons, arrived in G. S. L. City, under the direction of Capt. Noah T. Guyman.

—The American bark *Julia Ann* sailed from Sydney, N. S. W., Australia, with a company of Saints, under the direction

of Elders James Graham and John S. Eldredge, bound for America.

Mon. 10.—On this and the following day a large company of missionaries left G. S. L. City for Europe and the States.

Tues. 11.—Seth M. Blair's train of 45 wagons arrived in G. S. L. City with a few Saints from Texas.

Wed. 12.—W. W. Drummond was appointed successor to the late Leonidas Shaver as associate justice of Utah.

Thurs. 13. — The Horticultural Society was organized in G. S. L. City, with Wilford Woodruff as president. Various other societies were organized in the forepart of the year, among which were the "Universal Scientific Society", the "Polysophical Society", the Deseret Philharmonic Society and the "Deseret Typographical Association."

Sat. 22. — Elder A. Milton Musser and Truman Leonard left Kurrachee, India, for Bombay.

Sun. 23.—James W. Hunt, Wm. Behunin and Edward Edwards, of the Elk Mountain mission, were killed by Indians, who also wounded Pres. Alfred N. Billings, besides burning hay and stealing cattle. The following day the colonists left their fort and started for Manti, where they arrived Sept. 30th.

Tues. 25.—The fourth company of immigrating Saints of the season, under Capt. Richard Ballantyne (45 wagons, 402 souls), arrived in G. S. L. City.

Fri. 28.—The fifth company of immigrating Saints of the season, under Capt. Moses Thurston (33 wagons), arrived in G. S. L. City.

October Thurs. 4.—Elders John S. Eldredge and James Graham and 28 Saints emigrating to Utah from Australia, on board the ship *Julia Ann*, were wrecked on a coral reef near the Society Islands. Five persons were drowned and the rest barely escaped with their lives and landed on a barren and uninhabited island (Scilly Island), where they subsisted on turtle for six weeks, when they were rescued.

Sun. 14.—Carl G. Maeser, Edward Schoenfeld and two others were baptized by Apostle Franklin D. Richards, as the first fruits of the preaching of the gospel at Dresden, Germany.

Mon. 15.—Gov. Young ordered out part of the Utah militia, to protect the settlements in the eastern part of the Territory from the Indians.

—Elder Orson Spencer died in St. Louis, Mo.

Thurs. 18.—Elder Josiah W. Flemming was arrested at Sydney, N. S. W., Australia, on a false charge instigated by apostates. After spending the night in a miserable prison, he was acquitted and liberated the following day.

Sun. 21.—A branch of the Church, consisting of eight members, was organized at Dresden, Germany. Shortly afterwards the number increased to about twenty, including a few in Leipzig.

Wed. 24.—Capt. Milo Andrus' immigrant train, called the third P. E. Fund company of the season, arrived in G. S. L. City.

Mon. 29.—The sixth company of immigrating Saints of the season (39 wagons), under Capt. C. A. Harper, arrived in G. S. L. City.

—The First Presidency of the Church, in the "Thirteenth General Epistle," proposed that the Saints, who emigrated by the P. E. Fund, should cross the plains with handcarts.

November. *Fri. 2.*—Part of the seventh or last company of immigrating Saints for the season (38 wagons, 62 souls) arrived in G. S. L. City; Isaac Allred, captain. Some wagons, which had to stop over at Green river, arrived on the 13th.

Tues. 13.—John M. King, formerly a member of the Mormon Battalion, died in G. S. L. City.

Sun. 23.—Elders Wm. Walker and Leonard I. Smith, accompanied by 15 Saints, sailed from Algoa Bay, Cape Colony, Africa, on the *Unity*, bound for Utah. They arrived in London, England, Jan. 29, 1856.

—Elder Truman Leonard sailed from Bombay, India, for England.

Tues. 27.—A grand festival, in honor of the returned missionaries, was given by the First Presidency in the Social Hall, G. S. L. City. About seventy missionaries attended.

Fri. 30.—The ship *Emerald Isle* sailed from Liverpool, England, with 349 Saints, under the direction of Philemon C. Merrill. It arrived at New York Dec. 29th.

—Elder Allen Findlay, a missionary from England, who had assisted the American Elders in Bombay and vicinity for some time, sailed from Bombay, on his return to England.

December.—The Utah legislature passed a bill, authorizing an election of delegates to attend a Territorial convention, the object of which was to draft a State constitution, and petition Congress a second time for the admission of Utah into the Union.

Sat. 1.—Apostle Amasa M. Lyman arrived in G. S. L. City from California, and Wm. Fotheringham and Hugh Findlay from India.

Mon. 3.—Elder A. Milton Musser sailed from Bombay for Calcutta, India, where he arrived Jan. 22, 1856.

Mon. 10.—The Utah legislature (fifth annual session) met at Fillmore, Millard Co., the new capital of the Territory, and organized by electing Heber C. Kimball president of the Council, and Jedediah M. Grant speaker of the House.

Wed. 12.—The ship *John J. Boyd* sailed from Liverpool, England, with 508 Saints (437 Scandinavians, 41 British and 41 Italians), under the direction of Knud Peterson. It arrived at New York, Feb. 15, 1856. A part of the company remained in Iowa and Illinois for some time, while a portion continued to Utah the same season *via* St. Louis and Florence.

Mon. 31.—An able address on plural marriage, written by Apostle Parley P. Pratt, was read before the Utah legislature at Fillmore, Utah.

1856.

In the forepart of this year there was great scarcity of provisions in Utah. Many domestic animals died from starvation. Beaver County, Utah, was settled by pioneers from Parowan. A general reformation took place throughout the Church, most of the Saints renewing their covenants by baptism. This reformation extended to the several missionary fields in different parts of the world. Many of the Saints from Europe suffered severely in crossing the plains and mountains with handcarts. The practice of paying tithing was generally introduced among the Saints in Europe.

January. *Sat. 5.*—Box Elder, Cache, Greasewood, Humboldt, St. Mary's, Malad and Cedar Counties, Utah, were created by legislative acts, approved by Gov. Brigham Young.

Sat. 12.—An act, passed by the Utah legislature, creating Shambip County, Utah, was approved.

Fri. 18.—The Utah legislature adjourned.

Sat. 26.—At a mass meeting held in G. S. L. City, steps were taken for organizing the B. Y. Express Carrying Company, to carry a daily express from the Missouri river to California. In subsequent meetings shares were taken to stock a thousand miles of the road.

February.—Beaver County, recently created by legislative act, was settled by Simeon F. Howd and thirteen others from Parowan, who located Beaver City. The townsite was laid out April 17, 1856.

—The Indians stole many cattle and horses in Utah and Cedar Valleys. On Feb. 21st they killed two herdsmen west of Utah Lake, and on the 22nd a *posse* of ten men with legal writs called at an Indian camp in Cedar Valley to arrest the murderers. A fight ensued, in which one Indian and a squaw were killed and Geo. Carson, one of the *posse*, mortally wounded. He died on the 23rd. On that day (the 23rd) Gov. Brigham Young, by proclamation, ordered out part of the Utah militia to fight the Indians. This difficulty with the natives is known in history as the "Tintic War."

Wed. 6.—Elder Robert C. Petty, of Herriman, Utah, died on Grand river, Ind. Ter., where he labored as a missionary.

Fri. 8.—The Saints who were settling on Beaver creek, Beaver Co., Utah, were organized into a branch of the Church by Apostle Geo. A. Smith, with Simeon F. Howd as president.

Tues. 12.—The Seventies, now numbering 40 quorums commenced a jubilee in G. S. L. City, which lasted five days. Their hall, which had undergone a thorough improvement, was again dedicated.

Mon. 18.—The ship *Caravan* sailed from Liverpool, England, with 454 Saints, under the direction of Daniel Tyler. The company arrived at New York March 27th.

Sat. 23.—The first number of the *Western Standard*, a weekly paper published in the interest of the Church, was issued at San Francisco, Cal.; Geo. Q. Cannon, editor.

Tues. 26.—John Catlin and another man were killed, and Geo. Winn was mortally wounded, by Indians, near Kimball's creek, southwest of Utah lake. Capt. Peter Connover, with eighty men, soon afterwards crossed Utah lake on the ice and pursued the hostile tribe into Tintic Valley, where he recovered some of the stock stolen by the savages.

Wed. 27.—Elder Robert W. Wolcott, of G. S. L. City, died of smallpox at Northampton, England, where he labored as a missionary.

March. *Mon. 3.*—Elder A. Milton Musser sailed from Calcutta, for London, England, where he arrived July 19, 1856, after being 138 days at sea. He came by way of the Cape of Good Hope. Capt. Winsor, of the *Viking*, gave Elder Musser a free first-class passage.

Mon. 17.—A convention met in G. S. L. City to prepare a State constitution and memorialize Congress for the admission of Utah into the Union as the State of Deseret. The constitution and memorial were adopted on the 27th, and Apostles Geo. A. Smith and John Taylor were elected delegates to present the same to Congress.

Sun. 23.—The ship *Enoch Train* sailed from Liverpool, England, with 534 Saints, under the direction of James Ferguson. It arrived at Boston May 1st. From that city the emigrants traveled by rail *via* New York to Iowa City, Iowa, whence the journey across the plains this year was commenced by wagons and handcarts. Daniel Spencer acted as general superintendent of emigration on the borders, assisted by Geo. D. Grant, Wm. H. Kimball, James H. Hart and others.

Fri. 28.—Elder Hector C. Haight, president of the Scandinavian mission, was arrested and a conference meeting broken up by the police, at Malmø, Sweden.

April. *Sun. 6.*—On this and the following day the 26th annual conference of the Church was held in G. S. L. City. About two hundred Elders were called on foreign missions.

Sat. 19.—The ship *Samuel Curling* sailed from Liverpool with 707 Saints, under the direction of Dan Jones; it arrived at Boston May 23rd. From that city the emigrants traveled by rail to Iowa City.

Mon. 21.—Jacob Whitmer, one of the Eight Witnesses to the Book of Mormon, died near Richmond, Ray Co., Mo.

Tues. 22.—A large company of missionaries, including Apostles Orson Pratt, Geo. A. Smith, Ezra T. Benson and Erastus Snow, Elder Abraham O. Smoot and many other prominent men, left G. S. L. City, on missions to the States and Europe. They arrived at St. Louis, Mo., June 12th.

May. *Fri. 2.* — Elder Robert Skelton, after appointing James Patrick Meik to preside over the Saints in India, sailed from Calcutta, homeward bound. He was the last of the American Elders to leave India, which was now abandoned for the time being as a missionary field.

Sun. 4.—The ship *Thornton* sailed from Liverpool, England, with 764 Saints, under the direction of James G. Willie. It arrived at New York June 14th, and the emigrants, continuing the journey by rail, arrived at Iowa City, June 26th.

Sun. 25.—The ship *Horizon* sailed from Liverpool with 856 Saints, under the direction of Edward Martin. The company ar-

rived safely at Boston, and reached Iowa City by rail July 8th.

Wed. 28.—A small company of Australian Saints, under the direction of Augustus Farnham, sailed from Port Jackson, New South Wales, bound for Utah. The ship touched at Tahiti, Society Islands, June 22nd, Honolulu, Hawaii, July 16th, and arrived at San Pedro, Cal., Aug. 15th. From the latter place the emigrants traveled by teams to San Bernardino.

June. *Sun. 1.*—Weber County, Utah, was divided into four Bishops' Wards, and Erastus Bingham appointed Bishop of the First, James G. Browning of the Second, Chauncey W. West of the Third and Thos. Dunn of the Fourth Ward.

—The ship *Wellfleet* sailed from Liverpool, England, with 146 Saints, under the direction of John Aubray. It arrived at Boston July 13th. The emigrants remained in the States until the following season.

July. *Sat. 5.*—The ship *Lucy Thompson* sailed from Liverpool with fourteen Saints, under the direction of James Thompson. It arrived at New York Aug. 8th.

Sat. 19.—Six families from Mississippi, under the direction of Benjamin Matthews, arrived at G. S. L. City, as the first immigrants of the season. They brought small pox with them into the Valley.

Thurs. 24.—Pioneer day was celebrated on the headwaters of Big Cottonwood creek, where a temporary bowery had been erected for the occasion.

August.—Apostle Orson Pratt succeeded Apostle Franklin D. Richards in the presidency of the European Mission.

Mon. 18.—The last of Capt. Philemon C. Merril's company of Saints arrived at G. S. L. City.

Sat. 23.—Bishop Isaac Houston, of Alpine, Utah Co., died.

Mon. 25.—Col. Almon W. Babbitt's train loaded with government property and traveling west, was plundered by Cheyenne Indians, near Wood river, Neb. A. Nichols and two others were killed, and a Mrs. Wilson was carried away by the savages.

September. Cache County was settled by Peter Maughan and others, who located what is now the town of Wellsville.

—Col. Almon W. Babbit, Thos. Margetts and child, James Cowdy and wife and others were killed, and Mrs. Margetts carried away by Cheyenne Indians, east of Fort Laramie.

Tues. 2.—Capt. John A. Hunt's company of Saints, the last wagon train of the season, left Florence, Neb., for G. S. L. Valley, having commenced the journey from Iowa City a few months previous.

Thurs. 11.—Apostle Parley P. Pratt, accompanied by other Elders, left G. S. L. City on a mission to the States, from which he never returned.

Wed. 17.—A Female Relief Society was organized in the 14th Ward, G. S. L. City, with Phœbe Woodruff as president.

Sat. 20.—Elder Knud Peterson's wagon company of immigrants (mostly Scandinavians) arrived in G. S. L. City. This was called the second company of the season.

Fri. 26.—The first two companies of immigrating Saints, which crossed the plains with handcarts, arrived at G. S. L. City, in charge of Capt. Edmund Ellsworth and Daniel D. McArthur. They were met and welcomed by the First Presidency of the Church, a brass band, a company of lancers, and a large concourse of citizens. Capt. Ellsworth's company had left Iowa City June 9th, and McArthur's June 11th. When they started, both contained 497 souls, with 100 handcarts, 5 wagons, 24 oxen, 4 mules and 25 tents.

October. *Thurs. 2.*—Capt. John Banks' wagon company of immigrating Saints, and Capt. Edward Bunker's handcart company, which had left Iowa City June 23rd, arrived in G. S. L. City. The immigrants in the latter were mostly from Wales.

—The Deseret Agricultural and Manufacturing Society commenced its first exhibition in G. S. L. City, called the "Deseret State Fair."

Fri. 3.—W. M. F. Magraw, formerly mail contractor, wrote a defamatory letter to the President of the United States, about Utah affairs.

Sat. 4.—Apostle Franklin D. Richards, Daniel Spencer, John Van Cott, Wm. C. Dunbar, John D. T. McAllister, Nathaniel H. Felt, and a number of other missionaries, arrived in G. S. L. City, having left Florence Sept. 3rd.

Mon. 6.—The general semi-annual conference of the Church was commenced in G. S. L. City. It continued three days; 177 Elders were called to go on missions.

Tues. 7.—The Twentieth Ward, G. S. L. City, was organized with John Sharp as Bishop.

—Capt. Geo. D. Grant left G. S. L. City with a relief company to meet the immigration.

Sat. 11.—Capt. Croft's company of emigrants from Texas and the Cherokee Nation arrived in G. S. L City.

Fri. 17.—An ordinance was passed by the G. S. L. City council, organizing a Fire Department. Jesse C. Little was appointed chief engineer.

Tues. 28.—Capt. Edward Martin's handcart company, detained by the unusual early snow storms of the season, was met by Joseph A. Young, Daniel W. Jones and Abel Garr, at a point sixteen miles above the Platte bridge. Three days later the company arrived at Greasewood creek, where four wagons of the relief company, in charge of Geo. D. Grant, loaded with provisions and some clothing for the suffering emigrants were awaiting them.

November. *Sun. 9.* — Capt. James G. Willie's handcart company arrived in G. S. L. City, after great sufferings from scarcity of provisions, cold and over-exertion in the mountains. It left Iowa City, Iowa, July 15th, with 120 handcarts and six wagons, numbering about five hundred souls, of whom 66 died on the journey. Captain Abraham O. Smoot's wagon train arrived the same day.

Thurs. 13.—Joseph A. Young and Abel Garr arrived in G. S. L. City with the news that the last companies of emigrants were perishing in the mountains. More teams and provisions were immediately forwarded to help them in.

Tues. 18.—The ship *Columbia* sailed from Liverpool with 223 Saints, under the direction of J. Williams. It arrived at New York Jan. 1, 1857.

Thurs. 20.—The ladies of Cedar City, Iron Co., organized a Female Benevolent Society, with Mrs. Lydia Hopkins as president.

Sat. 22.—Heber Jeddie Grant was born in G. S. L. City.

Sun. 30.—Edward Martin's handcart company arrived in G. S L. City, after extreme suffering. Many of the emigrants had died in the mountains, and the handcarts had to be gradually abandoned as the relief teams from the Valley were met. When the company passed Florence, Neb., Aug. 25th, it consisted of 576 persons, 146 handcarts, 7 wagons, etc.

December. *Mon. 1.*—Jedediah M. Grant, second Counselor to Pres. Brigham Young, died in G. S. L. City.

Tues. 2.—About sixty mule and horse teams started from G. S. L. City to meet Capts. Hodgett's and Hunt's wagon companies.

Fri. 5.—David S. Laughlin, formerly a member of the Mormon Battalion, died in Cedar Valley, Utah.

Mon. 8.—The Utah legislature (sixth annual session) convened at Fillmore and organized by electing Heber C. Kimball president of the Council, and Hosea Stout speaker of the House. It then adjourned to G. S. L. City.

Wed. 10.—The First Presidency issued their "Fourteenth General Epistle" to the Church.

—On this and the following six days Capts. Wm. B. Hodgett's and John A. Hunt's companies of emigrants arrived in G. S. L. City, after much suffering, being helped in by the relief trains sent out from the Valley.

Thurs. 11.—Contractor Magraw failing to carry the mails through, Feramorz Little and Eph. K. Hanks left G. S. L. City with the mail, for the East.

Thurs. 18.—The Utah legislature convened in the Social Hall, G. S. L. City.

Wed. 24.—Pres. Brigham Young gave an entertainment in the "Lion House" to a large number of Elders, lately returned from foreign missions.

1857.

The winter of 1856-57 was excessively severe, snow falling to a depth of eight feet in various places in the valleys of Utah. The harvest of 1857 was the best Utah ever had up to that time. Influenced by falsehoods, circulated by Judge W. W. Drummond and others, the Federal government sent an army to Utah, when the citizens organized for self-defense. The Elders were called home from foreign missions, and the Saints who had settled in Carson Valley, on Salmon river, on Green river and in Southern California were advised to abandon their locations and return to places nearer the headquarters of the Church.

January. *Sun. 4.*—Daniel H. Wells was set apart as second Counselor to Pres. Brigham Young, in place of the late Jedediah M. Grant.

Fri. 9.—San Bernardino, Cal., was visited by a violent earthquake.

February. *Wed. 4.*—A reformation meeting was held in No. 42 Islington, Liverpool, England, and on the following day the presiding brethren of the British mission, including Apostles Orson Pratt and Ezra T. Benson, renewed their covenants by baptism. This was followed by a general renewal of covenants throughout the mission.

March.—The 43rd quorum of Seventy was organized in Tooele County, Utah, with John Shields, James Bevan, Thomas Lee, Francis D. St. Jeor, George Atkin, Hugh S. Gowans and Geo. W. Bryan as presidents.

Mon. 2.—The 41st Quorum of Seventy was organized in Salt Lake County, Utah, with John Van Cott, Wm. C. Dunbar, Knud Peterson, Thomas Morris, Leonard I. Smith, Wm. Casper and Levi N. Kendall as presidents.

Thurs. 12.—Reformation meetings were held at Swansea, Wales, after which the presiding Elders, and subsequently all the Saints in that mission, renewed their covenants by baptism.

Fri. 20.—Henry Mitchell Johnson, formerly a member of the Mormon Battalion, died in G. S. L. City.

Sat. 28.—The ship *George Washington* sailed from Liverpool, England, with 817 Saints, under the direction of James P. Park, bound for Utah *via* Boston.

Mon. 30.—Judge W. W. Drummond, in framing the letter of his resignation as chief justice of Utah, wrote the most wicked and abominable falsehoods against Gov. Brigham Young and the people of Utah, thereby influencing the government to send troops against the "Mormons."

April. *Sat. 4.*—Cache County, Utah, was organized; Peter Maughan, probate judge.

Mon. 6.—The 27th annual conference on the Church convened in G. S. L. City; it was continued till the 8th; 350 Elders were called on missions.

Wed. 15.—Feramorz Little, having arrived in the States, with the Utah mail, wrote a letter to the New York *Herald*, refuting Drummond's falsehoods.

Mon. 20.—The Nauvoo Legion held a grand parade in G. S. L. City; the election of officers took place, and a new system for the government of Utah militia was inaugurated.

Thurs. 23.—A company consisting of about seventy missionaries, bound for Europe and other parts of the world, left G. S. L. City with handcarts. They arrived at Florence, Neb., June 10th, making the trip to the Missouri river in 40½ traveling days. (They rested 7½ days.)

Fri. 24.—Pres. Brigham Young and many others started from G. S. L. City on a tour to the settlements on Salmon river, Oregon (now Idaho). They returned May 26th.

Sat. 25.—The ship *Westmoreland* sailed from Liverpool, England, with 544 Saints, mostly Scandinavians, under the direction

of Mathias Cowley. It arrived at Philadelphia May 31st, and the emigrants reached Iowa City by rail June 9th.

May.—The Tithing Office Block wall in G. S. L. City was finished.

—The 46th quorum of Seventy was organized at Payson and Santaquin, Utah Co., with James B. Bracken, John Thomas Hardy, Benjamin F. Stewart, Wm. Carrol McClellan, Geo. W. Hancock and Wm. B. Maxwell as presidents.

—A temporary settlement called Genoa, was located for the benefit of emigrating Saints, on Beaver Creek, near Loup Fork, Neb., about one hundred miles west of Florence. The settlers consisted mostly of Saints from the St. Louis branch (Mo.).

Wed. 6.—The Saints who were settling Washington, in southern Utah, were organized into a branch of the Church with Robert D. Covington as president. He was ordained a Bishop Aug. 1, 1858.

Sat. 9.—The 45th quorum of Seventy was organized at Provo, with Robert T. Thomas, James Goff, Robert C. Moore, Isaac Bullock, Lewis C. Sabrisky, Wm. Marsden and Charles Shelton as presidents.

Wed. 13.—Apostle Parley P. Pratt was murdered by Hector H. McLean, near Van Buren, Ark.

Fri. 15.—The 47th quorum of Seventy was partly organized at Ephraim, Sanpete Co., Utah, with Tore Thurston, James A. Lemmon, Joseph Clements and Nils Bengtsen as presidents. Most of the members of the new quorum were ordained Seventies on the 17th.

Sat. 16.—The 48th quorum of Seventy was organized at Manti, Sanpete Co., with Daniel Henrie as senior president.

Mon. 18.—The 49th quorum of Seventy was organized at Nephi, Juab Co., with John A. Woolf, Samuel Pitchforth, Timothy S. Hoyt, Geo. Kendall, Miles Miller, John Burrowman and David Webb as presidents.

Tues. 19.—The 50th quorum of Seventy was partly organized at Spanish Fork, Utah Co., with Dennis Dorrity as one of the presidents.

Wed. 20.—The 51st quorum of Seventy was organized at Springville, Utah Co., with Alexander F. McDonald, Noah T. Guyman, Lorenzo Johnson, Spicer W. Crandall, Abraham Day and Hamilton H. Kerns as presidents.

Thurs. 21.—The 52nd quorum of Seventy was organized at Provo, Utah, with Alfred D. Young as senior president. Quite a number of members were ordained on the 25th.

—On the same day the 44th quorum of Seventy was organized at American Fork, Utah Co., Utah, with Wm. Hyde, James McGaw, Shadrach Driggs, Wm. Greenwood, James W. Preston, Wm. Fothering-ham and Thomas Taylor as presidents.

Thurs. 28.—The U. S. 2nd dragoons, 5th and 10th infantry and Phelps' Battery of the 4th artillery—2,500 men—were ordered out as an expedition to Utah, by order of Gen. Winfield Scott.

Sat. 30.—The ship *Tuscarora* sailed from Liverpool, England, with 547 Saints, under the direction of Richard Harper. It arrived at Philadelphia July 3rd, and the emigrants continued by rail to Burlington, Iowa, in the vicinity of which most of them sought temporary employment.

June. *Sun.* 7.— The 53th and 54th quorum of Seventy were organized at Ogden, Utah, by Joseph Young and Albert P. Rockwood, with Rufus Allen and James Brown 3rd as senior presidents.

Fri. 12.—Senator Stephen A. Douglas, in a politcal speech,delivered at Springfield, Ill., characterized "Mormonism" as a loathsome ulcer of the body politic, and recommended that Congress should apply the knife and cut it out.

Sun. 14.—The 42nd quorum of Seventy was organized at Fillmore, Utah, with Hiram Mace, David N. Raney, Andrew Love, J. W. Radford, Edward Frost. Allen Russel and John Felshaw as presidents.

Sat. 27.—The American ship *Lucas* sailed from Sydney, N. S. W., Australia, with 69 Saints, in charge of Elder Absalom P. Dowdle, bound for Utah.

July.—The 55th quorum of Seventy was organized at Kaysville, and the 56th quorum at Farmington, Davis Co., Utah.

Sat. 11.—Alfred Cumming, of Georgia, was appointed governor of Utah.

Wed. 15.—Indian Agent Thomas S. Twiss wrote a libellous letter to the government at Washington, D. C., about the "Mormons."

Sat. 18.—The Tenth Infantry, the vanguard of the Utah expedition, took up the line of march from Fort Leavenworth for the West, under the command of Col. E. B. Alexander. The artillery and Fifth Infantry followed a few days later. The command of the whole expedition was given to Gen. W. S. Harney.

—The ship *Wyoming* sailed from Liverpool, England, with 36 Saints, under the direction of Charles Harman. It arrived safely at Philadelphia, Pa.

Fri. 24.—The people of G. S. L. City and vicinity celebrated the 10th anniversary of the arrival of the Pioneers by a feast,near the head of Big Cottonwood Canyon. While the festivities were going on, Abraham O. Smoot and Judson Stoddard arrived from Independence, Mo., without the mails, the postmaster there having refused to forward them. They reported that General Harney with 2,000 infantry, and a proportionate number of artillery and cavalry, were ordered to Utah.

August. *Sat.* 1.—The Utah militia was ordered to be kept in readiness for an expedition to the mountains, to prevent the entering of the approaching army, if necessary.

Fri. 7.—Apostles John Taylor and Erastus Snow and other missionaries arrived in G. S. L. City from the East

—The first part of the "Utah Army," consisting of the Tenth Infantry and Phelps' Battery,arrived at Fort Kearney.

Fri. 14.—Geo. Scholes, one of the Pioneers of 1847, died at Big Cottonwood, Salt Lake Co.

—A company of the Carson Valley settlers returned to G. S. L. City.

Sat. 15.—Col. Robert T. Burton and James W. Cummings left G. S. L. City for the East, with seventy men, for the purpose of protecting the emigrant trains and observing the movements of the approaching army.

Fri. 21.—Col. Burton's expedition arrived at Ft. Bridger; on the 30th it reached Devil's Gate.

Fri. 28.—Col. Albert Sidney Johnston was appointed successor to Gen. W. S. Harney as commander of the Utah expedition.

September. *Fri.* 4.—Part of Wm. Walker's company of immigrating Saints, including Thos. B. Marsh, formerly a member of the Twelve Apostles, arrived in G. S. L. City.

Tues. 8.—Capt. Stewart Van Vliet, of Gen. Harney's staff, arrived in G. S. L. City and the following day had an interview with President Young. After a few days' stay he returned to his escort on Ham's Fork, and thence proceeded to Washington, where he used his influence in favor of the Saints.

Fri. 11.—The Mountain Meadow massacre took place.

Sat. 12.—The last of Israel Evans' handcart company, cenisting of 154 souls and 31 handcarts, arrived in G. S. L. City.

—Jesse B. Martin's wagon company of immigrants arrived in G. S. L. City.

Sun. 13.—Chr. Christiansen's handcart company and Mathias Cowley's wagon company of immigrants arrived in G. S. L. City.

Mon. 14.—Delegate John M. Bernhisel started from G. S. L. City for Washington, D. C., in company with Capt. Stewart Van Vliet and others.

—Joseph A. Keating, with a company of Saints, sailed from Sydney, Australia, bound for Utah.

Tues. 15.—Gov Brigham Young declared the Territory of Utah under martial law and forbade the troops to enter G. S. L. Valley. Large numbers of armed militia were ordered to Echo Canyon and other points to intercept the soldiers and prevent their access to the Valley.

Thurs. 17.—Col. Philip St. George Cooke left Ft. Leavenworth with the second division of the "Utah Army." He arrived at Ft. Bridger Nov 19th.

Tues. 22.—Col Robt. T. Burton and three other men camped within half a mile of the "Utah Army" (Col. E. B. Alexander's command), near Devil's Gate.

Wed. 23.—Col. Burton's men met the advance companies of the "Utah Army, and from that time were their "immediate neighbors" until they arrived at Ham's Fork.

Sat. 26.—Capt. Wm. G. Young's train arrived in G. S. L. City with the last of this season's immigration. Among the returning Elders in this train was A. Milton Musser, who returned home from a five years' mission to India and England, during which he had circumnavigated the globe, traveling as a missionary "without purse and scrip."

Tues. 29.—General Daniel H. Wells left G. S. L. City for Echo Canyon, where he established headquarters. About one thousand two hundred and fifty men, from the several militia districts, were ordered to Echo Canyon, where they engaged in digging trenches across the canyon, throw ing up breast works, loosening rocks on the heights, etc., preparing to resist the progress of the army.

October.—The "Mormon" settlements in Carson Valley were broken up: most of the settlers returned to G. S. L. City in the beginning of November.

—Samuel W. Richards succeeded Apostle Orson Pratt as president of the European mission.

Mon. 5.—Lot Smith, with a small company of men, surprised and burned two trains of government stores, near the Big Sandy and Green river.

Sat. 10.—The officers of the Utah expedition held a council of war at Ham's Fork, and decided that the army should march to G. S. L. Valley *via* Soda Springs. The following day the march was commenced, but after several days of slow and exhaustive traveling, the expedition was forced to return.

Fri. 16.—Major Joseph Taylor and Wm. R. R. Stowell, of the Utah militia, were taken prisoners by the U. S. troops near Ft. Bridger.

November. *Wed. 4.*—Col. Albert Sidney Johnston joined his command on Ham's Fork, with a small reinforcement.

Fri. 6.—Five hundred animals perished from cold and starvation around the U. S. army camp on Black's Fork.

Mon. 16.—The "Utah Army" went into winter quarters at Camp Scott, two miles from the site of Ft. Bridger and 115 miles from G. S. L. City.

December. *Fri. 4.*—Capt. John R. Winder was appointed to take charge of a picket guard, to be stationed at Camp Weber, at the mouth of Echo Canyon, to watch the movements of the U. S. soldiers during the winter. Two weeks later, when deep snow fell in the mountains, this guard was reduced to ten men. The remainder of the militia returned to their homes for the winter.

Mon. 14.—The Utah legislature convened in G. S. L. City and organized by electing Heber C. Kimball president of the Council and John Taylor speaker of the House.

Mon. 21.—The Utah legislature unanimously concurred in the message, policy and actions of Gov. Brigham Young, in stopping the army, etc.

Tues. 22.—An act disorganizing Green River County and attaching it to G. S. L. County, was approved.

1858.

Awaiting the arrival of the Federal army from the East, the Saints in Utah abandoned G. S. L. City and all their northern settlements and moved south, but most of them returned after peace was restored. Nearly all the Elders who had been on foreign missions returned home. In the spring of this year Kane County, Utah, was settled by Joshua T. Willes at Toquerville, and in the fall by Nephi Johnson and six others, who located Virgin City. San Bernardino, Cal., was vacated by the

Saints, who removed to Utah. Most of them settled at Parowan and Beaver. An edition of the Book of Mormon was published by James O. Wright and Co., 337 Broadway, New York, for speculative purposes and unauthorized by the Church.

January. *Wed. 6.*—A memorial from the members and officers of the Utah legislature to the President and Congress of the United States, praying for constitutional rights, etc., was signed in G. S. L. City.

Sat. 16.—A large mass meeting of citizens was held in the Tabernacle, G. S. L. City. A petition and resolution, setting forth the true state of affairs in Utah, were adopted, and, on motion, sent to the U. S. government at Washington.

Tues. 19.—Apostles Orson Pratt and Ezra T. Benson, and Elders John Scott and John M. Kay arrived in G. S. L. City from missions to Europe, and Geo. Q. Cannon, Joseph Bull and three other Elders from California.

Fri. 22.—The Utah legislature adjourned, without the occurrence of a negative vote on any question or action during the session.

February. *Sat. 6.*—Thorit Peck, formerly a member of the Mormon Battalion, died at Pleasant Grove, Utah Co., Utah.

Fri. 19.—Sixty-four Saints, mostly returning Elders, under the direction of Jesse Hobson, sailed from Liverpool, England, on the ship *Empire*, which arrived at New York March 20th.

Wed. 24.—Col. Thomas L. Kane arrived in G. S. L. City by way of Southern California. He came voluntarily for the purpose of bringing about a peaceful solution of the existing difficulties between the United States and Utah. After conferring with Gov. Brigham Young and other leading citizens, he went out to the army, which was encamped at Ft. Scott (near Ft. Bridger). There he had an interview with the new governor, Alfred Cumming, who concluded to accompany him to G. S. L. City.

Thurs. 25.—Geo. McBride and James Miller were killed and five other brethren wounded by a large party of Bannock and Shoshone Indians, near Fort Limhi, Oregon (now Idaho).

March.—Asa Calkin succeeded Samuel W. Richards as president of the European mission.

Sun. 21.—The citizens of G. S. L. City and the settlements north of it agreed to abandon their homes and go south, all the information derived from Eastern papers being to the effect that the approaching formidable army was sent to destroy them. Their destination, when starting, was by some supposed to be Sonora.

Mon. 22.—The ship *John Bright* sailed from Liverpool, England, with about ninety Saints, mostly Scandinavians, under the direction of Iver N. Iversen. The company arrived at New York April 23rd and at Iowa City May 1st.

Wed. 31.—Lyman Wight, once a member of the council of Twelve Apostles, died in Texas.

—Bailey Lake, one of a small party from Salmon river, traveling south, was killed by Indians on Bannock creek. The Indians also robbed the company of eleven horses.

April. *Mon. 5.*—Gov. Alfred Cumming and Col. Thos. L. Kane, with a servant each, left the army at Ft. Scott for the Valley. They arrived in G. S. L. City on the 12th. The new governor was kindly received by Pres. Brigham Young and other leading citizens and treated everywhere with "respectful attention."

Sat. 10.—The Saints who were settling on Ash Creek, southern Utah, were organized into a branch of the Church, called Toquerville, with Joshua T. Willis as president.

Mon. 19.—Gov. Alfred Cumming and Col. Thos. L. Kane examined the Utah library, where James W. Cummings showed them the records and seal of the U. S. District Court, alleged to have been destroyed by the Mormons. This accusation was one of the reasons why the army was ordered to Utah. A few days later the governor sent a truthful report to the government in relation to the affairs in the Territory.

Tues. 20.—Joseph Adair, one of the first settlers of Utah "Dixie", died at Washington, Washington Co., Utah.

Sat. 24.—Henry Jones was killed at Salem, Utah Co., Utah.

May.—The citizens of Utah, living north of Utah County, abandoned their homes and moved southward, leaving only a few men in each town and settlement to burn everything, in case the approaching troops, on their arrival in the Valley, should prove hostile.

Wed. 5.—The *Deseret News* having been removed from G. S. L. City to Fillmore, Millard Co., the first number of the paper published at that place was issued.

Thurs. 13.—Gov. Cumming left G. S. L. City for Camp Scott, for the purpose of removing his wife to the city. When he returned, June 8th, he found the city deserted by its inhabitants.

—Elder Samuel Francis Neslen, of G. S. L. City, Utah, died of consumption, in Williamsburg, N. Y., returning from a mission to England. He was buried in the Cypress Hill cemetery.

Tues. 18.- John Whittaker Taylor was born at Provo, Utah.

June. *Fri. 4.*—Jens Jørgensen and wife, Jens Terkelsen and Christian E. Kjerulf were murdered by Indians in Salt Creek Canyon, while traveling unarmed on their way to Sanpete Valley.

Mon. 7.—Ex-Gov. L. W. Powell, of Kentucky, and Major Ben McCullough, of Texas, sent as peace commissioners by the Federal government, arrived in G. S. L. City.

Fri. 11.—The peace commissioners met with Pres. Brigham Young and others in the Council House, G. S. L. City, and the difficulties between the United States and Utah were peaceably adjusted.

Tues. 15.—Commissioners Powell and McCullough visited Provo. The next day Mr. Powell addressed an audience of about four thousand persons in the Bowery, at Provo, Utah Co.

Sat. 19.—Col. Thos. L. Kane arrived in Washington, D. C. Soon afterwards he reported the situation in Utah to Pres. Buchanan.

Mon. 21.—A company of Elders returned to G. S. L. City from their missions in Europe, Canada and the States. A number of these had sailed from Liverpool on the ship *Underwriter*, Jan. 21st and others on the ship *Empire* Feb. 19th.

Sat. 26.—The army, under Col. Albert Sidney Johnston, passed through G. S. L. City and camped on the west side of the Jordan river. It subsequently marched to Cedar Valley, and there located Camp Floyd, about forty miles from the city.

July. *Thurs 1.*—The First Presidency and a few others returned to their homes in G. S. L. City, from Provo. They were followed by most of the people, who likewise returned to their deserted city and settlements in the North, and resumed their accustomed labors.

Sat. 3.—Commissioners Powell and McCullough left G. S. L. City, *en route* for Washington, D. C.

Fri. 9.—A party of Elders, accompanied by a few immigrating brethren, arrived in G. S. L. City, under the leadership of Horace S. Eldredge.

August. *Thurs. 12.*—Eli Harvey Pierce, one of the Utah Pioneers of 1847, died in G. S. L. City.

Mon. 16.—Wm. Evans was killed by lightning near Beaver, Utah.

September. *Mon. 20.*—Iver N. Iversen's company of immigrating Saints arrived in G. S. L City.

Wed. 22.—The *Deseret News* resumed its publication in G. S. L. City, after publishing twenty numbers at Fillmore.

October. *Tues. 12.*—Policeman Wm. Cooke was shot and mortally wounded, in G. S. L. City, by a ruffian named McDonald. He died on the 18th. The murderer escaped.

Fri. 15.—The remains of Josiah Call and Samuel Brown, of Fillmore, Millard Co., were found in a state of decomposition, near Chicken creek bridge, Juab Co. They had been murdered by Indians, Oct. 7th.

Thurs. 28.—Jacob Hamblin, with eleven men, left the settlement of Santa Clara, in southern Utah, to visit the Moquis or Town Indians, on the east side of the Colorado river. This was the beginning of intercourse with the Indians on that side of the Colorado and of the exploration of the country, which opened the way for colonization by the Saints.

November. — Notwithstanding President Buchanan s "Proclamation of Pardon," Judge Chas. E. Sinclair, in the Third District Court, urged the prosecution of the leading "Mormons" for alleged treason.

Thurs. 4. — Associate Justice John Cradlebaugh arrived in G. S. L. City, and U. S. District Attorney A. Wilson the following day.

Mon. 22.—The police in G. S. L. City were attacked and fired upon by a party of rowdies. Disturbances of the peace, robberies and stealing occurred frequently in the city at that time.

December.—*Thurs. 2.*—A violent wind

storm visited G. S. L. Valley and did much damage to property. Samuel Leaver and Wm. Redman froze to death.

Mon. 13. — The Utah legislature convened in G. S. L. City and adjourned to meet at Fillmore.

Sat. 18.—The Utah legislature convened at Fillmore, and organized by appointing Wilford Woodruff president of the Council *pro tem*, and Aaron Johnson speaker of the house *pro tem*. It then passed a resolution to adjourn the assembly to G. S. L. City.

Mon. 27.—The Utah legislature convened in G. S. L. City and organized by electing Daniel H. Wells president of the Council and John Taylor speaker of the House.

1859.

The Federal judges in Utah exercised undue authority and caused considerable difficulty by instituting court proceedings against the leaders of the Church and others. A number of settlements were founded in Cache Valley, where a Stake of Zion was organized. Provo Valley, Utah, was settled at Heber, Midway and Charleston.

January.—*Sat. 1.*—The *Millennial Star* announced to the Saints in Europe that emigration to Utah was again open for those who had means to take them through.

Tues. 11.—A legislative act, changing the county seat of Washington County from Harmony to the town of Washington, was approved.

Wed. 19.—An act passed by the Utah legislature reorganizing Carson and Green River Counties and attaching St. Mary's and Humboldt Counties to Carson County, was approved. Genoa was made the county seat of Carson and Ft. Bridger of Green River County.

February.—The Deseret Alphabet was first introduced in Utah.

—The 58th quorum of Seventy was organized at Brigham City, Box Elder Co., Utah. Some time previously the 56th and 57th quorums had been organized.

Thurs. 3.—The 59th quorum of Seventy was organized by Joseph Young at North Willow Creek (Willard), Box Elder Co., Utah, with George J. Marsh, Thomas W. Brewerton, John M. McCrary, Richard J. Davis, Elisha Mallory, Mathew W. Dalton and Peter Greenhalgh as presidents.

Fri. 11.—The 60th quorum of Seventy was organized at Ogden, Weber Co., Utah, with Luman A. Shurtliff as senior president.

Fri. 25.—The 61st quorum of Seventy was organized at Mill Creek, G. S. L. Co., with John Scott, James Craigan, Wm. Casto, James P. Park, Andrew J. Rynearson, Dudley J. Merrill and Thurston Larson as presidents.

March.—Plain City, Weber Co., Utah, was settled by Jeppe G. Folkman, Christopher O. Folkman, Jens Peter Folkman, Joseph Skeen, Daniel Collett, John

Spiers, John Carver, Wm. Geddes and others.

Tues. 8.—Associate Justice John Cradlebaugh, in his charge to the grand jury, composed of "Mormons," at Provo, called them "fools", "dupes", "instruments af a tyrannical church despotism", etc. Provo was occupied by a detachment of U. S. troops.

Wed. 9.—A small company of Saints, under the leadership of Joseph Humphreys, sailed from Port Elizabeth, South Africa, bound for America. They arrived at Boston early in May, 1859.

Mon. 21.—A small company of Saints from Australia arrived at San Francisco, Cal., *en route* for G. S. L. City.

Tues. 22.—Howard O. Spencer, a Mormon youth, was assaulted and brutally beaten on the head by Sergeant Ralph Pike, of the U. S. army, in Rush Valley, Utah.

Sun. 27.—Gov. Cumming issued a proclamation against the presence of troops in Provo. About this time it was reported that certain U. S. officials had entered into a conspiracy to secure the arrest of Pres. Brigham Young, and that Col. Johnston had promised the assistance of U. S. troops under his command to effect the arrest. As a consequence Gov. Cumming notified General Daniel H. Wells to hold the militia in readiness to prevent the outrage, should it be attempted; 5,000 troops (militia) were placed under arms.

April.—*Mon. 4.*—The U. S. troops evacuated Provo.

Wed. 6.—The 29th annual conference of the Church was commenced at G. S. L. City. Benjamin L. Clapp, one of the presidents of the Seventies, was excommunicated from the Church on the 7th, for apostasy.

Mon. 11.—The ship *William Tapscott* sailed from Liverpool, England, with 725 Saints, under the direction of Robert F. Neslen. The company arrived at New York May 14th, and at Florence, Neb., May 25th.

May.—*Tues. 10.*—Gen. Albert Sidney Johnston promised protection to all persons who wished to leave the Territory of Utah.

Wed. 11.—Isaac Allred was assaulted and killed by Thomas Ivie, at Mount Pleasant, Sanpete Co., Utah.

Wed. 18.—Joseph Abbott was killed by lightning, while engaged in planting corn on the "Old Fort Square," G. S. L. City.

Thurs. 26.—James Johnson, a son of Luke S. Johnson, of Shambip County, was shot and mortallly wounded by Delos Gibson in G. S. L. City. Death ensued the following day. A number of other murders, principally among bad characters who infested the Territory, took place about the same time.

Sun. 29.—Leo Hawkins, clerk at the Historian's office, died in G. S. L. City.

June.—Logan, Cache Co., was first settled.

July.—*Sun. 10.*—Hon. Horace Greeley, editor of the New York *Tribune*, arrived at G. S. L. City *en route* for California.

—The ship *Antarctic* sailed from Liverpool, England, with 30 Saints, under the direction of James Chaplow. It arrived at New York Aug. 21st.

Thurs. 14.—Geo. W. Bradley was ordained Bishop of Moroni, Sanpete Co., which place had recently been settled.

August.—*Mon.1.*—Wm. H. Hooper was elected Utah's second delegate to Congress, Hon. John M. Bernhisel having served in that capacity since the organization of the Territory.

Thurs. 11.—Sergeant Ralph Pike, a U. S. soldier, was shot in G. S. L. City, in supposed retaliation for having cracked the scull of Howard O. Spencer with a musket, five months previously.

Mon. 15.—U. S. soldiers set fire to a hay stack at Cedar Fort, Cedar Valley, Utah, and fired upon the citizens in the night. The soldiers were excited over the killing of Sergeant Pike.

Sat. 20.—The ship *Emerald Isle* sailed from Liverpool, England, with 54 Saints, mostly Swiss, under the direction of Henry Hug.

Sat. 27.—The first number of the *Mountaineer,* a weekly newspaper, was published in G. S. L. City; Messrs. Blair, Ferguson & Stout editors and proprietors.

Mon. 29.—Captain James Brown's company of immigrants, which had left Florence June 13th, and consisted of 353 souls with 59 wagons, arrived at G. S. L. City.

September.—*Thurs. 1.*—Capt. Horton D. Haight's wagon company (called the Church train), bringing merchandise and 134 immigrants, arrived at G. S. L. City.

Sun. 4.—Capt. George Rowley's handcart company, which had left Florence, June 9th, with 235 souls, 60 handcarts, and 6 wagons, arrived in G. S. L. City.

Thurs. 15.—Capt. Robert F. Neslen's company of immigrants, consisting of 372 souls, with 58 wagons, which had left Florence June 26th, arrived in G. S. L. City.

Fri. 16.—Capt. Edward Stevenson's immigrating company, consisting of about three hundred and fifty souls, with 54 wagons, arrived at G. S. L. City. It had started from Florence June 26th.

Sat. 17. — Alexander Carpenter was shot and mortally wounded by Thomas H. Ferguson in G. S. L. City. Both were non-Mormons.

October. *Mon. 10.*—Smithfield, Cache Co., was settled by Seth Langton and Robert and John Thornley.

Fri. 28.—Thos. H. Ferguson, the murderer, was executed in G. S. L. City. This was the first execution of a criminal in Utah.

November. *Mon. 14.*—A Stake of Zion was partly organized in Cache Valley, Utah. Peter Maughan was appointed presiding Bishop in Cache Valley. Logan Ward was organized, with Wm. B. Preston as Bishop.

December. *Mon. 12.*—The ninth annual session of the Utah legislature convened in G. S, L. City and organized by electing Daniel H. Wells president of the Council and John Taylor speaker of the House.

This year Spring City, Sanpete Co., Utah, was resettled under the name of Little Denmark.

1860.

General Albert Sidney Johnston, left Utah with a part of the Federal army, which had been stationed at Camp Floyd, Cedar Valley, since 1858. A large immigration arrived in Utah from Europe.

January. *Wed. 25.*—John King was accidentally killed and buried in a snowslide, in Centreville, Canyon, Davis Co. Utah.

February. *Tues. 7.*—The Social Hall, G. S. L. City, was reopened for public amusements, which had been discontinued there for three years.

Wed 15.—Wm. Price was ordained the first Bishop of Goshen, Utah Co.

March. *Thurs. 1.*—Gen. Albert Sidney Johnston, commander of the "Utah Army," left Camp Floyd for Washington, D. C. He had never visited G. S. L. City since he passed through with his army on June 26, 1858. Philip St. George Cooke, formerly commander of the Mormon Battalion, succeeded Johnston in the command.

Sun. 4.—Levi Gifford, formerly a member of Zion's Camp, died at Moroni, Sanpete Co.

Mon. 19.—Dr. Wm. France died suddenly in G. S. L. City.

Sun. 25.—Apostle Ezra T. Benson moved to Logan, Cache Co., having been called to preside over the Saints in Cache Valley.

Fri. 30.—The ship *Underwriter* sailed from Liverpool, England. with 594 British and Swiss Saints, under the presidency of James D. Ross. It arrived at New York May 1st, and the emigrants continued to Florence, where Geo. Q. Cannon was acting as Church emigration agent this year, to arrange for the journey across the plains.

April.—Hyrum, Cache Co., Utah, was first settled by about twenty families. In the following month Calvin Bingham was appointed Bishop. Paradise, Cache Co., was settled about the same time.

Sat. 7.—The Saints who had settled on lower Beaver creek, Beaver Co., Utah, were organized into a Ward named Minersville, by Apostles Amasa M. Lyman and Charles C. Rich; James K. Rollins, Bishop.

—The first "Pony Express" from the West arrived at G. S. L. City, having left Sacramento, Cal., on the evening of April 3rd.

Mon. 9.—The first "Pony Express" from the East arrived at G. S. L. City, having left St. Joseph, Mo., on the evening of April 3rd.

—The Union Academy was opened in the building known as the Union Hotel (afterwards Deseret Hospital), with Orson Pratt as principal.

Fri. 13.—Thos. Miles was attacked and wounded by Indians, between Ogden and Kaysville. The savages proceeded to Brigham City, where they stole horses and insulted the citizens.

Mon. 16.—Hyde Park, Cache Co., was settled by several families from Utah County.

Fri. 27.—Jack Cole, a horsethief and outlaw, was mortally wounded at Spring.

ville, Utah Co., while resisting the officers of the law.

May.—A large number of the troops stationed at Camp Floyd, Utah, left, according to orders, for New Mexico and Arizona Territories.

—Nathaniel V. Jones and Jacob Gates succeeded Asa Calkin in the presidency of the European mission.

Thurs. 3.—John W. Brown was accidentally killed by the falling of a rock, near Draper, G. S. L. Co.

Sat. 5.—Niels Jensen, one of the early members of the Church in Denmark, died in G. S. L. City.

Tues. 8.—Jesse W. Johnson was accidentally killed at Snyder's Mill, in Parley's Park.

Fri. 11.—The ship *William Tapscott* sailed from Liverpool, England, with 731 Saints (including 312 Scandinavians), under the direction of Asa Calkin. During the voyage small pox broke out among the emigrants, who had to remain several days in quarantine after arriving at New York harbor. They finally landed June 20th and continued their journey to Florence, Neb., where they arrived July 1st.

Sat. 12.—G. S. L. City was visited by a heavy snow storm.

Mon. 28.—The Indians attacked the mail station at Deep Creek, Tooele Co., shot a man and stole several horses.

Thurs. 31.—Rees Jones Williams was accidentally killed in a saw mill, in Little Cottonwood Canyon.

June. *Sun. 3.*—The first train of merchandise from the East that season arrived in G. S. L. City.

July. *Sun. 22.*—Smithfield, Cache Co., was attacked by Indians. A fight ensued; John Reed and Ira Merrill and two Indians were killed, and several others wounded on both sides.

Tues. 24.—The day was celebrated by the citizens of G. S. L. County near the head waters of Big Cottonwook.

Sat. 28.—The remains of a woman, evidently killed by the departing soldiers, were found in Provo Valley, Wasatch Co.

August.—Apostles Amasa M. Lyman and Charles C. Rich succeeded Nathaniel V. Jones and Jacob Gates in the presidency of the European mission.

Thurs. 2.—Mrs. Ruth B. Clark, of the Sugar House Ward, Salt Lake Co., was bitten by a scorpion, while asleep, causing her death.

Sat. 4.—A terrible hailstorm visited Davis County, doing a great deal of damage.

Thurs. 9.—Capt. Warren Walling's train, the first company of immigrating Saints of the season, arrived in G. S. L. City, having left Florence, May 30th, with 160 persons and 30 wagons, mostly drawn by oxen.

Sun. 12.—The Indians made an attack upon the mail station at Egan Canyon, (Tooele Co.) and the following day on Shell Creek Station. A company of soldiers came to the rescue and killed 17 Indians.

Sun. 26.—Geo. Q. Cannon was ordained one of the Twelve Apostles, in G. S.L.City.

Mon. 27.—Capt. Daniel Robinson's handcart company (the first of the season), consisting of 233 persons, 43 handcarts, 6 wagons. 38 oxen and 10 tents, arrived in G. S. L. City. Pres. Brigham Young had sent out wagons with 2,500 lbs. of flour and 500 lbs. of bacon to help the company.

Thurs. 30.—Capt. J. E. Murphy's immigrant company, consisting of 279 persons, 38 wagons, 164 oxen and 39 cows, arrived at G. S. L. City, having left Florence June 19th.

September. *Sat. 1.*—Capt. John Smith's company of immigrants, consisting of 359 persons and 39 wagons, arrived in G. S. L. City.

Mon. 3.—Capt. James D. Ross' company of immigrants, consisting of 249 persons, 36 wagons, 142 oxen and 54 cows, which left Florence June 17th, arrived in G. S. L. City.

Tues. 4.—A portion of Capt. Franklin Brown's company of immigrants arrived in G. S. L. City.

Fri. 14.—Capt. Brigham H. Young's train of immigrants arrived in G. S. L. City.

Mon. 17.—Capt. John Taylor's company of immigrating Saints arrived in G. S. L. City, having left Florence July 3rd.

Mon. 24.—The second handcart company of the season, under Capt. Oscar O. Stoddard, arrived in G. S. L. City, having left Florence July 6th, with 126 persons and 22 handcarts. These were the last immigrants who crossed the plains with handcarts.

Wed. 26. — On this and the two following days a company of missionaries left G. S. L. City, among whom were Apostles Orson Pratt and Erastus Snow, for the United States and Geo. Q. Cannon on his way to England.

October.—Capt. Jacob Hamblin, left Santa Clara, southern Utah, with nine men, to visit the Moquis Indians.

Thurs. 4.—Hon. John F. Kinney arrived in G. S. L. City, having been reappointed chief justice of the Territory of Utah.

Fri. 5.—Capt. Wm. Budge's train, the last immigrant comany of the season, arrived in G. S. L. City, having left Florence July 20th, with over four hundred persons, 55 wagons, 215 oxen and 77 cows.

Sun. 21.—A branch of the Church was organized at Mountain Green, Weber Valley, Utah.

November. *Fri. 2.*—Geo. A. Smith, jun., (a son of Pres. Geo. A. Smith),one of Jacob Hamblin's exploring party, was killed by Navajo Indians, in New Mexico. The rest of the company were obliged to return, and barely escaped with their lives.

Mon. 12.—An extra session of the Utah legislature convened in G. S. L. City, for the purpose of assigning the Federal judges to the various districts, in obedience to a proclamation of Gov. Cumming.

Fri. 16.—A terrible storm visited Great Salt Lake, Weber and surrounding Counties, destroying considerable property.

December. *Mon. 3.*—Starling Graves Driggs, one of the Utah Pioneers of 1847, died in Parowan, Iron Co.

Tues. 4.—The Ute Indian Chief Arrapeen died in the mountains between Sevier Valley and Grass Valley, about sixty miles south of Manti.

Mon. 10.—The tenth annual session of the Utah legislature convened in G. S. L City and organized by electing Daniel H

Wells president of the Council, and John Taylor speaker of the House.

1861

Utah was divided, and the western part organized into the Territory of Nevada. A large number of teams were sent to the Missouri river for the poor Saints. The U. S. soldiers stationed at Camp Floyd were withdrawn from Utah. The overland telegraph line was completed from the States *via* G. S. L. City to California. In the fall of the year a large number of people were called from the middle and northern counties of Utah Territory to settle in southern Utah, on the Rio Virgen and Santa Clara. The city of St. George and the towns on the upper Rio Virgen were located and the resources of the country rapidly developed. A missionary field was opened in Holland.

January. *Tues. 1.*—The 13th Ward assembly rooms in G. S. L. City were dedicated.

Thurs. 3.—Capt. David R. Evans died at Brigham City, Box Elder Co.

Sat. 19.—The Utah legislature adjourned.

Tues. 29.—Wm. S. Champlin, a survivor of the Haun's Mill massacre, died at Lehi, Utah Co.

February.—The 62nd quorum of Seventy was organized at G. S. L. City, with James F. Cleary, Wm. L. Brundage, Richard Golightly, Francis Platt, Henry W. Naisbitt, J. D. Ross and Claude Clive presidents.

Sat. 2.—A band of thieving Indians (Goshutes) were taken prisoners by a posse of men, near Grantsville, Tooele Co., but a few days later they escaped, after shooting one of the guard.

Wed. 6.—By order of the commander the military post of Camp Floyd changed name to Fort Crittenden. Secretary of War John B. Floyd, after whom the camp originally was named, had allied himself with the South against the Union.

March. *Fri. 1.*—A branch of the Church was organized at Deseret, Millard Co., Utah, with Jacob Croft as president.

Sat. 2.—A bill, providing for the organization of Nevada Territory out of the western portion of Utah, was approved by President James Buchanan.

Mon. 4.—A branch of the Church was organized in Round Valley (now Scipio), Millard Co., Utah, with B. H. Johnson as president.

April. *Sat. 6.*—On this and the following day the 31st annual conference of the Church was held in G. S. L. City.

Sun. 14.—Logan, Cache Co., was divided into four wards, with Benjamin M. Lewis, Henry Ballard, John B. Thatcher and Thos. X. Smith as Bishops, respectively.

Tues. 16.—The packet ship *Manchester* sailed from Liverpool, England, with 380 Saints, under the direction of Claudius V. Spencer. They arrived at New York May 18th.

6

Tues. 23.—The clipper ship *Underwriter* sailed from Liverpool, with 624 Saints, under the presidency of Milo Andrus, Homer Duncan and Charles William Penrose. The company arrived at New York May 22nd, and at Florence June 2nd. From the 23rd to the 31st of this month upwards of two hundred Church wagons, with four yoke of cattle to each, carrying 150,000 pounds of flour, left G. S. L. Valley for the Missouri river to bring in the poor. They traveled in four companies under Capts. Joseph W. Young, Ira Eldredge, Joseph Horne and John R. Murdock.

Mon. 29.—Elder Reynolds Cahoon died at South Cottonwood. G. S. L. Co., of dropsy.

May. *Wed. 15.*—Pres. Brigham Young and others left G. S. L. City on a trip to the southern settlements, from which they returned June 8th. A little later the President visited Cache Valley.

Thurs. 16.—The packet ship *Monarch of the Sea* sailed from Liverpool, with 955 Saints of various nationalities, under the direction of Jabez Woodard, H. O. Hansen and Niels Wilhelmsen. The company arrived in New York June 19th.

Fri. 17.—Gov. Alfred Cumming and wife left G. S. L. City, quietly, for the States.

July.—The rest of the army at Camp Floyd, or Fort Crittenden, was ordered to the States. In consequence of this, government property and outfit at Camp Floyd was sold at extraordinarily low prices. It was estimated that $4,000,000 worth of goods was sold for $100,000.

August. *Mon. 5.*— Paul A. Schettler and A. W. Van der Woude arrived as missionaries in Rotterdam, Holland. After laboring several months, they succeeded in organizing a branch of the Church of 14 members.

Fri. 16.—The first company of immigrating Saints of the season, which had left Florence May 29th, under Capt. David H. Cannon's charge, arrived in G. S. L. City. The company consisted of 225 persons, with 57 wagons.

September. *Mon. 2.*—A company of settlers left G. S. L. City for the Uintah country, intending to locate a settlement, in which, however, they did not succeed.

Fri. 6.—Apostles Orson Pratt and Erastus Snow arrived in G. S. L. City from a mission of gathering the poor Saints in the Eastern States.

Thurs. 12.—Captains Milo Andrus and John R. Murdock arrived in G. S. L. City with their respective companies of immigrants.

Fri. 13.—Captains Joseph Horne and Homer Duncan arrived in G. S. L. City with their companies of immigrants. Horne's company left Florence July 1st.

Sun. 15.—Capt. Ira Eldredge's train of immigrants arrived in G. S. L. City, having left Florence June 30th.

Sat. 21.—Wm. Cockcroft, the murderer of Robert Brown, was executed in G. S. L. City.

Sun. 22.—Capt. Samuel A. Woolley arrived in G. S. L. City, with his company of immigrants, mostly Scandinavians.

Mon. 23.—The last Church train of the season arrived in G. S. L. City, under the direction of Capt. Ansel P. Harmon.

Fri. 27. — Capt. Sextus E. Johnson's company of immigrating Saints arrived in G. S. L. City, with about sixty wagons. This was the last company of immigrants that arrived this season.

October. *Thurs. 3.*—John W. Dawson was appointed governor of Utah.

Sun. 6.—The semi-annual conference of the Church was commenced in G. S. L. City. It was continued three days. A number of brethren were called to settle in southern Utah and turn their special attention to the raising of cotton.

Tues. 8.-- Parshall Terry died at Draper, G. S. L. Co.

Fri. 18.—The overland telegraph line was completed from the States to G. S. L. City. Pres. Brigham Young sent the first telegram, which passed over the line, to J. H. Wade, president of the company.

Thurs. 24.—The first telegram was sent from G. S. L. City to San Francisco by Pres. Brigham Young.

November. *Mon. 18.*—The Toquerville branch, southern Utah, was organized as a Ward, with Joshua T. Willis as Bishop.

Thurs. 28.—A company of Swiss Saints, under the leadership of Daniel Bonnelli, arrived at Santa Clara, southern Utah, having been called to settle there.

Fri. 29.—Apostles Geo. A. Smith and Erastus Snow, Elder Horace S. Eldredge and others left G. S. L. City for southern Utah, with a view to locating settlements in the valleys of the Rio Virgen and Santa Clara for the purpose of raising cotton.

December. *Wed. 4.*—At a meeting of southern Utah settlers who had arrived from the north, it was decided, on motion of Apostle Erastus Snow, to build a city to be called St. George.

Sat. 7.—John W. Dawson, Utah's third governor, arrived in G. S. L. City, accompanied by James Duane Doty, superintendent of Indian affairs.

Mon. 9.—Luke S. Johnson, once a member of the Twelve Apostles, died at Orson Hyde's residence, G. S. L. City.

—The 11th annual session of the Utah legislature convened in G. S. L. City, and organized by electing Daniel H. Wells president of the Council and John Taylor speaker of the House.

Fri. 13.—The Saints who were settling Grafton, southern Utah, were organized into a Ward, by Apostles Orson Pratt and Erastus Snow, with Franklin W. Young as Bishop.

Mon. 23.— Peteetneet, the famous Ute Indian chief, died near Fort Crittenden, Utah Co.

Tues. 31.—Gov. John W. Dawson, left G. S. L. City for the States, under peculiar circumstances. Secretary Frank Fuller succeeded him as acting governor.

1862.

The people of Utah petitioned the Federal government the third time for admission into the Union as a State. A large immigration arrived this year from Europe, and the Church sent teams to the Missouri river to bring most of them across the plains. In response to a call from the government a company of militia went eastward to protect the mail stations against the Indians. In the fall of this year the southern settlements in Utah were strengthened by the arrival of new settlers from the North. About one hundred thousand pounds of cotton was raised in Washington County. Jacob Hamblin, with a small party crossed the Colorado river, south of St. George, and went to the Moquis towns *via* the San Francisco Mountains. On the return trip three of the Moquis accompanied the party and visited G. S. L. City, where they had an interview with the leading men of the Church.

January. *Wed. 1.* — An important council of the Priesthood of the European mission was commenced in Birmingham, England; it was continued for six days.

Thurs. 16.—Lot Huntington, an outlaw, was killed by O. Porter Rockwell, near Ft. Crittenden, while attempting to escape from the officers. On the following day, while trying to effect their escape, John P. Smith and Moroni Clawson, two other outlaws, were killed in G. S. L. City.

Fri. 17.—The Utah legislature adjourned. Among the acts passed was one defining the boundaries of the Territory and its respective counties, after the creation of Nevada, etc. The counties were 17 in number, namely, Beaver, Box Elder, Cache, Davis, Great Salt Lake, Green River, Iron, Juab, Millard, Morgan, Summit, Sanpete, Tooele, Utah, Washington, Wasatch and Weber.

Sat. 18.—A flood did much damage in the Rio Virgen and Santa Clara Valleys, southern Utah.

Mon. 20.—A convention for the establishment of a State government, assembled in G. S. L. City.

Thurs. 23.—The convention of delegates, chosen by the people, adopted a State constitution for Utah and a memorial to Congress, praying the third time for the admission of Utah into the Union as a State with the name of Deseret. George Q. Cannon and Wm. H. Hooper were elected delegates to present them to Congress.

March. *Thurs. 6.*—The Salt Lake Theater, which had been erected the previous season, was dedicated. The building is 144 feet long and 80 feet wide.

Sat. 8.—The Salt Lake Theater was opened to the public. The pieces played at the opening performance were "Pride of the Market" and "State Secrets."

Sat. 22.—At a conference held in the new settlement of St. George, southern Utah, that town was divided into four Wards.

Wed. 26.—Salomon Chamberlain, an old member of the Church, and a Pioneer of 1847, died in Washington County, Utah.

April. *Sun. 6.*—The 32nd annual conference of the Church was commenced in G. S. L. City; it was continued until the 9th.

Tues. 8.—Mr. Morrill of Vermont, introduced a bill in the U. S. House of Representatives, at Washington, D. C., to punish and prevent the practice of bigamy in the Territories of the United States. It was read twice and referred to the committee on Territories. This bill also made it unlawful for any religious or charitable association in any of the U. S. Territories to own real estate worth more than $50,000.

Wed. 9.—The ship *Humboldt* sailed from Hamburg, Germany, with 323 Scandinavian Saints, under the direction of Hans Christian Hansen. The company arrived at New York May 20th and at Florence about the 1st of June.

Tues. 15.—The ship *Franklin* sailed from Hamburg, Germany, with 413 Scandinavian Saints, under the direction of Christian A. Madsen. The company arrived in New York harbor May 29th and at Florence June 9th. Between forty and fifty children died of measles on board the ship.

Mon. 21.—The ship *Athenia* sailed from Hamburg, Germany, with 484 Scandinavian Saints, under the direction of Ola N. Liljenquist. The company arrived at New York June 6th and at Florence June 19th.

Wed. 23.—The ship *John J. Boyd* sailed from Liverpool, England, with 701 Saints, under the direction of James S. Brown; it arrived at New York June 1st.

Mon. 28.—The Indians having destroyed the mail stations between Fort Bridger and North Platte, burned the coaches and mail bags, killed the drivers and stolen the stock. Adjutant-General L. Thomas, at Washington, D. C., made a call upon Pres. Brigham Young for a company of cavalry to protect the mail route.

May.—Two hundred and sixty - two wagons, 293 men, 2,880 oxen and 143,315 pounds of flour were sent from Utah to assist the poor of the immigration across the plains and mountains. They traveled in six companies under Captains Horton D. Haight. Henry W. Miller, Homer Duncan, Joseph Horne, John R. Murdock and Ansel P. Harmon.

—Col. Patrick Edward Connor was ordered to Utah with California volunteers. In July they took up their line of march.

Thurs. 1.—In obedience to the call of L. Thomas, a company of cavalry, numbering about one hundred men, left G. S. L. City for Independence Rock, under Capt. Lot Smith's command.

Tues. 6.—The ship *Manchester* sailed from Liveroool, with 376 Saints, under the direction of John D. T. McAllister; it arrived at New York June 12th.

Wed. 14.—The ship *Wm. Tapscott* sailed from Liverpool, with 808 Saints, under the direction of Wm. Gibson, John Clark and Francis M. Lyman. It arrived safely at New York.

Thurs. 15.—The ship *Windermere* sailed from Havre, France. with 109 Swiss and French Saints, under the direction of Serge L. Ballif, bound for Utah *via* New York.

Sun. 18.—The packet ship *Antarctic* sailed from Liverpool, England, with 38 Saints, under the charge of Wm. C. Moody.

June.—*Tues. 3.*—The anti-bigamy bill was passed by the U. S. Senate, considerably amended. The House afterwards concurred in the amendments.

Mon. 9.—Delegate John M. Bernhisel presented the constitution of the State of Des-

eret, and the accompanying memorial, in the U. S. House of Representatives. On the 10th the Vice-President presented the same in the Senate.

Thurs. 12.—An expedition, or marshal's *posse*, under Robert T. Burton, left G. S. L. City for the purpose of arresting Joseph Morris and others, encamped on the Weber river, a little below the mouth of the canyon.

Thurs. 12.—The Saints at Harrisburg, Washington Co., Utah, were organized into a branch of the Church, with James Lewis as president.

Fri. 13.—The expedition, under Capt. Robert T. Burton, which had been joined by men from the settlements in Davis County, arrived before Morris' Camp, on the Weber; and as the Morrisites refused to surrender, fire was opened on the camp, with fatal effect.

Sun. 15.—Joseph Morris, John Banks, and others were killed and the Morrisites taken prisoners.

Mon. 16.—The Morrisites were brought to G. S. L. City.

Wed. 18.—The Morrisite prisoners were on trial in G. S. L. City; some of them were fined and others admitted to bail.

Fri. 20.—President Abraham Lincoln approved the act of Congress prohibiting slavery in the Territories.

July. — Much property, including a great number of bridges, was destroyed in Utah by floods.

—Apostle George Q. Cannon succeeded Apostles Amasa M. Lyman and Charles C. Rich in the presidency of the European mission. Jacob G. Bigler had temporary charge of the mission during the absence of Elder Cannon.

Fri. 4.—Utah showed its loyalty to the Union by celebrating Independence day in grand style, while the rebellion was in progress in the East.

—John A. Ray died at Fillmore, Millard Co.

Mon. 7.—Stephen S. Harding, Utah's fourth governor, arrived in G. S. L. City. He had been appointed to the governorship March 31st

—Florence, Neb., where thousands of Saints were camped, was visited by a terrible storm, during which two brethren were killed by lightning, and Joseph W. Young was severely hurt.

Tues. 8.—The anti-bigamy law was approved by President Lincoln.

Fri. 11.—Associate Justices Chas B. Waite and Thos. J. Drake arrived in G. S. L. City.

Fri. 25.—Donald McNichols, a member of Captain Lot Smith's expedition, was drowned in Lewis Fork, about ten miles below the Three Tetons, Oregon (now Idaho), while pursuing a band of thieving Indians.

August.—*Fri. 29.*—Capt. Lewis Brunson's ox-train, which had left Florence June 17th with 212 Saints and 48 wagons, arrived in G. S. L. City.

September.—The first number of *Die Reform*, a monthly periodical published in the interest of the Church in the German language, was issued by John L. Smith, at Geneva, Switzerland.

Mon. 1.—Pres. Brigham Young and a.

company of Elders left G. S. L. City on a visit to southern Utah, from which they returned on the 25th. Later in the season the President visited the northern settlements.

Tues. 9.—Col. Patrick E. Connor arrived in G. S. L. City, his company of volunteers remaining in Ruby Valley, Nevada.

Tues. 16.—Apostle Amasa M. Lyman, and Charles C. Rich, accompanied by other Elders, arrived in G. S. L. City, from their missions in Europe.

Tues. 23.—The independent companies of Scandinavian Saints, under the direction of Captains Christian A. Madsen and Ola N. Liljenquist, which had left Florence July 14th, with about five hundred immigrants and eighty wagons, arrived in G. S. L. City.

Wed. 24.—Capt. Homer Duncan's Church train (first), which had left Florence July 22nd, arrived in G. S. L. City. This train had made the round trip from the Valley to Florence and back in 130 days.

Fri. 26.—Capt. James Wareham's independent company of immigrants arrived in G. S. L. City.

Sat. 27.—Capt. John R. Murdock's Church train (second), which had left Florence July 24th, with 65 wagons and about seven hundred immigrants arrived in G. S. L. City.

October. — *Wed. 1.* — Capt. Joseph Horne's Church train (third), which had left Florence July 20th, with about five hundred and seventy souls and 52 wagons, arrived in G. S. L. City.

Thurs. 2.—Capt. James S. Brown's independent company (third), which had left Florence July 28th, with 46 wagons and about two hundred immigrants, arrived n G. S. L. City.

Sun. 5.—Capt. Ansel P. Harmon's Church train (fourth) arrived in G. S. L. City, with about five hundred immigrants. About fifteen children died of measles, on the plains.

Thurs. 16.—Capt. Isaac A. Canfield's independent company of immigrants arrived in G. S. L. City, having been eleven weeks on the journey from Florence.

Fri. 17.—Capt. Henry W. Miller's Church train (fifth), which had left Florence Aug. 8th, with sixty wagons and about six hundred and sixty-five immigrants, arrived in G. S. L. City. The company had suffered considerably from sickness, and about twenty-eight persons died on the journey.

—Col. Patrick E. Connor's command of 750 California volunteers arrived at Ft. Crittenden, Cedar Valley, and on the following day marched to the Jordan river.

Sun. 19.—Capt. Horton D. Haight's Church train (sixth), in which there were about six hundred and fifty immigrants, arrived in G. S. L. City. Thirty persons died on the journey.

Mon. 20.—Col. Patrick E. Connor arrived in G. S. L. City with his command, and on the 22nd he located Camp Douglas, about three miles east of the city.

Wed. 29.—Capt. Wm. H. Dame's Church freight train, the last of the season, arrived in G. S. L. City.

November. *Sat. 15.*—The 65th quorum of Seventy was organized at G. S. L. City,

with John L. Dunyon, Thos. C. Armstrong, Jens. C. A. Welbye, Henry W. Brizzee, Gustaf A. Ohlson, Edward W. Tullidge and Jens Hansen as presidents.

Fri. 21.—The 66th quorum of Seventy was organized at Mt. Pleasant, Sanpete Co., with Levi B. Reynolds as one of the presidents.

Fri. 28.—The 68th quorum of Seventy was organized at Lehi, Utah Co., with John Brown, John R. Moyle, Wm. S. S. Willes, Orice C. Murdock, John C. Naegle, John R. Murdock and Israel Evans as presidents.

Sat. 29.—The 67th quorum of Seventy was organized at American Fork, Utah Co., with Samuel Mulliner, Stephen Chipman, Thomas Barrett, Washburne Chipman, Lewis Harvey, Calvin Moore and Wm. F. Reynolds as presidents.

December. *Mon. 8.*—The Utah legislature (12th annual session) convened in G. S. L. City, and organized by electing Daniel H. Wells president of the Council, and Orson Pratt speaker of the House.

Wed. 10.—Gov. Harding, who proved to be a bitter enemy to the people of Utah, delivered a very insulting message to the territorial legislature.

Fri. 19.—Joseph B. Haws, one of the early members of the Church, died at Spanish Fork, Utah Co.

—Elder Gustav Pegua, who labored as a missionary in Hamburg, Germany, was arrested and the following day banished from that city.

1863.

This year Sevier Valley, Utah, was settled at Richfield and Monroe. The Shoshone Indians were defeated on Bear river by Col. Connor's troops. Nearly four hundred wagons were sent to the Missouri river after the poor. In the fall Bear Lake Valley was settled by Apostle Charles C. Rich and others who founded Paris (now in Bear Lake Co., Idaho).

January.—*Fri. 16.*—The Utah legislature adjourned without being able to accomplish much, as Gov. Harding vetoed nearly all the bills.

Thurs. 29.—Col. Patrick E. Connor, with about two hundred troops, defeated a band of Shoshone Indians, numbering over four hundred, in a ravine on Beaver creek, near Bear River, 12 miles north of Franklin. About sixteen soldiers and some two hundred and twenty-five Indians were killed, including the chiefs Bear Hunter and Lehi. The savages were entirely defeated. This is known in history as the battle of Bear river.

February. *Sun. 15.*—Elder Nathaniel V. Jones, sen., died in G. S. L. City.

March.—The bitter feelings existing between the troops at Camp Douglas and the citizens of G. S. L. City came near terminating in a collision.

Tues. 3.—A large mass-meeting was held in the Tabernacle, G. S. L. City, at which protests were entered against the infamous course persued by Gov. Harding and Associate Justices Waite and Drake. A petition, asking for their removal, was drawn up,and subsequently was forwarded to President Abraham Lincoln, Washington, D. C.

—A Congressional act creating the territory of Idaho was approved. A portion of northeastern Utah was included in the new territory; later (July 25, 1868) this became a part of Wyoming.

Wed. 4.—John Taylor, Jeter Clinton and Orson Pratt, appointed in the mass meeting the day previous, waited on Gov. Harding and Judges Drake and Waite, asking them, in behalf of the people, to resign their official positions, which they refused to do.

Tues. 10.—Pres. Brigham Young was arrested on a charge of bigamy, under the anti-bigamy law of 1862, brought before Judge Kinney, and placed under $2,000 bonds.

Sat. 14.—The barque *Rowena* sailed from Port Elizabeth, Cape of Good Hope, Africa, with 15 Saints on board, under the direction of Robert Grant, bound for Utah.

Sun. 22.—The overland mail coach, with four passengers, was attacked by Indians, near Eight Mile Creek Station, Tooele Co. Henry Harper, the driver, was killed and one passenger wounded. Judge Mott, delegate to Congress from Nevada, who was in the coach, took the reins, drove for life and escaped.

Tues. 31.—Gov. Stephen S. Harding pardoned all the Morrisites, who had been convicted of resisting the officers, etc.

April. *Wed. 1.*—A fight took place between a small detachment of U. S. troops from Camp Douglas and a party of Indians, near Cedar Fort, Utah Co.

Sun. 5.—In Spanish Fork Canyon, Utah Co., 200 Indians were defeated by 140 cavalry, under Col. G. S. Evans. Lieut. F. A. Queale was killed in the battle.

Mon. 6.—The thirty-third annual conference of the Church was commenced in G. S. L. City; it was continued till the 8th; 47 missionaries were called.

Sun. 12.—A small party of soldiers from Camp Douglas had a fight with Indians at Pleasant Grove, Utah Co., during which several horses were killed.

Wed. 15.—Two companies of soldiers from Camp Douglas attacked a band of Indians in Spanish Fork Canyon, Utah Co. During the engagement several Indians were killed and wounded. Also a few of the soldiers were wounded.

Sat. 18.—The 63rd quorum of Seventy was organized at Cedar City, Iron Co., with Richard R. Birkbeck, Alexander G. Ingram, Christopher J. Arthur, Joseph H. Smith, John M. Macfarlane, Francis Webster and Robert W. Heyborne as presidents.

—The ship *Electric* sailed from Hamburg, Germany, with 336 Scandinavian Saints, under the direction of Søren Christophersen. The company arrived in New York June 5th and at Florence June 19th.

Mon. 20.—President Brigham Young left G. S. L. City, on another trip to the South. After visiting the principal settlements as far as St. George, he returned to the city on May 19th.

Mon. 27.—About ten mounted ruffians (soldiers) from Camp Douglas made an unsuccessful attempt to kidnap a young woman in G. S. L. City, and take her to camp.

—Hiram Kimball and Thos. Atkinson were killed by a steamboat explosion, at San Pedro, Cal. while on their way as missionaries to the Sandwich Islands.

Thurs. 30.—The ship *John J. Boyd* sailed from Liverpool, with 763 (or 766) Saints, under the direction of Wm. W. Cluff. The emigrants landed in New York June 1st, and arrived at Florence June 12th.

May.—Three hundred and eighty-four wagons, 488 men, 3,604 oxen, taking 235,-969 pounds of flour, started east to assist the poor of the immigration; 4,300 pounds of Utah grown cotton was sent east for sale, with the teams. The captains were John W. Woolley, John R. Murdock, Horton D. Haight, Peter Nebeker, Wm. B. Preston, Thomas E. Ricks, Rosel Hyde, John F. Sanders, Samuel D. White, and Daniel D. McArthur. Horace S. Eldredge acted as Church emigration agent in the States this year.

Fri. 8.—A small band of Indians made a raid on Box Elder Valley, four miles above Brigham City, killing William Thorpe and driving off several head of horses.

—The ship *B. S. Kimball* sailed from Liverpool, England, with 654 (or 657) Saints under the direction of Hans Peter Lund. The same day 38 Saints, under the direction of Anders Christensen, sailed on the *Consignment*. The emigrants on the *B. S. Kimball* landed in New York June 15th and thence continued by rail to Florence. The *Consignment* arrived at New York June 20th.

Tues. 19. — The stage from California was attacked by Indians, in Deep Creek Canyon, 150 miles west of G. S. L. City, and the driver, W. R. Simpson, was killed. Major Howard Egan, who was one of the passengers, caught the reins and drove away at full speed.

Fri. 22.—The *Farmer's Oracle*, a small semi-monthly paper published by Joseph E. Johnson, at Spring Lake Villa, Utah Co., Utah, was first issued.

Sat. 23.—The ship *Antarctic* sailed from Liverpool, England, with 483 Saints, under the direction of John Needham. The emigrants landed in New York July 10th and arrived safely at Florence a few days later.

Sat. 30.—The ship *Cynosure* sailed from Liverpool, with 754 Saints,under the direction of David M. Stuart. It arrived at New York harbor July 19th.

June. *Thurs. 4.*—The packet ship *Amazon* sailed from London, England, with 882 (or 895) Saints,under the direction of Wm. Bramall. It arrived in New York harbor July 18th, and the immigrants reached Florence a few days later.

Wed. 10.—The stage coach was attacked by mounted Indians between Fort Crittenden and the Jordan river, Utah Co.; the driver and another man were killed and their bodies fearfully mutilated by the savages.

Thurs. 11.—Gov. Stephen S. Harding, who was succeeded by James D. Doty, left G. S. L. City for the East.

Mon. 22.—James D. Doty, formerly superintendent of Indian affairs, took the oath of office as governor of Utah.

July. *Sat. 4.*—A fire destroyed $3,000 worth of property belonging to Daniel H. Wells, in G. S. L. City.

Wed. 8.—The Indians attacked Canyon Station, near Deep creek, 150 miles west of G. S. L. City, killing four soldiers and Wm. Riley, the station keeper.

Thurs. 30.—Gov. Doty and Gen. Connor made a treaty of peace with the Shoshone Indians at Brigham City.

August.—The troops under command of Capt. Smith killed twelve Indians, near Schell Creek station, Tooele Co., Utah.

Mon. 3.—John F. Kinney, formerly chief justice of Utah, was elected delegate to Congress from Utah.

Fri. 7.—John Titus, of Pennsylvania, successor to John F. Kinney as chief justice of Utah, arrived in G. S. L. City; he took the oath of office on the 12th.

Sat. 29.—Capt. John R. Murdock's train of immigrants, which had left Florence June 29th, with 375 souls, arrived at G. S. L. City.

September. *Fri. 4.*—Capt. Patterson's independent train of immigrants, which had left Florence June 30th, arrived at G. S. L. City.

Sat. 5.—Capt. John F. Sanders' Church train of immigrants, which had started from Florence July 6th, arrived at G. S. L. City.

Mon. 7.—Pres. Brigham Young's woolen factory, on Canyon creek, commenced running.

Thurs. 10.—Capt. W. B. Preston's train of immigrants, which had left Florence July 9th, with 55 wagons, arrived in G. S. L. City.

Sat. 12.—Capt. John R. Young's independent train of immigrants, which had started from Florence July 7th, arrived in G. S. L. City. Several of the immigrants were killed in a cattle stampede on the plains July 28th.

Fri. 25.—Capt. Peter Nebeker's Church train of immigrants, which had started from Florence July 25th, arrived at G. S. L. City.

Wed. 30.—Capt. James Brown, formerly of the Mormon Battalion and the founder of Ogden, died from the effects of an accident, at Ogden.

October. *Thurs. 1.*—Gov. James D. Doty, of Utah, and Gov. James W. Nye, of Nevada, formed a treaty of peace with the Indians at Ruby Valley.

Sat. 3.—Capt. Daniel D. McArthur's Church train of immigrants, which had started from Florence Aug. 6th, with about seventy-five wagons, arrived at G. S. L. City.

Sun. 4.—Capt. John W. Woolley's Church train of immigrants, which had left Florence Aug. 9th, and also Capt. Thomas E. Ricks' Church train of immigrants, which had started from Florence Aug. 10th, arrived at G. S. L. City.

—Capt. Horton D. Haight's Church train of immigrants arrived at G. S. L. City.

Mon. 12.—Charles Hopkins, formerly a member of the Mormon Battalion, died at Petersburg, Millard Co.

Tues. 13.—Capt. Rosel Hyde's Church

train of immigrants, which had left Florence Aug. 11th, arrived at G.S. L. City.

Thurs. 15.—Capt. Samuel D. White's Church train of immigrants, which left Florence Aug. 15th, arrived at G. S. L. City. This was the last Church train of the season.

November. *Mon. 2.*—Robert C. Egbert, formerly a member of the Mormon Battalion, died at Deseret, Millard Co.

Fri. 20.—The first number of the *Union Vidette*, a bitter anti-Mormon newspaper, was issued at Camp Douglas. Utah.

Mon. 23.—Seth Taft, a Pioneer of 1847, died in G. S. L. City.

December. *Sat. 5.*—Ira Jones Willes, formerly a member of the Mormon Battalion, and his son, were accidentally killed while crossing a creek, near Lehi, Utah Co.

Mon. 14.—The 13th session of the Utah legislature convened in G. S. L. City, and organized by appointing Daniel H. Wells president of the Council, and John Taylor speaker of the House.

Sat. 19.—Joseph Fielding, one of the first missionaries sent from America to England, died at Mill Creek, Salt Lake Co.

Thurs. 31.—Bishop David Pettigrew, once a member of the Mormon Battalion, died in G. S. L. City.

1864.

The Perpetual Emigrating Fund Company sent 170 wagons, 1,717 oxen and 277 men to the Missouri river after the poor this year. The first mining districts were located, the first mining companies incorporated and the first smelting furnaces built in the Territory. A number of new settlements were founded in Bear Lake Valley.

January. *Tues. 5.*—The *Daily Vidette* succeeding the *Union Vidette*, was first issued at Camp Douglas, Utah. Like its predecessor, it was a bitter anti-Mormon paper.

Sat. 16.—An act passed by the Utah legislature, creating Kane and Richland Counties, was approved.

February. *Wed. 10.*—Lewis Robbins was accidentally killed while quarrying rock near St. George, Utah.

March.—Circleville, Piute Co., Utah, was settled by about fifty families from Ephraim, Sanpete Co.

Thurs. 31.—Apostle Lorenzo Snow had a very narrow escape from drowning while attempting to land at Lahaina, Maui, Hawaiian Islands, with other Elders.

April. *Fri. 1.*—Thomas Pierce and Robert Spurgeon were killed in a snowslide at the head of Mill Creek Canyon. The body of the latter was not found until May 3rd.

Tues. 5.—A small company of Saints bound for Utah, sailed from Port Elizabeth, South Africa, under the direction of John Talbot.

Wed. 6.—On this and the four following

days the 34th annual conference of the Church was held in G. S. L. City.

Fri. 8.—At a council meeting held at Lahaina, Maui, Hawaiian Islands, attended by Apostles Ezra T. Benson and Lorenzo Snow and Elders Joseph F. Smith, Wm. W. Cluff and Alma L. Smith, Walter M. Gibson, who had usurped Church authority and imposed upon the native Saints, was excommunicated from the Church.

Sun. 10.—Elders Wm. Fotheringham and Henry A. Dixon, accompanied by a small company of Saints, sailed from Port Elizabeth, South Africa, in the barque *Susan Pardew*, which arrived at Boston after 60 day's voyage.

Thurs. 28.—The ship *Monarch of the Sea*, sailed from Liverpool, England, with 973 Saints, under the direction of Patriarch John Smith. It arrived at New York June 3rd, and the emigrants reached Wyoming, Neb., in safety.

Wyoming, a village seven miles north of Nebraska City, Neb., had been selected as the outfitting place for the emigrants, crossing the plains, instead of Florence. About one hundred and seventy Church teams were sent from Utah to the Missouri river this year, after the poor.

May. *Thurs. 12.*—The Saints who were settling Salina, Sevier Co., Utah, were organized as a Ward by Apostle Orson Hyde, with Peter Rasmussen as Bishop.

Sat. 21.—The ship *General M'Clellan* sailed from Liverpool, England, with 802 Saints, under the direction of Thos. E. Jeremy, Joseph Bull and Geo. G. Bywater, It arrived at New York June 23rd, and the company arrived at Wyoming July 3rd.

June. *Fri. 3.*—The ship *Hudson* sailed from London, England, with 863 Saints, under the direction of John M. Kay. The company arrived at New York July 19th, and at Wyoming Aug. 2nd.

July. *Mon. 4.*—The *Daily Telegraph*, a newspaper, was first issued, in G. S. L. City, Thos. B. H. Stenhouse proprietor and editor. October 8th, a semi-weekly edition was also commenced.

August. *Fri. 26.*—Capt. John R. Murdock's mule train arrived in G. S. L. City, with 78 passengers.

Wed. 31.—James Calvin Sly, once a member of the Mormon Battalion, died at Chicken Creek, Juab Co.

September.—Elder Joseph Greenwood, of American Fork, Utah, died on Bear river, from the effects of cold, on returning from a mission to the States.

—Daniel H. Wells succeeded Apostle Geo. Q. Cannon as president of the European mission.

Thurs. 1.—Pres. Brigham Young and others left G. S. L. City, on a trip to the southern settlements. They returned Sept. 29th, after visiting 37 settlements and holding 39 meetings.

Thurs. 15.—Capt. Wm. B. Preston's train of immigrants, consisting of about fifty wagons and four hundred passengers, arrived at G. S. L. City. This company also brought new fonts of type for the *Deseret News* office.

Tues. 20.—Capt. Joseph S. Rawlins' train of immigrants arrived at G. S. L. City.

Mon. 26.—Elder John M. Kay, returning

missionary from Europe, died on the Little Laramie, while crossing the plains in Capt. Warren S. Snow's train.

October. — The first number of the *Peep o'Day*, a magazine devoted to science, literature and art, and to opposing the "Mormons," was published by Elias L. T. Harrison and Edward W. Tullidge, at G. S. L. City.

Sat. 1.—Capt. John Smith's independent train of immigrants arrived at G. S. L. City.

Tues. 4.—Capt. Wm. 'S. Warren's train of immigrants, which had started from Wyoming July 19th, arrived at G. S. L. City.

Wed. 5.—Capt. Isaac A. Canfield's train arrived at G. S. L. City.

Mon 10.—The surviving members of Zion's Camp had a festival in the Social Hall, G. S. L. City, This was the first gathering of these veterans for 30 years; 54 men and 4 women were present out of the 63 then known to be in the Territory.

Wed. 26.—Capt. Wm. Hyde's train of immigrants arrived at G. S. L. City.

November. *Wed. 2.*—Capt. Warren S. Snow's train of immigrants, the last company of the season, arrived at G. S. L. City.

Wed. 16.—A destructive hurricane visited Davis and Weber Counties.

December. *Mon. 12.*—The 14th annual session of the Utah legislature convened in G. S. L. City and organized by electing Geo. A. Smith president of the Council and John Taylor speaker of the House.

Sat. 17.—A landing and site for a Church warehouse, afterwards known as Call's Landing, was selected by Anson Call, on the Colorado river, 125 miles from St. George, and the land along the Muddy found suitable to settle on. At that time the Church contemplated sending the emigrants from Europe, by way of Panama, the Gulf of California, and up the Colorado river, to this landing, which was the head of navigation on the Colorado.

Fri. 23.—Samuel H. Davis was accidentally killed in G. S. L. City, while engaged in walling up a well.

1865.

This year new settlements were founded by the Saints on the Muddy, Arizona (now Nevada). A long and desperate war between the settlers in Sanpete and Sevier Valleys and the Indians under the chief Black Hawk was commenced. Many of the settlers were killed and wounded.

January. *Sun. 8.*—The first Latter-day Saint settlers on the lower Muddy (now in Lincoln Co., Nev.) arrived there. Under the presidency of Thos. S. Smith they and other settlers, who followed, located St. Thomas.

Wed. 18.—Apostle Orson Pratt and Wm. W. Riter arrived as missionaries in Vienna, Austria, to open up the gospel door in that country.

Fri. 20.—The Utah legislature adjourned.

Mon. 23.—The legislature of the State of

Deseret met in G. S. L. City, attended to some business and adjourned.

Sat. 28.—The Church, through its agent, Francis A. Hammond, purchased the Laic plantation, consisting of 6,500 acres of land, on the island of Oahu, Sandwich Islands, for $14,000, of T. Dougherty. This place, which has since been a gathering place and mission headquarters for the natives of the Hawaiian Islands, is about thirty-two miles from Honolulu, the capital of the islands.

February.—A warehouse was erected at Call's Landing, on the Colorado river.

Sat. 4.—A company for building a canal from the Jordan river, near the Point of the Mountain south, to G. S. L. City was partly organized.

Mon. 13.—The 69th quorum of Seventy was partly organized at Parowan, Iron Co., with Silas S. Smith, sen., Zachariah B. Decker, Abraham Smith, Joseph K. Parramore, Horace Thornton, Edward Dalton and Wm. E. McGregor as presidents. Most of the ordinations took place Feb. 22nd.

Wed. 15.—James Lindley, James Wiles, John Mullcaron and Robert Nicholson were killed by a snowslide, while asleep in their tent in City Creek Canyon.

Thurs. 16.—Luther William Glazier, formerly a member of the Mormon Battalion, died at Provo, Utah Co.

Wed. 22.—Geo. Barzee and John Boice, jun., perished in the snow, near Franklin, Cache Valley.

March. The people in the Utah Dixie settlements suffered much for the want of breadstuff, and several of the northern counties were infested with the measles.

Sat. 4.—A grand celebration on the occasion of the re-inauguration of President Abraham Lincoln, was held in G. S. L. City.

Mon. 13.—Wm. Millard's house, in the 20th Ward, G. S. L. City, was destroyed by fire, and a little girl burned to death and buried in the ruins.

April. *Thurs. 6.*—The 35th annual conference of the Church convened in the Tabernacle, G. S. L. City, and continued until the 9th.

Sun. 9.—John Lowry had a quarrel with the Indian chief Jake, in Manti, Sanpete Co., Utah, the Indians boasting of having killed stock belonging to the citizens.

Mon. 10.—A small party of men from Manti was fired upon by the Indians, near Twelve Mile Creek, Sanpete Co., and young Peter Ludvigsen killed and mutilated by the savages. The same evening Elijah B. Ward and James Anderson were killed and scalped by the Indians, in Salina Canyon, Sevier Co., who also drove away considerable stock.

—A special conference, held in G. S. L. City, voted to erect a telegraph line through the settlements of Utah.

Wed. 12.—Col. Reddick N. Allred, with 84 men, who pursued the Indians, had a dangerous encounter with them in the mountains, about fifteen miles east of Salina, during which Jens Sorenson, of Ephraim, and William Kearns, of Gunnison, were killed. The company retreated to Salina.

—The brig *Mexicano* sailed from Port Elizabeth, South Africa, with 47 Saints on board, under the presidency of Miner G. Atwood, bound for Utah. The company arrived in New York, June 18th.

Sat. 15.—News having reached G. S. L. City of the assassination of President Abraham Lincoln, all business houses in the city were closed, and the whole municipality was placed in a state of mourning.

Mon. 17.—The dead bodies of Sørensen and Kearns were secured and brought to Salina.

Sat. 29.—The ship *Belle Wood* sailed from Liverpool with 636 Saints on board, bound for Utah, under the direction of Wm. H. Shearman. The company landed at New York June 1st, and arrived at Wyoming, Neb., on the 15th.

May. *Mon. 1.*—About sixty missionaries, called at the late conference, were set apart at the Historian's Office, G. S. L. City.

Wed. 3.—Pres. Brigham Young, accompanied by five of the Twelve and other brethren, left G. S. L. City on a trip to Cache Valley, from which they returned on the 11th.

Mon. 8.—The packet ship *B. S. Kimball* sailed from Hamburg, Germany, with 557 Saints, under the direction of Anders W. Winberg. The company landed in New York June 15th and arrived at Wyoming June 26th.

Wed. 10.—A company of 24 Saints, under the direction of Wm. Underwood, sailed from Liverpool on board the ship *David Hoadley*, bound for Utah.

Thurs. 18.—A company, consisting of nine missionaries, eleven women, eighteen children and six teamsters, left G. S. L. City, bound for the Hawaiian Islands. Geo. Nebeker was appointed captain; the company had ten wagons.

Sat. 20.—Elder Jesse Yelton Cherry, of Centreville, Davis Co., Utah, died of smallpox in Nottingham, England, where he labored as a missionary.

Mon. 22.—The missionaries bound for the East were organized, with Bishop Wm. B. Preston as captain.

Thurs. 25.—Jens Larsen, a sheep herder, was killed by Indians about four miles north of Fairview, Sanpete Co.

Fri. 26.—John Given, his wife and four children, were murdered and their bodies fearfully mangled by Indians, near Thistle Valley, about twelve miles north of Fairview, Sanpete Co.

Sun. 28.—The Saints who were settling St. Joseph, on the Muddy (now in Nevada), were organized as a branch of the Church, with Warren, Foote as president.

Mon. 29.—David Hadlock Jones, a member of the Mormon Battalion, was killed by Indians, about three miles northwest of Fairview, Sanpete Co.

June. *Thurs. 8.*—Col. O. H. Irish, superintendent of Indian affairs, made a treaty with the principal Indian chiefs in Utah, at Spanish Fork Reservation farm, in the presence of Brigham Young and other leading men.

Sun. 11.—Hon. Schuyler Colfax, speaker of the U. S. House of Representatives, and party, arrived in G. S. L. City. He remained until the 19th.

Mon. 12.—Schuyler Colfax and two of his companions, Lieut.-Gov. Bross, of Illinois, and Albert D. Richardson, war correspondent of the *Tribune*, addressed the citizens in front of the Salt Lake House.

Tues. 13.—Gov. James D. Doty died in G. S. L. City.

Sat. 17.—The Saints who had settled on Chalk creek, above Coalville, Summit Co., Utah, were organized as a branch of the Church, named Upton; Joseph Huff, president.

Sun. 18.—A petition was drafted to Andrew Johnson, President of the United States, asking for the appointment of Col. O. H. Irish to the governorship of Utah. It was signed by 250 leading citizens.

Sat. 24.—Patriarch Isaac Morley died at Fairview, Sanpete Co.

Thurs. 29.—Lars Petersen, a benevolent young man, who had assisted some twenty Danish Saints to emigrate, was drowned in a small stream, called the Weeping Waters, near Wyoming, Neb.

July. *Sat. 1.*—The 70th quorum of Seventy was organized in Davis Co., Utah, with Wm. H. Lee, L. S. Burnham, Samuel Bryson, sen., Andrew Dalrymple, A. D. Boynton, Henry Tingey and Israel Barlow, jun., as presidents. Nearly all the brethren who became members of the quorum resided in Bountiful and Centreville.

Tues. 4.—The national holiday was remembered in G. S. L. City, by a grand celebration.

—Hon. J. M. Ashley, of Ohio, chairman of the Committee on Territories, in Congress, arrived in G. S. L. City, on a visit.

Thurs. 6. — Francis A. Hammond and George Nebeker arrived at the Laie plantation, Hawaiian Islands.

Fri. 7.—Pres. Brigham Young, several of the Twelve and others left G. S. L. City on a missionary trip to Sanpete County, from which they returned on the 19th, having traveled about three hundred miles and held eighteen meetings.

Fri. 14.—Robert Gillespie and Anthony Robinson were killed by Indians, near Salina, Sevier Co.

Sat. 15.—Chas. Durkee, of Wisconsin, was appointed governor of Utah.

Tues. 18.—The militia under Warren S. Snow surprised a party of hostile Indians, killed twelve and routed the rest, in Grass Valley. The command then went east to Green river and suffered much by long marches and for want of supplies.

Mon. 24.—The people of southern Utah celebrated the day in the pines, 2½ miles above Pine Valley, Washington Co.

—Hon. J. M. Ashley addressed an audience in the Bowery, G. S. L. City, at the celebration of the Territorial anniversary.

Wed. 26.—The Indians attacked Glenwood, Sevier Co., Utah, wounded a man and drove off nearly all the stock belonging to the settlement.

Mon. 31.—A provost guard of soldiers, who for some time had been stationed in front of the Tabernacle, on the south side of South Temple Street, in G. S. L. City, was removed.

August.—Brigham Young, jun., succeeded Daniel H. Wells as president of the European mission.

Tues. 1.—Pres. Brigham Young and a party of brethren left G. S. L. City on a missionary trip to Cache Valley, returning on the 10th.

—After seven months' unsuccessful labors, Apostle Orson Pratt and William W. Riter left Vienna, Austria, on their return to England. They arrived at Liverpool Aug. 6th.

Thurs. 3.—James Davis, one of the Mormon Battalion, died suddenly in G. S. L. City.

Wed. 23.—A book, entitled "Joseph Smith the Prophet," by Lucy Smith, the Prophet's mother, published by Orson Pratt and Samuel W. Richards, in England, was condemned for its inaccuracy, by the First Presidency and Twelve Apostles.

Fri. 25.—Pres. Brigham Young and others left G. S. L. City on a missionary trip to Tooele County, from which they returned on the 27th.

September. *Mon. 4.*—Pres. Brigham Young and others left G. S. L. City on a trip to southern Utah. After holding a number of meetings in the intervening settlements, the company arrived in St. George on the 15th, and on the 29th returned to G. S. L. City.

Fri. 15.—An agricultural fair was held in St. George, Utah.

Mon. 18.—Col. O. H. Irish made a treaty with the Piede Indians, at Pinto, Washington Co., Utah.

Thurs. 21.—General Warren S. Snow had an engagement with the Indians, near Fish lake, 80 miles east of Circleville. Seven Indians were killed, and Snow and two of his men wounded.

Fri. 22.—Captain Miner G. Atwood's company of immigrating Saints was attacked by Indians west of Fort Laramie. Several of the brethren were wounded and one woman (Mrs. Grundtvig) carried away by the savages.

Sat. 30.—Charles Durkee, Utah's sixth governor, arrived in G. S. L. City. He took the oath of office Oct. 3rd.

October. *Sun. 1.*—The 71st quorum of Seventy was organized at Nephi, Juab Co., with Edward Oakey, Samuel Claridge, Edwin Harley, Daniel Miller, John Kienke, Charles Sperry and Benjamin Riches as presidents.

Sat. 7.—Pres. Daniel H. Wells, who had presided over the European mission, arrived in G. S. L City.

Sun. 8.—The semi-weekly *Deseret News* was first issued.

Tues. 10.—The surviving members of Zion's Camp had a feast in the Social Hall, G. S. L. City.

Tues. 17.—Morten Pedersen Kuhr and wife, Elizabeth Petersen, Wm. Thorpe, Søren N. Jespersen, Benj. J. Black and Wm. T. Hite were killed by Indians, under the chief Black Hawk, near Ephraim, Sanpete Co.

—A company of Saints, bound for Utah, sailed from Melbourne, Australia, on board the barque *Albert*.

Sun. 22.—Foster Gordon and wife were found murdered in Skull Valley. Four discharged soldiers were suspected of the crime.

November.—The first Hebrew marriage in G. S. L. City was celebrated.

Wed. 1.—Elder Geo. Simms, of G. S. L. City, returning home from a mission to England, was drowned in the Platte river.

Wed. 8.—Capt. Miner G. Atwood's company of immigrants, which had left Wyoming, July 31st, with 45 wagons and about four hundred souls, arrived at G. S. L. City.

Thurs. 9.—Pres. Brigham Young issued a circular to the Bishops and presiding Elders in the Church, calling upon them to assist in the erection of a telegraph line through the settlements.

—Capt. Henson Walker's company of immigrating Saints, which had started from Wyoming, Aug. 12th, arrived at G. S. L. City.

Thurs. 23.—Faust's livery stables, on 2nd South Street, G. S. L. City, were destroyed by fire.

Wed. 29.—Capt. Wm. S. S. Willis' ox train of immigrating Saints, which started from Wyoming, Aug. 15th, arrived at G. S. L. City. The women and children had arrived previously with relief teams, sent out about three hundred and fifty miles to meet the immigrants.

December. **Mon. 11.**—The fifteenth session of the Utah legislature convened in the State House, G. S. L. City, and organized by appointing Geo. A. Smith president of the Council, and John Taylor speaker of the House.

Thurs. 14.—Hon. Wm. H. Hooper, Utah's delegate to Congress, left G. S. L. City for Washington, D. C.

Mon. 18.—A number of Piede Indians, made a break on Kanab, Kane Co., Utah, and stole some horses.

Sat. 23.—Wm. Naylor, of West Jordan, Salt Lake Co., froze to death, while returning from Cottonwood mill.

Sun. 24.—John Singleton, of American Fork, Utah Co., froze to death, near Lehi. The winter of 1865-66 was very cold and severe in Utah.

1866.

The Indian war in southern Utah continued, and a number of the smaller settlements were abandoned by the settlers. Ten Church trains were sent to the Missouri river for the poor. The rock aqueduct on North Temple Street, G. S. L. City, was built. A meeting house, 36x24, feet, was erected by the Saints at Laie, Hawaiian Islands.

January. **Mon. 1.**—The first number of the *Juvenile Instructor* was published in G. S. L. City; George Q. Cannon, editor.

Tues. 2.—The members of the city council of G. S. L. City met for the first time in their new hall, or city building, recently erected on the corner of First East and First South streets.

Mon. 8.—Dr. James M. Whitmore and Robert McIntire were killed by Piede Indians, near the Pipe Springs' ranch Kane Co., Utah.

Sat. 20.—The dead bodies of Whitmore

and McIntire were found about four miles from the Pipe Springs herd house by a company of armed men, who also surprised the murderers camped in a narrow gulch, about twelve miles distant, and killed seven of them.

February. **Tues. 6.**—Titus Billings, a Church veteran, died at Provo.

Mon. 12.—At the municipal election, Daniel H. Wells was elected mayor of G. S. L. City.

March. **Sat. 3.**—The Utah Produce Company was organized in G. S. L. City, with Bishop Edward Hunter as chairman.

Sun. 4.—The 72nd quorum of Seventy was organized at Little Cottonwood, Salt Lake Co., with Daniel S. Cahoon, Robert Maxfield, Richard Maxfield, Henry W. Brown, Willis Smith, Nathan Tanner, jun., and Wm. James Panter as presidents.

Wed. 7.—Wm. Poulter was accidentally killed in Ogden Canyon, while logging.

Thurs. 8.—Carl Widerborg, president of the Scandinavian Mission, was arrested in Copenhagen, Denmark, on a trumped up charge of seduction. After five days' imprisonment he was released, and shortly after honorably acquitted.

April. **Mon. 2.**—Joseph and Robert Berry, and the latter's wife, were killed by Indians, about four miles from Maxfield's ranch, on Short Creek, Kane Co., Utah.

—S. Newton Brassfield was shot in G. S. L. City by some unknown person. He had seduced another man's wife. This caused quite an excitement among the anti-Mormons, and an attempt was made to have more troops forwarded to Utah.

Fri. 6.—The thirty-sixth annual conference convened in G. S. L. City and continued until the 8th.

Wed. 18.—The Indian chief Sanpitch was killed at the mouth of Birch Canyon, between Moroni and Fountain Green, Sanpete Co.

Fri. 20.—The Indians attacked Salina, Sevier Co., drove off about two hundred head of stock and killed two men, who were guarding them. Soon afterwards the settlers vacated Salina and removed to Gunnison, Sanpete Co.

Sun. 22.—Alfred Lewis was killed and three others were wounded by Indians, near Marysvale, Piute Co., Utah.

Fri. 27.—A gang of soldiers from Camp Douglas shot at and insulted a number of citizens in the east part of G. S. L. City.

Sun. 29.—Andrew Petersen was reported killed and Thos. Jones Avery wounded while on picket guard, near Fairview, Sanpete Co.

Mon. 30.—The ship *John Bright* sailed from Liverpool, England, with 747 (or 764) Saints, under the direction of C. M. Gillet. The company landed at New York June 6th, and arrived at Wyoming June 19th, traveling by way of New Haven (Conn.), Montreal (Canada), Detroit, Chicago, Quincy (Ill.) and St. Joseph (Mo.).

May.—The Church trains, which this year went to the Missouri river for the poor, left G. S. L. City in ten companies. They numbered 10 captains, 456 teamsters, 49 mounted guards, 89 horses, 134 mules, 3,042 oxen and 397 wagons: 62 wagons, 50 oxen and 61 mules were sent for.

—A company of armed militia from Salt Lake and Utah Counties was sent out to assist the settlers in Sanpete and Sevier Valleys in protecting themselves against the Indians.

—The 73rd quorum of Seventy was organized at South Cottonwood, G. S. L. Co., with James Winchester, Harvey E. Hullinger, Jonas Ericksen. Charles Wilkins, Thomas A. Wheeler, Peter Ericksen and James Maxfield as presidents.

—The settlers of Piute County moved into Circleville, because of Indian troubles.

Tues. 1.—President Brigham Young instructed the people in Sanpete, Piute and Sevier Counties to collect together in bodies of not less than 150 men, arm themselves well, protect their stock from the Indians, etc.

Wed. 2.—Mr. Thurston's three year old daughter was stolen by Indians, near Mendon, Cache Co. She was never recovered.

Sat. 5.—A Congressional act was approved, giving to Nevada a strip of country 60 miles wide, containing 20,850 square miles, which was formerly a part of Utah.

—The ship *Caroline* sailed from London, England, with 389 Saints, under the presidency of Samuel H. Hill. It arrived at New York June 11th, and the company continued the journey by steamboats and railroad to Wyoming.

Sun. 6.—At a conference held at St. George, Utah, the Saints residing in Pine Valley, at Pinto, Shoal Creek (Hebron), and Mountain Meadows, were organized as a Ward, called Pine Valley, with Robert Gardner as Bishop; the settlements in Long Valley, Kane Co., were organized into the Long Valley Ward, and the settlements in Clover, Meadow, Eagle and Spring Valleys, Nevada, were organized into a Ward, called Panaca, with John Nebeker as acting Bishop; Thos. S. Smith was sustained as president and Bishop of the settlements on the lower Muddy, (now in Nevada).

Wed. 16.—Christian Larsen, of Spanish Fork, Utah Co., was killed by Indians while herding cows.

Sun. 20.—A woman in Springville, Utah Co., shot and killed a man, who tried to seduce her.

Wed. 23.—The ship *American Congress* (third ship of the season from Europe) sailed from London, England, with 350 Saints, under the direction of John Nicholson; it arrived at New York July 4th, and the emigrants reached Wyoming July 14th.

Fri. 25.—The ship *Kenilworth* sailed from Hamburg, Germany, with 684 Scandinavian Saints, under the direction of Samuel L. Sprague. The company landed in New York July 17th and arrived at Wyoming July 29th.

Wed. 30.—The ship *Arkwright* sailed from Liverpool, England, with 450 Saints, under the direction of Justin C. Wixom. It arrived at New York July 6th.

—A small company of Saints (26 souls) sailed from London, England, on the ship *Cornelius Grinnel*, bound for Utah. They arrived at New York July 11th.

Thurs. 31.—The first circumcision of a Hebrew child in G. S. L. City took place.

June.—The settlements on the Sevier river, south of Richfield, were broken up, because of Indian troubles, and the inhabitants sought protection in the larger towns.

Fri. 1.—The ship *Cavour* sailed from Hamburg, Germany, with 201 Scandinavian Saints, under the direction of Niels Nielsen. The company arrived in New York, July 31st, and at Wyoming, Aug. 11th.

Sat. 2.—The ship *Humboldt* sailed from Hamburg, Germany, with 328 Scandinavian Saints, under the direction of Geo. M. Brown. The company arrived in New York, July 18th, and at Wyoming, Aug. 1st.

Wed. 6.—A severe wind storm did much damage in southern Utah.

—The ship *St. Mark* sailed from Liverpool, England, with 104 Saints, under the direction of A. Stevens. It arrived at New York, July 26th.

Sun. 10.—The Indians made a raid on Round Valley, Millard Co., driving away three hundred head of cattle and horses, and killing James Ivie and Henry Wright.

Mon. 11.—Gen. Daniel H. Wells and some militia started for Sanpete Valley, to protect the settlements in that and adjacent counties, against the Indians.

Sun. 24.—The Indians made a raid on Thistle Valley, Sanpete Co., killed Charles Brown, wounded Thos. Snarr and drove off 26 horses.

Tues. 26.—The Indians drove off a band of horses and cattle from Spanish Fork, Utah Co. A company of men followed and overtook the thieves; a battle ensued, in which Jonathan Edmiston, of Manti, was killed, and others were wounded. Most of the stock was recovered.

August. *Mon. 20.*—Elder C. M. Gillet died on the plains, 23 miles west of Fort Kearney, while returning from a mission to England.

Tues. 21.—A flood did great damage in Sevier County.

September. *Tues. 4.*—Capt. Thos. E. Ricks' train of immigrating Saints, consisting of 46 wagons and 251 passengers, arrived in G. S. L. City.

Wed. 5.—Capt. Samuel D. White's mule train, which had left Wyoming, July 7th, with 230 immigrants, arrived at G. S. L. City.

Sat. 15.—Capt. Wm. Henry Chipman's train of immigrants, which had left Wyoming July 13th, arrived at G. S. L. City. About one hundred head of cattle were stolen from this company by Indians, on the plains.

Tues. 25.—Capt. John D. Holladay's ox train of immigrating Saints, which had started from Wyoming July 19th, arrived in G. S. L. City.

Sat. 29.—Capt. Peter Nebeker's train of 62 wagons and nearly four hundred immigrants, which had started from Wyoming Aug. 4th, arrived at G. S. L. City.

—Capt. Daniel Thompson's ox train of immigrants, which had left Wyoming July 25th, with 84 wagons and about five hundred immigrants, arrived at G. S. L. City.

October. *Mon. 1.*—Capt. Joseph S. Rawlins' ox train of 65 wagons and over four hundred passengers, which had started

from Wyoming Aug. 2nd, arrived at G. S.
L. City.

Sun. 7.—Part of Capt. Arza E. Hinkley's relief train, which was sent back 450
miles to meet the last companies, returned
to G. S. L. City, with 87 passengers from
Capt. Abner Lowry's train.

Mon. 8.—Capt. Andrew H. Scott's ox
train, which had started from Wyoming,
Aug. 8th, with 49 wagons and about three
hundred immigrants, arrived at G. S. L.
City. About thirty of the immigrants
died on the journey.

Wed. 10.—The surviving members of
Zion's Camp had a reunion at the Social
Hall, G. S. L. City.

Mon. 15.—Capt. Horton D. Haight's train
of 65 wagons, bringing the wire for the
Deseret Telegraph Line, arrived at G.S.L.
City.

Mon. 22.—Captain Abner Lowry's train
of immigrating Saints, the last company
of the season, arrived at G. S. L. City. It
had started from Wyoming Aug. 13th. A
great number of immigrants died of
cholera on the journey.

—Dr. J. King Robinson was killed in G.
S. L. City.

Tues. 23.—John P. Lee's ranch, on South
creek, about eight miles from Beaver, was
attacked by Piute Indians, who fired the
house and wounded Joseph Lillywhite.

November. *Fri. 30.* — Elder Abel
Evans, missionary from Utah, died at
Merthyr Tydfil, Wales.

December. *Sat. 1.*—The Deseret Telegraph Line was opened between Salt
Lake City and Ogden. On the 8th it
was opened to Logan and on the 28th to
Manti.

Sun. 9.—The 16th session of the Utah
legislature convened at G. S. L. City and
organized by electing Geo. A. Smith president of the Council, and John Taylor
speaker of the House.

Thurs. 20.—In a letter, addressed to the
"Leaders of the Mormon Church", a number of Gentile merchants in G. S. L. City,
proposed to leave the Territory if Brigham
Young would buy them out. A character-
istic reply from Pres. Young the following
day was the result, and their proposition
was declined.

Thurs. 27.—"Dutch Charley", a burglar,
was shot and killed in G. S. L. City, while
in the act of stealing.

1867.

The Indian difficulties in the South,
known as the BlackHawk war, became more
serious; companies of militia were sent
from the North to protect the settlers; but
nearly all the settlements on the upper
Sevier and those in Kane County were deserted by their inhabitants, who moved to
the older and stronger towns for safety.
Grasshoppers destroyed the crops in different parts of the Territory. No Church
teams were sent this year to the Missouri
river for the poor, in consequence of

which the immigration was compara-
tively small.

January. — The Utah legislature petitioned Congress to repeal the anti-bigamy law of 1862, and the general assembly
of Deseret prayed for admission into the
Union as a State.

—The Indians made a raid on Pine Valley, Washington Co., and captured a band
of horses. Capt. Andrus, with a company of cavalry, followed them, recovered
most of the horses and killed seven Indians.

Mon. 7.—John Lowry,·sen., one of the
first settlers of Sanpete Valley, died at
Manti.

Tues. 15.—The Deseret Telegraph Line
was opened to St. George.

Wed. 23.—Amasa M. Lyman, in a communication addressed to the Latter - day
Saints in all the world, acknowledged his
doctrine, annulling the atonement of Jesus
Christ, to be false.

February. *Sun. 24.*—The Saints who
had settled west of the river Jordan, west
of G. S. L. City, were organized into a
Ward called Brighton, with Andrew W.
Cooley as Bishop.

Mon. 25.—Patriarch Mark Anthony
Coombs died at Beaver, Utah.

Tues. 26.—James W. Huntsman died at
Shoal Creek, Washington Co., Utah.

March. *Thurs. 21.*—The Deseret Telegraph Co., incorporated Jan. 18, 1867, was
organized, with Brigham Young as president.

—The Indians made a raid on the stock
of Richfield and Glenwood, Sevier Co.,
killing Jens Peter Petersen and wife
(Charlotte Amalie) and Miss Smith, all of
Richfield.

Fri. 29.—Geo. Davis was accidentally
killed near G. S. L. City.

April. *Sat. 6.*—The 37th annual conference of the Church was commenced in G.
S. L. City. It was continued till the 8th.

Sat. 20.—Richfield, Sevier Co., was deserted by its inhabitants because of Indian
trouble. About the same time the other
settlements in Sevier and those in Piute
County were abandoned for the same
cause, as well as the settlements of Berry-
ville, Winsor, Upper and Lower Kanab,
Shunesberg, Springdale and Northup, and
many ranches in Kane County; also the
settlements of Panguitch and Fort Sandford, in Iron County.

Mon. 22.—Pres. Brigham Young and
company left G. S. L. City, on a tour to
"Dixie," from which they returned May
15h, after traveling seven hundred miles.

June. *Sat. 1.*—Lois Lund was killed
and Jasper Robertson wounded, near
Fountain Green, Sanpete Co., by Indians,
who also drove off 40 horses.

—Twenty Saints sailed from London,
England, on the ship *Hudson*, bound for
Utah. The vessel arrived at New York
July 19th.

Sun. 2.—Major John W. Vance, of Al-
pine, Utah Co., and Heber Houtz, of G. S.
L. City, were waylaid and killed by
Indians on Twelve Mile creek,· Sanpete
Co., Utah.

Mon. 3.—Geo. W. Rogers was accidentally killed in G. S. L. City, by the falling of a bank of earth.

Fri. 14.—The Indians made a raid on Beaver, Utah, and captured a large herd of stock.

Fri. 21.—The steamship *Manhattan* sailed from Liverpool, England, with 480 Saints, under the direction of Archibald N. Hill. It arrived in New York July 4th, and the emigrants continued the journey to North Platte, a station on the Union Pacific Railroad, 391 miles west of Omaha. From that place the journey across the plains was commenced, Aug. 8th, with ox teams, under the direction of Capt. Leon-ard G. Rice, and the company arrived in G. S. L. City Oct. 5th.

July.—Apostle Franklin D. Richards succeeded Brigham Young, jun, as president of the European mission.

Sat. 6.—The Saints in Pine Valley, Washington Co., Utah, were organized into a separate Ward, with Wm. Snow as Bishop.

Fri. 19.—The grasshoppers appeared in vast numbers and did great damage to the crops in Utah during the following few weeks.

Sun. 21.—The Indians made a descent upon the stock on Little creek, near Parowan, Iron Co., but were driven back by a company of cavalry.

Wed. 24.—Brigham Willard Kimball, a son of Heber C. Kimball, died on Pole creek, while returning from a mission to England.

August. *Sat. 3.*—Robert Todd, sen., of Tooele, was found dead on the Jordan bottoms, G. S. L. Co.

Sun. 4.—Anson V. Call died on Laramie plains, while returning home from a mission to England.

Tues. 13.—The Indians made a raid on Springtown, Sanpete Co., killing James Meeks and Andrew Johansen. They also wounded another man and captured a band of horses.

Tues. 20.—The Harmony branch, Washington Co., Utah, was organized into a Ward by Apostle Erastus Snow, with Wilson D. Pace as Bishop.

Sat. 24.—The Provo meeting house (81 feet long and 47 feet wide, with a tower 80 feet high) was dedicated.

September. *Thurs. 5.*—John Hay, of Capt. Wm. L. Binder's company of militia, was killed by Indians, near Fayette, Sanpete Co.

Wed. 18.—The Indians made another raid on Beaver, and drove off two hundred head of horses and cattle.

October. *Sun. 6.*—The first conference held in the large Tabernacle, in G. S. L. City, was commenced. It continued until the 9th. This structure, which had just been completed, was 250 feet long and 150 feet wide, with its immense roof, arched without a pillar. Height of interior, 68 feet from floor to ceiling. During the conference 163 missionaries were called to strengthen the settlements in southern Utah, and the Saints were called upon to assist liberally the following year towards emigrating all the poor Saints from Great Britain. On the 8th Joseph F. Smith was chosen to fill the vacancy in the Council of

the Twelve Apostles, occasioned by the apostasy of Amasa M. Lyman.

Tues. 22.—Vilate Murray Kimball, wife of Pres. Heber C. Kimball, died in G. S. L. City.

November. *Wed. 13.*—The Union Pacific Railway was completed to Cheyenne.

Thurs. 21.—The first number of the *Deseret Evening News* was issued in G. S. L. City; Geo. Q. Cannon, editor.

December. *Sat. 1.*—Benjamin Stringham was appointed to preside over the Saints at Benniagton (now Leeds) and Harrisburg, Washington Co., Utah, as acting Bishop.

Tues. 17.—Bishop Caleb G. Edwards died at Ephraim, Sanpete Co.

Tues. 24.—Millersburgh and other small towns in southern Utah, on the Rio Virgen, were almost completely destroyed by a flood.

Wed. 25.—John James and wife, of Willard, Box Elder Co., were accidentally drowned in Sand creek.

1868.

During this year the grasshoppers did much damage to the crops in Utah, and many of the farmers, as well as others, sought employment on the Union Pacific Railroad, which was now being built through the Territory. Names changed to Salt Lake City and County. Church teams were sent east for the last time to bring in the immigration.

January. *Tues. 7.*—Geo. R. Galloway froze to death near Kamas, Summit Co., Utah.

Mon. 13.—The 17th annual session of the Utah legislature convened in G. S. L. City and organized by appointing Geo. A. Smith president of the Council, and John Taylor speaker of the House.

Fri. 17.—The first number of the *Utah Magazine* was published in G. S. L. City, Elias L. T. Harrison editor.

Wed. 22.—The first number of *Our Dixie Times*, a weekly paper, edited and published by Joseph E. Johnson, at St. George, Utah, was issued. In the following May it changed name to the *Rio Virgen Times*.

Wed. 29.—A legislative act was approved, changing the names of Great Salt Lake City and Great Salt Lake County to Salt Lake City and Salt Lake County. On the same day an act, changing the name of Richland County to Rich County (Utah), was approved.

February. *Thurs. 13.*—A legislative act incorporating Morgan City, Morgan Co., Utah, was approved.

Mon. 17.—Hiram B. Clawson and Wm. C. Staines, who had been appointed Church emigration agents this season, left Salt Lake City for the East, with $27,000 to be used for gathering the poor. This year about seventy thousand dollars was raised for the emigration of the poor Saints, mainly from Great Britain, an extra effort being made on the part of the Saints in Utah for that purpose.

March. *Sun. 29.*—The 74th quorum of

Seventy was partly organized at Farmington, Davis Co., with Lot Smith, James T. Smith, Oliver L. Robinson, John Leavit, Philander Brown, Elias Vanfleet and Charles Wm. Stayner as presidents.

April. Sat. 4.—Bishop Frederick Olson's company of settlers was attacked by Indians near the Rocky Ford of the Sevier river, between Salina and Richfield. During the fight which ensued, Lars Alex. Justesen and Charles Wilson were killed and others wounded.

Mon. 6.—The 38th annual conference of the Church, which was continued for three days, was commenced in Salt Lake City.

Mon. 13.—Heber M. Walker of Pleasant Grove, Utah Co., was accidentally killed by the stumbling of a horse.

May. Thurs. 7.—Four Indians made a raid on Scipio, Millard Co., and drove off fifteen head of horses.

Mon. 11.—The citizens of Salt Lake City commenced an organized warfare against the grasshoppers, which appeared in great numbers.

Sat. 16.—Samuel B. Reed, chief of construction on the Union Pacific Railroad, and Silas Seymour, constructing engineer, arrived in Salt Lake City, on business for their road. A few days later Pres. Brigham Young took a contract to do the grading on ninety miles of the road, and great numbers of men from the valleys turned out to labor on it. By this means money became more plentiful in the Territory.

Thurs. 21.—Jeremiah Willey, formerly a member of the Mormon Battalion, died at Bountiful, Davis C.

June.—The Union Iron Company commenced operations at Pinto, Iron Co.

—The Indians continued troublesome in Sanpete County, stole cattle and annoyed the settlers.

Thurs. 4.—The packet ship John Bright sailed from Liverpool, England, with 722 Saints (176 from Scandinavia), under the direction of James McGaw; the company arrived at New York July 13th, and at Laramie City, on the Union Pacific Railroad, 573 miles west of Omaha, July 23rd.

Mon. 8.—Joseph A. Young, Brigham Young, jun., and John W. Young left Salt Lake City for the head of Echo Canyon, as agents for Pres. Brigham Young, to let contracts for grading on the Union Pacific Railroad.

Tues. 9.—Ground was broken for the Union Pacific Railroad at Devil's Gate, in Weber Canyon.

Wed. 10.—A mass meeting in Salt Lake City passed resolutions in favor of assisting the Union Pacific Railroad through the Territory of Utah.

Sun. 14.—The Star of the West, a vessel owned by Mr. Meredith, was wrecked on the Great Salt Lake, in a storm, while used by a surveying party.

Mon. 15.—On this and the two following days, the Church teams, about five hundred in number, sent to the terminus of the Union Pacific Railroad this season for the poor, left Salt Lake City, under Captains Edward T. Mumford, Joseph S. Rawlins, John G. Holman, William S. Seeley, John R. Murdock, Daniel D. McArthur, John Gillespie, Horton D. Haight, Chester Loveland and Simpson M. Molen.

Wed. 17.—John Ager was found drowned in the Weber river, near Morgan, Utah.

Sat. 20.—The packet ship Emerald Isle sailed from Liverpool, England, with 876 Saints, under the direction of Hans Jensen Hals. It arrived at New York harbor, after an unpleasant voyage, Aug. 11th. The emigrants landed on the 14th and arrived at Benton, on the Union Pacific Railroad, about seven hundred miles west from Omaha, Aug. 25th. Thirty-seven deaths occurred on the ocean, and others died in the hospital in New York.

Mon. 22.—Heber C. Kimball, first Counselor to Pres. Brigham Young, died in Salt Lake City.

Tues. 23.—Latimer & Taylor's machine shops, in Salt Lake City, were destroyed by fire. Loss, $12,000.

Wed. 24.—The packet ship Constitution, the last sailing vessel which brought any large company of Saints across the Atlantic, sailed from Liverpool, England, with 457 British, Swiss and German Saints, in charge of Harvey H. Cluff. It arrived at New York Aug. 5th, and the immigrants continued by rail to Benton.

Thurs. 25.—Niels Christoffersen and Peter Smith, of Manti, Peter Nielsen of Fairview, Chr. Jensen and Chr. Nebellah, of Mount Pleasant, and Thos. Yeates, of Millville, all belonging to the Church trains, were drowned at Robison's ferry, on Green river, by the capsizing of a boat.

Tues. 30.—The steamship Minnesota, with 534 Saints, under the direction of John Parry, sailed from Liverpool, England. It arrived at New York July 12th, and the immigrants reached Laramie City July 22nd.

July. Sat. 4.—Water was first brought on the Provo bench, Utah Co., by means of a big canal just completed, from the Provo river.

Sat. 11.—The Indians made a raid on a horse herd, near Ephraim, Sanpete Co., driving off some twelve head of horses. The herdsman gave chase, had a fight with the savages and recovered most of the animals.

Tues. 14.—The steamship Colorado sailed from Liverpool, England, with 600 Saints, under the direction of Wm. B. Preston. It arrived at New York, July 28th, and the company reached Benton, Aug. 7th.

—Elder Ezra J. Clark, son of Ezra T. Clark, of Farmington, Davis Co., Utah, died near Fonda, Montgomery Co., N. Y., while returning from a mission to Great Britain, with the company of emigrants who crossed the Atlantic on the Minnesota.

August. Mon. 3.—At the annual election in Utah, Wm. H. Hooper was re-elected delegate to Congress.

Tues. 14.—David Fisher, of the 10th Ward, Salt Lake City, was accidentally killed while working on the Union Pacific Railroad, in Weber Canyon.

Tues. 18.—The settlement of St. Joseph, Arizona (on the Muddy), was partly destroyed by fire.

Wed. 19.—Col. F. H. Head, superintendent of Indian affairs, and Dimick B. Huntington, Indian interpreter, had a "big talk" with the Indians in Strawberry Valley, Uintah, and a treaty of peace was made with these Indians, who had raided the settlements in Sanpete Valley and other places.

—Capt. John R. Murdock's mule train, which left Laramie City, July 27th, with 50 wagons and about six hundred immigrants, arrived at Salt Lake City; six persons died on the journey.

—Robert C. Sharkey was killed by the discharge of a gun, in Salt Lake City.

Thurs. 20.—Capt. Chester Loveland's mule train of 40 wagons and about four hundred passengers, which left Laramie City, July 25th, arrived in Salt Lake City. Two deaths occurred on the journey.

—Capt. Joseph S. Rawlins' mule train, consisting of 31 wagons and nearly three hundred passengers, which left Laramie City, July 25th, arrived in Salt Lake City. Two died on the journey.

Mon. 24.—Capt. Horton D. Haight's mule train, which left Laramie City July 27th, with freight and 275 passengers, arrived in Salt Lake City. Six deaths occurred on the journey.

Sat. 29.—Capt. Wm. S. Seeley's ox train of 39 wagons, which left Laramie City August 1st, with passengers (272 souls) from Williamsburg, N. Y., and freight, arrived in Salt Lake City. Four deaths occurred on the trip.

September.—Albert Carrington succeeded Apostle Franklin D. Richards as president of the European mission.

Pres. Brigham Young spent most of the summer on preaching tours through the settlements.

Wed. 2.—Capt. Simpson M. Molen's ox train of 61 wagons, which left Benton Aug. 13th, with freight and about three hundred passengers, and Capt. Daniel D. McArthur's ox train of 61 wagons, which left Benton Aug. 14th with 411 passengers, arrived in Salt Lake City. One child died in the former and five children in the latter company, on the journey.

Tues. 15.—Capt. John Gillespie's ox train of 54 wagons and about five hundred immigrants, which left Benton Aug. 24th, arrived in Salt Lake City.

Sun. 20.—At a special conference held at Nephi, Juab Co., and attended by Pres. Brigham Young and other leading men, Nephi was organized into a Stake of Zion, with Jacob G. Bigler as president.

Thurs. 24.—Capt. Edward T. Mumford's mule train of 28 wagons, which left Benton Sept. 1st, arrived in Salt Lake City with 250 passengers.

Fri. 25.—Capt. John G. Holman's ox train of 62 wagons, which left Benton Sept. 1st, arrived in Salt Lake City, with about six hundred and fifty immigrants. A number of the Saints died on the journey.

October. *Thurs. 1.*—Apostle Franklin D. Richards and Chas. W. Penrose arrived in Salt Lake City from their foreign missions.

Tues. 6.—The general conference was commenced in Salt Lake City. It was continued three days. For the first time in Utah, a full quorum of the Twelve Apostles was present at conference. A number of missionaries were called to strengthen the southern settlements. On the 6th Geo. A. Smith was chosen as First

Counselor to Pres. Brigham Young, in place of the late Heber C. Kimball, and Brigham Young, Jun., was called to fill the vacancy caused thereby in the Council of Twelve Apostles.

Fri. 9.—Brigham Young, Jun., was set apart as one of the Twelve Apostles.

Wed. 14.—Henry Erikson was thrown from a wagon and killed, at Mill Creek, Salt Lake Co.

Thurs. 15.—Alexander Ott, an able and faithful Elder, died in Salt Lake City.

Fri. 16.—Zion's Co-operative Mercantile Institution commenced operation in Salt Lake City, with Brigham Young as president. Co-operative stores were shortly afterwards opened in most of the towns and settlements of the Territory.

Sat. 17.—Samuel Dennis White died in Salt Lake City.

Sat. 24.—A company of sixty-one immigrants, who had been left from some of the companies, in New York, because of sickness, arrived in Salt Lake City, in charge of Fred. C. Anderson, having left New York Oct. 3rd.

November. *Sun. 15.*—Agnes Taylor, wife of James Taylor and mother of Apostle John Taylor, died in Salt Lake City.

Fri. 27.—Christian Jørgensen, of Salt Lake City, was accidentally killed, while working on the Union Pacific Railroad, on the Weber.

December. *Tues. 8.*—Daniel Spencer, president of the Salt Lake Stake of Zion, died in Salt Lake City.

Wed. 9.—Leonora Taylor, wife of Apostle John Taylor, died in Salt Lake City.

Fri. 11.—Harlam P. Swett was killed near Lehi, Utah Co. The murderer escaped.

Sun. 20.—Patriarch Elisha H. Groves died at Kanarra, Iron Co.

Tues. 22.—David Grant, one of the Utah Pioneers of 1847, died at Mill Creek, Salt Lake Co., Utah.

Wed. 23.—Wm. Jennings' fine residence, in the 16th Ward, Salt Lake City, was dedicated.

Tues. 29.—Bishop Jonathan O. Duke died at Provo.

Wed. 30.—James Read and Richard Gibbs were accidentally killed, while laboring on the Union Pacific Railroad, above Round Valley, on the Weber.

1869

This year the Saints residing in Millard and Beaver Counties and in Bear Lake Valley were organized into Stakes of Zion. The great Pacific railroad was completed through the Territory and a branch road built from Ogden to Salt Lake City. Missionary labor was considerably revived in the United States.

January.—The first general directory of Salt Lake City was compiled by Edward L. Sloan.

Fri. 1.—The first number of *Der Stern*, a monthly 16-page octavo periodical, published in the interest of the Church in Switzerland, in the German language, was.

issued in Zurich; Karl G. Maeser, editor and publisher.

Mon. 11.—The 18th annual session of the Utah legislature convened in Salt Lake City and organized with Geo. A. Smith president of the Council and Orson Pratt speaker of the House.

Fri. 15.—Ira Ames, a true and faithful Elder, died at Wellsville, Cache Co.

—The end of the Union Pacific Railroad track reached Echo, Summit Co.

Tues. 19.—Elder John Mace, missionary from Utah, died in Leeds, England.

Thurs. 21.—An observatory was erected on the south-east corner of the Temple Block, Salt Lake City.

Sat. 23.—Miss Augusta St. Clair, a talented lecturess, died in Salt Lake City.

Fri. 29.—Chauncey W. Millard, a murderer, was executed at Provo.

February.—Patriarch Asahel Perry died at Springville, Utah Co.

Wed. 3.—Simeon Carter, formerly a member of Zion's Camp and prominent in the Church, died at Brigham City, Box Elder Co.

Mon. 15.—Rio Virgen County, Utah, was created by act of the Utah legislature.

Fri. 19.—The Utah legislature closed its 18th session.□

Thurs. 25.—The Navajo Indians invaded southern Utah and stole stock at Harrisburgh. A number of armed men from St. George and other settlements started in pursuit.

—Delegate Wm. H. Hooper, by an able speech in the House of Representatives, frustrated a plan to divide the Territory of Utah.

March.—*Mon. 1.*—Z. C. M. I. commenced business in the Eagle Emporium, Salt Lake City.

Mon. 8.—The Utah Central Railway company was organized, with Brigham Young as president.

—A United States land office was opened in Salt Lake City.

—The University of Deseret was opened in the Council House, Salt Lake City.

—The Union Pacific Railroad was completed to Ogden, and a celebration held there in honor of the event.

Tues. 9.—At a special conference held in the State House, at Fillmore, Millard Co., Utah, a Stake of Zion was organized in Millard County, by Pres. Geo. A. Smith and Apostles Erastus Snow and Joseph F. Smith, with Thos. Callister as president. Daniel Thompson was sustained as Bishop of Scipio (Round Valley), and Culbert King as Bishop of Kanosh.

Fri. 12.—The Saints residing in Beaver County, Utah, were organized into the Beaver Stake of Zion, by Apostles Geo. A. Smith and Erastus Snow, with John R. Murdock as president. The town of Beaver was divided into two Wards, with Marquis L. Shepherd as Bishop of the First and John Ashworth as Bishop of the Second Ward. The villages of Greenville and Adamsville were organized into a third Ward, with David B. Adams, of Adamsville, as Bishop. James McKnight was sustained as Bishop of Minersville.

—Elder Carl Widerborg died suddenly at Ogden.

Tues. 16.—Senator Pomeroy introduced

a bill in the U. S. Senate, to establish woman suffrage in Utah.

Sun. 21.—Franklin B. Woolley, son of Bishop Edwin D. Woolley, of Salt Lake City, was killed by Indians, on the Mohave river, near San Bernardino, Cal.

Thurs. 25.—Parowan, Iron Co., was divided into two Wards, with Herman D. Bayles as Bishop of the First and Samuel H. Rogers as Bishop of the Second Ward.

—Corinne, Box Elder Co., on the Central Pacific Railroad, was located by non-Mormons.

Sat. 27.—The 75th quorum of Seventy was organized at Ogden, with Archibald Macfarlane, David G. Nelson, Henry J. Newman, Joseph A. West, Sanford Bingham, jr., Wm. Stoker, Richard White and Ivar Isaacson as presidents.

—Indians made a raid on the stock near Scipio, Millard Co., and took about one hundred head of cattle and horses.

Sun. 28.—The 76th quorum of Seventy was organized in Weber County, with Wm. F. Critchlow, David H. Peery, Jeppe G. Folkman, Wm. Halls, James Barker, Enoch Farr and Edward Edwards as presidents.

April. *Thurs. 1.*—Major J. W. Powell finished his explorations of the Colorado river.

Sat. 3.—By action of the county court, St. Joseph, on the Muddy, was made the county seat of Rio Virgen County.

Mon. 5.—Three men were killed by a snowslide in Mill Creek Canyon, Salt Lake Co.

Tues. 6.—On this and the two following days the 39th annual conference of the Church was held in Salt Lake City; forty-six missionaries were called.

Wed. 14.—The dead body of John V. Long was found in a ditch, in Salt Lake City.

Tues. 20.—Apostle Orson Pratt left Salt Lake City for New York, to publish the Book of Mormon in the Deseret alphabet.

Sat. 24.—The Salt Lake *Daily Telegraph* was moved from Salt Lake City to Ogden.

May. *Mon. 10.*—The great Pacific Railroad was completed by the junction of the Union Pacific and Central Pacific Railroads, at Promontory, northwest of Ogden, Utah, where the last rail was laid and the last spike (gold) driven, in the presence of the chief officers of both roads, and a large concourse of people.

Mon. 17.—Ground was broken by Pres. Brigham Young at Ogden for the Utah Central Railway, a branch road soon afterwards built from Ogden to Salt Lake City.

June. *Tues. 1.*—The Provo Co-operative Woolen Manufacturing Company was organized; Brigham Young, president; Abraham O. Smoot, vice president. A site for the factory was also selected, and Nathan Davis appointed architect.

Wed. 2.—Elder Barnabas L. Adams, a Pioneer of 1847, died suddenly in City Creek Canyon, near Salt Lake City.

—The Guion & Co's. steamship *Minnesota* sailed from Liverpool, England, with 338 Saints, under the direction of Elias Morris. It arrived at New York June 14th.

Fri. 11.—Elder Heman Hyde died in Salt Lake City.

Sat. 12.—James Davidson and wife died from want of water on the desert, between St. George and the settlements on the Muddy.

Tues. 15.—Hon. B. Q. Wade, late president of the U. S. Senate, and Major-General Philip H. Sheridan and staff visited Salt Lake City.

Sun. 20.—The Saints residing in Bear Lake Valley were organized by Pres. Brigham Young into a Stake of Zion, with David P. Kimball as president.

Fri. 25.—The first company of Latter-day Saint immigrants who came all the way from the Missouri river by rail arrived in Ogden by the U. P. R. R., in charge of Elias Morris.

July. *Fri. 9.*—Senator L. Trumbull and the Chicago Commercial party arrived in Salt Lake City, on a visit.

Sat. 10.—The Chicago Commercial delegation, headed by Col. J. H. Bowen, called upon Pres. Brigham Young, in Salt Lake City.

Thurs. 15.—The steamship *Minnesota* sailed from Liverpool, England, with 598 Saints, mostly from Scandinavia, under the direction of O. C. Olsen. The company arrived at New York July 28th, and at Taylor's Switch, near Ogden, Aug. 6th.

Sun. 25.—The first shipment of Utah ore to California took place. It consisted of ten tons from the Monitor and Magnet mine, Little Cottonwood, shipped by Woodhull Bros. to T. H. Selby, San Francisco.

Mon. 26.—Thomas L. Frazier, formerly a member of the Mormon Battalion, died at Wanship, Summit Co., from the effects of stabbing inflicted a few days before by a Mr. Kilfoyle.

Wed. 28.—The fine steamship *Colorado* sailed from Liverpool, England, with 365 Saints, in charge of John E. Pace. The company arrived at New York about Aug. 10th, and at Ogden Aug 20th.

Sat. 31.—Woodhull Bros. made the first shipment of copper ore, ten tons, from the Kingston mine, Bingham Canyon.

August.—The grasshoppers destroyed a large portion of the growing crops in Cache, Washington, Kane and Iron Counties; other parts of the Territory escaped the visitation and gathered abundant crops.

Sat. 21.—The Joint Congressional Committee on retrenchment, including several distinguished statesmen, arrived in Salt Lake City, on a visit.

Wed. 25.—Frederick Woesner was killed by unknown parties, at Montpelier, Rich Co., Utah (now in Idaho).

—The steamship *Minnesota* sailed from Liverpool, England, with 443 Saints, in charge of Marius Ensign. The company arrived at New York Sept. 6th, and at Ogden Sept. 16.

Mon. 30.—Geo. Francis Train delivered an interesting lecture in the Theatre, Salt Lake City. The following evening he lectured on the subjects, "Doctor, Lawyer and Clergyman."

September. *Fri. 3.*—Apostle Ezra T. Benson died at Ogden, Utah.

Fri. 10.—John Goddard, son of Geo. Goddard, was accidentally drowned in the Jordan river, near Salt Lake City.

7

Sat. 18.—Bishop Wm. W. Wall died at Provo.

Mon. 20.—The Indians made a raid on Fairview, Sanpete Co., and stole eighteen head of horses.

Wed. 22.—Tracklaying was commenced on the Utah Central Railway at Ogden.

—The steamship *Manhattan* sailed from Liverpool, England, with 239 Saints, in charge of Joseph Lawson. The company arrived at New York Oct. 7th, and at Ogden Oct. 16th.

Sun. 26.—Apostle Orson Pratt arrived in Salt Lake City from his mission to the East.

October. *Sun. 3.* — Vice-President Schuyler Colfax and party arrived in Salt Lake City, en route from California to the East.

Tues. 5. — Vice-President Colfax delivered a speech from the portico of the Townsend House, Salt Lake City, in which he praised the industries of the Mormon people, but denounced polygamy. This led to an important open correspondence between Colfax and Apostle John Taylor.

—A company of 40 Saints from Georgia and other States arrived at Ogden, in charge of Jesse W. Crosby, jun.

Wed. 6.—The steamship *Minnesota* sailed from Liverpool, England, with 294 Saints, in charge of James Needham. The company, which was the sixth ship-load of the season sailing from Liverpool, arrived at New York Oct. 17th, and at Ogden Oct. 28th. By a collision with an express train, at Evanston, Oct. 27th, two of the immigrants were killed and others wounded.

Thurs. 7.—A mass meeting was held in Salt Lake City, with a view of again appealing to Congress for the admission of Utah into the Union as a State.

Fri. 8.—About one hundred and ninety missionaries were called at the general conference, held at Salt Lake City, to go on missions.

Sat. 9.—The surviving members of Zion's Camp had a party in Salt Lake City, arranged by Bishop Edward Hunter and Counselors.

Mon. 18.—John Walker, a survivor of the Haun's Mills massacre, died at Farmington, Davis Co., Utah.

Wed. 20.—The ground was broken for the Coalville and Echo Railway, in Summit County.

Mon. 25.—Elias L. T. Harrison, Wm. S. Godbe and Eli B. Kelsey were excommunicated from the Church, by the High Council, in Salt Lake City, for apostacy.

Sun. 31.—Indians made a raid on the town of Kanarra, Iron Co., Utah, and drove off horses.

November. *Sun. 7.*—At a conference held in St. George, the settlements in southern Utah were organized into a stake of Zion with Joseph W. Young as president, and Robert Gardner and Jas. G. Bleak as counselors; St. George was divided into four wards with David Milne, Henry Eyring, Walter Granger and Nathaniel Ashby as their respective bishops. Hebron and Clover Valley were organized into a Ward, with Geo. H. Crosby as Bishop.

Mon. 8.—Carpenters began work on the

gallery in the New Tabernacle, Salt Lake City.

Sun. 14.—The Saints who had settled on Cherry Creek, Malad Valley, Idaho, were organized into the Willow Springs branch of the Church, with Richard J. Davis as president.

Thurs. 18.—Miss Annie Lockhart, a favorite actress, died in Salt Lake City.

Mon. 22.—Ogden was decided upon as the junction of the Union Pacific and Central Pacific Railways.

Wed. 24.—Street lamps were first used in Salt Lake City.

Mon. 29.—Emer Harris, brother of Martin Harris, died at Logan, Utah.

December. *Mon. 6.*—The Utah Central Railway was permanently opened for trafic from Ogden to Farmington.

—Senator Aaron H. Cragin, of New Hampshire, introduced an anti-polygamy bill in the U. S.Senate.

Sat. 18.—The Deseret Telegraph Line was extended to Franklin, Idaho.

Sun. 19.—The "Godbeite Movement" began to take definite shape.

Thurs. 30.—Samuel Gould, formerly a member of the Mormon Battalion, died at Parowan, Iron Co.

1870.

The women of Utah were enfranchised. The Liberal Party was organized in Salt Lake City, and commenced its warfare against the "Mormons." The annual muster of the Utah militia was forbidden by Gov. Schaffer. Judge James B. McKean commenced his inglorious career in the Territory. Dr. Taggart, assessor of internal revenue, made a despicable attempt to compel the Church to pay an enormous tax on tithing, but failed in his scheme.

January.—*Sat. 1.*—The first number of the Ogden *Junction*, a semi-weekly newspaper, was issued at Ogden, by the Ogden Junction Publishing Company; Franklin D. Richards, editor. Later it was edited by Charles W. Penrose. The paper was continued under that name until Feb. 14, 1881.

—The first number of the *Mormon Tribune*, a weekly paper, was published by the Godbeites, in Salt Lake City.

Sun. 9.—Bishop Chauncey W. West, of Ogden, died at San Francisco, Cal.

Mon. 10.—The last rail of the Utah Central Railway was laid and the last spike driven, at Salt Lake City, by Pres. Brigham Young, in the presence of 15,000 people.

Tues. 11.—The nineteenth annual session of the Utah legislature assembled in Salt Lake City, and organized by electing Geo. A. Smith president of the Council, and Orson Pratt speaker of the House. It was an important session.

Wed. 12.—Woodhull Bros. shipped the first car-load of ore over the Utah Central Railway.

Thurs. 13.—A great mass meeting was held by the ladies of Salt Lake City, to protest against the passage of the Cullom anti-polygamy bill, which had been introduced in Congress. Similar meetings were subsequently held by the ladies in most of the settlements in the Territory.

—The first coal shipped by rail, direct to Salt Lake City, arrived there, consisting of two carloads from the Wasatch Coal Company's mines, consigned to Frederick A. H. F. Mitchell.

February.—The "Liberal Party" of Utah was formed by a union of the Gentiles and Godbeites of Salt Lake City.

Thurs. 10.—A political mass meeting, appointed by the "Liberal Party" of Salt Lake City and held in Walker's old store, was carried by the "People's Party."

Fri. 12.—An act passed by the legislature, conferring the elective franchise upon the women of Utah, was approved by Acting-Governor S. A. Mann.

Thurs. 17.—Some soldiers from Camp Douglas beat an Indian boy and fired on the police, who interfered with and arrested them.

Thurs. 24.—Pres. Brigham Young, accompanied by a number of leading men, left Salt Lake City on a trip to the southern settlements. They arrived at the Colorado river, at the mouth of the Rio Virgen, Arizona, March 16th.

March. *Wed. 2.*—Elder Jabez Woodard died at Milton, Morgan Co.

—The first number of the *Keepapitchinin*, a small semi-weekly periodical, devoted to fun and amusement, was issued in Salt Lake City, by Geo. J. Taylor and Joseph C. Rich.

Mon. 7.—Ole Bull, the great Norwegian violinist, arrived in Salt Lake City, on a visit. He gave two concerts in the theatre and left on the 10th.

Sun. 20.—Hon. J. Wilson Schaffer, seventh governor of Utah, arrived in Salt Lake City. He proved to be one of the most bitter officials that the Territory ever had.

Wed. 23.—Although Delegate Wm. H. Hooper made a very able speech in defence of religious liberty in Utah, the Cullom Bill was passed by the House of Representatives.

Tues. 29.—A company of 30 Elders returned to Salt Lake City from missions to the States.

Thurs. 31.—The citizens of Salt Lake City held an immense mass meeting to protest against the Cullom Bill, which had not yet passed the Senate. Afterwards mass meetings were held in the settlements for the same purpose, and a petition drafted and forwarded to the Senate.

April.—Sidney Alvarus Hanks, one of the Pioneers of 1847, froze to death in Parley's Park, Summit Co., Utah.

—The gallery in the large Tabernacle, Salt Lake City, was finished.

—Camp Rawlins, a military post, was established near Provo, Utah.

—An abandoned child was left at the door of Mrs. Prescinda L. Kimball—the first occurrence of the kind known in Salt Lake City.

Fri. 1.—The first number of the *Utah Pomologist and Gardener*, devoted to the orchard, vineyard, farm and garden, was issued by Joseph E. Johnson, at St. George, Utah.

Thurs. 7.—Elder Edward Stevenson preached in the Kirtland Temple, O.

. Tues. 12.—The resolutions adopted by the Salt Lake City mass meeting, on March 31st, were presented to the U. S. Senate and referred to the committee on Territories.

Wed. 13.—Elder Moroni Bigelow was killed on the steamboat *Mary McDonald* and thrown into the Missouri river, between Camden and Wellington, Mo. He was returning from a mission to the States.

Sat. 16.—Pres. Brigham Young and party returned to Salt Lake City, from a preaching trip to the southern settlements.

Thurs. 21.—The dead body of Sidney Alvarus Hanks was found near Silver Creek, Summit Co.

Wed. 27.—Patriarch John Young, Pres. Brigham Young's eldest brother, died in Salt Lake City.

May. *Thurs. 5.*—The 40th annual conference of the Church convened in Salt Lake City. It was continued until the 8th.

Sun. 8.—General Philip Henry Sheridan and staff arrived in Salt Sake City, on a visit.

—Rev. Geo. M. Pierce entered his field of labor as the first Methodist missionary in Salt Lake City.

Tues. 10.—A land-slide in Bingham Canyon resulted in the death of Charles A. Freeman and James Leicester.

Thurs. 12.—Amasa M. Lyman, once a member of the Twelve Apostles, was excommunicated from the Church for apostacy.

Fri. 13. — Geo. Knighton and Henry Langford were drowned in the Jordan river, northwest of Salt Lake City.

—Col. M. T. Patrick, U. S. Marshal for Utah, arrived in Salt Lake City.

Sat. 14.—Nathaniel H. Felt and Thos. Jackson arrived at Salt Lake City, with a small company of Saints from New York State.

Fri. 20.—Elder Wm. I. Appleby died in Salt Lake City.

Fri. 27.—James Taylor, Apostle John Taylor's father, died in Salt Lake City, 87 years of age.

Sat. 28.—The corner stones of the Provo Co·operative Woolen Factory were laid.

June.—The grasshoppers did much damage in the Territory.

—Horace S. Eldredge succeeded Albert Carrington as president of the European Mission.

Sun. 5.—The first number of the Salt Lake *Daily Herald* was issued; Wm. C. Dunbar and Edward L. Sloan, publishers; Edward L. Sloan, editor.

Mon. 13. — Johan C. Christensen was killed by lightning, while in the field irrigating, near Ephraim, Sanpete Co.

Fri. 17.—In the Probate Court at Manti, John Steward, of Fairview, Sanpete Co., was sentenced to be shot, for the killing of Sally Woodward, an Indian girl, some time previous.

Thurs. 23.—Fifteen wagons, loaded with machinery for a woolen factory at Beaver, left Salt Lake City.

Tues. 28.—A company of 20 Saints sailed from Liverpool, England, on the steamship *Colorado,* for the United States.

July. — Pres. U. S. Grant appointed James B. McKean chief justice and Vernon H. Vaughan secretary of Utah. They succeeded Judge Charles C. Wilson and Secretary S. A. Mann.

Sun. 3.—Albert Carrington was ordained one of the Twelve Apostles, in Salt Lake City.

Fri. 8.—James Hendricks, who was crippled at the Crooked River battle, Oct. 25, 1838, died at Richmond, Cache Co.

Tues. 12.—Lady Franklin, widow of Sir John Franklin, visited Ogden, on her return trip from searching for her lost husband. She afterwards visited Salt Lake City.

Wed. 13. — The steamship *Manhattan* sailed from Liverpool, England, with 269 British, German and Swiss Saints, in charge of Karl G. Maeser. The company arrived at New York July 26th, and at Salt Lake City Aug. 5th.

Wed. 20. — The steamship *Minnesota* sailed from Liverpool, England, with 357 Saints, mostly Scandinavians, in charge of Jesse N. Smith. The company arrived at New York Aug. 1st, and at Salt Lake City Aug. 10th.

Sat. 23.—Geo. Francis Train lectured in the Salt Lake Theatre, in defence of Brigham Young.

August. *Mon. 1.*—At the general election in Utah, Wm. H. Hooper received over twenty thousand votes for delegate to Congress, and Geo. R. Maxwell, the Liberal candidate, only a few hundred.

Fri. 12.—A discussion commenced in the large Tabernacle, Salt Lake City, between Apostle Orson Pratt and Dr. John P. Newman, chaplain of the U. S. Senate, on the question: "Does the Bible sanction Polygamy?" It was continued three days.

Sat. 13.—S. D. Woodhull, of the firm of Woodhull Bros., the earliest active mining operators in Utah, was shot in Little Cottonwood Canyon, in a difficulty over a claim. He died on the 14th.

Sat. 27.—The establishment of Paul Engelbrecht was broken up, and his stock of liquors destroyed under authority of Salt Lake City, because he sold liquor without a license.

—Pres. Brigham Young and party left Salt Lake City for southern Utah, from which he returned Sept. 24th.

Mon. 29.—Alderman Jeter Clinton and several police officers were arrested by the U. S. marshal for participation in the abatement of the Engelbrecht liquor establishment.

Tues. 30.—Martin Harris, one of the Three Witnesses to the Book of Mormon, arrived in Salt Lake City. He was 88 years old. In the ensuing conference he bore a faithful testimony to the truth of the Book of Mormon.

—Judge James B. McKean arrived in Salt Lake City.

September. *Fri. 2.*—The first number of the semi-weekly edition of the Salt Lake *Herald* was issued.

Mon. 5.—Chief Justice James B. McKean was assigned to the Third Judicial District, and forthwith commenced his in-famous official career in Utah.

Wed. 7.—The steamship *Idaho* sailed from Liverpool, England, with 186 Saints, in charge of Frank H. Hyde. The company arrived at New York Sept. 21st, and at Ogden Oct. 1st.

Fri. 9.—Messrs. Jones & Roblus began the erection of smelting works on the State Road, south of Salt Lake City.

Sat. 10.—A town site was located by Pres. Brigham Young at Kanab, Kane Co., and the following day a Ward organization was effected, with Levi Stewart as Bishop.

Wed. 14.—A company of Scandinavian Saints (19 souls), in charge of B. N. Walter, sailed from Liverpool, England, on board the steamship *Nevada*, bound for Utah.

Thurs. 15.—Gov. J. Wilson Schaffer issued a proclamation appointing Patrick E. Connor major-general of the Utah militia (Nauvoo Legion), and Wm. M. Johns assistant adjutant-general. On the same day he issued a proclamation prohibiting all drills, musters and militia gatherings, except upon his orders, or those of the U.S. marshal. He also ordered the delivery of all arms belonging to the Territory of Utah, or the United States (except those in possession of U. S. soldiers), to Col. Wm. M. Johns.

Tues. 20.—The first run of crude bullion was made at the first smelting works built in Utah, erected six miles south of Salt Lake City by Woodhull Brothers.

Thurs. 22.—On the night of this day a party of U. S. troops, stationed near Provo, made a raid on some of the citizens in that town, some of whom they abused shamefully.

☐ October. *Mon. 10.*—The surviving members of Zion's Camp and the Mormon Battalion had an enjoyable party at the Social Hall, Salt Lake City. Of the members of Zion's Camp 32 were present, and 63 of the Battalion boys participated.

Wed. 12.—The old arsenal building in Salt Lake City was burned to the ground.

Fri. 14.—A scientific exploring party from Yale College, under direction of Prof. Marsh, arrived in Salt Lake City.

Sun. 23.—The stage from Pioche was robbed near Nephi, Juab Co., by three men, who were afterwards caught and punished.

Mon. 31.—Gov. J. Wilson Schaffer died at his residence in Salt Lake City. Secretary Vernon H. Vaughan succeeded him as acting governor.

November. Fri. 4.—Prof. Ferdinand V. Hayden, United States geologist, arrived in Salt Lake City.

—In the Third District Court the jury returned a verdict against Salt Lake City, allowing Engelbrecht & Co., $59,063.25 damages. The case was appealed.

Tues. 8.—Gen. Chas. A. Washburn, U. S. minister to Paraguay, and Hon. Alvin Flanders, governor of Washington Territory, visited Salt Lake City.

Wed. 16.—A company of 59 Saints, in charge of Ralph Thompson, sailed from Liverpool, England, on the steamship *Manhattan*, which arrived at New York

Dec. 2nd. The company reached Salt Lake City, Dec. 11th.

Mon. 21.—The so-called "wooden gun rebellion" in the 20th Ward, Salt Lake City, occurred. Messrs. Charles R. Savage, Geo. M. Ottinger, John C. Graham, Charles and Archibald Livingstone, Wm. G. Phillips and Jas. Fennimore were arrested on a charge of treason and confined at Camp Douglas.

Wed. 23.—Charles R. Savage and the other prisoners were admitted to bail and liberated.

Fri. 25.—Pres. Brigham Young, Geo. A. Smith and Brigham Young, jun., left Salt Lake City for southern Utah, where they spent part of the winter.

December. Fri. 2.—Richard Soper and Anton Valardie (?), guilty of committing rape, were killed between Levan and Nephi, Juab Co., while trying to escape from the officers.

Wed. 14.—Six members of Levi Stewart's family were burned to death in Kanab, Kane Co., Utah.

Sat. 24.—No. 1 of the *Footlights*, a programme of the entertainments at the Theatre, in Salt Lake City, was issued.

Wed. 28.—Richard Brown was shot and killed at Provo by John J. Baum, whose niece Brown had seduced. Baum was subsequently arrested, tried and acquitted, on the ground of justifiable homicide.

1871.

This year Judge James B. McKean made himself obnoxious to the Saints in Utah by his absurd rulings and his judicial persecutions of the "Mormons". The settlements of the Saints on the Muddy, in Nevada, were vacated because of the excessive taxation. The people in Utah again subscribed liberally towards emigrating the poor Saints from Europe. The first Utah edition of the Book of Mormon was printed. Several hundred stands of the Italian honey-bee were imported into the Territory. The Utah Southern Railway was built to Draper, Salt Lake Co. Latter-day Saint Sunday Schools were organized in all the large branches of the Church in the Scandinavian mission.

January. Tues. 17.—The Utah Southern Railway Company was organized, with Wm. Jennings as president.

Thurs. 19.—Mary Phillips, one of the old Herefordshire (England) Saints, died at Kaysville, Davis Co.

February.—Judge McKean made some absurd rulings in the naturalization of foreigners, making their belief in polygamy a test question.

—The settlements of St. Joseph, St. Thomas and Overton, on the Muddy, were broken up, because of their being set off into Nevada, where taxation was oppressive.

Thurs. 2.—The nomination of Geo. L. Woods, of Oregon, for governor of Utah.

and Geo. A. Black, of Illinois, for secretary, was confirmed by the U. S. Senate.

Mon. 6.—The meeting house, tithing office and post office in Pleasant Grove, Utah Co., was burned.

Fri. 10.—Pres. Brigham Young and Geo. A. Smith arrived in Salt Lake City from their winter visit to St. George.

Sun. 19.—The new governor, Geo. L. Woods, arrived in Salt Lake City.

March.—Geo. R. Maxwell's infamous memorial, praying for a seat in Congress, as a contestant against Wm. H. Hooper, was presented to Congress.

Thurs. 9.—The Deseret Philharmonic Society was organized in Salt Lake City, with David O. Calder as president.

Mon. 13.—Bishop Alfred Cordon died at Willard City, Box Elder Co.

Sat. 18.—Commercial Street, Salt Lake City, was opened.

Mon. 27.—The Salt Lake fire department was reorganized.

Fri. 31.—The Emma mine, in Little Cottonwood Canyon, was sold for $1,500,000.

April. — Numerous grasshoppers appeared in the northern part of Cache County. During the summer these insects again damaged the crops considerably in various parts of the Territory.

Mon. 3.—Mary Champlin, a survivor of the Haun's Mill massacre, died in Salt Lake City.

—Gov. Alvin Saunders, of Nebraska, visited Salt Lake City.

Thurs. 6.—The 41st annual conference of the Church convened in Salt Lake City. It was continued until the 9th.

Sat. 15.—The first number of the Salt Lake *Daily Tribune* was issued instead of the *Mormon Tribune*, suspended.

Tues. 18.—Ralph Waldo Emerson, the eminent *littérateur*, arrived in Salt Lake City, on a visit.

Mon. 24.—Bishop Peter Maughan, one of the founders of the Cache Valley settlements, died

May.—The Corinne *Daily Journal*, an anti-Mormon paper, was first published at Corinne, Box Elder Co., Utah.

Mon. 1.—Ground was first broken for the Utah Southern Railway.

Wed. 3.—Major J. W. Powell, the Colorado explorer, and party arrived in Salt Lake City.

Wed. 10.—Elder Joseph Parry with ten Saints, sailed from Liverpool on the steamship *Wyoming*, bound for Utah.

June.—Apostle Albert Carrington succeeded Horace S. Eldredge as president of the European mission.

Sun. 11.—The first camp-meeting ever held in Utah, took place in Salt Lake City, under the auspices of the Methodists.

Wed. 14.—While shoveling snow in American Fork Canyon, Clark Thompson was accidentally killed and a companion wounded.

Wed. 21. — The steamship *Wyoming* sailed from Liverpool, England, with 248 Saints, under the direction of Robert F. Neslen and Geo. Lake. The company arrived at New York July 3rd, and at Salt Lake City July 12th.

Mon. 26.—Pres. Brigham Young, Geo. A. Smith and others left Salt Lake City, on a trip to the northern settlements, return-

ing in the latter part of July, after visiting Soda Springs, Bear Lake Valley, etc.

Wed. 28. — The steamship *Minnesota* sailed from Liverpool, England, with 397 Saints, in charge of Wm. W. Cluff. The company landed at New York July 13th, and arrived at Ogden July 21st.

Fri. 30.—Geo A. Black, acting-governor of Utah, issued a proclamation, forbidding the assembling of any of the militia of the Territory, to participate in the celebration of the 95th anniversary of American Independence, in Salt Lake City.

July. *Tues. 4.*—Notwithstanding Act.-Gov. Black's proclamation against the assembling of the Territorial militia, the day was celebrated in good style in Salt Lake City.

Mon. 10.—Hon. S. S. Cox, of New York, visited Salt Lake City.

Wed. 12. — The steamship *Colorado* sailed from Liverpool, England, with 146 Saints, under the direction of Hamilton G. Park. The company arrived in New York July 25th, and at Salt Lake City Aug. 4th.

Thurs. 20.—The Pioneer Mill, Ophir Mining District (the first stamp mill in Utah), commenced running; Walker Bros., proprietors.

Fri. 21.—The *Lady of the Lake*, a little steamer bought by John W. Young and intended for an excursion boat on the Salt Lake, arrived in Salt Lake City. It was launched in the Jordan on Aug. 2nd.

Sun. 23.—A meeting and dwelling house, erected by the Saints in Christiania, Norway, was dedicated.

Wed. 26.—The steamship *Nevada* sailed from Liverpool, England, with 93 Saints, under the direction of Lot Smith. The company arrived at New York Aug. 7th, and in Salt Lake City Aug. 16th.

August. *Tues. 1.*—M. T. Patrick, U. S. marshal, took possession of the Utah Penitentiary, under protest of Albert P. Rockwood.

Fri. 4. —Briant Stringham, one of the Pioneers of 1847, died in Salt Lake City.

Wed. 9. — The steamship *Minnesota* sailed from Liverpool, England, with 60 Saints, under the direction of Wm. Douglass. The company arrived at New York Aug. 21st, and at Ogden Aug. 30th.

Fri. 11.—Prof. J. D. Runkle, president of the Massachusetts Institute of Technology, visited Salt Lake City. He was engaged in extensive explorations in Utah and Nevada.

Wed. 23.—A company for building the Utah and Northern Railway was organized, with John W. Young as president and general superintendent.

Sat. 26. — Ground was broken for the Utah and Northern Railway, at Brigham City.

Mon. 28.—Wm. Hutchinson was shot and killed, in Coalville, Summit Co., in self-defence.

September.—At this time the U. S. officials in Utah acted more like bigoted missionaries than administrators of the law. Absurd rulings, illegal processes and packed juries characterized their proceedings.

Fri. 1.—The National Bank of Deseret commenced business on the corner of East Temple and First South Street, Salt Lake City.

Sat. 2.—U. S. Marshal Patrick made a demand of Warden Albert P. Rockwood to deliver up the prisoner Kilfoyle to the marshal's custody, which was refused on legal grounds.

—The Deseret Telegraph Company extended a branch line to Coalville, Summit Co.

Wed. 6.—The steamship *Nevada* sailed from Liverpool, England, with 263 Saints, under the direction of John I. Hart. The company arrived at New York Sept. 18th, and at Ogden Sep. 27th.

Fri. 8.—After several days' preliminary examination before Associate Justice C. M. Hawley, Marshal McAllister and Warden Rockwood (Salt Lake City) were held to bail in $1,000 each to await the action of the grand jury.

Mon. 11.—A detachment of U. S. cavalry surrounded the houses of Messrs. John J. Baum and H. L. Davis, near Provo, Utah Co., and fired several shots at the former. A packed grand jury had indicted Baum and Davis for murder.

Tues. 19.—Caleb Parry, missionary from Utah, died at Birmingham, England. He was buried in the same grave as James H. Flanigan, who died Jan. 29, 1851.

Fri. 22.—James Hendry was shot and fatally wounded at Hooperville, by the father and son of a girl, whom he had seduced.

Sat. 23.—The Utah Southern Railway was completed to Sandy.

Sun. 24.—The corner stones of the new Catholic Church, in Salt Lake City, were laid, the ceremonies being conducted by Rev. Patrick Walsh.

October. *Mon. 2.*—Pres. Brigham Young was arrested by U. S. Marshal Patrick, on an indictment charging him with lascivious cohabitation with his polygamous wives. The President was guarded in his own house for some time afterwards.

Tues. 3.—Daniel H. Wells was arrested by U. S. Marshal Patrick, on a charge of "lascivious and unlawful cohabitation," and placed under $5,000 bonds.

Sat. 7.—Geo. Q. Cannon and Henry W. Lawrence were arrested on charges of lascivious cohabitation; Cannon was placed under $5,000 bonds.

Mon. 9.—Pres. Brigham Young went into court. After several days' trial, Judge McKean (on the 12th) rendered a decision, admitting the defendant to bail in $5,000, and the case was postponed until the prosecution was better prepared for action. In delivering his opinion the judge said that while the case was called "The people versus Brigham Young, its other and real title is Federal Authority versus Polygamic Theocracy."

Tues. 10.—Hon. O P. Morton, senator from Indiana, accompanied by several distinguished ladies and gentlemen, arrived in Salt Lake City, on a visit. They used their influence against the Federal crusade, then being carried on in Utah.

Wed. 11.—A mass meeting convened in answer to the mayor of Salt Lake City, to adopt measures for the relief of the sufferers by the Chicago fire.

Thurs. 12.—A terrific wind storm visited Salt Lake City and vicinity.

Sat. 14.—Mayor Daniel H. Wells remitted $12,000 for the relief of the sufferers by the Chicago fire. He subsequently sent another amount.

Wed. 18.—The steamship *Nevada* sailed from Liverpool, England, with 300 Saints, in charge of Geo. H. Peterson. The company arrived at New York, Nov. 1st, and at Salt Lake City, Nov. 11th.

Mon. 23.—The Deseret Telegraph line was completed to Pioche, Nevada.

Tues. 24.—Pres. Brigham Young left Salt Lake City for St. George, with the intention of spending the winter there. It was soon afterwards extensively published that he had fled from justice.

Sat. 28.—Mayor Daniel H. Wells, Hosea Stout and W. H. Kimball were arrested on a trumped up charge of murder, the notorious outlaw, "Bill" Hickman, being their accuser, and committed to the military prison at Camp Douglas.

—Thomas Hawkins was sentenced by Judge McKean to three years' imprisonment and $500 fine, for adultery with his own wives. He appealed his case to the Territorial Supreme Court, but not being able to get $20,000 bonds, he was imprisoned.

Mon. 30.—In the Third District Court, Salt Lake City, Mayor Daniel H. Wells was admitted to $50,000 bail, for his appearance, when wanted, on the charge of murder.

November. *Thurs. 2.*—Captain Jacob Hamblin met in council with the principal chiefs of the Navejo Indians, at Ft. Defiance, and concluded a treaty of peace with them in behalf of the people of Utah.

Mon. 6.—James P. Brown, a member of the Mormon Battalion, died at Rockville, Kane Co.

Thurs 9.—The site for the St. George Temple was dedicated.

—The Deseret Telegraph Company opened an office at Paris, Bear Lake Co., Idaho.

Mon. 20.—Elder Caleb W. Haws, missionary from Utah, died at Barugh Bridge, near Barnsley, Yorkshire, England.

—The corner stones of the Methodist Episcopal Church, in Salt Lake City, were laid, Rev. Geo. M. Pierce officiating.

Wed. 22.—Ellen Sanders Kimball, one of the three Pioneer women of 1847, died near Salt Lake City, Utah.

—Salt Lake City was entered under the "Town site law".

Sun. 26.—The Roman Catholic Church in Salt Lake City was dedicated.

Mon. 27.—Through intense malice, Judge McKean called up the case of Pres. Brigham Young and thus compelled him to travel all the way from St. George to Salt Lake City in the dead of winter. The judge fixed the trial for Dec. 4th.

—The Summit County Railway Company was organized.

December.—The Salt Lake City authorities arrested a number of prostitutes, who subsequently were released by the Federal officials.

Wed. 13.—Alexander Burt, John L. Blythe, James Toms and John Brazier were arrested in Salt Lake City, accused of the murder of Dr. J. King Robinson in

1866. On the 19th Policeman Brigham Y. Hampton was arrested on a similar charge.

Mon. 18.—An examination of the Robinson murder case was commenced before Justice McKean, in chambers; it was continued for several days. On the 22nd Alexander Burt, one of the accused, was discharged from custody.

Fri. 22.—Harriet Page Wheeler Young, one of the three Utah Pioneer women of 1847, died in Salt Lake City.

Sat. 23.—Patriarch John Murdock died in Beaver, Utah.

Tues. 26.—Pres. Brigham Young arrived in Salt Lake City from St. George.

1872.

This year a secret society, called the "Gentile League of Utah," was organized in Salt Lake City, its alleged object being to break up "Mormon Theocracy." Court proceedings against leading men in the Church were continued. The people of Utah again petitioned Congress for admission into the Union as a State.

January.—The Salt Lake City Street Railway Company was organized.

—Judge James B. McKean refused to have Charles W. Baker arrested for perjury, notwithstanding the proof of his guilt.

Mon. 1.—Zera Pulsipher, formerly one of the seven presidents of the Seventies, died at at Hebron, Washington Co., Utah, over 82 years of age.

Tues. 2.—Pres. Brigham Young was in the Third District Court, but his case was continued until March. Judge McKean refused $500,000 bail for him, and the President was again guarded in his own house by U. S. Deputy marshals.

Wed. 3.—Charles W. Baker, the principal witness against Brigham Young and others, declared under oath that his testimony in court against the accused was utterly false.

Mon. 8.—The twentieth session of the Utah legislature convened in Salt Lake City and organized by electing Lorenzo Snow president of the Council, and Orson Pratt speaker of the House.

Mon. 15.—Elder James McGaw died at Ogden.

Sat. 20.—Alexander Burt was again arrested on the old charge of being connected with the Robinson murder case.

Wed. 24.—Charles W. Baker was arraigned before Justice Jeter Clinton, in Salt Lake City, for perjury. In default of $3,000 bail, he was sent to prison, awaiting the action of the grand jury.

Wed. 31.—James L. High, Deputy U. S. District Attorney, being directed by the U. S. Attorney General at Washington, D. C., and District Attorney Geo. C. Bates, to do so, requested the District Court to admit Brigham Young and other prisoners to bail. The court refused the application.

—A concurrent resolution was passed by the Utah legislature for the election of delegates to a convention, to adopt a State constitution.

February.—A "deadlock" existed in the Utah Federal courts for want of funds to defray expenses.

Thurs. 1.—At the first masquerade ball held in Utah (in Faust's Hall, Salt Lake City), a fearful row occurred, in which Police Officer Andrew Smith was considerably hurt.

Sun. 4.—The Japanese Embassy arrived in Salt Lake City. On the 6th a reception was given it in the City Hall.

Mon. 5.—Edward Samuels and Wm. Hamptou were killed by a snowslide in Big Cottonwood Canyon.

Wed 14.—Bishop Abraham Hoagland, of the 14th Ward, Salt Lake City, died.

Fri. 16.— The Utah legislature adjourned.

Sat. 17.—James G. Blair, of Missouri, delivered a powerful speech in defence of the people of Utah, in the House of Representatives, at Washington D. C.

Mon. 19.—A constitutional convention, for the adoption of proper measures for the admission of Utah into the Union, met in the City Hall, Salt Lake City.

—John Cradlebaugh, formerly associate justice of Utah, died in poverty, at Eureka, Lander Co., Nev.

Thurs. 22.—The Japanese Embassy left Salt Lake City for the East.

Wed. 28.—Patriarch William Cazier, one of the first settlers of Juab County, died at Nephi.

March. *Sat. 2.*—The constitutional convention adopted a constitution and memorial to Congress, asking for the admission of Utah into the Union as a State, and then adjourned *sine die.*

Wed. 6.—Thos. Fitch, Geo. Q. Cannon and Frank Fuller left Salt Lake City for Washington, D. C., as delegates from the late convention, to present to Congress the claims of the proposed State of Deseret.

Thurs. 7.—Wm. W. Phelps died in Salt Lake City.

Wed. 20.—A deputation of friends, mostly ladies, paid a visit of condolence to Hosea Stout, Brigham Y. Hampton and fellow-prisoners, at the City Hall, Salt Lake City.

Fri. 22.—Through malice, the prisoners (Hosea Stout, Brigham Y. Hampton, Alexander Burt, Wm. H. Kimball and John L. Blythe) were removed from the City Hall, Salt Lake City, to Camp Douglas, by order of U. S. Marshal Patrick.

Mon. 25.—Tracklaying was commenced on the Utah Northern narrow gauge railway at Brigham City, Box Elder Co.

April. *Tues. 2.*—The new constitution of the State of Deseret was presented to both houses of Congress, and referred to a special committee, who subsequently reported adversely to Utah's admission as a State.

Thurs. 4.—The members elected to the legislature of the State of Deseret met in Salt Lake City and proceeded to organize. During the session Wm. H. Hooper and Thos. Fitch were elected senators to Congress.

Sat. 6.—The 42nd annual conference of the Church convened in Salt Lake City. It was continued daily until the 9th, when it was adjourned to the 14th, then to the 21st and closed on the 28th.

Mon. 15.—A decision was rendered by the Supreme Court of the United States in the Engelbrecht case, overturning the judicial proceedings in Utah for the last eighteen months, and declaring null indictments against about one hundred and twenty persons, some of whom had been imprisoned for some time.

Thurs. 25.—Pres. Brigham Young was released from custody on a writ of *habeas corpus* from Elias Smith, probate judge of Salt Lake County.

Tues. 30.—Hosea Stout, Wm. H. Kimball, Brigham Y. Hampton, John L. Blythe, Alexander Burt and James Toms were released by the Third District Court, on the strength of the Supreme Court decision, at Washington, D. C. John Brazier had previously been released.

May. *Thurs. 2.*—Thomas Hawkins, of Lehi, was admitted to $5,000 bail, pending an appeal to the Supreme Court of the Territory, and liberated from prison.

Wed. 8.—Ira Reid was killed by lightning, at West Jordan, Salt Lake Co.

Fri. 17.—Columbus Delano, Secretary of the Interior arrived in Salt Lake City, on a visit.

Mon. 20.—Ground was broken for the American Fork (narrow gauge) Railroad, to run up American Fork Canyon.

Sat. 25.—The Salt Lake City Gas Works Company was organized.

June.—The first number of the *Woman's Exponent* was published in Salt Lake City, Miss Lulu L. Greene editor.

Sat. 8.—The first passenger train was run on the Utah Northern Railway.

Wed. 12.—The First Presidency, in a general circular, called on the people for aid to gather the poor Saints from abroad. The sum of $14,000 was donated during the year.

—The steamship *Manhattan* sailed from Liverpool, England, with 221 Saints, in charge of David Brinton. The company arrived at New York June 26th, and at Salt Lake City July 4th.

Sun. 16.—A company of about one hundred journalists from Iowa, arrived in Salt Lake City, on a visit.

—Niels Heiselt, jun., was killed on Twelve Mile creek, Sanpete Co., by Shiverute Indians, who also drove off considerable stock belonging to the settlers.

Wed. 26.—The steamship *Nevada* sailed from Liverpool, England, with 426 Saints, namely, 396 from Scandinavia, 28 from the British Isles and two from Holland, in charge of Eric Peterson. The company arrived at New York July 8th, and at Salt Lake City July 17th.

July. *Thurs. 4.*—Shadrach Roundy, one of the Utah Pioneers of 1847, died in Salt Lake City.

Sun. 28.—The Saints who had settled on Twin Creek, Bear Lake Co., Idaho, were organized into a branch of the Church, called the Georgetown branch, with Philemon C. Merrill as presiding Elder.

Wed. 31.— The steamship *Wisconsin* sailed from Liverpool, England, with 179 Saints, in charge of Geo. P. Ward. The company arrived at New York Aug. 12th, and at Salt Lake City Aug. 20th.

August. *Sat. 3.*—The "Gentile League of Utah", and others, armed to the teeth, held a political meeting in front of the Salt Lake Hotel, Salt Lake City.

Mon. 5.—Elder Geo. W. Grant died near Bountiful, Davis Co.

—At a general election in Utah for delegate to Congress, Geo. Q. Cannon received 20,969 and Geo. R. Maxwell 1,942 votes.

Thurs. 8.—The Rocky Mountain Conference of the Methodist Episcopal Church was organized in Salt Lake City.

Fri. 9. — The Utah Southern Railway commenced to run trains to the Point of the Mountain, south of Draper.

Mon. 12.—Gen. James A. Garfield, after a short visit, left Salt Lake City for Montana.

Sat. 17.—Gen. Henry A. Morrow, with a body of troops, left Camp Douglas for Sanpete Valley, where Indian difficulties of a serious nature existed.

Thurs. 22.—General Morrow made a treaty with Ute Indians, at Springville, Utah Co.

Sat. 24.—Gen. Geo. B. McClellan and party arrived in Salt Lake City, on a visit.

Thurs. 29.—An attempt was made to assassinate Officers Brigham Y. Hampton and Alexander Burt, in Salt Lake City.

—Two houses of ill fame, kept by Kate Flint and Cora Rubodo, were abated in Salt Lake City, under municipal authority, the furniture and other effects being demolished.

Sat. 31.—Indians make a raid on Spanish Fork, Utah Co., stealing horses.

September. *Mon. 2.*—The Walker House, in Salt Lake City, was formally opened.

Tues. 3.—Ground was broken for the Salt Lake City water works, up City Creek.

Wed. 4.—The steamship *Minnesota* sailed from Liverpool, England, with 602 Saints, in charge of Geo. W. Wilkins. The company landed in New York, Sept. 17th, and arrived at Salt Lake City, Sept. 26th.

Sat. 7.—A treaty of peace was concluded by Gen. Morrow with several Indian chiefs, at Mount Pleasant, Sanpete Co.

Tues. 10.—The Bingham Canyon and Camp Floyd Railway Company was organized.

Sat. 21.—Miss Phœbe W. Couzins, of St. Louis, and Miss Georgie Snow, daughter of Judge Zerubbabel Snow, of Salt Lake City, were admitted to the bar in the Third District Court—the first ladies thus admitted in Utah.

Mon. 23.—The Utah Southern Railway was completed to Lehi, Utah Co.

Thurs. 26. — Indians killed Daniel Miller, near Bernard Snow's mill, in Sanpete Valley, and wounded his little son.

October. *Fri. 4.*—Wool was carded at the Provo Woolen Factory for the first time.

Mon. 14.—The Wasatch and Jordan Valley Railway Company was organized. Ground was broken for the road, Nov. 4th.

Tues. 15.—Pres. George A. Smith left Salt Lake City on his trip to Palestine. He was accompanied by Feramorz Little and daughter, and Willis T. Fuller. Afterwards he was joined by others.

Wed. 16.—The steamship *Minnesota* sailed from Liverpool, England, with 203 Saints, in charge of Thos. Dobson. The company arrived at New York, Oct. 29th, and at Salt Lake City, Nov. 7th.

Thurs. 17.—A delegation of Ute Indians (Wanderodes, Antero, Tabiona and Kanosh), accompanied by Dr. Dodge, Indian agent, and Geo. W. Bean, interpreter, left Salt Lake City for Washington, D. C. There they had an interview with President U. S. Grant.

Sun. 20.—The Saints who had settled on the bench northwest of Richmond, Cache Co., Utah, were organized into a branch of the Church (now Lewiston), with Wm. H. Lewis as president.

November. *Wed. 6.*—Twenty-six Saints sailed from Liverpool, England, on the steamship *Nevada*, which, after several days' rough sailing, was forced to return to Liverpool.

Tues. 19.—The Palestine party, consisting of Pres. Geo. A. Smith, Apostle Lorenzo Snow, Elders Feramorz Little, Paul A. Schettler and Geo. Dunford, Sisters Eliza R. Snow and Clara S. Little, arrived in Liverpool, England, from New York.

Tues. 26.—General Thos. L. Kane, of Pennsylvania, arrived in Salt Lake City, on a visit.

—The Germania Smelting and Refining Works, the first of the kind in Utah, commenced operation on Little Cottonwood creek, below the State road.

—The American Fork Railroad was completed to Deer creek, in American Fork Canyon.

December. *Tues. 3.*—Bengt Swenson, of Santaquin, died at Nephi, from the effects of bodily injuries, inflicted by M. Daley, of Payson, at the coal bed in Sanpete County, Nov. 30th.

Wed. 4. — The steamship *Manhattan* sailed from Liverpool, England, with 35 Saints, including those who had returned with the *Nevada*. The company, which was in charge of Daniel Kennedy, arrived at New York Dec. 21st. and at Salt Lake City a few days later.

—Pres. Geo. A. Smith and party, having left London, Nov. 30th, arrived in Amsterdam, Holland, and Dec. 11th they arrived in Paris, France, after having visited Antwerp and Brussels, in Belgium.

Sun. 8.—Major J. W. Powell, chief of the Colorado Exploring Expedition, arrived in Salt Lake City, and reported that the exploration of the Grand Canyon of the Colorado was completed.

Tues. 17.—Pres. Geo. A. Smith and party visited Versailles and were admitted to the hall of the *Corps Legislatif*. In the evening they had an interview with M. Thiers, President of the French Republic.

Wed. 18.—John R. Clawson, a member of the Mormon Battalion, died in Salt Lake City.

Thurs. 19.—The Utah Northern Railway was opened to Mendon, Cache Co.

Mon. 23.—Pres. Brigham Young and party, including Gen. Thos. L. Kane, wife and two sons, arrived at St. George, to spend the winter, having left Salt Lake City about December 12th.

Thurs. 26.—A snowslide at Alta, Little Cottonwood Canyon, resulted in the loss of several lives.

Fri. 27.—Susannah L. Richards, relict of the late Willard Richards, died near Mill Creek, Salt Lake Co.

Sat. 28.—In the Probate Court, Salt Lake City, Charles W. Baker was sentenced to two years' imprisonment for perjury.

1873.

This year there was considerable railroad building in Utah. An unsuccessful attempt was made by a company of Saints to settle Arizona Territory. Pres. Geo. A. Smith and party visited Palestine and other countries.

January. *Wed 1.*—Elder Stephen Winchester died in Salt Lake City.

Fri. 17.—Professor John Tullidge died in Salt Lake City.

Thurs. 23.—David R. Allen, a prominent citizen, died at Sugar House Ward, Salt Lake Co.

Tues. 28.—Associate Justice C. M. Hawley liberated a number of criminals held by the Box Elder County officers for cattle stealing, at Corinne.

Fri. 31.—The Utah Northern Railway was completed to Logan.

February.—A daily anti-Mormon paper, called the *New Endowment*, was published in Salt Lake City, by W. J. Forbes.

Thurs. 6.—Pres. Geo. A. Smith and party arrived at Alexandria, Egypt. Since leaving Paris the party had visited Lyons, Marseilles, Genoa, Rome, Naples, Corfu and other large cities.

Fri. 21.—Major Wm. Pitt, the famous leader of the Nauvoo brass band, died in Salt Lake City.

Sun. 23.—Wm. W. Player, a respected veteran of the Church, died in Salt Lake City.

Tues. 25.—The Frelinghuysen anti-Mormon bill was passed in the U. S. Senate, but failed to come up before the House.

—The Geo. A. Smith Palestine party arrived at Jerusalem.

Thurs. 27.—Pres. Brigham Young returned to Salt Lake City, from St. George, where he had spent the winter. General Thos. L. Kane and family also returned from a trip to southern Utah.

Fri. 28.—The Palestine party visited the Dead Sea; they returned to Jerusalem on the 1st of March.

March. *Sun. 2.*—The Palestine party held solemn worship on the Mount of Olives. After having visited all the noted places in Jerusalem and vicinity, the party left that city March 5th, and journeyed northward, visiting the ancient sites of Shiloh, Shechem (now Nablous), Samaria, Nazareth, Cana, Tiberias, by the sea of Galilee, Bethsaida, Capernaum, Dan and Cesarea Philippi, at the foot of Mount Hermon, and arrived in Damascus, Syria, March 15th. From that city the journey was continued over the mountains of Lebanon to Beyrout, where they embarked on a steamer for Constantinople, Turkey, arriving there April 1st.

Wed. 5.—Elder Wm. C. Staines was set apart for his mission to attend to the emigration of the Saints in New York. He labored efficiently in that business until his death in 1881.

Thurs. 6.—Apostle Erastus Snow and others left Salt Lake City for Europe. They arrived in Liverpool, England, April 1st.

Sat. 8.—Quite a large number having been called by the authorities of the Church to plant colonies in Arizona, a general meeting was held in the Old Tabernacle, Salt Lake City, where they were instructed by Pres. Brigham Young and others concerning their mission.

Mon. 10.—The mason work was commenced on the St. George Temple.

Sat. 15.—Hon. Wm. H. Hooper arrived in Utah from Washington, D. C. He had served the Territory faithfully for ten years, as its delegate to Congress.

April. *Sun. 6.*—The 43rd annual conference of the Church convened in Salt City; it was continued for three days. Owing to infirmities incident to old age, Pres. Brigham Young resigned several minor official positions, and chose five additional Counselors, namely Lorenzo Snow, Brigham Young, jun., Albert Carrington, John W. Young, and George Q. Cannon.

Mon. 14.—Ground was broken for the Salt Lake, Sevier Valley and Pioche Railroad (afterwards the Utah and Nevada), in Salt Lake City.

Sun. 20.—A society for young men's mutual improvement was organized by Apostle Franklin D. Richards and others, at Ogden.

Mon. 21. Elder Calvin C. Pendleton died at Parowan, Iron Co.

May. *Sat. 3.*—The Wasatch and Jordan Valley Railway was completed to Granite, at the mouth of Little Cottonwood Canyon.

—The *Alta Daily Independent*, a newspaper, was first published at Alta, Little Cottonwood Canyon. It only lived a short time.

—On this and the following day an adjourned session of the 43rd annual conference of the Church was held in Salt Lake City.

Wed. 7.—John S. Eldredge, one of the Pioneers of 1847, died at Charleston Wasatch Co., Utah.

Sat. 10.—Elder James D. McCullough died at Panacca (Nevada).

Tues. 13.—James Edwards, a desperado, was killed at Sandy, Utah, after threatening the lives of several citizens.

Wed. 14.—The first car-load of coal was shipped from Coalville, over the Summit County Railway.

Thurs. 15.—Apostle Erastus Snow and son (Erastus W.) arrived in Copenhagen, Denmark, on a visit.

Sun. 18.—Pres. Geo. A. Smith and part of the Palestine party arrived in London, England.

Fri. 23.—James G. Blaine, speaker of the U. S. House of Representatives, arrived in Salt Lake City, on a visit.

—Cyril Call, an aged veteran, died at Bountiful, Davis Co.

Sun. 25.—Feramorz Little and daughter,

of the Palestine party, returned to Salt Lake City.

June. *Mon. 2.*—Lieut. Geo. M. Wheeler, of the U. S. Army, arrived in Ogden, for the purpose of erecting a military observatory at that place.

Wed. 4.—The steamship *Nevada* sailed from Liverpool, England, with 246 Saints, in charge of Charles H. Wilcken. The company arrived at New York June 16th, and at Salt Lake City June 26th.

Sat. 7.—Elder Joseph W. Young died at Harrisburg, Washington Co., Utah.

Mon. 9.—A branch of four miles of the Utah Northern Railway was completed to Corinne, from Brigham City Junction.

Wed. 18.—Pres. Geo. A. Smith returned to Salt Lake City, from his trip to Palestine.

Mon. 30.—Salt Lake City was first lighted with gas.

July. *Wed. 2.*—The steamship *Wisconsin* sailed from Liverpool, England, with 976 Saints, in charge of David O. Calder. The company arrived at New York July 15th, and at Salt Lake City July 24th.

Sat. 5.—Zion's Savings' Bank and Trust Company was organized; Brigham Young, president.

Thurs. 10.—The steamship *Nevada* sailed from Liverpool, England, with 283 Saints, in charge of Elijah A. Box. The company landed in New York July 23rd, and at Salt Lake City Aug. 1st.

Tues. 22.—The Arizona missionaries reached the Little Colorado river. A company of explorers, which was sent out, brought back a discouraging report of the country, whereby the company became disheartened, and returned home.

Wed. 23.—Sylvester H. Earl, one of the Pioneers of 1847, died at St. George, Utah.

Thurs. 24.—Gabriel L. Cotton and his two sons were killed by S. M. Butcher, near the mouth of Bingham Canyon, Salt Lake Co.

Wed. 30.—Severe shocks of earthquake were felt at Beaver.

August. *Fri. 1.*—The first number of the *Provo Daily Times* was issued at Provo, Utah Co. The following year it was changed to a tri-weekly publication called the *Utah County Times.* In 1876 it was discontinued, and the *Advertiser*, a semi-weekly paper, published in its place.

Tues. 5.—Nine stores in Ogden, Utah, were destroyed by fire.

Tues. 26.—A small company of immigrants arrived in Salt Lake City from Australia.

September.—A military post, afterwards known as Fort Cameron, was established near Beaver, Utah.

Wed. 3.—The steamship *Wyoming* sailed from Liverpool, England, with 510 Saints (291 British and 219 Scandinavian), in charge of John B. Fairbanks. The company, after barely escaping shipwreck near Sable Island, landed in New York, Sept. 20th, and arrived at Salt Lake City, Sept. 29th.

Thurs. 4.—Sarah Ann Kimball, widow of Heber C. Kimball, and daughter of the late Bishop Newel K. Whitney, died in Salt Lake City.

Tues. 23.—The Utah Southern Railway was opened for traffic to American Fork.

Sun. 28.—The Wasatch and Jordan Valley Railway made its terminus at Fairfield Flat, in Little Cottonwood Canyon.

October.—Lester J. Herrick succeeded Apostle Albert Carrington as president of the European mission.

Wed. 1.—Zion's Savings Bank and Trust Company commenced business in Salt Lake City. The sum of $6,000 was deposited the first day.

Wed. 15.—A. H. Bowen, chief of police in Provo, was shot by Harrison Carter, a notorious renegade, who escaped, but was afterwards caught in Nevada, brought to Salt Lake City and imprisoned.

Thurs. 16.—The Bingham Canyon Railway was opened for traffic.

Wed. 22.—The steamship *Idaho* sailed from Liverpool, England, with 522 Saints, in charge of John I. Hart. The company arrived at New York, Nov. 4th, and at Salt Lake City, Nov. 14th.

Fri. 24.—The Clift House in Salt Lake City was burned. Estimated loss: $70,000.

Tues. 28.—In the Supreme Court of Utah, Judge McKean reversed his former decision in the Third District Court against Thos. Hawkins.

Fri. 31.—Elder Isaac Laney, a respected citizen, who was wounded in the Haun's Mill massacre, died in the 10th Ward, Salt Lake City.

November. *Thurs. 6.*—John Mullett, of the 16th Ward, Salt Lake City, was accidentally shot and killed, while hunting ducks on the Jordan river.

Tues. 25.—A grand celebration was held in Provo, on the event of the Utah Southern Railway being completed to that city.

Wed. 26.—Geo. White Pitkin, a respected Church veteran, died at Millville, Cache Co., Utah.

Fri. 28.—Pres. Brigham Young and Geo. A. Smith and others left Salt Lake City for St. George, where they arrived Dec. 15th. They spent the winter there.

Sat. 29.—A man and woman were burned to death at Alta, Salt Lake Co.

December. *Mon. 1.*—Notwithstanding Geo. R. Maxwell's protest, Geo. Q. Cannon was permitted to take his seat in Congress.

Sat. 20.—The first number of *Utah Posten*, a weekly newspaper in the Danish-Norwegian language, was published by Peter O. Thomassen, in Salt Lake City. This was the first paper published in a foreign language in Utah.

1874.

The Utah Northern Railway was opened from Ogden to Franklin, Idaho. A large number of Indians joined the Church. Work on the St. George Temple was pushed forward with vigor. The United Order was introduced among the Saints.

January. *Fri. 2.*—Sally W. Phelps, relict of the late Judge Wm. W. Phelps, was killed by a skylight falling from a building near the Townsend House, Salt Lake City.

Mon. 12.—The Utah legislature (21st session) convened in Salt Lake City and organized by electing Lorenzo Snow president of the Council, and Orson Pratt speaker of the House.

Thurs. 29.—Bishop David H. Holliday, of Santaquin, Utah Co., died.

February. *Thurs. 5.*—The Utah Northern Railway was opened for traffic between Brigham City and Ogden.

Thurs. 12.—Bishop John Proctor, of the 10th Ward, Salt Lake City, died.

Mon. 16.—In the House of Representatives at Washington. D. C., Geo. Q. Cannon presented a memorial from the Utah legislature, asking Congress to appoint a commission to investigate Utah affairs, about which the anti-Mormons had made serious complaints.

Wed. 18. — Peter Van Valkenberg, of Union, Salt Lake Co., was shot and killed near his residence. The murderers were soon afterwards captured.

March.—Apostle Joseph F. Smith succeeded Lester J. Herrick as president of the European mission.

Mon. 2.—In the U. S. House of Representatives Geo. Q. Cannon introduced a bill for admitting Utah into the Union as a State.

Sat. 7.—Mrs. Judson, of Fillmore, was burned to death.

April. *Wed. 1.*—A box, containing valuable records, was deposited in the wall of the St. George Temple.

Sat. 4.— David Martin Perkins, formerly a member of the Mormon Battalion, died at Pleasant Green, Salt Lake Co.

Sat. 11.—Robert Lang Campbell, clerk at the Historian's Office, died in the 12th Ward, Salt Lake City.

Mon. 20.— Pres. Brigham Young and Geo. A. Smith, and party, arrived in Salt Lake City, from St. George, where they had spent the winter.

—A party of representative men from Australia visited Salt Lake City, on a tour of inspection.

May. *Sat. 2.*—The Fairview Coal Mining and Coke Company was incorporated.

Sun. 3.—Geo. D. Watt was excommunicated from the Church, at Kaysville, Davis Co., for apostacy.

Wed. 6.—The steamship *Nevada* sailed from Liverpool, England, with 155 Saints, in charge of Lester J. Herrick. The company arrived at New York May 21st, and at Salt Lake City May 30th.

Thurs. 7.—The 44th annual conference of the Church was commenced in Salt Lake City. The principal subject dwelt upon by the speakers was the "United Order", which was organized with Brigham Young as president. The conference was continued until the 10th.

Thurs. 14. — St. Mark's Cathedral (Episcopal) in Salt Lake City was consecrated.

Fri. 15.—Hon. Cyrus W. Field, originator of the Atlantic cable system, and Mr. Kingsley, an eminent English gentleman, accompanied by other men of prominence, arrived at Salt Lake City, on a visit.

Fri. 22.—General Alexander W. Doniphan, favorably known in Church History during the Missouri persecutions in 1838, visited Salt Lake City.

Sun. 24.—The Sevier Stake of Zion was partly organized by Apostles John Taylor and Orson Pratt, with Joseph A. Young as president and Albert K. Thurber as his first counselor.

—Mons. Henri Rochefort, the celebrated Communist leader, who had recently escaped from imprisonment in the French penal settlement, New Caledonia, arrived in Salt Lake City, on a visit.

Fri. 29.—A hurricane did much damage at Ogden.

June.—The Utah Educational Bureau was established in Salt Lake City, by Dr. John R. Park.

Tues. 2.—One hundred Goshute Indians were baptized by the Indian interpreter Wm. Lee in Deep Creek, Tooele Co., Utah. Hundreds of Indians were subsequently baptized at other places, and there was a general religious movement among the Lamanites.

Wed. 10.—Ex-Judge Solomon P. Mc-Curdy, an old and inoffensive man, was assaulted and abused by Thomas Hackett, a soldier.

Thurs. 11.—A party of soldiers from Camp Douglas, under command of Major Gordon, broke into the jail at Salt Lake City and rescued their comrade, Thomas Hackett, who had been confined there for assaulting Solomon P. McCurdy the previous day.

—The steamship *Nevada* sailed from Liverpool, England, with 243 Saints (131 British, 91 Swiss and German, 10 Dutch and 11 Icelandic), in charge of Joseph Birch. The company arrived at New York June 23rd, and at Salt Lake City July 2nd.

Tues. 23.—The so-called Poland bill, "in relation to courts and judicial officers in the Territory of Utah," was approved, having been passed by the U. S. House of Representatives and Senate.

Wed. 24.—The steamship *Idaho* sailed from Liverpool, England, with 806 Saints (about 700 Scandinavian and 110 British), in charge of P. C. Carstensen. The company arrived at New York July 6th, and at Salt Lake City July 15th.

July.—This month was remarkable for much lightning, thunder and rain storms in Utah.

Wed. 1.—Patriarch Thomas Kington died at Wellsville, Cache Co.

Sat. 4.—General Phil. H. Sheridan and party arrived in Salt Lake City, on a visit.

Wed. 8.—The steamship *Minnesota* sailed from Liverpool, England, with 81 Saints, in charge of John Keller. The company arrived at New York July 21st, and at Salt Lake City, July 30th.

Fri. 17.—Thomas Williams, treasurer of Z. C. M. I., and of the Salt Lake Theatre, died suddenly in Salt Lake City.

Sun. 19.—The Glenwood branch, Sevier Co., Utah, was organized as a Ward; Archibald T. Oldroyd, Bishop.

Fri. 24.—The anniversary of the entrance of the Pioneers into Salt Lake Valley was celebrated by a grand juvenile jubilee, in the large Tabernacle, Salt Lake City. Four thousand musicians and singers participated.

August. *Sun. 2.*—Edward L. Sloan, one of the founders of the Salt Lake *Herald*, died in Salt Lake City.

Mon. 3.—At the general election, Geo. Q. Cannon was re-elected Utah's delegate to Congress. He received 22,260 votes, and Robert N. Baskin, the Liberal candidate, 4,513.

—An attempt was made by the "Liberal Party" to get possession of the polls of election in Salt Lake City. U. S. Marshal Maxwell and a *horde* of armed assistants rendered aid. Mayor Daniel H. Wells was mobbed, and considerable rioting done at the City Hall, but the plot proved a failure.

Thurs. 20.—Loptur Johnson, a native of Iceland, was accidentally killed, near Spanish Fork, Utah Co.

Thurs. 27.—General John E. Smith, the new Camp Douglas commander, arrived in Salt Lake City. He succeeded Gen. Henry A. Morrow.

Sat. 29.—John McDonald, sen., fell from a haystack and was killed, in Salt Lake City.

September.—Wm. Fotheringham was arrested at Beaver on a charge of polygamy, and placed under $2,000 bonds.

Wed. 2.—The steamship *Wyoming* sailed from Liverpool, England, with 558 Saints, mostly British, Swiss and German, in charge of John C. Graham. The company arrived at New York Sept. 14th, and at Salt Lake City Sept. 23rd.

Fri. 11.—The U. S. marshal seized the county clerk's office of Tooele County, upon an order issued by Judge McKean.

Wed. 30.—A terrible fire destroyed considerable grain and hay, at Huntsville, Weber Co.

October. *Sun. 4.*—Jay Gould, accompanied by a distinguished party of wealthy railway gentlemen, arrived in Salt Lake City.

—Mrs. Elizabeth Adams, of Bountiful, Davis Co., was shot and killed by an unknown person, while engaged in reading in her own house.

Mon. 5.—Arthur Pratt, Fanny Stenhouse and others were excommunicated from the Church by the High Council, in Salt Lake City. On the 8th Andrew Cahoon was cut off. All these for apostacy.

Tues. 6.—Ephraim Green, formerly a member of the Mormon Battalion, died at Rockport, Summit Co.

Wed. 7.—Patriarch James Lake died at Oxford, Oneida Co., Idaho.

Sat. 10.—Ann Eliza Webb Young, one of Pres. Brigham Young's wives, was excommunicated from the Church.

Sun. 11.—Bishop Andrew H. Scott, of Provo (2nd Ward), Utah Co., died.

—The First Presbyterian Church in Salt Lake City was dedicated.

Wed. 14.—The steamship *Wyoming* sailed from Liverpool, England, with 155 Saints, under the direction of Wm. N. Fife. The company arrived at New York Oct. 26th, and at Salt Lake City Nov. 5th.

Thurs. 22.—The first number of the *Utah Scandinav*, an anti-Mormon weekly newspaper, was issued in Salt Lake City, in the Danish-Norwegian language. After about three years' run it ceased publication.

Mon. 26.—Geo. Reynolds, who had been indicted by the grand jury for polygamy appeared in court and was placed under $2,500 bonds, awaiting trial.

Thurs. 29.—Pres Brigham Young, who for some time had been unwell, left Salt Lake City for the South, accompanied by Geo. A. Smith and other prominent men. They arrived at St. George Nov. 11th.

November. *Thurs. 5.* — A frightful hurricane did considerable damage in Tooele County.

Mon 9.—John D. Lee, of Mountain Meadows celebrity, was arrested at Panguitch, Piute Co.

Thurs. 12.—Geo. Q. Cannon was arrested in Salt Lake City, on a charge of polygamy, and placed under $5,000 bonds.

Wed 25.—Phinehas Richards, brother of the late Pres. Willard Richards, and father of Apostle Franklin D. Richards, died in Salt Lake City.

December. *Fri. 4.*—Wm. Hepworth Dixon, a celebrated English author, visited Salt Lake City.

Wed. 9.—Major Edward P. Duzette, celebrated drummer of the Nauvoo brass band, died at Rockville, Kane Co.

Fri. 25.—The workmen of the St. George Temple had a Christmas assembly in the St. George Tabernacle.

Mon. 28.—Gov. Geo. L. Woods left Salt Lake City for the East, Samuel B. Axtell having been appointed his successor.

1875.

Young Men's Mutual Improvement Association work was made universal throughout the settlements of the Saints. Judge McKean and supporters became very aggressive and caused considerable bitter feeling between the Mormon and anti-Mormon elements in Utah; the judge, however, was superceded by David B. Lowe.

January. *Tues. 5.*—An act of the Idaho legislature, creating Bear Lake County, was approved; Paris was made the county seat.

Fri. 8.—Wm. Fotheringham, of Beaver, was arrested on a charge of "committing adultery with his wife," and placed under $300 bonds.

Sun. 10.—The Utah Western Railway (later the Utah and Nevada) was opened for traffic to Black Rock, on the shore of Great Salt Lake.

Mon. 11.—The explosion of a quantity of oil at the Utah Central Railway station, at Salt Lake City, did considerable damage to property.

—A terrible snowslide, resulting in the loss of four lives and much property, occurred in Little Cottonwood Canyon.

Sat. 16.—Albert Stickney was killed in Summit Canyon, Utah Co., by a snowslide.

Tues. 19.—Six persons were killed by a snowslide, near Alta, Little Cottonwood Canyon.

Wed. 20.—Thomas Broderick, Joseph Ferguson and four other men were killed by a snowslide in Big Cottonwood Canyon. Their bodies were not found until the following spring.

Sun. 24.—A delegation from Salt Lake City had an interview at Ogden with His Majesty Kalakaua, king of the Hawaiian Islands.

February. *Tues. 2.*—Samuel B. Axtell, ninth governor of Utah, arrived in Salt Lake City.

Tues. 16.—The Utah Southern Railway was completed to York, Juab Co.

Fri. 19.—Pres. Brigham Young, who had spent the winter in St. George, arrived in Salt Lake City.

Thurs. 25.—In the case of Brigham Young *vs.* Ann Eliza Young, Judge McKean decided that the defendant, Pres. Brigham Young, should pay $9,500 alimony.

March. *Wed. 3.*—W. G. Thomas was killed by a snowslide, in Little Cottonwood Canyon.

Sun. 7.—A branch of the Church was organized at West Porterville, Morgan Co.

Mon. 8.—Joseph S. Schofield, of Salt Lake City, died at Bellevue, southern Utah.

Tues. 9.—The case of Kate Flint, *vs.* Jeter Clinton *et al.*, for the abatement of her house of ill fame, by the Salt Lake City police officers, was commenced in the Third District Court. The jury disagreed.

Thurs. 11.—Pres. Brigham Young was sentenced to confinement in the Penitentiary, by Judge James B. McKean, for alleged contempt of court, in the Ann Eliza Young case.

Fri. 12.—After 24 hours' confinement, Pres. Brigham Young was released from the Utah Penitentiary.

Tues. 16.—Richard Fryer shot his wife and baby and Thomas Batty, and Fryer was killed by the sheriff, who attempted to arrest the insane murderer, at Toquerville, southern Utah. Mrs. Fryer died of her wounds the same day, Batty on the 17th, and the baby on the 18th.

Wed. 17.—Major Seth M. Blair died at Logan.

Thurs. 18.—Chief Justice James B. McKean, was superceded by the appointment of David B. Lowe, of Kansas.

Sat. 20.—About two hundred Indians from. the desert were baptized at St. George.

Thurs. 25.—William Kay, the founder of Kaysville, Davis Co., died at Ogden.

Wed. 31.—The trial of George Reynolds, for polygamy, was commenced in the Third District Court, in Salt Lake City. The following day (April 1st) the jury brought in a verdict of guilty.

April. *Fri. 2.*—The case of Geo. Q. Cannon, indicted for polygamy, was dismissed in the Third District Court.

Sat. 3.—Wm. H. Dame, indicted on a charge of having participated in the Mountain Meadows massacre in 1857, and who had been imprisoned since October, 1874, was taken out of the Utah Penitentiary and sent to Beaver.

Tues. 6.—The 45th annual conference of the Church was commenced in Salt Lake City. It was continued till the 10th.

Sat. 10.—Geo. Reynolds was sentenced to one year's imprisonment and a $300 fine for polygamy. The case was appealed, and the defendant admitted to bail in bonds of $5,000.

Wed. 14.—John D. Lee, who had been confined at Fort Cameron, was brought before the Second District Court, at Beaver, but the trial was continued for the term.

May. *Wed. 12.*—The steamship *Wyoming* sailed from Liverpool, England, with 176 Saints, under the direction of Hugh S. Gowans and others. The company arrived at New York May 24th, ;and at Salt Lake City June 3rd.

Fri. 14.—Elder John B. Fairbanks died at Payson, Utah Co.

—About two hundred and fifty aged people from Salt Lake County had a pleasant excursion to Dr. Clinton's Hotel, at Lake Point. on the Great Salt Lake. This was the beginning of the Old Folks' annual excursions.

June.—General James A. Garfield arrived in Salt Lake City, on a visit.

Sat. 5.—Elder Wm. Gibson died at Salt Lake City.

Mon, 7.—Elder Ralph Harrison died in Salt Lake City, from the effects of an accident a few days previous.

Tues. 8.—Geo. W. Emery, of Tennessee, was appointed governor of Utah, in place of Samuel B. Axtell, who was removed because of his friendship to the "Mormons."

Thurs. 10.—The first Young Men's Mutual Improvement Association was organized in the 13th Ward, Salt Lake City, with H. A. Woolley as president, and B. Morris Young and Heber J. Grant as counselors.

Tues. 15.—John Burns, a railroad employe, was accidentally killed on the Utah Western (now Utah and Nevada) Railway.

Wed. 16.—The steamship *Wisconsin* sailed from Liverpool, England, with 167 Saints, under the direction of Robert T. Burton. The company arrived at New York June 27th, and at Salt Lake City July 8th.

Sat. 19.—The Territorial Supreme Court reversed the decision in the case of George Reynolds, owing to the illegality of the grand jury that found the bill of indictment.

Mon. 23.—Bishop Culbert King baptized 85 Indians of Kanosh's band, at Kanosh, Millard Co. More than two thousand Indians had been baptized previous to this time.

Wed. 30.—The steamship *Idaho* sailed from Liverpool, England, with 765 Saints, under the direction of Christen G. Larsen. The company arrived at New York July 14th, and at Ogden July 22nd.

July. *Sat. 3.*—Geo. W. Emery, of Tennessee, successor to Samuel B. Axtell as governor of Utah, arrived in Salt Lake City.

Sat. 10.—Martin Harris, one of the Three Witnesses to the Book of Mormon, died in Clarkston, Cache Co., 92 years of age.

Fri. 16.—Philip Klingensmith, an important witness for the prosecution in the John D. Lee case, arrived at Beaver, from California.

Sat. 17.—Pres. Brigham Young, his Counselors and others renewed their covenants by baptism at Ephraim, Sanpete Co. This example was subsequently followed by the Saints generally.

—Emeline Free Young, wife of Pres. Brigham Young, died in Salt Lake City.

Thurs. 22.—Governor Samuel B. Axtell left Salt Lake City for New Mexico, where he had been appointed chief justice.

—The trial of John D. Lee, indicted for murder, was commenced at Beaver.

August. *Sun. 1.*—Geo. W. Hill baptized over three hundred Indians in Box Elder County, Utah, and many of them, who were sick, were miraculously healed under his administration.

Thurs. 5.—Elder Joseph A. Young died at Manti, Sanpete Co., and Amos Fielding died in Salt Lake City.

Sat. 7.—Bishop Wm. Miller, *alias* "Bogus Brigham," died at Provo, Utah Co., and Elder Alphonso Green died at his residence, between Lehi and American Fork, Utah Co.

—After a long trial in the case of John D. Lee, at Beaver, the jury disagreed.

Thurs. 12.—A band of peaceable Indians were driven from their grain fields and lodges on Bear river, by U. S. authority. This was evidently the result of a conspiracy on the part of the citizens of Corinne.

Thurs. 19.—Gen. Philip H. Sheridan and wife arrived in Salt Lake City, on a visit.

Wed. 25.—Robert E. Blard, one of the Utah Pioneers of 1847, died at Lynne, Weber Co., Utah.

September.—Apostle Albert Carrington succeeded Apostle Joseph F. Smith as president of the European mission.

Wed. 1.—Geo. A. Smith, first Counselor to Pres. Brigham Young, died at his home—the Historian's Office—Salt Lake City.

Wed. 15.—The steamship *Wyoming* sailed from Liverpool, England, with 300 Saints, in cl arge of Richard V. Morris. The company landed in New York, Sept. 27th, and arrived at Salt Lake City, Oct. 5.

Sat. 25.—Elizabeth Henriod suicided at. Nephi, Juab Co.

Mon. 27.—Elder Haden W. Church, who labored as a missionary in the Southern States, died at Shady Grove, Hickman Co., Tenn. He was formerly a member of the Mormon Battalion.

October. *Sun. 3.*—U. S. Grant, President of the United States, arrived in Salt Lake City, on a visit. He was met by Pres. Brigham Young and other prominent men at Ogden.

Mon. 4.—Pres. U. S. Grant and party left Salt Lake City for Denver, Colo.

Sat. 9.—At the general conference the large Tabernacle, in Salt Lake City, was dedicated. A large number of missionaries were called during the conference.

Thurs. 14.—The steamship *Dakota* sailed from Liverpool, England, with 120 Saints, in charge of Bedson Eardley. The company arrived at New York Oct. 24th, and at Salt Lake City Nov. 3rd.

Thurs. 28.—Nine buildings in Salt Lake City were destroyed by fire.

Fri. 29.—Pres. Brigham Young was arrested by U. S. Marshal Geo. R. Maxwell, by order of Judge Boreman, on a charge of contempt of court. He had not complied with the order to pay $9,500 alimony to Ann Eliza Young.

Sat. 30.—President Brigham Young deeded some valuable real estate for the B. Y. Academy, at Provo, to the trustees of that institution.

Sun. 31.—Baron Lionel de Rothschild and party arrived in Salt Lake City, on a visit.

November. *Mon. 1.*—The grand jury·

having found another indictment against George Reynolds for polygamy, he was again arrested and placed under $2,500 bonds.

Wed. 3.—Prince Frederick, of Wittgenstein, Count Turenne and Baron Rothschild paid a visit to Pres. Brigham Young, in Salt Lake City.

Mon. 8.—The Saints who had settled near the Sevier river, between Richfield and Glenwood, Sevier Co., Utah, were organized into the Prattville Ward, with Joseph K. Rogers as Bishop.

Tues. 16.—The First National Bank building in Salt Lake City was destroyed by fire; loss about $200,000.

Thurs. 18.—Pres. Brigham Young was discharged from the custody of the U. S. marshal, by order of Chief Justice J. Alexander White.

December.—The ladies of Utah sent a petition having 23,626 signatures to Congress, praying for the admission of Utah into the Union as a State, and the repeal of the anti polygamy laws.

Thurs. 9.—A second trial of George Reynolds for polygamy was commenced in the Third District Court, Salt Lake City.

Tues. 14.—A bill was presented to the U. S. House of Representatives, to enable the people of Utah to form a constitution and State government, and for the admission into the Union as a State.

Sun. 19.—Elder John Snider, one of the first missionaries to England, died in Salt Lake City.

—James McKnight was excommunicated from the Church for apostacy.

Tues. 21.—Geo. Reynolds was sentenced, in the Third District Court, to two years' imprisonment and to pay a $500 fine. Pending an appeal to the Supreme Court, at Washington, D. C., the defendant was admitted to bail in $10,000.

Sat. 25.—Another fatal snowslide occurred in Little Cottonwood Canyon.

1876.

Settlements of the Saints were founded on the Little Colorado river, Arizona. About four thousand persons from different parts of the world visited the Temple Block during this year. The *Utah Musical Times* was published by Calder & Careless, in Salt Lake City.

January. *Fri. 7.* — Daniel W. Jones and company of missionaries crossed the Rio Grande from El Paso Texas to Ciudad Juarez, Mexico, and commenced their labors as the first Latter-day Saint missionaries in that country.

Mon. 10.—The 22nd session of the Utah legislature convened in Salt Lake City, and organized by electing Lorenzo Snow president of the Council, and Orson Pratt speaker of the House.

—Father James Allred, 92 years old, died at Spring City, Sanpete Co.

Wed. 19.—Elder Isaiah M. Coombs, with a company of Saints (about twenty souls), sailed from Liverpool, England, on the steamship *Montana.* The company ar-

rived at New York Jan. 31st, and at Salt Lake City Feb. 6th.

Sun. 30. — Patriarch James Turnbull died in Salt Lake City.

February. *Thurs. 3.*—A number of missionaries, who had been called to locate settlements in Arizona, left Salt Lake City, with teams for that Territory.

Mon. 14.—At the municipal election, Feramorz Little was elected mayor of Salt Lake City.

Fri. 18.—The legislative assembly of Utah closed its session. It had labored diligently in the interest of the people, without compensation. The funds that should have paid its expenses had been appropriated by Congress to pay the expenses of the Federal courts.

Tues. 29.—Robert Harris, a member of the Mormon Battalion, died suddenly at Kaysville, Davis Co.

March. *Tues. 14.*— A fatal snowslide occurred at Ophir, Tooele Co.

—Seven prisoners escaped from the Penitentiary, after having overpowered the guards and fatally wounded Captain Bergher, who died on the 16th. The prisoners were all recaptured.

Fri. 17.—W. D. Phelps, one of the escaped convicts and murderers, was wounded with fatal effect by Sheriff John D. Holladay, who tried to capture him near Santaquin, Utah Co.

Mon. 20.—Elders Daniel W. Jones, Heldman Pratt, James Z. Stewart, Anthony W. Ivins and Wiley C. Jones, of the Mexican missionaries, left Ciudad Juarez for the interior of Mexico; they arrived at Chihuahua, the capital of Chihuahua, April 2nd.

Thurs 23.—The advance companies of Arizona settlers, (called from Utah), arrived at Sunset Crossing, Little Colorado river, Arizona. Others followed, and soon afterwards the settlements of Allen (St. Joseph), Obed, Sunset and Ballenger (Brigham City) were founded by them.

April. *Sat. 1.*—The new Z. C. M. I. building on Main Street, Salt Lake City, was opened for business.

Wed. 5.—Forty tons of powder in magazines on Arsenal Hill, north of Salt Lake City, exploded, resulting in the loss of four lives and great destruction of property. The shock was felt for miles around.

—The Mexican missionaries in the City of Chihuahua mailed about five hundred copies of Trejo's "Selectos" (extracts from the Book of Mormon, translated into Spanish by Milton G. Trejo) to prominent men in the principal cities of Mexico.

Thurs. 6.—The 46th annual conference of the Church convened in Salt Lake City; it was continued for four days.

Sat. 8.—By permission from Gov. Luis Terrazas, the Mexican missionaries held a meeting in the city of Chihuahua. About five hundred people attended. This was the first Latter-day Saint meeting ever held in the interior of Mexico.

Wed. 12.—Father Eleazer Miller, one of the early members of the Church, died in the 12th Ward, Salt Lake City.

Thurs. 13. — P. S. Gillmore, the celebrated music leader, gave a concert in the large Tabernacle, Salt Lake City.

Tues. 18.—The Mexican missionaries arrived at Gerero, at the base of the Sierra Madre Mountains. After holding one meeting there, they returned to the United States.

Sat. 22.—Dom Pedro, emperor of Brazil, and escort, arrived in Salt Lake City, on a visit. On the following day the emperor attended the services in the 14th Ward Assembly Rooms, after which he continued his journey to California.

Sun. 30.—A flood did considerable damage to property in the lower parts of Salt Lake City.

May. *Mon. 1.*—Pres. Brigham Young, accompanied by Daniel H. Wells and others, left Salt Lake City for St. George, where they arrived May 9th.

Mon. 8.—A company of immigrants, 27 souls, from Minnesota, arrived at Salt Lake City.

Thurs. 11.—After a long confinement Wm. H. Dame, John D. Lee and Geo. W. Adair were admitted to bail in the respective sums of $20,000, $15,000 and $10,000.

Wed. 17.—Daniel H. Wells and other Elders started from St. George, on a missionary trip to the new settlements in Arizona.

Wed. 24.—The steamship *Nevada* sailed from Liverpool, England, with 131 Saints, in charge of John Woodhouse. The company arrived at New York June 5th, and at Salt Lake City June 14th.

—Bishop Lorenzo W. Roundy, of Pres. Daniel H. Wells' missionary party, was drowned by the sinking of the ferry boat in the Colorado river, at Lee's ferry, and Pres. Wells and others barely escaped with their lives.

Sun. 28.—Michael Schaeffer, the newly appointed chief justice for Utah, arrived in Salt Lake City.

Tues. 30.—The mail coach was robbed near the Sevier river, in Juab County.

June.—Much property in Utah was destroyed by floods, caused by the sudden melting of snow in the mountains.

Thurs. 8.—The Old Folks of Salt Lake County had a pleasant excursion to Provo, Utah Co.

Mon. 12.—Pres. Brigham Young and party left St. George for Salt Lake City, where they arrived July 1st.

Tues. 13.—The case of George Reynolds, convicted and sentenced to the penitentiary under the anti-bigamy law, was argued before the Supreme Court of the Territory, on appeal.

Sun. 18.—Levi Richards, brother of the late Willard Richards, died in the 20th Ward, Salt Lake City.

Wed. 21.—Mrs. Ann Smart was killed by lightning in Franklin, Oneida Co., Idaho.

Thurs. 22.—The convicts at the Penitentiary, by a bold venture, took possession of the jail, and seven of the prisoners escaped.

Wed. 28.—The steamship *Idaho* sailed from Liverpool, England, with 628 British, Scandinavian and Swiss Saints, in charge of Nils C. Flygare. The company arrived at New York July 10th, and at Ogden July 18th.

July. *Thurs. 6.*—The Supreme Court of Utah confirmed the decision and proceedings of the lower court against Geo. Reynolds. The case was subsequently ap-

pealed to the Supreme Court of the United States.

—David Woolley Evans, Church phonographic reporter, and assistant editor of the *Deseret News*, died in Salt Lake City.

Fri. 14.—Sidney Rigdon, formerly prominent in the Church, died in Alleghany County, New York.

Mon. 17.—Four more convicts escaped from the Penitentiary.

Sun. 23.—Patriarch Levi Jackman, a prominent Elder in the Church and one of the Pioneers of 1847, died at Salem, Utah Co.

Wed. 26.—Samuel L. Evans, of the 6th Ward, Salt Lake City, having been indicted by the grand jury for polygamy, was arraigned in the Third District Court. He pleaded not guilty and was placed under $500 bonds.

Mon. 31.—In the Third District Court, Salt Lake City, Judge Michael Schaeffer rendered a decision in the case of Brigham Young *vs.* Ann Eliza Young, in which the alimony was reduced from $500 to $100 a month.

August. *Tues. 1.*—The first number of *Bikuben*, a weekly newspaper in the Danish language, was published in Salt Lake City, by Anders W. Winberg.

Tues. 8.—Elder Jonathan Pugmire died in Salt Lake City.

Wed. 9.—Wm. Diamond, of Richfield, Sevier Co., was killed by lightning, near that town.

Wed. 16.—Chauncey Loveland, one of the Utah Pioneers of 1847, died at Bountiful, Davis Co., Utah.

Mon. 21.—A band of Navajo Indians arrived in Salt Lake City on a visit.

September. *Sat. 2.*—The order of July 31st not having been complied with, $4,000 worth of property, belonging to Pres. Brigham Young, was attached to satisfy the order for alimony in the Ann Eliza case. The property, however, was not sold.

Sun. 10.—The Saints who had settled on Mink Creek, Oneida Co., Idaho, were organized into the Mink Creek branch of the Church, with Rasmus Rasmussen as president.

Wed. 13. — The steamship *Wyoming* sailed from Liverpool, England, with 322 Saints, in charge of Wm. L. Binder. The company arrived at New York Sep. 23rd, and at Salt Lake City Oct. 3rd.

Thurs. 14.—John D. Lee was again placed on trial in Beaver, Beaver County,for participation in the Mountain Meadows massacre. On the 20th he was convicted of murder in the first degree.

Wed. 20.—Geo. D. Grant, a brother of the late Jedediah M. Grant, died at Bountiful, Davis Co.

Fri. 29.—Earl Dufferin, governor-general of Canada, and party arrived in Salt Lake City, on a visit.

October.—Small pox prevailed in Salt Lake City and Ogden.

Tues. 3.—General Wm. T. Sherman and party arrived in Salt Lake City, on a visit.

Sat. 7.—At the general conference John W. Young, son of President Brigham Young, was sustained as First Counselor to Pres. Young, in place of the late Geo. A. Smith.

Sun. 8.—Lavina Walker, eldest daughter

·of Hyrum and Jerusha Smith, died at Farmington, Davis Co.

Tues. 10.—Judge Jacob S. Boreman sentenced John D. Lee to be shot on Jan 26, 1877.

Mon. 16.—The Brigham Young Academy was founded in Provo.

Wed. 25.—The steamship *Wyoming* sailed from Liverpool, England, with 118 Saints, in charge of Peter Barton. The company arrived at New York Nov. 4th, and at Salt Lake City Nov. 12th.

November. *Wed. 1.*—Pres. Brigham Young, Wilford Woodruff, Geo. Q. Cannon and Brigham Young, jun., accompanied by members of their families, left Salt Lake City for St. George, where they arrived Nov. 9th.

December. *Mon. 4.*—Archibald T. Gardner, son of Bishop Archibald Gardner, of West Jordan, Salt Lake Co., was killed by the explosion of a boiler, at a sawmill, in Little Cottonwood Canyon.

Fri. 8.—A central committe of the Y. M. M. I. Associations was organized at the Council House, Salt Lake City. Junius F. Wells was elected president; Milton H. Hardy and Rodney C. Badger were chosen counselors; John Nicholson, Richard W. Young and Geo. F. Gibbs, secretaries; and Mathoni W. Pratt, treasurer.

Mon. 18.—Elder Wm. S. Phillips, formerly a prominent missionary in Wales, died at Brigham City, Box Elder Co.

Fri. 29.—Two men were killed by a snow slide in Little Cottonwood Canyon.

1877

The first Temple built by the Saints in Utah was dedicated at St. George. The settlements of the Saints were more perfectly organized into Stakes of Zion. President Brigham Young died, and the Council of Twelve Apostles once more took charge of the affairs of the Church. Elders Louis Garff and Milton G. Trejo opened a mission in Sonoro, Mexico, and baptized five in Hermosilla, the capital of Sonoro. The publication of the History of Joseph Smith (Joseph Smith's Levnetsløb) was commenced in Salt Lake City by Elders Andrew Jenson and Joh. A. Bruun. This was the first book published in Utah in the Danish-Norwegian language.

January.—The first number of *Nord-stjernan*, a semi-monthly Church periodical, was published in Gøteborg, Sweden: John C. Sandberg, editor. After issuing a few numbers there, its publication was continued in Copenhagen, Denmark.

—Rich silver mines were discovered near Leeds, southern Utah.

Mon. 1.—The lower part of the St. George Temple was dedicated, under the direction of Pres. Brigham Young. There were present 1,230 persons.

Fri. 5.—Wm. M. Evans, a prominent Elder, died at Nephi, Juab Co.

Tues. 9.—The first ·ordinance for the

dead in the St. George Temple was administered.

Fri. 19.—Samuel Holmes was crushed to death at the Utah Central Railway depot, Salt Lake City.

February.—Garden City, Rich Co., Utah, was settled by Wright A. Moore and others, and organized as a branch of the Church, which became a Bishop's Ward in 1879.

Sat. 3.—Elder Wm. Stevenson died at Holden, Millard Co., Utah.

Sun. 4.—Amasa M. Lyman, once a member of the Council of Twelve Apostles, died at Fillmore, Millard Co.

Sat. 24.—The first number of the *Silver Reef Echo* was published at Silver Reef, Utah; Joseph E. Johnson, editor and publisher.

Sun. 25.—The Saints who had settled Redmond, Sevier Co., Utah, were organized into a Ward; John Johnson, Bishop.

March. *Thurs. 1.*—Thos. Heath was accidentally drowned in the Jordan river, near Salt Lake City. His body was not found until four weeks afterwards.

Tues. 6.—A company of Latter-day Saints from Utah, under the direction of Daniel W. Jones, arrived on Salt river, Arizona, and encamped near the present site of Lehi, Maricopa Co.

Wed. 7.—In the Second District Court, at Beaver, John D. Lee was re-sentenced to be executed March 23rd.

Sun. 11.—Matthew Ingram and Jared Pratt were killed by a snowslide, near Alta, Little Cottonwood Canyon.

Mon. 12.—Levi P. Luckey, who, on Feb. 13, 1877, had been appointed secretary for Utah, arrived in Salt Lake City.

Sun. 18.—Lyman Leonard, one of the early settlers, died at Salt Lake City.

Fri. 23.—John D. Lee was executed at the Mountain Meadows, southern Utah.

Thurs. 29.—Wm. P. Tippets, once a member of Zion's Camp, died at Three Mile Creek, Box Elder Co., Utah.

April. *Fri. 6.*—The 47th annual conference of the Church was commenced in the Temple at St. George. Pres. Brigham Young, his Counsleors, most of the Apostles and a number of leading Elders were present, and the Temple was fully dedicated. Pres. Daniel H. Wells offered the dedicatory prayer. A more perfect organization of the various Stakes of Zion was commenced, and John D. T. McAllister was (on April 7th) appointed president of the St. George Stake, with Thos. J. Jones and Henry Eyring as his counselors. A number of missionaries were called.

Fri. 13.—The Old Folks of the 20th Ward, Salt Lake City, were treated to a sumptuous supper at the meeting house. There was no general excursion arranged for the old folks this year.

—Elder Levi W. Riter died in Salt Lake City.

Wed. 18.—At a two days' meeting held at Kanab, Kane Co., the Kanab Stake of Zion was organized, with L. John Nuttall as president, and Howard O. Spencer and James L. Bunting as counselors.

Mon. 23.—At a two days' meeting held at Panguitch, Piute (now Garfield) Co., Utah, the Panguitch Stake of Zion was organized by Apostles John Taylor, Lorenzo

Snow and Erastus Snow, with James Henrie as president, and Geo.W. Sevy and Jesse W. Crosby, jun., as counselors.

Wed. 25.—The temple site at Manti, Sanpete Co., was dedicated. Pres. Brigham Young offered the dedicatory prayer.

—The military post recently located near Beaver City was named Fort Cameron, by order of Asst. Adjutant-General R. Williams.

Fri. 27.—Pres. Brigham Young and party returned to Salt Lake City from St. George.

—The case of Ann Eliza Young *vs.* Brigham Young was finally decided in the Third District Court, Salt Lake City, the alimony being disallowed.

Mon. 30—Ground was broken for the Manti Temple.

May. *Wed. 2.*—Elder Briant W. Nowland was accidentally killed at Mr. Black's sawmill, in Butterfield Canyon, Salt Lake Co.

Thurs. 3.—Elder Miles Romney, a prominent Elder, died at St. George, Utah.

Sun. 6.—The Saints who had founded Kingston, Circle Valley, Piute Co., were organized as a branch of the Church; Wm. King, presiding Elder.

Thurs. 10.—Bishop Aaron Johnson died at Springville, Utah Co.

Sun. 13.—At a special conference held in Salt Lake City, Angus M. Cannon was sustained as president of the Salt Lake Stake of Zion, with David O. Calder and Joseph E. Taylor as counselors.

Fri. 18.—The ground for the Logan Temple was dedicated. Apostle Orson Pratt offered the dedicatory prayer.

Sun. 20.—The first converts to "Mormonism" among the Pima Indians were baptized at Camp Utah, on Salt river, Ariz. Among them was the chief Che-eh-chum.

Mon. 21.—At a Priesthood meeting held in Logan, the Cache Stake of Zion was partly reorganized: Moses Thatcher, president; Wm. B. Preston and Milton D. Hammond, counselors. Pres. Brigham Young delivered a very important discourse on Priesthood.

Sun. 27.—At a special conference held at Ogden, Utah, the Weber Stake of Zion was partly reorganized; with David H. Peery, president; Lester J. Herrick and Charles F. Middleton, counselors.

—On this and the following day, Salt Lake City and Ogden was visited by an editorial excursion from Nevada.

Mon. 28.—The reorganization of the Weber Stake was completed by the appointment of Ward officers. Ogden was divided into four Wards, instead of three as heretofore, with Francis A. Brown as Bishop of the First, Robert McQuarrie of the Second, Winslow Farr of the Third and Nils C. Flygare of the Fourth Ward. The several settlements and districts in Weber County, which hitherto had existed only as branches of the Church, were organized, as Bishop's Wards, namely, Riverdale (Sanford Bingham, Bishop); Harrisville (Pleasant G. Taylor, Bishop); North Ogden (Amos Maycock, Bishop); Plain City (Lewis W. Shurtliff, Bishop); Slaterville (John A. Allred, Bishop); Lynne (Daniel F. Thomas, Bishop); Mar-

riott's (Jas. Ritche, Bishop); Mound Fort (David Moore, Bishop); Huntsville (Francis A. Hammond, Bishop); Eden (Josiah M. Ferrin, Bishop); West Weber (John I. Hart, Bishop); and Hooper, (Gilbert Belnap, Bishop).

Wed. 30.—Elders Helaman Pratt and George Terry commenced a short mission among the Yaquis Indians, Sonora, Mexico.

Thurs. 31.—Jerome B. Stillson, correspondent of the New York *Herald*, alleged that an attempt on his life had been made in Salt Lake City. The affair was investigated and resulted unsatisfactorily to Stillson.

June.—Apostle Joseph F. Smith succeeded Apostle Albert Carrington as president of the European mission.

Wed. 6.—The settlement of Santaquin, Utah Co., Utah, was organized as a Ward; Geo. Halladay, Bishop.

Thurs. 7.—The Saints at Gunlock, Washington Co., Utah, were organized as a branch of the Church; Dudley Leavitt, as president.

Mon. 11.—Alderman Walter Thomson died at Ogden.

Tues. 12.—Dr. Ezekiel Lee died in Salt Lake City.

Wed. 13.—The steamship *Wyoming* sailed from Liverpool, England, with 186 Saints, in charge of David K. Udall. The company arrived at New York June 23rd, and at Salt Lake City July 3rd.

Thurs. 14.—Benson Ward, Cache Co., was organized; Alma Harris, Bishop.

Sun. 17.—At a special conference, held at Farmington, a Stake of Zion was organized in Davis County, with Wm. R. Smith, of Centreville, as president, and Christopher Layton, of Kaysville, and Anson Call, of Bountiful, as counselors.

—At a special meeting held at West Jordan, Salt Lake Co., that Ward was divided into four Wards, namely: North Jordan, with Samuel Bennion as Bishop, West Jordan, with Archibald Gardner as Bishop, Fort Herriman, with James Crane as Bishop, and South Jordan, with Wm. A. Bills as Bishop.

Mon. 18.—The Pinto settlement, Washington Co., was organized as a Ward; Robert Knell, Bishop.

Wed. 20.—At a special meeting, held at Bountiful, that Ward was divided into three parts, namely: East Bountiful, West Bountiful and South Bountiful, with Chester Call, Wm. T. Muir and William Brown as their respective Bishops.

Sun. 24.—At a special meeting held at Tooele, Tooele Co., the Tooele Stake of Zion was organized, with Francis M. Lyman as president, and James Ure and Wm. Jeffries as counselors. Three new Wards were partly organized, namely, E. T. City (Wm. F. Moss, Bishop); Lake View (Moses Martin, Bishop), and Vernon (John C. Sharp, Bishop).

Tues. 26.—South Hooper, Davis Co., which formerly constituted a part of the Kaysville Ward, was organized as a separate Ward; Henry B. Gwilliams, Bishop.

Wed. 27.—The steamship *Wisconsin* sailed from Liverpool, England, with 714 Saints, in charge of John Rowberry. The company arrived at New York July 7th, and at Salt Lake City July 14th.

Fri. 29.—South Weber, which had formerly belonged to the Weber Stake of Zion, was organized as a Ward, with David S. Cook as Bishop, and attached to the Davis Stake of Zion.

July.—Elder John Jaques, who for six years past had occupied the position as assistant editor of the *Deseret News*, was appointed to take temporary charge of the Historian's office, during the absence of Historian Orson Pratt on a special mission to England. Elder Charles W. Penrose was appointed assistant editor of the *Deseret News*.

Sun. 1.—The Saints residing in Morgan County were organized as the Morgan Stake of Zion, with Willard G. Smith, as president, and Richard Fry and Samuel Francis, counselors. The following Wards were also organized: North Morgan, Wyman M. Parker, Bishop; South Morgan, Charles Turner, Bishop; Richville, Albert D. Dickson, Bishop; East Porterville, Joseph R. Porter, Bishop; Milton, Eli Whitear, Bishop; Enterprise, John K. Hall, Bishop; Croyden, John Hopkins, Bishop; and Weber (Peterson), Charles S. Peterson, Bishop.

—At a special conference held at Nephi, Juab Co., Utah, the Saints residing in Juab County were organized as the Juab Stake of Zion with George Teasdale as president. (This organization was a continuation of the Nephi Stake of Zion organized in 1868.) Nephi was divided into two Wards, with Joel Grover as Bishop of the South and Charles Sperry as Bishop of the North Ward. Levan and Mona, which previously had existed as branches of the Church, were organized into Wards, the former with Niels Aagaard and the latter with John M. Hawes as Bishop.

—South Cottonwood, Salt Lake Co., was divided into three Wards, namely, South Cottonwood, Union and Granite, with Joseph S. Rawlins, Ishmael Phillips and Solomon J. Despain as Bishops, respectively.

Wed. 4.—The Sanpete Stake of Zion was reorganized with Canute Peterson as president and Henry Beal and John B. Maiben as counselors. Eleven new Wards were partly organized, namely, Chester, Reddick N. Allred, Bishop; Fayette, John Bartholomew, Bishop; Thistle Valley (Indianola), Jefferson Tidwell, Bishop; Mayfield, O. C. Olsen, Bishop; Manti South Ward, Hans Jensen, Bishop; Manti North Ward, Wm. T. Reid, Bishop; Ephraim North Ward, Lars S. Andersen. Bishop; Ephraim South Ward, Carl C. N. Dorius, Bishop; Mt. Pleasant North Ward, Orange Seeley, Bishop; Mt. Pleasant South Ward, Wm. S. Seeley, Bishop; Pettyville (Sterling), Wm. G. Petty, Bishop, and Wales, John E. Reese, Bishop. Gunnison, Mayfield and Fayette, which formerly belonged to the Sevier Stake organization, were made a part of the Sanpete Stake.

Thurs. 5.—The eastern part of the Twentieth Ward, Salt Lake City, was organized as the Twenty-first Ward; Andrew Burt, Bishop.

Mon. 9.—The Saints residing in Summit County, Utah, were organized by Apostles John Taylor, Lorenzo Snow and Franklin D. Richards as the Summit Stake of Zion; Wm. W. Cluff, president; Geo. G. Snyder and Alma Eldredge, counselors. The organization of six new Wards was also provided for, namely: Echo (Elias Asper, Bishop); Henefer (Charles Richens, Bishop); Hoytsville (Andrew Hobson, Bishop); Parley's Park (Joseph H. Black, Bishop); Upton (Charles Staley, Bishop), and Rockport (Edward Bryant, Bishop.

Tues. 10.—Preston Thomas, sen., a prominent Elder was accidentally killed at Franklin, Oneida Co., Idaho.

Sun. 15.—East Mill Creek Ward (Salt Lake Co.), formerly the north part of Big Cottonwood Ward, was organized as a separate Ward; John Neff, Bishop.

—At a special conference held at Heber, Wasatch Co., Utah, the Wasatch Stake of Zion was organized by Apostles John Taylor and Franklin D. Richards, with Abram Hatch as president and Thomas H. Giles and Henry S. Alexander as counselors. Six new Wards were organized, namely, Centre (Benjamin Cluff, Bishop); Charleston (Nymphus C. Murdock, Bishop); Heber West Ward (Wm. Foreman, Bishop); Heber East Ward (Thos. Rasband, Bishop); Midway (David Van Wagener, Bishop, and Wallsburg (Wm. E. Nuttall, Bishop).

—At a special conference held at Richfield, Sevier Co., the Sevier Stake of Zion was reorganized by Apostles Orson Hyde and Erastus Snow, with Franklin Spencer as president; Albert K. Thurber and Wm. H. Seegmiller, counselors. Several new Wards were organized, namely, Richfield First Ward, Paul Poulsen Bishop; Richfield Second Ward, Tarleton Lewis, Bishop; Elsinore, Joshua W. Sylvester, Bishop; Central (Inverary), Wm. A. Steward, Bishop; Vermillion, Peter Gotfredsen, Bishop; Grass Valley, Joseph H. Wright, Bishop, and Joseph City, Gideon A. Murdock, Bishop.

Thurs. 19.—Dr. Jeter Clinton was arrested at Tooele, on a trumped up charge of murdering John Banks in 1862. He was brought to Salt Lake City and imprisoned in the Penitentiary.

Sun. 22.—At a special conference held at Fillmore, Millard Co., Utah, the Millard Stake of Zion was reorganized, with Ira N. Hinckley as president, and Edward Partridge and Joseph V. Robison as counselors. Fillmore was divided into two Wards called the North and South Ward, with Alexander Melville as Bishop of the North Ward. Meadow Creek, Holden and Oak Creek, which hitherto had existed as branches, were organized into Wards with Hyrum B. Bennett, David R. Stevens and Platte D. Lyman as their respective Bishops. Joseph S. Black was appointed Bishop of Deseret, which place had been resettled.

Mon. 23.—Farmers Ward, Salt Lake Co., was organized; Lewis H. Mousley, Bishop.

Tues. 24.—President Brigham Young deeded 9,642 acres of land in Cache Valley to the B. Y. College, at Logan.

Thurs. 26.—At a special conference held at Beaver, the Beaver Stake of Zion was organized; John R. Murdock, president; John Ashworth and Marcus L. Shepherd, counselors.

Tues. 31.—The first cremation in Salt Lake City took place, Dr. Chas. F. Winslow, who had died July 7th, having made provision for this disposition of his body, in his will.

August.—Geo. Q. Cannon and Brigham Young, jun., succeeded David O. Calder as editors and publishers of the *Deseret News*.

After the death of Willard Richards, the first editor of the *Deseret News*, in March, 1854, Albert Carrington occupied the position as editor of the paper till March, 1859, when he was succeeded by Elias Smith, whose name appeared as editor and proprietor until September, 1863, when Albert Carrington again became editor. In November, 1867, he was succeeded by Geo. Q. Cannon, whose name appeared as editor and publisher till August, 1873, when David O, Calder became editor and publisher, continuing thus till 1877.

Sat. 4.—After severe sufferings at the Penitentiary, Dr. Jeter Clinton was removed to the county jail, Salt Lake City. Some time afterwards he was set at liberty.

—Glendale, Kane Co., was organized as a Ward; James Leathead, Bishop.

Sun. 5.—At a Stake conference held at Panguitch, Piute Co., Kingston, Hillsdale, Clinton (afterwards named Cannonville), and Escalante were organized as Wards, with Wm. King, Seth Johnson, Jonathan T. Packer and Andrew P. Schow as their respective Bishops.

Tues. 7.—Johnson, Kane Co., was organized as a Ward; Sixtus E. Johnson, Bishop.

Thurs. 9.—Apostle Orson Pratt arrived at Liverpool England, to superintend, the republication of the Book of Mormon and the Doctrine and Covenants, but soon afterwards he was called home, on account of the death of Pres. Brigham Young.

Sun. 12.—Spring Lake branch, Utah Co., was organized as a Ward; Benjamin F. Johnson, Bishop.

Sun. 19.—At a special conference held at Brigham City, Utah, the Box Elder Stake of Zion was organized, with Oliver G. Snow as president, and Elijah A. Box and Isaac Smith as counselors. Brigham City was divided into four Wards, with Henry Tingey as Bishop of the First Ward, Alvin Nichols of the Second, John D. Burt of the Third, and John Welch of the Fourth. Bishops were also appointed for the smaller settlements, namely: Alonzo Perry, for Three Mile Creek; Geo. W. Ward, for Willard; Peder C. Jensen, for Mantua; Thos. Harper, for North Ward; Abraham Hunsaker, for Honeyville; John C. Dewey, for Deweyville; H. J. Faust for Corinne; Wm. Neeley, for Bear River City; Arnold Goodliffe, for Curlew (now Snowville); Samuel Kimball, for Grouse Creek; Oliver C. Hoskins, for Portage; Geo. Dunford, for Malad City, and Samuel Williams, for Samaria. The three last named Wards were in Malau Valley, Idaho; all the others in Box Elder Co., Utah.

Fri. 24.—A delegation of fifteen Navajo Indians, among whom was the principal chief of the tribe, arrived in Salt Lake City.

Sat. 25.—At a special conference held at Paris, Bear Lake Co., Idaho, the Bear Lake Stake of Zion was reorganized, with Wm. Budge as president, and James H. Hart and Geo. Osmond as counselors. Bishops for the different settlements in the Stake were also appointed, as follows: Henry J. Horne, Paris First Ward; Robt. Price, Paris Second Ward; Henry Lewis, Georgetown; Joseph Moore, Bennington; Henry H. Dalrymple, Preston; Peter Jensen, Ovid; Edwin N. Austin, Liberty; John A. Hunt, St. Charles, and Charles E. Robison Montpelier. At the continuation of the conference the following day (Sun. 26th), Wm. Hulme was sustained as Bishop of Bloomington, Robert Pope of Fish Haven, Ira Nebeker of Laketown, Joseph Kimball of Meadowville, Randolph S. Stewart of Randolph, and Wm. H. Lee of Woodruff.

Wed. 29.—Pres. Brigham Young died at his residence, in Salt Lake City.

September. *Sat. 1.*—Elder John Bennion died at North Jordan, Salt Lake Co.

Sun. 2.—The funeral of Pres. Brigham Young took place from the large Tabernacle, Salt Lake City.

Tues. 4.—The Twelve Apostles publicly assumed their position as the head of the Church of Jesus Christ of Latter-day Saints.

Wed. 5.—The first number of the *Territorial Enquirer* was issued at Provo, Utah Co.; John C. Graham, editor.

Wed. 12.—Apostles Orson Pratt and Joseph F. Smith (and family) and Franklin S. Richards sailed from Liverpool, England, bound for Utah. The affairs of the European mission were left in the temporary charge of Elder Henry W. Naisbitt.

—Elder John Hubbard, of Willard, Box Elder Co., Utah, died at the Wichita reservation, Kan.

Mon. 17.—The corner stones of the Logan Temple were laid.

Wed. 19.—The steamship *Wisconsin* sailed from Liverpool, England, with 482 Saints, in charge of Hamilton G. Park. The company landed at New York Sept. 30th, and arrived at Salt Lake City Oct. 6th.

Thurs. 27.—Apostles Orson Pratt and Joseph F. Smith arrived at Salt Lake City, from their missions to Europe.

Fri. 28.—The corner stones of the Salt Lake Assembly Hall were laid near the southwest corner of the Temple Block, Salt Lake City.

Sat. 29.—Hannah Fielding, widow of Joseph Fielding and one of the first who embraced the gospel in England, died at Ogden.

—O. Porter Rockwell was arrested and imprisoned in Salt Lake City, being charged with murder, said to have been committed about twenty years before. Oct. 5th, he was admitted to bail in the sum of $15,000.

October. *Sat. 6.*—On this and the following day, the semi-annual conference of the Church was held in Salt Lake City; John Taylor, presiding. John W. Young and Daniel H. Wells, formerly Counselors to Pres. Brigham Young, were sustained as Counselors to the Twelve Apostles.

Tues. 9.—Elder James T. Lisonbee, of Monroe, Sevier Co., died at Springville, Utah Co., on his way home from a mission to the Southern States.

Sat. 13.—The Utah Stake of Zion, (originally known as the Provo Stake), embracing the Saints residing in Utah County, Utah, was reorganized by Apostles John Taylor, Wilford Woodruff and Erastus Snow, with Abraham O. Smoot as president and David John and Harvey H. Cluff as counselors. Two new Wards were organized, namely: Provo Fifth Ward (Lake View), with Peter Madsen as Bishop, and Salem, with Robert H. Davis as Bishop.

Wed. 17.—The steamship *Idaho* sailed from Liverpool, England, with 150 Saints, in charge of Wm. Paxman. The company arrived at New York Oct. 29th, and at Salt Lake City Nov. 7th.

Tues. 23.—The Saints at Portage, Box Elder Co., were organized as a Ward of the Box Elder Stake of Zion; Oliver C. Hoskins, Bishop.

November. *Thurs. 1.*—Elder John S. Higbee, one of the Pioneers of 1847, died at Toquerville, Washington Co.

Wed. 7.—The first number of the *Amateur* was published by the Y. M. M. I. Association of Ogden; Joseph A. West, editor.

Tues. 13.—Patriarch Philip B. Lewis died at Kanab, Kane Co.

Sun. 18.—The Saints residing on the Weber river, below the mouth of Weber Canyon, Weber Co., were organized as the Easton Ward; Ira N. Spaulding, Bishop.

Thurs. 29.—A company of Latter-day Saint settlers from Utah arrived on the San Pedro river, Arizona. They became the founders of St. David.

December. *Sun. 9.*—The Saints who had settled at Almy, principally as coal miners, were organized as the Almy Ward; James Bowns, Bishop.

Sun. 16.—The Saints who had settled in Rabbit Valley (now Wayne Co.), Utah, were organized as a branch of the Church, called the Rabbit Valley branch; Jeremiah Stringham, president; the branch was organized as a Ward in 1878,with Geo. S. Rust as Bishop; still later it was named Loa.

Fri. 21.—Samuel Pitchforth, the first person baptized on the Isle of Man, died at Nephi, Juab Co,

—The woolen factory at Brigham City, Box Elder Co., was destroyed by fire.

Mon. 31.—The Saints at Dingle Dell, Bear Lake Co., Idaho, were organized as a branch of the Bear Lake Stake of Zion; Wm. Passey, presiding Elder

1878.

Settlements of the Saints were located in Castle Valley, Utah; San Luis Valley, Colo.; and on Salt river, Ariz. Two Stakes of Zion were organized in Arizona. The Book of Mormon was translated into the Swedish language by August W. Carlson, and published at Copenhagen, Denmark, by Nils C. Flygare.

January.—The first Latter-day Saint settlers at Mesa, Maricopa Co., Ariz., located.

Wed. 2.—The first number of the Salt Lake *Independent* was issued in Salt Lake City. It only continued its career about two months.

Mon. 14.—The 23rd session of the Utah legislature convened in Salt Lake City, and organized by appointing Lorenzo Snow president of the Council, and Orson Pratt speaker of the House.

Sun. 20.—Elder Llewellyn Harris arrived at a village of the Zuni Indians, in New Mexico. About four hundred of these Indians, who were suffering with small pox, were said to have been healed under his administration.

Fri. 25.—Ebenezer Brown, member of the Mormon Battalion, died at Draper, Salt Lake Co.

Sun. 27.—The Saints who had settled on the Little Colorado river, Apache Co., Arizona, were organized as a Stake of Zion, with Lot Smith as president, and Jacob Hamblin and Lorenzo H. Hatch as counselors. Geo. Lake was ordained Bishop of Brigham City (formerly Ballinger): Levi M. Savage, Bishop of Sunset. John Kartchner was appointed presiding Elder of Taylor, and John Bushman, acting Bishop of St. Joseph (formerly Allen). This was the first Stake of Zion organized in Arizona.

February. *Sat. 9.*—Capt. John Robinson died at Birch Creek, Weber Co.

March. *Fri. 15.*—Philip T. Van Zile took the oath of office as district attorney for Utah.

Sat. 16.—Major Howard Egan and Burr Frost, both Pioneers of 1847, died in Salt Lake City.

Sun. 17.—Col. Stephen Markham died at Spanish Fork, Utah Co.

Wed. 20.—Elder James Z. Stewart, of Draper, left Salt Lake City on a special mission to explore for a location, upon which the Saints, who emigrated from the Southern States, could settle. This mission led to the purchase of Mexican claims in Conejos County, Colorado, where settlements subsequently were made.

Sun. 24.—Adamsville, Beaver Co., was organized as a Ward of the Beaver Stake of Zion; Joseph Henry Joseph, Bishop.

April. *Wed. 3.*—The Utah Northern Railway was sold at auction in Salt Lake City, the Union Pacific Railroad Company being the purchaser. The name of the road was changed to the Utah and Northern.

Sat. 6.—The 48th annual conference of the Church was commenced in Salt Lake City. It was continued till the 8th.

Fri. 12.—Elder E. W. Street, a young missionary from Utah, died at Breachwood, Green Heath, Herts, England.

May. *Fri. 17.*—Bishop David Brinton died suddenly at Big Cottonwood, Salt Lake Co.

—Hon. E. B. Washburn and party arrived in Salt Lake City, on a visit.

Sun. 19.—Daniel R. Sellers and Mary A. Kirtland, with their respective families, arrived at a place near Los Cerritos, Conejos Co., Colo., as the first Saints from the

Southern States to settle in San Luis Valley, which had been selected by the authorities of the Chnrch as a gathering place for the Saints from the Southern States. Other families soon followed.

Sat. 25.—The steamship *Nevada* sailed from Liverpool, England. with 354 Saints, under the direction of Thos. Judd. The company arrived at New York June 5th, and at Salt Lake City June 13th.

June.—A small four-page paper called the St. George *Union* was first published at that place by J. W. Carpenter.

—Grasshoppers did considerable damage in Utah.

Sat. 1.—Berne, Bear Lake Co., Idaho, waⁱ organized as a branch of the Church, with John Kunz, sen., as president. The branch was organized into a Ward in 1890.

Mon. 3.—Isaiah Huntsman, a member of the Mormon Battalion, died at Annabella, Sevier Co.

Thurs. 6.—Richmond, Ray Co., Mo., was partly destroyed by a cyclone, in which a number of the old anti-Mormon mobocrats were injured and others killed.

Sat. 8.—Lydia Partridge, relict of the late presiding Bishop Edward Partridge, died at Oak City, Millard Co.

Sun. 9.—O. Porter Rockwell died in Salt Lake City.

Tues. 11.—About five hundred and fifty persons participated in the Salt Lake County Old Folks' excursion to Ogden, where the aged people had a splendid time.

Sat. 15.—The steamship *Montana* sailed from Liverpool, England. with 221 Saints, in charge of Theodore Brandley. The company arrived at New York June 25th, and at Salt Lake City July 3rd.

Wed. 19.—Wm. V. Morris, a painter of ability, died in Salt Lake City.

Sat. 22.—A party of eleven persons were accidently drowned in Funk's Lake, near Manti, Sanpete Co., while boat-riding.

Thurs. 27.—Elder Daniel S. Thomas died at Lehi, Utah Co.

Sat. 29.—The steamship *Nevada* sailed from Liverpool, England, with 569 Saints, in charge of John Cook. The company arrived at New York July 10th, and at Salt Lake City July 18th.

July. Tues. 2.—In a horse race, at St. Charles, Bear Lake Co., Idaho. Thomas G. Rich, son of Apostle Charles C. Rich, was accidentally killed.

Fri. 5.—Elder Joseph E. Hyde, who was returning from a mission to England, died on board the steamship *Nevada*.

Sat. 6.—William Budge, of Paris, Idaho, arrived in Liverpool, England, as successor to Apostle Joseph F. Smith in the presidency of the European mission.

Thurs. 11.—John Whitmer, one of the Eight Witnesses to the Book of Mormon, died at Far West, Caldwell Co., Mo.

August. Thurs 1.—A fire broke out in Alta, Little Cottonwood Canyon, destroying nearly the whole camp, except a few cabins. Loss: $100,000.

Fri. 16.—The tower of the St. George Temple was struck by lightning and slightly damaged.

September. Tues. 3.—Apostles Orson Pratt and Joseph F. Smith, accompanied by other Elders, left Salt Lake City on a special mission to the States.

Fri. 6.—Two small boys, sons of Joshua Terry, of Draper, Salt Lake Co., were buried in a sandbank and killed.

Mon. 9.—Apostles Orson Pratt aud Joseph F. Smith visited Far West, Mo., after previously visiting David Whitmer at Richmond. They afterwards visited Kirtland, O., and the hill Cumorah, N. Y.

Sat. 14.—The steamship *Wyoming* sailed from Liverpool, England. with 609 Saints, in charge of Henry W. Naisbitt. The company arrived at New York, Sept. 25th, and at Salt Lake City, Oct. 3rd.

Sat. 21.—A small company of Saints sailed from Liverpool, England, on the steamship *Nevada*, in charge of J. C. Christensen.

Tues. 24.—The Saints who were settling on Silver Creek, Apache Co., Ariz., were organized by Apostle Erastus Snow as a Ward; John Hunt, Bishop. The next day (Sept. 25th) Apostle Snow located the townsite, which was named Snowflake, in honor of Erastus Snow and Wm. J. Flake.

Wed. 25.—Joseph Farnsworth was accidentally killed, while working in a coal mine at Coalville, Summit Co.

Fri. 27.—Sam Kaealoi, a native of the Marquesas Islands, was accidentally killed on the Temple Block, Salt Lake City.

Sat. 28.—The Saints who had settled near the top of the Mogollon Mountains, Arizona were organized by Apostle Erastas Snow as the Forest Dale Ward; Oscar Mann, Bishop.

October. Sun. 6.—Bishop Hans Jensen and other brethren from Manti, Utah, arrived at Los Cerritos, Conejos Co.,Colo., on a special mission to help locate the Saints from the Southern States in the San Luis Valley.

Tues. 8.—The trial of Sylvanus Collett for the murder of the Aiken party in 1857 commenced at Provo. On the 16th, after a long trial, the jury returned a verdict of not guilty.

Sat. 12.—The Saints who were settling in the San Luis Valley. Colo., were organized as a branch of the Church with Bishop Hans Jensen as president, and John Allen and Søren E. Berthelsen as counselors. This was the commencement of settlements which afterwards became the San Luis Stake of Zion.

Fri. 18.—A destructive fire at the Ontario mine, near Park City, caused a loss of $100,000, and heavy consequential damage.

Sat. 19.—The steamship *Wyoming* sailed from Liverpool, England, with 145 Saints, in charge of Aurelius Miner. The company arrived at New York Oct. 29th, and at Salt Lake City Nov. 6th.

Fri. 25.—John Miles was arrested for bigamy or polygamy, CarollneOwen,claiming to be his first wife, being the principal witness. The defendant was admitted to bail in $1,500.

Thurs. 31.—After several days' preliminary examination before Commissioner Sprague, John Miles, accused of polygamy, was again placed under $1,500 bonds, to await the action of the grand jury.

November. Thurs. 14.—On this and the following day the case of Geo. Reynolds was argued before the Supreme Court of the United States.

Sat. 16.—A woman's mass meeting was

held in the Salt Lake Theater, numerously attended and addressed by prominent ladies. Resolutions were adopted with unanimity, in which the "Mormon" women claimed ability and the right to represent themselves.

Wed. 20.—James Fielding, a Church veteran, died in Salt Lake City.

Wed. 27.—A letter was sent by Pres. John Taylor, directing the division of the settlements of the Saints in Arizona into two Stakes, making Berardoes (now Holbrook) the dividing point between the Little Colorado Stake, on the West, and the Eastern Arizona Stake, on the East.

Thurs. 28.—Apostle Orson Hyde died at Spring City, Sanpete Co.

Sat. 30.—Washington Phipps was murdered by John H. Boynton, near Escalante, Iron Co.

December. *Mon. 9.*—Annie White and Mercy Robinson were burned to death at the Insane Asylum, near Salt Lake City.

Sat. 21.—Apostle Orson Pratt, accompanied by Elder Brigham S. Young, again arrived in Liverpool, England.

Tues. 24.—Isaac Sampson, one of the early members of the Church, died at Glenwood, Sevier Co.. Utah.

1879.

Settlements of the Saints were located on the San Juan river; in Ashley Valley, Utah; and in eastern Arizona. A branch of the Church was organized in Mexico.

January.—The Saints who had settled on Cottonwood, Ferron and Huntington creeks, Castle Valley, were organized into branches of the Church.

Sat. 4.—Elder Hugh Findlay arrived at Lerwick, to open the gospel door on the Shetland Islands. After encountering a number of difficulties, he succeeded, on March 31st, in baptizing two persons, as the first fruits of preaching the gospel on these islands.

Sun. 5.—Ex-Judge James B. McKean died in Salt City, of typhoid fever.

Mon. 6.—The Supreme Court of the United States unanimously confirmed the constitutionality of the anti-bigamy law of 1862, and confirmed the sentence of the lower courts upon George Reynolds.

Sat. 11.—A Ward organization was effected at Bunkerville, Lincoln Co., Nev., with Edward Bunker as Bishop.

Sat. 18.—Price Ward, near St. George, Utah, was organized, with Robert Gardner as Bishop.

Thurs. 30. — Norton Jacob, one of the Pioneers of 1847, died at Glenwood, Sevier Co.

February. *Sat. 1.*—Dimick B. Huntington, Indian interpreter, and formerly a member of the Mormon Battalion, died in Salt Lake City.

Mon. 3.—Elder Thomas R. King died at Kingston, Piute Co.

—At a meeting of the Saints in San Luis Valley, Colo., it was decided to locate a settlement there to be called Manassa.

The townsite was surveyed the following spring.

Mon. 10. — Henry Wadman, jun., was killed by Joseph Dudley, at Plain City, Weber Co.

Sun. 16.—Gunlock branch, Washington Co., Utah, was organized as a Ward; Joseph S. Huntsman, Bishop.

Thurs. 20.—The trial of Robert T. Burton, on a charge of murder during the Morrisite difficulty in 1862, was commenced in the Third District Court, Salt Lake City. On March 7th a verdict of not guilty was rendered.

March.—Joseph C. Fisher located with his family on Poole's Island, north of Eagle Rock, as the first Latter-day Saint settler in Snake River Valley, Idaho.

Sun. 23.—At a meeting held in Ogden, Utah, Lester J. Herrick and Chas. F. Middleton, of the Weber Stake presidency, organized a company of Saints to settle on Snake river, Idaho, with John R. Pool as president.

Fri. 28.—A company of Saints from Georgia and Alabama, in charge of Elder John Morgan, arrived at Alamosa, the end of the railroad track, and proceeded by wagons to the camp of the Saints, near Los Cerritos, Conejos Co., Colo., where they arrived the next day.

April. *Sun. 6.*—The 49th annual conference of the Church, which was continued three days, commenced in Salt Lake City. A number of Elders were called on foreign missions. Moses Thatcher was chosen as one of the Twelve Apostles to fill the vacancy in the Council of the Apostles caused by the death of Orson Hyde. He was ordained on the 7th.

Mon. 14.—The corner stones of the Manti Temple were laid.

Sat. 19.—The steamship *Wyoming* sailed from Liverpool, England, with 170 Saints, in charge of Chas. W. Nibley. The company arrived at New York April 30th, and at Salt Lake City May 8th.

Thurs. 24.—The first Utah wheat was shipped by ocean to Liverpool, England, from San Francisco, in the sailing vessel *Ivy*, by S. W. Sears.

Sun. 27.—Father Hezekiah Thatcher died in Logan, Cache Co.

Wed. 30.—Emma Smith, formerly the wife of Joseph Smith, the Prophet, died at Nauvoo, Ill.

May. *Thurs. 1.* — After several days' exertion in getting a jury suitable for the prosecution, the trial of John Miles for polygamy began in the Third District Court, Judge Emerson presiding.

Sat. 3.—Daniel H. Wells was sentenced by Judge Emerson to two days' imprisonment in the Territorial Penitentiary, for alleged contempt of court, in refusing to describe the endowment clothing.

Tues. 6.—Daniel H. Wells was released from prison, and there was a grand demonstration in his honor.

—John Miles was convicted of polygamy.

Fri. 16.—Wallace Wilkerson, a murderer, was executed in Provo.

Sat. 24.—The steamship *Wyoming* sailed from Liverpool, England, with 700 Saints, in charge of Alexander F. Macdonald. The company arrived at New York June 3rd, and at Salt Lake City June 11th.

Sat. 31.—Silas S. Smith and company of explorers and settlers arrived on the San Juan river, in southeastern Utah, with a view to locating a settlement of the Saints there.

June. *Sun. 1.*—At a special conference held in Ashley Valley, Utah, the Saints, who had settled on the Ashley fork of Green river, were organized into three districts, named Incline, Ashley Centre and Mountain Dell, with Fred. G. Williams, Jeremiah Hatch and Thos. Bingham as their respective presidents.

—Panguitch, Iron Co., was divided into two Wards, with Joseph C. Davis as Bishop of the First and Geo. W. Sevey as Bishop of the Second Ward.

Thurs. 5.—Elder Frederick Walter Cox, sen., died at Manti, Sanpete Co.

Fri. 13.—The Utah Southern Railway was opened to Juab, Juab Co.

—Suit was commenced in the Third District Court by a few of Pres. Brigham Young's heirs against the executors of the estate.

Sat. 14.—George Reynolds was re-sentenced in the Third District Court of Utah, and on the 16th he left Salt Lake City for Lincoln, Nebraska, to be confined there in the State Penitentiary.

Sat. 21.—Elder Jonathan Browning died at Ogden, Utah.

Tues. 24.—The Old Folks of Salt Lake County had a grand excursion to American Fork, Utah Co. Of the six hundred participants, 405 were over seventy years of age.

Sat. 28.—The steamship *Wyoming* sailed from Liverpool, England, with 622 Saints, in charge of William N. Williams. They arrived at New York July 8th, and at Salt Lake City, July 16th.

July. *Wed. 2.*—John A. Hunter, of Missouri, was appointed chief justice of the Supreme Court of Utah. He arrived in Salt Lake City Aug. 4th, following.

Thurs. 10.—The Deseret Sunday School Reader was issued from the press. It was the first effort of the Deseret Sunday School Union toward supplying the children of the Latter-day Saints with desirable and appropriate readers.

Sat. 12.—John Taylor, Geo. Q. Cannon, Brigham Young and Albert Carrington were arrested on an order issued by Judge Jacob S. Boremah, for contempt, in not having delivered certain Church property to Receiver Wm. S. McCornick.

Mon. 14.—The Saints in Park Valley, Box Elder Co., were organized as a Ward; Erastus D. Mecham, Bishop.

Thurs. 17.—Geo. Reynolds was returned to Utah, to be confined in the Territorial Penitentiary.

Mon. 21.—Joseph Standing was shot and killed by a mob, near Varnell's Station, Whitfield Co., Georgia, where he had labored as a missionary.

Thurs. 31.—The body of the martyred Joseph Standing arrived in Salt Lake City, in charge of Rudger Clawson.

August. *Sat. 2.*—Timothy Saben Hoyt, a member of the Mormon Battalion, died at Nephi, Juab Co.

Sun. 3.—The funeral services of Elder Joseph Standing were held in the large Tabernacle, Salt Lake City.

Mon. 4.—Geo. Q. Cannon, Albert Carrington and Brigham Young, executors of the estate of Pres. Brigham Young, were confined in the Utah Penitentiary, for alleged contempt of court.

Tues. 5.—The Trustee-in-Trust of the Church of Jesus Christ of Latter-day Saints commenced suit against the heirs, executors and receivers of the estate of Brigham Young, deceased.

Sat. 9.—Wm. M. Evarts, Secretary of State, issued his noted letter of instructions to diplomatic officers of the United States in various countries against "Mormon" emigration.

Sun. 10.—Apostle George Q. Cannon preached in the Penitentiary.

Sat. 16.—Apostle Orson Pratt left Liverpool, England, for Utah, having accomplished the work assigned him in procuring electrotype plates for new editions of the Book of Mormon and Doctrine and Covenants. He had been ably assisted in his labors by Joseph Bull, John Nicholson and others.

Thurs. 28.—The order of Judge Boreman, committing Geo. Q Cannon, Brigham Young and Albert Carrington to the Penitentiary for alleged contempt, was reversed by the Supreme Court of Utah and set aside; the prisoners were released.

September.—The first number of the *Logan Leader* was issued at Logan, Cache Co.

Mon. 1.—Bishop Daniel Daniels died at Malad, Oneida Co., Idaho.

Sat. 6.—Six men were suffocated in the Lavinia Mine, near Alta, Little Cottonwood Canyon.

—The steamship *Wyoming* sailed from Liverpool, England, with 336 Saints, in charge of Nils C. Flygare. The company arrived at New York Sept. 16th, and at Salt Lake City Sept. 24th.

Tues. 9.—Elder Elijah Fordham died in Wellsville, Cache Co., over 81 years of age.

Thurs. 25.—John T. Hilton was run over by railroad cars and killed, at Sandy, Salt Lake Co.

Sat. 27.—Martha Howell, relict of the late Wm. Howell (first Latter-day Saint missionary to France), died at Wellsville, Cache Co.

Sun. 28.—Major Chas. H. Hempstead died in Salt Lake City.

October. *Sat. 4.*—The first number of the *Contributor* was issued in Salt Lake City ; Junius F. Wells, editor.

—The suit of the heirs of the late Pres. Brigham Young *vs.* the administrators of the estate was settled by the Church paying the heirs $75,000.

Tues. 7.—Canute Peterson, Pres. of the Sanpete Stake of Zion, organized the Saints who had settled on Huntington creek, Castle Valley, Utah, as Huntington ; Ward Elias Cox, Bishop. On the same day, the Saints who had settled on Cottonwood creek, in the same valley, were organized by Pres. Peterson as Castle Dale Ward ; Jasper Petersen, Bishop.

Wed. 8.—Ernest I. Young, son of Pres. Brigham Young, died suddenly in Salt Lake City.

Thurs. 9.—The Saints who had settled on Ferron creek, Castle Valley, were organized as Ferron Ward, by Pres. Canute Peterson; Wm. Taylor, Bishop.

Fri. 10.—Phineas H. Young, brother of the late Pres. Brigham Young, and one of the Pioneers of 1847, died in Salt Lake City.

Sat. 18.—The steamship *Arizona* sailed from Liverpool, England, with 224 Saints, in charge of Wm. Bramall. The company arrived at New York Oct. 27th, and at Salt Lake City Nov. 5th.

Mon. 20.—The Saints who had settled on Bear river, northeast of Preston, Oneida Co., Idaho, were organized as the Riverdale branch of the Church; Abraham Peter Davis, president.

Tues. 21.—The Saints who had settled on Worm Creek, Oneida Co., Idaho, were organized as the Worm Creek Ward; Nahum Porter, Bishop. This settlement was subsequently named Preston, in honor of Presiding Bishop Wm. B. Preston.

Wed 22.—The murderers of Elder Joseph Standing were acquitted by the Circuit Court of Whitfield County, Georgia, after a short trial.

November. *Fri. 7.*—The steamship *Arizona, en route* from New York to Liverpool, and having four Utah Elders on board, collided with an iceberg and was greatly damaged, in consequence of which it had to seek shelter in St. Johns, Newfoundland, and lie up for repairs.

Tues. 11.—Job Rowland, one of the first Latter-day Saints who emigrated from Wales, died at Logan, Cache Co.

Sat. 15.—Apostle Moses Thatcher and Elders James Z. Stewart and Meliton G. Trejo arrived in the city of Mexico, as Latter-day Saint missionaries.

Sun. 16.—The Saints who had settled in Marsh Valley, Bingham Co., Idaho, were organized as Marsh Valley Ward; Melvin L. Gruce, Bishop.

Wed. 19.—The first Young Men's Mutual Improvement Association in Scandinavia was organized in Copenhagen, Denmark, with Andrew Jenson as president.

Thurs. 20.—The first Female Relief Society in Scandinavia was organized in Copenhagen, Denmark, with Johanne Christine Nordstrøm as president.

—Apostle Moses Thatcher baptized and confirmed Plotino Constantino Rhodacanaty and Silviano Artiago in the city of Mexico, as the first fruits of preaching the gospel in the interior of Mexico.

Sun. 23.—Elder Meliton G. Trejo baptized six persons in the city of Mexico, who together with the two previously baptized were organized into the first branch of the Church in Mexico, by Apostle Moses Thatcher and fellow-missionaries, with Plotino C. Rhodacanaty as president, and Silviano Artiago and Jose Ybarola as counselors. These three brethren were also ordained Elders.

Mon. 24. — Ammon M. Tenney was appointed by Apostle Wilford Woodruff to preside over the Saints who were settling at St. Johns, Apache Co., Ariz.

—Wm. Dykes, one of the Pioneers of 1847, died in Nebraska.

Tues. 25.—The city council of Salt Lake City adopted a resolution for constructing the Jordan River and Salt Lake City Canal.

Wed. 26. — Elder Albert P. Rockwood,

one of the First Seven Presidents of the Seventies, died in Sugar House Ward, near Salt Lake City.

December. *Thurs. 4.* — Elder Wm. Clayton died in Salt Lake City.

Thurs. 11.—Henry Hoskins, a member of the Mormon Battalion, died in Salt Lake City.

1880.

A number of settlements in Utah, Idaho, Arizona and Nevada were organized as Bishops' Wards. Three new counties were created by the Utah legislature. The Church celebrated its fiftieth anniversary with a grand jubilee, and successful missionary work was carried on by the Elders in foreign lands.

January. *Wed. 7.*—The first number of *Ungdommens Raadgiver,* a small monthly periodical, published in the interest of the young Latter-day Saints in Scandinavia, was issued in Copenhagen, Denmark; Andrew Jenson, editor.

Mon. 12.—The 24th session of the Utah legislature convened in Salt Lake City, and organized by appointing Lorenzo Snow president of the Council, and Orson Pratt speaker of the House.

February.—An act was passed by the Utah legislature, authorizing the city council of Salt Lake City to borrow money for the completion of the Jordan River and Salt Lake City Canal. Emery, San Juan and Uintah Counties were created by legislative acts.

Sun. 8.—The Saints who had settled on Otter creek, or the East Fork of the Sevier river, Piute Co., Utah, were organized as a branch of the Church called Wilmot; John D. Wilcox, presiding Elder.

Mon. 9.—The trial of parties charged with the murder of Dr. J. King Robinson, in 1866, was called, and, on motion of the prosecuting attorney, dismissed, notwithstanding the defendants demanded a trial.

Sun. 22.—The Saints who had settled on the Mesquite Flat, near Bunkerville, Nev., were organized as the Mesquite Ward; Wm. H. Branch, Bishop.

Sun. 29.—Eli H. Murray, the 11th governor of Utah, and successor of Gov. Geo. W. Emery, arrived in Salt Lake City.

March. *Wed. 3.*—James Whittaker, sen., died in Cedar City, Iron Co.

Thurs. 4.—The Salt Lake weekly *Herald* was first issued.

Sun. 14.—The Saints who had settled at Concho, Apache Co., Ariz., were organized as a branch of the Church with B. H. Wilhelm as presiding Elder.

Fri. 19.—John D. Rees, one of the first settlers of Brigham City, died at Malad, Idaho.

April. *Fri. 2.*—Col. Peter Litz, the first member of the Church in Virginia, died in Burke's Garden, Tazewell Co., Va.

Sun. 4.—Public meetings were held in the Salt Lake Assembly Hall for the first time.

Mon. 5.—Salt Lake City decided by vote, to build the Salt Lake and Jordan Canal.

—The co-operative store at Monroe, Sevier Co., was destroyed by fire.

—Bluff City, on the San Juan river, was settled by a company of Latter-day Saints from Iron County.

Tues. 6.—At a conference of the Y. M. M. I. Associations, held in the Salt Lake Assembly Hall, Wilford Woodruff was appointed general superintendent of all the associations in the Church, with Joseph F. Smith and Moses Thatcher as his counselors. Junius F. Wells, Milton H. Hardy and R. C. Badger were sustained as assistants to the general superintendency, Heber J. Grant as secretary, and Wm. S. Burton as treasurer.

—On this and three following days the 50th annual conference of the Church was held in Salt Lake City. It was voted to remit $802,000 of the indebtedness to the P. E. Fund, in favor of the worthy poor, and to distribute 1,000 cows and 5,000 sheep among the needy. The Saints were advised to be charitable and liberal toward one another, and make this a jubilee year by forgiving the worthy poor their debts, and thus relieve them from bondage. Wm. W. Taylor was sustained as one of the seven presidents of the Seventies, to fill the vacancy caused by the death of Albert P. Rockwood.

Sat. 10.—The steamship *Wyoming* sailed from Liverpool, England, with 120 Saints, in charge of James L. Bunting. The company arrived at New York April 21st, and at Ogden and Salt Lake City April 30th.

Tues. 13.—The Utah Central Railway depot and adjoining hotel, at Sandy, Salt Lake Co., was destroyed by fire.

Sun. 18.—Elder Wm. C. Martindale was appointed to preside over the Saints who had settled in Goose Creek Valley and vicinity, Cassia Co., Idaho.

Fri. 23.—Mary Parker, an aged lady, was outraged and cruelly murdered, near Rockville, Kane Co. Jared Dalton was subsequently arrested, suspected of the crime.

May. *Mon. 3.*—The corner stone of St. Paul's Chapel (Episcopal), Salt Lake City, was laid by the Masonic fraternity.

Tues. 4.—Rosewell Stevens, one of the Pioneers of 1847, died at Bluff, San Juan Co., Utah.

Sun. 9.—A branch of the Church was organized in Spring Basin, Cassia Co., Idaho, where a few families of Saints had located.

Sat. 15.—The Utah Southern Railway was opened to Milford, Beaver Co.

Mon. 24. — John Y. Greene, one of the Pioneers of 1847, died in Salt Lake City.

June. *Sat. 5.*—The steamship *Wisconsin* sailed from Liverpool, England, with 332 Saints, in charge of John G. Jones. The company arrived at New York June 15th, and at Salt Lake City June 25th.

Wed. 23.—The Utah Southern Railway was opened to Frisco.

Sat. 26. — A small company of Saints from Iceland sailed from Liverpool, England, bound for Utah.

July. *Sat. 3.*—John F. Turner, son of Sheriff John Turner, of Provo, was killed by Fred. Hopt (Welcome), at Park City, Summit Co. The body, which the murderer

conveyed to Echo Canyon, was found there July 10th.

Thurs. 8.—The Old Folks of Salt Lake County had a grand excursion to Black Rock, on the shore of Great Salt Lake.

Sat. 10.—The steamship *Wisconsin* sailed from Liverpool, England, with 727 Saints, in charge of Niels P. Rasmussen. The company landed at New York July 21st, and arrived at Salt Lake City July 29th.

Tues. 20.—According to the census return, Utah had a population of 143,690, showing an increase of 56,904 since 1870.

Sun. 25.—Fred. Hopt (Welcome), the murderer, arrived in Salt Lake City, in custody of Sheriff John Turner, who had arrested him at Cheyenne, Wyo., on the 23rd.

August.—Apostles Erastus Snow and Brigham Young and other prominent men visited Castle Valley, Emery Co., Utah, and appointed Christen G. Larsen to preside over the Saints who were locating in that part of the country.

Thurs. 5.—Under the administration of the Elders, Eliza Robinson, of the Birmingham branch, England, was instantly healed of ulcers, after fifteen years suffering.

Tues. 17.—A stately monument was erected on the grave of the martyred Joseph Standing, in the Salt Lake City cemetery.

Wed. 18.—Jonathan H. Holmes, a member of the Mormon Battalion, died at Farmington, Davis Co.

Thurs. 19.—Elders Serge L. Ballif, Morris D. Rosenbaum and John Kienke were arrested and imprisoned at Berlin, Germany, and on the following day ordered out of the country for preaching the gospel.

September.—The Saints who had settled on the San Juan river, southeastern Utah, were organized as Bluff Ward, by Apostles Erastus Snow and Brigham Young, Jens Nielsen, Bishop.

Sat. 4.—The steamship *Nevada* sailed from Liverpool, England, with 337 Saints, in charge of John Rider. The company arrived at New York Sept. 15th, and at Salt Lake City Sept. 25th.

Sun. 5.—Rutherford B. Hayes, President of the United States, Mrs. Hayes and party, visited Salt Lake City.

Sat. 11.—An electric light exhibition was given in Salt Lake City, in front of Z. C. M. I.

Sat. 18.—Bishop Jonathan Pugmire, a prominent Elder, died at St. Charles, Bear Lake Co., Idaho.

Tues. 21.—John Orson Angus, a prominent Elder, died at St. George, Utah.

Sun, 26.—Dr. Thos. De Witt Talmage, in a sermon at the "Brooklyn Tabernacle," N. Y., suggested the annihilation of the "Mormons" by the Ft. Douglas artillery.

—At a priesthood meeting held at Snowflake, Ariz., the Saints who had settled on the Gila river were organized as Smithville Ward; Joseph K. Rogers, Bishop.

—At a Stake conference held at Snowflake, Apache Co., Ariz., Bush Valley branch was organized as Alpine Ward; Edward A. Noble, Bishop. The Saints who had located in Round Valley, Apache

Co., Ariz., were organized as a Ward; Peter C. Christoffersen, Bishop. The Saints composing the Concho branch, Apache Co., Ariz., were organized as the Erastus Ward; Sixtus E. Johnson, Bishop. The Saints constituting the settlement of Woodruff, Apache Co., Ariz., were organized as the Woodruff Ward, with James C. Owens as Bishop; and the Saints who had settled above Snowflake were organized as the Walker (now Taylor) Ward; Henry Standifird, Bishop.

October. *Sun. 10.*—At the general conference held in Salt Lake City, the First Presidency of the Church was reorganized, with John Taylor as President, and Geo. Q. Cannon and Joseph F. Smith as Counselors. The vacancies thereby occurring in the Council of the Twelve Apostles were partly filled by the calling of Francis M. Lyman and John Henry Smith to the Apostleship. These two brethren were ordained Apostles Oct. 7th.

Sat. 23.—The first number of the *Bear Lake Democrat* was issued at Paris, Bear Lake Co., Idaho.

—The steamship *Wisconsin* sailed from Liverpool, England, with 258 Saints, in charge of John Nicholson, The company arrived at New York Nov. 2nd, and at Salt Lake City Nov. 11th.

Fri. 29. — At a special meeting held at Milford, Beaver Co., Utah, the Saints residing at that place were organized as Milford Ward, of the Beaver Stake of Zion; Wm. McMillan, Bishop.

Sat. 30.—Gordon S. Bills and another Elder were mobbed in Lawrence County, Ky.

Sun. 31.—The Willow Springs branch, Malad Valley, Idaho, was organized as the Cherry Creek Ward; John D. Jones, Bishop.

November. *Tues. 2.* — At the general election in Utah for delegate to Congress, Geo. Q. Cannon, the Peoples' Party candidate, received 18,568 votes; and Allen G. Campbell, the Liberal Party candidate, 1,357 votes.

Sat. 6. — Apostle Albert Carrington succeeded Wm. Budge as president of the European mission.

Sun. 7.- The mining town of Bingham, Bingham Canyon, Salt Lake Co., was partly destroyed by fire.

Mon. 8. — Hon. Jonathan C. Wright died at Brigham City.

December. *Mon. 6.*—Geo. H. Luke and Hans C. Madsen, of Manti, Sanpete Co., were accidentally killed, while working on the Denver and Rio Grande Railway, in Colorado.

Sat. 11. — The Utah Eastern Railway was completed from Coalville to Park City.

Tues. 14.—Elder Geo. Lamb died in St. George.

1881.

A number of prominent Elders in the Church died. Several new settlements were founded by the Saints, and there was general prosperity throughout the Church.

January. *Sat. 8.*—Notwithstanding the fact that Geo. Q. Cannon was elected delegate to Congress with 17,211 majority, Gov. Eli H. Murray issued a certificate of election to the minority candidate, Allen G. Campbell.

Sun. 9.—A branch of the Church was organized at Beaver Bottom, Millard Co., with Thos. Naylor as presiding Elder.

Wed. 12.—Between this date and the 17th fifteen lives were lost through snowslides in Little Cottonwood and American Fork canyons; $60,000 worth of property was also destroyed.

Sat. 15.—The Wasatch Flour Mill, on the State Road, Salt Lake Co., was destroyed by fire.

—The dead body of Charles Jensen, of Rush Valley, Tooele Co., was found. He had been murdered.

Thurs. 20.—Geo. Reynolds was released from the Penitentiary, his term of imprisonment having expired.

Sun. 23.—Freeborn Demill, one of the early members of the Church, died at Manti, Sanpete Co.

February. *Fri. 4.*—Z. C. M. I. store at Ogden was dedicated.

Tues. 15.—The Saints who had settled in Grand Valley, Utah, were organized as the Moab Ward, by Apostles Francis M. Lyman and Heber J. Grant; Randolph H. Stewart, Bishop.

Wed. 16.—The trial of Fred. Hopt (Welcome), for the murder of John F. Turner, was commenced in the Third District Court, Salt Lake City. On the 19th the jury returned a verdict of guilty.

Sun. 27.—Aurora Ward, Sevier Co., was organized; Jabez Durfee, Bishop.

March. *Thurs. 3.*—A number of men were killed by an explosion in a coal mine, at Almy, near Evanston, Wyoming.

Sat. 12.—Elder Samuel L. Evans died in Salt Lake City

April. *Sun. 3.*— On this and the following three days the 51st annual conference of the Church was held in Salt Lake City. A number of missionaries were called to go abroad and others to settle in Arizona.

Mon. 4.—Fred. Hopt, *alias* Welcome, the murderer, was sentenced to be shot on May 20th. The case was appealed.

—The U. S. Supreme Court reversed the decision of the Utah courts in the John Miles polygamy case, and a new trial was ordered.

Sun. 17.—James Drysdale was shot and killed by Peter Moore, at Hooperville, Weber Co.

—The steamship *Wyoming* sailed from Liverpool, England, with 186 Saints, in charge of David C. Dunbar. The company arrived at New York April 26th, and at Salt Lake City May 5th.

May. *Mon. 2.*—The first issue of the *Ogden Herald* was published in Ogden, Utah; John Nicholson, editor; Edward H. Anderson, business manager.

Sat. 21.—The steamship *Wyoming* sailed from Liverpool, England, with 278 Saints, in charge of Joseph R. Matthews. The company arrived at New York June 1st, and at Salt Lake City June 10th.

Mon. 23.—A company of 27 Saints from New Zealand arrived in Salt Lake City, in charge of George Batt.

Wed. 25.—The Old Mill, or Locust Farm,

containing 110 acres, was purchased by Salt Lake City, for a public park.

Thurs. 26.—The Union Pacific and Central Pacific transfer depot and twenty cars of merchandise, at Ogden, were destroyed by fire.

June.—Three railroads, namely, the Utah Central, Utah Southern and Utah Southern Extension, were consolidated as one corporation under the name of the Utah Central Railway, with a capital of $4,325,000. The new corporation commenced business July 1st.

Sat. 4.—Elder Henry Emery died in the 16th Ward, Salt Lake City.

Sat. 11.—Patriarch John Stoker died at Bountiful, Davis Co.

Sun. 12.—The Saints who had settled in the Tonto Basin and vicinity, Ariz., were organized as a Ward; Riel Allen, Bishop.

Wed. 22.—The Old Folks of Salt Lake County had a pleasant excursion to Ogden.

Sat. 25.—The steamship *Wyoming* sailed from Liverpool, England, with 775 Saints, in charge of Samuel Roskelley. The company arrived at New York July 7th, and at Ogden July 15th.

Mon. 27.—The Saints residing at Frisco, Beaver Co., were organized as a branch of the Church; Benjamin Bennett, presiding Elder.

July. *Sat. 16.*—Joseph Young, sen., brother of the late Pres. Brigham Young, and senior president of all the Seventies, died in Salt Lake City.

—Twenty-two Saints from Iceland, in charge of John Eyvindson, sailed from Liverpool, England, bound for Utah.

Mon. 18.—Two little girls, daughters of John C. Harper, were killed by lightning at Payson, Utah Co.

Sun. 24.—The Saints who had settled on the Provo river, northeast of Heber City, Wasatch Co., were organized as the Woodland Ward; Henry Moon, Bishop.

Wed. 27.—Senator John Sherman, of Ohio, General Benjamin Harrison, of Indiana, Judge Strong and Albert Bierstadt, the landscape painter, visited Salt Lake City.

Sat. 30.—Architect Obed Taylor died at Salt Lake City.

August *Mon. 1.*—Elder Niels Wilhelmsen, president of the Scandinavian mission, died at Copenhagen, Denmark. He was the first Elder from America who died in Scandinavia.

Wed. 3.—Elder Wm. C. Staines died in Salt Lake City.

Thurs. 4.—The corner stone of the Walker Opera House, Salt Lake City, was laid.

Tues. 16.—A Ward was organized at Clinton, Utah Co.; John Spencer, Bishop.

September. *Sat. 3.*—The steamship *Wyoming* sailed from Liverpool, England, with 644 Saints, in charge of James Finlayson. The company arrived at New York, Sept. 13th, and at Salt Lake City, Sept. 21st.

Sun. 11.—The Saints in Ashley Valley, Uintah Co., were organized into two Wards, namely, Ashley and Mountain Dell, with Jeremiah Hatch and Thos. Bingham as Bishops, respectively.

Sun. 18.—Apostle Orson Pratt delivered his last public discourse, in the Tabernacle, Salt Lake City.

Tues. 20.—Elder Solomon Angell died at Leeds, Washington Co.

Tues. 27.—Feramorz L. Young died of typhoid fever and was buried at sea, about one hundred miles from Havana, while returning from a mission to Mexico.

Wed. 28.—Hon. John M. Bernhisel died at his residence in Salt Lake City.

October. *Mon. 3.*—Apostle Orson Pratt died in Salt Lake City.

Mon. 10.—Geo. J. Belliston was killed by lightning at Nephi, Juab Co.

Fri. 14.—Bishop Edwin D. Woolley died in Salt Lake City.

Sat. 22.—The steamship *Wyoming* sailed from Liverpool, England, with 396 Saints, in charge of Lyman R. Martineau. The company landed in New York Nov. 2nd, and arrived at Ogden and Salt Lake City Nov. 11th.

Mon. 24.—George D. Watt, the first man baptized in the British mission, died at Kaysville, Davis Co.

Tues. 25.—After a lengthy trial in the Third District Court, Jack Emerson was adjudged guilty of the murder of John F. Turner, as an accomplice of Fred. Hopt.

Thurs. 27.—Joel Hinckley, railroad agent at Franklin, Oneida Co., Idaho, was murdered by two masked men, who subsequently were arrested.

Fri. 28.—Stephen Hales, an old member of the Church, died in the 16th Ward, Salt Lake City.

November. *Thurs. 10.*—Wm. Falconbridge, a centenarian, died in Salt Lake City. He was born Oct. 24, 1780.

Fri. 11.—David D. Morgan, of Salt Lake City, was accidentally killed, while working in a coal mine, in Pleasant Valley.

Wed. 23.—Robert Pixton, a member of the Mormon Battalion, died at Taylorsville, Salt Lake Co.

Fri. 25.—The Saints who had settled on Poole's Island, Snake River Valley, Idaho, were organized as a branch of the Church, by Marriner W. Merrill, of the Cache Stake presidency, with John R. Poole as presiding Elder.

Sat. 26.—Jacob M. Truman, a member of the Mormon Battalion, died at Hamblin, Washington Co.

Mon. 28.—Geo. Beebe died at Provo.

December. *Sun. 4.*—Elder Daniel A. Miller, of Farmington, Davis Co., died at Providence, Cache Co.

Thurs. 8.—Albert R. Carrington, conductor on the Utah Central Railway, was fatally hurt at the depot, in Salt Lake City. He died the following day.

Tues. 20.—Evan Morgan, one of the first who joined the Church at Swansea, Wales, died in the 21st Ward, Salt Lake City.

Thurs. 22.—The Saints who had settled in Pleasant Valley, Emery Co., were organized as a branch of the Church; David Williams, president.

1882.

The Edmunds anti-polygamy law was passed by Congress, which later introduced legal proceedings of an extraordinary character in Utah. New Stakes of Zion were organized in Castle Valley, Utah, and in Salt river, Ariz. The first branches of the Church were arganized in Cassia County, Idaho.

January. Mon. 2.—Pres. John Taylor moved into the Gardo House, Salt Lake City. A public reception was given, in which over two thousand people participated.

Sun. 8.—The Salt Lake Assembly Hall was dedicated.

Mon. 9.—The Utah legislature (25th session) met in Salt Lake City, and organized by electing Joseph F. Smith president of the Council,and Francis M. Lyman speaker of the House.

—Hans F. Petersen, the first Latter-day Saint missionary to Norway, died at Ephraim, Sanpete Co.

Tues. 10.—The Utah election case was argued in the U. S. House of Representatives, and, after a hot debate, deferred to the Committee on Elections.

Wed. 25.—Elizabeth Hoagland Cannon, wife of Geo. Q. Cannon, died in Salt Lake City, while her husband was attending to his public duties in Washington, D. C.

February.—The Latter-day Saint missionaries in the Southern States were subject to much persecution.

Mon. 13.—Wm. Jennings was elected mayor of Salt Lake City.

Wed. 15.—Elizabeth A. Whitney, widow of Bishop Newel K. Whitney, died in Salt Lake City, aged 81 years.

Thurs. 16.—The Edmunds anti-polygamy bill was passed by the U. S. Senate. As soon as this became known in Utah, three petitions, asking Congress to send a deputation to investigate affairs in the Territory, before undertaking any hostile legislation against the people, were prepared and received about 75,000 signatures. They were treated with indifference.

Fri. 17.—A family of seven, named Teckett, was killed by an avalanche in Big Cottonwood Canyon.

Fri. 24.—Elder William Henry Butler, of Kaysville, Davis Co., Utah, died at Birmingham,England, where he labored as a missionary.

Sat. 25.—After four hours' investigation, the U. S. Committee on Elections decided that neither Cannon nor Campbell was entitled to a seat in Congress.

March. Tues. 7.—Thos. B. H. Stenhouse, formerly prominent in the Church, died at San Francisco, Cal.

Fri. 10.—The Utah legislature adjourned after 60 days' session; 72 acts were passed, of which 16 were vetoed by Gov. Murray. Among the latter was one that appropriated $40,000 for the completion of the Deseret University. Garfield County was organized during this session.

Sun. 12.—Richard V. Morris, Bishop of the 19th Ward, died in Salt Lake City.

Tues. 14.—The Edmunds anti-polygamy bill was passed by the United States House of Representatives. A few days later it was signed by Pres. Chester A. Arthur, and thus became law.

Thurs. 16.—The first number of *Morgenstjernen,* afterwards the *Historical Record,* was issued in Salt Lake City; Andrew Jenson, editor.

April. Thurs. 6.—The 52nd annual conference was commenced in Salt Lake City; it was continued four days; 127 missionaries were called.

Mon. 10.—A constitutional convention, consisting of delegates from all the counties of Utah and authorized by the late legislature, met in Salt Lake City for the purpose of framing a State Constitution and again petitioning Congress to admit Utah into the Union as a State. Regular meetings were held until the 27th, when the "Constitution for the State of Utah" was adopted by unanimous vote.

Tues. 11.—A large company of missionaries left Salt Lake City, for the United States and Europe.

Wed. 12.—The steamship *Nevada* sailed from Liverpool, England, with 343 Saints, including 11 returning missionaries, under the direction of John Donaldson. The company arrived in New York, April 24th, and at Ogden and Salt Lake City, May 1st.

Wed. 19.—Hon. Geo. Q. Cannon delivered a powerful speech in the U. S. House of Representatives, in vindication of the people of Utah.

—On this and the following day the Utah election case was argued in the U. S. House of Representatives, and Geo. Q. Cannon was denied his seat in Congress on account of polygamy.

Sun. 23.—Professor James L. Barfoot, curator of the Deseret Museum, died in Salt Lake City.

May. Thurs. 4.—Anders Christensen a prominent Elder, died at Brigham City, Box Elder Co.

Wed. 17.—The steamship *Nevada* sailed from Liverpool, England, with 392 Saints, including a number of returning Elders, under the direction of Wm. R. Webb. They arrived in New York May 27th, and in Salt Lake City June 4th.

Mon. 22.—The constitution adopted by the constitutional convention was ratified by a general vote of the people of Utah Territory.

June.—Thurber Ward, Rabbit Valley, Utah, was organized by Apostles Francis M. Lyman and John H. Smith; Geo. Brinkerhoff, Bishop.

Sun 4.—The Saints at Burrville, Sevier Co., were organized as a Ward, by Apostles Francis M. Lyman and John Henry Smith; Wm. H. Cloward, Bishop.

Mon. 5. — The Walker Opera House, Salt Lake City, was opened with a concert by the Careless Orchestra.

Tues. 6.—The State convention again met in Salt Lake City and prepared a petition to Congress for Utah's admission into the Union. Wm. H. Hooper, John T. Caine, James Sharp, Wm. W. Riter, Franklin S. Richards, David H. Peery and Wm. D. Johnson, jun., were chosen as delegates to present the same to Congress.

Sat. 10.—Levi W. Hancock, one of the First Seven Presidents of the Seventies, died at Washington, Washington Co.

Sun. 11. — Dingle Dell branch, Bear Lake Co., Idaho, was organized as Cottonwood (later Dingle) Ward; Samuel A. Wilcox, Bishop.

Fri. 16.—Pres. Chester A. Arthur nominated Alex. Ramsey, of Minnesota, A. S. Paddock, of Nebraska, G. L. Godfrey, of Iowa, A. B. Carlton, of Indiana, and James R. Pettigrew, of Arkansas, as members of the Utah Commission, provided for in the Edmunds law.

Sat. 17.—Liberty Park, Salt Lake City, was formally opened to the public.

Wed. 21.—The steamship *Nevada* sailed from Liverpool, England, with 932 souls, in charge of Robert R. Irvine. They arrived at New York July 2nd, and at Ogden July 9th.

Sat. 24.—Nathan E. Tenney was shot and killed by Mexicans at St. Johns, Apache Co., Ariz., while endeavoring to act as peacemaker between contending parties.

Tues. 27.—Mary Angell Young, widow of Pres. Brigham Young, died in Salt Lake City.

Wed. 28.—The Old Folks from Salt Lake, Utah, Juab, Tooele, Davis and Weber Counties enjoyed a grand feast in Salt Lake City. The festivities were continued the following day.

July. *Sun. 9.*—The Saints who had settled on the bench lands west of North Ogden, Weber Co., Utah, were detached from the North Ogden Ward, and organized as Pleasant View Ward; Edward W. Wade, Bishop.

Sun. 16.—The Saints residing in Wilson school district, Weber Co., were separated from West Weber and organized as Wilson Ward; Brigham H. Bingham, Bishop.

Mon. 17.—The Deseret Hospital, Salt Lake City, was dedicated and opened for business in the 12th Ward.

—Harriet Whittaker Taylor, wife of Pres. John Taylor, died in Salt Lake City.

Wed. 19.—Elder Jacob Samuel Ferrin was killed by Indians, near San Carlos, Ariz.

Fri. 21.—The Clover Ward, Tooele Co., was organized; Francis De St Jeor, Bishop.

Sat. 22.—A company of Saints, comprising 13 Icelanders and 5 British, sailed from Liverpool, England, on the steamship *Arizona*, bound for Utah.

August. *Tues. 1.*—The first number of the *Utah Journal* was issued in Logan, Cache Co., Utah, in place of the *Logan Leader*, suspended.

Sun. 6.—J. D. Farmer, a merchant of Salt Lake City, was lost in the Great Salt Lake, while bathing; the body could not be found.

Tues. 8.—Edward Martin, a member of the Mormon Battalion, died in the 14th Ward, Salt Lake City.

—The U. S. Congress adjourned; the Senate amendment to the civil appropriation bill (commonly known as the Hoar amendment), authorizing the governor of Utah to fill offices, supposed to be vacant in that Territory, was one of the last acts passed.

Sun. 13.—At a special conference held at Castle Dale, Emery Co., attended by Apostles Erastus Snow and John H. Smith, the Emery Stake of Zion was more fully organized, with Christen G. Larsen as president and Orange Seeley and Rasmus Justesen counselors. Orangeville Ward was organized; Jasper Robertson, Bishop; Henning Olsen was ordained Bishop of the Castle Dale Ward.

Wed. 16.—David G. Bigler, a brakeman on the Utah Central Railway, was accidentally killed, near River Side Station.

Fri. 18.—The Utah Commission, consisting of five men, appointed by the President of the United States, arrived in Salt Lake City. They went to work almost immediately, preparing for the November election.

—Bishop Geo. W. Ward died at Willard, Box Elder Co.

Sun. 20.—The Saints residing in Parley's Canyon, Salt Lake Co., were organized as Mountain Dell Ward; Wm. B. Hardy, Bishop.

Wed. 23.—A large company of missionaries left Salt Lake City for the United States and Europe.

Tues 29.—The Presidency of the Church issued an epistle to the Saints, advising all who could legally register and vote under the Edmunds law, to do so.

September.—Branches of the Church were organized by Francis M. Lyman, president of the Tooele Stake of Zion, at Oakley, Little Basin, Albion, Cassia and Almo, Cassia County, Idaho, where a number of Saints had recently located. The several branches were organized as the Cassia Ward; Wm. C. Martindale, Bishop.

Sat. 2.—The steamship *Wyoming* sailed from Liverpool, England, with 662 Saints, including 16 returning missionaries, under the direction of William Cooper. The company arrived in New York Sept. 12th, and in Salt Lake City Sept. 21st.

Sun. 3.—Sandy Ward, Salt Lake Co., was organized out of a part of Union Ward; Ezekiel Holman, Bishop.

Sat. 16.—Gov. Eli H. Murray, on the strength of the Hoar amendment, issued a proclamation appointing a great number of men to fill local offices, claimed to be vacant on account of the August election not being held. The incumbents, who held over under the statute, however, refused to recognize the governor's appointees as their successors, and the case was taken into the courts.

October.—*Sun. 1.*—The west part of Brighton Ward, Salt Lake Co., was organized as Pleasant Green Ward; Lehi N. Hardman, Bishop.

Fri. 6.—The semi-annual conference of the Church, which continued three days, was held in Salt Lake City; 78 missionaries were called.

Mon. 9.—Abraham Hoagland Cannon was ordained one of the First Seven Presidents of Seventies.

Fri. 13.—George Teasdale and Heber J. Grant were chosen by revelation to fill the vacancies in the Council of Twelve Apostles, caused by the death of Orson Pratt and the recent re-organization of the First Presidency. Seymour B. Young was chosen by the same revelation as one of the First Seven Presidents of the Seventies. These three brethren were ordained on the 16th.

Tues. 17.—About sixty missionaries bound for the United States and Europe, left Salt Lake City.

Sat. 21.—The steamship *Abyssinia* sailed from Liverpool, England, with 416 Saints, including 28 returning missionaries, unde the direction of Geo. Stringfellow. They landed in New York Nov. 3rd, and arrived in Salt Lake City Nov. 10th.

Tues. 24.—Melvina H. Snow, widow of Willard Snow, died in Salt Lake City.

Sun. 29.—Francis M. Pomeroy, one of the Utah Pioneers of 1847, died at Mesa, Maricopa Co., Ariz.

November. *Sat. 4.* — An important political ratification meeting was held by the People's Party in the Salt Lake Theater.

Tues. 7.—A general election was held in Utah, in which the People's Party candidate, John T. Caine, received 23,039 votes, and the "Liberal" candidate, Philip T. Van Zile, only 4,884 votes.

Mon. 13.—The Utah Commission submitted their first report to the government on the situation in Utah.

Sat. 25.—Apostle John Henry Smith succeeded Apostle Albert Carrington as president of the European mission.

Tues. 28.—Gen. Phil. H. Sheridan arrived in Salt Lake City, on an inspection tour to the military posts in the Territory.

—The Coveville branch, near Richmond, Cache Co., was organized as Coveville Ward; John C. Larsen, Bishop.

—Riverdale branch, Oneida County, Idaho, was organized as a Ward; Peter Preece, Bishop.

December. *Wed. 6.*—The first Latterday Saint meeting house in Snake River Valley, Idaho, was completed at Egin (Parker).

Sun. 10.—The Saints who had located on Salt river, Maricopa Co., Ariz., were organized as the Maricopa Stake of Zion, by Apostles Erastus Snow and Moses Thatcher, with Alexander F. Macdonald as president, and Henry C. Rogers and Charles I. Robson as counselors. Jonesville (now Lehi), Mesa, and the Tempe branch were organized as Wards, with Thos. E. Jones, Elijah Pomeroy and David T. LeBaron as their respective Bishops.

Mon. 18.—Thos. E. Ricks, of Logan, Utah, was called to preside as Bishop over the Saints in Snake River Valley, Idaho. Soon afterwards they were organized as Bannock Ward.

Thurs. 21. — Artemesia Snow, wife of Apostle Erastus Snow, died in St. George.

Sat. 30.—Hon. Wm. H. Hooper died in Salt Lake City.

Sun. 31.— The Saints who had settled on the San Pedro river, Ariz., were organized by Apostle Erastus Snow and Moses Thatcher as St. David Ward; David P. Kimball, Bishop.

1883.

The Saints who had settled on the Gila river, Arizona, and vicinity, were organized as a Stake of Zion; and a Stake of Zion was organized in San Luis Valley, Colo. A number of settlements were founded by the Saints in Snake River Valley, Idaho. A successful missionary work was commenced among the Maoris in New Zealand.

January. *Tues. 9.*—The Saints at Leamington, Millard Co., Utah, were organized as a Ward; Lars N. Christiansen, Bishop.

Wed. 17.—Notwithstanding bitter opposition, John T. Caine was permitted to take a seat in Congress, to fill the unexpired term of the 47th Congress.

Fri. 19.—The thermometer stood about 35 degrees F. below zero, in Salt Lake City.

February. *Thurs. 1.*—Judge Jeremiah S. Black delivered a powerful speech before the Committee on the Judiciary, at Washington, D. C., pleading for Utah's constitutional rights.

Sat. 17.—Bishop Wm. Bringhurst, of Springville, died

Sun. 18.—John Van Cott, one of the First Seven Presidents of the Seventies, died at his residence, near Salt Lake City.

—A number of Saints who had founded a new settlement (north of Manassa, Conejos Co., Colo.), were organized as a branch of the Church, named Richfield, with Thos. N. Petersen as presiding Elder.

Sun. 25.—The Saints at St. David, Ariz., by their vote, accepted Christopher Layton as president of the St. Joseph Stake of Zion (which had just been organized by the First Presidency) with David P. Kimball and James H. Martineau as counselors.

Mon. 26.—Phil Robinson, the noted *litterateur*, and Mr. Sergeant Ballantyne, the eminent English barrister, visited Salt Lake City.

March. *Sun. 4.*—The Saints who had settled on Price river, Emery Co., were organized as a Ward; Geo. Frandsen, Bishop.

Sun. 11.—A townsite was selected in Snake River Valley, Idaho, and named Rexburg, in honor of Thos. E. Ricks.

Tues. 20.—Wm. Holt and David Barney, two loggers, sleeping under an overhanging rock, near Parowan, Iron Co., were killed by the rock falling on them.

Fri. 30.—The Denver and Rio Grande Western Railway was completed, and communication established between Salt Lake City and Denver by this route.

April. *Mon. 2.*—A Ward organization was effected at Meadows, near St. Johns, Ariz.; Peter Isaacson, Bishop.

Tues. 3.—About fifty "Mormon" immigrants arrived in Salt Lake City from the Southern States.

Fri. 6.—The 53rd annual conference of the Church, which was continued three days, commenced in Salt Lake City.

Sun. 8.—The Saints who had settled near Savoia, Valencia Co., New Mexico, were organized as the Navajo (now Ramah) Ward; Ernest A. Tietjen, Bishop.

Tues. 10.—About ninety missionaries left Salt Lake City for the United States and Europe.

—The constitutional convention met in Salt Lake City and received the report of the committee appointed to present the memorial and constitution, upon which was based Utah's application for admission as a State.

Wed. 11.—The steamship *Nevada* sailed from Liverpool, England, with 353 Saints, including 13 returning missionaries, under the direction of David McKay. The company arrived at New York April 22nd, and Salt Lake City April 30th.

Sun. 15.—A branch of the Church was organized at Marysvale, Piute Co., Utah, with Hugh D. Lisenbee as presiding Elder.

Mon. 23.—A terrible wind storm did much damage in Utah.

Tues. 24.—Wm. E. McLellin, formerly one of the Twelve Apostles, died at Independence, Jackson Co., Mo.

Mon. 30.—Fort Cameron Military Reservation buildings, near Beaver, were sold and the fort was abandoned as a military station.

May. Tues. 1.—O. F. Due, of Salt Lake City, was arrested on a charge of bigamy and placed under $2,500 bonds.

Sun. 13.—At a two days' meeting, held at Pima, Graham Co., Ariz., the Saints who had settled on the Gila river, Graham Co., Ariz., were organized into four Wards, namely, Pima, Thatcher, Graham, and Curtis, with Joseph K. Rogers, John M. Moody, Jørgen Jørgensen and Moses M. Curtis as their respective Bishops.

Wed. 16.—The steamship *Nevada* sailed from Liverpool, England, with 427 Saints, including 14 returning missionaries, under the direction of Ben. E. Rich. The company arrived in New York May 27th, and in Salt Lake City June 3rd.

Fri. 18.—Belle Harris was committed to the Utah Penitentiary for contempt of court, in refusing to answer questions before the grand jury of the Second District Court, at Beaver, in a supposed polygamy investigation.

Sat. 19.—James W. Cummings, a prominent Elder, died in Salt Lake City.

Tues. 22.—The Empire grist mill, up City creek, near Salt Lake City, was burned to the ground. Loss; $23,500.

Sun. 27.—Bishop Calvin Bingham was accidentally killed near St. David, Cochise Co., Ariz.

Mon. 28.—Richard Fowler was shot and fatally wounded by David Gallifant, in Salt Lake City. Fowler died May 30th, and the murderer was held under $5,000 bonds.

Tues. 29.—Elder Hans Peter Jensen, one of the early converts to "Mormonism" in Scandinavia,.died in Brigham City.

—Bishops Wm..B. Preston and Leonard W. Hardy arrived at Rexburg, Snake River Valley, Idaho. During the few following days they located the townsites of Teton, Wilford. Lyman, Burton and Parker.

Thurs. 31.—John T. Alexander, of Salt Lake City, who labored as a missionary in Georgia, was shot and severely wounded by three masked men, near Plainville, Gordon Co., Ga.

June. Thurs. 7.—Dr. J. B. Carrington, a non-Mormon, arrested for bigamy, was discharged by Commissioner Gilchrist, at Salt Lake City, notwithstanding the proof of his guilt.

Sun. 10.—Five young persons, ranging from 12 to 23 years of age, were accidentally drowned, while boating on Utah lake, near Benjamin.

—The Saints who had settled in San Luis Valley, Colo., were organized as the San

Luis Stake of Zion, with Silas S. Smith as president and Richard C. Camp and Wm. M. Christensen as counselors. The settlements of Manassa and Richfield were organized as Wards, with John C. Dalton and Thos. N. Petersen as their respective Bishops.

Fri. 15.—Theodore Thomas, the celebrated orchestral leader, gave a concert in the Tabernacle, Salt Lake City.

Wed. 20.—The steamship *Nevada* sailed from Liverpool, England, with 697 Saints, including 22 returning missionaries, under the direction of Hans O. Magleby. The company arrived in New York July 1st, and at Ogden July 7th.

—Mary B. Newell was miraculously healed under the administration of the Elders, at Johnsonville, Warren Co., Ind.

Thurs. 21.—The Council House and adjacent buildings, in Salt Lake City,were destroyed by fire and the explosion of powder. Loss: about $100,000.

—Bishop Leonard E. Harrington died at his residence, at American Fork, Utah Co.

Sat. 23.—David Evans, formerly Bishop of Lehi, Utah Co., died at Lehi.

Sun. 24.—Elder Shadrach Jones, of Willard City, Box Elder Co., died at Swansea, Wales, where he labored as a missionary.

July. Wed. 4.—Robert Ritter and William Ayers were drowned in Silver lake, Big Cottonwood Canyon, while boating.

Fri. 6.—A fatal powder magazine explosion occurred in Ogden Canyon.

—Joseph Toronto, once a missionary to Italy, died at Salt Lake City.

Tues. 10.—Gov. Thomas A. Hendricks, of Indiana, visited Salt Lake City.

—D. C. Rich and Rudolph Smith made an unsuccessful attempt to rob Zion's Savings Bank, in Salt Lake City, assaulting B. H. Schettler,the assistant treasurer. They were both arrested.

Wed. 11.—The Old Folks of Salt Lake City were treated to their annual excursion, this time going to Provo.

Sat. 14.—A company of Icelandic Saints sailed from Liverpool, England, on the steamship *Wisconsin*, in charge of John A. Sutton. The company arrived in Salt Lake City July 30th, and subsequently located at Spanish Fork, Utah Co.

Sat. 28.—R. S. W. Andrew, a street car driver, was accidentally shot and killed in Salt Lake City.

Sun. 29.—A terrific flood at Kanab, Kane Co., removed masses of earth, trees, etc., which it carried down stream, and partly destroyed the settlement.

August. Thurs. 2.—The Salt Lake City Council decided that all houses within the city should be numbered, as a preparatory step toward the anticipated free mail delivery.

Sun. 19.—Jeremiah S. Black, the celebrated statesman and lawyer, who defended the people of Utah so ably a few months previously, died in Washington, D.C.

Mon. 20.—Ellen G. Lewis, a young lady, was accidentally shot and killed in Provo, by a policeman on duty.

Tues. 21.—The notorious "Bill" Hickman died in Lander City, Sweetwater Co., Wyoming.

Sat. 25.—Bishop Andrew Burt, captain of the Salt Lake City police force, was killed by a negro, whom he was trying to arrest. Half an hour later the negro was lynched by a mob, in the jail yard.

Sun. 26.—Alvin Henson was accidentally shot and killed by his comrades, while hunting, near Tooele, Utah.

—Jack Murphy was taken out of the jail at Coalville and lynched at Park City, Summit Co., for the murder of M. Brennan, a few days previously.

—The first permanent branch of the Church among the Maoris was organized by Ira N. Hinkley, jun., at Papawai, Wairarapa Valley,North Island,New Zealand; Manihera, a native chief, was ordained a Priest and appointed president. This was the beginning of a great work among the Maoris.

The first Maori who joined the Church was a sailor, baptized by Elder Richard G. Lambert, near Honolulu, Hawaiian Islands, early in 1874. Oct. 18, 1881, Elder Wm. John McDonald, baptized Ngataki, at Auckland. He was the first Maori to join the Church in New Zealand. Toward the close of 1883, and in the beginning of 1884, a number of Maoris were baptized in the Waikato district through the instrumentality of Pres. Wm. M. Bromley, Wm. J. McDonald and Thos. L. Cox. These were organized as the Wautu branch by Elder Thos. L. Cox, Feb. 25, 1883, with Hare Te Katere as president. This was the first Maori branch of the Church organized; but most of its members proved unfaithful to the cause.

Wed. 29.—The steamship *Nevada* sailed from Liverpool, England, with 682 Saints, including 29 returning missionaries, in charge of Peter F. Goss. The company arrived at New York Sept. 7th, and at Salt Lake City Sept. 17th.

Fri. 31.—Belle Harris was released from custody, having been imprisoned since May 18th.

September. *Sun. 2.*—Muddy branch, Emery Co.,Utah, was organized as a Ward, with Casper Christensen as Bishop. The name of the settlement was afterwards changed to Emery.

☐*Mon. 3.*—Washakie, a little Indian town in Box Elder Co., was visited by a fire, which destroyed grain to the value of $3,000.

Thurs. 6.—Wm. G. Phillips was appointed marshal of Salt Lake City, in place of the late Andrew Burt.

—Feramorz Little transferred a two story brick building, which he had erected by the 13th Ward Assembly Rooms for the benefit of the poor, to Bishop Millen Atwood.

Tues. 11. — The celebrated Henry Ward Beecher lectured in the Salt Lake City Theatre.

Wed. 12.—About midnight Elders Stephen R. Marks and David Franklin Davis, of Salt Lake City, were cruelly mobbed, near Laurel, Franklin Co., Indiana, where they labored as missionaries.

Sat. 22. — General William T. Sherman arrived in Salt Lake City, on a visit.

Sun. 23.—At a conference held at Bluff, San Juan Co., Utah, the Saints who had located at Fruitland, near Farmington, San Juan Co., New Mexico, were organ-

ized as a Ward, named Burnham, with Luther C. Burnham as Bishop.

—The Saints constituting the Wilmot branch, Piute Co., Utah, were organized as the Marion Ward; Culbert King, Bishop.

Wed. 26.—Bishop Charles E. Robison, of Montpelier, Bear Lake Co., Idaho, died at Whittaker, South Carolina, where he labored as a missionary.

October. *Fri. 5.*—The semi-annual conference of the Church was commenced in Salt Lake City; it was continued three days; 92 missionaries were called; Apostle Wilford Woodruff was sustained as Church Historian.

Sat. 6.—King David Kalakaua visited the plantation of Laie, on the Hawaiian Islands, and addressed a conference of assembled Saints there.

Mon. 8.—John S. Fullmer, a prominent Elder in the Church, died in Springville, Utah Co., and Elder Henry Maiben died in Salt Lake City.

Tues. 16.—Presiding Bishop Edward Hunter died in Salt Lake City.

Sat. 27.—A fire destroyed Causey, Harkins & Co's. skating rink on West Temple Street, Salt Lake City. Loss: $10,000.

—The steamship *Wisconsin* sailed from Liverpool, England, with 369 Saints, including 20 returning missionaries, in charge of John Pickett. The company arrived at New York, Nov. 7th, and at Ogden, Nov. 14th.

Sun. 28.—The Neeleyville Ward, Oneida County, Idaho, was organized; Wm. Neeley, Bishop.

November. *Thurs. 1.*—Lewis Robison, prominent in the early history of Utah, died in Salt Lake City, 67 years of age.

Sat. 17.—Apostle Charles C. Rich died at Paris, Bear Lake Co., Idaho, 74 years of age.

Sun. 18.—The Saints who had settled in Luna Valley, Socorro Co., N. M., were organized as a Ward, with Geo. C. Williams as Bishop.

Wed. 21.—David Patten Kimball, counselor to Pres. Christopher Layton, of the St. Joseph Stake of Zion, Ariz., died.

Thurs. 22.—Bishop Wm. Davis died at Brigham City, Utah.

Wed. 28.—The Saints who had located on Portneuf creek, Bingham Co., Idaho, were organized as a branch of the Church; Judson A. Tolman, presiding Elder.

December. *Thurs. 13.*—Marshal Wm. G. Phillips, of Salt Lake City, reported to the postmaster that all the public streets in the city had been named and all the houses numbered.

Fri. 21.—Elder Lorenzo M. Richards died in Ogden.

Mon. 24.—A monument was raised on the grave of the late Pres. Niels Wilhelmsen, on "Assistents Kirkegaard," Copenhagen, Denmark.

Wed. 26.—Gen. Thos. L. Kane, favorably known in Church history, died at his home, in Philadelphia, Pa.

1884.

Two Stakes of Zion were organized in Idaho. The Logan Temple was dedicated. Several new Quorums of Seventy were or-

9

ganized. The prosecutions under the Edmunds law were commenced.

January. Tues. 1.—A fire broke out in the Utah Central coal mines, at Pleasant Valley, Emery Co., whereby John McLean and his son were suffocated.

Mon. 14. — The 26th session of the Utah legislature convened in Salt Lake City, and organized by electing Wm. W. Cluff president of the council, and James Sharp speaker of the house.

Fri. 25. — Elders Wm. H. Crandall and John W. Galley were mobbed in Jasper County, Mississippi.

Sun. 27.—The Brigham Young Academy in Provo was destroyed by fire.

—Plymouth Ward, Box Elder Co., Utah, was organized; Myron J. Richards, Bishop.

Mon. 28.—Senator Hoar introduced another anti-Mormon bill in the U. S. Senate, which was passed June 18th.

February. Mon. 4—The Bannock Ward, Snake River Valley, Idaho, was organized as the Bannock Stake of Zion; Thos. E. Ricks, president.

Wed. 6. — Peter Carlson and son were killed in a snowslide, near Logan.

Mon. 11. — At the municipal election in Salt Lake City, James Sharp was elected mayor.

Wed. 13.—The members of the Wyoming legislature and a number of others from that Territory arrived in Salt Lake City, on a visit. They remained two days, during which they visited the Utah legislature then in session; speeches were made by both bodies.

Mon. 18.—Elders Wm. H. Crandall and Thomas Davis were shot at by a mob in Jones County, Miss.

Sun. 24.—Portions of the North Jordan and Brighton Wards, Salt Lake Stake, were organized as Granger Ward; Daniel McRae, Bishop.

Mon. 25.—Elder Henry C. Fowler died in Salt Lake City.

March. Sun. 2.—The Saints who had settled near Safford, Graham Co., Ariz, were organized as Layton branch; John Walker, presiding Elder.

Fri. 7.—Ten men and two women were killed in a snowslide, at the Emma mine, Little Cottonwood Canyon.

Fri. 14.—The Utah legislature adjourned.

Mon. 17.—Bishop Silas Richards died at Union, Salt Lake Co.

Sat. 22.—Daniel Mathison died at Parowan, Iron Co.

Sun. 30.—Elder Thomas Biesinger was arrested and imprisoned at Prague, Bohemia, for preaching the gospel.

April. Tues. 1.—The world-renowned Adelina Patti, assisted by an excellent company, sang in the Tabernacle, in Salt Lake City.

Fri. 4.—Ebenezer Hanks, a member of the Mormon Battalion, died at Graves' Village, Piute Co.

—Patriarch John Rowberry died at Tooele, Tooele Co.

—On this and the three following days the 54th annual conference of the Church was held in Salt Lake City.

Wed. 9.—The steamship *Nevada* sailed

from Liverpool, England, with 319 Saints, including 17 returning missionaries, in charge of Christian D. Fjeldsted. It arrived in New York harbor April 19th, and the company reached Ogden, Utah, April 27th.

Tues. 15.—A large company of missionaries left Salt Lake City for the United States and Europe.

Thurs. 17.—Presidents John Taylor and Geo. Q. Cannon, accompanied by a number of others, left Salt Lake City, to visit the Iron Works in southern Utah.

Sun. 20.—The 77th quorum of Seventy was organized by Wm. W. Taylor at Ogden, with John Crawford, Louis F. Monch, Fred. Foulger, Chas. C. Brown and Henry W. Gwilliams as presidents. Ludvig Ehrnstrøm and Ephraim H. Nye were afterwards added to the council.

Thurs. 24.—Rudger Clawson was arrested in Salt Lake City, on a charge of polygamy, and placed under $3,000 bonds.

Sun. 27.—At the first quarterly conference of the Bannock Stake of Zion, held at Rexburg, Idaho, the Saints at Rexburg were organized as a Ward; Thos. E. Ricks, jun., Bishop.

—The 78th quorum of Seventy was organized by Wm. W. Taylor, at Oakley, Cassia Co., Idaho; Robert Wilson, John Alexander, Moroni F. Fairchilds, George S. Grant, John J. Millard, Thomas Taylor and Edward D. Hoagland, presidents. The two last named were ordained a day or two later.

—Pere Hyacinthe, renowned French orator, who was in Salt Lake City on a visit, attended the services in the Tabernacle.

—A branch of the Church was organized at Eureka, Juab Co.; John Beck, president.

Mon. 28.—Christian D. Fjeldsted, of Logan, was ordained one of the First Seven Presidents of Seventies, to fill the vacancy caused by the death of John Van Cott.

Tues. 29.—A third trial of the murderer Fred Hopt was commenced in the Third District Court, Salt Lake City. He was convicted May 5th, and sentenced on the 9th to be shot June 13th.

May. Mon. 12.—The 79th quorum of Seventy was organized by Abraham H. Cannon, in Bear Lake County, Idaho; Charles H. Bridges, John Bunney, Christian Hogansen, Carl F. Hellstrom, Herbert Horsley, Charles R. Clark and Brigham L. Tippetts, presidents.

Tues. 13.—David Gallifant, of Salt Lake City, was sentenced to five years' imprisonment for killing Richard Fowler on May 28, 1883.

—Ole U. C. Mønster, the first person baptized by Erastus Snow, in Denmark, died at Pettyville, Sanpete Co.

Sat. 17.—The Logan Temple was dedicated, under the direction of Pres. John Taylor.

—The steamship *Arizona* sailed from Liverpool, England, with 287 Saints, including 13 returning missionaries, in charge of Ephraim H. Williams. On the 26th they arrived in New York, and reached Salt Lake City June 1st.

Wed. 21.—The first marriages in the Logan Temple were solemnized. E. Y.

Taylor and Rida Colebrook, Frank Y. Taylor and Elizabeth Campbell, Matthias F. Cowley and Abbie Hyde were the contracting parties.

—Ground was broken for a new building for the B. Y. Academy at Provo.

Thurs. 22.—Nellie White, who refused to answer certain questions in the Third District Court, was sent to the Penitentiary.

Thurs. 29. — Edward Wallace East, a prominent Elder, died at Pima, Arizona.

—Elders Wm. C. A. Smoot, jun., and James E. Jennings, who labored as missionaries in Bavaria, were expelled from that country.

Fri. 30.—In Christiania, Norway, Elders N. C. Skaugaard and Peter Olsen were sentenced to pay a fine of 40 "Kroner" and costs of suit, each, for performing the ordinance of baptism.

June.—A missionary field was opened in Ireland by Elders Robert Marshall and Geo. Wilson. At the end of the year 47 had been baptized.

Sun. 1.—The Oneida Stake of Zion was organized by Apostle Moses Thatcher; Wm. D. Hendricks, president; Solomon H. Hale and Geo. C. Parkinson, counselors. The Wards and branches embraced in the new organization had formerly belonged to Cache and Box Elder Stakes.

Thurs. 5. — The Chesterfield branch Bingham Co., Idaho, was organized as a Ward; Parley P. Willey, Bishop.

—The Saints at Lyman, Snake River Valley, Idaho, were organized as a Ward; Sidney Weeks, Bishop.

—The Logan 6th and 7th Wards, Cache Co., were organized; Anthon L. Skanchey and Isaac Smith, Bishops.

Sun. 8.—Elder Christian H. Steffensen was released from prison in Drammen, Norway, where he had been confined five days for administering the Sacrament.

Mon. 9.—The Saints at Wilford, Snake River Valley, Idaho, were organized as a branch of the Church.

—The building known as the "Cock Pit," at Preston, England, in which the first "Mormon" missionaries to England held meetings in 1837, tumbled down.

Tues. 10.—The Saints at Teton, Snake River Valley, Idaho, were organized as a Ward; John Donaldson, Bishop.

—Elders Wm. Willes, Henry F. McCune, Milson R. Pratt and Geo. H. Booth, left Salt Lake City, on a mission to India.

Wed. 11.—The Saints at Parker, Snake River Valley, Idaho, were organized as a Ward; Wyman M. Parker, Bishop.

Fri. 13.—By a reprieve, issued by Acting-Governor Arthur L. Thomas, the execution of the murderer Fred Hopt (Welcome) was postponed.

Sat. 14.—The steamship *Arizona* sailed from Liverpool, with 531 Saints, including 25 returning missionaries, in charge of Ephraim H. Nye. They arrived in New York June 23rd and at Ogden June 29th.

Sun. 15.—At a Stake conference held at Mesa, Maricopa Co., Ariz., Tempe branch was organized as a Ward, Samuel Openshaw Bishop; and Alma Ward was organized, with Oscar M. Stewart as Bishop.

Tues. 17.—Martin H. Peck died in Salt Lake City.

Sun. 29.—Nicholas Groesbeck died in Salt Lake City.

July. *Thurs 3.*—David O. Calder, Counin the Salt Lake Stake presidency, died at Lake Point, Tooele Co.

Sun. 6.—A fearful tornado visited Summit County, Utah, doing much damage and causing the death of a little girl.

Mon. 7.—Nellie White, who had been confined in the Penitentiary since May 22nd, was restored to liberty.

Thurs. 17.—The Deseret Hospital was removed from the 12th to the 17th Ward, Salt Lake City.

Sun. 20.—The Fairview branch of the Church, near Franklin, Idaho., was organized as a Ward; Heman Hyde, Bishop.

Tues. 22.—About five hundred of the Old Folks of Salt Lake County had their annual excursion, going to American Fork, Utah Co.

Thurs. 31.—Leonard W. Hardy, first Counselor to the Presiding Bishop of the Church, died in Sugar House Ward, Salt Lake Co., and Orson K. Whitney, one of the Pioneers of 1847, died in Salt Lake City.

August. *Fri. 1.*—Wm. W. Taylor, son of Pres. John Taylor, and one of the First Seven Presidents of the Seventies, died in Salt Lake City.

—Elders Wm. Willes, Henry F. McCune, Milson R Pratt and Geo. H. Booth, arrived, as missionaries, in Calcutta, India.

Sat. 2.—Fourteen Saints sailed from Liverpool, England, in charge of H. W. Attley, on the steamship *Nevada.* They landed in New York Aug. 13th and arrived at Salt Lake City Aug. 18th.

Thurs. 7.—The 80th quorum of Seventy was organized by Seymour B. Young, at Spring City, Sanpete Co.; Thos. B. Allred, Jos. F. Ellis, John Larsen, James Christensen, Mads Nielsen, Lauritz Rasmussen and Joseph Downard, presidents.

Fri. 8.—James Roskelley, who labored as a missionary in the Southern States, was shot and wounded in the arm by a negro, in Lee Valley, Tenn.

Sat. 9.—J. R. Henson and family, because of their being "Mormons," were fired upon by a mob in Decatur County, Tennessee, and shortly after compelled to leave their homes, to escape mob violence.

Sun. 10.—Elders Wm. S. Berry, of Kanarra and John H. Gibbs, of Paradise, and Martin Condor and John Riley Hudson, of Tennessee, were murdered by a mob on Cane Creek, Lewis Co., Tenn., while holding religious services.

Fri. 15.—The first number of the *Sevier Valley Echo*, a weekly newspaper, was published in Richfield, Sevier Co., by James T. Jakeman. It was continued until May 1, 1885, when it was superseded by the *Home Sentinel*, published in Manti, Sanpete Co.

—Joseph H. Coult, of Salt Lake City, was drowned at Calder's Farm.

Sat. 16.—Bishop Wm. H. Dame died suddenly at Paragoonah, Iron Co.

Sun. 17.—At a quarterly conference held at Rexburg, Idaho, the Menan (Cedar Buttes) and Louisville Wards were partly organized, the former with Robert L.

Bybee and the latter with Richard F.
Jardine as Bishop.
—Elder Jesse J. Fuller, an elderly mis-
sionary, was whipped by a mob in Lauder-
dale County, Ala.
Fri. 22.—The remains of Elders Wm. S.
Berry and Geo. H. Gibbs arrived in Salt
Lake City from Tennessee.
Sat. 23.—Under the direction of the Old
Folks' Committee, the orphan children of
Salt Lake County had a free excursion to
Black Rock.
Wed. 27.—The St. John Ward (formerly
a part of the Malad Ward), Oneida Co.,
Idaho, was organized; James Harrison,
Bishop.
Sat. 30.—The steamship *Wyoming* sailed
from Liverpool, England, with 496 Saints,
including 31 returning missionaries, under
the direction of Benjamin Bennett. They
arrived at New York Sept. 9th, and at
Ogden Sept. 16th.
Sun. 31.—The Saints residing on Ferron
creek, east of Ferron, Emery Co., were
separated from Ferron Ward and organ-
ized as Molen Ward; Lyman S. Beach,
Bishop.
September.—The 81st quorum of Seven-
ty was organized by Seymour B. Young in
Emery County; Noah T. Guyman, Wm. H.
Branch, J. P. Wimmer, Peter R. Petersen,
Abner Buckley and James C. Jensen,
presidents.
Mon. 1.—Margaret T. Smoot, wife of
Abraham O. Smoot, died in Provo, Utah,
Co.
—Charles S. Zane, recently appointed
chief justice of Utah, took the oath of
office and was assigned, by proclamation
of Gov. Eli H. Murray, to the Third Dis-
trict Court.
Tues. 2. Piute County, Utah, was visited
by a fearful hail storm.
Wed. 3.—The Saints who had settled on
Rock Creek, Oneida Co., Idaho, were or-
ganized as Rockland Ward, of the Box
Elder Stake; Isaac Thorn, Bishop.
Sat. 6.—Wilford branch, Snake River
Valley, Idaho, was organized as a Ward;
Thos. S. Smith, Bishop.
Tues. 9.—The Saints who had settled on
the Mancos river, Colo., were organized
as a branch; James H. Duncan, presiding Elder.
Mon. 15.—Ashley Ward, Uintah Co.,
was divided, and two new districts, Merrill and Glines, organized, with Geo. A.
Davis and James H. Glines as their respective acting Bishops.
—Wm. C. A. Smoot, jun., missionary in
Germany, was arrested in Kiel, for bap-
tising a woman. He was held a prisoner
until Oct. 7th, when he was acquitted, but
nevertheless banished from the city.
Mon. 22.—Elder John Nicholson delivered a lecture in the Salt Lake Theatre
on the subject: The Tennessee massacre
and its causes; showing that it was the result of inflamatory articles in the Salt
Lake *Tribune*, circulated by sectarian ministers in Tennessee.
Sat. 27.—The first open venire grand
jury in Salt Lake City was impanneled by
Judge Zane.
October.—Severe persecutions continued against the Elders in the Southern

States, and also in Indiana, Michigan and
other places.
Wed. 1.—The 82nd quorum of Seventy
was organized in Grass Valley, Piute Co.,
Utah, by Seymour B. Young; Geo. A.
Burr and Ole E. Olsen, presidents. Chap-
man Duncan, Wm. E. Stringham and
Geo. A. Hatch were set apart as presidents
afterwards.
Tues. 7.—John Morgan was ordained
one of the First Seven Presidents of the
Seventies, to fill the vacancy caused by
the death of Wm. W. Taylor.
Tues. 14.—Bishop Marius Ensign died at
Santa Clara, Washington Co.
Wed. 15.—The trial of Rudger Clawson
for polygamy was commenced in the
Third District Court, Salt Lake City, and
continued several days, during which
Presidents John Taylor, Geo. Q. Cannon
and other prominent men were subpoenaed
as witnesses.
Tues. 21.—The jury, which could not
agree on a verdict in Rudger Clawson's
case, was discharged, and preparations
were made for a new trial.
Thurs. 23.—The steamship *City of Berlin* sailed from Liverpool, England, with
93 Saints, including nine returning Elders
in charge of Carl August Ek. The company arrived at New York Nov. 2nd, and
at Salt Lake City Nov. 9th.
Fri. 24.—Lydia Spencer, Rudger Clawson's alleged second wife, having been arrested, a new trial was commenced, and
Lydia Spencer, who refused to testify,
was sent to the Penitentiary.
Sat. 25.—In the Third District Court,
Lydia Spencer, by her husband's consent,
acknowledged that she was Rudger Clawson's wife, and the jury, after 17 minutes'
consultation, returned a verdict of guilty
against Clawson.
Fri. 31.—After several days' trial in the
Third District Court, John Connelly was
acquitted on the charge of polygamy, his
case being barred by the statute of limi-
tations.

November.   *Sat. 1.*—The steamship
Arizona sailed from Liverpool, England,
with 163 Saints, including 20 returning
missionaries, in charge of Joseph Alma
Smith. The company arrived at New
York Nov. 11th, and at Salt Lake City
Nov. 19th.
Mon. 3.—Hans Ottesen was murdered in
Manti, Sanpete Co.
—In the Third District Court (Judge
Zane), Rudger Clawson was sentenced to
four years' imprisonment and $800 fine for
polygamy and unlawful cohabitation. The
case was appealed, but bail was refused
and Clawson taken to the Penitentiary.
—Paul A. Schettler, treasurer of Salt
Lake City, died.
Tues. 4.—At the general election, John
T. Caine, the People's Party candidate for
delegate to Congress, received 22,120 votes
and Ransford Smith, the Liberal Party
candidate, 2,215.
—Layton branch, Graham Co., Ariz.,
was organized as a Ward; John Welker,
Bishop.
Wed. 5.—The trial of Joseph H. Evans,
indicted for polygamy and unlawful cohabitation, was commenced in the Third Dis-

trict Court, and the following day the jury returned a verdict of guilty.

Sat. 8.—The news of the Democratic victory in the election of Grover Cleveland for president of the United States having reached Salt Lake City, a grand jolification meeting was held by the Salt Lake City Democrats, in front of the City Hall.

—In the Third District Court (Judge Zane), Joseph H. Evans was sentenced to three and a half years' imprisonment in the Penitentiary and $250 fine.

Thurs. 13.—Eighty Latter-day Saint emigrants from the Southern States mission, and nine returning Elders, left Chattanooga, Tenn., bound for Colorado and Utah.

Fri. 14.—Rudger Clawson was brought before the Supreme Court of Utah on a writ of *habeas corpus*, and on the following day the decision of the lower court, in refusing him and Joseph H. Evans bail, pending an appeal to the higher courts, was affirmed.

Wed. 19.—Frederick W. Schoenfeld and Rudolph Hochstrasser, in the District Court of Zofingen, Canton Aargau, Switzerland, were sentenced to pay a fine of 100 francs each, and banished from the canton, for preaching the gospel in Niederwyl.

Sat. 22.—Horace Kimball Whitney, one of the Pioneers of 1847, died in Salt Lake City.

Sun. 23.—At a Stake conference held in Rexburg, Idaho, the Saints who had settled on the Teton island, near Rexburg, were organized as Salem Ward; Geo. H. B. Harris, Bishop.

Tues. 25.—John Aird, jun., of Salt Lake City, was arrested on a charge of unlawful cohabitation. The following day he was placed under $3,000 bonds, to await action of the grand jury.

December. *Thurs. 4.*—Ole L. Hansen, of Brighton, Salt Lake Co., was arraigned before U. S. Commissioner Wm. McKay, Salt Lake City, charged with polygamy.

Fri. 5.—Ammon M. Tenney, Peter J. Christoffersen. and Christopher J. Kempe, tried and convicted of polygamy, were each sentenced by Judge Howard, at Prescott, Ariz., to three years, and six months' imprisonment in the House of Correction at Detroit, Mich., and $5.00 fine. Their offence was unlawful cohabitation, but this was construed by the court as polygamy. Wm. J. Flake and Jens N. Skousen, who plead guilty to u. c. (unlawful cohabitation), were each sentenced to six months' imprisonment at Yuma, Ariz., and $500 fine.

Sun. 7.—Ammon M. Tenney, Peter J. Christoffersen and Christopher J. Kempe left Prescott, Ariz., for the prison at Detroit, Mich., and Wm. J. Flake and Jens N. Skousen for Yuma prison.

Sat. 13.—John Olsen, of Salt Lake City, was arrested on a charge of u. c. and placed under $1,000 bonds.

Sun. 14.—The 83rd quorum of Seventy was partly organized by Seymour B. Young, at St. Johns, Apache Co., Ariz.

Wed. 31.—Elder Jacob Spori arrived as a Latter-day Saint missionary at Constantinople, Turkey.

1885.

The prosecutions under the Edmunds anti-polygamy law were carried on with great hostility by the Federal officials and courts in Utah and Idaho. A large number of polygamists were imprisoned and many others went into exile, some going into Mexico.

January.—The Saints who had settled at different points on the Fremont river (Dirty Devil), east of Rabbit Valley, were organized as Blue Valley Ward; Henry Giles, Bishop.

—Peter Olsen, missionary in Norway, was imprisoned five days on bread and water, for preaching the gospel.

Tues. 6.—After several days' examination, the Seventh School District lawsuit (Salt Lake City) was submitted to Judge Charles S. Zane, who two days later gave his decision in favor of the district trustees.

Thurs. 8. — Alexander F. Macdonald, Christopher Layton and John W. Campbell arrived at Corralitos, Chihuahua, Mexico, to rent or buy land, on which to locate such families of Saints as were being driven into exile, because of their family relations in the United States.

Sat. 10.—Bingham County, Idaho, was created out of a small part of Oneida County, by an act of the Idaho legislature.

Mon. 12.—Addison Everett, a prominent Elder of the Church and a Pioneer of 1847, died at St. George.

—Mary Ann Fielding, widow of Joseph Fielding, died in Salt Lake City.

—Elders Ferdinand F. Hintze and Anton Lauritzen were mobbed at Ribe, Denmark.

Tues. 13.—George S. Grant, son of the late Pres. Jedediah M. Grant, was accidentally shot and killed in Oakley, Cassia Co., Idaho.

Fri. 16.—The Morgan smelter, situated a few miles south of Salt Lake City, was destroyed by fire.

Sun. 18.—The Saints who had settled on the lower Muddy, Lincoln Co., Nev., were organized as Overton Ward; Isaiah Cox, Bishop.

Mon. 19.—The U. S. Supreme Court confirmed the action of the Utah courts in refusing to admit Rudger Clawson to bail.

Tues. 20.—Pres. Angus M. Cannon was arrested in Salt Lake City. on a charge of u. c.

—Alexander F. McDonald and companions returned to Corralitos, Chihuahua, Mexico, from an exploring tour to some of the valleys lying on the east slope of the Sierra Madre Mountains, and found several families of exiles who had arrived from the United States.

Fri. 23.—Rudger Clawson's sentence for polygamy was confirmed by the Supreme Court of Utah. The case was appealed to the United States Supreme Court.

—Jacob S. Boreman qualified as associate justice, in place of Stephen P. Twiss, resigned.

Sat. 24.—After several days' examination before Commissioner McKay, Pres.

Angus M. Cannon was placed under $1,500 bonds.

—Daniel H. Wells succeeded Apostle John H. Smith as president of the European mission, the latter sailing for America.

Wed. 28.—Royal B. Young, of Salt Lake City, was arrested on a charge of polygamy and u. c.

Thurs. 29.—Royal B. Young was placed under $2,000 bonds, after his preliminary examination before Com. McKay.

Fri. 30.—Agnes McMurrin, Royal B. Young's alleged plural wife, was on trial in the Third District Court, on a charge of perjury.

Sat. 31.—Jacob S. Boreman was appointed judge of the Second Judicial District of Utah.

February.—A difficulty between the land owners in Utah County and the several canal companies of Salt Lake County, caused by the overflow of Utah lake, was settled by arbitration.

Sun. 1.—Pres. John Taylor delivered his last public discourse in the Tabernacle, Salt Lake City. In the evening, he and Pres. Geo. Q. Cannon secreted themselves, in order to avoid the Federal officials, who were carrying on their high handed judicial proceedings in the Territory. Elder L. John Nuttall accompanied them as private secretary, Charles H. Wilcken as driver, and Charles H. Barrell as general aid.

Tues. 3.—A law passed by the Idaho legislature, prohibiting all "Mormons" from voting, was approved by Gov. Bunn.

Sun. 8.—Col. Heber P. Kimball died in Salt Lake City.

—Elders Matts S. Mattson and H. Persson were mobbed in Aabyholm, Sweden.

Mon. 9.—Ogden experienced a hot political contest at the election, but the Peoples' Party succeeded in getting a majority of votes for their candidates.

—The Trenton branch, Cache Co., was organized as a Ward; James B. Jardine, Bishop.

—A number of Saints going into exile because of their family relations, left Snowflake, Ariz., for Mexico. On their arrival at Luna Valley, New Mexico, on the 15th, they were organized into a traveling company, with E. A. Noble as captain. The company had increased to about seventy souls.

Tues. 10.—Thomas Bullock, one of the Pioneers of 1847, and formerly Pres. Brigham Young's secretary, died at Coalville, Summit Co.

Wed. 11. — Pres. Angus M. Cannon was arraigned before the Third District Court and allowed until the following Friday to plead. He then plead not guilty.

Thurs. 12. — Elder William Willes returned to Salt Lake City, from his mission to India.

—Elders Niels W. Petersen and Mads P. Madsen were mobbed, while holding a meeting in Kallundborg, Denmark.

Fri. 13.—Alta, Little Cottonwood Canyon, was almost entirely destroyed by a snowslide, and about fifteen persons were killed.

Tues. 17.—Dr. John D. M. Crockwell died in Salt Lake City.

Fri. 20.—Ferdinand F. Hintze's case was

called in the Third District Court, and the prosecutors discovered that the absent defendant was not under bonds.

Wed. 25.—Elder Francis M. Lyman, jun., who was arrested the day previous, was arraigned before the court at Weinhem, Germany, accused of holding a meeting and preaching "Mormonism," and sentenced to one day's imprisonment, after suffering which he was banished from the country.

March.—The impossibility of securing a fair trial in the Utah Federal courts caused a number of leading men to voluntarily go into exile.

—Wm. Fotheringham, of Beaver, was indicted by the grand jury, arrested and placed under bonds, being charged with u. c.

Sun. 1.—Apostle Moses Thatcher and other prominent men arrived at the camp of the Saints on the Casas Grandes river, Chihuahua, Mexico. Soon afterwards explorations were made in the surrounding country.

Mon. 2.—Parley P. Pratt, son of the late Apostle Parley P. Pratt, was arrested in Salt Lake City, charged with u.c.

—The free mail delivery system was introduced in Salt Lake City.

—The first number of the *Salt Lake Evening Democrat*, a daily anti-Mormon newspaper, was published in Salt Lake City, by the Salt Lake Democrat Company.

—Elders Wm. F. Garner and Christian F. Christensen had a narrow escape from being lynched by a mob in Mitchell County, North Carolina, where they labored as missionaries.

Wed. 4.—Ole L. Hansen, of Brighton, Salt Lake Co., charged with u.c., was arraigned before the Third District Court and plead not guilty.

Fri. 6.—Wm. H. Pitts, of the firm of Godbe, Pitts & Co., died in Salt Lake City.

Sat. 7.—Captain Noble's company of Arizona exiles, arrived at a point on the Casas Grandes river, near Ascencion, Chihuahua, Mexico, where they formed a temporary encampment.

Sun. 8.—Elders Charles W. Penrose, Lorenzo Waldram, jun., and Wm. W. Burton arrived at Liverpool, England, as missionaries from Utah.

—Bishop John Hunt's wife was burned to death at Snowflake, Ariz.

—The first Latter-day Saint Sunday School in Mexico was commenced at Corralitos, Chihuahua; James Gale, supt.

Wed. 11.—The Church blacksmith shop at the mouth of Little Cottonwood Canyon, was burned.

Thurs. 12.—The jury returned a verdict of guilty against Thos. Simpson for polygamy.

Fri. 13.—The Gardo House, Salt Lake City, was searched by U. S. deputy marshals, who subpœnaed a number of witnesses.

Sat. 14.—In the Third District Court, Thos. Simpson was sentenced to two years' imprisonment for polygamy and taken to the Penitentiary.

—The case against Laban Morrill,of Circle Valley, Utah, for u. c., was dismissed in the Second District Court, at Beaver.

Mon. 16.—Thomas Holland was drowned at Baker's Spring, near Utah Lake.

Tues. 17.—John Nicholson, associate editor of the *Deseret News*, was arrested, charged with u. c., and placed under $1,500 bonds, to answer before the grand jury.

Thurs. 19.—U. S. deputy marshals raided the houses of Geo. Q. Cannon, Geo. Dunford and Mrs. J. C. Little, in an unsuccessful search for witnesses in polygamy cases.

Sun. 22.—The U. S. Supreme Court rendered a decision annulling the test oath formulated by the Utah Commission. By this ruling a number of persons were restored to the elective franchise.

Tues. 24.—Parley P. Pratt was arrested in Salt Lake City on a charge of polygamy and u. c.

—The jury in the Second District Court (Beaver) rendered a verdict of not guilty in the case of Mr. Pace, who had been charged with u. c.

—Joseph Pidcock, of Ogden, was found dead near Montpelier, Bear Lake Co., Idaho.

Wed. 25.—A grand musical concert, under the direction of Prof. Geo. Careless, was given in the Salt Lake Theatre.

Fri. 27.—Eli B. Kelsey died in Salt Lake City.

Sat. 28.—Elder Abraham Coon died in Salt Lake City.

Mon. 30.—Orson P. Arnold, of Salt Lake City, was arrested on a charge of u. c. and placed under $1,500 bonds.

April.—A number of flowing artesian wells were made in Salt Lake City and vicinity.

—A. Milton Musser was arrested in Salt Lake City, on a charge of u. c., and placed under $1,000 bonds.

Thurs. 2.—The Utah Commission made a verbal report to President Cleveland at Washington, D. C., on their work in Utah.

Fri. 3.—Jacob S. Boreman was appointed judge of the First Judicial District of Utah, the second time.

Sat. 4.—John Pack, one of the Pioneers of 1847, died in Salt Lake City.

—Wm. W. Roundy was appointed to preside in the camp of the Saints, located north of the town of Casas Grandes, Chihuahua, Mexico.

—The 55th annual conference of the Church convened in Logan, Utah, Franklin D. Richards presiding. It was continued three days. On the second day (April 5th), an epistle from the First Presidency was read, and a committee was appointed to draft a petition to the President of the United States, praying for protection against the tyrannical acts of the Federal officials in Utah.

Tues. 7.—Charles I. Robson, counselor to the president of the Maricopa Stake, and Bishop Oscar M. Stewart, of Alma, were each sentenced to ninety days' imprisonment, at Yuma, Ariz., for u. c.

Thurs. 9.—The Saints encamped on the Casas Grandes river, Mexico, were ordered to leave the State of Chihuahua, in fifteen days.

—The Tennessee legislature passed a law, forbidding the teaching of polygamy in that State.

Fri. 10.—In the District Court at Phœnix, Ariz., the jury returned a verdict of guilty against A. P. Spilsbury, indicted for u. c.

Sat. 11.—At Phœnix, Ariz., A. P. Spilsbury and Geo. T. Wilson were each sentenced to six months' imprisonment, and Chas. I. Robson, Hyrum S. Phelps, Oscar M. Stewart and James Wilson to three months' imprisonment each for u. c. The following day (April 12th), they were taken to Yuma prison.

—The steamship *Wisconsin* sailed from Liverpool with 187 "Mormon" passengers, including 19 returning missionaries, in charge of Louis P. Lund; it arrived in New York April 22nd, and the company reached Salt Lake City, on the 28th.

Mon. 13.—Orson P. Arnold, of Salt Lake City, plead guilty to the charge of unlawful cohabitation, in the Third District Court, and, promising to obey the law in the future, was discharged on paying $300 fine.

—Elders Wm. F. Garner, of North Ogden, and Christian F. Christensen, of Kanosh, were arrested in Carter County, Tenn., accused of preaching polygamy.

Tues. 14.—James Thompson, of Salt Lake City, was arrested on a charge of u. c.

—Elders Wm. F. Garner and Christian F. Christensen were imprisoned at Elizabethtown, Tenn.

Wed. 15.—Edward Brain, of the 20th Ward, Salt Lake City, was arrested on a charge of u.c., and placed under $2,000 bonds.

—Apostle George Teasdale and other Elders arrived at the City of Chihuahua, Mexico, to plead the cause of the Saints encamped on the Casas Grandes river. The next day (16th) they had an interview with the governor, who referred the question of ejectment to the Federal government.

Thurs. 16.—Judge Zane rendered a decision declaring the Territorial liquor law valid and sustaining the action of the county court against certain liquor dealers.

Fri. 17.—Clara D. Young, wife of John W. Young, died in Salt Lake City.

—Emil O. Olsen, of Salt Lake City, was arrested on a charge of u.c. and placed under $1,000 bonds.

Sun. 19.—Pres. Wm. D. Hendricks, of the Oneida Stake, Idaho, was arrested in Logan, Utah, on a charge of u.c.

Mon. 20.—Wm. A. Rossiter, of Salt Lake City, was arrested on a charge of u.c. and placed under $1,000 bonds.

—The U. S. Supreme Court sustained the decision of the Utah courts, in Rudger Clawson's polygamy case, but decided in favor of giving the murderer Fred Hopt a fourth trial.

Tues. 21.—David E. Davis, of Clover, Tooele Co., was arrested on a charge of u. c., and placed under $1,500 bonds.

Wed. 22.—Samuel H. B. Smith, of Salt Lake City, was arrested on a charge of u. c., and placed under $1,500 bonds.

Fri. 24.—U. S. deputy marshals searched the Temple Block for the purpose of making arrests, but found no one they wanted.

—Bishop Hiram B. Clawson, of Salt Lake City, was arrested on a charge of u. c., and placed under $1,500 bonds.

—The first number of the *Home Sentinel*, a weekly newspaper, was published by

Jakeman & Harrington, at·Manti, Sanpete Co.

Mon. 27.—The trial of Pres. Angus M. Cannon was commenced in the Third District Court, Salt Lake City.

Tues. 28.—Abraham H. Cannon, of Salt Lake City, was arrested on a charge of u. c., and placed under $1,500 bonds.

—The jury returned a verdict of guilty against Pres. Angus M. Cannon, for u. c.

—Bishop James C. Hamilton, of Mill Creek, Salt Lake Co., was arrested on a charge of u. c. and polygamy, brought to Salt Lake City, and placed under $1,500 bonds.

Thurs. 30.—The trial of A. Milton Musser was commenced in the Third District Court.

—John Aird, who plead guilty to the charge of u. c., promised to obey the law and was sentenced to $300 fine; in default of payment he was sent to the Penitentiary.

May.—The 84th quorum of Seventy was organized by Seymour B. Young in the Bannock Stake, Idaho; Swen Jacobs, sen., Walter Paul, Arvis C. Dille, Joseph H. Brown, L. E. Shurtliff, Walter G. Paul and Wm. H. Walker, presidents.

—Marcus L. Shepherd and David Levi were arrested at Beaver, Utah, on a charge of u. c.

—Apostles Brigham Young and Moses Thatcher visited the City of Mexico, and obtained permission from the Federal government for the Saints to remain in Chihuahua.

—Elder Niels Hansen, who labored as a missionary in Frederikshavn, Denmark, was ordered out of the country.

Fri. 1.—Claudius V. Spencer, who had been indicted for u. c., plead guilty in the Third District Court, and, promising to live within the law, Judge Zane suspended sentence.

Sat. 2.—A grand mass meeting was held in the Tabernacle, Salt Lake City, to protest against the oppressive course of the Federal officials in the Territory. A declaration of grievances and protest, addressed to the President and people of the United States, were adopted, and John T. Caine, John W. Taylor and John Q. Cannon were chosen as a delegation to proceed to Washington with the documents. Similar mass meetings were held in the various cities and towns of the Territory.

—The jury in the Third District Court returned a verdict of guilty against A. Milton Musser, James C. Watson and Parley P. Pratt. The latter, who had been indicted for u. c., plead guilty to the charge and was sentenced to six months' imprisonment and $300 fine, and taken to the Penitentiary.

Mon. 4.—O. L. Hansen, of Brighton, indicted for u. c., was acquitted in the Third District Court.

Fri. 8.—Wm. D. Newsom, of the 11th Ward, Salt Lake City, was arrested on a charge of polygamy, and the preliminary examination commenced before Com. McKay. Lucy Devereau, defendants' plural wife, one of the witnesses in the case, was taken to the Penitentiary for refusing to testify.

Sat. 9. — Pres. Angus M. Cannon, A.

Milton Musser and James C. Watson were each sentenced to six months' imprisonment and $300 fine for u. c., and taken to the Penitentiary.

—Samuel Humphreys was arrested at Nounnan Valley and Chas. Simpson at another place in Bear Lake Co., Idaho, on a charge of polygamy. They were both taken to Blackfoot for examination.

—Wm. D. Newsom was admitted to $3,000 bail, and Lucy Devereau released from custody, being placed under $200 bonds.

Sun. 10.—Eight armed deputy marshals arrested Wm. D. Pratt, of Wilford, and John L. Roberts, of Rexburg, Bingham Co., Idaho, in the night, on a charge of u. c., or polygamy, and started for Blackfoot the following day. Both plead guilty and were sentenced to imprisonment May 23rd following.

Mon. 11.—U. S. Marshal Fred. T. Dubois, of Idaho, and five assistants, armed to the teeth, visited Paris, Bear Lake Co. Idaho, in search of polygamists.

Wed. 13.—The Utah delegation (Caine, Cannon and Taylor) had an interview with President Cleveland, at Washington, D. C.

—Isaac Groo, of Salt Lake City, was arrested on a charge of u. c., and placed under $1,500 bonds, after pleading guilty to the charge before Com. McKay.

—J. D. Jones, of Idaho, was sentenced to $300 fine for u. c., and promised to obey the law in the future.

Thurs. 14.—After several days' trial, the jury in the Third District Court returned a verdict of not guilty in the case against Officer Thomas F. Thomas, who had been accused of assaulting the negro, who killed Capt. Andrew Burt, Aug. 25, 1883.

—James Taylor, of Ogden, was arrested on a charge of u. c., and placed under $1,500.

Fri. 15.—Moroni Brown and Francis A. Brown, of Ogden, were arrested on the charge of u. c., and each placed under $1,500 bonds.

Sat. 16.—Job Pingree, of Ogden, was arrested on a charge of u. c. and placed under $1,500 bonds.

—Wm. Fotheringham was adjudged guilty of u. c. by the jury in the Second District Court, Beaver, after a lengthy trial, although no proof of his guilt had been produced, except for "holding out."

—The steamship *Wisconsin* sailed from Liverpool, with 174 Saints, including 15 returning missionaries, under the direction of N. M. Hodges. On the 27th it arrived in New York, and the company arrived in Salt Lake City, June 2nd.

Tues. 19.—Lucy Devereau was again sent to the Penitentiary for refusing to answer certain questions before the grand jury in the Third District Court.

—Joseph M. Phelps, of Montpelier, Bear Lake Co., Idaho, was arrested in Salt Lake City, on a charge of u. c.

Wed. 20.—In the Second District Court (Judge Boreman), Wm. Fotheringham was sentenced to three months' imprisonment and $300 fine, and taken to the Penitentiary.

Thurs. 21.—Aurelius Miner, of Salt Lake City was arrested on a charge of u. c.

—Hiram B. Clawson, Bishop of the 12th

Ward, Salt Lake City, was arrested on a charge of u. c., and placed under $1,500 bonds.

—David Lee, who plead guilty to the charge of u. c., was discharged on paying a fine of $300.

—Elder John P. Ibsen, while preaching the gospel in a private house on Bornholm, Denmark, was arrested and brought to Rønne, where he was tried and imprisoned three days for preaching. Soon afterwards he was sent as a prisoner to Copenhagen.

Fri. 22.—The grand jury having found an indictment against Isaac Groo, of Salt Lake City, for u. c., he was re-arrested and placed under $1,500 bonds, to await trial.

Sat. 23.—In the District Court at Blackfoot, Idaho, Judge Morgan sentenced Bishop George Stuart, of Malad, Wm. J. Pratt, of Wilford, and John T. Roberts, of Rexburg, each to four months' imprisonment in the Boise Penitentiary and $300 fine; John Winn, an old man, of Battle Creek, Oneida Co., and Charles W. Simpson, of Montpelier, each to a fine of $300, and Samuel Humphreys to six months' imprisonment and $300 fine.

—Elder August Valentine, who labored as a missionary on Bornholm, Denmark, was arrested for preaching the gospel. He was brought to Copenhagen, and there imprisoned for five days, after which he was banished from the country.

Sun. 24.—Joseph S. Staker was ordained the first Bishop of Annabella Ward, Sevier Co., Utah.

Mon. 25.—Apostle Franklin D. Richards returned from a trip to the East, during which he visited Pueblo, Independence, Richmond (Mo.), Carthage, Nauvoo (Ill.) and other places known in Church history.

—Peter Nebeker died at Willard, Box Elder Co., Utah.

- Elders Wiley G. Cragun and Franklin A. Fraughton were mobbed in South Carolina; Fraughton received forty lashes with a whip and Cragun was shot in the chin.

Wed. 27.—Charles Seal, of the 16th Ward, Salt Lake City, was arrested on a charge of u. c., and placed under $1,000 bonds.

—The case of James Taylor, of Ogden, was dismissed for the time being, because of an error in the indictment.

Thurs. 28.—After a preliminary examination before Com. McKay, Charles Seal was arraigned on two charges of polygamy and bound over in $3,000 bonds, to await the action of the grand jury.

—Alfred Best, of Mill Creek, was arrested in Salt Lake City, on a charge of u. c. and placed under $1,000 bonds.

—Elder Aug. Valentine left Copenhagen for England, being the first Elder banished from Denmark for preaching the gospel.

Sun. 31.—Elder John P. Ibsen was imprisoned in Copenhagen, Denmark, awaiting his banishment from the country.

June.—Diphtheria was raging in Salt Lake City and vicinity.

—Edmund Ellsworth, of Arizona, was sentenced to $300 fine, for u.c., and, not being able to pay it, was imprisoned at Yuma.

—Wm. J. Flake, having served his sentence in the Yuma prison, Ariz., was released.

—Elders Ferdinand F. Hintze, Christian N. Lundsten, Jens Nielsen and Neils Hansen, missionaries from Utah, were banished from Jutland, Denmark, for preaching the gospel.

Tues. 2.—James H. Nelson was arrested in Ogden, on a charge of u.c. Deputy Marshals Ferkins and Brown, who attempted to enter Nelson's house, without a search warrant, received rough treatment from Mrs. Nelson.

Thurs. 4.—The first number of *Svenska Harolden* (a weekly), the first Swedish newspaper in Utah, was issued in Salt Lake City, by the Swedish Publishing Company, recently organized.

—The grand jury having found an indictment against Alfred Best, of Mill Creek, he was re-arrested and placed under $1,000 bonds.

—Elder John P. Ibsen was brought on board the steamer *Milo*, at Copenhagen, Denmark, by the police-officers, having been banished from the country for preaching the gospel.

Sat. 6.—Wm. Wilding died in the 17th Ward, Salt Lake City, 102 years of age.

—Bishop Dennison L. Harris, died at Monroe, Sevier Co.

Tues. 9.—N. P. Jeppesen, of Logan, and two others, were drowned in Salmon river, Idaho, by being carried over the falls.

Wed. 10.—The 85th quorum of Seventy was partly organized by Jacob Gates and Edward Steverson at Kanab, Kane Co., Utah; Reuben Broadbent, Chas. S. Cram, William J. Jolly, Svend M. Anderson and William H. Clayton, presidents.

Thurs. 11.—The motion for new trials in in the cases of Pres. Angus M. Cannon and A. Milton Musser was argued in the Supreme Court of Utah.

Fri. 12. — Brett's Circus performed in Salt Lake City.

—Isaac B. Nash, of Franklin, Oneida Co., Idaho, was arrested on a charge of u. c., and, after a preliminary examination before Commissioner House, at Oxford, placed under $1,500 bonds.

Sat. 13.—The Supreme Court of Utah affirmed the decision of the court below, against Thomas Simpson for polygamy.

—Andrew W. Cooley, of Brighton, Salt Lake Co., who had been indicted for u. c., gave himself up to the marshal and was put under $1,000 bonds.

—The 86th quorum of Seventy was partly organized by Jacob Gates and Edward Stevenson, at Panguitch, Garfield Co.; John W. Norton, Albert W. Norton, Albert H. Riding and S. A. Johnson, presidents.

Thurs. 18.—Policeman Andrew Smith, of Salt Lake City, was arrested on a charge of u.c. and placed under $1,500 bonds.

Sat. 20.—Charles L. White, of the 19th Ward, Salt Lake City, was arrested on a charge of u.c. Elizabeth Ann Starkey, one of the witnesses, was fined $50 and sentenced to one day's imprisonment for refusing to answer certain questions before the Commissioner.

—The steamship *Wisconsin* sailed from

Liverpool, with 541 Saints, including 30 returning missionaries, under the direction of Jørgen Hansen. They arrived at New York July 1st, and at Salt Lake City July 7th.

Sun. 21.—In the Parowan Stake quarterly conference, the two Parowan Wards were united into one Ward, with Charles Adams as Bishop.

—The 87th quorum of Seventy was organized by Abraham H. Cannon, at Plain City, Weber Co.; Wm. Geddes, J. P. Folkmann, Alonzo Knight, Charles Featherstone, William S. Geddes and Hans Poulsen, presidents.

Mon. 22.—The examination of Charles L. White's case was continued before Commissioner McKay; the defendant was placed under $2,000 bonds, and Miss Starkey, who still refused to answer, taken back to the Penitentiary.

—Benjamin F. Steward, presiding Elder at Benjamin, Utah Co., was killed by lightning, while sitting in his carriage near his residence.

Tues. 23.—Under the management of the Old Folks Committee, the aged people of Salt Lake County had an excursion to Garfield, on the southern shore of the Great Salt Lake.

Wed. 24.—Samuel Ensign, an eighty year old veteran, fell from the Temple walls, in Salt Lake City, and was instantly killed.

—The polygamy case against Charles L. White was dismissed, and he was held under $500 bonds to answer to the charge of u.c. Miss Starkey was brought before the grand jury and Judge Zane, but as she still refused to answer certain questions, she was taken back to the Penitentiary.

Thurs. 25.—Frederik H. Hansen, of Pleasant Green, Salt Lake Co., was arrested on a charge of u. c. and placed under $500 bonds.

—Septimus W. Sears, of Salt Lake City, was arrested in Chicago, Ill., on a charge of u.c. He was released on $3,000 bonds.

Sat. 27.—John Nicholson, Andrew Smith, Geo. Romney and John Connelly, all of Salt Lake City, were arrested, charged with u.c. They each gave bonds in $1,500, to appear for trial in September.

—The Supreme Court of Utah affirmed the decision of the Third District Court against Pres. Angus M. Cannon.

Sun. 28.—Wm. W. Drummond, once associate justice of Utah, was sentenced to the House of Correction for stealing postage stamps, in Chicago, Ill.

Mon. 29.—Joseph W. McMurrin, of Salt Lake City, was arrested on a charge of u.c. and gave bonds in $1,500, to await trial.

—In the Third District Court, Wm. D. Newsom, John Connelly, John Daynes, Geo. Romney and Andrew Smith plead not guilty to the charges against them, while John Nicholson refused to plead.

Tues. 30.—In the First District Court, at Ogden, Francis A. Brown, being on trial for u. c., read an able plea in his own defence.

July.—A number of artesian wells were obtained in Salt Lake City.

Thurs. 2.—Apostle John Henry Smith

was arrested in Salt Lake City, charged with u. c., but after the preliminary examination before Com. McKay, he was released for lack of evidence.

—Gov. Wm. M. Bunn, of Idaho, a bitter anti-Mormon, resigned his office.

Sat. 4.—The flag on the City Hall, County Court House and Z. C. M. I., Salt Lake City, was placed at half mast, in token of mourning over the condition of affairs in Utah. Great excitement ensued, and threats of violence by anti-Mormons were made.

—Edward Brain, of Salt Lake City, was arrested a second time, taken to the Penitentiary and later in the day placed under $2,500 bonds, to await the action of the grand jury, being charged with the crime of resisting the officers.

Tues. 7.—In the First District Court at Ogden, Job Pingree, of Ogden, was convicted of u. c.

Sat. 11.—Francis A. Brown and Moroni Brown, of Ogden, were each sentenced to six months' imprisonment and $300 fine, for u. c., and taken to the Utah Penitentiary.

—A "Liberal" mass meeting, held in Salt Lake City, for the purpose of condemning the half mast affair, proved unsuccessful to its instigators.

Mon. 13.—In the First District Court at Ogden, Job Pingree, was sentenced to five months in the Penitentiary and a fine of $300, for u. c.

—N. Porter of Preston, Idaho, was arrested, charged with u. c., taken to Oxford and placed under bonds.

Tues. 14.—The election for school trustees in the various school districts in Utah resulted in victory to the Peoples' Party.

Wed. 15.—The Insane Asylum at Provo was opened.

Thurs. 16. — Lovinia Careless, wife of Professor Geo. Careless, and one of the finest singers in the Territory, died from the effects of poison, in Salt Lake City.

—Charles F. Middleton, of the presidency of the Weber Stake, was arraigned before the District Court in Ogden, charged with u. c.

—Sarah A. Nelson, of Ogden, was arrested, charged with having resisted the officers on June 2nd.

—Pres. Hugh S. Gowans, of the Tooele Stake, and John Bowen, of Tooele, were arrested and brought to Salt Lake City, charged with polygamy and u. c.

Fri. 17.—Pres. Hugh. S. Gowans and John Bowen, of Tooele, were each placed under $1,500 bonds, to await the action of the grand jury,

—Thomas Burningham, of Bountiful, Davis Co., was arrested on a trumped up charge of threatening to kill, brought to Salt Lake City and acquitted, but placed under $1,500 bonds, charged with u. c.

—Acting on the suggestion of General O. O. Howard, Pres. Cleveland ordered U. S. troops ready for action, in case of an outbreak in Salt Lake City on the coming 24th of July.

Sun. 19.—The Improvement Associations of the Sevier Stake held a large conference at Fish lake.

Mon. 20.—A monster mass meeting was held in Paris, Bear Lake Co., remonstrating against the political oppression in that county, and petitioning Pres. Cleveland for redress.

Tues. 21.—Thomas Porcher, of the 21st Ward, Salt Lake City, was arrested on a charge of u. c. After the preliminary examination, he was admitted to bail in $1,000 bonds.

Wed. 22.—Truman O. Angell, jun., assistant Church architect, was arrested, charged with u. c., and placed under $1,500 bonds.

Thurs. 23.—Thomas Walton, of Bountiful, Davis Co., Utah, was arrested, charged with violating the Edmunds law, brought to Salt Lake City, tried before Com. McKay and discharged.

—John Penman, of Bountiful, was also arrested on a charge of u. c., but escaped from the officers, by strategy, on the way to Salt Lake City.

Fri. 24.—Although the rabid anti-Mormons were so enraged because the Mormons of Salt Lake City raised the flag on half mast on July 4th, and threatened direful consequences, if the act was repeated on the 24th, yet on this eventful day, all the citizens, anti-Mormons as well as Mormons, put the flag at half mast in token of mourning over the demise of Ex-President U. S. Grant, who died at Mt. McGregor, N. Y., the day before (July 23rd).

Sat. 25.—Florence A. Clawson, daughter of Henry Dinwoodey, sued for and obtained a divorce from her husband, Rudger Clawson, who was confined in the Penitentiary.

August. — Seventeen emigrants from New Zealand arrived in Box Elder County, Utah.

—Gas wells were bored in Salt Lake City, and the driving for flowing artesian wells was continued successfully.

—Elder Thomas Biesinger was again expelled from Bavaria.

Sun. 2.—Joseph Weatherell, of Santaquin, Utah Co., was drowned in the Jordan river, near Salt Lake City; the body was found on the 5th.

Mon. 3.—The general election in Utah for members to the legislative assembly resulted in victory to the People's Party, except in Summit County, which was carried by the Liberals.

Tues. 4.—Wm. Fotheringham was released from the Penitentiary.

—Joseph M. Weiler, of the 3rd Ward, Salt Lake City, died.

Fri. 7.—John W. Snell, of Salt Lake City, was arrested on a charge of u. c.

Sat. 8.—Morris D. Rosenbaum, of Brigham City, died suddenly at Franklin, Idaho.

Sun. 16.—The notorious apostate Wm. Jarman made an unsuccessful attempt to break up a conference meeting of Saints in Sheffield, England. A mob numbering several thousands followed the Elders, hooting and yelling. The police, however, protected the brethren from assault.

Mon. 17.—Eliza Shafer was sentenced to 24 hours in the Penitentiary and a $25 fine by Commissioner McKay for alleged contempt of court.

Wed. 19.—Judge Zane having sustained McKay's decision, Eliza Shafer was sent to the Penitentiary.

Thurs. 20.—The Utah Commission refused to investigate the election frauds in Summit County, and to count the votes cast for Orson F. Whitney as Territorial Superintendent of District Schools.

—Wm. R. Judd, a prominent citizen of Tooele County, died at Grantsville.

Fri. 21.—Elizabeth Ann Starkey, the alleged second wife of Chas. L. White, was released from the Penitentiary, after two months' imprisonment for contempt of court.

—Eliza Shafer, who had been released from the Penitentiary after one day's imprisonment, was again arrested and put under $700 bonds to appear before the grand jury in September.

Sun. 23.—The Saints who had settled on and near Green river, Uintah Co., Utah, were organized as the Riverdale district; Nathan Hunting, acting Bishop.

Wed. 26.—U. S. deputy marshals made a raid upon the settlement of Oakley, Cassia Co., Idaho.

Fri. 28.—About four hundred orphan children, from Salt Lake City, were treated to a free excursion to Garfield, under the auspices of the Old Folks Committee.

—Miss Elizabeth Ann Starkey was again arrested and sentenced by Commissioner McKay to another term of imprisonment, but a writ of *habeas corpus* and a hearing by Judge Zane procured her release.

Sat. 29. — Of four applicants John W. Snell, jun., was chosen as the Utah candidate to West Point.

—The steamship *Wisconsin* sailed from Liverpool with 329 Saints, including 16 returning Elders, under the direction of John W. Thornley. The company arrived in New York Sept. 8th, and at Salt Lake City Sept. 14th.

September.—Diphtheria raged in Gunnison, Sanpete Co.

Thurs. 3.—Wm. H. Lee, of Tooele, was arrested for u. c., taken to Salt Lake City and, after examination before Com. McKay, placed under $1,500 bonds.

Sat. 5.—Wm. W. Willey, of Bountiful, Davis Co., was arrested on a charge of u. c.

Mon. 7.—Twenty-two participants in the Rock Springs massacre were arrested and jailed at Green river.

—Wm. W. Willey had an examination before Com. McKay and was placed under $1,500 bonds.

Wed. 9.—Deputy marshals made a raid on Heber, Wasatch Co., and arrested Joseph Moulton, John W. Witt and John Duke, charged with u. c. The prisoners were brought to Salt Lake City with subpoenaed witnesses.

Thurs. 10.—John W. Witt and John Duke, after preliminary examination before Com. McKay, were each placed under $1,500 bonds to await the action of the grand jury.

Fri. 11.—Joseph Moulton was discharged, after the usual examination before Com. McKay, there being no testimony to hold him.

Tues. 15.—Miss Elizabeth Ann Starkey and Miss Eliza Shafer were sent to the Penitentiary by Judge Zane, of the Third District Court, for refusing to answer certain questions before the grand jury.

Wed. 16.—Judge Zane, in his instructions to the grand jury, interpreted the law in such a way, that persons found guilty of u. c. could be imprisoned for life. This was the commencement of the segregation policy.

Thurs. 17.—The annual Primary Fair opened in the Social Hall, Salt Lake City, and was continued three days.

Fri. 18. — Bishop John Sharp plead guilty to the charge of u. c. and promised to obey the law; he was fined $300 and costs.

Sat. 19.—Edward Thomas, of Beaver, was arrested for u. c. and placed under $1,500 bonds.

Sun. 20.—Marvin Allred, of St. Charles, Bear Lake Co., Idaho, was arrested at Montpelier, on a charge of u. c.

Mon. 21.—The fourth trial of Fred. Hopt (Welcome) for the murder of John F. Turner was commenced in the Third District Court.

Tues. 22.—Wm. Pickett, of Tooele, was discharged, the grand jury not being able to get testimony against him for u. c.

Wed. 23.—Judge Orlando W. Powers, in his charge to the grand jury of the First District Court, stated that an indictment could be found against a man guilty of co-habitation for every day.

—Elders Wm. F. Rigby and Alexander Leatham were arrested at Rexburg, Idaho, for u. c. and taken to Eagle Rock.

Mon. 28.—The jury of the Third District Court returned a verdict of guilty of murder in the first degree against Fred. Hopt (Welcome).

Tues. 29.—In the Third District Court (Judge Zane), Bishop Hiram B. Clawson was sentenced to six months' imprisonment and $300 fine, for u. c.

—Septimus W. Sears and Truman O. Angell, jun., charged with u. c., promised to live within the law, and were let off with fines, the former $300, and the latter $150.

—In the Second District Court (Judge Boreman), Beaver, John Lang, of Beaver, was sentenced to three months' imprisonment and $200 fine for u. c.

October.—Alonzo Johnson and Samuel Moody, two "Mormon" missionaries, were mobbed in Tolono, Champaign Co., Illinois.

Thurs. 1.—In the Third District Court (Judge Zane), John Daynes plead guilty to the charge of u. c., and promising to obey the law, Judge Zane discharged him on paying a $150 fine. The jury also returned a verdict of guilty against Wm. A. Rossiter for u. c.

Fri. 2.—Edward Brain of the 21st Ward, Salt Lake City, was found guilty of u. c. and sentenced to six months' imprisonment and $300 fine; he was taken to the Penitentiary.

Sat. 3.—Elder John Nicholson, assistant editor of the *Deseret News*, waived his right as a defendant and testified for the prosecution, which resulted in the jury bringing in a verdict of guilty against him for u. c. Aurelius Miner entered a plea of not guilty to the charge of u. c. Alfred Best, of Mill Creek, and Emil O. Olsen, of Salt Lake City, testified against them-

selves and were found guilty of u. c. by the jury.

Mon. 5.—In the Third District Court (Judge Zane), Isaac Groo and Charles Seal, of Salt Lake City, Alfred Best, of Mill Creek, David E. Davis, of Clover, Tooele Co., and Andrew W. Cooley, of Brighton, were each sentenced to six months' imprisonment and $300 fine. The prisoners were taken to the Penitentiary the same day.

Tues. 6.—The general conference of the Church was commenced at Logan, Cache Co. It was continued until Friday 9th.

—Charles L. White plead guilty to a charge of u. c. and was sentenced to six months' imprisonment and a fine of $300. This caused the release of his alleged wife, Miss Elisabeth Ann Sharkey, who had been confined in the Penitentiary since Sept. 15th. John Connelly plead guilty to the charge of u. c. and was sentenced by Judge Zane to six months' imprisonment and $300 fine.

Wed. 7.—Aurelius Miner, of Salt Lake City, was found guilty of u. c. by the jury, after a two days' trial. The jury also returned a verdict of guilty against Andrew Smith for u. c.

Thurs. 8.—Wm. D. Newsom was found guilty, by the jury in the Third District Court, of polygamy and u. c. Frederik H. Hansen was declared guilty of u. c.

—A. L. Blackburn was arrested at Rexburg, Idaho, charged with u. c.

Fri. 9.—Three jurymen (Moritz, Davis and Clayton) were discharged from the grand jury, in the Third District Court, because they refused to find indictments for u. c. against A. Milton Musser and others, who were then serving sentences for the same offense.

Sat. 10.—In the Third District Court (Judge Zane), Salt Lake City, Wm. A. Rossiter and Geo. Romney were each sentenced to six months' imprisonment and $300 fine for u. c. Thos. Porcher and Robt. H. Swain plead guilty to the same charge, but sentence was deferred because of the defendants being poor.

Mon. 12.—A. Milton Musser and James C. Watson were released from the Penitentiary, having served their term of imprisonment.

Tues. 13.—John Nicholson, Andrew Smith and Emil O. Olsen were each sentenced to six months' imprisonment and $300 fine, and taken to the Penitentiary.

Thurs. 15.—John Penman, of Bountiful, was re-arrested in Parley's Canyon, on a charge of u. c. (See July 23rd.)

—Parley P. Pratt was released from the Penitentiary.

Sat. 17.—In the Third District Court (Judge Zane), Wm. D. Newsom was sentenced to three years' and six months' imprisonment and $800 fine, for polygamy and u.c., and Aurelius Miner to six months' imprisonment and $300 fine for u. c. Both were taken to the Penitentiary; but, previous to their confinement there, Newsom was brutally treated by deputy marshals.

—Gov. Eli H. Murray, in his annual report to the Secretary of the Interior, grossly misrepresented the situation in Utah.

Mon. 19.—Bishop W. A. Follett died at Smithville, Graham Co., Ariz.

Tues. 20.—Thomas Simpson, a non-Mormon, who seven months' previous was sentenced to two years' imprisonment for polygamy, was pardoned by President Cleveland and released from the Penitentiary.

—John Penman and his alleged plural wife, Mary E. Hodgson, obtained bail and were released from prison.

—The Utah Commission submitted an unfavorable and partly untrue report to the Secretary of the Interior.

Wed. 21.—Isaac B. Nash, Andrew A. Biørn and Arthur Peck were on trial before Judge Hayes, at Blackfoot, Idaho, charged with u.c. The jury returned a verdict of guilty, as charged.

Thurs. 22.—U. S. deputy marshals made an unsuccessful raid on the Forest Farm, near Salt Lake City.

Fri. 23.—The 88th quorum of Seventy was partly organized by Seymour B. Young and Christian D. Fjeldsted, at Oxford, Oneida Co., Idaho; John H. Clark, Henry Dixon and B. H. Hunt, presidents.

—The first number of the *Southern Idaho Independent* was issued in Paris, Bear Lake Co., Idaho, instead of *The Bear Lake Democrat*, suspended.

Sat. 24.—Joseph H. Sissom, of Sandy, Salt Lake Co., was arrested on a charge of u. c.

—The steamship *Nevada* sailed from Liverpool with 313 Saints (162 British, 119 Scandinavian, 6 Swiss and German and 26 returning missionaries) in charge of Anthon H. Lund. They arrived at New York Nov. 4th and at Salt Lake City Nov. 10th.

Mon. 26.—Henry Grow was arrested on the Temple Block, Salt Lake City, on a charge of u. c.

—A fire destroyed 100 tons of tithing hay in Monroe, Sevier Co.

Tues. 27.—Price Ward, Emery Stake, was reorganized; Geo. Frandsen, Bishop.

Wed. 28.—In the Third District Court, Judge Zane made a decision in favor of U. J. Wenner, one of the governor's appointees, for the position of probate judge of Salt Lake County. The case was appealed.

Thurs. 29.—Gen. John B. Clark, the notorious Mormon persecutor of 1838, died at Fayette, Howard Co., Mo.

Sat. 31.—Herbert J. Foulger, of the 21st Ward, Salt Lake City, was arrested on a charge of u. c.

—Aurelius Miner was brought from the Penitentiary to the Third District Court, and was requested to promise to live within the law, which he declined.

November.—Apostle Albert Carrington was excommunicated from the Church for lewd and lascivious conduct and adultery.

Mon. 2.—Robert H. Swain was sentenced to six months' imprisonment and $300 fine for u. c., and taken to the Penitentiary.

—The "Millard Stake Academy" was formally opened in Fillmore, Millard Co., Utah.

Thurs. 5.—Frederik H. Hansen, found guilty of u. c., was sentenced to six months' imprisonment and $300 fine, and forthwith sent to the Penitentiary.

—John W. Keddington, of the 10th Ward, Salt Lake City, was arrested on a charge of u. c.

Fri. 6.—Thos. C. Jones, of the 10th Ward, Salt Lake City, was arrested on a charge of u. c.

Sat. 7.—Henry Grow, John W. Keddington and H. J. Foulger were arraigned before the Third District Court, the grand jury having found indictments against them for u. c. Grow plead not guilty and was put under $1,500 bonds, Keddington plead guilty and was kept on $1,500 security, formerly given, and Foulger, against whom three indictments had been found, plead not guilty and was put under $3,500 bonds.

—John P. Ball, of the 3rd Ward, Salt Lake City, was arrested on a charge of u. c., and put under bonds.

—By Judge Hayes, at Blackfoot, Idaho, Jos. M. Phelps, of Montpelier, Bear Lake Co., Alexander Leatham, of Rexburg, Bingham Co., Andrew A. Biørn and Arthur Peck, of Gentile Valley, Oneida Co., were each sentenced to six months' imprisonment, $300 fine and $100 costs of court; A. L. Blackburn (who pleaded guilty) to six months' imprisonment and $300 fine; Isaac B. Nash, of Franklin, Oneida Co., to three months' imprisonment; N. Porter, of Preston, Oneida Co., to three months' imprisonment and $150 fine—all for u. c. Geo. C. Parkinson, of Oxford, Bingham Co., was sentenced to one year's imprisonment, $300 fine and $100 costs of court, for being accused of secreting a friend from deputy marshals. The charge was false. The prisoners were started towards Boise City the same evening.

Sun. 8.—The Saints who had settled on the Provo bench, north of Provo, Utah Co., were organized as the Timpanogas Ward; Peter M. Wentz, Bishop.

Mon. 9.—William Cowan, of the 8th Ward, Salt Lake City, was arrested on a charge of u. c.

—The case against Elder Christian F. Christensen, for preaching in Tennessee, was dismissed.

Tues. 10.—Phœbe W. Woodruff, wife of Apostle Wilford Woodruff, died in Salt Lake City.

—Martha Taylor, of the 20th Ward, Salt Lake City, was accidentally burned to death.

—Deputy Sheriff Andrew Burt and Deputy Marshal H. F. Colin had an altercation on Main Street, Salt Lake City, for which Burt the following day was fined $25 in the police court.

Wed. 11.—By the explosion of gas in the Salt Lake Brewery, 10th Ward, Louis Boersig was instantly killed, and Jacob Kraut (who died November 18th) fatally injured.

Thurs. 12.—John P. Ball, of the 10th Ward, and Thomas C. Jones, of the 3rd Ward, Salt Lake City, plead not guilty to indictments for u. c. brought against them by the Third District grand jury.

—James Moyle, of the 15th Ward, Salt Lake City, was arrested on a charge of u. c. The following day he gave bonds in $1,500, to await the action of the grand jury.

Fri. 13.—Charles W. Nibley, of Logan, Utah, was arrested at Pocatello, Idaho, on a charge of u. c., and brought to Salt Lake City the following day.

Sat. 14.—Judge Zane, in the Third District Court, rendered a decision disbarring Aurelius Miner, and sentenced Andrew Burt to five days' imprisonment and $150 fine for his collision with Deputy Marshal Collin on the 10th inst.

Tues. 17.—Charles W. Nibley was discharged in Com. McKay's court, Salt Lake City, his arrest being illegal.

—Job Pingree, of Ogden, was released from the Penitentiary.

Wed. 18.—James Moyle, of Salt Lake City, was re-arrested, the grand jury having found three indictments against him for u. c.; a plea of not guilty was entered and bail given in the sum of $2,200.

Thurs. 19.—A number of U. S. deputy marshals came in collision with a number of young men, in Franklin, Oneida Co., Idaho.

Fri. 20.—Apostle Lorenzo Snow was arrested by seven deputies at his residence in Brigham City, on a charge of u. c., and brought to Ogden.

Sat. 21.—John W. Keddington and Thomas Porcher were sentenced to six months' imprisonment and $300 fine, each, for u. c. and forthwith taken to the Penitentiary.

—Deputy Marshal Oscar C. Vandercook and U. S. Commissioner Charles E. Pearson was arrested by the Salt Lake City police officers, on charges of lewd and lascivious conduct, and taken to the City Hall; each gave bonds in the sum of $500.

—Lorenzo Snow plead not guilty in the First District Court, in Ogden, and was admitted to bail.

Mon. 23.—Assistant District Attorney Sam. H. Lewis and W. H. Yearian, anti-Mormon merchant in Salt Lake City, were rrrested by the city police, on charges of lewd and lascivious conduct; $500 bail was given by each.

—Bishop David M. Stuart, of Ogden, was arrested on a charge of u. c., taken before Com. Black and placed under bonds.

—Deputy Marshal Vandercook was taken from the police officers to the Third District Court on a writ of *habeas corpus*.

Fri. 27.—In the *habeas corpus* case of Oscar C. Vandercook, Judge Zane decided in his favor and set the prisoner free.

Sat. 28.—Joseph W. McMurrin was shot and dangerously wounded by Deputy Marshal Collin, back of the Social Hall, Salt Lake City. The Federal officers refused to give up the would-be assassin to the city officers.

Sun. 29.—U. S. deputy marshals visited Manti, Sanpete Co., Utah, in search of polygamists.

Mon. 30.—Because of Judge Zane's decision, the cases against Sam. H. Lewis, Charles E. Pearson and W. H. Yearian for lewd and lascivious conduct was dismissed in the police court.

December.—Some of the Saints who had been encamped on the Casas Grandes river, Chihuahua, Mexico, located on the Peadres Verdes river, near the present site of Juarez, where lands had been purchased by the Church for a settlement.

Tues. 1.—Lorenzo and Seth Wright were killed by Indians, near Layton, Graham Co., Arizona, in their attempt to rescue stolen horses.

—Elders S. C. Nilson, M. P. Madsen and Thos. C. Schrøder were arrested in Aalborg, Denmark, for preaching the gospel.

Fri. 4.—U. S. Deputy Marshal Oscar C. Vandercook, Attorney Sam. H. Lewis and Charles E. Pearson were again arrested in Salt Lake City for immoral conduct.

Mon. 7.—A provost guard, consisting of about forty-five U. S. soldiers, was established in Salt Lake City.

—A company of artillery arrived at Fort Douglas, Utah, from Fort Omaha, Neb.

—Brigham Y. Hampton, one of the Salt Lake City officers, who had aided in detecting anti-Mormons guilty of immoral conduct, was arrested, charged with conspiracy etc., the grand jury having found four indictments against him.

—The City Council of Salt Lake City, after a thorough investigation, found that there was not the least danger of a "Mormon" uprising, and that telegraphic dispatches, sent to Washington, D. C., by Federal officials, were entirely false.

—Hon. John T. Caine had an interview with Pres. Cleveland, in Washington, D. C., explaining to him the true situation in Utah.

Tues. 8.—Brigham Y. Hampton plead not guilty in the Third District Court and was placed under $3,600 bonds.

—Oscar C. Vandercook was again taken from the Salt Lake City officers on a writ of *habeas corpus*.

—Geo. H. Taylor, of the 14th Ward, Salt Lake City, was arrested on three indictments, found against him by the grand jury, for u. c.

—Senator Edmunds introduced another anti-polygamy bill in the U. S. Senate.

Thurs. 10.—Judge Zane gave, as his decision, that the city had jurisdiction in cases for immoral conduct, which remanded Vandercook back to the city authorities.

Fri. 11.—In the Salt Lake City police court, Attorney Sam H. Lewis was sentenced to three months' imprisonment and $299 fine for immoral conduct; an appeal was taken.

Sat. 12.—In the police court, Salt Lake City, Com. Charles E. Pearson and Joe Bush were each sentenced to three months' imprisonment and $299 fine for immoral conduct. Appeals were taken. Vandercook was released a third time on writ of *habeas corpus*.

—Emily Crane, Delilah Clark and Sarah Hulet, of Parowan, Iron Co., were subpœnaed as witnesses and taken to Beaver in the night.

Mon. 14.—The appealed case against Sam. H. Lewis was dismissed in the Third District Court.

—Ed. L. Butterfield, a land agent, was arrested by the police officers in Salt Lake City for lewd and lascivious cohabitation.

—Pres. Angus M. Cannon, who had been imprisoned some two months longer than his sentence called for, awaiting the court decision from Washington, D. C., in his appeal case, was released from the Utah Penitentiary.

—Francis Platt, counselor to Bishop Atwood of the 13th Ward, died in Salt Lake City.

—The Supreme Court of the United States affirmed the judgment of the Supreme Court of Utah, against Pres. Angus M. Cannon.

Tues. 15.—Father Henry Gale, of Beaver, was sentenced by Judge Boreman, in the Second District Court, to six months' imprisonment and $300 fine for u. c. He was placed in the Penitentiary on the 17th.

Wed. 16.—Deputy Marshal H. F. Collin, who had been guarded in Ft. Douglas most of the time since shooting Joseph W. McMurrin, was admitted to bail.

Thurs. 17.—Mary A. T. Reynolds, wife of George Reynolds,died in Salt Lake City.

—Susanna W. Hunter, relict of Bishop E. Hunter, died in Salt Lake City.

—Bishop David K. Udall, of St. Johns, Ariz., who on a trumped up charge of perjury had been sentenced to imprisonment in Detroit, Michigan, was pardoned by Pres. Cleveland and immediately released.

Fri. 18.—Frank Foote was found guilty in the police court of immoral conduct and sentenced to three months' imprisonment and $299 fine. The case was appealed.

—D. J. Griffith was arrested by the police officers of Salt Lake City, for immoral conduct.

Sat. 19.—Eliza Shafer, who had been imprisoned since Sept. 15th for refusing to answer certain questions, was admitted to bail and released from custody.

—S. B. Guion, founder of the Guion Steamship Line, died in Liverpool, England.

Mon. 21.—Nicholas H. Groesbeck, of Springville, Utah Co., was arrested on a charge of u.c., brought to Salt Lake City, where he plead guilty before Com. McKay, and was placed under $1,500 bonds.

Tues. 22.—In the Second District Court (Judge Boreman), Beaver, Bishop Culbert King, of Marion Ward, Garfield Co., and James E.Twichel, of Indian Creek, Beaver Co., were each sentenced to six months' imprisonment and $300 fine. They were both placed in the Penitentiary on the 25th.

Thurs. 24.—After three days' trial the jury in the Third District Court brought in a verdict of guilty against Brigham Y. Hampton for conspiracy.

Wed. 30.—In the Third District Court, Judge Zane sentenced Brigham Y. Hampton to one year's imprisonment in the Salt Lake County jail.

Thurs. 31.—After two days' trial in the First District Court, at Ogden, the jury returned a verdict of guilty against Lorenzo Snow for u.c. in 1885, notwithstanding the evidence introduced had proven him innocent.

1886.

The prosecutions under the Edmunds law for polygamy and unlawful cohabitation were continued, and nearly every settlement of the Saints were raided by U. S. deputy marshals, in search of polyga-

mists. Fearing the impossibility of a fair trial, hundreds of the brethren and many families went into exile, some of whom sought refuge in Mexico and others in Canada. Nearly all the leaders of the Church were in hiding, and the situation thoroughout Utah was truly critical.

January.—The new *Herald* Company was incorporated, the capital stock of the company being $100,000, divided into $1,000 shares.

—The Logan Electric Light and Power Company was incorporated.

Mon. 4.—In the Second District Court, Ogden, Bishop David M. Stuart, of Ogden, was sentenced to six months' imprisonment, $300 fine and costs of suit, for u. c.

Tues. 5.—Pres. Grover Cleveland nominated Wm. C. Prowe postmaster of Salt Lake City.

—In the First District Court, at Ogden, the jury brought in another verdict of guilty against Lorenzo Snow for u. c. in 1884 and part of 1883, in conformity with the segregating policy.

Wed. 6. — Samuel F. Ball, of the 19th Ward, Salt Lake City, was arrested on a charge of u. c.

—James Taylor, of Ogden, was convicted of u. c., in the First District Court, Ogden.

Fri. 8. — A bill, known as the new Edmunds bill, was passed by the U. S. Senate.

—Paris, Bear Lake Co., Idaho, was raided by U. S. marshals, who arrested J. Lewis, sen., C. H. Wright and H. Duffin, charged with u. c. Peter Jacobson, of Bloomington, was arrested on a similar charge.

Mon. 11.—The twenty-seventh session of the Utah legislature convened in the City Hall, Salt Lake City, and organized by electing Elias A. Smith president of the Council, and Wm. W. Riter speaker of the House.

—Bishop Wm. M. Bromley and Wm. Grant, of American Fork, Utah Co., were arrested by U. S. marshals on charges of u. c., and taken to Salt Lake City.

Tues. 12.—Isaac Langton, of Salt Lake City, was arrested on a charge of u. c., taken before Com. McKay, and placed under $1,000 bonds.

—Bishop Wm. M. Bromley and Wm. Grant, of American Fork, waived examination before Com. McKay, and each were placed under $1,500 bonds.

—Gov. Murray's insulting message to the legislature was read in joint session.

—Henry Cummock, Wm. Horsley, Frank Mason, Enoch Thomas, Robert Murdock, John H. Hood, Joseph Evans, William Evans, John Peak, Ellis Gridgeman, John Hunter and two boys lost their lives by a disastrous explosion in a mine, at Almy, Wyoming.

Wed. 13.—Francis A. Brown and Moroni Brown, of Ogden, were liberated from the Penitentiary.

—Wm. J. Jenkins, F. A. Cooper, Hyrum Goff and James O. Poulson, of West Jordan, were arrested, charged with u. c.,and taken to Salt Lake City.

Thurs. 14.—Charles Livingston, of Salt

Lake City, was arrested on a charge of u. c., and placed under $1,500 bonds.

Fri. 15.—Hon. Wm. Jennings died at his residence in Salt Lake City.

Sat. 16.—In the First District Court, Ogden, Apostle Lorenzo Snow was sentenced to eighteen months' imprisonment, $900 fine and costs, for u. c. James H. Nelson was sentenced to six months' imprisonment and $300 fine for the same offense, while James Taylor, who promised to obey the law in the future, was let off with $300 fine. Nelson was taken to the Penitentiary, but Lorenzo Snow was given ten days in which to prepare his appeal, being placed under $15,000 bonds.

—Elder James Standing died in Box Elder County, Utah.

Tues. 19.—In search of polygamists, the 17th Ward meeting house was raided by U. S. deputy marshals; but no arrests were made.

Wed. 20.—The first number of the *Historical Record* was published by Andrew Jenson, Salt Lake City, as a continuation of *Morgenstjernen.*

—The tent of John E. Forsgren, on the 10th Ward bench, Salt Lake City, was burned.

—Bishop Alonzo Winters, of Hoytsville, Summit Co., died.

Thurs. 21.—John Lang was released from the Penitentiary.

—A. O. Patterson and wife and a miner named Thornstrom were killed by snowslides, near Park City, Utah.

Fri. 22.—County Collector Nathaniel V. Jones, of Salt Lake City, and Frank M. Treseder were arrested on a charge of bribery.

Sun. 24.—John Jolley, of Franklin, Oneida Co., Idaho, was arrested on a charge of u. c.

Mon. 25.—After several days examination before Com. McKay, in Salt Lake City, Deputy Marshal Collin, who attempted to kill Joseph W. McMurrin some time previous, was discharged.

Tues. 26—After two days' examination before Com. McKay, Nathaniel V. Jones was placed under $10,000 and Frank M. Treseder under $3,000 bonds, to appear before the grand jury.

—General David R. Atchison, who treated the Saints with consideration during the Missouri persecutions, died in Clinton County, Mo.

Sun. 31.—The first meeting was held in the new meeting ·house erected by the Latter-day Saint settlers on the Peadres Verdes river (Juares) Chihuahua, Mexico. This was the first house of worship built by the Saints on Mexican soil.

Februrary. *Mon. 1.*—The Saints who had located in the upper end of Rabbit Valley, Utah, were organized as Spencer branch; James A. Taylor, president.

—Hannah Cooper, wife of Fred A. Cooper, died in West Jordan, Salt Lake Co., in childbed, as a victim of the unholy crusade, her husband being under bonds on a charge of u. c.

Tues. 2.—The Saints who had settled on Bulberry creek and other streams, near the Fremont river, east of Rabbit Valley, Utah, were organized as Teasdale Ward; George Coleman, Bishop.

Wed. 3.—A grand jury was packed for the Third District Court February term, the special venire system being renewed.

Fri. 5.—Gov. Eli H. Murray vetoed the new jury bill passed by the legislature.

Sat. 6.—The Utah Supreme Court sustained Judge Powers' decision against Apostle Lorenzo Snow, but granted the defendant twenty days in which to perfect an appeal to the Supreme Court of the United States. It also sustained the decision of the Third District Court against Brigham Y. Hampton.

Sun. 7.—Deputy marshals made a raid on the Cannon Farm, near Salt Lake City.

—Nephi Stewart, of Payson, Utah Co., was accidentally killed, near Tintic, Juab Co.

Mon. 8.—The biennial Salt Lake City municipal election resulted in a great majority for the People's Party, Francis Armstrong being elected mayor.

—W. G. Saunders, of Uintah, Weber Co., was arrested, charged with u. c., and taken to Ogden.

—Marshal Ireland offered a reward of $500 for the apprehension of Pres. Geo. Q. Cannon.

—About twenty deputy marshals raided the Gardo House, Church Offices, Tithing Yards and the Historian's Office, searching for Prests. John Taylor and Geo. Q. Cannon, but did not find them.

Tues. 9.—Andrew L. Gibbons, one of the Pioneers of 1847, died at St. Johns, Apache Co., Ariz.

—Samuel H.B. Smith was adjudged guilty by the jury in the Third District Court, although he, in every respect, according to the testimony given, had complied with the Edmunds law since its passage.

—Desdemona Wadsworth Fullmer Smith, a widow of Joseph Smith, the Prophet, died in the 6th Ward, Salt Lake City.

—Joseph W. McMurrin, of Salt Lake City, and Wm. H. Lee, of Tooele County, waived their rights as defendants and testified against themselves. The jury returned a verdict of guilty.

Wed. 10.—In the Third District Court, Robert Morris plead guilty to a charge of u. c. Wm. W. Willey, of East Bountiful, Davis Co., acknowledged his wives, was found guilty and sentenced to five months' imprisonment in the Penitentiary and $200 fine. Thomas Burningham, of East Bountiful, acknowledged his relationship with his wives, and was pronounced guilty. John Penman, of Bountiful, indicted for polygamy, was declared guilty and sentenced to two years in the Penitentiary and $125 fine. He and Willey were taken to the Penitentiary the same day.

—Deputy marshals visited the old Church Farm, south of Salt Lake City, searching for Pres. Geo. Q. Cannon.

Thurs. 11.—Pres. Hugh S. Gowans, of Tooele, and Herbert J. Foulger, of the 21st Ward, Salt Lake City, who waived their rights as defendants, were pronounced guilty of u. c., in 1883. Two other and similar indictments against each of them were continued for the term.

Fri. 12.—In the Third District Court, the jury returned a verdict of guilty against John P. Ball and John Y. Smith, of Salt Lake City, for u. c. They both testified in their own cases. Thomas C. Jones, against whom three indictments had been found, also testified in his own case and was pronounced guilty of u.c. for 1883, two other indictments against him being continued for the term.

Sat. 13.—In the Third District Court the jury returned a verdict of guilty against James Moyle and Geo. H. Taylor for u. c.; they both testified in their own cases, and two other indictments against each of them were continued for the term.

—Utah's Supreme Court sustained the decision of Judge Powers, in the Lorenzo Snow case.

—Pres. Geo. Q. Cannon was arrested at Humboldt, forty miles west of Winnemucca, Nevada. On the way to Salt Lake City he fell from the car platform and was considerably bruised.

Sun. 14.—Elder Zera Cole died in Salt Lake City.

Mon. 15.—In the Third District Court, Samuel F. Ball, and James O. Poulson, charged with u.c., testified in their own cases, and were each adjudged guilty by the jury. Two other indictments against each of them were continued for the term. After trial, in which Eliza Shafer was forced to testify, the jury returned a verdict of guilty against John W. Snell. Robert Morris was sentenced by Judge Zane to six months' imprisonment and $150 fine, and taken to the Penitentiary. Martha T. Cannon, wife of Pres. Geo. Q. Cannon, was insulted in court.

Tues. 16.—In the Third District Court Hyrum Goff and Wm. J. Jenkins, of West Jordan, testified in their own cases, and were adjudged guilty by the jury. Another indictment against Jenkins, and two against Goff, were continued for the term. In the case of Isaac Langton, after trial, the jury returned a verdict of not guilty.

—In the First District Court, at Ogden, W. G. Saunders was sentenced to six months' imprisonment and $250 fine, for u.c. He was taken to the Penitentiary on the 18th.

Wed. 17.—In the Third District Court (Judge Zane), Thos. Burningham, of Bountiful, and John Bowen, of Tooele, were each sentenced to six months in the Penitentiary and $300 fine. They were both taken to the Penitentiary in the afternoon.

—Pres. Geo. Q. Cannon arrived in Salt Lake City as a prisoner, under guard of a company of soldiers. He was immediately taken to the marshal's office and placed under $45,000 bonds.

Thurs. 18.—The jury gave a verdict of guilty against Oluf F. Due for u. c., the charge of polygamy being dismissed. Joseph H. Sissom, who promised to obey the law, was fined $200, but not being able to pay this amount he was taken to the Penitentiary.

Fri. 19.—Against Charles F. Middleton, of Ogden, who was arraigned in the Second District Court on a charge of u. c., the jury returned a verdict of not guilty.

Sat. 20.—In the Third District Court, Judge Zane sentenced Samuel H. B. Smith to six months' imprisonment and $300 fine, for u. c. In the case of Isaac Langton,

who finally was acquitted, the legal wife was compelled, contrary to law, to testify.

—Elder Thomas Grover, one of the Pioneers of 1847, died in Farmington, Davis Co.

—Solomon Edwards, of American Fork, who had been arrested at Eagle Rock, Idaho, on a charge of polygamy, was incarcerated in the Penitentiary.

Mon. 22.—In front of the Continental Hotel, Salt Lake City, District Attorney Wm. H. Dickson was attacked and hit one or two blows by young Hugh J. Cannon, whose mother Dickson had insulted in court. The boy and two others who were with him were arrested.

Tues. 23.—Henry Dinwoodey and Joseph W. McMurrin, of Salt Lake City, were each sentenced to six months' imprisonment and $300 fine, by Judge Zane, in the Third District Court. They were both taken to the Penitentiary.

—In the First District Court, at Ogden, Amos Maycock, of North Ogden, and W. G. Childs, of Ogden, were sentenced by Judge Powers, the former to five months' imprisonment and $300 fine, and the latter to $300 fine.

—U.S. Deputy Marshals John G. Gleason and Wm. Thompson, jun., made a night raid at Greenville, Beaver Co., where they acted shamefully towards several ladies.

Thurs. 25.—In the First District Court (Ogden). Judge Powers sentenced Charles H. Greenwell, of Ogden, to six months' imprisonment and $300 fine, and Helon H. Tracy, of Marriott's Ward, to six months' imprisonment, both for u. c. They were incarcerated in the Penitentiary the following day.

Fri. 26.—Pres. Hugh S. Gowans and Wm. H. Lee, of Tooele, and Herbert J. Foulger, of Salt Lake City, were each sentenced by Judge Zane to six months' imprisonment and $300 fine, for u. c., and taken to the Penitentiary.

—The glass factory, lately erected near the Warm Springs, Salt Lake City, commenced operations.

Sat. 27.—In the Third District Court, Judge Zane sentenced John P. Ball, Thos. C. Jones and John Y. Smith each to six months' imprisonment and $300 fine for u. c.

March. *Mon. 1.*—In the Third District Court, Judge Zane sentenced James Moyle, Geo. H. Taylor, Samuel F. Ball, James O. Poulson and O. F. Due each to six months' imprisonment and $300 fine, for u. c. They were taken to the Penitentiary the same day. The jury returned a verdict of guilty against Fred. A. Cooper, of West Jordan, for the same offence.

—Mr. Woodburn, of Nevada, introduced another anti-Mormon bill in the U. S. House of Representatives.

Tues. 2.—In the Third District Court, the jury gave a verdict of guilty against Solomon Edwards, indicted for u. c.

—Bishop Hiram B. Clawson was discharged from the Penitentiary.

—Huldah A. Winters was arrested at Pleasant Grove, Utah Co., as a witness against Pres. Geo. Q. Cannon, brought to Salt Lake City and placed under $5,000 bonds.

Wed. 3.—In the Third District Court,

10

130 CHURCH CHRONOLOGY—1886.

Judge Zane sentenced Hyrum Goff and Wm. J. Jenkins, both of West Jordan, to six months' imprisonment and $300 fine each, for u. c.; both were taken to the Penitentiary.

Fri. 5.—In the Third District Court, sentence was suspended against Solomon Edwards, who promised to live with his first wife.

—Edward Brain was discharged from the Penitentiary.

—Senator Collum, of Illinois, offered a resolution in the U. S. Senate to deprive the Utah legislature of its pay.

—Elder Chester Loveland died at Call's Fort, Box Elder Co.

—*Sat. 6.*—The ladies of Salt Lake City held a large mass meeting in the Theatre, to protest against the abuse heaped upon their sex in the Federal courts.

Mon. 8.—Alfred Best was discharged from the Utah Penitentiary.

—In the Third District Court, Fred A. Cooper, of West Jordan, was sentenced to six months' imprisonment and $300 fine, for u.c.

Tues. 9.—Martin Garn, of the Sugar House Ward, was arrested for u.c., taken before Com. Critchlow, in Salt Lake City, and placed under $1,500 bonds.

—In the Third District Court, John W. Snell was sentenced by Judge Zane to six months' imprisonment and $300 fine, for u.c.

Wed. 10.—Almira Covey, who for many years was regarded as the oldest living member of the Church, died in the 12th Ward, Salt Lake City.

Fri. 12.—Apostle Lorenzo Snow voluntarily went to prison, in order to have his case brought before the U. S. Supreme Court speedily.

—The Utah legislature adjourned after a sixty days' session, during which 46 bills were presented in the Council, and 88 in the House. Of these 72 were not passed, 62 were sent to the governor, 37 were signed, 15 vetoed and 10 ignored by him.

Sat. 13.—John Nicholson, George Romney and Wm. A. Rossiter were discharged from the Penitentiary.

—Gov. Murray issued a proclamation appointing Arthur Pratt to be Territorial Auditor of Public Accounts, and Territorial Librarian and Recorder of Marks and Brands; Bolivar Roberts, Territorial treasurer; Parley L. Williams, superintendent of district schools.

Mon. 15.—Geo. C. Lambert, of Salt Lake City, was arrested on a charge of u. c. and placed under bonds in the sum of $1,500.

—By telegram from the Secretary of the Interior, Gov. Eli H. Murray was asked to resign his position as governor of Utah.

Wed. 17.—In the Third District Court the case of Pres. Geo. Q. Cannon was called, but as the defendant did not appear, his bail was declared forfeited.

—In the Third District Court (Judge Zane), Abraham H. Cannon was sentenced to six months' imprisonment and $300 fine, for u. c., and taken to the Penitentiary.

—After several days' trial, in the Second District Court, at Beaver, Marcus L. Shepherd. charged with u. c., was acquitted.

Thurs. 18.—In the Third District Court, Judge Zane sentenced Robert M. McKen-

drick, of Tooele, to six months' imprisonment and $300 fine for u. c. He was taken to the Penitentiary.

—In the First District Court (Provo), John Duke, of Wasatch County, indicted for u. c., testified in his own case, and was adjudged guilty.

—J. J. Williams, Charles Josephson and Joseph Harris were arrested in Malad Valley, Idaho, charged with u. c.

Fri. 19.—Suit was commenced in the Third District Court, by Arthur Pratt and others, for possession of the offices assigned them by the proclamation of Gov. Murray.

—Henry W. Naisbitt, of Salt Lake City, was arrested on a charge of u. c.; and placed under $1,500 bonds.

—In the Second District Court (Beaver), Marcus L. Shepherd was held on another indictment and put under $1,500 bonds.

—Lorenzo D. Watson, of Parowan, against whom three indictments had been issued, testified in his own case, and the jury returned a verdict of guilty on one indictment, two other indictments being dismissed.

Sat. 20.—Aurelius Miner was discharged from the Penitentiary.

Sun. 21.—The 89th quorum of Seventy was organized by Seymour B. Young, at Pima, Graham Co., Ariz. John M. Moody, James R. Welker, Patrick C. Thanie, James M. Larson, Frank Tyler, Joseph East and Oliver C. Wilson, presidents.

—The Saints settling on the Peadres Verdes river, Chihuahua, Mexico, held a grand celebration, raised a flag pole, cheered the Mexican flag and named their townsite Juarez.

Mon. 22.—The grand jury having found three indictments against Henry W. Naisbitt, for u.c. he was re-arrested and placed under $3,000 bonds. Five witnesses were also placed under heavy bonds.

Tues. 23.—Stanley Taylor, of the 16th Ward, Salt Lake City, was arrested for u. c., and placed under $1,500 bonds.

Wed. 24.—Thos. E. Taylor, of the 14th Ward, was arrested on a charge of u. c., and placed under $1,500 bonds.

—Marinda N. Hyde, relict of Apostle Orson Hyde, died in Salt Lake City.

—Bishop John Parker, of Virgin City, Washington Co., died.

Thurs. 25.—Robert Easton, arrested on a charge of u. c., was placed under $1,500 bonds.

—In the Second District Court (Judge Boreman), Lorenzo D. Watson was sentenced to six months' imprisonment and $300 fine. He was imprisoned in the Penitentiary on the 27th.

Fri. 26.—Joseph H. Dean, of the 19th Ward, and John Bergen, of the 13th Ward, Salt Lake City, were arrested, charged with u. c., and placed under bonds.

Sat. 27.—The grand jury having found four indictments against each, Stanley Taylor and John Bergen were re-arrested and placed under heavy bonds.

Sun. 28.—The 90th quorum of Seventy was organized by Seymour B. Young, at Mesa, Maricopa Co., Ariz.; Geo. Passey, Solomon F. Kimball, George F. Ellsworth, Talma E. Pomeroy, Joseph E. Johnson and Wm. S. Johnson, presidents.

Mon. 29.—After several days' preliminary examination before Com. McKay, Jos. H. Dean was placed under $3,000 bonds, although there was no evidence against him.

—Territorial Treasurer James Jack and Auditor Nephi W. Clayton filed their answers to the complaints of Bolivar Roberts and Arthur Pratt.

Wed. 31.—Patriarch John Boice died at Oxford, Idaho.

— Elders Joseph M. Tanner and Francis M. Lyman, jun., arrived at Yaffa (Joppa), Palestine, on a visit to the Holy Land.

April. — Bishop Chistopher Gardner, of Cherry Creek, Malad Valley, Idaho, was arrested on a charge of u. c., and placed under bonds.

—Wm. J. Cox, George Hales, James Farrer and a Mr. Jones of Adamsville, Beaver Co., were arrested, charged with u. c., and placed under bonds.

Thurs. 1.—Geo. C. Wood of South Bountiful, Davis Co., was arrested on a charge of polygamy, brought before Com. McKay and placed under $3,000 bonds.

—L. Loveridge, of Provo, who had been subpœnaed to Salt Lake City as a witness in a polygamy case, was himself arrested in the marshal's office on a charge of u. c., and placed under $1,500 bonds.

—Elders Joseph M. Tanner and Francis M. Lyman, jun., missionaries from Utah, visited Jerusalem, Palestine.

Fri. 2.—James Townsend, of Salt Lake hotel fame, died at the Warm Springs, Salt Lake City.

Sat. 3.—Thomas E. Taylor, of the 14th Ward, Salt Lake City, was arrested on three indictments, charging him with u.c., and placed under $3,000 bonds. Joseph H. Dean, of the 19th Ward, was arrested on a similar charge (two indictments) and put under bonds.

Sun. 4.—The fifty-sixth annual conference of the Church convened at Provo, Utah Co.; it was continued until the 7th. On the 6th an important epistle from the First Presidency was read.

Mon. 5.—John P. Wright, one of the first settlers of Cache Valley, Utah, died at Paradise.

Thurs. 8. — Martin Garn, of the Sugar House Ward, Salt Lake Co.,was re-arrested on a charge of u. c. and placed under $1,500 bonds.

—David E. Davis, Chas. Seal, Andrew W. Cooley and Isaac Groo were discharged from the Penitentiary.

Fri. 9.—Chas L. White was discharged from the Penitentiary.

—Geo. B. Bailey, Jens Hansen and Andrew Jensen, of Mill Creek, Salt Lake Co., were arrested, charged with u. c., brought to Salt Lake City and each placed under $1,000 bonds.

Mon. 12. — The *habeas corpus* case of John Connelly was argued in the Third District Court, and he was ordered back to prison until his fine was paid.

—Elias Morris, of Salt Lake City, was arrested on a charge of u. c., taken before Com. McKay, and placed under $1,000 bonds.

Tues. 13.—Ludvig H. Berg, of the 11th Ward, Salt Lake City, was arrested on a charge of u. c., taken before Com. McKay, and placed under $1,000 bonds.

—In the First District Court, at Provo, Bishop Wm. M. Bromley, of American Fork, was sentenced to ten months' imprisonment and $900 fine; Nephi J. Bates, of Monroe, to three months' imprisonment and $100 fine; Wm. Grant, of American Fork, to four months' imprisonment, and John Duke, of Heber City, to $300 fine —all for u. c. Brothers Grant and Bates were taken to the Penitentiary, but Bishop Bromley took an appeal and was released on $7,000 bonds.

Fri. 16.—Andrew Smith and Emil O. Olsen were discharged from the Penitentiary.

—Emma Rawlins Young, a witness in Royal B. Young's case, was arrested and placed under $2,500 bonds.

—Elder Edwin Spencer died at Randolph, Rich Co.

Sat. 17.—David W. Leaker and Charles Denney, both of the 11th Ward, Salt Lake City, were arrested, charged with u. c., taken before Com. McKay and each placed under $1,000 bonds.

—John Bergen, who was already under bonds charged with u. c., was arrested in the 13th Ward, Salt Lake City, on a charge of polygamy.

—Elder Reuben Kirkham died at Logan.

—The steamship *Nevada* sailed from Liverpool, England, with 179 Saints, under the direction of Elder E. T. Woolley. The company arrived at New York on the 27th, and at Salt Lake City, May 4th.

Sun. 18.—Timothy B. Foote, one of the first settlers of Juab County, died at Nephi.

Mon. 19.—Charles Denney had a preliminary examination before Com. McKay, Salt Lake City, and was still kept under bonds.

Tues. 20.—Several houses at American Fork, Utah Co., were raided by U. S. deputy marshals, who arrested Wm. Wagstaff, Wm. R. Webb, John P. Kelly and John Durrant, and subpœnaed a number of witnesses. All were brought to Salt Lake City, where the defendants were each placed under $1,500 bonds.

Wed. 21.—Royal B. Young, of Salt Lake City, was again arrested on a charge of u. c., three new indictments having been found against him. He was released on $5,000 bonds.

Sat. 24.—Elder August F. Thomstorff died in Salt Lake City.

—The Supreme Court of Utah rendered a decision which practically endorsed lewd and lascivious conduct and set Wm. H. H. Yearian and others free.

Mon. 26.—Some houses at Payson, Utah Co., were raided by U. S. deputy marshals.

—After trial in the Third District Court, John Bergen was sentenced to six months' imprisonment and $300 fine for u. c., and taken to the Penitentiary.

Tues. 27.—After trial in the Third District Court, Geo. C. Wood, of Bountiful, Davis Co., was adjudged guilty of u. c.

—The Kanesville Ward, Weber Co., was organized; Peter B. Petersen, Bishop.

—Pres. Ihaia Te Whakamairu, a prominent native Elder, died at Mainaia, Wairarapa, New Zealand.

Wed. 28.—In the Third District Court, the jury disagreed in the case of Joseph H. Dean, who was on trial for u. c. Ludvig H. Berg was convicted of u.c.

Thurs. 29. — Frank J. Cannon was arraigned before the Third District Court, charged with battery on District Attorney Wm. H. Dickson. On May 1st, he plead guilty to the charge.

—The case of Lorenzo Snow was argued in the U. S. Supreme Court.

Fri. 30.—After trial in the Third District Court, Henry W. Naisbitt was convicted of u. c.

—In Bristol, England, William Ratcliff was fined 40 shillings for disturbing a "Mormon" meeting.

May.   Sat. 1.—Geo. C. Lambert, who testified in his own case, Geo. B. Bailey, Jens Hansen and Andrew Jensen were adjudged guilty of u. c.

—Joshua Thomas Willis, formerly Bishop of Toquerville, died in Arizona.

Sun. 2.—Thomas Alfred Judd died in Salt Lake City.

Tues. 4.—After a trial in the Third District Court, Edward Brain was adjudged guilty of resisting a U. S. deputy marshal.

Wed. 5.—Utah's new governor, Caleb Walton West, arrived in Salt Lake City.

Thurs. 6.—Robert H. Swain was discharged from the Penitentiary.

—Orson P. Arnold, of Salt Lake City, was arrested on a charge of u.c. and placed under bonds.

Fri. 7.—The municipal government of Salt Lake City tendered Governor West a brilliant reception in the Theatre.

—In the Third District Court, after trial, Royal B. Young was adjudged guilty of u.c. The charge of polygamy against him was dismissed.

Sat. 8.—In the Third District Court, the perjury case against Agnes McMurrin, of the 8th Ward, Salt Lake City, was dismissed.

Sun. 9.—Agnes McMurrin, a witness in Royal B. Young's case, was arrested by deputy marshals and placed under bonds.

Mon. 10.—In the Third District Court Stanley Taylor, Andrew Jensen and Geo. B. Bailey were each sentenced by Judge Zane to six months' imprisonment and $300 fine, for u.c. and taken to the Penitentiary. Frank J. Cannon was sentenced to three months' imprisonment in the county jail and $150 fine, for battery.

—The Supreme Court of the United States dismissed the three Snow polygamy cases for "want of jurisdiction," and also set aside its former judgment in the Angus M. Cannon polygamy case. This left the polygamists to the mercy of the Utah Federal courts, with all the horrors of the segregating policy.

Tues. 11.—In the Third District Court Geo. C. Lambert and Henry W. Naisbitt were each sentenced to six months' imprisonment and $300 fine, for u.c.

Thurs. 13.—Wellsville, Cache Co., was raided by U. S. Deputy marshals, who arrested Levi Minnerly and Reuben C. Smith on charge of u.c.

—Pres. Joel Grover died at Nephi, Juab, Co.

—Gov. West, accompanied by Secretary Arthur L. Thomas and others, visited the

Penitentiary and offered amnesty to all the "brethren" imprisoned there for violation of the Edmunds law, on condition that they would "promise to obey the law as interpreted by the courts."

Fri. 14.—Joseph Matthews, one of the Utah Pioneers of 1847, died near Pima, Ariz.

Sat. 15.—Wm. G. Bickley was arrested, at Beaver, on a charge of u. c.

—At Logan, the United Order Foundry machine shops were destroyed by fire.

—Elders Isaac C. Gadd and Richard R. Fry sailed from Liverpool, England, in charge of fifteen Icelandic Saints, bound for Utah.

Sun. 16.—A. J. Kershaw, of Ogden, and John C. Thompson, of Riverdale, Weber Co., were arrested for u. c. and placed under bonds.

Tues. 18.—Amos Maycock, Helon H. Tracy and John Bergen were taken from the Penitentiary to Ogden for arraignment. Joseph H. Dean and Geo. C. Wood, were re-arrested.

—John A. Flowers, of the 11th Ward, Salt Lake City, shot and fatally wounded his wife and mother-in-law (Annie L. Decker), after which he shot and killed himself.

Wed. 19.—Annie L. Decker, shot the day before by her son-in-law, died.

—In the First District Court, at Ogden, W. G. Saunders, Helon H. Tracy and Amos Maycock, who were serving one term of imprisonment, were sentenced to six months' imprisonment each on additional indictments for u. c., and taken back to the Penitentiary.

—The Saints who had settled northwest of Parker Ward, Snake River Valley, Idaho, were organized as Brighton Ward; Reuben Hiatt, Bishop.

Fri. 21.—In the Second District Court, at Beaver, a packed jury brought in a verdict of guilty against Geo. Hales, for libel. On the 27th he was fined $100 and costs.

—The Saints who had settled on the east end of Poole's Island, Snake River Valley, were organized as Cleveland (later La Belle) Ward; Winslow F. Walker, Bishop.

Sat. 22.—In the First District Court, at Provo, Nicholas H. Groesbeck was sentenced by Judge Powers to nine months' imprisonment and $450 fine. Pending an appeal to the Territorial Supreme Court the defendant was admitted to $5,000 bail.

—The Saints who had settled southeast of Louisville, Snake River Valley, Idaho, were organized as the Rigby Ward; Geo. A. Cordon, Bishop.

—The steamship *Nevada* sailed from Liverpool, England, with 279 emigrating Saints on board, under the direction of Moroni L. Pratt. They arrived at New York June 2nd, and at Salt Lake City on the 8th by the D. & R. G. Ry.

Sun. 23.—Franklin Thursten was killed by Indians near Pima, Graham Co., Ariz.

—The Saints who had settled on Sand creek, Snake River Valley, Idaho, were organized as Iona Ward, of the Bannock Stake, James E. Steele, Bishop.

Mon. 24.—The brethren imprisoned in the Utah Penitentiary framed a respectful reply to Gov. West, showing their reasons for not accepting his offer.

—In the First District Court, at Ogden, Levi Minnerly and Reuben C. Smith, of Wellsville, were sentenced to imprisonment for u. c., the former to five months and the latter to six months. They were taken to the Penitentiary the following day.

—In the District Court at Blackfoot, Idaho, the following brethren were sentenced to imprisonment at Detroit, Mich., for u. c.: Andrew Jacobsen, of Bloomington, Bear Lake Co.; John J. Williams of Malad,Oneida Co.; Christopher Gardner,of Cherry Creek, Oneida Co.;Niels J. Jørgensen, of Gentile Valley, Bingham Co.; Rasmus Nielsen, of Weston, OneidaCo.; Thos. H. Wilde, Hans Rasmussen and Niels Graham, of Mink Creek, Oneida Co.; John Jolley, of Franklin,Oneida Co.; and Wm. Handy, of Whitney, Oneida Co. They all left Blackfoot as prisoners on the 26th, and arrived at Detroit the following Saturday (May 28th).

Tues. 25.—Thomas Porcher and John W. Keddington were discharged from the Penitentiary.

Wed. 26.—In the First District Court, at Ogden, Ambrose Greenwell, sen., of West Weber, was sentenced by Judge Powers to one year's imprisonment and $300 fine for u. c., and taken to the Penitentiary.

Thurs. 27. — In the Second District Court, at Beaver, Marcus L. Shepherd, Wm. J. Cox and Wm. G. Bickley, of Beaver, and Peter Wimmer, of Parowan, were each sentenced to six months' imprisonment and $300 fine, for u.c.

Fri. 28.—Wm. Y. Jeffs, of the 16th Ward, Salt Lake City, was arrested on a charge of u. c., brought before Com. McKay, and placed under $1,000 bonds.

Sat. 29.—Willard L. Snow, of Farmers Ward, Salt Lake Co., was arrested for u. c., taken before Com. McKay and placed under $1,000 bonds.

—In the First District Court, at Ogden, Geo. C. Wood, who plead guilty to the charge of polygamy, was sentenced to five years' imprisonment and $500 fine and taken to the Penitentiary.

June. *Tues. 1.*—In the Third District Court, Royal B. Young, agreeable to the segregation policy, was sentenced by Judge Zane to one and a half years' imprisonment and $900 fine, and Charles Denney and Ludvig H. Berg to six months' imprisonment and $300 fine each, all for u. c. They were taken to the Penitentiary.

Wed. 2.—In the Third District Court. Jens Hansen, of Mill Creek, was sentenced by Judge Zane to six months' imprisonment and $300 fine, for u. c., and imprisoned. Geo. C. Wood was brought in from the Penitentiary and sentenced to three months' imprisonment and $300 fine, for u. c.

—Hyrum P. Folsom, of the 19th Ward, Salt Lake City, was arrested on a charge of u. c., brought before Com. McKay, and placed under $1,000 bonds.

Thurs. 3.—Homer Duncan, of the 11th Ward, was arrested on a charge of u. c., taken before Com. McKay and placed under $1,000.

Fri. 4.—U. S. deputy marshals raided

Hooperville, Davis Co., and arrested Wm. W. Galbraith on a charge of u. c. He was taken to Salt Lake City and placed under bonds.

Sat. 5.—In the First District Court, at Ogden, Wm. Stimpson, of Riverdale, was sentenced by Judge Powers to eight months' imprisonment and $300 fine, for u. c., and taken to the Penitentiary.

Sun. 6.—The 91st quorum of Seventy was organized by Christian D. Fjeldsted, at Orangeville, Emery Co.; Erastus Curtis, P. R. Petersen, Abner Buckley, Boie P. Petersen, Frederick Andersen, Parker A. Childs-and Svend Larsen, presidents.

Mon. 7.—Andrew Hansen and Carl Janson, of West Jordan, Salt Lake Co., were arrested, charged with u. c., taken before Com. McKay in Salt Lake City, and placed under $1,000 bonds each.

Tues. 8.—Some reidences at Brigham City, Box Elder Co., were raided by U. S. deputy marshals, who arrested James May on suspicicn and took him to Ogden.

Wed. 9.—Wm. Felstead,of the 1st Ward, Salt Lake City, was arrested on a charge of u. c. and polygamy, brought before Com. McKay and placed under bonds.

—A powder mill, at the mouth of Ogden Canyon, Weber Co., was destroyed by the explosion of powder, and James Hoxer fatally injured.

Thurs. 10.—Elder John H. Berry died at Cottonwood, Bear Lake Co., Idaho.

—The Edmunds new anti-polygamy bill was reported to the House from the Judiciary Committee, greatly modified and amended.

Fri. 11.—Seymour B. Young, of the 12th Ward, Salt Lake City, was arrested on a charge of u. c., but escaped from the officer.

Sat. 12.—Pres. David John and Edward Peay, of Provo, were arrested, charged with u. c., taken to Salt Lake City, arraigned before Com. McKay and placed under bonds.

—Albert Gray, of the 16th Ward, Salt Lake City, was accidentally killed at Ogden.

—The Saints who had settled northeast of Payson and northwest of Spanish Fork, Utah County, were organized into two Wards, namely, Benjamin, Andrew J. B. Stewart, Bishop, and Lake Shore, Lorenzo Argyle, Bishop.

Mon. 14.—Some houses at Tooele, Tooele Co., were raided by U. S. deputy marshals, who arrested Richard Warburton, James Dunn and Jonas E. Lindberg, for u. c.: also residences at Pleasant Grove, Utah Co.,were raided by U. S. deputy marshals, who arrested Orlando F. Herron, Wm. Wadley and Victor Sandgren,charged with u. c. The defendants from both places were taken to Salt Lake City and arraigned before Com. McKay,with a number of witnesses, and after preliminary examination placed under bonds.

Tues. 15.—Charles M. Bergstrom, of the 11th Ward, Salt Lake City, was arrested for u. c. and placed under $1,000 bonds.

Thurs. 17.—Frank H. Dyer assumed the position of U. S. marsbal for Utah, in place of Elwin A. Ireland, retired.

—Patriarch Abraham Washburn died at Monroe, Sevier Co.

Fri. 18.—Louisa F. Wells, wife of Daniel H. Wells, died in Salt Lake City.

Sat. 19. — The Supreme Court of Utah rendered a decision in favor of the governor's appointees for Territorial treasurer and auditor. The case was appealed.

Sun. 20.—The first Latter-day Saint Y. L. M. I. A. in Mexico was organized in the camp of the Saints near Ascencion, Chihuahua, with Virona Whiting as president.

Mon. 21. — Henry Gale, of Beaver, was discharged from the Penitentiary.

Wed. 23.—Rebecca Van Zante Miller, relict of Eleazer Miller, died at Coalville, Summit Co.

Thurs. 24.—In the First District Court, at Ogden, Wm. H. Pidcock plead guilty to the charge of u. c.

Fri. 25.—Lorin Farr, of Ogden, was arrested on a five-count indictment, charging him with u. c., and placed under bonds.

—On this and the following day, the 92nd quorum of Seventy was organized by John Morgan in the San Luis Stake of Zion, Conejos Co., Col., with Christen Jensen as senior president. The members of the quorum were mostly young Elders from the Southern States.

Sat. 26.—The steamship *Nevada* sailed from Liverpool, England, with 426 emigrating Saints on board, in charge of Elder Christian F. Olsen. The company arrived at New York, July 7th, and at Ogden on the 12th. The emigrants were subjected to the most rigid questioning and examination by the officers at Castle Garden, because they were "Mormons."

Mon. 28.—Culbert King and James E. Twichel were discharged from the Penitentiary.

—Elder Wm. A. Cowan and another missionary were abused by an armed mob, consisting of about one hundred men, in Alabama.

Tues. 29.—The Old Folks of Salt Lake County were treated to a free excursion to American Fork, Utah Co.

—James Eardley, of the 3rd Ward, Salt Lake City, and Thos. F. H. Morton, of Farmers Ward, Salt Salt Co., were arrested for u.c., taken before Com. McKay and each placed under $1,000 bonds.

—Nephi J. Bates was discharged from the Penitentiary.

Wed. 30.—In the First District Court, at Ogden, Wm. H. Pidcock, was sentenced to thirteen months' imprisonment, for u.c. and taken to the Penitentiary.

—Francis A. Brown, of Ogden, was arrested on a new charge of u.c., and placed under $2,000 bonds.

—Amanda Smith, of Haun's Mill massacre fame, died at Richmond, Cache Co.

—John Irving, of West Jordan, was arrested for u. c., taken to Salt Lake City, examined before Com. McKay and discharged, there being no evidence against him. Geo.C.Watts was arrested on the same charge, taken before Com. McKay, plead guilty and was placed under $1,000 bonds.

July. *Thurs. 1.*—The Supreme Court of Utah reversed the action of the First District Court, by refusing a new trial in Barnard White's u.c. case.

—James May, of Call's Fort, Box Elder Co., who had been held to await the action

of the grand jury, was arrested on an indictment containing five counts alleging u. c. He was released on $3,000 bonds.

Fri. 2.—Amos H. Neff, of East Mill Creek, who had been arrested on a charge of u.c., was placed under $1,500 bonds, after preliminary examination before Com. McKay.

Sat. 3.—John W. Tate, sen., of Tooele, who had been arrested the day previous, charged with u.c., had an examination before Com. McKay, in Salt Lake City, and was placed under bonds.

Sun. 4.—The prisoners in the Penitentiary were permitted to celebrate Independence day.

Tues. 6.—Bishop James Crane died at Herriman, Salt Lake Co.

Wed. 7.—Fred W. Ellis, of North Ogden, Weber Co., who had been arrested on a charge of u.c., testified before the grand jury, at Ogden.

Thurs. 8.—Bishop James W. Loveless, of Provo, was arrested on a Utah Central Ry. train, charged with u.c.

—David M. Stuart was discharged from the Penitentiary, but was immediately re-arrested on a new charge for u.c. and placed under $1,500 bonds.

Fri. 9.—Alonzo E. Hyde, of the 17th Ward, Salt Lake City, was arrested for u.c.

—Elijah A. Box, of Brigham City, was arrested on a charge of u.c., taken to Ogden and placed under $1,500 bonds.

Sat. 10.—The Y. M. M. I. A. of the Sevier Stake held an interesting conference at Fish Lake.

—A small company of Icelandic Saints, bound for Utah, sailed from Liverpool, England. They arrived at New York July 18th.

Mon. 12.—Elder E. T. Mumford died at Pleasant Grove, Utah Co.

Fri. 16.—Gov. West issued a proclamation, warning the "Mormons" against disobeying the Edmunds law.

—Richard Jones, telegraph operator at Provo, was accidentally killed by the discharge of a gun, in Provo Canyon, Utah Co.

—Sister Clarinda Stanton died at Panacca, Nev., 92 years of age. She was one of the oldest members in the Church, having been baptized by Oliver Cowdery, Nov. 3, 1830.

Sat. 17.—Bishop Alexander McRae, of the 11th Ward, was arrested on a charge of u. c. and placed under $1,000 bonds by Com. McKay.

Sun. 18.—Robert Morris was discharged from the Penitentiary.

Mon. 19.—Wm. W. Willey, of Bountiful, was discharged from the Penitentiary.

—Isaac R. Pierce was arrested in Commissioner McKay's office, in Salt Lake City, on a charge of u. c.

Tues. 20.—James H. Nelson was discharged from the Penitentiary.

—After preliminary examination before Com. McKay, Bishop Alexander McRae and John Gillespie (of Tooele), accused of u. c., were discharged.

—Pres. Cleveland nominated Henry P. Henderson, of Michigan, to be associate justice of the Supreme Court of Utah.

Fri. 23.—Samuel H. B. Smith was discharged from the Penitentiary.

—Wm. Clifton was accidentally killed at Big Cottonwood, Salt Lake Co.

Sat. 24.—A solemn assembly was held in Salt Lake City, in commemoration of the entrance of the Pioneers into Salt Lake Valley.

—Mark Lindsay was arrested at Ogden, on a charge of u. c., and placed under $1,500 bonds.

—Wm. Grant, of American Fork, was discharged from the Penitentiary.

—The G. A. R. (Grand Army of the Republic) commenced a series of meetings in the Skating Rink, Salt Lake City.

Mon. 26.—Charles O. Card was arrested at Logan, charged with u. c., but escaped from the officers by jumping from the train.

—Henry Dinwoodey was discharged from the Penitentiary.

Wed. 28.—Wm. Geddes, of Plain City, was arrested on a charge of u. c., taken to Ogden and placed under $2,000 bonds.

—John D. Jones, of Cherry Creek, Oneida Co., Idaho, was arrested for u. c., taken to Malad City and placed under $1,500 bonds. Erik M. Larsen, of Malad City, was arrested on the same charge and put under bonds.

Thurs. 29.—At the G. A. R. meeting held at the Skating Rink, Salt Lake City, the crowd was treated to a series of bitter anti-Mormon harangues.

—Charles H. Greenwell was discharged from the Penitentiary.

Fri. 30.—James G. Burton, of Nephi, Juab Co., was accidentally kicked to death by a horse in Grantsville, Tooele Co.

—General John A. Logan and others spoke at the G. A. R. Camp meeting in Salt Lake City.

—The rock work on the Manti Temple was completed.

Sat. 31.—The last of the G. A. R. camp meetings was held in the Skating Rink. In these meetings the most abominable falsehoods were uttered against the "Mormon" people.

August.—Elder Jacob Spori arrived at Haifa, Palestine, as a Latter-day Saint missionary to that country. He came from Constantinople.

Sun. 1.—Rhoda Maria Carrington, wife of Albert Carrington, of Salt Lake City, died at Georgetown, Idaho.

Mon. 2.—The general election in Utah resulted in victory to the People's Party in all the counties.

—Nicholas H. Groesbeck, of Springville, was taken to the Penitentiary to serve nine months' imprisonment for u. c.

Tues. 3.—Bishop Wm. M. Bromley, of American Fork, Utah Co., commenced his term of imprisonment, for u.c., in the Penitentiary.

Wed. 4.—Geo. H. Taylor and James Moyle were discharged from the Penitentiary.

Fri. 6.—John Douglas was arrested at West Weber, Weber Co., on a charge of u. c., taken before Com. Duane W. Felshaw and placed under $1,500 bonds.

Sat. 7.—Søren L. Petersen was arrested at Ogden, on a charge of u. c., and gave bonds in the sum of $2,000.

Sun. 8.—Thomas Jackson was drowned in the Jordan river, at Salt Lake City.

—New Wards of the Church were organized at Bluff Dale and Riverton, Salt Lake Co.; Lewis H. Mousley and Orrin P. Miller, Bishops.

Tues. 10.—Bishop John C. Dewey, of Deweyville, Box Elder Co., was arrested for u. c. He was taken to Ogden the next day and placed under $1,500 bonds.

—Clyde Cranney was accidentally drowned in the Logan river, Cache Co.

Wed. 11.—Samuel M. Parkinson, of Franklin, Idaho, was taken prisoner by deputy marshals, near Ogden.

Thurs. 12.—James Higgins was arrested at West Jordan, Salt Lake Co., on a charge of u. c. After spending the night in the Penitentiary, he was admitted to $2,500 bail the following day.

Fri. 13.—The grand jury in the Third District Court reported that they had found 45 indictments for polygamy and u. c.

Sat. 14.—The first Latter-day Saint Primary Association in Mexico was organized in the camp of the Saints, near Casas Grandes. Chihuahua; Hannah H. Romney, president.

Mon. 16.—Dr. Samuel L. Sprague died in Salt Lake City, of old age.

Tues. 17.—Apostle John W. Taylor was arrested at Pocatello, Idaho, on a charge of treason.

—Mrs. Elizabeth James was killed and Mrs. Walter Williams and child hurt by a runaway team in Salt Lake City.

—Mary Foreman Higgins, the alleged plural wife of James Higgins, was arrested at West Jordan, Salt Lake Co.

—Pres. Abraham H. Cannon was discharged from the Penitentiary.

Wed. 18.—An excursion party, consisting of journalists from Nebraska, arrived in Salt Lake City, on a visit.

—Apostle John W. Taylor appeared before U. S. Commissioner J. C. House, at Oxford, Idaho, and gave bonds in the sum of $5,000.

—Elder Oliver L. Robinson died at Farmington, Davis Co.

—Peter Petersen, of Morgan County, was arrested on a charge of u. c., taken to Ogden and placed under $1,500 bonds.

Thurs. 19.—John Gillespie, of Tooele County, was arrested on a charge of u. c., taken to Salt Lake City the next day and placed under $1,500 bonds.

Fri. 20.—John Bowen and Thomas Burningham were discharged from the Penitentiary.

Sat. 21.—The steamship *Wyoming* sailed from Liverpool, England, with 301 emigrating Saints on board, in charge of David Kunz. The company arrived in New York on the 31st. Forty-five of the emigrants were detained there by Com. Stephenson on pretended charges of pauperism. Finally all were permitted to continue their journey, except a woman and three children, who were sent back to England. The remainder of the company arrived in Salt Lake City Sept. 7th.

Tues. 24.—Henry Reiser, of the 6th Ward, Salt Lake City, was arrested for u. c. and placed under $1,000 bonds by Com. McKay.

—Wm. D. Johnson, jun., commenced to survey a townsite (Diaz) on land which had been purchased of P. G. del Campe, north of La Ascencion, Chihuahua, Mexico.

Wed. 25.—Bishop Wm. Thorn, of the 7th Ward, Salt Lake City, was arrested on a charge of u. c. and placed under $1,000 bonds.

Thurs. 26.—U. S. deputy marshals raided some of the settlements west of the Jordan river, Salt Lake Co., and arrested Rasmus Nielsen, of Hunter, on a charge of u. c.

—Joseph W. McMurrin, of the 8th Ward, Salt Lake City, was discharged from the Penitentiary.

Fri. 27.—Elder Samuel R. Jewkes died from the effects of an accident, at Orangeville, Emery Co.

Sat. 28.—Herman F. F. Thorup, of the 1st Ward, Salt Lake City, was arrested for u. c., taken before Com. McKay, and placed under $1,000 bonds.

—Henry P. Henderson, recently appointed assistant justice of the Territory, arrived in Salt Lake City, and took the oath of office.

Sun. 29.—Elder Jacob Spori baptized Johan Geo. Grau, a German, at Haifa, Palestine. This is believed to have been the first baptism by divine authority in that country in this dispensation.

Mon. 30.—Wm. H. Foster and Bedson Eardley, of the 7th Ward, Salt Lake City, were arrested, charged with u. c., and placed under $1,000 bonds each by Com. McKay.

—John Y. Smith, Hugh S. Gowans, and Thos. C. Jones were discharged from the Penitentiary, but Com. McKay refused to discharge Herbert J. Foulger, Wm. H. Lee, and John P. Ball without paying their fines, which they declined to do.

—Richard Henry Sudweeks, of Kingston, Piute Co., charged with u. c., and Maria Elder, his supposed wife, were both arrested and brought to Beaver, where they on the following day were arraigned before Com. J. W. Wilkins and placed under bonds.

Tues. 31.—Isaac Brockbank, of the 8th Ward, Salt Lake City, was arrested for u. c., and placed under $1,000 bonds.

September. *Wed. 1.*—Ezra T. Clark, Wm. H. Watson and Leonard G. Rice, of Farmington, Davis Co., were arrested on charges of u. c., taken to Salt Lake City and placed under bonds.

—Willard S. Hansen, who was under arrest for u. c., escaped from Deputy Marshal Steele, while waiting for the train at Collinston, Box Elder Co.

—Forty-four Latter-day Saint emigrants just arrived from Europe on the steamship *Wyoming*, were detained by Commissioners Starr and Stephenson, at New York, by a strained application of the statute in relation to foreign paupers.

Thurs. 2.—Mark Bigler was arrested at Collinston, Box Elder Co., for u. c., taken to Ogden and placed under $1,000 bonds.

—Herbert J. Foulger, John P. Ball and Wm. H. Lee were discharged from the Penitentiary, only the first named paying his fine.

Fri. 3.—Harvey Murdock, of Harrisville,

Weber Co., was arrested on a charge of polygamy, brought before Com. Black, at Ogden, and placed under $4,000 bonds.

Sat. 4.—Samuel F. Ball was discharged from the Penitentiary.

—Abraham Chadwick, of North Ogden, and Thomas Bennett Helm, of Pleasant View, Weber Co., were arrested for u. c., brought to Ogden and placed under bonds.

Mon. 6. — Oluf F. Due was discharged from the Penitentiary.

—Most of the "Mormon" emigrants detained at New York were released on writs of *habeas corpus* by Judge Andrews of the Supreme Court of the State of New York, and started for Utah.

Tues. 7.—Hyrum Goff, Wm. J. Jenkins and James O. Poulson, who had served their terms in the Penitentiary, were brought before Com. McKay, in Salt Lake City. Jenkins and Poulson were liberated, but Goff was returned to the Penitentiary, not being allowed to take the oath required, in order to avoid paying fine and costs of suit.

—Peter Anderson and N. C. Mortensen, of Huntsville, Weber Co., were arrested for u. c., brought to Ogden and placed under bonds.

Wed. 8.—Deputy marshals raided houses in the 8th Ward, the Church Farm and other places, in quest of victims for the anti-polygamy crusade.

—Henry Tribe was arrested on a charge of u. c., taken before Com. Black, at Ogden, and placed under $1,500 bonds.

—John Waters, of Springville, Utah Co., was arrested on a charge of u. c., taken to Salt Lake City, with four witnesses, and placed under $1,000 bonds.

—Elder Isaac C. Haight died at Thatcher, Graham Co., Ariz.

Thurs. 9.—After a hearing before Judge Zane, in the Third District Court, on a writ of *habeas corpus*, Hyrum Goff was released from imprisonment, by paying his fine.

Fri. 10.—Henry Saunders, sen., of Provo, was arrested on a charge of u. c., brought to Salt Lake City, arraigned before Com. McKay and placed under $500 bonds.

—James McFarland, of West Weber, Weber Co., was arrested for u. c., taken before Com. Black, at Ogden, and placed under $1,000 bonds.

Sat. 11.—Frederick A. Cooper, of West Jordan, was discharged from the Penitentiary. Immediately afterwards he was arrested on another indictment charging him with u. c. and placed under $1,500 bonds.

—Myron W. Butler was arrested at Trenton, Cache Co., and Willard Bingham, at Wilson, Weber Co., charged with u. c. They were brought to Ogden and placed under bonds.

Mon. 13.—Peter S. Barkdull, of Farmington, Davis Co., was arrested on a charge of u. c., brought to Salt Lake City, arraigned before Com. McKay, and placed under $1,500 bonds.

—Elder Leonard G. Rice died suddenly at Farmington, Davis Co. He was under bonds for u. c.

Tues. 14.—In the Third District Court, William Felstead, of the 1st Ward, Salt Lake City, who had plead guilty to a charge of polygamy and u. c., was sentenced by Judge Zane to three years and six months' imprisonment, and $300 fine, and taken to the Penitentiary. Brother Felstead was seventy-two years old.

Wed. 15.—Bernhard H. Schettler, of Salt Lake City, was arrested on a charge of u. c., taken before Com. McKay, and placed under $1,500 bonds.

—Laura Nebeker Smith died in the 17th Ward, Salt Lake City.

—Hon. Morrison R. Waite, Chief Justice of the Supreme Court of the United States, who was on a visit to Salt Lake City, was given a reception at the governor's mansion, after which the distinguished judge visited Fort Douglas and the Penitentiary. At the latter place he had a conversation with Apostle Lorenzo Snow.

Thurs. 16.—Henry B. Gwilliam, of South Hooper, Davis Co., was arrested on a charge of u. c., taken before Com. Black, at Ogden, and placed under $1,500 bonds.

—John Cartwright, of the 8th Ward, Salt Lake City, was arrested for u. c., taken before Com. McKay, and placed under $1,000 bonds.

Sat. 18.—The First District Court, at Ogden, was opened with the recently appointed judge, Henry P. Henderson, on the bench.

—John B. Førster, of the 13th Ward, Salt Lake City, was arrested on a charge of u.c. and placed under $1,000 bonds by Com. McKay.

—Robert M. McKendrick was discharged from the Penitentiary.

—Richard H. Sudweeks, arrested some time previously on three indictments, was again arrested on another charge of u. c., at Beaver.

Mon. 20.—In the Third District Court, Richard Warburton, of Tooele, was sentenced by Judge Zane to six months' imprisonment and $300 fine, and Jonas E. Lindberg, also of Tooele, to eighteen months' imprisonment and $300 fine, both for u.c., and taken to the Penitentiary. They both plead guilty.

—Elder Andrew N. Macfarlane died in the 21st Ward, Salt Lake City.

—Charles Jameson, who was wounded at the Haun's Mill massacre with four balls, and also served in the Mormon Battalion, died at Minersville, Beaver Co.

Tues. 21.—Maria Sudweeks was arrested in Beaver, on a charge of having resisted the officers, when they arrested her husband. She was released on giving a $250 bond.

—After trial, in the Third District Court, the jury returned a verdict of guilty against C. M. Bergstrøm, charged with u. c.

Wed. 22.—W. J. Hooper was arrested in Salt Lake City for u.c. and placed under $1,000 bonds.

—In the Third District Court, Wm. W. Galbraith, of South Hooper, charged with u c., plead guilty, and was sentenced by Judge Zane to six months' imprisonment and $300 fine. Wm. Y. Jeffs, charged with the same offense, who also plead guilty, was sentenced to eighteen months' imprisonment and $300 fine. After trial, the jury returned a verdict of guilty against James Higgins and Carl Janson, of West Jordan,

for u. c. Hyrum P. Folsom plead guilty to the same charge.

Thurs. 23.—The Gardo House was raided by U. S. deputy marshals, in search of Pres. John Taylor.

—In the Third District Court, James Dunn, of Tooele, charged with u.c., plead guilty and was sentenced by Judge Zane to one year's imprisonment and $300 fine; Thomas F. H. Morton plead guilty to the same charge. After trial, James Eardley, also accused of u.c., was acquitted. Fred. A. Cooper, of West Jordan, who had served six months in the Penitentiary for u.c., promised to obey the Edmunds law in the future, and thus escaped going to prison a second time.

Fri. 24.—After a two days' trial in the Third District Court, Joseph H. Dean was convicted of u.c. Willard L. Snow, of Farmers Ward, plead guilty to the same charge.

—James I. Steele, of Lake View, Tooele Co., was arrested for u.c., brought to Salt Lake City and placed under $1,000 bonds.

—The Utah Commission made their annual report of Utah affairs to the Secretary of the Interior.

Sat. 25.—Hannah Tapsfield King died in Salt Lake City.

—In the Third District Court, Salt Lake City, Hyrum P. Folsom was sentenced by Judge Zane to six months' imprisonment and $300 fine for u. c. In the case of C. M. Bergstrøm, who promised to obey the law, sentence was suspended. The trial of Nathaniel V. Jones and Frank M. Treseder, charged with bribery, was commenced.

—In the Second District Court, at Beaver, Wm. Robinson, who plead guilty to u. c., was sentenced to four months' imprisonment and $100 fine; Geo. Hales, Thomas Scofield and James Farrer were each sentenced to four months and $300 fine; Richard H. Sudweeks to eight months and $600 fine. These brethren were imprisoned in the Penitentiary the following day.

Mon. 27.—In the Third District Court, Joseph H. Dean, of Salt Lake City, was sentenced by Judge Zane to six months' imprisonment and $300 fine, and Anders Hansen, of West Jordan, to eighteen months' imprisonment and $300 fine, for u. c.

—Ground was broken for the new Union Depot building at Ogden.

Tues. 28.—After trial in the First District Court, at Provo, the jury returned a verdict of guilty against Robert C. Kirkwood, charged with u. c. A motion for a new trial was made. The case against L. Loveridge was dismissed.

—After a lengthy trial the jury returned a verdict of guilty against Nathaniel V. Jones and Frank M. Treseder for bribery, contrary to the evidence given.

Wed. 29.—After a trial in the Third District Court, David W. Leaker, of the 11th Ward, Salt Lake City, was adjudged guilty of u. c. W. H. Watson and Ezra T. Clark, of Farmington, plead not guilty to the same charge.

—After trial in the First District Court, at Provo, the jury returned a verdict of guilty against Bishop James W. Loveless, for u. c.

—Lorenzo D. Watson, of Parowan, and Levi Minnerly, of Wellsville, were discharged from the Penitentiary.

—Joseph M. Phelps, of Montpelier, Idaho, was accidentally shot and killed near Cokeville, Uintah Co., Wyo.

Thurs. 30.—In the Third District Court, after trial, John Gillespie was sentenced by Judge Zane to six months' imprisonment and $300 fine, and James Higgins and Carl Janson, both of West Jordan, to eighteen months' imprisonment and $400 fine each. After trial, the jury also returned a verdict of guilty against Amos H. Neff—all for u. c.

—The Home Fire Insurance Company was incorporated in Salt Lake City, with Heber J. Grant as president.

—Elder August Wilcken died in Salt Lake City.

October.—The "Manuscript Found," a romance written by Rev. Solomon Spaulding, and which gave rise to the ridiculous Spaulding Story in connection with the origin of the Book of Mormon, was published by the Deseret News Company, Salt Lake City.

—Gov. Caleb W. West, in his report on Utah affairs to the Secretary of the Interior, suggested quite drastic measures against the Mormons.

—Bishop Niels Hansen, of Providence, and Thomas W. Kirby, of Hyde Park, Cache Co., were arrested for u. c. and placed under bonds.

—Charles O. Card and a company of explorers, acting under instructions from Pres. John Taylor, visited British Columbia and Alberta, Canada, for the purpose of selecting a tract of land on which to locate a colony of Saints.

Fri. 1.—In the Third District Court, after trial, the u. c. case against Thomas Lee, of Tooele County, was dismissed, there being no evidence against the defendant. A verdict of guilty was rendered against Homer Duncan for u. c. John R. Forster, of Salt Lake City, and Thos. F. H. Morton, of Farmers Ward, were sentenced by Judge Zane to six months' imprisonment and $300 fine each, and Willard L. Snow, of Farmers Ward, to eighteen months' imprisonment and $300 fine, all for u. c. They were taken to the Penitentiary.

—Bishop Geo. D. Snell and Sylvester Bradford, of Spanish Fork, were arrested on charges of u. c.

Sat. 2.—O. L. Brown succeeded G. N. Dow as warden of the Utah Penitentiary.

—In the Third District Court, after a long trial, the jury returned a verdict of guilty against Orson P. Arnold for u. c.

Mon. 4.—In the Third District Court, Rasmus Nielsen plead guilty to a charge of u. c.

Tues. 5.—In the Third District Court, Wm. J. Hooper plead not guilty to a charge of u. c.

Wed.6.—In the Third District Court, David W. Leaker was sentenced by Judge Zane to six months' imprisonment and $300 fine for u. c.

—Thos. B. Cardon was arrested at Logan, Cache Co., on a charge of u. c. and placed under bonds.

—The semi-annual conference of the Church was commenced in Coalville, Summit Co., Apostle Franklin D. Richards presiding. It continued until the 8th.

Thurs. 7.—John Q. Cannon was arrested near Salt Lake City, on a charge of polygamy, and placed under bonds.

—Geo. C. Parkinson, having served his term of imprisonment in the Boise City Penitentiary, Idaho, was released from prison.

Sat. 9.—In the Third District Court, Isaac R. Pierce, of Salt Lake City, was sentenced to fifteen months' imprisonment and $100 fine, the indictment against him being divided into five counts.

—John P. Mortensen, of the 8th Ward, Salt Lake City, was arrested for u. c., and placed under $1,500 bonds.

Mon. 11.—In the Third District Court, Amos H. Neff was sentenced by Judge Zane to six months' imprisonment and $300 fine, and taken to the Penitentiary. Sentence was suspended in the case of Homer Duncan.

—James C. Watson, of Salt Lake City, who had served one term in the Penitentiary for living with his wives, was again arrested on a charge of u. c., but after a rigid examination before Com. McKay, he was acquitted.

—The body of J. D. Farmer, who was drowned Aug. 6, 1882, was found on the shores of Great Salt Lake, eight miles west of Garfield, Tooele Co.

Tues. 12.—John W. Hoffman, of the 21st Ward, Salt Lake City, was arrested on a charge of u. c., and, after spending the night in prison, brought before Com. McKay the following day and placed under $1,000 bonds.

Wed. 13.—In the Third District Court, suit was commenced against Horace S. Eldredge and Francis Armstrong for the payment of $20,000 bonds, forfeited in the case of Pres. Geo. Q. Cannon.

—Chas. Franks, of Logan, Cache Co., was arrested on a charge of u. c., brought before Com. Goodwin, and placed under $1,000 bonds.

—The steamship *British King* sailed from Liverpool, England, with a company of Saints, in charge of Joshua Greenwood. The company arrived at Philadelphia, Oct. 27th, and at Salt Lake City, Nov. 1st.

—Christopher J. Kempe, Peter J. Christoffersen and Ammon M. Tenney who had been wrongfully imprisoned at Detroit, Mich., since December, 1884, received the pardon of Pres. Cleveland and were set free.

Thurs. 14.—In the Third District Court, James I. Steel, of Pine Canyon, Tooele Co., convicted of u c. on a two-count indictment, was sentenced by Judge Zane to one year's imprisonment in the Penitentiary and $600 fine.

Fri. 15.—Bishop Wm. E. Bassett, of the 20th Ward, Salt Lake City, was arrested for u. c. and placed under $1,500 bonds.

—Prince Louis Napoleon, grand nephew of Napoleon Bonaparte, arrived in Salt Lake City on a visit from the West. He left for the East the following day.

Sat. 16.—W. H. Haigh, of West Jordan, was arrested on a charge of u. c., brought before Com. McKay, in Salt Lake City, and placed under bonds. On the same day Geo. W. Thatcher and Wm. Palmer, of Logan, and John C. Gray were arrested for u. c., and put under bonds.

Sun. 17.—The first Latter-day Saint Y. M. M. I. A. in Mexico was organized at Juarez, Chihuahua; Joseph Cordon, president.

—Hon. John R. Pettigrew, a member of the Utah Commission, died at Waco, Texas.

Mon. 18.—Bishop Wm. E. Bassett had an examination before Com. McKay, after which he was placed under $15,000 bonds, being charged also with polygamy.

Tues. 19.—Stephen R. Marks was arrested in Salt Lake City, for u. c.

Wed. 20.—Herman Grether, of the 10th Ward, Salt Lake City, was arrested on a charge of a. c., and, after examination before Com. McKay, placed under $3,000 bonds.

—Bishop Lewis H. Mousley, of Bluff Dale, Salt Lake Co., was arrested, for u. c., taken to Salt Lake City, and placed under $1,500 bonds, by Com. McKay.

Thurs. 21.—The motion for a new trial in the Third District Court being overruled, Orson P. Arnold was sentenced by Judge Zane to fifteen months' imprisonment and $450 fine and sent to the Penitentiary.

—After preliminary examination before Com. McKay, Stephen R. Marks was put under $3,000 bonds.

—Bishop James W. Loveless (sentenced in the First District Court, at Provo, to six months' imprisonment and $300 fine), and John Durrant and Hans Jensen (sentenced to six months' imprisonment and $100 fine, each) were taken to the Penitentiary.

Fri. 22.—In the Third District Court, a writ of *habeas corpus* was applied for in the case of Apostle Lorenzo Snow, who was confined in the Penitentiary. The application was refused and the case taken before the U. S. Supreme Court.

—Charles Hardy,of Provo, who had been convicted in the First District Court, at Provo, for resisting Deputy Marshal Redfield, was sentenced to imprisonment for one day in the Penitentiary.

Sat. 23.—The new political party of Idaho, consisting mainly of "Mormon" citizens and known as the Independent Party, held a Territorial convention at Franklin, Oneida Co., where a platform and resolutions were adopted.

—Enoch, Iron Co., was raided by U. S. deputy marshals and John P. Jones arrested for u. c. John L. Jones, his eldest son, and an alleged plural wife were also arrested.

Sun. 24.—Reuben C. Smith was discharged from the Penitentiary.

Mon. 25.—Elder John Nebeker, a prominent Elder, of Salt Lake City, died at Lake Town, Rich Co.

Tues. 26.—Geo. B. Wallace, of Granger, Salt Lake Co., was arrested on a charge of u.c., taken before Com. McKay and placed under $1,000 bonds.

—After a new trial in the First District Court, the jury returned a verdict of guilty against Robert C. Kirkwood, for u.c.

—Pres. Cleveland appointed Abner B. Williams, of Arkansas, a member of the Utah Commission, in place of John R. Pettigrew, deceased.

Wed. 27.—Marcus L. Shepherd, of Beaver, was discharged from the Penitentiary.

—Thomas Butler, of the 14th Ward, Salt Lake City, was arrested on a charge of u.c. and placed under $1,000 bonds.

—Five "Mormon" emigrants, who were sent back to England by the bigoted action of the emigrating commissioners at New York, arrived at Salt Lake City. Having arrived at Liverpool they were placed on another steamer bound for New York, and their religious belief not being suspected, they were landed in New York without further trouble.

Thurs. 28.—Apostle John W. Taylor was indicted at Blackfoot, Idaho, on a charge of inciting to acts of lawlessness in a sermon delivered by him at Oxford, Oneida Co., Idaho, Aug 1, 1886.

Sat. 30.—In the Third District Court, John C. Gray, of Salt Lake City, who plead guilty to the charge of u.c., was sentenced by Judge Zane to six months' imprisonment and $50 fine, and taken to the Penitentiary. Herman Grether, John P. Mortensen, Geo. B. Wallace and Bishop Lewis H. Mousley plead not guilty to the same charge.

—Elder John H. Evans, of the 15th Ward, Salt Lake City, died.

—A small company of Saints sailed from Liverpool, England, bound for Utah.

Sun. 31.—Elder Wm. M. Palmer, by permission, held a meeting with and administered the Sacrament to the brethren incarcerated in the Detroit House of Correction, Mich.

November.—The Saints who had been encamped on the Casas Grandes river, near Ascencion, Chihuahua, moved to the new townsite (Diaz).

Mon. 1.—Wad El Ward, a Jew, lectured in the Salt Lake Theatre.

—Hon. Geo. T. Curtis addressed an able letter to Hon. L. Q. C. Lamar, Secretary of the Interior, on Utah affairs, polygamy and cohabitation.

Tues. 2.—Geo. F. Gibbs, of the 20th Ward, Salt Lake City, was arrested on a charge of u. c. examined before Com. McKay and discharged for want of evidence.

—At the general election in Utah, John T. Caine, the People's Party nominee, was re-elected delegate to Congress, receiving 19,605 votes, while the Liberal candidate, William M. Ferry, only received 2,810 votes.

Wed. 3.—Wm. A. Morrow, an ex-Mormon, of Granger, Salt Lake Co., was arrested for u. c., and imprisoned in the Penitentiary for the night. The following day he was placed under $1,500 bonds by Com. McKay.

—Timothy Parkinson, of Wellsville, Cache Co., was arrested at Piedmont, Wyo., charged with u. c., taken to Ogden and placed under $1,500 bonds.

—Thomas Richardson, a member of the Mormon Battalion, died at Richmond, Cache Co.

Thurs. 4.—Thomas Jenkins, of the 4th Ward, Salt Lake City, was arrested on a charge of u. c., and placed under $1,500 bonds, by Com. McKay.

—The Historian's Office, Salt Lake City, was raided by U. S. deputy marshals, searching for Prests. Taylor and Cannon.

—John Aird died in Salt Lake City.

—Andrew J. Kershaw, who. had been arrested in Evanston, Wyo., was placed under $3,000 bonds to answer to a charge of u. c.

Fri. 5. — Centreville, Davis Co., was raided by U. S. deputy marshals, who arrested John Adams, on the charge of u. c., and took him to Salt Lake City. The next morning he was arraigned before Com. McKay, who put him under $1,000 bonds.

Sat. 6.—James Newton, of the 10th Ward, Salt Lake City, was arrested on a charge of u. c., brought before Com. McKay and placed under $1,500 bonds.

—Lorenzo Stutz, of Mill Creek, Salt Lake Co., was arrested on a charge of u. c.

Sun. 7.—Panguitch, Garfield Co., was raided by U. S. deputy marshals, who arrested a supposed plural wife and brought her to Beaver.

Mon. 8.—Gideon M. Mumford, of Mill Creek, was arrested on a charge of u. c., brought before Com. McKay, in Salt Lake City, and placed under $1,500 bonds. Lorenzo Stutz, of Mill Creek, was placed under $1,500 bonds.

—U. S. deputy marshals made an unsuccessful raid on houses at Paragoonah, Iron Co.

—Rasmus C. Rasmussen, of Mink Creek, Oneida Co., Idaho, who had served his term of imprisonment in the Boise Penitentiary, arrived home.

Tues. 9.—Jos. H. Thurber, accused of polygamy, who had been confined in the Beaver jail, secured bonds and was liberated.

—Wm. Fry, of the Morgan Stake presidency, was arrested on a charge of u. c., taken to Ogden, and placed under $1,500 bonds.

—Wm. D. Johnson was set apart to preside as Bishop at Diaz, Chihuahua, Mexico.

Wed. 10.—Stanley Taylor, Andrew Jensen and George B. Bailey were discharged from the Penitentiary.

—George Crismon, of Sugar House Ward, and Andrew W. Cooley (imprisoned before), of Brighton, were arrested for u. c., taken before Com. McKay and each placed under $1.000 bonds. Crismon plead guilty, Cooley waived examination.

Thurs. 11.—Edward Schoenfeld, of Brighton, was arrested in Salt Lake City, on a charge of u. c., brought before Com. McKay and placed under $1,500 bonds.

—Geo. C. Lambert and Henry W. Naisbitt were discharged from the Penitentiary.

—Matthew Pickett, of Tooele, Bishop Ishmael Phillips, of Union, and Thomas Allsop, of Sandy, were arrested, charged with u. c., brought to Salt Lake City and placed under bonds.

Sat. 13.—In the Third District Court, Nathaniel V. Jones and Frank M. Treseder were each sentenced by Judge Zane to three years' imprisonment, for alleged bribery, and taken to the Penitentiary, the motion for a new trial having been overruled.

—After a lengthy trial in the First District Court, at Provo, the jury returned a verdict of guilty of voluntary manslaughter, against H. H. Pearson, who killed Forest Green at Nephi, Jan 10, 1886.

Tues. 16.—Patriarch Wm. G. Perkins died in St. George.

Wed. 17.—John H. Rumel, sen., was arrested in Salt Lake City, on a charge of u. c., taken before Com. McKay and placed under $1,000 bonds.

Thurs. 18.—The Saints residing at Eagle Rock, Idaho, were organized as the Eagle Rock Ward, of the Bannock Stake; James Thomas, Bishop.

—Joseph Hogan, of Bountiful, was arrested for u. c., taken before Com. McKay and placed under $1,000 bonds.

—In the Third District Court, after trial, the jury returned a verdict of guilty against Henry H. Hawthorne, a "Gentile" polygamist.

—In the District Court, at Blackfoot, Idaho, Samuel R. Parkinson was sentenced to six months' imprisonment in the Boise Penitentiary and $300 fine for u. c.

Sat. 20.—Bishop Appollos G. Driggs, of Sugar House Ward, was arrested on a charge of polygamy. He was brought to Salt Lake City and finally discharged,after an examination before Com. McKay.

Mon. 22.—In the First District Court, in Ogden, Timothy Parkinson, who plead guilty to a charge of u. c., was sentenced to six months' imprisonment and $100 fine.

Tues. 23.—John W. Snell was liberated from the Penitentiary, having served two months and thirteen days more than his time.

—Thomas Fenton, of the 6th Ward, Salt Lake City, was arrested on a charge of u. c., taken before Com. McKay and placed under $1,000 bonds.

—In the Third District Court, H. H. Hawthorne, the "Gentile" polygamist, was sentenced to four years' imprisonment and $100 fine,and taken to the Penitentiary.

—Phillip Pugsley was arrested in Salt Lake City on a charge of u. c. After examination before Com. McKay, he was discharged.

Wed. 24.—George Dunford, of Salt Lake City, charged with u. c., gave himself up to the officers, plead guilty, and was sentenced by Judge Zane to six months' imprisonment and $150 fine. He was taken to the Penitentiary.

—Anders W. Winberg, of the 19th Ward, Salt Lake City, was arrested on a charge of u. c., taken before Com. McKay and placed under $1,500 bonds.

—Pres. Angus M. Cannon was arrested near Salt Lake City, on a charge of u. c., taken before Com. McKay and placed under $10,000 bonds.

—Jonathan Campbell, a member of the Mormon Battalion, died at North Ogden, Weber Co.

Thurs. 25.—After a lengthy trial in the First District Court, at Oden, the jury returned a verdict of not guilty in the case of Lorin Farr, charged with u. c.

—Christian P. Christiansen, of Monroe, Sevier Co., was arrested on a charge of u. c. Subsequently he was taken to Beaver and placed under bonds.

Fri. 26.—In the Third District Court, Lorenzo Stutz, of Mill Creek, plead guilty to a charge of u. c. Thos. Jenkins promised to obey the law, and sentence in his case was suspended.

—Wm. H. Tovey, of the 20th Ward, Salt Lake City, was arrested on a charge of u. c., brought before Com. McKay and placed under $1,000 bonds. Joseph Blunt, of the 21st Ward, was arrested and placed under bonds, charged with the same offense.

Sat. 27.—In the Third District Court, Wm. A. Morrow, a non-Mormon, charged with u. c., promised to obey the law, and sentence was suspended.

—In the First District Court, at Ogden, the jury returned a verdict of guilty against Wm. Geddes, of Plain City, for u. c.

Sun. 28.—Wilford H. Halliday shot and killed Joseph Dobson, the seducer of the former's wife, at Kanab, Kane Co.

Mon. 29.—Wm. J. Cox and Wm. G. Bickley, of Beaver, and Peter Wimmer, of Parowan, were discharged from the Penitentiary.

—In the Third District Court, Lorenzo Stutz was sentenced by Judge Zane to one year's imprisonment, and $100 fine, for u. c.

—In the First District Court, at Ogden, John Stoddard was sentenced by Judge Henderson to six months' imprisonment and $300 fine. Francis A. Brown, charged again with u. c., was acquitted.

—Walter M. Craner, of Tooele, was arrested on a charge of u. c., taken to Salt Lake City, examined before Com. McKay and discharged.

Tues. 30.—In the Third District Court, John H. Rumel, sen., promised to obey the law, and sentence was suspended.

—In the First District Court, at Ogden, sentence was suspended in the case of Susan Parry, wife of Joseph Parry; she was charged with perjury.

—George Naylor, of Kamas, was arrested on a charge of u. c. The following day he was brought to Salt Lake City. Charles Burgess, of Salt Lake City, was also arrested on the same charge and placed under $1,500 bonds.

December.—The "Loyal League" of Utah was organized, its object being the destruction of "Mormonism."

Wed. 1.—George Nebeker, a prominent Elder, died in Salt Lake City.

—Myron W. Butler, of Ogden, and Thos. H. Bullock, of Salt Creek, Weber Co., were imprisoned in the Penitentiary, for u.c.

—Charles Denney and Amos Maycock were discharged from the Penitentiary.

Thurs. 2.—Ludvig H. Berg and Jens Hansen were discharged from the Penitentiary.

—Brigham H. Roberts, of the Salt Lake *Herald* editorial staff, was arrested on a charge of u.c. and placed under $1,000 bonds. When called for examination the next day, the defendant did not appear, and his bonds were declared forfeited.

Fri. 3.—In the Third District Court, Salt Lake City, Geo. Naylor plead guilty to a charge of u.c., and was sentenced by Judge Zane to six months' imprisonment

and $300 fine, and taken to the Penitentiary.

—Philo Farnsworth, sen., of Pine Creek, Beaver Co., was arrested on the charge of u.c., taken to Beaver and placed under bonds.

Mon. 6.—Wm. Geddes, of Plain City, was imprisoned in the Penitentiary for u.c.

Tues. 7.—Geo. Chandler, of Ogden, was imprisoned in the Penitentiary for u.c.

—Wm. L. Binder, of the 15th Ward, Salt Lake City, was arrested on a charge of u.c., and placed under $1,000 bonds. After examination the next day before Com. McKay, he was discharged.

—Chas. Harmon, jun., of the 16th Ward, Salt Lake City, was arrested on a charge of u.c., taken before Com. McKay, examined and discharged.

—Several houses at Lehi, Utah Co., were raided by U. S. deputy marshals, who arrested Bishop Thos. R. Cutler, Edwin Standring, James Kirkham, George Kirkham, John L. Gibb, Samuel James, John Hart and William Yates, for u.c.

Wed. 8.—Secretary Arthur L. Thomas was nominated a member of the Utah Commission by Pres. Cleveland.

—The Lehi prisoners (except Wm. Yates, who was sick) were brought to Salt Lake City and placed under bonds, after examination before Com. McKay.

Thurs. 9.—John England, of Tooele, was arrested for u. c., taken to Salt Lake City and placed under $1,500 bonds, after examination before Com. McKay.

Sat. 11.—Daniel Corbett, of the 2nd Ward, Salt Lake City, was arrested for u.c., and placed under $1,500 bonds.

Mon. 13.—Pres. Angus M. Cannon was arraigned in the Third District Court, where he was arrested again on three more charges, two for u. c. and one for polygamy.

—John P. Sørensen, of Salt Lake City, was arrested, charged with polygamy, brought before Com. McKay and placed under bonds.

—In the First District Court (Judge Henderson), at Ogden, James May, of Calls' Fort, Box Elder Co.; Fred. W. Ellis, of Pleasant View, Weber Co.; Thomas B. Helm and Henry B. Gwilliam, of South Hooper, were, each, sentenced to six months' imprisonment in the Penitentiary and $100 fine.

Tues. 14.—In the Third District Court, Thomas Allsop, of Sandy, who plead guilty to a three count indictment for u. c., was sentenced by Judge Zane to fifteen months' imprisonment and $50 fine, and sent to the Penitentiary.

Wed. 15.—After a lengthy examination before Com. McKay, all the charges against Pres. Angus M. Cannon were dismissed, and he was discharged.

Thurs. 16. — Edward M. Dalton was foully murdered by U. S. Deputy Marshal Wm. Thompson, jun., at Parowan, Iron Co. The murderer was arrested.

—Matthew Pickett, of Tooele, was arraigned in the Third District Court, charging him with u. c. He plead not guilty.

—Thomas Jeremy and Peter Gillespie, of the 16th Ward, Salt Lake City were arrested, charged with u.c. and placed under bonds.

Fri. 17.—Under the auspicies of the Old Folk's Committee, the "Old Folks," widows and orphans, of Salt Lake County, were treated to a free entertainment in the Theatre, Salt Lake City, the Home Dramatic Club playing "Confusion."

Sat. 18.—After examination before Com. McKay, the polygamy case against John P. Sørensen was dismissed for lack of evidence.

Mon. 20. — After the usual examination before Com. McKay, the u. c. case against Peter Gillespie, of Tooele, was dismissed, and the defendant discharged.

. *Tues. 21.*—In the Second District Court, at Beaver, the grand jury indicted the murderer, Wm. Thompson, jun., for manslaughter.

—Bishop Wm. E. Bassett, of the 20th Ward, Salt Lake City, was arrested and placed under $10,000 bonds, being indicted by the grand jury for polygamy.

Fri. 24. — Elder John Horspool died at Ogden.

Sun. 26. — Elder John Hindley died at American Fork, Utah Co.

Mon. 27.—John P. Jones and John Lee Jones, of Enoch, Iron Co., and Joseph H. Thurber, of Greenwich, Piute Co., were imprisoned in the Penitentiary, the two former for u. c., and the latter for polygamy and u. c., all having been sentenced by Judge Boreman in the Second District Court, at Beaver.

—The 18th Ward (Salt Lake City) Independent School House was formally opened.

Tues. 28.—In the First District Court, at Ogden, after trial, the jury returned a verdict of guilty against Abraham Chadwick, of Ogden, and N. C. Mortensen, of Huntsville, for u. c.

Wed. 29.—Helon H. Tracy, of Ogden, was discharged from the Penitentiary.

—Brigham Y. Hampton, having served his term of imprisonment for alleged conspiracy, was released from the county jail.

Thurs. 30.—Mary M. D. Nebeker, relict of Peter Nebeker, died at Willard City, Box Elder Co.

—Peter Petersen, of Richville, Morgan Co., was imprisoned in the Penitentiary, having been sentenced by Judge Henderson, in the First District Court at Ogden, to six months' imprisonment and $100 fine for u. c.

1887.

During this year nearly two hundred of the brethren were imprisoned in the Utah Penitentiary, besides a number in Idaho, for infractions of the provisions of the anti-polygamy laws. The settlements of the Saints in Mexico and Canada were greatly strengthened by "Mormon" exiles from the United States. Under the provisions of the Edmunds-Tucker law the government, through its receiver, took possession of the Church offices, and a wholesale confiscation of Church pro-

perty was threatened. President John Taylor died in exile, and the Council of Twelve Apostles was sustained as the Presidency of the Church.

January.—The Saints who had settled at Juarez, Chihuahua, Mexico, moved to a new townsite which had been surveyed two miles west of the first location. The first townsite was found to be outside of the land purchased by the Saints.

Mon. 3.—In the First District Court (Judge Henderson), at Ogden, Wm. Palmer, Hugh Adams and Thomas McNeill, of Logan, who had plead guilty to a two-count indictment, each; Peter Andersen, of Huntsville, who had plead guilty to a three count indictment; and Robert Henderson, of Logan, who had plead guilty to a one-count indictment, were each sentenced to six months' imprisonment in the Penitentiary and a fine of $100 for u. c. Harvey Murdock, of Huntsville, who three weeks previous plead guilty to an indictment charging him with polygamy, was sentenced to five years' imprisonment and $500 fine.

—William Crackles, of Salt Lake City, was arrested on a charge of u. c., brought before Com. McKay and placed under $500 bonds.

—Søren C. Petersen, of Elsinore, Sevier Co., was arrested on a charge of u. c. He was subsequently taken to Beaver, and placed under bonds.

—Mary Jenson, wife of Andrew Jenson, died in Salt Lake City.

Tues. 4.—Levi North and Hyrum B. North, of Provo Valley, Wasatch Co., were arrested at Mill Creek, Salt Lake Co., charged with u. c., taken before Com. McKay, and each placed under $1,000 bonds.

Thurs. 6.—After a two days' trial in the First District Court, at Ogden, Bishop Wm. E. Bassett, of Salt Lake City, was adjudged guilty of polygamy and sentenced to five years' imprisonment and $500 fine. An appeal was taken to the Territorial Supreme Court.

Fri. 7.—After a two-days' trial, the anti-Mormon jury, in the First District Court (Beaver), gave a verdict of "not guilty" in the case of Wm. Thompson, jun., who murdered Edward M. Dalton at Parowan, Dec. 16, 1886.

Sat. 8.—In the First District Court, at Ogden, Thos. W. Kirby, of Hyde Park, Cache Co., who plead guilty to a three-count indictment charging u. c., was sentenced by Judge Henderson to six months' imprisonment and $100 fine. John Marriott, of Marriott, and Charles Franks, of Logan, received similar sentences. Niels C. Mortensen, of Huntsville, Abraham Chadwick and Joseph Parry, of Ogden, were sentenced to six months' imprisonment and $300 fine, each. The prisoners were all taken to the Penitentiary the same evening.

Mon. 10.—U. S. Deputy Marshal Wm. Hopson and *posse* raided Poole Island, Idaho, and arrested Charles Shipping, on a charge of u. c.

Wed. 12.—The Edmunds-Tucker bill was

passed by the U. S. House of Representatives.

Thurs. 13.—A bill repealing the anti-Mormon test oath in Arizona was passed by the Council branch of the Arizona legislature. The House passed it the following day, and the governor signed it on the 15th.

—The Edmunds-Tucker bill was referred to a conference committee by the U. S. Senate.

—Wm. Yates, of Lehi, Utah Co., who was arrested about a month previous for u. c., appeared before Com. McKay, in Salt Lake City, and was placed under $1,500 bonds.

Fri. 14.—Ex Gov. Eli H. Murray was admitted to the bar of the Territorial Supreme Court, as an attorney, while Lieut. Richard W. Young, a prominent lawyer of extensive practice in the East, was refused admittance because he was a "Mormon."

—Hong Hop, a Chinese merchant, married Nellie Adlard, a white woman, in Salt Lake City. This peculiar matrimonial incident was said to be the first of its kind in Utah.

Tues. 18.—Hans J. Petersen, of Kanesville, Weber Co., was arrested on a charge of u. c., taken to Ogden and placed under bonds.

Wed. 19. — Elder Wm. Ringwood, over ninety years old, died in the 20th Ward, Salt Lake City.

Thurs. 20.—The Lorenzo Snow *habeas corpus* case was argued before the Supreme Court of the United States, where Hon. Franklin S. Richards, of Utah, made an able argument against the segregation policy instituted by the Utah courts.

Sat. 22.—Elder Wm. A. McMaster died in the 11th Ward, Salt Lake City.

—George Saville, of the 18th Ward, Salt Lake City, was arrested on a charge of u. c., taken before Com. McKay and placed under $1,500 bonds.

Sun. 23.—A. P. Anderson, of Chesterfield, Idaho, was arrested on a charge of u. c., brought to Blackfoot and placed under $2,000 bonds.

Mon. 24.—Houses at Farmington, Davis Co., and Brigham City, Box Elder Co., were raided by deputy marshals.

—Peter Madsen, of Willard, Box Elder Co., was arrested for u. c. and placed under $1,500 bonds.

Tues. 25.—Richard Collett and Edwin Rawlins, of the 19th Ward, Salt Lake City, and Eric Hogan, of Bountiful, Davis Co., were arrested on a charge of u. c., brought before Com. McKay and placed under $1,500 bonds, each. After a preliminary examination in the evening, Hogan was discharged.

Wed. 26.—John D. Lang, of the 15th Ward, Salt Lake City, was arrested for u. c. After a preliminary examination before Com. McKay, he was found "innocent" and consequently discharged.

—Andrew J. Kershaw was arrested by deputy marshals at Randolph, Rich Co., for u. c.

Thurs. 27.—Elder Nathaniel H. Felt, of the 17th Ward, Salt Lake City, died.

—T. B. Lewis, of Ogden, was arrested, accused of u. c., and placed under $1,500 bonds.

Fri. 28.—Houses at Deseret, Millard Co. were raided by deputy marshals, in search of polygamists.

—R. G. Slater and Alexander Edwards, of Salt Lake City were arrested, charged with u. c., brought before Com. McKay and placed under $1,500 bonds, each.

—Jens P. C. Winter and John Petersen, of Huntsville, Weber Co., were arrested on a charge of u. c., brought to Ogden and placed under bonds.

Sat. 29.—Thomas Brunker, of the 11th Ward, Salt Lake, was arrested on a charge of u. c., arraigned before Com. McKay and discharged.

Mon. 31.—Charles Edler, of Tooele, was arrested on a charge of u. c., brought to Salt Lake City, arraigned before Com. McKay and finally discharged for lack of evidence.

—Houses at Kanosh, Millard Co., were raided by deputy marshals, who arrested Bishop Abram A. Kimball on a charge of u. c.

February. — Apostle George Teasdale succeeded Daniel H. Wells in the presidency of the European mission.

Tues. 1.—Allen Hunsaker was arrested for u. c., and shot at by deputy marshals, at his ranche on the Malad river, Box Elder Co. James Woods, of Tooele, was arrested on the same charge, brought to Salt Lake City, with part of his family, and placed under $1,500 bonds.

—George E. Steele, a member of the Mormon Battalion, died at Lehi, Maricopa Co., Ariz.

Thurs. 3.—Mrs. Sarah Rawlins Grow, a witness in an u. c. case against Henry Grow, was arrested in Salt Lake City, and placed under $750 bonds.

—Wm. Poole, an old gentleman, of Ogden was arrested on a charge of u. c., and placed under bonds.

Fri. 4.—Elder John E. Metcalf, sen., died at Fayette, Sanpete Co.

Sat. 5.—Mary Bishop, of the 10th Ward, Salt Lake City, died of old age, being in her 101st year. She was born in Crewkerne, Somersetshire, England, Sept. 24, 1786.

Mon. 7.—Bishop James C. Hamilton, of Mill Creek, was arrested on a charge of u.c., brought to Salt Lake City, and placed under $1,500 bonds. After a preliminary examination before Com. McKay, the following day, he was discharged.

—The U. S. Supreme Court reversed the decision of the Utah courts in Apostle Lorenzo Snow's *habeas corpus* case, and declared the "segregation policy" illegal.

Tues. 8.—Apostle Lorenzo Snow and Nicholas H. Groesbeck, agreeable to the decision of the U. S. Supreme Court, were released from the Penitentiary. They had served considerably longer than their term, awaiting the decision of the court.

—Bishop Harrison Sperry, of the 4th Ward, Salt Lake City, was arrested for u.c., taken before Com. McKay and placed under $1,500 bonds.

—Josiah Richardson was arrested near Malad City, Oneida Co., Idaho, for u.c.

Wed. 9.—As a further result of the U. S. Supreme Court decision, Wm. H. Pidcock, Ambrose Greenwell, Wm. M. Bromley, and Isaac R. Pierce were released from the Penitentiary.

Thurs. 10.—Royal B. Young, having served one term of imprisonment, was released from the Penitentiary, in accordance with the Supreme Court decision.

Fri. 11.—Marshal Frank H. Dyer, assisted by Deputies John W. Greenman, Oscar C. Vandercook, Arthur Pratt, Bowman Cannon, Samuel L. Sprague, John G. Gleason, C. H. M. y Agramonte and W. B. Parker, Detectives E. A. Franks, Sam. H. Gilson and many others made a raid on the Church buildings (Tithing Office, Historian's Office and Gardo House), searching for Prests. John Taylor and Geo. Q. Cannon and others; none of them were found.

—James Hansen, of Brigham City, Box Elder Co., was shot at by Deputy Marshal Whetstone, who tried to arrest him, but he escaped into the hills.

—David B. Ward, an aged man of Beaver Co., was arrested for u. c.

Mon. 14.—Notwithstanding the strenuous efforts of the "Liberals," the "People's Party" gained a handsome majority at the municipal election at Ogden.

—In the Third District Court, Salt Lake City, Bishop Ishmael Phillips, of Union, and Henry Reiser, of Salt Lake City, were each sentenced by Judge Zane to six months' imprisonment and $300 fine, for u. c. The cases against Wm. H. Haigh, of West Jordan, and John Tate, of Tooele, were continued for the term. Wm. J. Hooper plead guilty by saying, "If it is a crime to support my family, I am guilty of u. c." Joseph Blunt also plead guilty.

Tues. 15.—In the Third District Court, Isaac Brockbank, of Salt Lake City, was sentenced to six months' imprisonment and $300 fine, for u. c.

Wed. 16.—In the Third District Court, Wm. H. Foster and Bedson Eardley, of Salt Lake City, and Wm. H. Watson, of Farmington, plead guilty to u. c.

Thurs. 17.—In the Third District Court, the case against John Cartwright for u. c. was dismissed. The jury returned verdicts of guilty against Henry Grow and Ezra T. Clark, for u. c.

—In search of Presidents John Taylor and Geo. Q. Cannon the Gardo House and Pres. Taylor's residences, in the 14th Ward, Salt Lake City, were raided by Marshal Dyer and his assistants.

—The report of the Conference Committee on the Edmunds-Tucker bill was adopted by the U. S. House of Representatives, by 202 votes against 39. On the 18th it was adopted, also, in the Senate by 37 votes against 13. The act became law without the signature of President Cleveland.

Fri. 18.—In the Third District Court, James Wood, of Tooele, plead not guilty; Herman Grether, of Salt Lake City, Bishop Lewis H. Mousley, of Bluff Dale, and Andrew W. Cooley, of Brighton, plead not guilty to the charge of u. c. After trial for u. c., Geo. B. Wallace, of Granger, was acquitted. The grand jury ignored the cases against Alonzo H. Raleigh, Thos. Jeremy and Daniel Corbett, who were charged with u. c.

Sat. 19. — By Judge Zane in the Third District Court, Bishop Lewis H. Mousley, of Bluff Dale, Rasmus Nielsen, of Hunter,

John P. Mortensen, of Salt Lake City, Bishop Apollos G. Driggs, of the Sugar House Ward, and Henry Whittaker, of Salt Lake City, were each sentenced to six months' imprisonment and 300 fine, for u. c. and sent to the Penitentiary. The jury returned a verdict of guilty against John Adams, of Centreville, Davis Co., for u. c.

—Thos. H. Morrison, of the 17th Ward, Salt Lake City, was arrested for u. c., taken before Com. McKay, and placed under $1,500 bonds.

Sun. 20.—At a special meeting held at Draper, Salt Lake Co., the Seventies residing in Sandy, Union and Granite were organized, by Abraham H. Cannon, as the 93rd quorum of Seventy; Thos. Hewlett, Thos. H. Smart, Wm. Thompson and Wm. R. Scott, presidents.

Mon. 21.—In the Third District Court, Judge Zane sentenced to six months' imprisonment and $300 fine each: Wm. H. Foster and Bedson Eardley, of the 7th Ward, Salt Lake City; Wm. H. Watson, Ezra T. Clark, and Peter S. Barkdull, of Farmington, Davis Co.; Herman Grether, of the 10th Ward, Salt Lake City; John Adams, of Centreville, Davis Co.; Joseph Hogan, of Bountiful, Davis Co., (who plead guilty the same day); and Jos. Blunt, of the 21st Ward, Salt Lake City. They were taken to the Penitentiary. Wm. H. Tovey, of the 20th Ward, Salt Lake City, was found guilty of u. c.

—Wm. Y. Jeffs was discharged from the Penitentiary.

Tues. 22.—Houses at Kaysville, Davis Co., were raided by U. S. deputy marshals, who arrested John R. Barnes and Wm. Blood. The prisoners were taken to Salt Lake City, brought before Com. McKay, and placed under $1,500 bonds, each.

Wed. 23.—In the Third District Court (Judge Zane), Wm. J. Hooper, of Salt Lake City, Matthew Pickett, of Tooele, and Levi North, of Mill Creek, Salt Lake Co., were each sentenced to six months' imprisonment and $300 fine for u. c., and taken to the Penitentiary. After trial, the jury returned a verdict of guilty against Anders W. Winberg and Thomas Butler, of Salt Lake City.

Thurs. 24.—Joseph Booth, of the 1st Ward, Salt Lake City, was arrested on a charge of u.c., brought before Com. McKay, and discharged after examination.

—In the Third District Court, Hyrum B. North, of Midway, Wasatch Co., was sentenced by Judge Zane to six months' imprisonment and $300 fine, and sent to the Penitentiary.

—The murderer, Wm. Thompson, jun., who, after his acquittal at the Beaver trial, again had been appointed a U. S. deputy marshal, commenced suit against the Deseret News Company for damages ($25,000), because of certain articles reflecting upon his character, published in that paper.

—Geo. Taylor and G. H. Peterson, of Almy, Uinta Co., Wyo., were arrested for u.c., and, after a preliminary examination before Judge Corn, of Evanston, admitted to bail in the sum of $300 each. These were the first cases under the Edmunds law in Wyoming.

Fri. 25.—The Tithing Office and several residences in the 17th Ward, Salt Lake City, were raided by deputy marshals, searching for polygamists.

—James C. Watson and H. H. Evans, of the 6th Ward, and Edwin Rushton, of the 5th Ward, Salt Lake City, were arrested for u.c., taken before Com. McKay and placed under bonds.

Sat. 26.—The Supreme Court of Utah sustained the decision of the District Court against Bishop Wm. E. Bassett.

Sun. 27.—Sophia Whittaker Taylor, wife of Pres. John Taylor, died in Salt Lake City.

Mon. 28.—In the Third District Court, Anders W. Winberg, Thomas Butler and Harrison Sperry, all of Salt Lake City, were sentenced by Judge Zane to six months' imprisonment and $300 fine each, for u.c. All three were taken to the Penitentiary.

March. *Tues. 1.*—In the Third District Court, Edward Schoenfeld, Wm. H. Tovey and Thos. H. Morrison, of Salt Lake City, and Andrew W. Cooley, of Brighton Ward, were each sentenced by Judge Zane to six months' imprisonment in the Penitentiary, and fines, for u.c.

—Houses at Bountiful, Davis Co., were raided by U. S. deputy marshals, who subpœnaed a number of witnesses. In search of Pres. Taylor, the Deseret Paper Mill, at the mouth of Big Cottonwood Canyon, was raided.

Wed. 2.—William Douglas, of Smithfield, Cache Co., was arrested at Logan, for u.c., and placed under $1,500 bonds.

Thurs. 3.—N. P. Peterson, of Logan, was arrested for u.c. and placed under bonds.

Fri. 4.—Peter Olsen was arrested for u.c., and, not being able to raise $500 security, was sent to the Penitentiary.

Sun. 6.—The first marriage under the provisions of the Edmunds-Tucker law was celebrated in Salt Lake City, Wm. T. Pike, of Mill Creek, and Miss Hannah Christine Wallen, of Salt Lake City, being united in matrimony by Chief Justice Charles S. Zane.

Mon. 7.—In the Third District Court, George Crismon, of Sugar House Ward, was sentenced to six months' imprisonment and $50 fine, for u.c. The new test oath was administered to the petit jurors serving in the Third District Court. Several "Mormons" refused to take the oath and were excused from serving.

—Carl Janson was discharged from the Penitentiary.

—David John and Robert C. Kirkwood, of Provo, and William R. Webb, of American Fork, each sentenced in the First District Court, at Provo, to six months' imprisonment and a fine of $300, and Edward Peay, of Provo, Christian P. Christiansen, of Monroe, and Søren C. Petersen, of Elsinore, each sentenced to six months' imprisonment, were incarcerated in the Penitentiary.

—The first election in Utah under the new Edmunds-Tucker law was held in Brigham City, Box Elder Co. Much to the disappointment of the anti-Mormons, the brethren subscribed to the test oath, polled their votes and carried the election.

—Jens Hansen, of Brigham City, was arrested at Three Mile Creek, Box Elder Co., on a charge of u.c., brought to Ogden and placed under $1,500 bonds.

Tues. 8.—After trial in the Third District Court, John England, of Tooele, was convicted of u.c.

—Peter Olsen, having raised the $500 bonds required of him, was released from the Penitentiary.

—P. A. Nielsen, of Logan, was arrested on a charge of u.c. and placed under $1,000 bonds.

Wed. 9.—Frederik Petersen, of the 2nd Ward, Salt Lake City, was arrested on a charge of u.c., brought before Com. McKay, and placed under $1,000 bonds.

Thurs. 10.—Samuel Anderson, of Salt Lake City, was arrested on a charge of u.c., brought before Com. McKay, and placed under $1,000 bonds.

—After examination before Com. McKay, at Salt Lake City, Cyrus Rawson, of Kaysville, Davis Co., who had been arrested on a charge of u.c., was acquitted.

Fri. 11.—Bountiful, Davis Co., was again raided by U. S. deputy marshals, but no polygamists were found.

Sat. 12.—At the Davis Stake quarterly conference, held at Bountiful, U. S. deputy marshals put in their appearance, searched the meeting house, but found nobody they wanted.

—Daniel Johnson, of Logan, was arrested for u.c. and placed under $1,000 bonds.

Mon. 14.—In the Third District Court, Herman F. F. Thorup was sentenced by Judge Zane to six months' imprisonment and $25 fine, for u.c.

—Solomon A. Wixom, of Granite, Salt Lake Co., was arrested on a charge of u.c., imprisoned in the Penitentiary for the night and the next day brought before Com. McKay. Wixom plead guilty and was placed under $1,000 bonds.

—Ralph Smith, of Logan, Cache Co., was arrested for u.c., and placed under $2,500 bonds.

Tues. 15.—John Connelly, who had previously served a term in the Penitentiary for u.c., was again arrested on the same charge, and placed under $1.500 bonds, after a preliminary examination before Com. McKay.

—Wm. C. Browe, postmaster of Salt Lake City, died.

—Joseph H. Evans, who had been pardoned by Pres. Cleveland, was released from the Penitentiary. He had been imprisoned there since Nov. 8, 1884.

Thurs. 17.—Archibald N. Hill, of the 19th Ward, Salt Lake City, was arrested on a charge of u.c. but slipped away from the officers.

Sat. 19.—In the Third District Court, Salt Lake City, Henry Grow, of Salt Lake City, was sentenced to five months' imprisonment and $50 fine by Judge Zane, for u.c.

—Andrew Jacobson, John J. Williams, Christopher Gardner, Niels J. Jørgensen, Rasmus Nielsen, Thos. H. Wilce, Hans Rasmussen, Niels Graham, John Jolley and Wm. Handy were released from their imprisonment at Detroit, Mich., and started for home. They were liberated, five days before their sentence expired,

11

through the decision of the U. S. Supreme Court.

Sun. 20.—At a meeting held at South Jordan, the Seventies residing in Riverton, Bluff Dale and Herriman were separated from the 33rd quorum of Seventy, and organized by Abraham H. Cannon as the 94th quorum; Wm. H. Freeman, Geo. Miller, Timothy Gilbert, John M. Bowen, Alexander B. Kidd and Charles M. Nokes, presidents. On the same occasion the 95th quorum was organized with Edwin D. Holt, James Oliver, Isaac J. Wardle, Albert Holt, Andrew Amundsen, Henry B. Beckstead and Alexander Bills as presidents. The members of this quorum resided in South Jordan Ward.

—James W. Loveless, Hans Jensen, Orson P. Arnold and John Durrant were discharged from the Penitentiary.

Mon. 21.—In the Third District Court, Salt Lake City, John England, of Tooele, was sentenced by Judge Zane to six months' imprisonment and $150 fine, for u. c.

—Richard Warburton was discharged from the Penitentiary.

—Ebenezer Woodford, of the 12th Ward, Salt Lake City, was arrested on a charge of adultery with his plural wife. He was finally placed under bonds for u. c.

—Wm. Harrison and Albert Singleton, of Provo, Geo. Kirkham and James Kirkham, of Lehi, R. M. Rogers, of Pleasant Grove, Wm. Unthank, of Cedar City, and Wm. Dally and James Dally, of Summit, Iron Co., were incarcerated in the Penitentiary, the five first having been sentenced in the First District Court (Judge Henderson), at Provo, and the three last in the Second District Court (Judge Boreman), at Beaver, to six months' imprisonment each and various fines, for u. c.

—The Mancos branch, Montezuma Co., Colo., was organized as a Ward; Geo. Halls, Bishop.

Tues. 22.—Jonas E. Lindberg was discharged from the Penitentiary.

Wed. 23.—James Dunn was released from the Penitentiary.

Thurs. 24.—John Bergen was discharged from the Penitentiary, but was placed under $8,000 bonds, to await the result of the polygamy charge pending against him.

Sat. 26.—Geo. Hales, James Farrer, Wm. Robinson, Thos. Schofield and Richard H. Sudweeks were discharged from the Penitentiary.

—Wm. S. Muir, of Bountiful, Davis Co., and Lars Hansen, of Logan, Cache Co., were arrested on the charge of u. c., and placed under bonds.

Sun. 27.—The two Wards formerly existing in Panguitch, Garfield Co., were united; Allen Miller, Bishop.

—Paragoonah, Iron Co., was raided by U. S. deputy marshals, who arrested Bishop Wm. Jones on a charge of u. c.

Mon. 28.—Joseph H. Dean, of Salt Lake City, and Andrew Hanson, of West Jordan, were discharged from the Penitentiary.

—In the First District Court, at Provo, the jury returned a verdict of guilty against six of the men who lynched Joseph Fisher at Tintic, Juab Co., July 7, 1886.

—The Latter-day Saint meeting house at Hoytsville, Summit Co., was burned.

Tues. 29.—John C. Gray was discharged from the Penitentiary.

—Kingston Ward, Piute Co., was disorganized, and two new Wards were organized in its place, namely, Circleville Ward, with James E. Peterson as Bishop, and Junction Ward, with Rufus C. Allen as Bishop.

Thurs. 31.—John Gillespie, of Tooele, was released from the Penitentiary.

April. Fri. 1.—Herriman, Salt Lake Co., was raided by U. S. deputy marshals; nearly every house in the village was searched, but no arrests were made.

Sat. 2.—Elder John A. Halverson, of the 4th Ward, Salt Lake City, died.

—South Jordan, Salt Lake Co., was raided by U. S. deputy marshals, who arrested Alexander Bills and Henry Beckstead for u. c.

Mon. 4.—Ole Hansen, of Logan, was arrested for u. c. and placed under $1,500 bonds.

Tues. 5.—Karl G. Maeser, of Provo, was arrested on a charge of u. c. Lars Nielsen and John Felt, of Huntsville, Weber Co., were arrested on the same charge, taken to Ogden and placed under bonds.

Wed. 6.—Knud Emmertsen, of Huntsville, was arrested for u. c.

—David W. Leaker was discharged from the Penitentiary.

—Springville, Utah Co., was raided by U. S. deputy marshals, who arrested Jacob Houtz and Jesse Gardner for u. c.

—The 57th annual conference of the Church was commenced in the new Tabernacle, at Provo, Utah Co., Lorenzo Snow, presiding. It was continued until the 10th.

Sun. 10.—Elder Daniel Carter died at Bountiful, Davis Co.

Tues. 12.—Edwin Booth, the renowned actor, appeared in the Salt Lake Theater, for the first time.

—In the First District Court, at Provo, Don Carlos Snow and J. T. Arrowsmith, of Provo, John L. Gibb, of Lehi, and Sanford Fuller, of Springville, were sentenced by Judge Henderson to six months' imprisonment and a fine of $100 each; Edwin Standring, of Lehi, and Geo. D. Snell, of Spanish Fork, to six months' imprisonment and $200 fine each, and Edwin Lucius Whiting, of Springville, to six months' imprisonment and $50 fine—all for u. c.

Wed. 13.—Amos H. Neff was discharged from the Penitentiary.

—Samuel Ridout, of Hooper, was arrested on a charge of u. c.

—Ira Judd, of Panguitch, arrived at Beaver, in charge of a U. S. deputy marshal, having been arrested on a charge of u. c.

Thurs. 14.—James I. Steel was discharged from the Penitentiary.

Fri. 15.—Jens P. Holm, of Salt Lake City, was arrested on a charge of u. c., but, after a preliminary hearing before Com. McKay, was acquitted.

—Thos. Harding, of Provo, was arrested on a charge of u. c.

—Wm. H. Dickson, prosecuting attorney for Utah, resigned his office, by request of the Attorney General, and his successor

Geo. S. Peters, of Ohio, was appointed the day following.

Sat. 16.—John Needham, of the 11th Ward, Salt Lake City, was arrested on a charge of u. c. After a hearing before Com. McKay, he was acquitted.

—Geo. H. Peterson was tried at Evanston, Wyo., on a charge of u. c., and discharged.

—The steamship *Nevada* sailed from Liverpool, England, with 194 Saints, including 13 returning missionaries. in charge of Daniel Porter Callister. The company arrived at New York April 29th and at Salt Lake City May 4th.

Sun. 17.—Alex. Perry, of Willard, Box Elder Co., was arrested on a charge of u. c., and placed under $1,500 bonds.

Mon. 18.—The Zion's Board of Trade buildings, at Logan, Cache Co., were destroyed by fire.

Tues. 19.—Bishop Samuel Carter, of Porterville, Morgan Co., was arrested on a charge of u. c., taken to Ogden and placed under $1,500 bonds.

—U. S. deputy marshals made an unsuccessful raid at Salem, Utah Co., in search of polygamists.

Wed. 20.—Peter Jacob Lammers, of Ogden, was arrested on a charge of u. c., and placed under $1,500 bonds.

—The first Latter-day Saint settlers arrived at Corralles Basin, Chihuahua, Mexico, where Colonia Pacheco subsequently was founded.

Fri. 22.—Timothy Parkinson was discharged from the Penitentiary.

—John T. Gerber, of Granger, was arrested by U. S. deputy marshals, on a charge of of u. c., but ran away from the officers. He, however, gave himself up the following day.

Sat. 23.—Amos Howe, of Salt Lake City, was arrested on a charge of u. c., and placed under $1.500 bonds. He was subsequently acquitted.

—Charles Richens and John Harris, of Pleasant Grove, Utah Co., were arrested on a charge of u. c.

—Geo. Dunford was discharged from the Penitentiary.

Wed. 27.—H. C. Hansen, of Plain City, Weber Co., was arrested for u. c., taken to Ogden and placed under $1,500 bonds.

—Charles O. Card and three companions selected a place for a settlement on Lee's creek, Alberta, Canada — the present Cardston—where other "Mormon" settlers from Cache County, Utah, arrived a few days later. Plowing was commenced May 3rd.

Thurs. 28.—In the Third District Court, Solomon A. Wixom, of Butler Precinct, Salt Lake Co., was sentenced by Judge Zane to six months' imprisonment and $300 fine, for u.c.

—Joseph Parry was arrested at Brighton, Salt Lake Co., on a charge of u. c., imprisoned in the Penitentiary for the night and the following day put under $1,000 bonds.

Fri. 29.—Queen Kapiolani, of the Sandwich Islands, and company, passed through Salt Lake City, going east over the D.& R. G. Ry.

—Charles McCarthy, of American Fork, Utah Co., was arrested on a charge of u.c.

Sat. 30.—In the Third District Court, Salt Lake City, Richard Collett and Alexander Edward, of Salt Lake City, were each sentenced by Judge Zane to six months' imprisonment and $300 fine for u.c. and taken to the Penitentiary.

—In the First District Court, Provo, Geo. T. Peay, of Provo, was sentenced by Judge Henderson to six months' imprisonment and $100 fine, for u.c.

—Harvey H. Cluff, of Provo, was arrested on a charge of u. c. and placed under $1,500 bonds. Rodney C. Badger, of Salt Lake City, and George Harmon, of Taylorsville, Salt Lake Co., were arrested on a similar charge.

—Prince Leopold, of Prussia, visited Salt Lake City.

May. *Sun. 1.*—The Seventies residing in Midway, Charleston and Wallsburg, Wasatch Co., were separated from the 20th quorum of Seventy and organized by Abraham H. Cannon as the 96th quorum. Elijah Alder, Emanuel Richman, Robert Cook, George Wilson, James Price, Ulrich Probst and John Morton, presidents.

Mon. 2.—George Naylor was released from the Penitentiary.

—Miles Williams, of North Point, Salt Lake Co., was arrested for u. c., and the following day placed under $1,500 bonds.

—In the District Court, at Blackfoot, Idaho, the trumped up charge of treason against Apostle John W. Taylor was dismissed.

Tues. 3.—Hans Madsen, of Salt Lake City, was arrested on a charge of u. c., and placed under $2,500 bonds.

—Thomas Colburn, a Church veteran, of Peterson, Morgan Co., died in Salt Lake City.

Wed. 4.—Andrew Hammer, of Union, Salt Lake Co., was arrested on a charge of u. c., and after a hearing before Com. McKay, discharged.

—Andrew Hamer, of Mill Creek, was arrested on a charge of u. c., and placed under bonds.

Thurs. 5.—William Geddes, of Weber County, was released from the Penitentiary.

—George S. Peters, the newly appointed District-Attorney for Utah, arrived in Salt Lake City.

Sat. 7.—James Bishop, of the 16th Ward, Salt Lake City, was arrested on a charge of u. c., and placed under $1,000 bonds.

Mon. 9.—The Saints in Ashley Valley, Uintah Co., were organized by Apostles John Henry Smith and John W. Taylor, as the Uintah Stake of Zion; Samuel R. Bennion, president; and Reuben S. Collett and James Hacking, counselors. At the time of the organization, the Stake consisted of six Wards, namely, Ashley, (Vernal), Merrill's, Mill, Glines, Riverdale (Jensen), and Mountain Dell, with the following named Bishops: Geo. Freestone, Thos. J. Caldwell, Wm. Shaffer, Peter Abplanalp, Nathan Hunting and Silas Jerome Merrill.

—In the Third District Court, Judge Henry P. Henderson refused to grant papers of citizenship to several persons because of their belief in polygamy.

Tues. 10.—Elder Miner G. Atwood died in Salt Lake City.

Wed. 11.—Monroe, Sevier Co.,was raided by U. S. deputy marshals, who arrested Bendt Larsen, Christian Anderson and C. C. Brown, for u. c.

—Peoa, Summit Co., was visited by U. S. deputy marshals, who arrested James Welsh and John A. Marchant, for u. c.

Thurs. 12.—Geo. Wardell, of Peoa, was arrested for u. c.

—James May, of Call's Fort, Box Elder Co.,was discharged from the Penitentiary.

Fri. 13.—Thos. Allsop was discharged from the Penitentiary.

Sat. 14.—After a lengthy trial in the Third District Court, Salt Lake City, the jury returned a verdict of not guilty in the case of Joseph H. Dean, charged with polygamy.

—Alexander Brown, of the 16th Ward, R. J. Caffall, of the 21st Ward, and Thos. C. Griggs, of the 15th Ward, Salt Lake City, were arrested, charged with u. c., and placed under bonds. Hans Hansen and Gustav Anderson, of Hyrum, Cache Co., were arrested on a similar charge.

Mon. 16.—James M. Fisher, of East Mill Creek, and Jesse R. Turpin, of South Cottonwood, Salt Lake Co., were arrested for u. c.

Tues. 17.—Fred. W. Ellis, of North Ogden, Weber Co., was discharged from the Penitentiary.

Wed. 18.—James Lawson, of the 16th Ward, Salt Lake City, was arrested on a charge of u. c., and placed under bonds.

Fri. 20.—Wm. S. Lewis, of Ogden, had an examination on the charge of u._c., and was placed under $1,000 bonds.

Sat. 21.—In the First District Court, at Ogden, Allen Hunsaker, of Bear River City, was sentenced by Judge Henderson to six months' imprisonment and $200 fine, and James W. Burton, of Marriott, to six months' imprisonment and $100 fine, for u. c.

—The steamship *Nevada* sailed from Liverpool, England, with the second company of this season's emigration from Europe, consisting of 187 souls, including 8 returning Elders, in charge of Edward Davis. The company arrived in New York June 1st. From that city the emigration route this year was by the Old Dominion Steamship Line to Norfolk, Virginia, thence by the Norfolk & Western Ry. to Bristol, thence *via* Chattanooga, Memphis and Kansas City to Salt Lake City, where Elder Davis' company arrived June 8th.

Mon. 23.—John Swenson fell from a load of hay in Salt Lake City, and was killed.

—Carl C. N. Dorius of Ephraim, Sanpete Co., was arrested on a charge of u. c., taken before Com. Jacob Johnson, at Spring City, and placed under bonds.

Tues. 24.—Manti, Sanpete Co.,was raided by U. S. deputy marshals, who also ransacked the Temple, in search of polygamists, but no arrests were made.

Wed. 25.—Bishop Wm. E. Jones and Jos. P. Barton, of Paragoonah, Iron Co., Samuel Worthen, of Panguitch, Piute Co., and Alex Orton, of Parowan, Iron Co., were imprisoned in the Penitentiary, having each been sentenced by Judge Boreman in the Second District Court, at

Beaver, the day previous, to six months' imprisonment and $300 fine, for u. c.

—William Openshaw, of the 16th Ward, Salt Lake City, was accidentally killed and his body frightfully mangled on the Utah & Nevada Railway, at Brighton.

Thurs. 26.—Jeremiah H. Kimball, of the 17th Ward, Salt Lake City, fell off the railway train and was killed, while traveling through Missouri, *en route* for Europe, whither he had been called on a mission. His body was brought back to Salt Lake City, and buried there June 1st.

—Thos. H. Smart, of Union, Salt Lake Co., was arrested on a charge of u. c., and placed under $1,500 bonds.

Fri. 27.—James Lattimer was arrested at Nephi, Juab Co., on a charge of u. c., and the following day he started in custody of the officers for Beaver.⚊

Sat. 28.—Edward Brain, of the 20th Ward, Salt Lake City, and Thomas A. Wheeler, of South Cottonwood, were arrested for u. c., and placed under bonds.

—In the First District Court, at Ogden, Hans C. Høgsted, Daniel B. Rawson and Levi J. Taylor, of Harrisville, Willard Bingham, of Wilson, and John J. Dunn, of Three Mile Creek, were each sentenced by Judge Henderson to six months' imprisonment and $100 fine; and Joseph W. Wadsworth, of Hooper, and Ralph Douglas, of Ogden, to six months' imprisonment each—all for u. c. They were all taken to the Penitentiary the same day.

Sun. 29.—The Fourth Ward, Ogden, Utah,was divided into two Bishops' Wards, and the new Ward, named Ogden Fifth Ward, organized;Thos. J. Stevens, Bishop.

Tues. 31.—Lorenzo Stutz, of Mill Creek, and John Stoddard, of Ogden, were discharged from the Penitentiary.

—Frank Stanley was arrested at Woods Cross, Davis Co., on a charge of u. c., taken to Salt Lake City, and placed under bonds. After a preliminary examination, June 3rd, he was discharged.

June. Wed. 1.—John Cottam, of the 16th Ward, Salt Lake City, was arrested on a charge of u. c., and placed under $1,500 bonds.

Thurs. 2. — Wm. Palmer, of Logan, Cache Co., was discharged from the Penitentiary.

—Pres. Wm. Budge, of Bear Lake County, Idaho, was arrested at Ogden, without a warrant, and held in custody,contrary to law, until he was finally released on $3,000 bonds.

Sat. 4.—In the First District Court, at Ogden (Judge Henderson), Wm. L. Walters, of Wellsville, was sentenced to six months' imprisonment and $300 fine; Jens P. Jensen, of Logan, to six months' imprisonment and $200 fine;and Peter Madsen, of Willard, to six months' imprisonment and $100 fine, all for u. c.

—The steamship *Wyoming* sailed from Liverpool, England,with the third company of this season's emigration from Europe, consisting of 159 souls, including 14 returning missionaries, in charge of J. C. Nielsen. The company arrived in New York on the 15th, and in Salt Lake City on the 23rd.

Sun. 5.—Graham Ward, Kane Co., Utah, was organized; Franklin B. Snow, Bishop

—The Saints at Juarez, Chihuahua, Mexico, were organized as a Ward by Apostle Erastus Snow; Geo. W. Sevey, Bishop.

—The Saints who were settling on Lee's creek, Alberta, Canada, held their first meeting on the site of Cardston; the meeting was held in a tent.

Mon. 6.—Huntsville, Weber Co., was raided by U. S. deputy marshals, who arrested Andrew C. Berlin, Christian Petersen and Andrew J. Strømberg on charges of u. c. and adultery. The prisoners were taken to Ogden and placed under bonds.

Tues. 7.—Zion's Choral Union rendered the popular cantata, "Belshazzar," in the Tabernacle, Salt Lake City.

Wed. 8.—U. S. deputy marshals made an unsuccessful raid on Spring City. Sanpete Co., in search of polygamists.

Thurs. 9.—Amasa M. Barton was shot and fatally wounded by a Navajo Indian, at Bluff City, San Juan Co. He died on the 16th.

Fri. 10.—The first number of the *Nephi Ensign,* a weekly newspaper, was issued at Nephi, Juab Co.; James T. Jakeman, publisher.

Sat. 11.—John P. Wright, of Mill Creek, was arrested on a charge of u. c., taken to Salt Lake City, and placed under $2,000 bonds.

Sun. 12.—The first Latter-day Saint Sunday School in Alberta, Canada, was organized on Lee's creek; Jonathan E. Layrel, superintendent.

Mon. 13.—Henry B. Gwilliam and Thomas Bennett Helm were discharged from the Penitentiary.

—Isaac Farley, of Mount Fort, Weber Co., was arrested on a charge of u. c., placed under bonds.

Tues. 14.—The Spencer branch, Rabbit Valley, Utah, was organized as the Fremont Ward; James A. Taylor, Bishop.

—John Farrell, of Eden, Weber Co., was arrested for u. c., and placed under bonds.

Wed. 15.—Bishop James Hansen, of Brigham City, was arrested on a charge of u. c., brought to Ogden and placed under bonds.

Thurs. 16.—A. Milton Musser, of Salt Lake City, was again arrested on a charge of u. c., and placed under bonds. After a preliminary examination, July 5th, he was discharged.

Fri. 17.—Levan, Juab Co., was raided by U. S. deputy marshals, who arrested H. A. Petersen on a charge of u. c.

Sat. 18.—The steamship *Nevada* sailed from Liverpool, England, with 111 Saints, in charge of Elder Quincy B. Nichols. The company arrived in New York on the 28th, and in Salt Lake City July 7th.

Sun. 19.—Elder Alma L. Smith died at Coalville, Summit Co.

Mon. 20.—In the Third District Court, Salt Lake City, Geo. Wardell, of Peoa, was sentenced by Judge Zane to a fine of $50 and costs, for u. c. He promised to obey the law.

—Bishop Henry Hughes, of Mendon, Cache Co., was arrested on a charge of u. c., brought to Ogden and placed under bonds.

Tues. 21.—In the First District Court, at

Ogden, Knud Emmertsen, of Huntsville, and Hans J. Petersen, of Kanesville, were sentenced by Judge Henderson to six months' imprisonment and $200 fine each; Jens P. C. Winter, of Huntsville, and Wm. Butler, of Marriott, to six months' imprisonment, and $300 fine; Jens Frandsen, of Huntsville, Peter J. Lammers, of Ogden, Wm. Douglas, of Smithfield, Lars C. Petersen, of Hyde Park, Hans Jensen, of Hyrum, and Lars Nielsen, of Huntsville, were each sentenced to six months' imprisonment and $100 fine; Albert G. Slater, of Huntsville, Elisher Campbell, of Hyrum, and Gustav Anderson, of Hyrum, to six months' imprisonment and $50 fine, each, and Samuel Carter, of Porterville, to four months' imprisonment and $100 fine —all for u. c.

Wed. 22.—The Old Folks of Salt Lake County had their annual excursion, this year going to Ogden, where they spent a very pleasant day.

—Manti, Sanpete Co., was raided by U. S. deputy marshals, who arrested John Buchannan and Richard Hall on the charge of u. c.

Thurs. 23.—Elder Jesper Petersen, of Castle Dale, Emery Co., died at Odense, Denmark, where he labored as a missionary. He was the second missionary from Utah who died in Scandinavia.

Fri. 24.—In the Third District Court, the murderer, Fred. Hopt, was sentenced to be shot on the 11th of August next.

—Bishop Critchlow and James H. Nelson, of Ogden, were arrested on the charge of u. c. and placed under bonds.

Sat. 25.—A large and enthusiastic meeting was held in the Theater, Salt Lake City, in favor of Utah's Statehood.

Sun. 26.—Elder Samuel W. Musser died in the 1st Ward, Salt Lake City.

Mon. 27.—John P. Jones and John Lee Jones, of Iron County, were discharged from the Penitentiary.

Tues. 28.—Aaron Hardy, of Moroni, Sanpete Co., was arrested on a charge of u. c., taken to Spring City and placed under bonds.

Thurs. 30.—The State constitutional convention met in Salt Lake City and continued its labors until July 7th, when a constitution was adopted.

July.—The Salt Lake *Democrat,* an anti-Mormon newspaper published in Salt Lake City, succumbed for the want of support, after struggling for existence a little over two years.

—James Ipsen, of Mantua, G. F. Hampson and James Eywater, of Brigham City, and Peter Løvgren, of Huntsville, were arrested on the charge of u. c.

Fri. 1.—James Lloynd, of Farmington, Davis Co., was arrested on a charge of u. c. The following day he had a hearing and was bound over in the sum of $1,000.

—Pres. Joseph F. Smith and wife, accompanied by Elder Wm. W. Cluff, sailed from Honolulu, Hawaiian Islands, per steamship *Mariposa,* bound for Utah. They arrived at San Francisco, Cal., July 9th. Pres. Smith had spent nearly two years and five months in Hawaii, as an exile.

Mon. 4.—The Tabernacle, Salt Lake City, took fire from the alighting of a toy balloon, from the fire works, on the roof, but the flames were promptly put out by the fire brigade before doing much damage.

Tues. 5.—The State Convention adopted an anti-polygamy clause, to be inserted in the new constitution.

—Thomas McNeil and Hugh Adams, of Logan, were discharged from the Penitentiary.

Wed. 6.—Geo. Morris, of the 17th Ward, Salt Lake City, was arrested on a charge of u. c., and placed under $1,500 bonds.

Thurs. 7.—The first Latter-day Saint Relief Society in Mexico was organized at Juarez, Chihuahua; Elizabeth Hawkins, president.

—Wm. C. Brown and Andrew J. Kershaw, of Ogden, were arrested for u. c. and placed under bonds.

Fri. 8.—Hyrum H. Barton, arrested the previous day on a charge of u. c., had a hearing before Com. Norrell and was placed under $1,500 bonds.

—Thomas W. Kirby and Abraham Chadwick were discharged from the Penitentiary.

Mon. 11.—Edward Brain, of the 20th Ward, Salt Lake City, was arrested on a charge of polygamy and placed under bonds.

—In the election of school trustees in Salt Lake City, the non-Mormons elected a trustee in each of the following districts: the 7th, 8th, 12th, 13th and 14th.

Wed. 13.—Thomas Henderson, a resident of Emigration Canyon, and Charles Balmforth, of Salt Lake City, were arrested on the charge of u. c., and placed under bonds. The latter was discharged the following day.

—Henry Reiser was discharged from the Penitentiary.

Thurs. 14.—The 97th quorum of Seventy was organized by Abraham H. Cannon at Ashley, Uintah Co., Utah; Matthew Caldwell, Joseph H. Gardner, David Bingham and Geo. Hislop were set apart as presidents.

—Isaac Brockbank was released from the Penitentiary.

—Richard M. Humphreys, of Salina, Sevier Co., was arrested on a charge of u. c.

Fri. 15.—Pres. Joseph F. Smith and party arrived at American Falls, Idaho, where they were met by a conveyance in charge of Elder Albert W. Davis, and started for Utah by team.

Sat. 16.—William Henry Walker, of Wasatch County, was arrested on a charge of u. c., taken to Park City and placed under bonds.

Sun. 17.—The Petersboro branch, Cache Co., was organized as a Ward; Willard D. Cranney, Bishop.

Mon. 18.—Apollos G. Driggs, Lewis H. Mousley and John P. Mortensen were discharged from the Penitentiary.

—John T. Lambert, of Spring City, Sanpete Co., was arrested for u. c.

—Pres. Joseph F. Smith and party arrived at Kaysville. Davis Co., where they met Prests. John Taylor and Geo. Q. Cannon and others, who were faithful watchers at the bedside of Pres. Taylor. He was very sick.

Wed. 20.—Ezra T. Clark, Joseph Hogan

and William H. Foster were discharged from the Penitentiary.

—Brigham Willard Young, of Salt Lake City, died of fever, at Nuhaka, New Zealand, where he labored as a missionary.

Thurs. 21.—James W. Ure, of the 15th Ward, Salt Lake City, was arrested on a charge of u. c. His case was dismissed on the 23rd.

—Patriarch Zebedee Coltrin, once a member of Zion's Camp, died at Spanish Fork; Utah Co.

—After a thorough examination before Com. Rogers, at Ogden, the u. c. case against James H. Nelson was dismissed.

Fri. 22.—Bishop Wm. T. Reid was arrested at Manti, Sanpete Co., on a charge of u. c.

Sat. 23.—Seymour B. Young, against whom there was a charge of u. c., surrendered himself to Marshal Dyer and was placed under bonds. His case was subsequently dismissed.

—The St. Johns Stake of Zion, Ariz., was organized out of the eastern part of Eastern Arizona Stake, by Apostles Francis M. Lyman and John Henry Smith; with David K. Udall as president, and Elijah N. Freeman and Wm. H. Gibbons as counselors. At the time of its organization the St. Johns Stake consisted of seven Wards, namely, Ramah, Erastus, St. Johns, Union, Nutrioso, Alpine and Heber (Luna Valley).

Sun. 24.—Henry Grow was discharged from the Penitentiary.

Mon. 25.—Pres. John Taylor died as an exile at the house of Thos. H. Rouche, at Kaysville, Davis Co., in the presence of Geo. Q. Cannon, Joseph F. Smith, L. John Nuttall, Samuel Bateman, James Malin, H. C. Barrell and others.

Wed. 27.—Wm. R. Smith, president of the Davis Stake of Zion, was arrested at Centreville, on a charge of u. c., taken to Salt Lake City, and placed under bonds.

—Bishop Harrison Sperry was discharged from the Penitentiary.

Thurs. 28.—John Oborn, of Union, Salt Lake Co., was arrested on a charge of u.c., taken to Salt Lake City, and placed under $1,000 bonds.

Fri. 29.—The funeral of Pres. John Taylor took place in Salt Lake City. After the funeral services, Geo. Q. Cannon, Joseph F. Smith, Wilford Woodruff, Lorenzo Snow, Franklin D. Richards, Moses Thatcher, Heber J. Grant and Daniel H. Wells (just returned from England) met in council in Salt Lake City, and decided that the Counselors to the late Pres. John Taylor should preside until the members of the Council of the Twelve Apostles got together.

—Joseph A. Taylor, of Harrisville, Weber Co., was arrested on a charge of u. c. and placed under $1,000 bonds.

Sat. 30.—In the Supreme Court of Utah, suit was commenced against the Church and the Perpetual Emigrating Fund Company, according to the provisions of the Edmunds-Tucker law.

Sun. 31.—Edward Schoenfeld. Thos H. Morrison and Andrew W. Cooley were discharged from the Penitentiary.

August.—General Alexander W. Doniphan, favorably known in early Church history, died in Missouri.

Mon. 1.—Pres. Joseph F. Smith met with his family for the first time since September, 1884, when he went into exile.

—Olaus Johnson, of South Cottonwood, Salt Lake Co., was arrested on a charge of u. c., taken to Salt Lake City, and placed under bonds.

—By the general election in Utah, 10 of the 12 members of the Council branch, and 21 of the 24 members of the House branch of the Utah legislature, were elected by the "People's Party." This result was very satisfactory to the Saints, as the Utah Commission, aided by the governor, had redistricted the Territory without proper consideration of geographical consistency, and arranged the legislative districts so as to place all the anti-Mormon strongholds together. The new constitution of the State of Utah, voted upon at the same time, received over 13,000 affirmative votes; the negatives numbered less than 500.

Wed. 3.—Counselors Geo. Q. Cannon and Joseph F. Smith, eight of the Council of Twelve Apostles (Wilford Woodruff, Lorenzo Snow, Franklin D. Richards, Moses Thatcher, Francis M. Lyman, John Henry Smith, Heber J. Grant and John W. Taylor), and Counselor Daniel H. Wells, met in council in Salt Lake City. Geo. Q. Cannon and Joseph F. Smith were reinstated in their former positions in the Council of the Twelve and an epistle, written by Pres. Wilford Woodruff to the Church, was approved.

—Bishop Wm. Brown, of South Bountiful, Davis Co., was arrested on a charge of u. c., brought to Salt Lake City and placed under bonds. Francis Greenwell was arrested at Ogden on the same charge.

Sat. 6.—Walter M. Gibson, the deposed prime minister of the Hawaiian Kingdom, arrived in San Francisco.

—Pres. David John, Edward Peay, Søren C. Petersen and Christian P. Christiansen were discharged from the Penitentiary.

Thurs. 11.—The murderer Fred. Hopt was executed in the Penitentiary, by shooting.

Sat. 13.—Herman F. F. Thorup was discharged from the Penitentiary.

—John E. Page was arrested at St. George on a charge of u. c.

—Pres. Canute Petersen, of the Sanpete Stake, was arrested at Ephraim, Sanpete Co., on a charge of u. c., but, after a hearing before Com. Johnson, in Spring City, the following Saturday, he was discharged.

Sun. 14.—Ex-Mayor Feramorz Little died in Salt Lake City.

Mon. 15.—Bishop Ishmael Phillips was discharged from the Penitentiary.

Tues. 16.—Wm. G. Baker, of Richfield, was arrested at Monroe, Sevier Co., on a charge of u. c. He was taken to Beaver for examination.

Thurs. 18.—Byron W. King, of East Bountiful, Davis Co., was arrested on a charge of u. c., taken to Salt Lake City and placed under bonds.

Fri. 19.—John A. Carlson, of Salt Lake City, was arrested on a charge of u. c., but after examination was discharged.

—Elder Brigham W. Young, of Salt Lake City, died in New Zealand, where he labored as a missionary. His remains were sent home.

—Elder John Bullock, from Utah, died in England, whither he had gone to visit relatives.

Sat. 20.—The remains of Pres. John Taylor were transferred to a granite sepulchre in the Salt Lake City cemetery.

—Nathan Hanson, of North Point, was arrested on a charge of u. c. and placed under $1,500 bonds.

Sun. 21.—At a Stake conference held at Rexburg, Idaho, that town was divided into three Wards, with Thos. E. Ricks, jun., as Bishop of the First, and Casper Steiner as Bishop of the Second Ward; Timothy J. Winter was chosen as Bishop of the Third Ward. On the same occasion the Lyman Ward was divided, and the north part organized as the Burton Ward; Geo. U. Smith, Bishop.

Mon. 22.—Bedson Eardley, Joseph Blunt, Herman Grether, Wm. H. Watson, Peter S. Barkdull and John Adams were discharged from the Penitentiary.

Tues. 23.—Matthew Pickett, Levi North and Wm. J. Hooper were discharged from the Penitentiary.

Wed. 24.—Toquerville, Washington Co., was raided by U. S. deputy marshals, who arrested Levi Savage on a charge of u. c.

—Hyrum B. North was discharged from the Penitentiary.

—Joseph H. Ridges, of the 19th Ward, Salt Lake City, was arrested on a charge of u. c. and placed under bonds.

Thurs. 25.—Alexander Burt, of the 6th Ward, Salt Lake City, was arrested on a charge of u. c. and placed under bonds.

Fri. 26.—Isaac Riddle, of Beaver, was arrested on a charge of u. c.

Sat. 27.—The steamship *Wisconsin* sailed from Liverpool, England, with over four hundred Saints in charge of John I. Hart. The company arrived in New York Aug. 27th and in Salt Lake City Sept. 15th.

—By an explosion at a saw mill on Lake creek, Wasatch County, J. M. Alexander was killed and two others wounded.

Mon. 29.—Anders W. Winberg and Thos. Butler were discharged from the Penitentiary.

Tues. 30.—Elder Edward Hanham died in the 17th Ward, Salt Lake City.

September.—Wm. Severn, of Montpelier, Bishop Dalrymple, of Preston, and John Johnson, of Ovid, were arrested for u. c.

Thurs. 1.—Charles H. Bassett, of the 2nd Ward, Salt Lake City, was arrested on a charge of u. c., and placed under $1,500 bonds.

—Elder Joseph M. Tanner was surprised and robbed by a band of eight Bedouins, near Yaffa, Palestine.

Wed. 7.—William R. Webb was discharged from the Penitentiary.

Sun. 11.—J. T. Arrowsmith, Edwin Standring, Sanford Fuller, Bishop Geo. D. Snell, Don C. Snow and John L. Gibb were discharged from the Penitentiary.

—The Seventies residing in Marriott, Lynne and Mound Ford Wards, Weber Co., were organized by Seymour B. Young and Abraham H. Cannon as the 98th quorum of Seventy, with Simon F. Halverson, Walter W. Crane, Samuel P. Richards, Wm. Barker, Alonzo O. Perry, Hans Madsen and John Maddock as presidents.

Mon. 12.—David B. Bybee, of Hooper, was arrested at Taylor's Mill, Weber Co., on a charge of u. c. Sam. M. Butcher, who resided near Bingham Canyon, Salt Lake Co., was arrested on a similar charge.

Wed. 14.—In the Third District Court, Salt Lake City, John Connelly was fined $100 and George Harmon $50 for u. c., both promising to obey the law in the future.

Thurs. 15.—Nicholas Sommer, who had just returned with an immigrant company from a mission to Switzerland, was arrested at Ogden on a charge of u. c. and placed under bonds. He was subsequently discharged.

Sat. 17.—Phoebe Soper Pratt, widow of Apostle Parley P. Pratt, died at Provo, Utah Co.

Mon. 19.—In the Third District Court, Salt Lake City, Thomas H. Smart, of Union, was tried and convicted,on a charge of u. c., and sentenced by Judge Zane to six months' imprisonment and $300 fine. James A. Woods, of Tooele, for the same "offence," was sentenced to six months' imprisonment and $100 fine. The jury returned a verdict of guilty in the case of Miles L. Williams, for u. c.

Tues. 20.—After trial, in the Third District Court, the jury returned verdicts of guilty in the cases of Andrew Homer and James M. Fisher, for u.c. Alexander Bills, of South Jordan, was sentenced by Judge Zane to six months' imprisonment and $100 fine, for u. c.

—Christian Hansen, of Box Elder County, was arrested on a charge of u. c.

Wed. 21.—In the Third District Court, George Wilding, sen., was sentenced by Judge Zane to six months' imprisonment and a fine of $100, for u. c.

—Joseph Clark, of Provo, was imprisoned in the Penitentiary, having been sentenced by Judge Henderson, at Provo, to six months' imprisonment and $300 fine, for u. c.

—John England, James Dalley, William Dalley and William Unthank were discharged from the Penitentiary.

—M. D. Pierson, of Plymouth, was arrested on a charge of u. c., taken to Logan and placed under bonds.

—The Saints who had settled on Swift creek, Star Valley, Wyo., were organized as the Afton Ward; Charles D. Cazier, Bishop.

Thurs. 22.—In the Third District Court, the jury returned a verdict of guilty in the u. c. case of Frederik Petersen, notwithstanding the testimony introduced proving that the defendant had lived strictly within the law.

—James Smith was imprisoned in the Penitentiary for u. c., having been sentenced to six months' imprisonment and $300 fine.

—John Warwood, of Nephi, Juab Co., was arrested on a charge of u. c. and placed under bonds.

—In the Second District Court, at

Beaver, the jury returned a verdict of not guilty in the case of David Ward, charged with u. c.

—Bishop Hans Funk, of Newton, and Perrigrine Sessions, of Bountiful,were arrested for u. c.

Fri. 23.—In the Third District Court, after trial, the jury returned a verdict of not guilty in the case of James Bishop, of Salt Lake City, and Wm. H. Hague, of Taylorsville.

—Elder John Roylance, a member of the Mormon Battalion, died at Springville, Utah.

—Elder John P. Sørensen, of Salt Lake City, was banished from the Island of Als, Schleswig, where he labored as a missionary.

Mon. 26.—In the ·Third District Court, Henry Beckstead, of South Jordan, was sentenced to six months' imprisonment and $100 fine; and Joseph H. Ridges, of Salt Lake City, to six months' imprisonment and $25 fine, for u.c. After trial, the case against Elias Morris for a similar "offense" was dismissed.

Tues. 27.—After a lengthy trial in the Third District Court the jury returned a verdict of guilty in the case of Thomas F. Harris, a non-Mormon, for polygamy.

—Frangott Stumph, of Mendon, was arrested on a charge of u. c.

Wed. 28.—In the Third District Court, Ebenezer Woodford, who promised to obey the law, was fined $150 for u.c.

—In the Second District Court, at Beaver, Charles Wilkinson, charged with u.c., was acquitted.

—J. C. Gasberg was arrested at Richmond, Cache Co.,on a charge of u.c. About the same time Paul Poulsen was arrested on a similar charge.

Thurs. 29.—In the Third District Court, Salt Lake City, John Cottam, of the 16th Ward, Salt Lake City, James M. Fisher, of East Mill Creek, and Daniel Harvey, of Kaysville, were each sentenced by Judge Zane to six months' imprisonment, for u.c. Fines were also imposed. John Tate, of Tooele, who promised to obey the law, was fined $50 for a similar "offense."

—Alexander Edwards, Richard Collett and Geo. T. Peay were discharged from the Penitentiary.

—Jacob Miller, of Providence,Cache Co., was arrested on a charge of u. c.

—In the Second District Court, at Beaver, Levi Savage, of Toquerville, and Isaac Riddle, of Marion, were sentenced by Judge Boreman to six months' imprisonment and $300 fine each, for u.c. Wm. Lefevre was fined $100 for a similar "offense."

Fri. 30.—Bishop Samuel Carter was released from the Penitentiary.

—In the Third District Court, William Blood, of Kaysville, was sentenced by Judge Zane to six months' imprisonment and a fine of $150,and John A. Marchant, of Peoa, to six months' imprisonment and $100 fine, and John P. Wright, of Mill Creek, and Joseph C. Perry, of Brighton, to six months' imprisonment and $50 fine, each,for u.c. These four brethren, together with Levi Savage and Isaac Riddle,just arrived from Beaver, were taken to the Penitentiary.

October.—The first number of the *Palantic*, a monthly journal devoted to the interests of the Saints, was published in Salt Lake City; A. Milton Musser, editor and proprietor. One volume of twelve numbers was published.

Sat. 1.—Elder John Preece died in the 4th Ward, Salt Lake City.

—Robert Parker, of Washington, Washington Co., was arrested on a charge of polygamy, but the prisoner made his escape by getting through a window.

—Sine Madsen, of Washington, Washington Co., was arrested in Salt Lake City, being wanted in a polygamy case.

Mon. 3.—In the Third District Court (Judge Zane), Edwin Rushton, of the 5th Ward, Salt Lake City, was sentenced to four months' imprisonment and $50 fine, and Hyrum Henry Evans, of the 6th Ward, Salt Lake City, to six months' imprisonment and $50 fine, both for u. c. The jury returned a verdict of guilty against Rodney C. Badger; Thomas C. Griggs was acquitted. The charges in all these cases were u.c.

Tues. 4.—In the Third District Court, Frederik Petersen, of the 2nd Ward, Salt Lake City, was sentenced by Judge Zane to six months' imprisonment and $100 fine, for u.c. After trial, Edward Brain, also charged with u.c., was acquitted.

—Mrs. Hodson and daughter, the latter the alleged plural wife of John Penman, were imprisoned in the Penitentiary in default of bail.

Wed. 5.—In the Third District Court, Thomas G. Labrum, of Union, was sentenced by Judge Zane to three months' imprisonment and $25 fine, for u.c.

Thurs. 6.—John C. Graham, of Provo, was arrested on a charge of u.c.

—The general semi-annual conference of the Church was commenced in Salt Lake City; it was continued until the 9th.

—Charles Rondquist, of Hooper, who had been arrested on a charge of u.c., had a hearing before Com. Rogers, at Ogden, and was discharged.

Fri. 7.—In the Third District Court, John Oborn, of Union, was sentenced by Judge Zane to six months' imprisonment and to pay a fine of $50, for u.c.

Sat. 8.—The State constitutional convention, which had re-assembled in Salt Lake City, adopted a memorial prepared by a special committee.

—The steamship *Nevada* sailed from Liverpool, England, with the sixth and last company of this season's emigration from Europe, numbering 278 souls, including 23 returning missionaries, in charge of Joseph S. Wells. The company arrived at New York on the 18th, and in Salt Lake City on the 25th.

Tues. 11.—In the Third District Court, John T. Gerber, of Granger, was sentenced by Judge Zane to six months' imprisonment and $100 fine; James C. Watson, of Salt Lake City, to six months' imprisonment and $300 fine, and Charles Burgess, of Salt Lake City, to six months' imprisonment and $25 fine, for u.c. Miles L. Williams, of North Point, who promised to obey the law, was fined $50.

—Elder Andrew W. Cooley died at Brighton, Salt Lake Co.

—John Squires, of Salt Lake City, was arrested on a charge of u.c.

Wed. 12.—In the Third District Court, Samuel Anderson, of Salt Lake City, was sentenced by Judge Zane to six months' imprisonment and $50 fine; Wm. S. Muir, of Bountiful, to six months' imprisonment and $100 fine; John Penman, of Bountiful, to three months' imprisonment and $25 fine; James Loynd, of Farmington, to six months' imprisonment and $50 fine, and Nathan Hansor, of North Point, to six months' imprisonment and $100 fine, all for u.c.

Thurs. 13.—In the First District Court, at Provo, William Yates, of Lehi, and Lars Jacobsen, of Provo, were sentenced by Judge Henderson to six months' imprisonment and $50 fine, each; Victor Sandgren, of Pleasant Grove, was sentenced to six months' imprisonment and $100 fine, and Charles McCarthy, of American Fork, to six months' imprisonment and a fine of $300, all for u.c.

Fri. 14.—In the Third District Court, Salt Lake City, Jesse R. Turpin, of South Cottonwood, and Charles Livingston, of the 11th Ward, Salt Lake City, were each sentenced by Judge Zane to six months' imprisonment and $100 fine, and Andrew Homer, of Mill Creek, to five months' imprisonment and a fine of $100, all for u.c.

—In the First District Court, at Provo, Aaron Hardy, of Moroni, and John T. Lambert, of Spring City, were sentenced by Judge Henderson to six months' imprisonment each, for u.c.; Niels P. Madsen and Edward Cliff, of Mt. Pleasant, were sentenced to six months' imprisonment and a fine of $200, each, for similar "offenses."

Sat. 15.—In the Third District Court, Salt Lake City, James Welsh, of Coalville, Summit Co., was sentenced by Judge Zane to six months' imprisonment and $50 fine, for u.c.

Sun. 16.—Elder Truman O. Angell, sen., Church architect and one of the Utah Pioneers, died at his residence in Salt Lake City.

—The first Latter-day Saints Y. M. M.I. A. in Canada was organized on Lee's creek, Alberta; O. L. Robinson, president.

Mon. 17.—In the Supreme Court of Utah, arguments were commenced in the suits of the United States vs. the Church of Jesus Christ of Latter-day Saints.

Tues. 18.—John Winnell, an aged resident of Kaysville, Davis Co., who had been arrested on a charge of u. c., had a hearing in Salt Lake City, and was placed under bonds.

—Daniel L. Macfarlane was arrested at Cedar City, Iron Co., on a charge of u. c.

Wed. 19.—Payson, Utah Co., was raided by U. S. deputy marshals, who arrested Henry G. Boyle, Joseph Jones, Germand Ellsworth, John Staehle, C. C. Schramm, Samuel Francom and Ferdinand Oberhansle, for u. c.

Thurs. 20.—In the Utah Supreme Court, Hon. James O. Broadhead presented a masterly argument in opposition to the appointment by the court of a Receiver, in the suit of the United States vs. the Church, etc.

Fri. 21.—Pres. Jesse W. Crosby, jun., of Panguitch, Piute Co., was arrested on a charge of u. c. About the same time Elijah M. Steers, of Washington, Washington Co., was arrested on the same charge.

Sat. 22.—In the Third District Court, Salt Lake City, Byron W. King, of Bountiful, was sentenced by Judge Zane to six months' imprisonment and $50 fine, for u.c.

Mon. 24.—In the Third District Court, Perrigrine Sessions, a pioneer settler of Davis County, was fined $150 for u. c.

—In the First District Court, at Provo, Henry Beal, of Ephraim, Sanpete Co., was sentenced by Judge Henderson to imprisonment for three months' and a fine of $300; Peter M. Petersen, of Ephraim, to three months' imprisonment, and Peter C. Hansen, of Gunnison, who promised to obey the law, to two months' imprisonment.

Tues. 25.—In the Third District Court, David B. Bybee, of South Hooper, Davis Co., was sentenced by Judge Zane to six months' imprisonment and $50 fine for u. c.

—In the First District Court, at Ogden, Andrew C. Berlin, of Huntsville, was sentenced by Judge Boreman to six months' imprisonment and $200 fine, and Christian Petersen, of Huntsville, to six months' imprisonment and $300 fine, for u. c. They were taken to the Penitentiary the same day.

Thurs. 27.—In the First District Court, at Provo, Orlando F. Herron, of Pleasant Grove, was sentenced by Judge Henderson to six months' imprisonment and a fine of $50, for u. c. In Ogden, Christian Hansen, of Brigham City, was sentenced to six months' imprisonment and $300 fine, and Andrew G. Strømberg, of Huntsville, to six months' imprisonment and $50 fine for similar "offences." The latter was also accused of adultery with his plural wife and sentenced to six months' additional on that account.

Sun. 30.—Geo. Holyoak was arrested on his farm, near Parowan, Iron Co., on a charge of u. c., and taken to Beaver the following day for examination.

Mon. 31.—Nils J.Gyllenscog was arrested at Smithfield, Cache Co., on a charge of u. c.

November. *Tues. 1.*—Bishop Daniel F. Thomas, of Lynne,was arrested on a charge of u. c., taken to Ogden and bound over in the sum of $2,000.

Wed. 2.—Elder Brigham H. Roberts met the apostate Wm. Jarman in public discussion in London, England.

Thurs. 3.—In the First District Court at Provo, Hans Christian Hansen, of Gunnison, Sanpete Co., was sentenced by Judge Henderson to six months' imprisonment, and John Harwood, of Nephi, to six months' imprisonment, for u. c.

Sat. 5.—The Supreme Court of Utah rendered a decision in favor of appointing a Receiver to take charge of Church property.

—F. A. Petersen, of Levan, was imprisoned in the Penitentiary, to serve 18 months for "adultery."

Sun. 6.—The Saints residing in Springdale, Washington Co., were organized as the Springdale Ward; Wm. R. Crawford Bishop.

—The Saints who had located on Garden creek and vicinity, in Marsh Valley, Bingham Co., Idaho, were organized as the Garden Creek Ward; Joseph E. Capell, Bishop.

Mon. 7.—Marshal Frank H. Dyer was appointed Receiver, to take charge of Church property, by the Supreme Court of Utah.

—Henry Jones, of Bountiful, fell down an embankment near the Warm Springs, Salt Lake City, and was killed. His body was found the next day.

Tues. 8.—James G. Brown, of the 17th Ward, Salt Lake City, was arrested on a charge of u. c., and placed under $1,500 bonds.

—The Utah Supreme Court issued a decree giving Receiver Dyer extraordinary powers in handling Church property. He was required to give $250,000 bonds.

Wed. 9.—In the Utah Supreme Court, a demurrer introduced by the defence in the Church suits, was overruled.

—Isaac Farley, of Ogden, who had been sentenced by Judge Boreman in the First District Court, at Ogden, to six months' imprisonment and $300 fine, was taken to the Penitentiary.

Thurs. 10.—Receiver Dyer filed his bond of $250,000 with the clerk of the Supreme Court. His bondsmen were Wm. S. McCornick, John E. Dooley, Boyd Park, Louis Martin, John J. Daly, Horace S. Eldredge, John Sharp, Andrew Brixen, Matthew Cullen, Jacob Moritz, Charles Beal, J. C. Glenfield and Wm. L. Pickard.

Fri. 11.—Receiver Dyer took possession of the Tithing Office, Salt Lake City, but did not interfere with the regular business.

Sat. 12.—Levi Curtis,an aged gentleman, of Springville, Utah Co., was arrested on a charge of u. c.

—Isaac Bullock, of Provo, who had been sentenced in the First District Court (Judge Henderson), at Provo, to two months' imprisonment and $300, for u. c., was incarcerated in the Penitentiary.

Mon. 14.—In the Third District Court, Salt Lake City, Thomas Henderson was sentenced by Judge Zane to six months' imprisonment and $100 fine, for u. c.

Tues. 15.—Receiver Dyer took possession of the Historian's Office and the Gardo House. The Tithing Office and Historian's Office were leased to the Church. The marshal demanded the President's Office delivered to him.

—Henry H. Petersen, of Hyrum, Cache Co., was arrested on a charge of u. c.

Wed. 16.—Jens Petersen,of Petersboro, Cache Co., was arrested for u. c., taken to Logan and bound over in the sum of $1,000.

Thurs. 17.—Marshal Dyer filed his bond of $50,000 as Receiver in the suit of the United States against the Perpetual Emigrating Fund Company.

—In the First District Court (Judge Henderson), at Provo, Ferdinand Oberhansle, and Germand Ellsworth, of Payson, were each sentenced to six months' imprisonment, for u. c. Fines were also imposed. They were taken to the Penitentiary the same day.

Fri. 18.—Receiver Dyer took posession of the property belonging to the Perpetual Emigrating Fund Company.

—After a lengthy trial in the Third District Court, the jury returned a verdict of not guilty in the case against Alfred H. Martin for the killing of John H. Burton, May 29, 1887.

—In the District Court at Blackfoot, Idaho, Judge Hays on the bench, Josiah Richardson, of Malad, Austin G. Green and Sidney Weeks, of Bingham County, and Wm. Severn, of Montpelier, Bear Lake Co., were sentenced to six months' imprisonment in the Sioux Falls (Dakota) Penitentiary, for u. c., and three years additional for alleged adultery with their wives. Charles Shippen, A. P. Anderson, Elijah Wilson, Alexander N. Stephens, of Menan, Wm. Woodward and J. H. Denning were each sentenced to six months' imprisonment in the Boise City Penitentiary, for u. c. Milo Andrus, for a similar "offence," was fined $300.

Sat. 19.—In the First District Court, at Ogden, John Jenkins and Hans Funk, of Newton, and Richard Fry, of Morgan, were sentenced to six months' imprisonment and $300 fine each, for u. c.; Oluf Hansen, of Logan, to five months' imprisonment and a $100 fine.

—At a special conference held at Oakley Cassia Co., Idaho, Cassia Ward, embracing the Saints who had settled in Goose Creek Valley and vicinity, were organized as the Cassia Stake of Zion; Horton D. Haight, president.

Sun. 20.—Apostle John W. Taylor and Elder Seymour B. Young organized the Saints constituting the Oakley branch, Cassia Co., Idaho, as a Ward; John L. Smith, Bishop.

—The first Relief Society and the first Primary Association, inaugurated by Latter-day Saints in Canada, was organized at Lee's creek, Alberta, with Mary L. Woolf and Sarah B. Daines as their respective presidents.

Mon. 21.—James W. Burton, of Marriott, was discharged from the Penitentiary.

—In the Third District Court (Judge Zane), Rodney C. Badger, of Salt Lake City, was sentenced to six months' imprisonment and a fine of $100, for u. c.

—In the First District Court, at Ogden, (Judge Boreman), John Martin was sentenced to pay a fine of $100 for u. c.; Peter Barton, of Clarkston, and Ralph Smith, of Logan, were sentenced to six months' imprisonment and a fine of $100 each, also for u. c.

—The Saints residing northwest of Oakley, Cassia Co., Idaho, were organized as the Marion Ward; Adam G. Smith, Bishop.

Tues. 22.—Thomas A. Harris, of Salt Lake City, was arrested on a charge of u, c., but was acquitted after a hearing before Com. Norrell.

—James Hardy, of Provo, was arrested on a charge of u. c. and placed under bonds. After a preliminary trial the following Saturday, he was acquitted.

—R. Hochstrasser, of Providence, who had been sentenced by Judge Boreman in

the First District Court, at Ogden, to six months' imprisonment and $100 fine, was incarcerated in the Penitentiary.

—At a special meeting held at Spring Basin, Cassia Co., Idaho, the branch of the Church previously established there was organized as a Ward; Enoch R. Dayley, Bishop.

—The first Latter-day Saint Y. L. M. I. A. in Canada was organized on Lee's creek, Alberta; Zina Y. Card, president.

Wed. 23.—Wm. Felstead, who was serving a long term of imprisonment for polygamy, was released from the Penitentiary, having been pardoned by Pres. Cleveland.

—Receiver Dyer took formal possession of the President's office, leaving two deputies in charge.

—Robert Hazen, of Brighton, Salt Lake Co., was arrested on a charge of u. c. and placed under $1,000 bonds.

—The Saints at Albion, Cassia Co., Idaho, were organized as a Ward of the Cassia Stake; Thos. Taylor, Bishop.

Thurs. 24.—The Elba branch of the Church, Cassia Co., Idaho, was organized as a Ward; Thos. Taylor, Bishop.

Fri. 25.—Bishop Wm. Jones, Joseph P. Barton, Samuel Worthen and Alexander Orton were discharged from the Penitentiary.

—Elder Richard T. Booth, of Alpine, Utah Co., died in Kansas City, Mo., while laboring as a missionary in the States.

—The Almo branch, Cassia Co., Idaho, was organized as a Ward; Thos. O. King, Bishop.

Sat. 26.—Henry Hughes, of Mendon, Cache Co., was imprisoned in the Penitentiary, having been sentenced by Judge Henderson, in the First District Court, to six months' imprisonment and $100 fine, for u.c.

—In the Third District Court, Samuel M. Butcher, of Herriman Precinct, who promised to obey the law in the future, was fined $50 for u. c.

Mon. 28.—John J. Dunn and Hans C. Høgsted were released from the Penitentiary.

—Joseph B. Forbes and S. Glenwood, of American Fork, Utah Co., were arrested for u.c.

Tues. 29.—William H. Tovey, who had already served one term of imprisonment in the Penitentiary for u.c., was again arrested on a charge of u. c. and placed under $1,500 bonds.

Wed. 30.—Judge E. T. Sprague was appointed examiner in the forfeiture suits against the Church.

—Thomas F. Harris, a non-Mormon, was sentenced to six months' imprisonment for polygamy, in the Third District Court. An appeal was taken and the defendant released on $1,000 bail.

December. *Thurs. 1.*—Joseph H. Byington and Austin G. Green, of Menan, Sidney Weeks, of Lyman, and W. Severn, of Montpelier, Idaho, who had been sentenced to three years and six months' imprisonment, each, (except Elder Weeks who got three years) for u.c.,left Idaho, in charge of Marshal Baird, for Sioux Falls Penitentiary.

Mon. 5.—Eliza R. Snow, president of all

the Latter-day Saint Relief Societies, died in Salt Lake City.

—Ephraim Briggs was arrested at Bountiful on a charge of u. c., taken to Salt Lake City, and placed under bonds.

—Receiver Dyer demanded the Weber Stake property delivered over to him, but was refused.

—In the First District Court, at Ogden, Joseph A. Taylor, who promised to obey the law, was fined $50 for u.c. In the case against James C. Petersen, of Logan, sentence was suspended by his promising to obey the law in the future.

Tues. 6.—A church building in Pleasant Valley, Union Co., Ill., in which Latter-day Saint Elders were holding meetings, was burned by a mob.

Wed. 7.—Receiver Dyer seized the President's office and carried off books, some of which never belonged to the Church.

Thurs. 8.—Bishop David Udall, of Nephi, Juab Co., was arrested on a charge of u.c.

—Elder William W. McGuire died in Plain City, Weber Co.

Fri. 9.—In the First District Court, Thomas Young, of Brigham City, was sentenced to six months' imprisonment and $50 fine, for u. c. Herman D. Pearson convicted for a similar "offence," but who promised to obey the law, was sentenced to pay costs of prosecution.

Sat. 10.—In the First District Court, at Ogden, for u. c., Jens Hansen, of Brigham City, was sentenced by Judge Henderson to six months' imprisonment and $300 fine; Charles O. Dunn, of Millville, John Lewis Jones, of Calls Fort, Jens Petersen, of Huntsville, and Wm. Wheeler, of Mendon, to six months' imprisonment and $150 fine, each; Frederick Jensen, of Logan, to six months' imprisonment and a fine of $100, and Nils J. Gyllenscog, of Smithfield, who promised to obey the law, to sixty days' imprisonment. These brethren were taken to the Penitentiary the same day.

Sun. 11.—A Ward organization was effected at North Point, Salt Lake County, with Levi W. Reid as Bishop.

Mon. 12.—Rudger Clawson,who had been pardoned by Pres. Cleveland, was released from the Penitentiary, where he had been imprisoned since Nov. 3, 1884.

—Wm. F. Rigby, of Idaho, was arrested on a charge of u. c.

—Several anti-polygamic measures were introduced in the U. S Senate

Tues. 13.—Elder William K. Barton died in Manti, Sanpete Co.

—James Kemp, of Lewiston, who had been sentenced by Judge Henderson in the First District Court, at Ogden, to six months' imprisonment and $200 fine, was incarcerated in the Penitentiary.

Wed. 14.—Harrison Severe, of Grantsville, was arrested on a charge of u. c., taken to Salt Lake City and placed under bonds. Jonathan Gledhill was arrested at the Deseret Woollen Mills, Salt Lake Co., on a similar charge.

Thurs. 15. — Charles Livingston was released from the Penitentiary, having been pardoned by Pres. Cleveland.

—In the First District Court, at Ogden, H. R. McBride, charged with u. c., promised to obey the law, and sentence in his case was suspended.

Sat. 17.—Wm. J. Lewis was arrested in Provo, on a charge of u. c., and placed under bonds.

—In the First District Court (Ogden), H. N. Petersen and M. C. Jensen were sentenced by Judge Henderson to pay a fine of $100, each; Gustaf Thomson, of Logan, and Andrew Madsen, of Brigham City, to six months' imprisonment and a fine of $100, each; Wm. Chugg, of Providence, to six months' imprisonment and a fine of $200; Lars Mortensen, of Brigham City,to four months' imprisonment,and $150 fine; M. P. Mortensen, of Brigham City, to four months' imprisonment and to pay a fine of $100, and Jacob Miller, of Providence, to two months' imprisonment. Frangott Stumph, of Mendon, was sentenced to two years' imprisonment for polygamy.

Sun. 18. — Showlow, Taylor, Snowflake and Woodruff Wards, which formerly belonged to the Eastern Arizona Stake, and St. Joseph, Moan Coppy and Tonto Wards, constituting the remnant of the defunct Little Colorado Stake, were organized by Apostle John H. Smith as the Snowflake Stake of Zion; Jesse N. Smith, president; Lorenzo H. Hatch and Joseph H. Richards, counselors. The so called Snowflake Camp, located near the top of the Mogollon Mountains, was organized as the Pinedale Ward; Niels Petersen, Bishop.

Mon. 19.—The new constitution of Utah, with accompanying memorial, was presented in the U. S. Senate.

Tues. 20.—Andrew Anderson, of Hyrum, against whom an indictment was out for u. c., gave himself up to the officers of the law.

Wed. 21. — Peter J. Lammers, Jens Frandsen, Albert G. Slater, Wm. Butler, Hans Jensen, Knud Emmertson and Jens P. C. Winter were discharged from the Penitentiary.

—Wm. Williams, of Logan, was arrested on a charge of u. c.

Thurs. 22.—Hans J. Petersen, of Kanesville, Weber Co., was discharged from the Penitentiary.

—In the Second District Court (Judge Boreman), Stephen S. Barton of Paragoonah,David Chidester,of Leeds,Elijah M. Steers,of Washington, George Holyoak,of Parowan, and Daniel L. Macfarlane, of Cedar City, were sentenced to six months' imprisonment and a fine of $300 and costs, each, for u. c. The next day they were imprisoned·in the Penitentiary.

—In the First District Court, at Ogden, Ferdinand F. Hansen of Brigham City, was sentenced by Judge Henderson to four months' imprisonment and to pay a fine of $100, for u. c.

—John B. Johnson was arrested at East Mill Creek, Salt Lake Co., on a charge of u. c. John Burt, of Clarkston, Cache Co., was arrested at Logan, and Fred. Theurer at Providence on the same charge.

Fri. 23.—In the First District Court, at Ogden, Wm. F. Rigby, of Newton, was sentenced by Judge Henderson to six months' imprisonment; John L. Andersen, of Brigham City, to three months' imprisonment; James Christensen,of Newton, to six months' imprisonment and $300 fine;

Andrew W. Stratford, of Brigham City, to six months' imprisonment and to pay a fine of $100; Francillo Durfee, of Dewey-ville, to six months' imprisonment and $300 fine; Lars C. Larsen, of Brigham City, to six months' imprisonment and $50 fine, and Peter Bensen, of Newton, to six months' imprisonment and a fine of $100, all for u. c.

—John Bergen, of Salt Lake City, commenced to serve a sentence of three years for polygamy, in the Penitentiary.

Sat. 24.—In the Third District Court, Salt Lake City, Walter C. Brown, of the 16th Ward, Salt Lake City, indicted for u.c., plead guilty, promised to obey the law and was sentenced to pay a fine of $50.

Tues. 27.—The company of soldiers, which had been stationed in Salt Lake City as a provost guard for some time, was removed to Fort Douglas.

Sat. 31.—Because of the persecution and legal proceedings against the Church, all the workmen on the Temple Block, Salt Lake City, were discharged, and work on the building was suspended.

1888.

The year, generally speaking, was a prosperous one for the Saints in Utah and surrounding Territories, although more arrests and imprisonments for conscience sake took place this year than during any previous season since the prosecutions under the Edmunds law commenced. A good harvest was gathered in nearly all the settlements of the Saints, although water was somewhat scarce in many places. The missionaries abroad were quite successful in their labors, especially on "the islands of the sea," including Samoa, where the fulness of the gospel was introduced in 1888.

January. *Sun. 1.*—Isaac Bullock was discharged from the Penitentiary.

Mon. 2.—Hans Christian Hansen was arrested at Logan for u.c. and placed under $1,000 bonds.

Wed. 4.—Elder Lewis Brunson died in Millard County, Utah.

Thurs. 5.—George Taylor was arrested at Provo, for u.c.

Sun. 8.—Henry Beal and Peter M. Petersen were discharged from the Penitentiary.

Mon. 9.—The 28th session of the Utah legislature met in Salt Lake City and organized by electing Elias A. Smith president of the Council and Wm. W. Riter speaker of the House.

Tues. 10.—James H. Clinger, of Lake View, Utah Co., was arrested for u.c.

—Delegate John T. Caine presented the constitution of the proposed State of Utah, with a memorial asking for admission into the Union, in the U. S. Congress. The measure met with much opposition in the House, and was bitterly opposed by Geo. F. Edmonds in the Senate.

Wed. 11.—Bishop James A. Allred, of

Spring City, Sanpete Co., was arrested for u. c. After examination before Com. Johnson be was discharged on the 12th. Frederick Yeates, of Millville, Cache Co., was also arrested for u. c.

Thurs. 12.—Joseph Dover, of the 21st Ward, Salt Lake City, and Lorenzo Argyle, of Lake Shore, Utah Co, were arrested for u. c. and placed under bonds.

—Edwin Rushton was discharged from the Penitentiary.

Fri. 13. Speaker Wm. W. Riter introduced a bill in the Utah legislature, providing a penalty for polygamy.

—Thomas Pierpont, of the Fifteenth Ward, Salt Cake City, and George B. Bailey, of Mill Creek, Salt Lake Co., were arrested for u. c. and placed under bonds. Bailey was discharged after examination before Com. Norrell on the 19th.

Sat. 14.—Bishop Wm. H. Hickenlooper, of the Sixth Ward, Salt Lake City, died.

—Fred. A. Newberger, of Logan, Cache Co., and William Gallup, of Springville, Utah Co., were arrested for u. c.

Mon. 16.— Carl Capson, of Mill Creek, Salt Lake Co., was arrested for u. c.

Tues. 17.—George Davis, of Three Mile Creek, Box Elder Co., was arrested on a charge of u. c. and placed under $1,000 bonds.

Wed. 18.—Wm. Shin Wardsworth, one of the Pioneers of 1847, died at Springville, Utah Co.

—The Supreme Court of Utah denied an appeal to the U. S. Supreme Court, in the case of appointing a Receiver for Church property.

—Samuel Smith and Henry Tingey, of Brigham City, and Gibson A. Condie, of Springville, Utah Co., were arrested for u. c.

Thurs. 19.—Bishop Peder C. Jensen, Jens Keller Jens Christensen and — Bradshaw were arrested at Mantua, Box Elder Co., for u. c.

—Caroline Harris, widow of the late Martin Harris (one of the Three Witnesses to the Book of Mormon) died at Lewisville, Bingham Co., Idaho.

—Hans C. Hansen was discharged from the Penitentiary.

Sat. 21.—Walter M. Gibson, once a member of the Church, and ex Premier of the Hawaiian Islands, died in San Francisco, Cal.

Wed. 25.—David Whitmer, the last survivor of the Three Witnesses to the Book of Mormon, died at Richmond, Ray Co., Mo.

Thurs. 26.—The Supreme Court of Utah rendered a decision, which restricted the jurisdiction of U. S. Commissioners, in civil cases, to that of justices of the peace.

Fri. 27.—Andrew Hansen was arrested at Newton, Cache Co., for u. c.

Sat. 28.—George C. Watts, of South Cottonwood, was arrested for u. c.

Sun. 29.—The first meeting house built by Latter-day Saints in Canada, was dedicated on Lee's creek, Alberta.

Mon. 30.—John H. Butler, of Spring Lake, Utah Co., was arrested on a charge of u. c., and placed under bonds.

—Niels P. Madsen was discharged from the Penitentiary.

—Arthur Pratt succeeded O. S. L. Brown as warden of the Penitentiary.

Tues. 31. — Peter Svendsen, of Hyde Park, Cache Co., was arrested on a charge of u. c.

—Nils J. Gyllenscog was discharged from the Penitentiary.

February. Sun. 5.—Ole A. Jensen and Alfred Atkinson, of Clarkston, Cache Co., were arrested for u. c.

—Capt. John Douglas, commander of the Guion Line steamship *Nevada*, who had brought many companies of Saints across the sea, died at New York.

Mon. 6.—The People's Party convention, in Salt Lake City, tendered four places on the municipal ticket to the Liberals, which were accepted by the more conservative Liberal element.

—Hans Sørensen and J. H. Barker, of Newton, and James Archibald, of Clarkston, Cache Co., were arrested for u. c.

—Jacob Miller was discharged from the Penitentiary.

Tues. 7.—A. D. Rogers, of Ogden, John Marriott, of Marriott, Weber Co., and Charles A. Andersen, of Hyrum, Cache Co., were arrested for u. c. About the same time Hans P. Hansen, of Hyrum, was arrested on the same charge.

Wed. 8.—Bishop William H. Warner, of Nephi, Juab Co., was arrested for u. c.

Fri. 10.—The anti·fusion Gentiles, in a disorderly meeting, held in Salt Lake City, opposed the municipal fusion ticket adopted by the People's Party, and the more radical Liberals nominated a full city ticket of their own. Gov. West and others, favoring the fusion movement, were grossly insulted.

—John Squires, William H. Tovey, Joseph Dover and Alexander Burt, of Salt Lake City, were arrested, charged with u. c. When arraigned next day Joseph Dover promised to obey the law. The others plead not guilty.

Sat. 11.—Apostle Joseph F. Smith, who had been appointed to preside over the affairs of the Church in the East, left Salt Lake City, for Washington, D. C. He was joined by Charles W. Penrose at Spanish Fork. They arrived at Washington on the 17th. For several months they labored there in the interest of Statehood, assisted by John W. Young and Franklin S. Richards. L. John Nuttall, as secretary to Delegate John T. Caine, and Geo. F. Gibbs, as stenographer, also rendered efficient aid.

Sun. 12.—At a special conference held at West Portage, Box Elder Co., the Malad Stake of Zion was organized out of portions of the Box Elder and Cache Stakes, with Oliver C. Hoskins as president. The new Stake, at the time of its organization, consisted of the following named Wards: Plymouth, Washakie, Portage, Cherry Creek, Samaria, Malad, St. John, Rockland and Neelyville.

Mon. 13.—At the biennial municipal election in Salt Lake City, the fusion ticket, containing four Liberals, was elected; Francis Armstrong, mayor.

—In the First District Court, at Ogden, the following brethren were sentenced by Judge Henderson for breaking the Edmunds law: Alvin Crocket of Logan, to

four months' imprisonment; Wm. Williams, of Hyrum, to six months' and $100 fine; Mads Christensen, of Farmington, to eight months; Carl M. Borgstrøm, of Brigham City, to four months and $100 fine; Wm. H. Griffin, of Newton, to three years and six months and $300 fine; Mariner W. Merrill, jun., of Richmond, to five months; Gehart Jensen to $50 fine; James Hansen, of Brigham City, to six months and $100 fine; Charles A. Andersen, of Hyrum, to two months; Ira Allen, of Hyrum, to six months and $300 fine; Hans Peter Hansen, of Hyrum, to six months and $200 fine, and Ulrick Stauffer, of Willard, to six months.

—Thos. Henderson was discharged from the Penitentiary.

Tues. 14.—Bishop Wm. A. Bringhurst, of Toquerville, Washington Co., was arrested for u. c.

Wed. 15.—After trial in the Third District Court, Salt Lake City, George Morris, charged with u. c., was acquitted.

—Francis A. Berg, of Logan, was arrested on a charge of adultery.

Thurs. 16.—In the Third District Court, Salt Lake City, John Weinel, of Kaysville, 74 years old, was sentenced by Judge Zane to pay a fine of $200 for u. c.

—John H. Linck, a real ·state speculator form Colorado, Alma H. Winn. of Salt Lake City, and other land jumpers, who, on the previous Monday and following days, had attempted to jump and steal the lands belonging to Salt Lake City, on Arsenal Hill, were forcibly ejected from their pretended claims by the city marshal and police.

Sat. 18.—Andrew Homer, of Mill Creek, was discharged from the Penitentiary.

—The question of Utah's admission into the Union as a State was argued before the Senate committee on Territories; John T. Caine and Franklin S. Richards delivered excellent speeches in favor of admission.

Mon. 20.—The Seventies residing in Price, Wellington and Spring Glen Wards, Emery Co., Utah, were organized as the 101st quorum of Seventy, with Wm. H. Branch as senior president. On the 21st, Laurentius M. Olson, George W. Eldredge, Albert Bryner, Samuel Cox, Wm. J. Hill and John D. Lee were set apart as presidents, and 26 members were ordained.

—Abraham H. Cannon, of Salt Lake City, and Chester V. Call, of Bountiful, were arrested for u. c. After examination before Com. Norrell on the 24th, Elder Cannon was discharged.

—Alexander Bills was discharged from the Penitentiary.

Thurs. 23.—Isabella Adamson, of American Fork, Utah Co., who refused to testify in a case under the Edmunds law, was imprisoned in the Penitentiary, for contempt of court.

Fri. 24.—In the Third District Court, Salt Lake City, John B. Johnson of East Mill Creek, was sentenced by Judge Zane to six months' imprisonment and a fine of $150, for u.c.

Sat. 25.—John Andrews, of Logan, and Niels C. Andersen, of Hyrum, were arrested for u.c.

· —George Parker Dykes, once a prominent Elder in the Church and a member of the Mormon Battalion, died at Zenos, Maricopa Co., Ariz.

Sun. 26.—Judge Zane decided against the land jumpers in Salt Lake City.

—Charles Allen Burke, one of the Pioneers of 1847, died at Minersville, Beaver Co.

—Henry Beckstead was released from the Penitentiary.

—Daniel Jones, of Salt Lake Co., Marcus Funk and John Tanner, of Washington, Washington Co., and Dr. Silas G. Higgins, of St. George, were arrested on the charge of u.c.

Mon. 27.—In the Third District Court, Salt Lake City, Edward Cox, of the Sixteenth Ward, was sentenced by Judge Zane to six months' imprisonment and a fine of $50 for u. c.

—John Thorp, of Logan, was arrested for breaking the Edmunds law.

Tues. 28.—At a meeting held at East Bountiful, Davis Co., the 100th quorum of Seventy was organized by Seymour B. Young, with Joseph L. Holbrook as senior president.

—The city council of Salt Lake City, decided to present a portion of the corporation lands on Arsenal Hill to the Territory for State Buildings.

Wed. 29—Gov. West, Mayor Armstrong and a committee from the legislature and city council selected a site for the erection of State Buildings on Arsenal Hill, to be known in future as Capitol Hill.

—In the Third District Court, Salt Lake City, Olaus Johnson,of South Cottonwood, was sentenced by Judge Zane to six months' imprisonment and $50 fine, and Bernhard H. Schettler to six months' imprisonment and $300 fine, for u.c.

—In the First District Court, at Provo, Søren N. Sørensen, of Ephraim, was sentenced by Judge Henderson to four months' imprisonment and $50 fine, and Chr. L. Thorp, of Ephraim, to four months and $100 fine, for u.c.

—John A. Marchant, Isaac Riddle, Wm. Blood and James M. Fisher were discharged from the Penitentiary.

March. *Thurs. 1.*—Thomas Pierpont, of Salt Lake City, was sentenced by Judge Zane, in the Third District Court, to six months' imprisonment and a fine of $300, for u. c.

Sat. 3.—William J. Jenkins, of West Jordan, was arrested on a charge of u. c. and placed under $1.000 bonds.

—Hyrum H. Evans and John Harwood were discharged from the Penitentiary.

Sun. 4.—Aaron Hardy was discharged from the Penitentiary.

Mon. 5.—Elder John B. Johnson died in the Penitentiary, where he was confined for conscience sake.

—In the Third District Court, Salt Lake City, Charles H. Bassett, who promised to live with his legal wife, was sentenced to pay a fine of $50, for u. c.

Tues. 6.—The city council of Salt Lake City decided to offer the Tenth Ward Square to the Territory for fair grounds. The Territory accepted of it on the 9th.

—In the First District Court, at Provo, Samuel Allred, of Ephraim, was sentenced by Judge Henderson to six months' imprisonment and Wilson M. Allred, of Ephraim, to six months' imprisonment and $100 fine, for u. c.

—John Penman was discharged from the Penitentiary, having served out a sentence of two years for polygamy and three months for u. c.

Wed. 7.—John Oborn was discharged from the Penitentiary.

Thurs. 8.—John L. Andersen was discharged from the Penitentiary.

Sat. 10.—The Utah legislature closed its session. The most important bills which became law were those providing for the bonding of the Territory to the amount of $150,000; for the establishment of a Reform School, in Weber County, and an Agricultural College in Cache County; uniformity in county and municipal governments, and appropriating means for the completion of the Deseret University, including a department for the deaf mutes. The municipal authorities of Salt Lake City, having given to the Territory a beautiful site for capitol grounds, on Arsenal Hill, an appropriation was made for its improvement. To erect permanent fair buildings on the Tenth Ward Square (also tendered the Territory by Salt Lake City), an appropriation of $20,000 was made by the legislature.

—In the First District Court, at Provo, Carl C. N. Dorius, of Ephraim, was sentenced by Judge Henderson to six months' imprisonment and $100 fine; Wm. T. Reid, of Manti, to three months and $300 fine; Joseph S. Jones. of Payson, to six months and $100 fine, and John J. Walser, of Payson, to six months, all for u. c.

Sun. 11.—James C. Watson and Charles Burgess were discharged from the Penitentiary.

Mon. 12.—In the Third District Court, Salt Lake City, James S. Brown, of the Seventeenth Ward, was sentenced by Judge Zane to three months' imprisonment and $100 fine, for u. c.

—Nathan Hanson and James Loynd were discharged from the Penitentiary.

Tues. 13.—In the Third District Court, Salt Lake City, Thomas Allsop, of Sandy, was sentenced by Judge Zane to three months' imprisonment and $50 fine, for u.c.

—Lars Jacobsen and Wm. Yates were discharged from the Penitentiary.

Wed. 14.—Alonzo Norton and E. Wright, of Brigham City, Box Elder Co., were arrested on the charge of u. c.

—John T. Lambert, of Spring City, was discharged from the Penitentiary.

Thurs. 15.—In the Third District Court, Salt Lake City, Ephraim Briggs, of Bountiful, was sentenced by Judge Zane to six months' imprisonment and to pay a fine of $25, for u. c.

—John W. Hess, of Farmington, was arrested on a charge of u. c.

Fri. 16.—In the First District Court, at Provo, Bendt Larsen, of Monroe, was sentenced by Judge Henderson to six months' imprisonment and $50 fine, for u. c.

Mon. 19.—John Woods and Thomas H. Smart were discharged from the Penitentiary.

Tues. 20.—Elder Erastus W. Snow, son of Apostle Erastus Snow, died in Salt Lake City.

—D. Spillsbury, of Toquerville, was arrested at Silver Reef, for u. c.

Wed. 21.—Albert K. Thurber, president of the Sevier Stake, died at Ephraim, Sanpete Co.

—Joseph Clark and George Wilding were discharged from the Penitentiary.

Thurs. 22.—James Smith was discharged from the Penitentiary.

Fri. 23.—The Driving Park grounds at Ogden were granted to the Reform School.

—John Bergen was discharged from the Penitentiary.

Sat. 24.—In the First District Court, at Provo, Thomas Harding, of Provo, was sentenced by Judge Henderson to six months' imprisonment; Robert T. King, of American Fork, to six months; George Farnsworth to pay a fine of $200; Henry Hamilton, of Spanish Fork, to six months and $100 fine; L. Loveridge, of Provo, to six months and $50 fine; James Lattimer, of Nephi, to six months and $300 fine; Levi Curtis, of Springville, to six months and $100 fine; James G. Higginson, of Spanish Fork, to six months; Joseph Lunceford, of Lake View, to six months and $50 fine; Joshua Adams, of American Fork, to six months and $100 fine; Karl G. Maeser to pay a fine of $300; Henry G. Boyle, of Payson, to six months and $100 fine, and Thomas R. Cutler (in whose case a new trial was granted and he admitted to bail), of Lehi, to six months, and $300 fine; all for breaking the Edmunds law.

—James Hendrickson, a member of the Mormon Battalion, died in Star Valley, Wyo., aged 65 years and four months.

Sun. 25.—William A. Bringhurst, of Toquerville, Dr. Silas G. Higgins, of St. George, Marcus Funk and John Tanner, of Washington, and Hyrum S. Church, of Panguitch, who had been sentenced by Judge Boreman, in the Second District Court, at Beaver, to six months' imprisonment and $300 fine, each, the day previous, for transgression of the Edmunds law, were imprisoned in the Penitentiary.

Mon. 26.—In the Third District Court, Salt Lake City, Alexander Burt was sentenced by Judge Zane to six months' imprisonment, for u.c.

—Joseph H. Ridges was discharged from the Peditentiary.

—The U. S. Senate Committee on Territories, to whom was referred the Utah State constitution and accompanying memorials, reported unfavorably for Utah's admission into the Union, and was discharged from its further consideration.

Tues. 27.—James E. Mitchel, of Riverdale, Weber Co., was arrested for u.c.

—Orlando F. Herron was discharged from the Penitentiary.

Wed. 28.—Levi Savage and John Cottam were discharged from the Penitentiary.

Fri. 30.—Joseph C. Perry and John P. Wright were discharged from the Penitentiary.

Sat. 31.—In the Third District Court, Salt Lake City, William R. Smith, pres. of the Davis Stake, was sentenced by Judge Zane to six months' imprisonment and $300 fine, for u.c.

April. *Mon. 2.*—Moroni F. Sheets, a witness in the Church suits before the Territorial Supreme Court, was adjudged guilty of contempt of court for refusing to answer certain questions in relation to Church property, and imprisoned in the Penitentiary. He appealed his case to the Supreme Court of the United States.

—Peter Andersen, of Huntsville, Weber Co., was arrested on a charge of u.c.

Ferdinand F. Hansen was released from the Penitentiary.

Tues. 3.—John Durrant, of American Fork, and Søren Jacobsen, of Bountiful, Davis Co., were arrested for u.c.

—Charles A. Andersen and Isabella Adamson were discharged from the Penitentiary.

Wed. 4.—John Harwood, Frederik Petersen, Wm. D. Newsom, Peter S. Barton and Daniel Harvey were discharged from the Penitentiary. Newsom and Barton had been pardoned by President Cleveland.

Thurs. 5.—The Fifty-eight annual conference convened in Salt Lake City. It was continued on the 6th and it was very well attended. A general board of education to superintend Church schools was sustained, consisting of Wilford Woodruff, Lorenzo Snow, George Q. Cannon, Karl G. Maeser, Horace S. Eldredge, Willard Young, George W. Thatcher, Anthon H. Lund and Amos Howe.

Fri. 6.—Jens P. Holm, of Salt Lake City, was arrested for u. c., and placed under bonds. After examination on the 9th he was discharged.

Tues. 10.—The city council committee in Salt Lake City reported favorably on sewerage.

—Søren Christophersen was arrested at Manti, Sanpete Co., for u. c.

Wed. 11.—In the Third District Court, Salt Lake City, Daniel Jones, of Salt Lake County, was sentenced by Judge Zane to six months' imprisonment and $300 fine for u. c.

—John T. Gerber was discharged from the Penitentiary.

Thurs. 12.—William S. Muir and Samuel Anderson were discharged from the Penitentiary.

Fri. 13.—Charles McCarthy and Victor Sandgren were discharged from the Penitentiary.

Sat. 14.—In the First District Court, at Provo, Harvey H. Cluff, of the Utah Stake presidency, was sentenced by Judge Henderson to six months' imprisonment and $300 fine, and Charles Monk, of Spanish Fork, to four months, both for u. c.

—Jesse R. Turpin and Edward Cliff were discharged from the Penitentiary.

Mon. 16.—James Welsh was discharged from the Penitentiary.

Tues. 17.—William J. Parkin was arrested at Bountiful, and R. Bird at Springville, for u. c.

—Germand Ellsworth was discharged from the Penitentiary.

Wed. 18.—Hans Olsen, of Millville, Cache Co., was arrested at Marsh Valley, Idaho, on a charge of polygamy, and Lars C. Christiansen at Hyde Park, and Niels P. Olsen and Ole Olsen at Smithfield, Cache Co., charged with u. c.

Thurs. 19.—Richard Fry, John Jenkins

and Ferdinand Oberhansle were discharged from the Penitentiary.

Sat. 21.—In the Third District Court Salt Lake City, Williams J. Jenkins, of West Jordan, and William H. Tovey, of Salt Lake City, were sentenced by Judge Zane to a second term of six months in the Penitentiary, and to pay a fine of $50; Geo. C. Watts, of South Cottonwood, to three months' imprisonment and $50 fine—all for u. c.

—Rodney C. Badger and Ralph Smith were discharged from the Penitentiary.

Sun. 22.—R. Hochstrasser was discharged from the Penitentiary.

Mon. 23.—John Harris and Byron W. King were discharged from the Penitentiary.

Wed. 25.—Andrew C. Berlin, Christian Petersen, Oluf Hansen and David B. Bybee were discharged from the Penitentiary.

Thurs. 26.—Hans E. Nielsen, of Hyrum, Cache Co., was arrested for u.c.

—Henry Hughes was discharged from the Penitentiary.

Fri. 27.—Christian Hansen and Andrew J. Strømberg were discharged from the Penitentiary, but Strømberg was immediately sent back to serve another term.

—Jens Hansen, of Mill Creek, and David West, of Pleasant Grove, Utah Co., were arrested for u.c.

Sat. 28.—The Matthews Ward, Graham Co., Ariz., was organized; David H. Matthews, Bishop.

—Lars Mortensen and M.P. Mortensen were discharged from the Penitentiary.

—The steamship *Wyoming* sailed from Liverpool, England, with 74 Saints, under the direction of Franklin B. Bramwell. The company reached New York May 10th, and arrived in Salt Lake City May 17th.

Mon. 30.—In the Third District Court, John R. Barnes, of Kaysville, was sentenced by Judge Zane to three months' imprisonment and $300 fine, for u.c.

May. Wed. 2.—The Utah Supreme Court ruled that the Tithing Office and certain personal Church property should be turned over to the Receiver. Chief Justice Zane dissented from this opinion.

—Moroni M. Sheets was brought into court from the Penitentiary, where he had been imprisoned for a month, for refusing to answer questions in regard to Church suits. He now answered the questions and was released.

—Hans C. H. Beck, of Chester, Sanpete Co., was arrested on a charge of u. c.

Thurs. 3.—Bernhard H. Schettler, having been pardoned by Pres. Cleveland, was liberated from the Penitentiary.

—Nathaniel V. Jones in whose case the Supreme Court of Utah had ordered a new trial, was released from the Penitentiary.

Sat. 5.—"Mormons" were excluded from the Democratic Territorial convention at Ogden.

Wed. 9.—Isaac Farley, of Ogden, was discharged from the Penitentiary.

—Friedrick Hirth, a prominent Chinese doctor, visited Salt Lake City.

Thurs. 10.—Wm. Wheeler was discharged from the Penitentiary.

Fri. 11.—W. H. Kelsey and Lorin Harmer, of Springville, Utah Co., were arrested for u. c. Charles W. Nibley was arrested at Logan, on the same charge. After examination, he was discharged, a few days later.

—Simon Webb, of Richmond, Cache Co., who had been sentenced to six months' imprisonment and $50 fine for u. c., was imprisoned in the Penitentiary.

Sat. 12.—In the First District Court, at Ogden, Edwin R. Miles, of Smithfield, was sentenced by Judge Henderson to six months' imprisonment and $50 fine, for u. c.

Mon. 14.—Deputy marshals demanded the Latter-day Saint tabernacle at Logan as Church property, but were refused.

Tues. 15.—William Kelly, of American Fork, Utah Co., was arrested for u. c.

Wed. 16.—Christian P. Nielsen, of Mocharge of u. c. Albert Haws, of Provo, and John Walton, of Alpine, Utah Co., roni, Sanpete Co., was arrested on a were arrested on the same charge. in Provo Valley.

Thurs. 17.—Andrew Madsen was discharged from the Penitentiary.

Fri. 18.—In the First District Court, at Ogden, Fred. Yeates, of Millville, was sentenced by Judge Henderson to six months' imprisonment and a fine of $100, for u. c.

Sat. 19.—Bishop Ezekiel Holman, of Sandy, was arrested on a charge of u. c.—

—Hans Funk, of Newton, was discharged from the Penitentiary.

—The steamship *Wyoming* sailed from Liverpool, England, with 137 Saints, in charge of William Wood. The company arrived at New York May 30th, and at Salt Lake City June 6th.

Mon. 21.—The Temple at Manti, Sanpete Co., was dedicated. This was the third Temple completed in Utah, and with its surroundings is the finest structure erected in the Rocky Mountains. Its entire cost, including the terraces, when finished, is estimated at $1,000,000.

—Bishop William West, of Paris, Bear Lake Co., Idaho, was arrested for u. c.

Wed. 23.—Wm. F. Rigby and Lars C. Larsen (of Brigham City) were discharged from the Penitentiary.

Thurs. 24.—Peter Bensen and Alvin Crocket were discharged from the Penitentiary.

Fri. 25.—In the First District Court, at Ogden, Christopher S. Winge, of Hyrum, and Elijah Seamons, of Hyde Park, were each sentenced by Judge Henderson, to six months' imprisonment and $50 fine, for u. c. Both men were taken to the Penitentiary.

—Geo. L. Graehl, of Brigham City, who the day previous had been sentenced by by Judge Henderson to pay $10 fine, was incarcerated in the Penitentiary for u. c., in default of payment. He promised to obey the same.

—Edward Davis, of South Cottonwood, Salt Lake Co., having been arrested on a charge of u. c., was placed under bonds. His wife lost her reason because of the prosecution.

—A. C. Nielsen, Engebregt Poulsen and John F. F. Dorius were arrested at Ephraim, Sanpete Co., for u. c.

Sat. 26.—In the First District Court, at Ogden, Jens Christensen, of Hyde Park, was sentenced by Judge Henderson to six months' imprisonment and $50 fine; Lorenzo Waldron, of North Ogden, to six months' imprisonment and $300 fine, and Winslow Farr, jun., of Ogden, to six months' imprisonment and $300 fine; all for u. c.

—Bishop Wm. T. Reid, of Manti, was discharged from the Penitentiary.

Sun. 27.—Apostle Erastus Snow died in Salt Lake City.

Mon. 28.—James S. Brown, of Salt Lake City, was discharged from the Penitentiary.

—Amos W. Haws fell a distance of thirty eet from the Woollen factory at Provo, Utah Co., and was killed.

—In the First District Court, at Ogden, James Bywater, of Brigham City, was sentenced by Judge Henderson to six months' imprisonment and $50 fine; Samuel Taylor, of Ogden, to three months, Thomas Harper, of Calls Fort, and Niels C. Andersen, of Hyrum, to six months and $300 fine each; for u. c.

—Thomas E. Ricks, president of the Bannock Stake, Idaho, was arrested at Logan, for u. c. After preliminary examination he was discharged.

Tues. 29.—Thomas Allsop, of Sandy, was discharged from the Penitentiary.

Wed. 30.—In the Manti Temple, which had just been opened for ordinance work, a number of marriages were solemnized. Janne M. Sjödahl and Christine Christoffersen were the first couple married in the building; Apostle Francis M. Lyman officiated.

—The new buildings of the Utah Penitentiary were opened for the accommodation of the prisoners.

Thurs. 31.—In the Third District Court, Salt Lake City, John Squires, of Salt Lake City, was sentenced by Judge Zane to six months' imprisonment and $300 fine, for u. c.

—In the First District Court, at Ogden, Daniel F. Thomas, of Lynne, was sentenced by Judge Henderson to three months' imprisonment and $300 fine, for u. c.

—James B. Hayes, chief justice of Idaho, and a bitter anti-Mormon, died at Boise City.

June. *Fri. 1.*—In the Second District Court, at Beaver, Wm. Carter, Warren Hardy, Walter Granger and Casper Bryner, of St. George, Jacob Bastion, of Washington, and Mark Burgess, of Panguitch, were each sentenced by Judge Boreman to six months' imprisonment and $300 fine, for u. c.

—The Salt Lake and Fort Douglas Railway was opened.

Sat. 2.—In the First District Court, at Ogden, Thos. B. Helm, of Pleasant View, Weber Co., and John Jardine, of Clarkston, Cache Co., were each sentenced to six months' imprisonment and $300 fine, for u. c., and taken to the Penitentiary.

—Alma Fairfield, of Eureka, Juab Co., was arrested for u. c.

—The steamship *Wisconsin* sailed from Liverpool, England, with a company of Saints, in charge of Charles R. Dorius. The company arrived at New York June

13th, and part of the emigrants in Salt Lake City June 19th.

Sun. 3.—Bishop Hans Jensen and William Braithwait, of Manti, and J. C. Frost, of Ephraim, were arrested for u. c.

Mon. 4.—Andrew Anderson, of Union, was arrested on a charge of u. c. D. A. Sanders, of Farmington, Davis Co., indicted for polygamy, was arrested, but succeeded in getting away from the officer during the following night.

Wed. 6.—A railway car, loaded with products of Utah, left Salt Lake City, on an advertising tour through the country. It bore the following inscription: "Utah Palace Exposition Car; the Resources of Salt Lake City, the Gem of the Rocky Mountains. Free Exhibit sent out under the auspices of the Salt Lake Chamber of Commerce."

Thurs. 7.—P. J. Rasmussen and William Roundy, of Milton, Morgan Co., were arrested for u. c.

Fri. 8.—James Turner, of West Jordan, Salt Lake Co., was arrested for u. c.

Sat. 9.—The steamship *Nevada* sailed from Liverpool, England, with a company of Saints, in charge of Elder Charles H. Haderli. The company arrived in New York on the 20th, and part of them in Salt Lake City about the 27th.

—Thomas Young and Søren N. Sørensen were discharged from the Penitentiary.

Mon. 11.—John Irving, of North Jordan, Salt Lake Co., was arrested for u. c.

—Fred. Jensen, Jens Hansen, Charles O. Dunn, Jens Petersen and John R. Jones were discharged from the Penitentiary.

Tues. 12.—Christian L. Thorp was discharged from the Penitentiary.

—Two million government shad, imported from Lake Superior, were put into Utah Lake.

Wed. 13.—The dead body of Lewis Bishop, who was drowned the previous April in the Sevier River, near Deseret, was found three miles below where he fell in.

—William H. Griffin and James Kemp were discharged from the Utah Penitentiary.

Thurs. 14.—John C. Ostler, of Nephi, Juab Co., was arrested for u. c.

Fri. 15.—Father Graves, of Provo, was arrested for u. c.

Sun. 17.—A fire on East Temple Street, Salt Lake City, destroyed property worth $50,000.

—Pleasant Valley Ward, Emery County, Utah, was divided into two Wards, namely, Winter Quarters and Scofield, with John T. Ballantyne and Thos. J. Parmley as their respective Bishops.

Mon. 18.—Gustaf Thomassen, Marriner W. Merrill, jun., and William Chugg were discharged from the Penitentiary.

—Dr. Milford B Shipp surrendered himself to the officers at Salt Lake City, to answer to a charge of u. c.

—Elder Joseph H. Dean (with wife and child) arrived on the Samoan Islands, to open up a new missionary field among the natives of that group.

Wed. 20.—In the Third District Court, Salt Lake City, Alexander Brown was sentenced to one month's imprisonment for alleged adultery.

—James Loynd, of Farmington, Davis Co., was arrested on a charge of u. c. He had already served one term for living with his wives.

Fri. 22.—Daniel S. Macfarlane, George Holyoak, Stephen S. Barton, David Chidester, Elijah Steers, and John R. Barnes were discharged from the Penitentiary, having served terms for u. c. The latter was pardoned by Pres. Cleveland.

Sat. 23.—In the First District Court, at Ogden, John Henry Bott, of Brigham City, was sentenced by Judge Henderson to six months' imprisonment and $100 fine; Alexander Baird, of Deweyville, to six months and $50 fine; Christian H. Monson, of Richmond, to six months' imprisonment and $200 fine; Henry W. Manning, of Hooper, Weber Co., to four months and $300 fine; Axel Christensen, of Brigham City, to four months and $100 fine; Hans C. Hansen, of Logan, to six months and $100 fine, and C. F. Schade, of Huntsville, to $300 fine; all for u. c.

—Andrew W. Stratford, James Christensen and Francillo Durfee were discharged from the Penitentiary.

—John Alma Pace was arrested at Thistle Station, and N. P. Nielsen at Hyrum, Cache Co., for u. c.

—The steamship *Wyoming* sailed from Liverpool, England, with 118 Saints, in charge of Henry E. Bowring. The company arrived at New York July 3rd, and at Salt Lake City July 11th.

Sun. 24.—Judge Elias Smith died in Salt Lake City.

Mon. 25.—Joseph Brundish was arrested near Thistle Station, Utah Co., for u.c.

—C.M. Borgstrøm and George L. Graehl were discharged from the Penitentiary.

—Elder Joseph H. Dean baptized his first convert in Samoa, on the little island of Aunuu. By the 1st of July thirteen souls had been baptized.

Wed. 27.—James Howard, of South Bountiful, was arrested for u. c.

Sat. 30.—In the First District Court, at Ogden, Frank Greenwell, of Ogden, was sentenced by Judge Henderson to five months' imprisonment for u.c.

July. *Wed. 4.*—Elder Orville S. Cox, died in Fairview, Sanpete Co.

Thurs. 5.—Houses at Kanosh, Millard Co., were raided by U. S. marshals, who arrested Bishop Abram A. Kimball, Baldwin H. Watts, John T. Prows and Albert Nadauld, for u.c.

Fri. 6.—Andrew Amundsen, of South Jordan, and William B. Bennett, of West Jordan, Salt Lake Co., were arrested for u.c.

—The Church farm,in Salt Lake County was turned over to Receiver Dyer.

Sat. 7.—Seventy-five school teachers from Colorado and Indiana visited Salt Lake City.

—A small company of Icelandic Saints sailed from Liverpool, England, in charge of Robert Lindsay, bound for Utah.

Mon. 9.—Receiver Frank H. Dyer petitioned the Supreme Court of Utah to have $157,666.15 worth of Church property delivered to him.

—The election for school trustees in Salt Lake City resulted in victory for the Liberals in the Eighth, Ninth, Twelfth, Thirteenth and Fourteenth districts.

—Henry Arnold, of Salt Lake City, was arrested on a charge of u.c.

—President Cleveland nominated Elliott Sandford, of New York, to be chief justice of the Supreme Court of Utah, and John W. Judd, of Tennessee, to be the fourth associate justice. These nominations were confirmed by the Senate July 20th.

Tues. 10.—Considerable Church property was turned over to Receiver Dyer on compromise, pending appeal to the U. S. Supreme Court.

—The city council of Salt Lake City, provided for the issuance of five per cent bonds for corporate purposes.

Thurs. 12.—The Old Folks of Salt Lake County had their annual excursion, this time going to Lehi, Utah Co.

Fri. 13.—Ira Allen and H. P. Hansen, of Hyrum, Cache Co., and Ulrich Stauffer, of Willard, Box Elder Co., were discharged from the Penitentiary.

Sat. 14.—The Iowa Press Association, numbering about two hundred persons, visited Salt Lake City.

Mon. 16.—Lorenzo D. Watson, of Parowan, Iron Co., was arrested for u. c., but got away from the officer on the road to Beaver.

Tues. 17.—Patriarch John Andrews died at Nephi, Juab Co., from injuries received the day before.

—U.S. deputy marshals raided a number of houses at Richfield, Sevier Co., and arrested Ole P. Borg and Niels M. Petersen for u. c.

—Frangott Stumph was discharged from the Penitentiary.

Fri. 20.—U. S. deputy marshals raided places at Spring City, Sanpete Co., and arrested N. C. Jenson for u. c.

—Alexander Brown was discharged from the Penitentiary.

Sat. 21.—Pres. William R. Smith, of Davis Co., was released from the Penitentiary, having been pardoned by Pres. Cleveland.

Wed. 25.—Charles Monk was discharged from the Penitentiary.

Fri. 27.—Seymour B. Young was arrested in Salt Lake City, and Charles Sperry, at Nephi, Juab Co., for u. c.

—Edward Cox was discharged from the Penitentiary.

Sat. 28.—The steamship *Wyoming* sailed from Liverpool, England, with 136 Saints, under the direction of Hans J. Christiansen. The company landed in New York, Aug. 8th, and arrived in Salt Lake City, Aug. 15th.

August.—Elder Alma P. Richards, of Morgan County, Utah, who labored as a missionary in the Southern States, was murdered, near Russell Station, on the A. G. S. Ry., Miss. His body, which was found June 3, 1889, was shipped to Utah.

—A very large number of arrests under the Edmunds law were made in Utah, during this month.

Wed. 1.—Thomas Pierpont was discharged from the Penitentiary.

—James P. Freeze was arrested in Salt Lake City, on a charge of u. c., but dis-

charged the following day, after examination before Com. Norrell.

Thurs. 2.—Howard O. Spencer was arrested in Salt Lake City, for u. c.

Fri. 3.—George Godfrey, of Clarkston,
Cache Co., was arrested for u. c.

Mon. 6. — Samuel Allred and Geo. C.
Watts were discharged from the Penitentiary.

—The election for county officers in
Utah resulted in victory to the People's
party, except in Summit County, which
was carried by the Liberals.

Tues. 7.—Howard O. Spencer (already
under arrest for u. c.) was arrested for
murder, being accused of killing Ralph
Pike, Aug. 11, 1859.

Wed. 8.—Samuel Cluff, of Provo, was
arrested for u. c.

Fri. 10.—Carl C. N. Dorius, John J. Wal-
ser and Joseph S. Jones were discharged
from the Penitentiary.

Sat. 11.—The steamship *Wisconsin* sailed
from Liverpool, England, with 155 Saints,
in charge of Levi Naylor. The emigrants
landed in New York, August 24th, and arrived in Salt Lake City, Sep. 1st.

Sun. 12.—James H. Hart was arrested at
Bloomington, Idaho, for u. c.

—A Latter-day Saint meeting was dis-
turbed and broken up by the apostate Wm.
Jarman, at Swansea, Wales.

Mon. 13.—William Williams, James Hansen and Samuel Taylor completed their
term in the Penitentiary and were discharged.

—Elder Edmund Z. Taylor, of Ogden,
died near Loch Laird, Rockbridge Co.,
Virginia, where he labored as a missionary.
His body was sent to Utah for burial.

Wed. 15.—After a lengthy examination
before Com. Norrell, Howard O. Spencer,
accused of killing Ralph Pike, was admitted to bail in the sum of $6,000.

—Ephraim Briggs was discharged from
the Penitentiary.

—Erik Eliasen, of Millville, Cache Co.,
was arrested for u. c.

Thurs. 16.—Samuel Obray was arrested
at Paradise, Cache Co., for u. c.

—Daniel F. Thomas was discharged from
the Penitentiary.

Fri. 17.—The Territorial Reform School
Commissioners located the site for the
buildings on the Driving Park grounds,
Ogden, which had been donated for the
purpose.

Sun. 19.—At a Stake conference held at
Lewisville, Snake River Valley, Idaho,
three new Wards were organized in the
Bannock Stake, namely, the Taylor Ward,
with Wm. Priest as Bishop; Willow Creek
Ward, Alfonso B. Simmons, Bishop; and
Basalt Ward, Andrew O. Ingelstrøm,
Bishop.

Mon. 20.—John D. Jones was arrested
at Cherry Creek, Idaho, for u. c.

Tues. 21.—Rasmus Nielsen, of Hunter,
Salt Lake Co., was arrested for u. c.

—The Saints who had settled on the
bench, south of Springville, Utah Co., were
organized as a Ward called Mapleton;
Edwin L. Whiting, Bishop.

Thurs. 23.—John W. Judd, of Tennessee,
Utah's new associate justice, arrived at
Ogden.

Fri. 24.—Thomas Harding, Robert T.

King, Joshua Adams, James G. Higginson
and L. Loveridge were discharged from
the Penitentiary.

—Bishop John Kienke, of Mona, Juab
Co., was arrested for u. c.

—A Democratic political club was organized in Salt Lake City.

Sat. 25.—A Republican political club was
organized in Salt Lake City.

Sun. 26.—The Hunter branch, Salt Lake
Co., was organized into a Ward; William
Miller, Bishop.

—Elliot Sanford, recently appointed
chief justice for Utah, arrived in Salt Lake
City. On the 27th he took the oath of
office and superseded Judge Charles S.
Zane.

Mon. 27.—Alexander Burt was discharged
from the Penitentiary.

Wed. 29.—Olaus Johnson and Levi Curtis
were discharged from the Penitentiary.

Thurs. 30.—The court house at Beaver,
Beaver Co., was burned. Loss $15,000.

Fri. 31.—Bishop James C. Hamilton, of
Mill Creek, Salt Lake Co., was arrested
for u. c.

September. *Sat. 1.* — Bishop John
Spencer, of Indianola, Sanpete Co., was
arrested for u. c.

—The steamship *Wyoming* sailed from
Liverpool, England, with 83 Saints, in
charge of Abraham Johnson. The company arrived in New York Sept. 11th, and
at Salt Lake City the 19th and 20th.

Sun. 2.—Elders Elias S. Wright, Thos.
Holt, Azahel L. Fuller and two others
were dragged from their beds and fearfully beaten by a masked mob, near Bell's
Station, Tennessee, for preaching the
gospel.

Mon. 3.—Bishop Archibald McKinnon,
of Randolph, Rich Co., was arrested for
u. c.

—Mads Christensen was discharged from
the Penitentiary.

—Elder Henry Beckstead died at South
Jordan, Salt Lake Co.

Tues. 4.—Apostle Moses Thatcher was
arrested at Logan. On the 7th, after examination, he was discharged for lack of
evidence.

Thurs. 6.—Wilson M. Allred was discharged from the Penitentiary.

—Horace S. Eldredge, one of the First
Seven Presidents of the Seventies, died in
Salt Lake City.

—Elders Andrew Jenson, Edward
Stevenson and Joseph S. Black left Salt
Lake City for the East, to visit the "waste
places of Zion," in the interest of Church
history.

Fri. 7.—After examination before Com.
Norrell, Seymour B. Young was discharged for lack of evidence.

Tues. 11.—An excursion party of Dakota
editors visited Salt Lake City.

—Daniel Jones was discharged from the
Penitentiary.

Fri. 14.—Harvey H. Cluff was discharged
from the Penitentiary.

Sat. 15.—The steamship *Wisconsin* sailed
from Liverpool, England, with 145 Saints,
in charge of William G. Phillips. The
company arrived at New York Sept. 25th,
where twenty of the emigrants were
arbitrarily detained by the officers, on the
pretence that they were paupers. The

rest of the company arrived in Salt Lake City Oct. 2nd.

Sun. 16.—Bendt Larsen was discharged from the Penitentiary.

Mon. 17.—Apostle George Q. Cannon, who had been hiding for some time, surrendered himself to U. S. Marshal Dyer, plead guilty to two indictments charging him with u.c., and was sentenced by Judge Sanford in the Third District Court to 175 days' imprisonment and to pay a fine of $450. On the same occasion. Archibald N. Hill, of Salt Lake City, and Wm. J.Parkin, of Bountiful, were sentenced to 50 days' imprisonment and $50 fine, each, and Samuel H. Hill, of Salt Lake City, to 60 days and $75 fine; all for u.c.

—In the Swansea police court, Wales, William Jarman,who had incited the populace to riot against the Mormons, was placed under £100 bonds, to keep the peace for three months.

Tues. 18.—In the Third District Court, Salt Lake City (Judge Sanford), James Turner, of West Jordan, was sentenced to 50 days' imprisonment and $50 fine; Daniel Lewis, of Kamas, to 60 days and $60 fine;Milford B.Shipp,of Salt Lake City, to 75 days and $65 fine, and Edwin L. Davis, of South Cottonwood, to 75 days and $70 fine; all for u.c.

—Bishop George Coleman, of Teasdale, Sevier Co., was arrested for u.c.

Wed. 19.—In the First District Court, at Provo, Francis C. Boyer, of Springville, was sentenced by Judge Judd to two months' imprisonment and $200 fine, and Jesse Gardner, of Springville, to three months' imprisonment, for u.c.

—Benjamin Perkins was arrested on Carcass Creek, near Teasdale (now Wayne Co.), for u.c.

Fri. 21.—In the First District Court, at Provo, Niels L. Petersen, of Ephraim, was sentenced by Judge Judd to five months' imprisonment, for u.c.

Sat. 22.—In the First District Court, at Provo, Thomas Barrett, of American Fork, was sentenced to four months imprisonment; Joseph B. Forbes, of American Fork, to four months' and $100 fine; Elijah Bourne, of American Fork, to five months; Christian P. Nielsen, of Moroni, to three months; Wm. J. Lewis, of Provo, to five months; Ebenezer Hunter, of American Fork, to two months and Richard Bird, of Springville, to pay a fine of $100; all for u. c.

—John M. Dunning, of Cannonville, Garfield Co., was sentenced by Judge Boreman, in the Second District Court, Beaver, to six months' imprisonment and $300 fine, for u. c. He was taken to the Penitentiary on the 26th.

Sun. 23.—The Nephi Ward, Maricopa Co., Arizona,was organized; Samuel Openshaw, Bishop.

Mon. 24.—Elder Henry Arnold died in Salt Lake City.

—In the Third District Court, Salt Lake City, James Woolstenhulme, of Kamas, Summit Co., was sentenced by Judge Sanford to 65 days imprisonment and $65 fine; and Edwin Rawlins, of Salt Lake City, to 75 days and $75 fine; both for u. c.

—In the First District Court, at Provo, Lewis Olsen, of Ephraim, and Paul Poul-

son,of Richfield, were sentenced by Judge Judd to four months' imprisonment and $200 fine each; Lars Larsen, of Spanish Fork to three months and $100 fine; and Daniel King, of Spanish Fork, Samuel Wagstaff, of American Fork, and Reddick N. Allred, of Chester, Sanpete Co., to 60 days and $50 fine each; all for u. c. Lars Frandsen, of Piute County, was sentenced to six months' imprisonment for alleged bigamy.

—Henry Hamilton, Joseph Lunceford, Silas G. Higgins, Wm. H. Bringhurst,Marcus Funk, John Tanner and Hyrum S. Church were discharged from the Penitentiary.

Wed. 26.—In the First District Court, at Provo, James Butler, of Spring Lake, Utah Co., was sentenced by Judge Judd to five months' imprisonment, and Mons Nilson, of Ephraim, to four months and $200 fine, both for u. c.; and Baldwin H. Watts, of Kanosh, to one-year's imprisonment, for alleged adultery.

Thurs. 27.—Judge Zerubbabel Snow died in Salt Lake City.

—A. G. Strømberg, of Huntsville, Weber Co., was discharged from the Penitentiary, having served two sentences for breaking the Edmunds law.

—David A. Sanders was arrested at Farmington, Davis Co., for u. c.

—In the First District Court, Parley R. Young, of Fairview, was sentenced by Judge Judd to six months' imprisonment and $150 fine, and Hans Jensen, of Manti, to five months' imprisonment; both for u. c.

—David H. Cannon, of St. George, gave himself up to a U. S. deputy marshal, being charged with u. c. After examination the following day, before Com. Julius Jordan, at Silver Reef, he was discharged.

Fri. 28.—Sarah Ann Down, an alleged plural wife from Davis County, was arrested for "fornication."

—John Homer, of Marion, Cassia Co., Idaho, was accidentally shot by his hunting companions, being mistaken for a deer.

Sat. 29.—In the First District Court, at Provo, Lorenzo D. Argyle, of Lake Shore, Utah Co., was sentenced by Judge Judd to six months' imprisonment and $150 fine; John W. Gardner, of Pleasant Grove, to five months' imprisonment; Christian Sørensen, of Mt. Pleasant,to 90 days; Wm. Beeston, of Fillmore, to four months and $200 fine; Christian Borregaard, of Fillmore, to 60 days and $50 fine; Niels M. Petersen, of Richfield, and David Broadhead to $150 fine, each; all for u.c. Ole P. Borg, of Richfield, was sentenced to nine months, and John Durrant, of American Fork, to 18 months' imprisonment, for alleged adultery.

October. *Mon. 1.*—John Squires, imprisoned in the Penitentiary for u.c., was pardoned by President Cleveland.

—Twenty emigrants detained by the officers at New York, through malice, were released, and continued their journey to Utah.

—Thirteen Utah probate judges were confirmed by the U. S. Senate.

Tues. 2.—In the First District Court, at Provo, Søren C. Christensen, of Mt.

Pleasant, was sentenced by Judge Judd to 60 days' imprisonment for u.c.

Wed. 3.—Henry W. Manning was discharged from the Penitentiary.

Thurs. 4.—Samuel C. Pratt, of Salt Lake City, fell into the Hot Springs, at Wadsworth, Nev., and was scalded to death.

Fri. 5.—The Fifty-ninth semi-annual conference of the Church commenced in Salt Lake City. It was continued until the 7th, on which day Brigham H. Roberts was sustained as one of the First Seven Presidents of the Seventies, Horace S. Eldredge being deceased.

—John Squires was discharged from the Penitentiary.

Sat. 6.—The steamship *Wyoming* sailed from Liverpool, England, with 123 Saints in charge of Niels P. Lindelof. The company arrived in New York Oct. 15th, and in Salt Lake City Oct. 23rd.

Sun. 7.—At the first conference held by Latter-day Saints in Alberta, Canada, the Saints, who had located on Lee's creek, were organized by Apostles Francis M. Lyman and John W. Taylor as a Ward, which was named Cardston, in honor of Charles O. Card, the president of the colony; Anthony Woolf, Bishop.

Mon. 8.—Statement of facts in Church confiscation case was agreed upon and submitted in the Utah Supreme Court; decree was entered and notice of appeal given.

Tues. 9.—In the First District Court, at Provo, Gibson Condie, of Springville, was sentenced by Judge Judd to four months' imprisonment and to pay a fine of $200; Rasmus Nielsen, of Spanish Fork, to four months and $200 fine; Andrew R. Andersen, of Lehi, to four and a half months and $50 fine; Charles Hawkins, of Benjamin, to four months and $100 fine; John Walton to four months and $50 fine; Niels Nielsen, of Ephraim, to four and a half months; Fred. J. Christiansen, of Mayfield, to four months and $50 fine; Engebregt Poulsen, of Ephraim, to five months; Rasmus Henningson of Manti, to 90 days; Lars Svendsen, of Moroni, to 90 days and $50 fine; Peter Westenskov, of Manti, to four months and $200 fine, and John P. R. Johnson, of Provo, to four months; all for u.c.

Wed. 10.—The hearing in the Idaho test case was commenced before Judge C. H. Berry, at Blackfoot, Idaho. The decision rendered the following day was practically to the effect that no "Mormons" hereafter could vote in Idaho.

Thurs. 11.—Bishop Elijah F. Sheets, of Salt Lake City, indicted for u. c., gave himself up to the officers of the law.

—Elder William F. Carter died at Santaquin, Utah Co.

Fri. 12.—In the Third District Court, Salt Lake City, James C. Hamilton, of Mill Creek, Salt Lake County, was sentenced by Judge Sandford to 75 days' imprisonment and to pay a fine of $150, for u. c.

—In the First District Court, at Ogden, Bishop Pleasant G. Taylor, of Harrisville, was sentenced to three months' imprisonment and $300 fine.

—Edwin R. Miles was discharged from the Penitentiary.

Sat. 13.—In the Third District Court, Salt Lake City, Bishop Elijah F. Sheets, of Salt Lake City, was sentenced by Judge Sandford to 80 days' imprisonment and $100 fine.

—In the First District Court, at Provo, Lars C. Larsen, of Mayfield, was sentenced by Judge Judd to 120 days' imprisonment; Jens Anderson, of Ephraim, to three months and $50 fine; Archibald T. Oldroyd, of Glenwood, to four months and $50 fine, and Nils H. Borresen, of Spring City, to 60 days; all for u. c. Isaac Clark was sentenced to six months' imprisonment for adultery.

Mon. 15.—N. A. Lindquist, of Logan, was arrested for u. c.

—Elders Andrew Jenson, Edward Stevenson and Joseph S. Black returned from their trip to the East, having visited Independence, Richmond, Far West, the Haun's Mill massacre ground, Adam-ondi-Ahman, and Liberty, Mo.; Palmyra, the hill Cumorah, and Fayette township, N. Y.; Kirtland, Ohio; Nauvoo and Carthage, Ill.; Montrose, Iowa, and many other places of historic interest to the Saints.

Thurs. 18.—In the Third District Court, Salt Lake City, John Irving, of West Jordan, was sentenced by Judge Sandford to four and a half months' imprisonment and $250 fine; Charles M. Nokes, of Riverton, to 85 days' imprisonment and $150 fine; and Dr. Oliver C. Ormsby, of Logan, to 75 days' imprisonment and $200 fine; all for u. c.

Fri. 19.—George Manwaring, of Big Cottonwood, was arrested for u. c.

—Thos. R. Cutler, of Lehi, Utah Co., was imprisoned in the Penitentiary, for u. c.

—At Blackfoot, Idaho, Martin Jacobson, of St. Charles, and Joshua Hawks and Edmund Bulkley, of Franklin, were each sentenced to four months' imprisonment in the Boise Penitentiary, and $100 fine; and Jonathan Smith, of Weston, to four months' imprisonment and $100 fine; all for u. c.

Sat. 20.—In the First District Court, at Provo, Hans P. Petersen, of Moroni, was sentenced by Judge Judd to four months' imprisonment and $100 fine, and Lewis Larsen, of Ephraim, to 90 days and $100 fine; both for u. c.; and Sidney R. Carter, of Joseph, Sevier Co., to six months, for alleged adultery.

—The steamship *Wisconsin* sailed from Liverpool, England, with 125 Saints in charge of John Quigley. The company arrived in New York harbor Oct. 30th, and in Salt Lake City Nov. 7th.

Mon. 22.—Wm. J. Jenkins and Wm. H. Tovey were discharged from the Penitentiary.

Tues. 23.—Houses at Springville, Utah Co., were raided by U. S. deputy marshals, who arrested Lucius Whiting and his plural wife, for u. c.

—Andrew J. Kershaw, of Ogden, was imprisoned in the Penitentiary, having been sentenced by Judge Henderson to 18 months' imprisonment for adultery.

Wed. 24.—In the First District Court, at Provo, Jens C. N. Breinholt, of Redmond, was sentenced by Judge Judd to 90 days' imprisonment, for u. c.

Fri. 26.—Bishop Wm. H. Maughan was arrested at Wellsville, Cache Co., for u. c.

—Elder Vincent Pugmire, of St. Charles, Bear Lake Co., Idaho, died in Coffee County, Alabama, where he labored as a missionary. His remains were shipped to Utah.

Sat. 27.—In the First District Court, at Provo, Bishop George Halliday, of American Fork, was sentenced by Judge Judd to 75 days' imprisonment; Henry Nebeker, of Vermillion, Sevier Co., to six months, and Søren C. Thyggersen, of Ephraim, to nine months; all for u. c.

Mon. 29.—William Smith was arrested at Springville, Utah Co., for u. c.

—Delaney R. Eccles, chief justice of Utah from 1857 to 1860, died at Green Castle, Ind.

Tues. 30.—At Blackfoot, Idaho, A. S. Anderson, of Rexburg, was sentenced to one year's imprisonment for alleged perjury, and Bishop Dalrymple, of Preston, Bear Lake Co., Idaho, to five months and $250 fine, for u. c.

Wed. 31.—In the First District Court, at Provo, Charles Frampton, of Fillmore, a non-Mormon, was sentenced to nine months' imprisonment, for adultery.

—Abraham Zundell, of Willard, Box Elder Co., charged with u. c., surrendered himself to the officers.

—Hans J. Nielsen, of Logan, was arrested for u. c.

November.—Marshal Frank H. Dyer demanded $25,000 for his services as Receiver. So far, $750,000 worth of Church property had been placed in his charge.

Thurs. 1.—Peter Nielsen, of Logan, was arrested for u. c.

Sat. 3.—In the Third District Court, at Provo, James Mellor, jun., of Fayette, was sentenced by Judge Judd to five months imprisonment; Bishop Abram A. Kimball, of Kanosh, to eight months; Gustave Turnburg, to seven months; Robert G. Frazer, of Gunnison, to $100 fine; Eli B. Hawkins, of Benjamin, to five months' and $200 fine; and Joseph Clark, of Provo, to six months and $300 fine; all for breaking th Edmunds law.

—Axel Christensen was discharged from the Penitentiary.

Sun. 4.—William Grant, of American Fork, and John Hart, of Lehi, were arrested for u. c.

Mon. 5.—The corner stone of the new Union Depot was laid in Ogden.

—Frank Greenwell and W. J. Parkin were discharged from the Penitentiary.

—John G. Holman, one of the Pioneers of 1847, died at Rexburg, Idaho.

Tues. 6.—David P. Rainey, a member of the Mormon Battalion, died in Richmond, Cache Co.

—James Turner, of West Jordan, was discharged from the Penitentiary.

—The general election throughout the United States gave a Republican victory, and Benjamin Harrison was elected President. In Utah, the election for delegate to Congress resulted in 10,117 votes for John T. Caine, 3,484 for Robert N. Baskin, 561 for Samuel R. Thurman and 6 scattering votes. In Idaho, a number of the brethren, who had withdrawn from the Church, voted, but nevertheless Mr.

Fred. T. Dubois, a bitter anti Mormon Republican, was elected delegate to Congress from Idaho.

Thurs. 8.—Ten car-loads of potatoes were shipped to Fort Worth, Texas, from Salt Lake City.

Fri. 9.—In the Third District Court, at Ogden, Daniel B. Hill, of Wellsville, was sentenced by Judge Henderson to six months' imprisonment and $100 fine; and Thomas Duce, of Hyde Park, to three months and $100 fine; both for u. c.

Sat. 10.—In the First District Court, at Provo, William R. Webb, of American Fork, was sentenced by Judge Judd to 18 months' imprisonment, for adultery.

—Jollification meetings were held in Salt Lake City and Ogden, over the result of the late election.

Wed. 14.—George B. Bailey, of Mill Creek, Bishop Joseph S. Tanner, of Payson, and Thomas R. Jackson, of Nephi, were arrested for u. c.

Thurs. 15.—Samuel H. Hill and Archibald N. Hill were released from the Penitentiary.

—William Crane was shot and killed by Pardon Dodds, a U. S. Commissioner, at Vernal, Uintah Co.

Fri. 16.—E. T. Harper, of Payson, Utah Co., was arrested for u. c.

—Ex-Judge Charles S. Zane appeared in Utah Supreme Court, as an attorney in behalf of the schools, to oppose exorbitant fees to Receiver and counsel.

Sat. 17.—A small company of Saints, in charge of Louis F. Monch, sailed from Liverpool, England, bound for Utah.

Mon. 19.—In the First District Court, at Provo, the following named brethren were sentenced by Judge Judd for u. c. and alleged adultery: Hans Nielsen, of Chester, to three months' imprisonment and $300 fine; Randolph H. Stewart, of Moab, Emery Co., to seven months; Jens Hansen, of Gunnison, to three months and $50 fine; Eli A. Day, of Fairview, to five months and $150 fine; John F. F. Dorius, of Ephraim, to four months and $50 fine; Oluf C. Larsen, of Ephraim, to five months; Wm. Christiansen, of Pleasant Grove, to three months; John Spencer, of Indianola, to four months; Samuel S. Cluff, of Provo, to four months and $50 fine; Alfred Turner, of Lehi, to 30 days and $50 fine; Richard Jenkins, of Nephi, to 120 days and $50 fine; Oluf J. Andersen, of Castle Dale, to 120 days and $50 fine; Albert Jones, of Provo, to 14 months and $200 fine; Orlando F. Herron, of Pleasant Grove, to 60 days; Søren C. Jensen, of Mt. Pleasant, to four months and $50 fine; Lorin Harmer, of Springville, to four months and $100 fine, and Wm. Gallup, of Springville, to 90 days. Erik Eriksen, Peter M. Andersen and Niels L. Christiansen promised to obey the law and were sent home free.

—Fred Yeates and Francis C. Boyer were discharged from the Penitentiary.

Tues. 20.—In the First District Court, at Ogden, Niels P. Nielsen, of Logan, was sentenced by Judge Henderson to four months' imprisonment and $23 fine, for u.c.

—Wm. W. Drummond, ex-chief justice

of Utah, died in a grog-shop in Chicago, Ill., as a drunken pauper.

Wed. 21.—"Father" John Leishman died in Wellsville, Cache Co.

—In the First District Court, at Ogden, Lars C. Sørensen, of Smithfield, was sentenced by Judge Henderson to 30 days' imprisonment for u.c.

Thurs. 22.—In the First District Court, at Ogden, Poul Poulsen, of Richmond, Cache Co., was sentenced by Judge Henderson to nine months' imprisonment, for adultery.

—Ebenezer Hunter, of American Fork, was discharged from the Penitentiary.

Sat. 24.—In the First. District Court, at Ogden, Hans J. Petersen, of Smithfield, was sentenced by Judge Henderson to four months' imprisonment; Chas. Bailey, of Wellsville, to four months and $100 fine: Willard Hansen, of Brigham City, to four months and $200 fine, and Robert Baxter to $50 fine; all for u.c.

—In the Third District Court, Salt Lake City, George B. Bailey, of Mill Creek, was sentenced by Judge Sandford to a second term of six months' imprisonment for u. c.

—In the First District Court, at Ogden, Henry Stander, of Brigham City, was sentenced by Judge Henderson to six months' imprisonment for adultery; Samuel W. Obray to $200 fine, and Thomas Obray, of Paradise, to five months; all for u.c.

—Asahel L. Fuller, of Mill Creek, was arrested, for u.c.

—Bishop Winslow Farr, Christopher S. Winge, Elijah Seamons, Jens Christensen and Lorenzo Waldron were discharged from the Penitentiary.

—In the First District Court, at Provo, Judge Judd sentenced Albert Haws, of Provo, to 95 days' imprisonment and $50 fine, for u.c.

Tues. 27.—In the First District Court, at Provo, Jens Sørensen, of Glenwood, was sentenced to 95 days imprisonment and $50 fine, for u.c.

—James Woolstenhulme was discharged from the Penitentiary.

Wed. 28.—Bishop Thomas Harper, James Bywater and Niels C. Anderson were discharged from the Penitentiary.

Fri. 30.—In the First District Court, at Ogden, Ole A. Jensen, of Clarkston, was sentenced to six months' imprisonment and $100 fine, and John A. Halgren, of Richmond, to 30 days; both for u.c.

—Søren C. Christensen was discharged from the Penitentiary.

December. *Sat. 1.*—Mark Burgess, Bishop Walter Granger, William Carter, Casper Bryner, Warren Hardy, Jacob Bastion, Milford B. Shipp and Edwin L. Davis were discharged from the Penitentiary.

—Thos. Gunderson, of Mill Creek, was arrested for u.c.

—In the First District Court, at Ogden, Christian Jensen, of Hyrum, was sentenced by Judge Henderson to two months' imprisonment and $150 fine; Richard Thorn, of Three Mile Creek, Box Elder Co., to four months and $100 fine; James H. Brown, of Logan, to four months, and $200 fine; Phineas W. Cook, of Logan, to one month; George Davis, of Three

Mile Creek, to three months, and John Thorp, of Logan, to six months and $100 fine; all for u.c.

Mon. 3.—Bishop John Jardine, Thos. B. Helm and Robert G. Frazer were discharged from the Penitentiary.

—Peter Anderson, of Logan, was arrested for u. c.

Wed. 5.—In the First District Court, of Ogden, Robert Davidson, of Logan, was sentenced by Judge Henderson to four months' imprisonment and $100 fine, for u. c.

Thurs. 6.—In the First District Court, at Ogden, Charles H. Berrett, of Pleasant View, Weber Co., was sentenced by Judge Henderson to three months' imprisonment, for u. c.

Fri. 7.—Lewis Larsen and Edwin Rawlins were discharged from the Penitentiary.

Sat. 8.—In the First District Court, at Ogden, Andrew Hansen, of Newton, was sentenced by Judge Henderson to six months' imprisonment, for u. c.

Mon. 10.—In the Third District Court, Salt Lake City, William H. Hill, of Mill Creek, was sentenced by Judge Sanford to 75 days' imprisonment and $100 fine, for u. c.

—In the First District Court, at Ogden, Frederick A. Newberger, of Logan, was sentenced by Judge Henderson to six months' imprisonment and $100 fine; Jacob Fuhrman, of Providence, to three months and $50 fine; and Christian Andersen, of Newton, and Herbert Savage, of Brigham City, to pay a fine of $50 each; all for u. c.

Tues. 11.—Nils H. Børresen was discharged from the Penitentiary.

—The U. S. Supreme Court set the Church cases for Jan. 14, 1889.

Wed. 12.—Apostle Francis M. Lyman surrendered himself to the U. S. marshal in Salt Lake City, and was placed under $1,500 bonds to answer to a charge of u. c.

—"Mormon" legislators were expelled from the Idaho legislature.

Thurs. 13.—Edward Stevenson, of Salt Lake City, was arrested for u. c.

—In the First District Court, at Ogden for breaking the Edmunds law, the following named brethren were sentenced by Judge Henderson as follows: Peter A. Forsgren, of Brigham City, to three months' imprisonment; Jeppe Jepsen, of Brigham City, to three months; Peter C. Andersen, of Huntsville, to eighteen months; Henry Tingey, of Brigham City, to four months and $200 fine; James Keller, of Mantua, to six months; Peder C. Jensen, of Mantua, to six months and $100 fine; Peter Jørgensen, of Mantua, to three months, and James Monroe Wade, of Pleasant View, to four months; all for u.c.

Fri. 14.—Christian Sørensen was discharged from the Penitentiary.

Sat. 15.—Patriarch Joel Ricks died in Logan, Cache Co.

Mon. 17.—Daniel Lewis was discharged from the Penitentiary.

Tues. 18.—In the Second District Court, at Beaver (Judge Jacob S. Boreman), John T. Covington, of Orderville, Thomas Chamberlain, of Graham, Kane Co., Cornelius McReavy, of Washington, Andrew

Anderson, of Koosharem, James H. Langford, of Junction, Piute Co., and Benjamin Perkin, of Carcass Creek, Piute Co., were each sentenced to six months' imprisonment and $300 fine; all for u. c.

Wed. 19.—In the Third District Court Salt Lake City, Judge Sanford sentenced Andrew Amundsen, of South Jordan, to 80 days' imprisonment and $65 fine; Samuel Bateman, of West Jordan, to 85 days' and $75 fine, and Samuel W. Woolley, of Iron City, Iron Co., to 90 days' and $80 fine; all for u. c.

Thurs. 20.—The Secretary of the Interior ruled that the salt shores of Great Salt Lake could not be located as placers.

—Lars C. Sørensen was discharged from the Penitentiary.

—Elder Ferdinand F. Hintze arrived at Haifa, Palestine, from Asia Minor, on a missionary tour to the Holy Land.

Fri. 21. — Twenty-six Idaho legislators visited Salt Lake City.

Sat. 22.—Rasmus Henningsen, Redick N. Allred, Daniel King and Samuel Wagstaff were discharged from the Penitentiary.

—In the Second District Court, at Beaver, Sylvester F. Jones, of Enoch, Iron Co., Lorenzo D. Watson, of Parowan, Wm. R. Butler, of Escalante, Joseph S. Barney, of Escalante, Francis Webster of Cedar City, and Simon Thornton Topham, of Paragoonah, were each sentenced by Judge Boreman to six months' imprisonment and $300 fine, for u. c.

Sun. 23.—U. S. deputy marshals raided houses at Lehi, Utah Co., and arrested William Gurney, Mons Andersen, A. D. Rhodes and S. Briggs, for u. c.

—Hans C. Hansen, Christian H. Monson, John H. Bott, and Alexander Baird, were discharged from the Penitentiary.

Mon. 24.—William Strong, a member of the Mormon Battalion, died in Salt Lake City.

—In the First District Court, at Ogden, for u. c., Judge Henderson sentenced John Ash, of Logan, to six months imprisonment; Matthew B. Wheelwright, of Ogden, to four months; Niels P. Rasmussen, of Brigham City, to six months and $100 fine; Alonzo Norton, of Honeyville, to two months and $50 fine; Peter Svendsen, of Hyde Park, to four months and $100 fine; Stephen Nye, of Huntsville, to three months; Archibald McKinnon, of Randolph, to three months; William H. Lee, of Woodruff, to four months and $150 fine; Robert Crawshaw, of Wellsville, to three months, and Elijah A. Box, of Brigham City, to six months and $300 fine.

Tues. 25. — Bishop James C. Hamilton was discharged from the Penitentiary.

Thurs. 27.—Bishop Abram A. Kimball, (pardoned by Pres. Cleveland) was released, and Christian P. Borregaard was discharged, from the Penitentiary.

Fri. 28.—Bishop Pleasant G. Taylor was discharged from the Penitentiary.

Sat. 29.—John A. Halgren was discharged from the Penitentiary.

Sun. 30.—Apostle Joseph F. Smith, accompanied by Franklin D. Richards and Geo. F. Gibbs, left Salt Lake City for Washington, D. C., in the interests of the people of Utah.

—Judge Ezra T. Sprague died in Salt Lake City.

Mon. 31.—The Old Folks, widows and orphans were treated to a free entertainment at the Theatre.

—Elijah F. Sheets and Oliver C. Ormsby were discharged from the Penitentiary.

—Pres. Cleveland pardoned A. G. Green, Jonah Richardson, J. H. Byington, Wm. Severn and Sidney Weeks, who were imprisoned at Sioux Falls for u. c, and they were released.

1889.

By the Saints in Utah 1889 will be remembered as the year when the question whether or not the Church to which they belonged could be robbed of its property by the government with the sanction of the supreme tribunal of their country; and also the question whether they could be robbed of civil and political rights as individual citizens, because of their religious belief. Abroad the missionaries met with considerable success, and a few were baptized in Asia Minor and Palestine. In New Zealand large numbers of natives embraced the gospel, and the progress in Europe is shown by the fact that, during the year, 321 were baptized in Great Britain, 572 in Scandinavia, 219 in Switzerland and Germany, and 77 in Holland. The Book of Mormon was translatnd into the modern Jewish and Maori languages. In Salt Salt Lake City, Ogden, and other places in Utah the political developments toward the close of the year will always be remembered as being very significant and demonstrative.

January.—This month was the coldest January known for years in Utah.

Tues. 1.—Phineas W. Cook was discharged from the Penitentiary.

Wed. 2.—Thomas Barratt was discharged from the Penitentiary.

—In the U. S. Senate, Geo. F. Edmunds introduced a protest from Gentile women in Utah against Utah's admission into the Union as a State.

Thurs. 3.—In the First District Court, at Ogden, William H. Maughan, of Wellsville, Cache Co., was sentenced by Judge Henderson to 2½ years' imprisonment, for alleged adultery.

Fri. 4.—Jesse Gardner was discharged from the Utah Penitentiary.

Sat. 5.—Clara Decker Young, widow of Pres. Brigham Young, and one of the three Pioneer women of 1847, died in Salt Lake City.

—Apostles Joseph F. Smith and Franklin S. Richards arrived at Washington, D. C., where they spent several weeks working in the interest of Statehood for Utah, assisted by John W. Young, Charles W. Penrose and others. Franklin S. Richards and Charles W. Penrose visited nearly all the Congressmen in the capitol and had several interviews with Pres. Cleveland; Isadore Morris, a non-Mormon, from Salt Lake City, who went to Washington at his own expense, also used his influence with the President and other leading men in behalf of the "Mormon" people.

—Elder William C. Morris, of Salt Lake City, died in New York from the effects of inhaling gas escaping through a defective tap.

Mon. 7.—In the First District Court, at Ogden, Bishop Sanford Bingham,of Riverdale, Weber Co., was sentenced by Judge Henderson to two months' imprisonment and $100 fine, for u. c.

—Christian P. Nielsen was discharged from the Penitentiary.

Tues. 8.—In the First District Court, at Ogden, Charles S. Hall, of Portage, was sentenced by Judge Henderson to two years' imprisonment, for alleged adultery and u. c., and Frederick G. Ralph to four months, for u. c.

—Alley Thatcher, of Hyrum, relict of the late Hezekiah Thatcher and mother of Apostle Moses Thatcher, died in Salt Lake City.

—Andrew J. Kershaw, George Halliday and Lars Larson were discharged from the Penitentiary.

Thurs. 10.—Peter F. Goss, of Eureka, Juab Co., charged with u. c., gave himself up to the U. S. marshal in Salt Lake City, and was placed under bonds.

—John Hill, of West Jordan, Salt Lake Co., was arrested for u. c.

Fri. 11.—In the First District Court, at Ogden, Mrs. Hester Hendrickson was committed to the Penitentiary for refusing to testify against her husband. She was imprisoned the following day.

Sat. 12.—The hearing on Utah's Statehood before the House Committee on Territories was commenced at Washington, D. C. Franklin S. Richards delivered an able address in favor of Statehood. The hearing was continued daily until the 22nd. Franklin S. Richards was ably assisted by Judge Jeremiah M. Wilson, Delegate John T. Caine and others. Among those who opposed Statehood for Utah, before the Committee, were Robert N. Baskin, John R. McBride and E. P. Ferry.

Sun. 13.—Elders Nephi Y. Schofield and John Morgan were roughly handled by a mob of nearly a thousand men, at Ashton, England.

Mon. 14.—In the Third District Court, Salt Lake City, Apostle Francis M. Lyman was sentenced by Judge Sanford to 85 days' imprisonment and to pay a fine of $200, for u. c.

—Elder Azmon Woodruff, brother of Pres. Wilford Woodruff, died in Farmers Ward, Salt Lake Co., 86 years old.

—Thomas C. Anderson, of Iowa, was nominated for associate justice for Utah, to succeed Jacob S. Boreman.

Thurs. 17.—In the John Hendrickson *habeas corpus* case the Supreme Court of Utah confirmed the action of Judge Henderson in sending a legal wife (Mrs. Hester Hendrickson) to prison for refusing to testify against her husband. The following

day she was taken to Ogden, and there answered the questions required of her.

—Orlando F. Herron and Alfred Turner were discharged from the Penitentiary.

Fri. 18.—The U. S. House of Representatives passed the Springer's omnibus Territorial bill, providing for the admission of several Territories into the Union.

Sat. 19.—Preston Lewis, of Big Cottonwood, was arrested for u. c.

—In the U. S. Supreme Court,arguments were heard in the Church escheat suits.

Sun. 20.—Gibson Condie, Peter Westenskov, John P. R. Johnson, Rasmus Nielsen, Lars Larson and Frederik J. Christiansen were discharged from the Penitentiary.

Mon. 21.—In the Third District Court, Salt Lake City, Thomas Gunderson, of Mill Creek, was sentenced by Judge Sanford to 80 days' imprisonment and $100 fine, for u. c.

—Lars Svendsen was discharged from the Penitentiary.

Tues. 22.—Francis Boggs, one of the Pioneers of 1847, died at Washington, Washington Co.

—In the First District Court, at Ogden, Peter C. Geertsen, of Huntsville, was sentenced by Judge Henderson to six months' imprisonment, for u. c.

Wed. 23.—Elders John E. Hansen and James L. Wrathall were attacked by a mob in Hardin County, Ky., and prevented from filling their appointment for preaching.

—Elder Janne M. Sjødahl arrived at Haifa, Palestine, on a missionary visit to the Holy Land. Soon afterwards he and Elder Ferdinand F. Hintze made a tour of the country, on which they visited Nazareth, Tiberius, Samaria, Nablous, Jerusalem, Jericho, the Dead Sea, Bethlehem, Hebron, Yaffa, etc.

Thurs. 24.—Archibald T. Oldroyd, of Glenwood, Sevier Co., was discharged from the Penitentiary.

Fri. 25.—T. A. Petersen, Thos. Duce, Niels Andersen and Wm. R. Webb were discharged from the Penitentiary.

—In the First District Court, at Ogden, Oliver C. Hoskins, president of the Malad Stake, Idaho, who plead guilty to a charge of u. c., was sentenced by Judge Henderson to three months' imprisonment and $100 fine.

—James Carlisle, of Mill Creek, charged with u. c., gave himself up to the officers of the law and was placed under bonds.

Sat. 26.—Peter J. Rasmussen, of Milton, Morgan Co., was arraigned in the First District Court, at Ogden, for u. c. He promised to obey the law, and sentence was suspended.

Sun. 27.—Niels L. Petersen was discharged from the Penitentiary.

Mon. 28.—Jens Andersen, Nils Peterson and Elijah Bourne were discharged from the Penitentiary.

—Thomas Palmer was arrested at Ogden for u. c.

Tues. 29.—Bishop Henry Ballard, of Logan, charged with u. c., was placed under bonds.

February. *Fri. 1.*—Joseph B. Forbes, Andrew R. Andersen, James Butler,

Christian Jensen and Wm. Gallup were discharged from the Penitentiary.

Sat. 2. — Bishop Hans Jensen was discharged from the Penitentiary.

Sun. 3.—John W. Gardner was discharged from the Penitentiary.

Mon. 4.—Paul Poulson, of Richfield, and Lewis Olsen were discharged from the Penitentiary.

—In the First District Court, at Provo, Charles R. Ockey was sentenced by Judge Judd to four months' imprisonment for u. c.

Tues. 5.—Jens C. L. Breinholt, and Mons Nilson were discharged from the Penitentiary.

Wed. 6.—In the Third District Court, Salt Lake City, Peter Barton, of Kaysville, was sentenced by Judge Sandford to fifteen months' imprisonment, for u. c.

—Joseph Foster, of Smithfield, Cache Co., was arrested for u. c.

—The House Committee on Territories recommended Statehood for Idaho, Wyoming and Arizona, but not for Utah.

Fri. 8.—In the First District Court, at Ogden, William Watterson, of·Logan, was sentenced by Judge Henderson to three months' imprisonment and $300 fine; Henry Ballard, of Logan, to two months; David Buttons, of Clarkston, Cache Co., to pay a fine of $100, and John Welch, of Paradise, Cache Co., to four months; all for u.c.

—William Beeston, of Fillmore, was discharged from the Penitentiary.

—Patriarch Alexander Hill died at Mill Creek, Salt Lake Co.

Sat. 9.—Houses at Scipio, Millard Co., were raided by U. S. deputy marshals, who arrested Bishop Thomas Yates and Benjamin Johnson, sen.

—Charles Nokes was discharged from the Penitentiary.

Sun. 10.—John Irving was discharged from the Penitentiary.

—At the Stake conference, Coalville, Summit Co., Utah, was divided into three Wards, namely, Coalville East, Coalville North and Coalville South, with Joseph Wright, Wm. Hudson and Geo. Beard as their respective Bishops.

Mon. 11.—In the Third District Court, Salt Lake City, James Howard, of South Bountiful, was sentenced by Judge Sandford to 90 days' imprisonment and $100 fine, for u. c.

—At the Ogden city election the Liberals gained the victory, having a fraudulent majority of over four hundred votes.

Tues. 12.—Engebregt Poulsen was discharged from the Penitentiary.

Wed. 13.—Ole A. Jensen, of Clarkston, Cache Co., was discharged from the Penitentiary.

Thurs. 14.—In the First District Court, at Ogden, Wm. C. Rounds, of Milton, Morgan Co., was sentenced by Judge Henderson to four months' imprisonment, for u. c.

—Lucius N. Scovil, a prominent Elder in the Church, died at Springville, Utah Co.

Fri. 15.—In the Third District Court, Salt Lake City, Hyrum B. Barton, of Salt Lake City, was sentenced by Judge Sandford to three months' imprisonment and $100 fine, for u. c.

—Elder John Rowe Moyle died at Alpine, Utah Co.

Sat. 16.—In the Third District Court, Salt Lake City, Henry Rampton, of East Bountiful, Davis Co., was sentenced by Judge Sandford to 90 days' imprisonment and $100 fine; and in the First District Court, at Ogden, Jens Mortensen, of Brigham City, by Judge Henderson to four months' imprisonment; both for u.c.

Mon. 18.—In the Third District Court, Salt Lake City, Charles W. Mann, of West Bountiful, Davis Co., was sentenced by Judge Sandford to fifteen months' imprisonment, for alleged adultery; and in the First District Court, at Provo, Peter C. Christensen, of Mayfield, was sentenced by Judge Judd to 90 days' imprisonment, for u. c.

—After a lengthy examination of the official doings of Receiver Dyer, in the Church suit before Examiner R. K. Harkness, "nothing" was found against him.

Tues. 19.—In the Third District Court, Salt Lake City, Martin Garn, of Sugar House Ward, was sentenced by Judge Sandford to four months' imprisonment and·$200 fine, for u. c.

—Chas. H. Berrett, Charles Hawkins and John Walton were discharged from the Penitentiary.

—Bishop Hyrum F. Stoddard, of Uintah, Weber Co., died.

Wed. 20.—In the Third District Court, Salt Lake City, Peter F. Goss, of Eureka, Juab Co., was sentenced by Judge Sandford to 85 days' imprisonment and $75 fine, for u. c.

Thurs. 21.—Pres. George Q. Cannon was discharged from the Penitentiary.

Fri. 22.—William H. Hill was discharged from the Penitentiary.

—Pres. Cleveland signed the bill providing for admitting North Dakota, South Dakota, Montana and Washington as States into the Union.

Sat. 23.—In the Third District Court, Salt Lake City, David A. Sanders, of Farmington, Davis Co., was sentenced by Judge Sandford to 100 days' imprisonment and $150 fine; Warren F. Reynolds, of South Cottonwoon, to 50 days and $50 fine; Søren Jacobsen, of East Bountiful, to 85 days and $75 fine; and Preston Lewis, of Big Cottonwood, Salt Lake Co., to 100 days and $100 fine; all for u. c.

—Jacob Fuhrman was discharged from the Penitentiary.

Sun. 24.—Charles W. Mann was discharged from the Penitentiary.

Tues. 26.—Jeppe Jeppesen and Lars Frandsen were discharged from the Penitentiary.

—The Salt Lake City council passed a resolution granting a franchise to the Salt Lake City Railway Company.

Wed. 27.—In the First District Court, at Ogden, Matthew S. Bell, of ·Richmond, and Peter Anderson, of Morgan County, were sentenced by Judge Henderson to six months' imprisonment, each, for u.c.

—Joseph B. Thurber, who had been pardoned by Pres. Cleveland, was liberated from the Penitentiary, where he had been imprisoned for polygamy and u.c. Loren Harmer, Samuel C. Cluff, John Spencer and William J. Lewis were discharged from the Penitentiary.

Thurs. 28.—In the First District Court

at Ogden, James Ritchie, of Marriott, was sentenced by Judge Henderson to four months' imprisonment and $200 fine, for u.c.

—Peter C. Andersen, of Huntsville, and Niels P. Nielsen, of Logan, were discharged from the Penitentiary.

March. *Fri. 1.*—The Liberal city council, at Ogden, attempted to gain possession of the Tabernacle square belonging to the Church.

Sat. 2.—In the Third District Court, Salt Lake City, George Manwaring, of Salt Lake City, was sentenced by Judge Sandford to four months' imprisonment, and Joseph Carlisle, of Mill Creek, to 85 days and $100 fine; both for u.c.

—Hans P. Nielsen and Niels Nielsen were discharged from the Penitentiary.

—Elder Hosea Stout died at Big Cottonwood, Salt Lake Co.

—The Supreme Court of Utah rendered a decision, fixing the compensation of Receiver Dyer and his attorneys at $27,365.63 for one year's services.

—Chairman Wm. M. Springer, of the U.S. House Committee on Territories, reported the bill for Utah's admission into the Union, recommending "that it be placed on the calendar for consideration and action thereon by the House."

—Charles W. Penrose, who was under indictment for u. c., was pardoned by Pres. Cleveland, at the solicitation of friends.

Sun. 3.—Samuel W. Woolley was discharged from the Penitentiary.

Mon. 4.—In the First District Court, at Provo, Henry W. Sanderson, of Fairview, Sanpete Co., was sentenced by Judge Judd to 85 days imprisonment and $100 fine; Joseph D. Reynolds, of Springville, and August Svendsen, of Spanish Fork, to 75 days and $50 fine each; and Mads Jensen to a fine of $50; all for u. c.

—Hans J. Petersen, Charles R. Bailey and Willard S. Hansen were discharged from the Penitentiary.

Tues. 5.—In the First District Court, at Provo, the following named brethren were sentenced by Judge Judd, for breaking the Edmunds law: John Frantzen, of Spring City, Sanpete Co., to 13 months' imprisonment; Joseph S. Horne, of Richfield, to 18 months; Andrew Nielsen, of Richfield, 60 days; Gotlieb Ence, of Richfield, to 85 days and $50 fine; Niels P. Nielsen, of Richfield, to three months' imprisonment and $50 fine; Lars P. Christensen, of Richfield, to 85 days and $50 fine; John Oberg, of Richfield, to 85 days and $50 fine; James Sellars, of Richfield, to 18 months; Thomas Ogden, of Richfield, to 19 months; Reuben Gurr, of Richfield, to 12 months; Hans Christensen, of Richfield, to 16 months; William C. Prows, of Kanosh, to 65 days; James P. Hansen, of Ephraim, to 50 days; Carl Olsen, of Emery, to 75 days and $50 fine; Mons Rosenlund, of Mayfield, to 85 days; Andrew Poulsen to $110 fine, and Shadrach T. Driggs to $10 fine.

Wed. 6.—In the First District Court, Provo, George Kendall was sentenced by Judge Judd to a fine of $10 for u. c. The case for adultery and u. c. against F. C. Christensen, who promised to obey the law, was dismissed. Sentence was also

suspended in the case of William Braithwaite, charged with u. c., the defendant promising to obey the law.

—Wm. Christiansen, Jens Hansen and Hans Nielsen were discharged from the Penitentiary.

Fri. 8.—Apostle Joseph F. Smith and Elder Charles W. Penrose returned to Salt Lake City from their special mission to Washington, D. C.

—Andrew Amundsen was discharged from the Penitentiary.

Sat. 9.—In the First District Court, at Provo, Jacob Hafen, of Mt. Pleasant, was sentenced by Judge Judd to 85 days' imprisonment and $50 fine, and Thos. Cloward, of Payson, to 50 days' imprisonment; both for u. c.

—Archibald McKinnon and James Mellor, jun., were discharged from the Penitentiary.

—Frank H. Dyer tendered his resignation as U. S. marshal for Utah to Pres. Cleveland.

Tues. 12.—In the First District Court, at Provo, Thos. Didriksen, of Spanish Fork, was sentenced by Judge Judd to 65 days' imprisonment, and Hans Nielsen (who had just served a term in the Penitentiary, for u. c.) to 125 days' imprisonment, for "adultery." Nielsen petitioned for a writ of *habeas corpus*, representing that he was being punished twice for the same offence. The writ was refused, and the case appealed to the Supreme Court of the United States.

—George Davis and Richard Thorn were discharged from the Penitentiary.

Wed. 13.—In the First District Court, at Provo, Charles Hampshire, of Mt. Pleasant, was sentenced by Judge Judd to 120 days' imprisonment and $50 fine, for u. c.

—In the Second District Court, at Beaver, John G. Jørgensen, of Grass Valley, and Christian Nielsen, of Koosharem, were each sentenced by Judge Boreman to six months' imprisonment and $300 fine, for u. c.

—Samuel Bateman and Isaac Clark were discharged from the Penitentiary.

Thurs. 14.—In the First District Court, at Provo, Frands C. Christiansen, of Mt. Pleasant, was sentenced by Judge Judd to 75 days' imprisonment, for u. c.

—Albert Haws, of Provo, was discharged from the Penitentiary.

Fri. 15.—In the Third District Court, Salt Lake City, John Groves, of Sugar House Ward, was sentenced by Judge Sandford to 50 days' imprisonment and $75 fine; and in the First District Court, at Provo, Andrew Rasmussen, of Fairview, was sentenced by Judge Judd to 50 days; both for u. c.

Sat. 16.—Ole P. Borg was discharged from the Penitentiary.

Tues. 19.—Judge Philip H. Emerson died at Ogden.

—Bishop Thos. R. Cutler, of Lehi, was discharged from the Penitentiary.

Wed. 20.—Sidney R. Carter, of Joseph, Sevier Co., was discharged from the Penitentiary.

—Thos. J. Anderson, the newly appointed associate justice for Utah, arrived in Salt Lake City.

Thurs. 21.—In the First District Court

at Ogden, George Facer, of Willard, was sentenced by Judge Henderson to four months' imprisonment and $50 fine, for u. c.

—Bishop H. H. Dalrymple. of Preston, Bear Lake Co., Idaho, was discharged from the Boise City Penitentiary.

Fri. 22.—Judge Thomas J. Anderson commenced his official career in Utah and was assigned to the Second District.

Sat. 23.—In the First District Court, at Provo, the following named brethren were sentenced by Judge Judd for breaking the Edmunds law: Joseph Clark, of Provo, to three years and six months' imprisonment; Michal Vaughan, of Lehi, to nine months; Niels Aagaard, of Levan, to 50 days; Martin Bushman, of Lehi, to 90 days; William Gurney, of Lehi, to 85 days; Mons Andersen, of Lehi, to 12 months; Isaac W. Fox, of Lehi, to 35 days; William Ball of Lehi, to 85 days; John Jacobs to 10 months; William Hutchings, of Lehi, to 11 months; Stephen Mott, of American Fork, to 75 days; John W. Gardner to 125 days, and John Hart, of Lehi, to 18 months.

—John M. Dunning was discharged from the Penitentiary.

—The first number of the *Wasatch Wave,* a weekly newspaper, was published in Heber City, Wasatch Co., Utah, by a company.

Sun. 24.—James M. Wade was discharged from the Penitentiary.

Mon. 25.—Joseph Dean, of Salt Lake City, was arrested for u.c.

Tues. 26.—In the First District Court, at Provo, B. W. Brown, of Lehi, was sentenced by Judge Judd to three years' imprisonment and to pay a fine of $1,000 for alleged perjury.

—Alonso Norton was discharged from the Penitentiary.

—George W. Bean, of Richfield, Sevier Co., was arrested for u.c.

Wed. 27.—Oluf J. Andersen and Henry Nebeker were discharged from the Penitentiary.

—J. M. Hansen, of Newton, Cache Co., was arrested on a charge of u. c.

Thurs. 28.—In the First Distrist Court, at Provo, J. H. Turner was sentenced by Judge Judd to two years' imprisonment, and Jens Jørgensen, of Mount Pleasant, to 12 months, for alleged adultery.

—Richard Jenkins, Peter Jørgensen and Peter A. Forsgren were discharged from the Penitentiary.

—Adolphus R. Whitehead, of St. George, was arrested in Salt Lake City, and Jens Sørensen, at Richmond, Cache Co., for u. c.

Fri. 29.—Parley R. Young, John F. F. Dorius and Søren C. Jensen were discharged from the Penitentiary.

Sat. 30.—Lorenzo D. Argyle was discharged from the Penitentiary.

—Joseph Clark was brought into the First District Court, at Provo, from the Penitentiary, and sentenced a third time for breaking the Edmunds law, this time to three years' imprisonment, to commence at the expiration of the term he was serving for alleged adultery.

Sun. 31.—The Twenty-second Ward, Salt Lake City, was organized out of the west portion of the Nineteenth Ward; Alfred Solomon, Bishop.

April.—*Mon.* 1.—In the First District Court, at Ogden, Anthony Heiner, of Morgan, was sentenced by Judge Henderson to three months' imprisonment and $200 fine, for u. c.

—Thomas Obray, of Paradise, was discharged from the Penitentiary.

Tues. 2.—Thomas H. Winter, who had been sentenced by Judge Judd, at Provo, the day previous, to one year's imprisonment for polygamy, was incarcerated in the Penitentiary.

Thurs. 4.—Bishop Wm. H. Lee and M. B. Wheelwright were discharged from the Penitentiary.

Sat. 6.—The 56th annual conference of the Church commenced in Salt Lake City, continuing until the 8th.

—Sandford Bingham, of Riverdale, Weber Co., was discharged from the Penitentiary.

Sun. 7.—In the general conference of the Church, held in Salt Lake City, a First Presidency was sustained, consisting of Wilford Woodruff, President; George Q. Cannon, First Counselor, and Joseph F. Smith, Second Counselor. Franklin D. Richards was sustained as Church Historian and General Church Recorder.

This was the fourth time in the history of the Church that the First Presidency was organized.

Mon. 8.—Apostle Francis M. Lyman, Eli B. Hawkins, Robert Crawshaw, Henry Ballard and Stephen Nye were discharged from the Penitentiary.

Tues. 9.—Daniel B. Hill, of Wellsville, was discharged from the Penitentiary.

—Elder John B. Reid and a missionary companion were seized by a mob and expelled from their field of labor in Georgia.

Wed. 10.—Pres. Oliver C. Hoskins was discharged from the Penitentiary.

Thurs. 11.—James H. Brown was discharged from the Penitentiary.

Sat. 13.—In the First District Court, at Ogden, Jacob I. Naef, of Providence, was sentenced by Judge Henderson to three months' imprisonment for u. c.

—Wm. F. Reynolds was discharged from the Penitentiary.

Sun. 14.—The Saints who had settled on the Casas Grandes river, opposite Casas Grandes, Chihuahua, Mexico, were organized as a branch of the Church, called San Francisco; Frederic W. Jones, president.

Mon. 15.—Bishop Robert Davidson, of Logan, was discharged from the Penitentiary.

—Elder Arza Adams died at American Fork, Utah Co.

Tues. 16.—Madame Albani, the world-renowned lyric artist, sang in the Salt Lake Theater for the first time.

Sat. 20.—In the First District Court, at Provo, the following named brethren were sentenced by Judge Judd, as follows: Wm. Grant, of American Fork, to 20 months' imprisonment, for alleged adultery; John C. Harper to five months and $200 fine, for u.c.; Sylvester Bradford to 100 days and $25 fine, for u. c.; James Smuin to 85 days and $50 fine, for u. c.; Thomas R. Jackson, of Salt Lake City, to 12 months' imprisonment, for alleged adultery; James H. Tidwell to 60 days, for u. c.; Joseph C. Stickney to six months, for alleged adultery; and Joseph S. Murdock, of Heber, to 35 days, for u. c. George H. Brimhall and John Adams, who promised to obey the law, went free.

Mon. 22.—Thomas Wilson, of Ogden, was arrested for u. c.

—Franklin S. Richards delivered a very able argument before the U. S. Supreme Court, in the Hans Nielsen *habeas corpus* case.

Tues. 23.—Bishop Henry Tingey and Willard Watterson were discharged from the Penitentiary.

Wed. 24.—Eli H. Day and Oluf C. Larsen were discharged from the Penitentiary.

Thurs. 25.—Elder Joseph S. Allen, a member of Zion's Camp, died in Huntington, Emery Co.

Fri. 26.—In the First District Court, at Ogden, Samuel Oldham, of Paradise, was sentenced by Judge Henderson to six months' imprisonment and $100 fine, for u. c.

—James Howard, George B. Bailey and Isaac W. Fox were discharged from the Penitentiary.

Sat. 27.—A company of 26 Saints, including two returning Elders, bound for Utah, sailed from Amsterdam, Holland.

—Thomas P. Cloward was discharged from the Penitentiary.

Mon. 29.—Elder David Garner, a member of the Mormon Battalion, died at North Ogden, Weber Co.

—Andrew Anderson, was arrested at Huntsville, Weber Co., for u. c.

Tues. 30.—Hyrum B. Barton was discharged from the Penitentiary.

May.—Elders John F. Chidester and George E. Burgess, were assaulted and banished from their field of labor by a mob in South Carolina, where they labored as missionaries.

Wed. 1.—In the Third District Court, Salt Lake City, Brigham H. Roberts was sentenced by Judge Sandford to four months' imprisonment and $200 fine, for u. c.

—Henry Rampton, of East Bountiful, was discharged from the Penitentiary.

Fri. 3.—Martin Garn and Peter C. Christensen were discharged from the Penitentiary.

Sat. 4.—Peter Svendsen was discharged from the Penitentiary.

—A small company of Saints from the Netherlands, in charge of Martinus Krumperman, and bound for Utah, sailed from Liverpool, England. They arrived at New York May 15th.

Sun. 5.—Elder Sylvester Collett died in the City of Mexico, where he had labored as a missionary.

Mon. 6.—Arthur L. Thomas was appointed governor of Utah, as successor to Caleb W. West.

—Samuel Brannan, formerly a prominent Elder in the Church and at one time a wealthy real estate owner in California, died in Sonora, Mexico.

Tues. 7.—Elijah Sells was appointed secretary and Ellsworth Daggett surveyor-general of Utah.

Fri. 10.—Thos. Gunderson was discharged from the Penitentiary.

Sat. 11.—After a lengthy trial in the Third District Court, Salt Lake City, Howard O. Spencer, accused of killing Sergeant Ralph Pike Aug. 11, 1859, was acquitted.

—In the First District Court, at Ogden, Bendt Petersen was sentenced by Judge Henderson to four months' imprisonment and $100 fine, and Thomas Bullock, of Salt Creek, near Plain City, to a similar term with fine, both for u.c.

—Bedson Eardley, of Salt Lake City, and his plural wife, were arrested on a charge of adultery.

— Dr. O. C. Ormsby, of Logan, was arrested for u.c.

—Niels Aagaard, of Levan, was discharged from the Penitentiary.

Mon. 13.—Bishop Peder C. Jensen and James Keller, of Mantua, was discharged from the Penitentiary.

—The U. S. Supreme Court reversed the decision of the First District Court of Utah, in the Hans Nielsen *habeas corpus* case, and decided that a man cannot be convicted of two different offences (adultery and u.c.) which are covered by the same transaction, etc.

Tues. 14.—Alvin W. Saunders, of Nebraska, was appointed a member of the Utah Commission, to succeed Arthur L. Thomas.

—Hans Nielsen, whose case had been carried to the U. S. Supreme Court, on a writ of *habeas corpus*, was released from the Penitentiary.

Wed. 15.—P. F. Goss, was discharged from the Penitentiary.

—In the Manchester police court, England, Wm. H. Nichols and Adolphus D. Bolitho, confederates of William Jarman, the anti-Mormon lecturer, were fined 20 shillings and costs, each, for disturbing a "Mormon" meeting the previous Sunday.

Thurs. 16.—In the First District Court, at Ogden, James L. Sørensen was sentenced by Judge Henderson to three months' imprisonment, for u. c.

—In the Second District Court, at Beaver, Christopher J. Arthur, of Cedar City, and Frank W. Young, of Fremont, Piute Co., were sentenced by Judge Anderson to six months' imprisonment and $300 fine each, for u.c.

—Arthur L. Thomas took the oath of office and succeeded Caleb W. West as governor of Utah.

—Randolph H. Stewart, Charles R. Oakey and Ole P. Berg were discharged from the Penitentiary.

Fri. 17.—Joseph D. Reynolds and August Svendsen were discharged from the Penitentiary.

Sat. 18.—Thomas Chamberlain was discharged from the Penitentiary.

—The steamship *Wisconsin* sailed from Liverpool, England, with 142 Saints on board, including eight returning missionaries, in charge of Mayhew H. Dalley. The company arrived in New York on the 29th and in Salt Lake City June 4th.

Mon. 20.—John Welch and F. G. Ralph were discharged from the Penitentiary.

Tues. 21.—In the Second District Court,

at Beaver, Martin B. Cutler was sentenced by Judge Anderson to six months' imprisonment and $300 fine, for u. c., and John F. Maxwell to six months, for alleged adultery.

Wed. 22. — Enos Stookey, of Clover, Tooele Co., died suddenly in Salt Lake City.

Thurs. 23.—In the First District Court, at Ogden, Severin N. Lee, of Brigham City, was sentenced by Judge Henderson to three months' imprisonment and $100 fine, for u. c.

—Jens P. Hansen, of Ephraim, was discharged from the Penitentiary.

Fri 24.—Judge Zane was reappointed chief justice for Utah, by Pres. Harrison.

—In the Third District Court, Salt Lake City, Joseph Dean was sentenced by Judge Sanford to 110 days' imprisonment and $200 fine, for u. c.

—Joseph S. Murdock, Elijah A. Box and John Ash, sen., were discharged from the Penitentiary.

Sat. 25.—In the First District Court, at Ogden, Knud Emmertsen, of Huntsville, was sentenced by Judge Henderson to six months' imprisonment, and Jens N. Hansen, of Newton, to two months, both for u. c.

—Joseph Carlisle was discharged from the Penitentiary.

Sun. 26.—Wm. C. Rounds was discharged from the Penitentiary.

Mon. 27.—In the First District Court, at Ogden, Richard Jessup, of Millville, Cache Co., was sentenced by Judge Henderson to two months' imprisonment; and Rasmus N. Jeppeson was sentenced to pay a fine of $50; both for u. c.

Tues. 28.—The Board of Trade was organized in Salt Lake City.

—Jens Mortensen, of Brigham City, was discharged from the Penitentiary.

—William M. Palmer was arrested at Nephi, on a charge of u. c.

June. Sat. 1.—In the First District Court, at Ogden, Thomas Godfrey, of Clarkston, was sentenced by Judge Henderson to four months' imprisonment and $100 fine; Thomas Griffin, of Clarkston, to six months' and $100 fine, and Wm. T. Reed, of Woodruff, to four months' and $100 fine; all for u. c.

Mon. 3.—Chief Justice Charles S. Zane qualified and went on the bench, succeeding Judge Sandford.

—Andrew Nielsen and Andrew Rasmussen were discharged from the Penitentiary.

—The body of Alma P. Richards, of Morgan County, Utah (murdered about the 2nd of August, 1888), was found near Russell Station, on the A. G. S. Ry., Mississippi. It was exhumed, placed in a metallic coffin and shipped to Utah, where it arrived in charge of Elder John Morgan, June 8th.

Wed. 5.—Stephen Mott, of American Fork, and Martin Bushman were discharged from the Penitentiary.

Thurs. 6.—Joseph A. A. Bunot was arrested in Ogden, for u. c.

—Elder Simeon Atwood died from the effects of an accident, at Benjamin, Utah Co.

Fri. 7.—William C. Prows, of Kanosh, was liberated from the Penitentiary.

Sat. 8.—James Ritchie was discharged from the Penitentiary.

—The steamship *Wyoming* sailed from Liverpool, England, with 359 Scandinavian, Swiss and German Saints, including 18 returning missionaries, in charge of Elder Lars S. Andersen. The company arrived in New York on the 19th, and in Salt Lake City on the 26th.

Sun. 9.—Whitney branch, north of Franklin, Idaho, was organized as a Ward; James Chadwick, Bishop.

—Bishop Joseph S. Black was arrested at Deseret, Millard Co., for u. c.

—The body of Elder Alma P. Richards, killed in Mississippi, was re-interred in Morgan County, Utah. Nearly the whole county turned out in honor of the deceased.

Mon. 10.—Hoyt Sherman, jun., was appointed Receiver of the Salt Lake Land Office.

—Fred. A. Newberger, of Logan, was discharged from the Penitentiary.

Tues. 11.—A grand concert was given in the Tabernacle Salt Lake City, to aid the Johnstown, Pa., flood sufferers.

Wed. 12.—George Manwaring, of Salt Lake City, and Søren C. Thyggersen were discharged from the Penitentiary.

Fri. 14.—Thomas Didriksen, of Spanish Fork, was discharged from the Penitentiary.

Sat. 15. — Preston Lewis, David A. Sanders, William Ball, William Gurney and Anthony Heiner were discharged from the Penitentiary.

—Three young men (William Laing, Harry Heusner and John W. Sullivan) were drowned by the capsizing of a boat during a heavy wind storm on the Great Salt Lake, near Syracuse. Their bodies were subsequently found.

Mon. 17.—In the First District Court, at Ogden, Bishop Isaac E. D. Zundell, of Washakie, Box Elder Co., was sentenced by Judge Henderson to four months' imprisonment and $100 fine; Wm. McNeil of Logan, to three months and $100 fine, and Frank Whitehead, of Richmond, to three months; all for u. c.

—Benjamin Perkins, Andrew Anderson, John T. Covington, Cornelius McReavy, James H. Langford, Carl Olsen, Søren Jacobsen and Charles Frampton were discharged from the Penitentiary.

Tues. 18.—Andrew Andersen, of Huntsville, was arrested for u. c.

Fri. 21.—Jacob Hafen, Joseph S. Barney, Lorenzo D. Watson, Wm. R. Butler, Francis Webster, Sylvester F. Jones, Simon F. Topham and Niels Nielsen were discharged from the Penitentiary.

Sat. 22.—The steamship *Wisconsin* sailed from Liverpool, England, with 172 souls, including 12 Hollanders and nine returning Elders. The company arrived in New York harbor July 3rd, landed on the 5th, and arrived in Salt Lake City on the 12th.

—Peter C. Geertsen was discharged from the Penitentiary.

Mon. 24.—The Supreme Court of Utah ordered the Church farm leased to John R. Winder for $401 per month.

—Niels P. Rasmussen was discharged from the Penitentiary.

Tues. 25.—In the First District Court, at Ogden, Andrew W. Stratford, of Brigham City, was sentenced by Judge Henderson to six months' imprisonment, for u. c.

Wed. 26.—The Old Folks of Salt Lake County were given a free excursion to Ogden, where the citizens treated them with great kindness and hospitality.

—John Oberg, Henry W. Sandersen and Frands C. Christiansen were discharged from the Penitentiary.

—Mrs. Jerusha Gibbs Fox, wife of Jesse W. Fox, sen., died in Salt Lake City.

Thurs. 27.—John Groves, Lars P. Christensen, Mons Rosenlund and Gotlieb Ence were discharged from the Penitentiary.

—Bishop James Watson, of the 19th Ward, Salt Lake City, died.

Sat. 29.—Patriarch Wm. Box died at Brigham City, Box Elder Co.

July. *Mon. 1.*—The Saints who had settled on Stump Creek, Star Valley, Wyoming, were organized as the Auburn Ward; Wm. Corbridge, Bishop; and others who had settled on the east side of Salt river, north of Afton, were organized as the Grover Ward; James Jensen, Bishop.

—Elder Charles H. Hales died in Spanish Fork, Utah Co.

—Bishop George Facer and J. I. Naef were discharged from the Penitentiary.

Tues. 2.—The Saints comprising the Cottonwood branch of the Afton Ward, Star Valley, Wyo., were organized by Apostle Heber J. Grant as Cottonwood Ward, with Wm. Parsons as Bishop; and the Fairview branch of the Afton Ward was organized as Fairview Ward; John C. Dewey, Bishop.

—Gen. George R. Maxwell died in Salt Lake City.

—John D. T. McAllister, of St. George, was arrested at Milford, Beaver Co., for u. c.

Sun. 7.—Elder George Manwaring died in Salt Lake City.

Mon. 8.—The School election was held in Salt Lake City; the Liberals carried eight districts, namely, the 4th, 7th, 8th, 9th, 12th, 13th, 14th and 20th; the last named by gross fraud.

—Poul Poulsen, of Richmond, Cache Co., was discharged from the Penitentiary, having served a nine months' term for polygamy.

Tues. 9.—In the First District Court, at Ogden, James Hywater, of Brigham City, was sentenced by Judge Henderson to six months' imprisonment and $150 fine, for u. c.

Wed. 10.—Bishop Lars S. Andersen, of Ephraim, Sanpete Co., was arrested on charges of u. c. and polygamy.

—A large number of editors and representatives of the press from Nebraska visited Salt Lake City.

Thurs. 11.—Sylvester Bradford was discharged from the Penitentiary.

Fri. 12.—Pres. Harrison appointed Elias H. Parsons marshal and Charles S. Varian district attorney for Utah.

Sat. 13.—In the contest for the office of sheriff of Bingham County, Idaho, Judge Berry decided against the "Mormons," throwing out a sufficient number of votes cast by alleged seceders from the Church to effect his purpose.

Sun. 14.—Mrs. Rachel Terry and daughter were burned to death in the Nineteenth Ward, Salt Lake City.

Thurs. 18.—Elias H. Parsons succeeded Frank H. Dyer as U. S. marshal for Utah.

—James H. Tidwell was discharged from the Penitentiary.

—Father James Burgon, of Union, Salt Lake Co., died, being 96 years old.

Sat. 20.—Peter Barton and Charles Hampshire were discharged from the Penitentiary.

Fri. 26.—Baldwin H. Watts, of Kanosh, was discharged from the Penitentiary.

—Elder Wilson Lund died at Paragoonah, Iron Co., and Elder Stephen Robert Wells died at St. George, Utah.

Sat. 27.—Capt. Joseph Amos succeeded Arthur Pratt as warden of the Penitentiary, the latter having filled the office since Jan. 30, 1888.

—Richard Jessop and Matthew F. Bell were discharged from the Penitentiary.

Wed. 31.—The Union Depot at Ogden was opened with a banquet.

August. *Fri. 2.*—James L. Sørensen was discharged from the Penitentiary.

Sun. 4.—Peter Okelberry, of Goshen, was arrested for u. c.

Mon. 5.—At the election in Utah for selectmen and Territorial officers, the "Mormon" vote was 14,161 against 6,166 cast by Gentiles; the Liberals were 41 votes ahead in Salt Lake City. To serve in the Council branch of the Utah legislature the People's Party elected 10 and the Liberals 2 members; of members in the House the People's Party elected 18 and the Liberals 6.

Tues. 6.—Sander Sandersen was arrested in Salt Lake City for u. c.

Thurs. 8.—The first experiment of running a street car by electricity in Salt Lake City was successfully made.

Fri. 9.—Severin N. Lee, of Brigham City, was discharged from the Penitentiary.

Mon. 12.—The Lawrence Ward, Emery Co., Utah, was organized; Calvin W. Moore, Bishop.

—Samuel P. Hoyt, a Pioneer of Weber Valley, died near Kamas, Summit Co.

—James Smuin was discharged from the Penitentiary.

Tues. 13.—Herman F. F. Thorup was arrested in Salt Lake City.

Wed. 14.—Dr. Henry I. Doremus died in Salt Lake City.

—William Butler, of Marriott, Weber Co., was arrested for u. c.

Thurs. 15.—The Church purchased a ranch in Skull Valley, Tooele Co., for the benefit of the Hawaiian Saints who had emigrated to Utah.

Fri. 16.—Elder Wm. Spry was arrested at Chattanooga, Tenn., being taken for Franklin Haymore, against whom there was a warrant of arrest. He was released on bonds the next day.

Sat. 17.—Samuel R. Thurman was arrested at Provo for u. c.

—The steamship *Wyoming* sailed from Liverpool, England, with 191 Saints (mostly Scandinavians), in charge of Jens C. A. Weibye. The company arrived in New York on the 27th, and in Salt Lake City Sept. 3rd.

Tues. 20.—James Hack, of Bountiful, Davis Co., was arrested for u. c.

Wed. 21.—Receiver Dyer leased 29,756 Church sheep at an average of 43 cents per head.

Thurs. 22.—The Saints who had settled in the Teton Basin, Idaho, were organized as the Aline Ward, of the Bannock Stake; Mathoni W. Pratt, Bishop.

Sat. 24.—Jens N. Hansen was discharged from the Penitentiary.

Sun. 25.—Judge Thomas J. Black died at Ogden.

Mon. 26.—Peter Anderson and John C. Harper were discharged from the Penitentiary.

—Patriarch Wm. Morrison died in Clear Creek Canyon, Sevier Co.

Wed. 28—The Hawaiian Saints from Salt Lake City, in charge of Pres. Harvey H. Cluff, arrived at the Skull Valley ranch, Tooele Co., and founded the Iosepa colony.

Fri. 30.—The 18th Ward, Salt Lake City, Seminary, was dedicated.

Sat. 31.—The steamship *Wisconsin* sailed from Liverpool, England, with 172 Saints, including nine returning missionaries, and 10 visitors, in charge of Wm. P. Payne. The company arrived in New York Sept. 11th, and continued the journey by rail the following day. The train on which they traveled over the Norfolk, and Western Ry., was wrecked early in the morning of Sept. 15th, near Lynchburg. Va.; several of the emigrants were hurt, but none killed. The company arrived in Salt Lake City Sept. 20th.

September. *Sun. 1.*—The Saints residing north of Kaysville, Davis Co., Utah, were separated from Kaysville Ward, and organized as the Layton Ward; Daniel B. Harris, Bishop.

Mon. 2.—Albert Singleton, of Provo, was arrested for u. c.; and John Cox, of Woodruff, was arrested at Lake Town, Rich Co., for u. c.

—Frank Whitehead was discharged from the Penitentiary.

Tues. 3.—Judge Judd, of the Supreme Court of Utah, resigned his office.

—Jacob Gates was arrested at Provo, for u. c.

—Elder Chandler Holbrook, a member of Zion's Camp, died at Fillmore.

Thurs. 5.—The Utah Sugar Company was incorporated, with a capital stock of $15,000; Elias Morris, president; Francis Armstrong, vice president; James Jack, treasurer, and Arthur Stayner, secretary and manager.

Mon. 9.—Bishop Samuel Bennion died at North Jordan, Salt Lake Co.

Tues. 10.—Brigham H. Roberts and Wm. T. Reed (of Woodruff) were discharged from the Penitentiary.

Thurs. 12.—John G. Jørgensen and Christian Nielsen were discharged from the Penitentiary.

—Elder Geo. J. Woodbury died at St. George, Utah.

—In the Third District Court, in Idaho, Samuel D. Davis was sentenced to pay a fine of $500 for having voted at a late election, being a "Mormon," as all "Mormons" in Idaho had been disfranchised. The case was appealed to the Supreme Court of the United States.

Fri. 13.—Thos. S. Higham was arrested in Salt Lake City for u. c.

Wed. 18.—Frederick Jensen, of Logan, was arrested for u. c.

—The Salt Lake City Railroad Company commenced running electric cars from Main Street to the 21st Ward.

Fri. 20.—In the First District Court, at Provo, John Powell, of Fillmore, was sentenced by Judge Judd to 75 days' imprisonment, and Benjamin Barney, of Monroe, to 85 days; both for u. c.

—In the Second District Court, at Beaver, Andrew P. Schow, of Escalante, was sentenced by Judge Anderson to six months' imprisonment and $300 fine, for u. c. An appeal was taken and the defendant released on $1,500 bonds.

—Joseph C. Stickney was discharged from the Penitentiary.

Sat. 21.—In the First District Court, at Provo, Thomas Yates, of Scipio, and James M. Paxton, of Kanosh, were each sentenced by Judge Judd to ten months' imprisonment, for alleged adultery.

—Joseph Dean, Thos. H. Bullock and Bendt Petersen were discharged from the Penitentiary.

—The steamship *Wyoming* sailed from Liverpool, England, with 113 Scandinavian, Swiss and German Saints, including nine returning Elders, in charge of Rasmus Larsen. The company arrived in New York Oct. 1st, and in Salt Lake City Oct. 10th.

—Elder John A. Richards, formerly a resident of Utah, died in the Indian Territory.

Sun. 22.—Salim Inzil and Pharez Randure were baptized below the Egyptian colony, Yaffa, Palestine, by Elder C. U. Locander. They were confirmed the same day, the first named by Elder J. M. Sjødahl and the latter by Elder Locander. These were the first Arabs who joined the Church in Palestine. A few Germans had previously been baptized.

Mon. 23.—In the First District Court, at Provo, John L. Butler, of Elsinore, was sentenced by Judge Judd to eight months' imprisonment, and Christian Andersen, of Fillmore, to 17 months, both for alleged adultery; and E. P. Marquardsen, of Elsinore, was sentenced to 120 days, for u. c.

Tues. 24.—In the First District Court, at Provo, the following named brethren were sentenced by Judge Judd, as follows: Charles Jensen, of Koosharem, to five months' imprisonment and $200 fine, for alleged adultery; Jens L. Bruun, of Richfield, to seven months, for alleged adultery; Hans C. Nielsen, of Salina, to five months and $200 fine, for u. c.; John Quarnberg, of Scipio, to six months', for alleged adultery; Niels Anderson, of Ephraim, to 75 days, for u. c.; Peter Ahlstrøm, of Manti, to 75 days, for u. c.; Thomas Johnson, of Glenwood, to six months, for alleged adultery; Jens C. Jørgensen, of Redmund, to 55 days, Elias A. Beckstrand, of Meadow Creek, to 85 days, and Peter L. Quist, of Monroe, to four months and $100 fine, all three for u. c.

—Bishop A. A. Kimball died at Kanosh, Millard Co.

Wed. 25.—The Bear Lake and River Water Works and Irrigation Co. (other-

13

wise known as the Bothwell Canal Company) was incorporated at Ogden.

Thurs. 26.—Hyrum Jensen was shot and killed in Blacksmith Fork Canyon, Cache Co., being mistaken for a deer.

Fri. 27.—In the First District Court, at Provo, Carl F. Carlson, of Manti, was sentenced by Judge Judd to one year's imprisonment, for alleged adultery.

—The Utah Commission made their annual report of Utah affairs to Secretary John W. Noble.

Sat. 28.—In the First District Court, at Provo, Stephen H. Allred, of Salina, was sentenced by Judge Judd to 87 days' imprisonment, for u. c.

—Bishop Isaac E. D. Zundell, of Washakie, Box Elder Co., was discharged from the Penitentiary.

—John A. McClernand, of the Utah Commission, submitted a minority report to the Secretary of the Interior, not agreeing with the other members of the commission in their recommendation of harsh measures toward the people of Utah.

Mon. 30.—In the Third District Court, Salt Lake City, Thomas S. Higham, of Salt Lake City, was sentenced by Judge Zane to six months' imprisonment and $300 fine.

—In the First District Court at Provo, Jens L. Jensen, of Central, Sevier Co., was sentenced by Judge Judd to 62 days' imprisonment, for u. c.; Haas Jensen, of Goshen, to two years, and Hans Sørensen, of Aurora, to six months, both for alleged adultery; and Terry Thurston, 70 years old, to a fine of $25, for u. c.

October.—People's Party political clubs were organized in the various Wards in Salt Lake City.

—The walls of the Council House, on the corner of East and South Temple Streets, Salt Lake City, which had been standing in ruins since the fire of June 21, 1883, were taken down.

Tues. 1.—In the First District Court, at Provo, John W. Jackson, of Glenwood, was sentenced by Judge Judd to 10 months' imprisonment, for u. c.

Wed. 2.—In the Third District Court, Salt Lake City, Walter E. Wilcox was sentenced by Judge Zane to six months' imprisonment, for u. c.

—William McNeil was discharged from the Penitentiary.

Fri. 4.—Perry Fitzgerald, ore of the Pioneers of 1847, died at Draper, Salt Lake Co.

—In the Third District Court, Salt Lake City, Bedson Eardley was sentenced by Judge Zane to 18 months' imprisonment; and in the First District Court, at Provo, Otis L. Terry, of Fairview, was sentenced by Judge Judd to nine months, both for alleged adultery.

—The semi-annual general conference of the Church was commenced in Salt Lake City, continuing until the 6th. On the last day the three vacancies existing in the Council of the Twelve Apostles were filled by the calling of Marriner W. Merrill, Anthon H. Lund and Abraham H. Cannon to the Apostleship. John Jaques was sustained as Assistant Church Historian and General Church Recorder.

Sat. 5.—Lorenzo H. Durrant, a returning missionary, and Miss Adeline Allen

and Miss Patience Bennett, who had been detained at Lynchburg, Va., because of injuries received in the train wreck, arrived in Salt Lake City.

—The steamship *Wisconsin* sailed from Liverpool, England, with 142 Saints, namely, 104 English, 13 Hollanders, 12 Bohemians (supposed to be the first Saints from Bohemia), nine returning Elders and four visitors, in charge of Edward Bennett. The company arrived in New York on the 17th, and in Salt Lake City on the 25th.

Wed. 9.—A Scandinavian People's Party political club was organized in Salt Lake City; Andrew Jenson, president.

—Abraham Chadwick, of North Ogden, was arrested for u. c.

Thurs. 10.—In the First District Court, at Provo, a number of brethren were sentenced by Judge Judd, as follows, for breaking the Edmunds law: Joseph S. Black, of Deseret, to 75 days' imprisonment; Henry Mower to 45 days; Jesse B. Martin, of Scipio, to 50 days; Joseph L. Jolly, of Moroni, to 100 days and $50 fine; Levi S. Dunham, of Moroni, to 16 months; James Andersen, of Spanish Fork, to 75 days and $50 fine; William McKellar, of Leamington, to one year; L. H. Newman, of Monroe, to 60 days; John F. Beck, of Spanish Fork, to five months; Hans Jespersen, of Goshen, to five years; George Curtis, of Payson, to 60 days; Newman Van Leuven, of Aurora, to 120 days; Thomas Cooper to $250 fine, and Wm. M. Palmer to $75 fine.

—Thos. Godfrey, of Clarkston, was discharged from the Penitentiary.

—Wm. D. Newsom was arrested in Salt Lake City, for u. c.

Fri. 11.—In the First District Court, at Provo, Lars J. Larsen was sentenced by Judge Judd to two years' imprisonment, for alleged adultery; and George W. Bean was fined $50, for u.c.

—Robert Allen was arrested in Salt Lake City, for u.c.

—Pres. Harrison appointed John W. Blackburn associate justice of the Supreme Court of Utah.

Mon. 14.—In the First District Court, at Provo, Thomas Broadbent, of Elsinore, was sentenced by Judge Judd to 3½ months' imprisonment and $100 fine, and Jacob Gates, of Provo, to pay a fine of $50, both for u.c.

Wed. 16.—George W. Bartch was appointed probate judge of Salt Lake County, *vice* Judge Marshall, resigned. Mr. Bartch took the oath of office on the 22nd.

—William H. Maughan and Charles S. Hall were discharged from the Penitentiary.

Thurs. 17.—Judge John W. Blackburn succeeded Hon John W. Judd on the bench of the First District Court, at Provo.

Fri. 18.—The Students' Society of the Latter-day Saints' College was organized in Salt Lake City.

Mon. 21.—David W. Leaker was arrested in Salt Lake City, for u. c.

Tues. 22.—The City Council of Salt Lake City ordered the police to be uniformed in 30 days.

—In the First District Court, at Provo, Kelsey Bird, of Benjamin, Utah Co., was sentenced by Judge Blackburn to six months' imprisonment and $300 fine, for u. c.

—Martin B. Cutler and John F. Manwell were discharged from the Penitentiary.

—John J. R. Hicks, of South Cottonwood, was arrested for u.c.

Wed. 23.—Charles Bailey was arrested at Paradise and Wm. S. Gibby at Mill Creek, for u.c.

Thurs. 24.—David James was arrested in Salt Lake City, for u.c.

—Christopher J. Arthur was discharged from the Penitentiary.

Fri. 25.—At Blackfoot, Idaho, Thomas E. Ricks was convicted of u.c.

Sat. 26.—In the First District Court, at Provo, Thomas C. Stephensen, of Holden, was sentenced by Judge Blackburn to six months' imprisonment, for u.c.

—Bishop Samuel Oldham, of Paradise, was discharged from the Penitentiary.

—The steamship *Wyoming* sailed from Liverpool, England, with 161 Saints, namely 116 from Scandinavia, 6 from Holland, 24 from Great Britain, 12 returning Elders and three returning visitors, in charge of A. L. Skanchy. The company arrived in New York in due course of time and in Salt Lake City Nov. 13th.

Mon. 28.—Jens P. Holm was arrested in Salt Lake City, and Edward A. Bagley at Greenwich, Piute Co., for u.c.

Wed. 30.—In the Third District Court, Salt Lake City, William C. Dunbar was refused citizenship because he believed in polygamy. Elder Dunbar had lost his citizen's papers, which he obtained many years before.

Thurs. 31.—The Reform School, at Ogden, was opened.

—In the First District Court, at Provo, Richard M. Humphreys, of Salina, was sentenced by Judge Blackburn to 90 days' imprisonment and $300 fine, for u.c.

November.—The Endowment House on the Temple Block, Salt Lake City, was taken down. This historic building was erected in 1855.

Sat. 2.—A Liberal torchlight parade took place in Salt Lake City; 2000 men were in line.

—Truman O. Angell was arrested in Salt Lake City, for u. c.

—George C. Wood, of Bountiful, Davis Co., having been pardoned by Pres. Harrison, was released from the Penitentiary.

Mon. 4.—In the Third District Court, Salt Lake City, Robert Allen, who promised to obey the law, was fined $100, for u. c.

—George W. Hancock was arrested in Payson on a charge of murder, committed 32 years ago.

Wed. 6.—In the Third District Court, Salt Lake City, John T. R. Hicks, of South Cottonwood, was sentenced by Judge Anderson to six months' imprisonment and $300 fine; and in the First District Court, Oluf A. Andelin, of Dover, Sanpete Co., was sentenced by Judge Blackburn to four months' imprisonment and $300 fine; both for u. c.

—Samuel G. Spencer, of Pleasant Green, wanted on a charge of u. c., gave himself up and was admitted to bonds.

Fri. 8.—Albert Jones, of Provo, and Michael Vaughan, of Lehi, were discharged from the Penitentiary.

—In the First District Court, at Ogden, Judge Henderson rendered a decision which gave the Latter-day Saint meeting house at Woodruff, Rich Co., to the district school trustees.

Mon. 11.—In the Third District Court, Salt Lake City, Judge Anderson refused to admit a number of applicants to citizenship because they were "Mormons."

—Spring Glen Ward, near Price, Emery Co., was organized; Heber J. Stowell, Bishop. The Saints who resided at Castle Gate were organized into a branch of the Church; Wm. T. Lamph, presiding Elder.

Thurs. 14.—In the Third District Court, Salt Lake City, the extraordinary proceedings, in which John Moore and other "Mormons" were refused citizenship on the pretence that they had subscribed to a certain secret and disloyal oath in the Endowment House, was commenced before Judge Thos. J. Anderson. Proceedings were continued day by day until the 25th.

Sat. 16.—The steamship *Nevada* sailed from Liverpool, England, with 11 Saints, including four returning Elders and one visitor, in charge of Richard Morse.

Sun. 17.—Patriarch Gardner Snow died in Manti.

Wed. 20.—Charles W. Penrose, who had testified as a witness in the naturalization case before Judge Anderson in the Third District Court, was committed to the Penitentiary for refusing to answer an impertinent question with reference to his family affairs.

Mon. 25.—In the First District Court, at Ogden, Goudy Hogan, of Richmond, Cache Co., was sentenced by Judge Henderson to 30 days' imprisonment, for u. c.

—Andrew Stratford and Knud Emmertsen were discharged from the Penitentiary. On the same day Charles W. Penrose was released from the Penitentiary. The testimony and arguments in the naturalization cases before Judge Anderson having been completed and the case submitted, there was no excuse for his further detention.

Tues. 26.—In the First District Court, at Ogden, Fred. Jensen, of Logan, was sentenced by Judge Henderson to six months' imprisonment and $100 fine, for u. c.

Thurs. 28.—Elder John Lyon died in Salt Lake City.

—James Bywater was discharged from the Penitentiary.

Fri. 29.—The second grand parade of the Liberals occurred in Salt Lake City; it was the greatest affair of the kind ever witnessed in Utah.

—Jesse B. Martin, of Scipio, was discharged from the Penitentiary.

Sat. 30.—Judge Anderson, in the Third District Court, rendered a decision to the effect, that "Mormon" aliens could not be admitted to citizenship.

—Joseph Clark, of Provo, was discharged from the Penitentiary.

December. — In the Third District Court, Charles L. White, of Salt Lake City, was sentenced by Judge Anderson to six months' imprisonment, for u. c.

—Thos. Griffin was discharged from the Penitentiary.

Mon. 2.—In the First District Court, at Ogden, Sidney B. Kent, of Lewiston, Cache Co., was sentenced by Judge Henderson to two months' imprisonment, for u. c.

Tues. 3.—John Jacobs was discharged from the Penitentiary.

Thurs. 5. — The second grand Liberal rally in the season's municipal campaign was held in the Opera House, Salt Lake City.

Fri. 6.—Elder David Williams died at Price. Emery Co.

Sat. 7.—In the First District Court, at Ogden, Charles Frank, of Logan, was sentenced by Judge Henderson to one year's imprisonment, for adultery, and Bishop Anthon L. Skanchy, of Logan, to four months and $100 fine, for u. c.

—Peter Ahlstrøm, Niels Andersen and Frank. W. Young were discharged from the Penitentiary.

Sun. 8.—George Curtis was discharged from the Penitentiary.

Mon. 9.—The sale of city lots by auction was commenced in Salt Lake City.

—On this and the following day the case of Samuel D. Davis, who had been sentenced by an Idaho court for voting at an election, being a "Mormon," was argued in the U. S. Supreme Court.

—Elder Benjamin Franklin Taylor died at Levan, Juab Co.

Tues. 10.—In the Second District Court, at Beaver, Christian L. Christensen, of Teasdale, was sentenced to six months' imprisonment and $300 fine, for u. c.

—The Idaho test oath case was argued before the U. S. Supreme Court.

Wed. 11.—In the First District Court, at Ogden, Hyrum Petersen was sentenced to six months' imprisonment and $100 fine, for alleged fornication.

Thurs. 12.—Joseph E. Taylor was arrested in Salt Lake City, for u. c.

—In the First District Court, at Ogden, John Christophersen, of Richmond, was sentenced by Judge Henderson to three months' imprisonment for breaking the Edmunds law.

Fri. 13.—John Groves, of Sugar House Ward, was arrested for u. c.

—Benjamin Barney was discharged from the Penitentiary.

Sat. 14.—In the Second District Court, at Beaver, William Robinson, of Beaver, was sentenced to one year's imprisonment, for alleged adultery, and Thomas J. Jones, of Cedar City, to six months and $300 fine, for u. c. Hans Thurgesen, of Koosharem, was sentenced to $50 fine, and Joseph P. Barton, of Paragoonah, to $300 fine, both for u. c. Not being able to pay, they were sent to the Penitentiary. Edward A. Bagley, who promised to obey the law, was fined $100, for u.c.

—John Durrant, of American Fork, was discharged from the Penitentiary.

Mon. 16.—Mayor Francis Armstrong and other municipal officials were arrested, in Salt Lake City, on a trumped-up charge of misappropriation of public funds and conspiracy. It was done for political effect.

Tues. 17.—Arthur L. Thomas was con-

firmed as governor, and Elijah Sells as secretary of Utah, by the U. S. Senate.

Wed. 18.—Judge Zane denied the People's Party mandamus against the Salt Lake City registrars, some of whom were charged with crooked work in their official capacity, calculated to harm the People's Party and favor the Liberals at the approaching election.

—Elder Henry G. Bywater died in Salt Lake City.

—In the First District Court, at Provo, William Gee, of Dover, Sanpete Co., was sentenced by Judge Blackburn to six months' imprisonment and costs.

—Jens Jørgensen, of Redmond, Sevier Co., was discharged from the Penitentiary.

Thurs. 19.—The Utah Commission sustained the registrars in their discrimination against "Mormon voters" and adjourned.

Fri. 20.—In the Second District Court, at Beaver, Joseph W. McAllister was sentenced to six months' imprisonment and $300 fine, for u.c.

Mon. 23 —This day was observed as a day of fasting and prayer by the Latter-day Saints generally, agreeable to a circular issued by the First Presidency a few days before.

—Bishop Joseph S. Black and Stephen H. Allred were discharged from the Penitentiary.

Tues. 24.—In the First District Court, at Ogden, Jens P. Jensen, of Logan, was sentenced by Judge Henderson to 18 months' imprisonment, for alleged adultery, and Anton A. Janson, of Brigham City, to three months' imprisonment, for u.c.

Wed. 25.—Goudy Hogan, of Richmond, was discharged from the Penitentiary.

Thurs. 26.—In the First District Court, at Ogden, Andrew Madsen, of Brigham City, was sentenced by Judge Henderson to eight months' imprisonment, for alleged adultery.

—The Liberals raised a 110 foot flag pole and had a grand rally in Salt Lake City.

Fri. 27.—James Leatham was arrested in Salt Lake City, for u.c.

Sat. 28.—William Hutchings, of Lehi, was discharged from the Penitentiary.

Sun. 29.—Elder Francis Cope died in Salt Lake City.

Mon. 30.—James P. Park, a member of the Mormon Battalion, died at Fairfield, Utah Co.

—Jens L. Jensen, of Central, Sevier Co., was discharged from the Penitentiary.

Tues. 31.—Joseph L. Jolly, of Moroni, was discharged from the Penitentiary.

1890.

Salt Lake City passed from the hands of the People's Party to those of the Liberals, or anti-Mormon element. Nearly all the civil rights left to the Saints were threatened by proposed anti-Mormon legislation. President Woodruff issued his manifesto, suspending plural marriage.

January. *Wed. 1.*—The Liberals of Salt Lake City gave a grand daylight parade.

Thurs. 2.—David James was arrested in Salt Lake City for u.c.

—John Powell, of Fillmore, was discharged from the Penitentiary.

Sun. 5.—Elder Andrew K. Andersen, of Ephraim, Utah, died in Aalborg, Denmark, where he labored as a missionary.

Mon. 6.—Joseph Derbidge, of the 19th Ward, Salt Lake City, was arrested for u. c.

—The U. S. Supreme Court decided that the offices of Territorial Treasurer and Auditor of Public Accounts, held respectively by James Jack and Nephi W. Clayton, should be turned over to Bolivar Roberts and Arthur Pratt, the men appointed by the governor of Utah.

Tues. 7.—L. H. Newman, of Monroe, was discharged from the Penitentiary.

Wed. 8.—James Bywater, of Brigham City, was discharged from the Penitentiary.

—George L. Woods, ex-Governor of Utah, died at Portland, Oregon.

Thurs. 9.—Andrew J. Kershaw, of Ogden, was discharged from the Penitentiary.

—Charles S. Zane's re-appointment as chief justice of Utah was confirmed by the U. S. Senate.

Fri. 10.—The People's Party held their first grand parade in Salt Lake City, notwithstanding the heavy snow storm. The procession numbered several thousands.

—In the First District Court, at Ogden, Albert M. Baker was sentenced by Judge Henderson to one month's imprisonment, for u. c.

Sun. 12.—Isabella Hay Hunter, one of the first members of the Church in Scotland, died in the Twenty-first Ward, Salt Lake City.

Mon. 13.—The Utah legislature convened in Salt Lake City, and organized by electing Franklin S. Richards president of the Council, and James Sharp speaker of the House.

—Hans Thurgesen, of Koosharem, Piute Co., emerged from the Penitentiary.

—John W. Stewart, of Vermont, introduced a bill in the House of Representatives to disfranchise all " Mormons."

—Idaho's admission as a State and the test oath were argued in the U. S. Senate Committee on Territories. The argument was continued the following day, when "Mormons" were heard.

Tues. 14.—The Liberals of Salt Lake City held their municipal convention in the Opera House and nominated George M. Scott for mayor. The other men on the ticket were mostly questionable characters and were nominated as a reward for their peculiar work against the "Mormons" during the campaign.

Thurs. 16.—A great Liberal ratification meeting was held at the Walker Opera House, Salt Lake City.

—Elias A. Beckstrand, of Meadow Creek, Millard Co., was discharged from the Penitentiary.

Fri. 17.—Fredonia, a new settlement, in Arizona, near Kanab, Kane Co., Utah, was organized as the Fredonia branch; Thos. P. Jensen, presiding Elder.

Sat. 18.—Robert H. Ford fell from a win-

dow on the Temple, Salt Lake City, thirty feet to the ground, receiving fatal injuries, from the effects of which he died on the 23rd.

Mon. 20.—Judge Charles S. Zane took the oath of office as chief justice of the Supreme Court of Utah.

Tues. 21.—The Supreme Court of Utah decided against the election of aldermen for Salt Lake City.

Wed. 22.—James Anderson was discharged from the Penitentiary.

Thurs. 23.—Mons Anderson, of Lehi, was discharged from the Penitentiary.

Sat. 25.—The People's Party of Salt Lake City had their second parade in a heavy rainstorm.

—William R. Webb, of American Fork, was discharged from the Penitentiary, where he had served a term for alleged adultery.

Sun. 26.—The Saints who were employed in the mines at Mammoth, Tintic, Juab Co., were organized as a branch of the Church, with Lewis W. Stout as president.

—Orson J. Spencer and George A. Peart were arrested at Randolph, Rich Co., for u. c.

Mon. 27.—The People's Party municipal convention convened in the Theatre, Salt Lake City, and the following day agreed upon a ticket, headed by Spencer Clawson as candidate for mayor.

—William McFarland, sen., a Church veteran, 95 years old, died at West Weber, Weber Co.

—Elder Samuel M. Lee died at Panaca, Nevada.

Tues. 28.—John Frantzen was discharged from the Penitentiary, where he had served a thirteen months' sentence, for alleged adultery.

Wed. 29.—An enthusiastic People's Party ratification meeting was held in the Theatre, Salt Lake City.

—Thomas Breadbent emerged from the Penitentiary.

Thurs. 30.—Charles S. Varian was confirmed as U. S. attorney for Utah.

—In the First District Court, at Ogden, William Archibald, of Clarkston, Cache Co., was sentenced by Judge Henderson to 2½ months' imprisonment and $50 fine, for u. c.

February. *Sun. 2.*—Sidney B. Kent was discharged from the Penitentiary.

Mon. 3.—The new baptismal font, located in the basement of the southwest portion of the Tabernacle, Salt Lake City, was dedicated.

—A grand go-as-you-please parade of the Salt Lake City Liberal club took place.

—Henry W. Naisbitt was arrested in Salt Lake City, for u. c.

—The Supreme Court of the United States rendered an opinion affirming the constitutionality of the Idaho test oath, in the case of Samuel D. Davis.

Tues. 4.—Elder Edgar D. Simmons, of Salt Lake City, who labored as a missionary in the Turkish mission, died at Aintab, Syria, Asia Minor.

—The appointment of Elsworth Daggett, as surveyor general of Utah, was confirmed.

—Reuben Gurr was discharged from the Penitentiary.

Wed. 5.—Peter L. Quist was discharged from the Penitentiary.

Fri. 7.—An outdoor People's Party meeting was held in front of the City Hall, Salt Lake City. It was the largest political meeting ever held in Utah.

—The last Liberal parade of the campaign took place in Salt Lake City.

—Joseph P. Barton, of Paragoonah, was discharged from the Penitentiary.

Sat. 8.—The third and last parade of the People's Party in Salt Lake City, took place.

Sun. 9.—Elder Alexander S. Izatt died at Logan.

Mon. 10.—The municipal election in Salt Lake City, for which so much planning had been done, resulted in victory to the Liberals, who through the grossest frauds managed to obtain possession of the city government.

—Albert M. Baker was discharged from the Penitentiary.

Tues. 11.—Salt Lake City Railroad Company was granted a franchise by the city Council.

Wed. 12.—Richard M. Humphreys, of Salina, was discharged from the Penitentiary.

—Elder Russel K. Homer died at Clarkston, Cache Co.

—In the First District Court, at Ogden, Orson J. Spencer, of Randolph, Rich Co., was sentenced by Judge Henderson to three months' imprisonment and $100 fine, for u. c.

Thurs. 13.—John F. Beck, of Spanish Fork, was discharged from the Penitentiary.

Fri. 14.—John H. Tippetts, one of the Pioneers of 1847, died at Farmington, Davis Co.

Sat. 15.—Ex-Judge Orlando W. Powers was banquetted by the Liberals in Salt Lake City, and presented with $10,000 as a reward for manipulating the Liberal municipal campaign.

Mon. 17. — Newman Van Leuven, of Aurora, was discharged from the Penitentiary.

—Bishop Geo. L. Farrell, of Smithfield, Cache Co., was arrested, for u. c.

Tues. 18.—The Liberals took possession of the municipality of Salt Lake City.

Wed. 19.—J. H. Van Natta was arrested in Salt Lake City, for u. c.

—There was a grand Liberal jollification, with parade and fireworks, in Salt Lake City.

Thurs. 20.—John Dunn, an aged man of Three Mile Creek, Box Elder Co., was arrested in Salt Lake City, for u. c.

Fri. 21.—Judge Zane rendered a decision that prisoners under the Edmunds law could not be held over their term of sentence for costs alone.

—Thomas R. Jackson was discharged from the Penitentiary.

Sat. 22.—Jens Jørgensen, of Mt. Pleasant, was discharged from the Penitentiary.

Mon. 24.—John Quarnberg, Thos. Johnson and Charles W. Mann were discharged from the Penitentiary.

Tues. 25.—Bishop Joseph Pollard, of the Fifteenth Ward, Salt Lake City, died.

—In the First District Court, at Provo, Teancum Pratt, of Spring Glen, was sentenced by Judge Judd to six months' imprisonment and $100 fine; Jens C. A. Weibye, of Manti, to six months; both for u. c.; Henry Teeples, of Burrville, was sentenced to 18 months, for alleged adultery.

Thurs. 27.—The appointment of John W. Blackburn as associate justice of Utah was confirmed. March 8th, following, he took the oath of office at Provo, and succeeded John W. Judd on the bench.

Fri. 28.—Elder Heber K. Perkins died in the Seventeenth Ward, Salt Lake City.

—Peter C. Andersen, of Huntsville, Weber Co., was discharged from the Penitentiary, having served an 18 months' sentence for alleged adultery.

March.—The Old Constitution Building, Salt Lake City, was torn down to make room for a new five story brick building, erected soon afterwards.

—The remains of the late Willard Richards and others were removed from the family burial ground, east of the Deseret Museum, in Salt Lake City, and placed in the cemetery.

Sat. 1.—Bishop Charles Jensen, Hans C. Nielsen and Hans Sørensen, having served their terms of imprisonment in the Penitentiary, for u.c., were set at liberty.

Sun. 2.—Walter E. Wilcox was discharged from the Penitentiary.

Mon. 3.—Elder John C. Hall died at Rockville, Washington Co.

Tues. 4.—The Utah Supreme Court made an order terminating the lease of the Gardo House and hereafter renting it to the highest bidder. The following day the lease of the Tithing Office grounds was terminated the same way.

—J. Bartch, probate judge of Salt Lake Co., rendered a decision. In the case of the Orson Pratt estate, to the effect that polygamous children could inherit.

Wed. 5.—The Salt Lake Clearing House Association was organized.

Fri. 7.—In the First District Court, at Provo, Andrew O. Anderson, of Glenwood, and Henry M. Payne, of Aurora, Sevier Co., were each sentenced by Judge Blackburn to six months' imprisonment and $300 fine; and William A. Stewart, of Central, to four months and $50 fine; all for u.c.

Sat. 8.—Bishop Anton A. Janson, of Brigham City, emerged from the Penitentiary.

Mon. 10.—The Gardo House was rented to Bishop John R. Winder for $450 per month, he being the highest bidder. Thus the building remained in the hands of the Church for the time being.

—John W. Young's railroads in Utah were incorporated under the name of the Utah Central Railway.

Tues. 11.—Father William Park, of Mill Creek, Salt Lake Co., died.

—William Henry Halliday, of Pleasant Grove, Utah Co., who was laboring as a missionary in the Southern States, died near Mocksville, Davie Co., North Carolina. □ His remains were sent home.

Wed. 12.—The Tithing Office grounds and Historian's Office were rented to

Bishop John R. Winder, for $500 per month.

Thurs. 13.—Territorial Auditor Arthur Pratt and Treasurer Bolivar Roberts took possession of their respective offices.

—Elder John A. Quist, of Big Cottonwood, Salt Lake Co., died at Wingåker, Sweden, where he labored as a missionary.

Fri. 14.—Pres. Angus M. Cannon was arrested in Salt Lake City, for u. c., and placed under $1,500 bonds.

—Edwin Crowther, of Coalville, Summit Co., who had previously been pardoned by Pres. Cleveland, was on trial before Com. McKay, in Salt Lake City, for u. c. He disowned his plural wife.

Sat. 15.—After sitting 56 hours over the specified time, the Utah legislature adjourned; Gov. Thomas had vetoed a number of important bills.

—Bishop Isaac M. Stewart died at his residence in Draper, Salt Lake Co.

—In the First District Court, at Ogden, Michael Stanley, of Lewiston, Cache Co., was sentenced by Judge Henderson to 18 months' imprisonment, for alleged adultery, and incarcerated in the Penitentiary.

—Moses Harris, a Church veteran, died at Glendale, Kane Co.

Sun. 16.—Hans P. Iverson, of Washington, Utah, was imprisoned in the Penitentiary, having been sentenced, in the Second District Court, at Beaver, the day before, to six months and $300 fine.

Mon. 17.—John C. Weston, in heroic self defence, shot and killed a robber in Salt Lake City, and mortally wounded another.

—Amos Pease Stone, an old Pioneer, died at Ogden.

—Oluf A. Andelin, of Dover, Sanpete Co., emerged from the Penitentiary.

—Nicholas Muhlestein was arrested by drunken U. S. marshals at Provo, for u. c.

Tues. 18.—Bishop Anthon L. Skancky, of Logan, was discharged from the Penitentiary.

Wed. 19.—Bryce Ward, Graham Co., Ariz., was organized; Nelson A. Mattice, Bishop.

Thurs. 20.—Niels Hansen, of Brigham City, was discharged from the Penitentiary.

Sat. 22.—William H. Folsom was arrested in Salt Lake City, for u. c.

—After a lengthy trial in the First District Court, at Provo, Joseph Hancock, indicted for the murder of Henry Jones, of Payson, in 1858, was adjudged guilty of murder in the second degree. Motion was made for a new trial.

Sun. 23.—Charles Crismon, one of the early settlers of Utah, died of old age in Mesa, Maricopa Co., Ariz.

—John Bergen emerged from the Penitentiary, where he had been confined since Dec. 23, 1887, for polygamy.

Mon. 24.—William McKay, the notorious anti-Mormon, was summarily removed from his position as assistant U. S. district attorney, by Pres. Harrison.

Tues. 25.—Father David James died at Paradise, Cache Co.

—James L. Thompson, a veteran in the Church, died in Henrieville, Garfield Co.

—Peter Wimmer, of Parowan, was im-

prisoned in the Penitentiary, having been sentenced in the Second District Court to one month's imprisonment for "adultery."

—In the First District Court, at Provo, H. S. Palmer, of Rabbit Valley, was sentenced to one month's imprisonment for u. c.; John A. Burr, of Teasdale, Piute Co., to one month for alleged adultery; Mads Jørgensen, of Provo, and Peter Okelberry, of Goshen, six months each, for u. c.

Wed. 26.—In the Third District Court, Salt Lake City, Samuel Hamer, of the Sixteenth Ward, was sentenced by Judge Anderson to imprisonment for 90 days, for u. c.

—Thomas C. Stephensen was discharged from the Penitentiary.

Sun. 30.—Jens L. Bruun, of Richfield, was discharged from the Penitentiary.

Mon. 31.—Thomas S. Higham, of Salt Lake City, was discharged from the Penitentiary.

—William Negus, of Plain City, Weber Co., was accidentally drowned near that place.

April. *Tues. 1.*—The Liberal city council of Salt Lake City raised the salaries of all the city officials, besides creating a number of new and unnecessary offices.

Thurs. 3.—Father John Wardrobe died in Salt Lake City.

—In the First District Court, at Provo, Wm. C. Sampson, of Glenwood, was sentenced to three months' imprisonment for u. c.

—The bill providing for the admission of Idaho into the Union as a State was passed by the U. S. House of Representatives, with its anti-Mormon test oath clause.

—The noted election conspiracy cases of Idaho, in which 52 ex-Mormons were indicted for alleged illegal voting, were dismissed at Malad.

Fri. 4.—The 60th annual conference of the Church was commenced in Salt Lake City, continuing until the 6th. In the voting for the general authorities of the Church on the 5th, Geo. Reynolds was sustained as one of the First Seven Presidents of the Seventies, to fill the vacancy caused by the calling of Abraham H. Cannon to the Apostleship.

Sat. 5.—Hans Christensen, of Richfield, was discharged from the Penitentiary.

Mon. 7.—The first general conference of the Relief Societies was held in Salt Lake City.

Wed. 9.—In the First District Court, at Provo, Nicholas Muhlenstein, of Provo, was sentenced by Judge Blackburn to two months' imprisonment, for u. c.

Thurs. 10.—Thos. Allsop, of Sandy, was arrested, for alleged adultery, and placed under $2,500 bonds.

—Shelby M. Cullom, of Illinois, introduced a bill, in the U. S. Senate, for the total disfranchisement of all Mormons.

Fri. 11.—Isaac S. Struble, of Iowa, introduced a bill, in the U. S. House of Representatives, to disfranchise the "Mormons;" it was referred to the Committee on Territories.

—The Canadian Parliament, in session at Ottowa, amended the criminal law of the Dominion as to make polygamy punishable with five years' imprisonment, instead of two, as heretofore. This was undoubtedly done with a view to reach the "Mormons," who had settled in Alberta.

Sun. 13.—John L. Butler, of Elsinore, was discharged from the Penitentiary.

Mon. 14.—James Leatham, of Salt Lake City, was sentenced in the Third District Court, by Judge Zane, to six months' imprisonment, for u.c.

Tues. 15. — Patriarch Thomas Oakey died at Paris, Bear Lake Co., Idaho.

Thurs. 17.—Elias H. Parsons was confirmed U. S. marshal for Utah, succeeding Frank H. Dyer.

Sat. 19.—The steamship *Wisconsin* sailed from Liverpool, England, with the first company of this season's emigration of European Saints, numbering 52 souls, including nine returning Elders, in charge of Orson H. Worthington. They arrived in New York on the 24th, and reached Salt Lake City May 7th.

Sun. 20.—Milburn Ward, Sanpete Co., was organized; James Wm. Stewart, Bishop.

—Pleasant Grove, Utah Co., was divided into three Wards, by Apostle Abraham H. Cannon, Counselor John W. Young and the Utah Stake Presidency, with Joseph E. Thorne as Bishop of the First Ward, James Cobley of the Second and Knud Svendsen of the Third.

Mon. 21.—Kelsey Bird, of Benjamin, was discharged from the Penitentiary.

Tues. 22.—Nathaniel V. Jones, of Salt Lake City, was arrested for u.c.

—In the First District Court, at Provo, George W. Hancock was sentenced to ten years' imprisonment, for murder in the second degree. Pending an appeal to the Supreme Court of Utah, the defendant was admitted to bail.

Wed. 23.—Delegate John T. Caine delivered a speech, before the U. S. House Committee on Territories, in opposition to the Struble anti-Mormon bill.

Thurs. 24.—I. A. Benton was appointed postmaster in Salt Lake City, in place of C. R. Barratt.

Fri. 25.—Peter Wimmer, H. S. Palmer and John A. Burr were discharged from the Penitentiary.

Sat. 26.—Judge Jeremiah M. Wilson delivered a powerful argument against the Struble bill, before the U. S. House Committee on Territories.

Sun. 27.—The Saints who had located at McCammon and its vicinity, in Marsh Valley, Oneida Co., Idaho, were organized as McCammon branch.

—Orson J. Spencer, of Randolph, was discharged from the Penitentiary.

Tues. 29.—Geo. Hales, proprietor of the *Richfield Advocate*, was arrested on a charge of violating the Edmunds law.

May. Thurs. 1.—John Halgreen, of Richmond, Cache Co., was arrested for u. c.

Fri. 2.—David J. Evans, of Pleasant View, Weber Co., was arrested for u. c.

—Charles L. White emerged from the Penitentiary.

Sat. 3.—Bishop James C. Hamilton, of Mill Creek, Salt Lake Co., was arrested, for u. c.

—The steamship *Wyoming* sailed from Liverpool, England, with 156 Saints, mostly Scandinavians, in charge of Adolph

Anderson. The company arrived in New York on the 13th, and in Salt Lake City on the 21st.

Mon. 5.—Bishop David S. Cook died at South Weber, Davis Co.

—The Rapid Transit Street Railway Company was granted a franchise in Salt Lake City.

Tues. 6.—John T. R. Hicks, of South Cottonwood, was discharged from the Penitentiary.

Wed. 7.—Svante Johansen, of Santaquin, Utah Co., was found dead in the mountains, east of that town.

—Elder Robert G. Berrett died at North Ogden, Weber Co.

Mon. 12.—The Seventies residing at Woodruff, Randolph, Laketown, Meadowville and Garden City, in the Bear Lake Stake of Zion, were organized by Seymour B. Young as the 102nd quorum of Seventy; Charles South, senior president.

—Wellington Ward, near Price, Emery Co., was organized; Albert E. McMullin, Bishop.

—In the Third District Court, Salt Lake City, Henry W. Naisbitt was sentenced by Judge Zane to six months' imprisonment for u. c., and taken to the Penitentiary.

—Thomas McLelland died in Farmers Ward, Salt Lake Co.

—Sister Harriet A. Snow, wife of Apostle Lorenzo Snow, and president of the Relief Societies of Box Elder Stake, died at Brigham City.

Wed. 14.—Wm. Archibald, of Clarkston, Cache Co., and Hyrum Petersen were released from the Penitentiary.

—Geo. F. Edmunds introduced another bill in the U. S. Senate, providing for the entire disfranchisement of the "Mormons."

Thurs. 15.—In the Third District Court, Salt Lake City, J. H. Van Natta, of that city, was sentenced to pay a fine for u. c.

—Henry Sudweeks was imprisoned in the Penitentiary, having been sentenced, in the Second District Court, at Beaver, to three years' imprisonment for alleged incest.

Fri. 16.—In the Third District Court, Salt Lake City, William D. Newsom was sentenced by Judge Zane to six months' imprisonment and $300 fine, for u. c.

Sun. 18.—Henry Dinwoodey's furniture store, in Salt Lake City, was burned.

—William Gee, of Dover, Sanpete Co., was discharged from the Penitentiary.

—Andrew P. Schow, of Escalante, Garfield Co., was incarcerated in the Penitentiary, having been sentenced on the 14th by Judge Anderson in the Second District Court, at Beaver, to six months' imprisonment and $300 fine, for u. c.

Mon. 19.—After trial on a charge of u.c., in the Third District Court, Salt Lake City, Joseph E. Taylor was acquitted.

—The U. S. Supreme Court rendered a decision declaring those sections of the Edmunds-Tucker bill escheating Mormon Church property valid and constitutional.

—The Cullom bill providing for the disfranchisement of all "Mormons" was agreed to in the U. S. Senate Committee on Territories, where Delegate John T. Caine and Frank J. Cannon opposed the bill.

Tues. 20.—Otis L. Terry, Bishop Joseph

S. Horne and James Sellers were discharged from the Penitentiary.

— James V. Turvesen, of Smithfield, Cache Co., was arrested for u. c.

Wed. 21.—Milford railway depot, Beaver Co., was destroyed by fire.

Thurs. 22.—The corner stone of the Board of Trade building was laid in Salt Lake City.

Fri. 23.—In the Third District Court, Moses Wilkinson, of East Mill Creek, was sentenced by Judge Zane to six months' imprisonment and $150 fine, for u. c.

—Elder Edward Brain died in Salt Lake City.

—Elder James David Hirst died at Paradise, Cache Co.

—George Francis Train, returning from his 60 days' trip around the world, delivered an interesting speech to a number of ladies and gentlemen from Salt Lake City, in his special car at Pocatello, Idaho.

Sat. 24.—In the First District Court, at Ogden, Thomas L. Obray, of Paradise, Cache Co., was sentenced ay Judge Henderson to three months' imprisonment, for u. c., and Jens C. Christensen, of Hyde Park, who promised to obey the law, to 15 days, for alleged adultery.

—"Edward Isaacson," an apostate Jew, who came to Utah two years ago, joined the Church, married a "Mormon" girl and made great pretensions, was fined $50 in the justice's court, at Provo, Utah Co., for theft. Soon afterwards he left Utah.

—The steamship *Wisconsin* sailed from Liverpool, England, with 122 British and Dutch Saints, in charge of John H. Hayes. The company arrived in New York June 4th, and in Salt Lake City June 11th.

Mon. 26.—Fred. Jensen, of Logan, was discharged from the Penitentiary.

Wed. 28.—David H. Workman and B. Bird were accidentally drowned near Vernal, Uintah Co., while in the act of rendering aid to Hon. J. P. Wimmer, who was saved.

Thurs. 29.—Charles Crabtree, of Wellsville, was placed in the Penitentiary, having been sentenced, in the First District Court, at Ogden, to three months' imprisonment, for u, c.

Sat. 31.—Two boys were accidentally drowned in the Weber river, near Morgan, Morgan Co.

—In the First District Court, at Ogden, Albert G. Slater, of Huntsville, was sentenced by Judge Henderson to two years' imprisonment, for u. c.

June.—Elder Janne M. Sjödahl finished the revision of the German hymn book, at Bern, Switzerland.

—The first number of the *Brigham Bugler*, a weekly newspaper, was published at Brigham City, Box Elder Co.

Sun. 1.—Bishop Thomas Yates and James M. Paxton were discharged from the Penitentiary.

—Elder Hugh D. Lisonbee died at Marysvale, Piute Co., Utah.

Mon. 2. — Harvey Murdock was discharged from the Penitentiary, where he had served a five years' term for polygamy.

Wed. 4.—Isaac J. Wardle, of South Jordan, Salt Lake Co., was arrested for u. c.

—Elder Wm. Marsden died at Parowan, Iron Co.

—The first number of the *County Register*, a weekly newspaper, was published at Ephraim, Sanpete Co.

Thurs. 5.—Elder Robert Campbell, clerk of the Seventies, died in Salt Lake City.

Fri. 6.—Charles Johns, of Portage, Box Elder Co., was arrested, for u. c., taken to Ogden and placed under bonds.

—The U. S. grand jury at Blackfoot, Idaho, reported 153 indictments, mostly against "Mormons," for alleged illegal voting, on the part of such as had withdrawn from the Church and voted at an election held about a year previous.

Sat. 7.—Captain John Hart and Jens C. Christensen were discharged from the Penitentiary.

—The steamship *Wyoming* sailed from Liverpool, England, with 304 Scandinavian, Swiss and German Saints, in charge of Elder Erastus C. Willardsen. The company arrived at New York June 19th, and at Salt Lake City on the 26th.

Mon. 9.—Father Royal Barney died in Salt Lake City.

—Christian L. Christensen and William Sampson were discharged from the Penitentiary.

—Mormon Mixer met with a terrible accident at Midway, Wasatch Co., from the effects of which he died the following day.

Tues. 10.—Geo. F. Edmunds introduced another anti-Mormon bill in the U. S. Senate, providing for the disposition of the escheated Church property.

Wed. 11.—John W. Jackson, of Glenwood, Sevier Co., was discharged from the Penitentiary.

Thurs. 12.—Monroe Allred, of Spring City, Sanpete Co., was arrested in Emigration Canyon, near Salt Lake City, on a charge of adultery with his plural wife.

Fri. 13.—Thomas J. Jones, president of the Parowan Stake, was discharged from the Penitentiary. Thomas Ogden, of Richfield, Sevier Co., after serving a term of 19 months for living with his wives, and William H. Grifin, of Newton, Cache Co., after serving a long term for polygamy, were also discharged.

Sat. 14.—J. B. Rosborough was appointed a special commissioner to examine the administration of Receiver Dyer.

—At Blackfoot, Idaho, for breaking the Edmunds law, Jonah Evans was sentenced to six months' imprisonment in the Boise Penitentiary and $300 fine; William C. Martindale to six months and $200 fine, and William Higginson to four months and $200 fine. The following were sentenced to imprisonment at Sioux Falls, South Dakota: Stephen Jones, to two years; Hyrum Skinner, one year; L. D. Wilson, one year; Niels C. Christensen, one year. The cases of most of these brethren were appealed, but bail was refused.

Tues. 17.—M. H. Silver was drowned in Bear River, near Smithfield, Cache Co.

—William A. Stewart was discharged from the Penitentiary.

Wed. 18.—Jens Frandsen, of Huntsville, Weber Co., was arrested for u. c.

—William C. Sampson, of Glenwood, Sevier Co., was discharged from the Penitentiary.

Thurs. 19.—Joseph W. McAllister, of St.

George, was discharged from the Penitentiary.

Fri. 20.—The population of Salt Lake City, as enumerated under the direction of the city council, was announced to be 52,-732.

—William Hinscock was arrested at Clarkston, Cache Co., for u. c..

—Pres. Harrison nominated James A. Miner, of Michigan, to be associate justice of the Supreme Court of Utah, and successor to Judge Henderson.

Mon. 23. — Charles Frank, of Logan, Cache Co., who was serving a term in the Penitentiary, for infraction of the Edmunds law, was pardoned by Pres. Harrison and set at liberty.

—Samuel Hamer was discharged from the Penitentiary.

Wed. 25.—The Co-operative Store in Willard City, Box Elder Co., was burned.

—Aaron Hardy, sen., and Jens E. J. Knop, were arrested at Moroni, Sanpete Co., for u. c.

Fri. 27.—The bill providing for the admission of Wyoming into the Union as a State, was passed by the U. S. Senate, by a party vote.

Sat. 28.—The steamship *Wisconsin* sailed from Liverpool, England, with 113 Saints, including five returning missionaries, in charge of Abraham Maw. The company arrived in New York on the 10th, and in Salt Lake City July 16th. A woman died on the railway journey.

Mon. 30.—Jens M. Krogh was arrested in Salt Lake City, for u. c.

July. *Tues.* 1.—The carnival train from New Orleans arrived at Ogden, where a carnival was held during the following few days.

—Patriarch Thos. S. Smith died at Wilford, Bingham Co., Idaho.

Wed. 2.—The corner stones of the Oneida Stake Academy building were laid at Preston, Idaho.

Thurs. 3.—Pres. Harrison signed the bill admitting Idaho as a State into the Union.

—Elder David William Savage was murdered by Mexican herders near Adairville, Apache Co., Ariz.

Fri. 4.—Walkers "Grand Opera House," Salt Lake City, was destroyed by fire in the night between the 3rd and 4th. A number of other smaller fires in the city destroyed considerable property, the cause being carelessness in using combustable articles in celebrating the Fourth.

Sat. 5.—Joseph A. A. Bunot, of Henefer, Utah, was arrested for u. c.

Mon. 7.—Receiver Dyer made a report on Church property for Examiner Rosborough.

Thurs. 10.—Peter A. Bergquist, of Salt Lake City, was arrested for u. c.

—The Wyoming Admission bill was signed by Pres. Harrison.

Fri. 11.—Jas. E. Caine, son of Hon. John T. Caine, was assaulted by two foot pads, in Salt Lake City, and struck in the head by one of them, from the effects of which he died Aug. 13, 1890.

Sat. 12.—Gustaf Thomassen, Fred. A. Newberger, and William Neve, of Cache County, were arrested for u. c., together with their alleged plural wives.

About the same time Jens Christian-

sen, of Newton, Cache Co., David Lewis, Hans J. Nielsen and John Andrews, together with their alleged plural wives, were arrested on the same charge.

Sun. 13.—Pocatello branch of the Church, Bingham Co., Ihaho, was organized as Pocatello Ward; Carl J. Cannon, Bishop.

Mon. 14. — The election of a board of school trustees for Salt Lake City, under the new law, resulted in the election of eight "Liberals" and four People's Party men; but the latter were kept out of their offices for some time, while the court tried the case.

—Frank H. Dyer resigned his office as Receiver of the confiscated Church property.

Tues. 15.—M. M. Stone was appointed examiner of the administration of Receiver Dyer, in place of Rosborough.

Wed. 16.—The Utah Supreme Court appointed Henry W. Lawrence Receiver of the escheated Church property, in place of Frank H. Dyer, resigned.

—William H. Freeman was arrested in Salt Lake City, for u. c.

Thurs. 17.—Anders Madsen, of Mantua, was discharged from the Penitentiary.

Sat. 19.—John Morgan, of Mill Creek, Salt Lake Co., and John W. Snell, of Salt Lake City, were arrested for u. c.

Sun. 20.—"Dr. Edward Isaacson," who had quietly returned to American Fork, Utah Co., was attacked by a number of disguised residents, who intended to inflict summary punishment upon him, but he escaped and soon left the town for good.

Thurs. 24.—Utah's Pioneer day was generally and heartily celebrated throughout the Territory.

Fri. 25.—Jens C. A. Welbye, of Manti, Sanpete Co., was discharged from the Penitentiary.

Sun. 27.—Carl F. Carlson, of Manti, was discharged from the Penitentiary.

Mon. 28.—The Utah Supreme Court, in the matter of the estate of George Handley, deceased, rendered a decision to the effect that polygamous children could not inherit from the father.

Tues. 29.—Receiver Henry W. Lawrence was ordered by the Utah Supreme Court to sell the Church sheep in his possession.

—Michael Clark, of Kaysville, Davis Co., was arrested for u. c.

August.—Burglars did effectual work in Salt Lake City, and "hold-ups" were an almost everyday occurrence.

—*Valkyrien*, a Danish paper, published in Salt Lake City, suspended publication.

Fri. 1.—B. W. Brown, of Lehi, was discharged from the Penitentiary, on cummutation of sentence by Pres. Harrison.

Sat. 2.—The steamship *Wisconsin* sailed from Liverpool, England, with 86 Saints, in charge of Leonard J. Jordan. The company landed in New York on the 13th, and arrived in Salt Lake City a few days later.

Sun. 3.—At the quarterly conference held at Logan, Cache Co., Orson Smith was sustained as president of the Cache Stake of Zion, with Simpson M. Molen, of Hyrum, and Isaac Smith, of Logan, as counselors.

Mon. 4.—The election of county officers in Salt Lake County resulted in the election by the People's and Workingmen's Independent Party of recorder, sheriff and treasurer. The other officers elected were "Liberals."

Tues. 5.—George M. White, of Mill Creek, Salt Lake Co., was killed by falling from a hay stack.

Thurs. 7.—Andrew O. Anderson, of Glenwood, was discharged from the Penitentiary.

—John Hendrickson and Thomas Kirby were arrested in Cache County, for u. c.

Sat. 9.—Thomas L. Obray, of Paradise, Cache Co., was discharged from the Penitentiary.

—Joseph Moser, of Logan, and Fred. Theurer, of Providence, Cache Co., were arrested for u. c.

Sun. 10.—Elder Wandle Mace died at Kanab, Kane Co.

—William McKellar, of Leamington, Millard Co., was discharged from the Penitentiary.

Tues. 12.—Cleveland Ward, Emery Co., was organized by Apostles Anthon H. Lund and Abraham H. Cannon; Lars Peter Oveson, Bishop.

Thurs. 14.—Caleb Crabtree, of Wellsville, was discharged from the Penitentiary.

Fri. 15.—Frank Gooch, of Logan, was arrested on a charge of fornication.

Sat. 16.—The steamship *Wyoming* sailed from Liverpool, England, with a company of emigrating Saints, in charge of Jonas Ostlund. The company arrived in New York Aug. 26th, and in Salt Lake City Sept. 3rd.

Mon. 18.—Mrs. Catherine Singleton, 77 years old, of American Fork, Utah Co., was struck by a Utah Central Ry. train, while crossing the track, and instantly killed. A similar fate befell Mrs. Clara Hewitt, while crossing the U. P. Ry. track near Ogden.

—Hiram H. Webb was discharged from the Penitentiary.

Tues. 19.—William A. Empey, one of the Pioneers of 1847, died at St. George, Utah.

—James Pitkin, of Cache County, and John Sutton, sen., of Montpelier, Bear Lake Co., Idaho, were arrested for u. c.

Wed. 20.—Nathan Hanson, of North Point, Salt Lake Co., was arrested for u. c.

—William Grant, of American Fork, Utah Co., was discharged from the Penitentiary.

Thurs. 21.—Joseph H. Felt, of Salt Lake City, was arrested for u. c.

Mon. 25.—The Saints composing the new settlement of Monticello, San Juan Co., Utah, were organized into a Ward; Fred. I. Jones, Bishop.

—Peter Okelberry, Mads Jörgensen and Teancum Pratt were discharged from the Penitentiary.

—Elder Orrin N. Woodbury died at St. George, Utah.

Fri. 29.—In the Third District Court, Salt Lake City, Judge Zane decided in favor of John H. Rumel, the People's Party candidate for the Salt Lake County recordership, as against H. Page, the Liberal candidate; and a certificate of election was given Rumel.

Sun. 31.—At a special meeting held at Afton, Uinta Co., Wyo., the 103rd quorum of Seventy was organized by Seymour B. Young, with the following named brethren as presidents: Samuel Henderson, Charles G. Cazier, Wm. V. Bonderson, Ole Jensen, Levi Richardson, John J. Corbridge and Isaac Lee.

—Anson Call, an old and prominent Elder in the Church, died at Bountiful, Davis Co.

—John Killian was discharged from the Penitentiary.

September.—Numerous complaints and protests were entered against Assessor E. R. Clute, of Salt Lake City, because of his exorbitant assessments.

—Ex-Senator Isaac P. Christiancy, who years ago used his influence against the Saints, died at Lansing, Michigan, in perfect obscurity.

—Apostle Brigham Young succeeded Apostle George Teasdale in the presidency of the European mission.

Mon. 1.—The new county officers, elected for Salt Lake County, filed their bonds and entered upon their duties of office.

Tues. 2.—The Salt Lake City Council passed the building and medical ordinances.

Thurs. 4.—John Warwood was arrested at Bountiful, Davis Co., for u. c.

—The Agricultural College at Logan was dedicated.

—Twenty-five Missouri editors visited Salt Lake City.

About the same time, Henry Hughes and Frangott Stumph, of Mendon, Brigham Pond, of Lewiston, Elrick Trapper, of Providence, and Benjamin Hemms, of Hyde Park, were arrested for u. c.

Sat. 6.—Bishop H. M. Payne, of Aurora, Sevier Co., was discharged from the Penitentiary.

—The steamship *Wisconsin* sailed from Liverpool, England, with a company of British, Swiss and German Saints, including six returning missionaries. The emigrants arrived in Salt Lake City on the 24th.

Mon. 8.—In the Third District Court, Salt Lake City, Herman F. F. Thorup was sentenced by Judge Zane to imprisonment for six months, for u.c.

Fri. 12.—Pres. Wm. Budge was arrested at Paris, Bear Lake Co., Idaho, on a trumped-up charge of conspiracy.

—Benjamin W. Driggs, of Pleasant Grove, Utah Co., was arrested at Montpelier, Idaho, for alleged adultery.

Sat. 13.—In the Second District Court, at Beaver, Wm. B. Pace, of St. George, was sentenced by Judge Anderson to one year's imprisonment, for alleged adultery; G. M. Crawford, of Washington, to six months and $300 fine, both for alleged adultery; and Wilson D. Pace, of Harmony, to six months and $300, for u. c.

Sun. 14.—James Leatham was discharged from the Penitentiary.

Mon. 15.—Hans P. Iversen, of Washington, was discharged from the Penitentiary.

Wed. 17.—The motormen and conductors of the Salt Lake City Ry. struck for higher wages. This was the first genuine strike in Salt Lake City. It lasted several days.

—Judge Charles S. Zane rendered a decision to the effect that Richard W. Young, the People's Party nominee, and not Parley L. Williams, a Liberal, had been elected a member of the city board of education, at the election held July 14, 1890.

—Elder Thos. Adair died at Show Low, Apache Co., Ariz.

Thurs. 18.—The Thatcher Opera House, Logan, was opened, the Salt Lake Home Dramatic Club playing " Held by the Enemy.

Fri. 19.—In the First District Court, at Provo, Mahonri M. Bishop, of Deseret, Niels H. Børreson, of Spring City, and James M. Stewart,were each sentenced by Judge Blackburn to six months' imprisonment, for breaking the Edmunds law.

—Elder Thos. Harris died in Salt Lake City.

Sat. 20.—In the First District Court, at Provo, Charles A. Terry was sentenced by Judge Blackburn to two years' imprisonment for alleged adultery; Isaac Whicker to six months, for the same offence; and H. B. Bennett, to one year, for u. c.

—The steamship *Wyoming* sailed from Liverpool, England, with 197 Saints, including a number of returning missionaries, in charge of Jens Jensen. They arrived in New York harbor Oct. 1st, and in Salt Lake City, Oct. 9th.

Mon. 22.—Christian Ottesen was imprisoned in the Penitentiary, having been sentenced in the First District Court, at Provo, to one month's imprisonment, for u. c.

Wed. 24.—A manifesto was issued, signed by Pres. Wilford Woodruff, in which the Saints were advised "to refrain from contracting any marriage forbidden by the laws of the land."

—The tithing yard buildings at Provo, Utah Co., were destroyed by fire and about two hundred tons of hay burned.

Fri. 26. — Martha Bowker Young, widow of Pres. Brigham Young, died in Salt Lake City.

—Elder Daniel C. Thomas died at Plain City, Weber Co.

October.—The " Old Eagle " was temporarily removed from its perch over the gateway leading to Canyon Road, Salt Lake City.

—Charles Ellis, a non-Mormon, delivered a number of pointed and interesting lectures in the theatre, Salt Lake City, in defence of the " Mormons."

Fri. 3.—The annual report of Governor Thomas, of Utah, to the Secretary of the Interior, was published. It contained recommendations for harsh measures against the " Mormons."

Sat. 4.—The semi-annual conference of the Church commenced in Salt Lake City. It was continued for three days. On the 6th Pres. Woodruff's manifesto was accepted by unanimous vote of the conference.

—In the First District Court, at Provo, James H. Jenkins, of Goshen, was sentenced by Judge Blackburn to two years' imprisonment; John A. Powell to one year; Zachariah S. Taylor to six months and $50 fine, and Lauritz B. Miller, of Spanish Fork, to six months and $50 fine; all for breaking the Edmunds law.

Sun. 5.—A general Primary Conference was held in the Assembly Hall, Salt Lake City.

Mon. 6.—In the First District Court, at Provo, Charles W. Rawlinson was sentenced by Judge Blackburn to one month's imprisonment and $25 fine,for alleged adultery; Arthur H. Campbell to 18 months, for alleged adultery; Aaron Hardy, of Moroni, to six months and $300 fine, for u. c.; and Rasmus Justesen, of Spring City, to two years, for alleged adultery.

Tues. 7.—In the Third District Court, Judge Zane ruled that membership in the Mormon Church should no longer be a barrier to aliens being admitted to citizenship.

Wed. 8.—C. C. Goodwin, editor of the Salt Lake *Tribune*, was nominated for delegate to Congress, by the Liberal convention, held in Salt Lake City.

Thurs. 9.—The People's Party Territorial convention re-nominated John T. Caine for delegate to Congress.

—In the First District Court, Hyrum S. Crane was sentenced by Judge Blackburn to one year's imprisonment, for breaking the Edmunds law.

Fri. 10.—Elder Hans C. Hansen, one of the Pioneers of 1847, died in Salina, Sevier Co.

—Elder John R. Jones, of Johnson Springs, Iron Co., met with a serious accident, from the effects of which he died the following day.

Sat. 11.—The steamship *Wisconsin* sailed from Liverpool, England, with a company of Saints, including several returning Elders, in charge of S. P. Jensen. The company arrived in New York Oct. 23rd, and in Salt Lake City a few days later.

Sun. 12.—Henry W. Naisbitt was discharged from the Penitentiary.

Mon. 13.—In the Third District Court, Salt Lake City, James E. Clark, of Kaysville, Davis Co., was sentenced by Judge Zane to pay a fine of $100, for u.c. In consideration of the manifesto just issued, no imprisonment was imposed.

—Samuel F. Miller, a member of the U. S. Supreme Court, who had always been a friend to the "Mormons," died in Washington, D. C.

Tues. 14.—Elder Evan Williams, of the 16th Ward, Salt Lake City, died.

—Wm. Robinson, of Beaver, was discharged from the Penitentiary.

Thurs. 16.—Elder John P. Ball died in the Third Ward, Salt Lake City.

Fri. 17.—Col. Thomas L. Snead, a friend of the "Mormons," died in New York.

Sun. 19.—The new Latter-day Saint meeting house in the Twelfth Ward, Salt Lake City, was dedicated.

Mon. 20.—Dr. John Farnham Boynton, once an Apostle in the Church, died in Syracuse, N. Y.

—In the First District Court, at Provo, Warren B. Smith, of American Fork, was sentenced by Judge Blackburn to six months' imprisonment and $200 fine, for u. c.

Wed. 22.—James Stewart fell between railway cars and was cut in two near Morgan, Morgan Co.

—Christian Ottesen was discharged from the Penitentiary.

—Elisha Averett, a member of the Mormon Battalion, died at Glendale, Kane Co.

Fri. 24.—William Howard, John Brasher, Thomas Stalworthy and H. T. Stalworthy were arrested at Huntington, Emery Co., for u. c.

⌐*Mon. 27.*—John Larsen was arrested at Salt Lake City, for u. c.

Tues. 28.—Joseph H. Turner was discharged from the Penitentiary, having served a term of two years, for alleged adultery.

Wed. 29.—George Staples was killed by a Holstein Bull, at Elsinore, Sevier Co.

—Ira S. Hatch was killed, through mistake, by a sheriff in the Zuni Mountains, N. M.

November. *Sat. 1.* — Evan Stephens succeeded Ebenezer Beesley as leader of the Tabernacle choir, Salt Lake City.

— Elder George Barber died in Mexico.

Sun. 2.—Elder William Willes, a prominent missionary and Sunday School worker, died in Salt Lake City.

Mon. 3.—A contract was signed for the erection of the first beet sugar plant in Utah, to cost $400,000.

—Elder Andrew Frantzen died in the Sugar House Ward, Salt Lake Co.

—Milton Dalrymple was killed by a runaway at Preston, Bear Lake Co., Idaho.

Tues. 4.—The election for delegate to Congress resulted in 16,353 votes for John T. Caine, the People's candidate, and 6,906 for C. C. Goodwin, Liberal. There were 28 scattered votes. Caine's majority was 9,419.

Wed. 5.—U. S. District Attorney Varian filed two suits for the forfeiture of the Temple Block under the escheat law, in the Third District Court.

Thurs. 6.—John Sholdebrand died in Salt Lake City.

Sat. 8.—In the Third District Court, Salt Lake City, Bishop James C. Hamilton, of Mill Creek, was fined $100 for u. c.

—The Sevier branch of the Rio Grande Western Ry. was completed to Fairview, Sanpete Co.

Sun. 9.—Elder Rasmus Petersen, one of the first members of the Church in Denmark, died at Pleasant Grove, Utah Co.

Tues. 11.—Joseph W. McMurrin, connected with the Collins affair, Nov. 28th, 1885, gave himself up to the officers of the law, in Salt Lake City.

Thurs. 13.—Andrew P. Schow was discharged from the Penitentiary.

Fri. 14.—J. W. Abbott lost both his hands by the explosion of a blast, in Ogden Canyon, Weber Co.

Sat. 15.—William D. Newsom, of Salt Lake City, and Christian Andersen, of Fillmore, were discharged from the Penitentiary.

—Martin Weight was arrested at Fremont, Piute Co., for u. c.

Sun. 16.—Jay Gould secured control of the Union Pacific Railroad.

Mon. 17.—D. G Brian was arrested in Piute County, for u. c.

Wed. 19.—Father Samuel Turnbow died in Salt Lake City.

—The first number of the *Korrespond-*

enten, a Swedish weekly, was published in Salt Lake City, by Charles V. Anderson and Otto Rydmar.

Thurs. 20.—In the First District Court, at Ogden, Levi H. Wheeler, of North Ogden, was sentenced by Judge James A. Miner to twenty days' imprisonment, for u. c.

Fri. 21.—The Salt Lake Hot Springs Ry. Company was organized.

Sat. 22.—Tarlton Lewis, one of the Pioneers of 1847, died at Teasdale, Piute Co.

—Levi S. Dunham, of Moroni, was discharged from the Penitentiary.

Sun. 23.—The Sevier branch of the Rio Grande Western Ry. was completed to Mount Pleasant, Sanpete Co.

—Elder Ebenezer Russell Young died at Wanship, Summit Co.

Mon. 24.—Henry Mower was discharged from the Penitentiary.

—In the First District Court, at Provo, Luke Sherwood was sentenced by Judge Blackburn to two months' imprisonment, for alleged adultery.

Tues. 25.—Hebər W. West, son of the late Bishop Chauncey W. West, was shot and killed at Pocatello, Idaho.

Thurs. 27.—In the First District Court, at Provo, Nicholas H. Groesbeck was sentenced by Judge Blackburn to 18 months' imprisonment, for alleged adultery. This was his second term of imprisonment for the same offense.

Fri. 28.—John Cunnington, one of the early merchants in Salt Lake City, died at San Mateo, Cal.

Sat. 29.—Dr. Orlando D. Hovey died in the Nineteenth Ward, Salt Lake City.

—Jesse B. Martin, of Scipio, was discharged from the Penitentiary.

Sun. 30.—The west part of Harrisville Ward, Weber Co., was organized as Farr West Ward; Wm. A. Taylor, Bishop.

December. *Mon. 1.*—In the Third District Court, Salt Lake City, Judge Zane sentenced Paul E. B. Hammer to a fine of $300, for u.c. John W. Snell was acquitted.

—In the First District Court, at Ogden, Lars Nielsen, of Lewiston, Cache Co., was sentenced by Judge Miner to 20 days' imprisonment, for alleged adultery.

Wed. 3.—The Hotel Templeton was opened in Zion's Savings Bank Building, Salt Lake City.

—In the Second District Court, at Beaver, Judge Thomas J. Anderson re-affirmed his former ruling, that alien "Mormons" were not entitled to American citizenship, he having no faith in the manifesto.

—Father John Hamilton died at Hamilton Fort, Iron Co.

Thurs. 4.—Moses Wilkinson was discharged from the Penitentiary.

Fri. 5.—Charles W. Rawlinson was discharged from the Penitentiary.

Sun. 7.—Niels Anderson and Peter Ahlstrøm were discharged from the Penitentiary.

Mon. 8.—Elder Jas. Moyle, superintendent of construction of the Salt Lake Temple, died in Salt Lake City.

—Herman F. F. Thorup was discharged from the Penitentiary.

—Elder Edwin Whiting died, in Springville, Utah Co.

—The first legislature of the State of Idaho met.

Tues. 9.—At a session of the Salt Lake City council, Recorder Louis Hyams, who had appropriated public money to his own use, resigned his position This was the first case of embezzlement by a Salt Lake City officer. He had been an ardent anti-Mormon political worker.

Wed. 10.—Levi H. Wheeler was discharged from the Penitentiary.

—In the Second District Court, at Beaver, Geo. H. Crosby was sentenced by Judge Anderson to three months' imprisonment; and Peter E. Olsen, to nine months; both for alleged adultery.

Thurs. 11.—An artesian well, 595 feet deep, and giving 95 gallons of water per minute, was completed on the corner of Third West and Eighth South Street, Salt Lake City.

Fri. 12.—In the First District Court, at Ogden, James Butcane, of Logan, was sentenced by Judge Miner to 60 days' imprisonment, for alleged adultery.

—George W. Beckstead, of South Jordan, Salt Lake Co., died at San Bernardino, Cal.

Sat. 13.—In the First District Court, at Ogden, Fred. W. Ellis, of North Ogden, was sentenced by Judge Miner to 60 days' imprisonment; Lars P. Johnson, of Hooper, to 60 days; and Henry J. Newman, of Ogden, to five months and $300 fine; all for u. c.

—The Sevier branch of the Rio Grande Western Ry. was completed to Ephraim, Sanpete Co.

Tues. 16.—J. F. Jack was appointed city recorder of Salt Lake City, in place of Louis Hyams, resigned.

—A franchise was granted to the Salt Lake and Hot Springs Ry. Company.

Wed 17.—Bishop Millen Atwood, of the 13th Ward, Salt Lake City, one of the Utah Pioneers of 1847, died in Salt Lake City.

Thurs. 18.—The Idaho legislature elected Gov. Shoup and W. J. McConnell to the U. S. Senate for the unexpired terms, and ex-Delegate Dubois for the six years' term commending March 4, 1891.

Sun. 21.—Lars Nielsen was discharged from the Penitentiary.

Mon. 22.—The U. S. Supreme Court rendered a decision in William E. Bassett's case, reversing the decision of the Utah courts, and declaring it illegal for a lawful wife to testify against her husband.

Tues. 23.—Joseph S. Black and H. B. Bennett were discharged from the Penitentiary.

Fri. 26.—Three men in Salt Lake City were held up and robbed by footpads, and a store was also burglarized. Lawlessness of that kind happened almost daily under the Liberal administration.

—The corner stone of the Sugar Factory at Lehi, Utah Co., was laid.

Mon. 29.—Elder Alfred H. Caine died in Salt Lake City.

—An indignation meeting was held in the Methodist Church, Salt Lake City, to protest against the vice and wickedness existing in the city.

—In the First District Court, at Ogden, John Archibald, of Clarkston, was sentenced by Judge John A. Miner to three months' imprisonment, for u. c.

—The Sevier branch of the Rio Grande Western Ry. was opened to Manti.

Wed 31.—Joseph L. Jolly was discharged from the Penitentiary.

—The famous Castle Gardens, known to so many immigrating Saints from Europe, as their landing place, was turned over to the New York City authorities.

1891.

The People's Party in Utah was dissolved and most of its members united with the two great national parties—Democrats and Republicans. Under the Liberal rule Salt Lake City became a regular rendezvous for foot pads, burglars and thieves. Immorality, wickedness and lawlessness had full sway; taxation was made oppressive and unjust.

January.—The Deseret Museum was removed from its old quarters, opposite the south gate of the Temple Block, Salt Lake City, to Zion's Saving Bank building (Templeton building).

Mon. 5.—Emma Abbott, the celebrated American opera singer, died suddenly in Salt Lake City.

Tues. 6.—In the First District Court, at Ogden, John Halgren, of Richmond, was sentenced by Judge Miner to 45 days' imprisonment; Fred. Yeates, of Millville, to 45 days; Ira Allen, of Hyrum, to 10 days; Wm. Popleton, of Wellsville, to 45 days, and Archibald McFarland, of Ogden, to three months; all for u. c.

Wed. 14.—Geo. Hancock's case of alleged murder came up on appeal from the First District Court, before the Supreme Court of Utah, which finally granted him a new trial.

Fri. 16.—Ira Allen was discharged from the Penitentiary.

Sat. 17.—In the First District Court, at Ogden, Utah, Thos. Stirland, of Providence, was sentenced by Judge Miner to 2½ years' imprisonment and $75 fine, for breaking the Edmunds law.

Sun. 18.—The Saints who had settled on or near the Provo river, northeast of Provo, Utah Co., were organized as the Pleasant View Ward; Alexander Gillispie, Bishop.

Mon. 19.—The U. S. Supreme Court rendered a decision, that polygamous children born within one year after the passage of the Edmunds law were legitimate and entitled to inherit after their fathers, thus reversing the findings of the Supreme Court of Utah.

Tues. 20.—The First Ward meeting house at Ogden was destroyed by fire.

Sat. 24.—Lucy Decker Young, widow of Pres. Brigham Young, and one of the first three Pioneer women of Utah, died in Salt Lake City.

—Luke Sherwood was discharged from the Penitentiary.

Mon. 26.—Elder Wm. Greenwood died at American Fork, Utah Co.

Tues. 27.—Mayor Geo. M. Scott's report for 1890, submitted to the city council of Salt Lake City, exhibited an enormous squandering of public funds in the city since the Liberals came into power.

February. *Mon. 2.*—The Deseret Museum was reopened in the Zion's Savings Bank building; James E. Talmage, curator.

Wed. 4.—The Supreme Court of Utah granted George W. Hancock (accused and convicted of killing Henry Jones, at Salem, Utah Co., April 24, 1858,) a new trial.

Thurs. 5.—The old Deseret Museum building, in Salt Lake City, was removed to make room for a new street (Richards Street).

Mon. 9.—The municipal election at Ogden, Utah, resulted in victory to the Citizens' Party, composed of "Mormons" and the better class of Liberals.

Tues. 10.—James Butcane, of Logan, was discharged from the Penitentiary.

Wed. 11.—Pres. Harrison commuted to four months the sentence of two years' imprisonment imposed on James H. Jenkins, of Goshen, Utah Co., who was dying at the Penitentiary. He was released the following day.

—Wilson D. Pace, Fred. W. Ellis and Lars P. Johnson were discharged from the Penitentiary.

—Lewis C. Bidamon (husband of Emma Smith, widow of the Prophet Joseph) died at Nauvoo, Ill.

Thurs. 12.—The Saints who had settled in the Corralles Basin, Chihuahua, Mexico, were organized as the Pacheco Ward; Jesse N. Smith, jun., Bishop.

—Stephen S. Harding, ex-governor of Utah, died at Milan, Ind.

Fri. 13.—The former residence of Geo. Q. Cannon on South Temple Street, and other valuable property in Salt Lake City, were seized by the U. S. marshal, under the pretence that it was escheated Church property.

Sat. 14.—A new place of amusement, called Wonderland, was opened in Salt Lake City.

Tues. 17.—In the Third District Court, Salt Lake City, Benjamin F. Knowlton was sentenced by Judge Judd to pay a fine of $150; Charles J. Lusty, of Coalville, to $100 fine; Thos. Beard, of Coalville, to $75 fine, and Thos. Copley and John W. Simester, both of Coalville, to $100 fine each; all for u. c. They promised to obey the law. Thos. Beard was imprisoned, not being able to pay his fine.

—In the First District Court, at Provo, Thos. Woolley, of Pleasant Grove, Utah Co., was sentenced by Judge Blackburn to one month's imprisonment and $200 fine, for u. c.

—Niels H. Børresen, Mahonri M. Bishop and James M. Stewart were discharged from the Penitentiary.

—Geo. Dunford died in Salt Lake City.

Wed. 18.—In the First District Court, at Provo, Jonas Ostler, James Shanks, Wm. McDonald, Wm. Foreman, Robert S. Duke and Wm. N. Casper were sentenced by Judge Blackburn to pay a fine of $100 each, for u. c.

—Isaac Whicker was discharged from the Penitentiary.

Thurs. 19.—In the First District Court, at Ogden, August J. Hansen, of Logan, was sentenced by Judge Miner to six months' imprisonment, for alleged adultery.

Fri. 20.—John Halgren, Fred. Yeates and Wm. Popleton were discharged from the Penitentiary.

—Elder Isaac H. Losee died at Clifton, Garfield Co.

Mon 23.—Geo. H. Crosby was discharged from the Penitentiary.

Tues. 24.—Gec. W. Hill. Indian interpreter, and a prominent Elder, died in Salt Lake City.

Wed. 25.—Elder Samuel Mulliner, an aged Church veteran, died at Lehi, Utah Co.

Thurs. 26.—Reuben McBride, a member of Zion's Camp, died at Fillmore, Millard Co.

—John D. Parker, another member of Zion's Camp, died at Kanarra, Iron Co.

March. *Tues. 3.*—Samuel Gompers, president of the American Federation of Labor, visited Salt Lake City.

—In the First District Court, at Provo, John A. Mower, of Fairview, was sentenced by Judge Blackburn to three months' imprisonment, for alleged adultery.

Wed. 4.—The Old Folks, widows and orphans of Salt Lake County, were treated to a free entertainment in the Salt Lake Theatre.

Thurs. 5.—Zachariah S. Taylor was discharged from the Penitentiary.

Sun. 8.—Elder Geo. W. Bradley, ex-Bishop of Moroni, Sanpete Co., died there.

Mon. 9.—Henry M. Stanley, the great African explorer, lectured in the Salt Lake Theatre.

Wed. 11.—Jens P. Jensen was discharged from the Penitentiary.

Thurs. 12.—Geo. H. Crawford was discharged from the Penitentiary.

Sun. 15.—James Butler was discharged from the Penitentiary.

Mon. 16.—Elder Isaac Bullock died at Provo, Utah Co.

—Thomas Woolley was discharged from the Penitentiary.

Wed. 18.—In the First District Court, at Provo, Richard Jenkins, of Nephi, was sentenced by Judge Blackburn to three months' imprisonment, and Thomas Featherston, of American Fork, to one month's imprisonment; both for u.c.

Thurs. 19.—In the First District Court, at Provo, Samuel Linton, of Nephi, was sentenced by Judge Blackburn to three months' imprisonment, for u.c.

Sat. 21.—Deseret, Millard Co., Utah, was divided into three Wards. Oasis and Hinckley, the two new Wards thereby created, were organized with John Styler and Wm. H. Pratt as their respective Bishops.

Sun. 22.—Archibald McFarland was discharged from the Penitentiary.

Tues. 24.—Pres. Daniel H. Wells died in Salt Lake City.

Thurs. 26.—At a meeting of the Salt County Court it was decided to erect a joint city and county building on Washington Square, Salt Lake City.

Fri. 27.—John A. Powell was discharged from the Penitentiary.

Sat. 28.—In the First District Court, at Provo, John B. Wasden was sentenced by Judge Blackburn to one year, and Orlando F. Herron, of Pleasant Grove, to four months' imprisonment; both for u. c. Herron had previously served two terms for infractions of the Edmunds law.

Sun. 29.—John Archibald was discharged from the Penitentiary.

April. *Thurs. 2.*—Nicholas H. Groesbeck was discharged from the Penitentiary.

Sat. 4.—The 61st annual conference of the Church convened in Salt Lake City; continuing till the 6th.

—Lauritz B. Miller was discharged from the Penitentiary.

Sun. 5.—Aaron Hardy was discharged from the Penitentiary.

Fri. 10.—Benjamin W. Driggs, of Pleasant Grove, Utah Co., was taken to the Penitentiary, having been sentenced by Judge Blackburn, at Provo, to six months' imprisonment, for alleged adultery.

Mon. 13.—Wm. B. Pace was discharged from the Penitentiary.

Fri. 17. — Patriarch Thos. E. Jeremy died in Salt Lake City.

Sat. 18. — Thos. Featherston was discharged from the Penitentiary.

Sun. 19.—Chauncey M. Depew, Cornelius Vanderbilt and other railroad magnates arrived in Salt Lake City on a visit.

Mon. 20. — Warren B. Smith was discharged from the Penitentiary.

Tues. 21.—In the First District Court, at Provo, John M. Murdock was sentenced by Judge Blackburn to one month's imprisonment, for u. c.

Sun. 26.—Elder Wm. C. Rawson died at Farr-West, Weber Co.

Thurs. 30.—Hans Jensen was discharged from the Penitentiary.

May. *Sat. 2.* — In the First District Court, at Ogden, Niels Peter Christensen, of Randolph, Rich Co., was sentenced by Judge Miner to one year's imprisonment, for alleged adultery.

Tues. 5.—In the First District Court, at Ogden, Charles L. White was sentenced by Judge Miner to four months' imprisonment, for u. c. This was his third term of imprisonment for the same offence. He was taken to the Penitentiary the following day.

Sat. 9.—Benjamin Harrison, President of the United States, and escort, arrived in Salt Lake City, on a visit, and was received with great enthusiasm by the populace, all classes joining in the demonstration.

Sun. 10.—Henry Teeples was discharged from the Penitentiary.

Sun. 17. — Henry Harriman, one of the First Seven Presidents of the Seventies, died at Huntington, Emery Co.

—Susan Bayless Richards, relict of the late Willard Richards, died at Farmington, Davis Co.

Mon. 18.—In the First District Court, at Ogden, John Thomas, of Logan, was sentenced by Judge Miner to sixty days' imprisonment; and Niels C. Andersen, of Hyrum, to pay a fine of $50; both for u. c. Both were taken to the Penitentiary, as Andersen, who had been imprisoned once before for the same offence, was unable to pay his fine.

Tues. 19.—John A. Mower was discharged from the Penitentiary.

Wed. 20.—At a mass meeting held in the Salt Lake Theatre, it was decided to organize the Republican Party of Utah.

Thurs. 21.—John Murdock was discharged from the Penitentiary.

Mon. 25.—The U. S. Supreme Court rendered a decision, that the escheated Church property should still remain in the hands of the Receiver, and the Utah Supreme Court should take further action in the case.

—A Republican political club was organized in Salt Lake City.

Wed. 27.—In the First District Court, at Ogden, Charles S. Hall, of West Portage, was sentenced by Judge Miner to 30 days' imprisonment, and Jens Frandsen, of Huntsville, was fined $100; both for u. c. They had previously served one term in the Penitentiary for the same offence.

Fri. 29.—At a meeting of the chief officers of the People's Party, held in Salt Lake City, it was decided to disorganize the People's party and advise its members to join the national parties.

—At a Liberal rally held in Salt Lake City, bitter opposition was manifested to the division on national party lines, and the "Mormons" were accused of insincerity.

Sat. 30.—Michael Stanley was discharged from the Penitentiary.

June. *Mon. 1.*—The first number of the *Lehi Banner* was published at Lehi, Utah Co.

Wed. 3.—The Knutsford hotel on State Street, Salt Lake City, was opened to the public.

—Richard Jenkins, of Nephi, was discharged from the Penitentiary.

Thurs. 4. — Samuel Linton was discharged from the Penitentiary.

Sat. 6.—Miss Emma Thursby sang at the musical festival given in the Tabernacle, Salt Lake City.

Wed. 10.—At a meeting of the Territorial Central Committee of the People's Party, resolutions were adopted dissolving the People's Party of Utah, leaving its members free to unite with the great national parties, according to individual preferences.

Mon. 15.—Plymouth, Box Elder Co., was divided into two Wards, and the northern portion organized as Pierson Ward; Thos. Archibald, Bishop. The residents of the new Ward, however, soon changed its name to North Plymouth.

Tues. 16.—Catharine Campbell Steele, one of the Pioneer women of Utah, and mother of the first white child born in Great Salt Lake Valley, died at Toquerville, Washington Co.

Wed. 17.—The Saints who had settled at Freedom, in Lower Salt River Valley, on the boundary line between Idaho and Wyoming, were organized as Freedom Ward; Arthur B. Clark, Bishop.

Thurs. 18.—The Old Folks of Salt Lake County were treated to a free excursion to Springville, Utah Co.

—Niels C. Andersen was discharged from the Penitentiary.

—The Saints who had settled in Lower Salt River Valley, Wyo., on the east side of the river, were organized as Glencoe Ward; John W. Titensor, Bishop.

Sat. 20.—At a political meeting held in Salt Lake City, the Territorial Democratic Central Committee passed resolutions favoring division on national party lines.

—Bishop Alexander McRae died in Salt Lake City.

—The track on the Sevier branch of the Rio Grande Western Ry. was finished to Salina, Sevier Co.

Fri. 26.—Elizabeth Gilbert, relict of the late Algernon Sidney Gilbert (who died of cholera in Missouri in 1834), died at Minersville, Beaver Co.

Sat. 27.—Jens Frandsen and Henry Sudweeks were discharged from the Penitentiary.

Sun. 28.—Farmers branch,Cache Co.,was organized as a Ward; Charles O. Dunn, Bishop.

Mon. 29.—Katie Eliza Hale Merrill, wife of Elder Joseph H. Merrill, of Smithfield, Utah, died in childbed at the mission house at Fagalii, Samoa. Her baby boy died the same day.

July. *Wed. 1.* — The Utah Supreme Court appointed Judge Charles F. Loofbourow to take testimony in the Church suits as a master of chancery.

Sun. 5.—The Saints who had settled south of Paradise, Cache Co., were organized as the Avon Ward; Henry W. Jackson, Bishop.

Mon. 6.—A Democratic convention, held in Salt Lake City, placed the first Democratic ticket for Salt Lake County officers in the field, after the division of the People's Party on party lines.

Wed. 8.—The Republicans of Salt Lake County held a convention in Salt Lake City and placed the first Republican ticket for county officers in Salt Lake County in the field, after the division of the People's Party on party lines.

—Orlando F. Herron was discharged from the Penitentiary.

Fri. 10.—At a large mass meeting held in Salt Lake City, resolutions were passed favoring division on national party lines, and denouncing the actions of the Liberals who were determined to continue the local warfare.

Tues. 14.—The Salt Lake County Liberals held a convention in Salt Lake City and placed candidates for county officers in the field.

Wed. 15.—Elders Brigham Smoot and Alva J. Butler arrived at Nukualofa, Tongatabu, Tonga, or the Friendly Islands, as the first Latter-day Saint Elders sent to that group.

Thurs. 16.—A Democratic convention was held in Salt Lake City, which nominated candidates for the Utah legislature.

Fri. 17.—Alfred G. Jackson and John Thomas were discharged from the Penitentiary.

Sat. 18.—The San Francisco branch, near Casas Grandes, Chihuahua, Mexico, was organized as Dublan Ward; Winslow Farr, Bishop.

Sun. 19.—August J. Hansen was discharged from the Penitentiary.

Mon. 20.—A Territorial Democratic convention met in Salt Lake City, passed resolutions and effected a complete Territorial organization.

—Benjamin W. Driggs was discharged from the Penitentiary.

Tues. 21.—Albert G. Slater was discharged from the Penitentiary.

Wed. 22.—Republican conventions were held in the various legislative districts of Utah, at which candidates were nominated for the Utah legislature, to be voted for in August following.

Fri. 24.—Peter E. Olsen was discharged from the Penitentiary.

Sun. 26.—The Saints residing on the uplands, northeast of Logan, Cache Co., were organized as Greenville Ward; Nicholas W. Crookston, Bishop.

Mon. 27.—John B. Wasden, Hans Jespersen and Charles A. Terry were discharged from the Penitentiary.

August. *Mon. 3.*—The election in Utah for members of the legislature resulted in the election of eight Democratic members for the Council and sixteen for the House, while the Liberals elected four for the Council and eight for the House. The Republican vote was small. In Salt Lake County the Liberals elected nearly the entire county ticket.

Wed. 5. — Dr. T. De Witt Talmage lectured in the Salt Lake Theatre.

Thurs. 6.—Samuel R. Axtell, formerly governor of Utah, died at Morristown, N. J.

—Rasmus Justesen was discharged from the Penitentiary.

Sun. 9.—Hyrum S. Crane was discharged from the Penitentiary.

Sat. 15.—Philander Colton, a member of the Mormon Battalion, died at Vernal, Uintah Co.

—Charles L. White was discharged from the Penitentiary.

Thurs. 20.—The first number of the Springville *Independent* was issued at Springville, Utah Co.

—Bishop John Spencer died at Indianola, Sanpete Co.

Fri. 21.—Elder John Pulsipher died at Hebron, Washington Co.

Sat. 22.—Jay Gould, the railroad magnate, and party, visited Salt Lake City.

Sun. 23.—The Saints who had settled in Castilla County, Colo., were organized as a branch of the Church, with Simeon A. Dunn as president.

Mon. 24.—Mary Ann Pratt, widow of Apostle Parley P. Pratt, died at Pleasant Grove, Utah Co.

Sun. 30.—Return Jackson Redden, one of the Utah Pioneers of 1847, died at Hoytsville, Summit Co.

September.—The Utah Commission formulated a misleading report about the "Mormons" and the situation in Utah, to the Secretary of the Interior (John W. Noble). Gen. John A. McClernand prepared a minority report, dissenting from the other Commissioners.

14

Wed. 2.—A Territorial Republican convention met in Salt Lake City, adopted a platform, appointed delegates, etc.

Sun. 6.—At the Stake conference, held at St. Johns, Ariz., the 104th quorum of Seventy was organized by John Morgan, with Charles G. D. Jarvis, Samuel D. Moore, W. C. Davis, Frithoff G. Nielsen, J. W. Brown, A. E. Cheeney and W. D. Rencher as presidents.

Tues. 15.—A great Irrigation Congress was opened and organized at the Exposition building, Salt Lake City, with 450 delegates present. Sixteen States and Territories were represented. The congress elected C. C. Wright, of California, chairman, and continued its sessions for three days.

Wed. 16.—The Irrigation Congress was addressed by Presidents Wilford Woodruff and Geo. Q. Cannon.

Fri. 18.—Members of the Irrigation Congress, accompanied by Presidents Wilford Woodruff and Geo. Q. Cannon, visited Lehi, Provo and other places.

Sun. 20.—Samuel H. Rogers, a member of the Mormon Battalion, died at Snowflake, Ariz.

Wed. 23.—In the First District Court, at Provo, John L. Butler, of Elsinore, and Josiah Bennett were each sentenced by Judge Blackburn to ten days' imprisonment, for u. c.

Fri. 25.—Judge U. G. Wenner died at his lonely retreat on Fremont Island, in the Great Salt Lake.

Sun. 27.—Pres. Joseph F. Smith, who had not appeared in public for several years, addressed the congregation at the Tabernacle, Salt Lake City.

Wed. 30.—Elder Joseph A. Allred died at Spring City, Sanpete Co.

October. *Sat. 3.*—Josiah Bennett was discharged from the Penitentiary.

Sun. 4.—The general semi-annual conference of the Church was commenced in Salt Lake City, continuing for three days.

Mon. 5.—The annual Territorial fair was opened in Salt Lake City.

—A tin box, containing a number of papers and periodicals, was deposited in the base of one of the pillars of the Eagle Gate, which was in course of re-construction, in Salt Lake City.

Tues. 6.—The general conference of the Church in Salt Lake City passed a number of resolutions, condemnatory of the false reports which the Utah Commission had forwarded to the Secretary of the Interior.

Thurs. 8.—The Latter-day Saints' College building in the Seventeenth Ward, Salt Lake City, was dedicated and opened.

Sat. 10.—A Democratic Territorial convention, in Salt Lake City, condemned the report of the Utah Commission.

Mon. 12.—The new school building of the Central Seminary of the Salt Lake Stake of Zion, in Mill Creek, was dedicated.

—The Lehi sugar factory commenced operations.

Tues. 13.—In the First District Court, at Provo, Chris. Anderson, of Monroe, was sentenced by Judge Blackburn to six months' imprisonment, for alleged adultery. ·

—Arthur H. Campbell was discharged

from the Penitentiary, his sentence having been commuted to one year.

Wed. 14.—In the Third District Court, at Provo, James M. Allred, of Fairview, Sanpete Co., was sentenced by Judge Blackburn to two months' imprisonment, for alleged adultery.

—Duckworth Grimshaw, of Beaver, who had been sentenced in the Second District Court, to one year's imprisonment for alleged adultery, was incarcerated in the Penitentiary.

Thurs. 15.—In the Third District Court, Salt Lake City, Robert Bowman was sentenced by Judge Zane to six months' imprisonment, and fined $100 for u. c.

Sat. 17.—The first car load of granulated sugar from the Utah sugar factory, near Lehi, Utah Co., reached Salt Lake City, assigned to Cunnington & Co.

Mon. 19.—Judge Charles F. Loofbourow, as a master in chancery, commenced taking testimony in the Church cases, with a view to deciding what charitable uses the escheated Church property should be applied to. Presidents Wilford Woodruff and George Q. Cannon testified as witnesses.

Tues. 20.—Joseph H. Felt was arrested in Salt Lake City, on a charge of violating the Edmunds' law, examined and discharged for lack of evidence.

Sat. 24.—In the First District Court, at Provo, Amasa Tucker, of Fairview, John Warwood, of Nephi, and Fred. W. Cox, of Manti, were each sentenced by Judge Blackburn to 20 days' imrisonment, for alleged adultery.

Tues. 27.—In the Third District Court, at Salt Lake City, Judge Charles S. Zane decided that the Whitney property of the Tithing Office block, the Cannon House on South Temple street, the Council House corner, Salt Lake City, were exempt from confiscation, as well as the Tabernacle square and other property, at Ogden.

November. *Sun. 1.*—Nathan B. Baldwin, a member of Zion's Camp, died at Fillmore, Millard Co.

—At a meeting held in the Sugar House Ward, Salt Lake Co., the Seventies residing in that locality were organized as the 105th quorum of Seventy, with Martin Garn, John M. Whitaker and Thomas Alston as presidents.

Tues. 10.—James K. Ingall was discharged from the Penitentiary.

Wed. 11.—After a lengthy investigation in the Third District Court, Salt Lake City, Judge Charles S. Zane rendered a decree escheating the Tithing Office, the Gardo House, Historian's Office, and Church farm to the government.

Fri. 13.—In the Third District Court, Salt Lake City, John R. Howard, of Logan, was sentenced by Judge Zane to one year's imprisonment, for alleged adultery.

—Amasa Tucker, John Warwood and Fred W. Cox were discharged from the Penitentiary.

Sun. 15.—The Saints who had settled on Fall River, Fremont Co., Idaho, were organized as Fall River Ward; Hyrum Brown, Bishop. On the same occasion Egin Ward was organized; Harry H. Smith, Bishop.

—The South Iona branch, Bingham Co.,

Idaho, was organized as a Ward; A. M. Rawson, Bishop.

Tues. 17.—Thomas Stirland was discharged from the Penitentiary, part of his sentence having been commuted.

Thurs. 19.—Father John B. Lewis, 95 years old, died in Salt Lake City.

Fri. 20.—In the First District Court, at Ogden, Henry Yates, of Clarkston, was sentenced by Judge Miner to three months' imprisonment, for alleged adultery.

Sun. 22.—The Saints composing parts of the Brighton and North Point Wards, lying west of the Jordan river and of Salt Lake City, were organized as Center Ward; Albert W. Davis, Bishop.

Fri. 27.—In the First District Court, at Provo, Wm. Bench, of Manti, was sentenced by Judge Blackburn to twenty days' imprisonment, for alleged adultery.

Sat. 28.—In the First District Court, at Ogden, Nils O. Wahlstrøm and Edwin Lambourne, of Lake Town, and S. C. Putnam, of Woodruff, were sentenced by Judge Miner to 30 days' imprisonment each; Christopher S. Winge, of Hyrum, to nine months; Peter Nielsen, of Smithfield, to six months; and James Bywater, of Brigham City, to two years and three months; all for breaking the Edmunds law. Bywater had previously served two terms and Winge one term, for u.c.

—The first number of the *Central Utah Press* was issued at Salina, Sevier Co., Utah; W. W. Wallace, editor.

December. *Tues. 1.*—The Gardo House, Salt Lake City, was vacated by the Church as escheated property.

Fri. 4.—Elder Isaac N. Canfield died at Preston, Idaho.

Sat. 5.—Elder Allen Taylor died at Loa, Piute Co.

—In the First District Court, at Ogden, Thomas H. Bullock, of Plain City, was sentenced by Judge Miner to 18 months' imprisonment, for alleged adultery. He had previously served two terms for u.c.

Fri. 11.—By invitation of the First Presidency, a number of prominent men met at the Lion House, Salt Lake City, to discuss the advisability of erecting a monument in honor of Brigham Young and the Utah Pioneers.

Sat. 12.—In the First District Court, at Ogden, N. C. Mortensen, of Huntsville, was sentenced by Judge Miner to one year's imprisonment, for alleged adultery. He had previously served a term in the Penitentiary for u. c.

Sun. 13.—Payson, Utah Co., was divided into two Wards, namely, Payson First and Payson Second Wards, with John E. Hulsh and Jonathan S. Page as their respective Bishops.

—The Twenty-third Ward, Salt Lake City, was organized; Geo. R. Jones, Bishop.

Mon. 14.—James M. Allred was discharged from the Penitentiary.

Tues. 15.—Patriarch Charles W. Hyde died in Salt Lake City.

—Robert Bowman was discharged from the Penitentiary.

Thurs. 17.—General Patrick Edward Connor died at the Walker House, Salt Lake City.

—Wm. Bench was discharged from the Penitentiary.

Sun. 20.—Spanish Fork, Utah Co., was divided into four Wards, named respectively, the First, Second, Third and Fourth Wards; Henry Gardner, Geo. D. Snell, Marinus Larsen and Andrew E. Nielsen, Bishops.

Wed. 23.—Bishop John Sharp died in Salt Lake City.

Sun. 27.—Franklin M. Anderson was accidentally killed in Salt Lake City, by a railway train.

—Edwin Lambourne was discharged from the Penitentiary.

Mon. 28.—Nils O. Wahlstrøm and S. C. Putnam were discharged from the Penitentiary.

1892.

A number of prominent Church people died this year. Missionary work was recommenced on the Society and Tuamotu Islands. Home Rule was proposed for Utah instead of Statehood. Respectable Gentiles in Salt Lake City united with "Mormons" to terminate Liberal rule, etc.

January. The Gardo House, Salt Lake City, was rented by the Receiver for a "Keeley Institute."

Fri. 1.—The branch of the Rio Grande Western railway, commencing at Springville and running around the south end of Utah lake to Eureka, Tintic Valley, Juab Co., was opened for traffic.

Sat. 2.—In the U. S. District Court at Boise City, Idaho, indictments against nearly a hundred "Mormons," accused of violating the election laws by registering and voting in 1888, were dismissed.

Mon. 4.—The new Brigham Young Academy building at Provo, Utah Co., was dedicated.

Tues. 5.—The "Home Rule Bill" for Utah was introduced in both houses of Congress. Charles D. Faulkner introduced it in the Senate and Delegate John T. Caine in the House.

Wed. 6.—In the Territorial Supreme Court, Salt Lake City, Henry W. Lawrence asked for $300 as a monthly compensation for his services as Receiver of escheated Church property; his attorney asked for $150 per month for his own services.

Fri. 8.—The Tuscarora Club of Utah was organized at a Liberal meeting, held at the Walker House, Salt Lake City, with Orlando W. Powers as grand sachem.

Sun. 10.—The first Latter-day Saint Deaf Mute Sunday School was organized in the 19th Ward, Salt Lake City, by the Salt Lake Stake Sunday School superintendency. Henry C. Barrell, Supt.; Laron Pratt, (a deaf mute,) asst. supt. and secretary.

Mon. 11.—The 30th session of the Utah legislature convened in Salt Lake City and organized with Wm. H. King as president of the Council and Wm. H. Seegmiller speaker of the House.

—A large excursion, consisting of members of the International League of Press

'Clubs, arrived in Salt Lake City on a visit. A musical concert was given in their honor in the Tabernacle and a reception at the Knutsford hotel.

Tues. 12.—In the House branch of the Utah legislature, Luther T. Tuttle introduced a bill prohibiting polygamy, etc.

Wed. 13.—In the Council branch of the Utah legislature, Peters, of Brigham City, introduced a bill providing for the punishment of polygamy, fornication, etc.

Fri. 15.—Master in Chancery, Charles F. Loofbourow, filed his report in the Church case, in the Territorial Supreme Court, and recommended that the escheated Church property be devoted to the benefit of public schools.

—Elder Daniel Allen, a Church veteran, died at Escalante, Garfield Co.

Sat. 16.—The Salt Lake Natural Gas Co. filed its articles of incorporation with the clerk of the Third District Court.

Mon. 18.—In the U. S. Senate, Henry M. Teller, of Colorado, introduced a bill providing for the admission of Utah into the Union as a State.

Tues. 19.—Elder Cornelius Green died in Mill Creek, Salt Lake Co.

Thurs. 21.—Fanny Young Thatcher died in Salt Lake City.

Sat. 23.—Susan Smith Adams, of Mormon Battalion fame, died at Harrisburgh, Washington Co., Utah.

Sun. 24.—Elder Geo. C. Riser, the pioneer shoemaker of Utah, and Harriet H. Phelps, wife of the late Judge Wm. W. Phelps, died in Salt Lake City.

Thurs. 28.—Elders Joseph W. Damron and Wm. A. Seegmiller, arrived at Papeete, Tahiti, from Samoa, being sent to reopen the Society Islands mission.

Sun. 31.—Patriarch Robert Logan died at Orangeville, Emery Co.

February. *Mon. 1.* — Prescindia L. Huntington Kimball died in Salt Lake City, and Addison Greene, once a member of Zion's Camp, died at Newbern, Jersey Co., Illinois.

Tues. 2.—Elder Geo. W. Price, died in the Fifteenth Ward, Salt Lake City.

Wed. 3.—A bill providing for the Fourth Judicial District in Utah was passed by the U. S. Senate.

Thurs. 4.—Bishop Niels Aagaard died of pneumonia, at Levan, Juab Co.

Fri. 5.—Henry Yates was discharged from the Penitentiary.

Mon 8.—The municipal election in Salt Lake City resulted in victory for the Liberals, except in the Third Precinct, which was carried by the Democrats.

Wed. 10.—The "Home Rule Bill" was again argued before the House Committee on Territories, at Washington, D. C.

Thurs. 11.—The Old Folks of Salt Lake County were tendered a free entertainment in the Salt Lake Theater, where the Lyceum Dramatic Company played "The Banker's Daughter."

—The Congressional enactment, authorizing the creation of the Fourth Judicial District in Utah, became law.

Fri. 12.—Col. O. J. Hollister, a bitter anti-Mormon, died in Salt Lake City.

Sat. 13.—During the proceedings before the U. S. Senate Committee, in reference to the "Home Rule Bill," an application

for amnesty for polygamists signed by the First Presidency and the Apostles and dated Salt Lake City, Dec. 19, 1891, was presented. The application was endorsed by Gov. Arthur L. Thomas and Judge Charles S. Zane.

Su n. 14.—The Seventies residing in the southern part of the Bannock Stake, Idaho, were organized as the 106th quorum of Seventy; Emil Bochman, Wrol C. Olsen, Lorenzo R. Thomas, George E. Hill, sen., Brigham H. Ellsworth and Joseph Empey, presidents.

Tues. 16.—John Fitzgerald, a Pioneer of 1847, died at Draper, Salt Lake Co.

Wed. 17.—Elder Wm. King, president of the Hawaiian settlement in Skull Valley, died at the Deseret Hospital, Salt Lake City. and Daniel B. Rawson, a member of the Mormon Battalion, died near Ogden, Weber Co.

Sat. 20.—At a meeting of the Brigham Young Memorial Association in Salt Lake City, the model offered by C. E. Dallin, of Springville, Utah Co., for a statue of Pres. Brigham Young, was accepted, and the southeast corner of the Temple Block suggested as a site for the monument.

—Thos. H. Bullock, of Plain City, was discharged from his third term of imprisonment in the Penitentiary.

Thurs. 25.—Elder Daniel Davis died at Bountiful, Davis Co.

Sun. 28.—Robert T. Thomas, one of the Utah Pioneers of 1847, died at Provo, Utah Co., and Patriarch John Duggan Gibbs, died at Portage, Box Elder Co.

March.—Mormon Elders were mobbed in Denmark, principally on Sjælland. Elders Niels J. Hendricksen and Ole Sørensen, jun., who labored on the islands of Falster and Møen, were banished from the country.

Tues. 1.—In the First District Court, at Provo, Joseph Dilworth was sentenced to one month's imprisonment, for "adultery.'

Wed. 2.—Niels Peter Christensen, who had been imprisoned since May 2, 1891, was discharged from the Penitentiary.

Thurs. 3.—In the First District Court, at Ogden, Judge James A. Miner commuted the sentence passed Nov. 20, 1891, upon Christopher S. Winge for six months' imprisonment, to twenty days' imprisonment.

Sat. 5.—Christopher S. Winge was discharged from the Penitentiary.

Sun. 6.—Bishop William Andrew Taylor died at Farr West, Weber Co.

Wed. 9.—Nicholas H. Groesbeck was arrested at Springville, Utah Co., on a charge of adultery.

Thurs. 10.—A new school law, passed by the Utah legislature, was approved; also a new election law, providing for holding all general and local elections in the Territory, on the Tuesday following the first Monday in November, 1892, and biennially thereafter.

Sat. 12.—The Utah legislature adjourned. Among the bills passed and approved was one creating Grand County.

—Chr. Anderson, who had been imprisoned since Oct. 13, 1891, was discharged from the Penitentiary.

Tues. 15.—The taking of depositions of

"Mormons" regarding the ownership of the Temple lot at Independence, Mo., was commenced at the Templeton hotel, Salt Lake City, before John M. Orr, a special commissioner, appointed by the U. S. Circuit Court for the Western Division of the State of Missouri. It was part of a suit "brought by the Reorganized church, commonly called Josephites, against the Church of Christ, commonly called Hedrickites, to obtain possession and title to a piece of land in Independence, Jackson Co., Mo., known as the Temple Lot."

Wed. 16.—The Rock Springs branch, Wyo., was organized as a Ward by Apostle John H. Smith; Joseph Soulsby, Bishop.

—Professor Charles William Elliot, president of the Harvard University, visited Salt Lake City. He addressed a large assembly in the Tabernacle in the evening.

Thurs. 17.—The *Deseret News* published a communication from the First Presidency, declaring that the rumors of their directing members of the Church which political party they should support were false and without foundation in fact. The Presidency had no disposition to direct in such matters, but desired the people to choose for themselves.

—The 50th anniversary of the organization of the Relief Society, at Nauvoo, Ill., was celebrated throughout the Church. In Salt Lake City, services were held in the Tabernacle, and the congregation was addressed by Zina D. H. Young, Abraham H. Cannon, Joseph F. Smith, Bathsheba W. Smith, Romania B. Pratt and others.

—In the First District Court, at Provo, John A. Mower was sentenced to ten days' imprisonment, for u.c.

⌐ *Sat. 19.*—An act, passed by the Utah legislature, organizing a fourth judicial district in Utah, comprising Weber, Box Elder, Cache, Rich and Morgan Counties, was approved.

Wed. 23.—General Russel A. Alger and family arrived in Salt Lake City on a visit; a banquet was given in his honor at the Templeton hotel.

--The examination in the Independence, Jackson Co., Mo., Temple lot case, at the Templeton hotel, Salt Lake City, was terminated.

Fri. 25.—Ex U. S. Marshal Frank H. Dyer died in Salt Lake City.

—Elder John R. Young was severely wounded and his grandchild killed by a gun accident, near Demming, New Mexico.

Sat. 26.—Dr. John Riggs, a Church veteran, died at Provo, Utah Co.

—John A. Mower was discharged from the Penitentiary.

Sun. 27.—Beaver Dams branch, Box Elder Co., was organized as a Ward; Francello Durfee, Bishop.

Tues. 29.—Gov. Arthur L. Thomas appointed Nelson A. Empey, R. Macintosh and R. C. Chambers World's Fair Commissioners for Utah.

Wed. 30.—The U. S. House Committee recommended the passage of the "Home Rule Bill" for Utah.

Thurs. 31.—Elder Wm. Glover died at Farmington, Davis Co.

—Elder Wm. C. Winder and a missionary companion were expelled by a mob from Stanley County, N. C., for preaching the gospel.

April. *Fri. 1.*—Joseph Dilworth was discharged from the Penitentiary.

Sun. 3.—The 62nd annual conference of the Church was commenced in Salt Lake City, continuing till the 6th.

Wed. 6.—In the general conference of the Church, the Priesthood was arranged in the stands and auditorium. Pres. Lorenzo Snow explained the order of ceremony at the laying of the capstone of the Temple and trained the congregation in shouting hosannah, after which remarks were made by Pres. Wilford Woodruff. The congregation then proceeded to the Temple in procession, when the capstone of the Temple was laid amid great enthusiasm and rejoicing, Pres. Woodruff pressing the electric button, which caused the stone to be lowered to its place. After the shouting of hosannah, the vast congregation, on motion of Apostle Francis M. Lyman, voted that the Temple should be finished by April 6, 1893. About forty thousand people were present and participated in the ceremonies.

Thurs. 7.—This evening the statue of the angel Moroni, on the main east tower, and the spire on the middle west tower of the Temple, in Salt Lake City, were beautifully illuminated with incandescent lights, for the first time.

Sun. 10.—Springville, Utah Co., was divided into the First, Second, Third and Fourth Wards, with John Tuckett, Loren Harmer, Geo. R. Hill and Joseph Loynd as their respective Bishops.

Mon. 11.—Edward Hunter, formerly a Bishop and a member of the Mormon Battalion, died at Grantsville, Tooele Co.

Tues. 12.—Elder Julian Moses died at East Mill Creek, Salt Lake Co.

—Jacob Albertson was arrested at Spanish Fork, Utah Co., for u. c.

—The Salt Lake City council refused to enforce the city ordnance forbidding saloon-keepers to sell liquor on Sunday.

Thurs. 14.—Jacob Gates, one of the First Seven Presidents of Seventies, died at Provo, Utah Co.

Fri. 15.—Elder Robert Bodily, a highly respected Church veteran, died at Kaysville, Davis Co.

Sat. 16.—Elder Thos. Butler, of Richfield, Sevier Co., died in Salt Lake City, on his way home from a mission to Virginia.

Mon. 18.—Elder Lester J. Herrick, a Church veteran, died at Ogden, Weber Co.

—The taking of depositions in the suit for the possession of the Temple lot at Independence, Jackson Co., Mo., was commenced at Independence.

Wed. 20.—Lars J. Augustson, of Vernal, Uintah Co., Utah, was arrested for u.c., taken before Com. James T. McConnell, at Fort Duchesne, and placed under $600 bonds.

Fri. 22.—Samuel Thompson, a member of the Mormon Battalion, died at Vernal, Uintah Co.

Mon. 25.—In the Third District Court, Salt Lake City, Henry Tuckett was sentenced to six months' imprisonment, for u.c.

Thurs. 28.—Peter Nielsen, of Smithfield, was discharged from the Penitentiary.

Fri. 29.—The first cattlemen's congress held in the United States, convened at Ogden. Fifteen States were represented.

May. Sun. 1.—This day was observed by the Latter-day Saints generally as a special day of fasting and prayer.

Mon. 2. — Elder Charles Lambert, a Church veteran, died in Salt Lake City.

Sat. 7.—Elder Lars N. Larsen died at Moroni, Sanpete Co.

Mon. 9.—In the Second District Court, Beaver, John Baird was sentenced to four months' imprisonment, for alleged adultery.

Tues. 10.—Dr. Jeter Clinton, a Church veteran, died in Salt Lake City.

Thurs. 12.—After trial in the First District Court, at Ogden, the case of Lars C. Christensen, charged with u.c., was dismissed.

Fri. 13.—The Salt Lake City council passed a bill authorizing bonding the city for $600,000 for corporate purposes.

Sat. 14.—The Utah Democrats, assembled in Territorial convention at Ogden, adopted a party platform.

—Elder Wm. D. Kartchner died at Snowflake, Ariz.

Sun. 15.—About seven hundred Presbyterians, chiefly preachers, arrived in Salt Lake City, *en route* to a convention in California. They attended services in the Tabernacle.

Mon. 16.—The visiting Presbyterians held a union missionary meeting in the Theatre, Salt Lake City.

Tues. 17.—In the Third District Court, Salt Lake City, Frank Meldrum was sentenced to six months' imprisonment, for "adultery."

Thurs. 19.—The first number of the Spanish Fork *Sun*, a newspaper, was issued at Spanish Fork, Utah Co.

Sat. 21.—Elder Seth Langton died at Logan, Cache Co., Utah.

Mon. 23.—In the Third District Court, Salt Lake City, Geo. E. Cozier was sentenced to one year's imprisonment, for "adultery."

Thurs. 26.—After trial in the First District Court, at Ogden, the jury returned a verdict of "not guilty" in the case of John L. Jones, charged with adultery.

—In the Third District Court, Salt Lake City, Nicholas H. Groesbeck was sentenced to one year's imprisonment for alleged adultery.

Fri. 27.—Dr. Foster R. Kenner died at Manti, Sanpete Co.

Sat. 28.—In the U. S. House of Representatives it was proposed that the so-called Industrial Christian Home of Utah" (which was founded some years previously as a refuge for Mormon wives who abandoned polygamy) be summarily disposed of by Congress, by granting the entire premises to the Territory as a site for a Territorial school for deaf and dumb. The proposition, however, was not sustained.

Mon. 30.—Leo Haefeli, a Utah journalist, died in Salt Lake City.

Tues. 31.—Benjamin W. Rolfe, a Utah Pioneer of 1847, died in Salt Lake City.

—Elijah Sells, acting governor of Utah,

issued a proclamation, ordering that "the regular terms of court in the Fourth Judicial District" be held at Ogden, and that the first term convene there June 1. 1892.

June. Wed. 1.—In the Fourth District Court, at Ogden, Wm. H. Dopp and Thos. W. Obray were each sentenced by Judge James A. Miner to four months' imprisonment, and Nils C. Erickson to one year's imprisonment, all for "adultery."

—James S. Brown and two other Elders from Utah arrived at Papeete, Tahiti, as missionaries to the Society Islands. Soon afterwards the mission was successfully reopened.

Mon. 13.—Dr. Karl G. Maeser delivered the first of a series of Sunday School lectures in the Assembly Hall, Salt Lake City.

Sun. 19.—Elder Noah L. Shurtliff was accidentally killed in a well, at Cardston, Alberta, Canada.

Tues. 21.—Elder Lot Smith, famous in the early history of Utah, was killed by Indians, at Tuba, near Moan Coppy, Ariz.

Wed. 22.—Hyrum Naegle was terribly mangled by a bear near Colonia Pacheco, Mexico, from the effects of which he soon afterwards died.

Wed. 29.—The Old Folks of Salt Lake City and County were treated to a free excursion to Payson, Utah Co.

July. Fri. 8.—The Utah Supreme Court made an order directing the Receiver, in the suits of the government against the Church, to turn over to the Secretary of the Interior all Church property declared confiscated. This included the Tithing House property, the Church farm, coal lands, the Historian's office and the Gardo House.

—The Utah "Home Rule Bill" was passed by the U. S. House of Representatives.

Sun. 10.—W. M. Allred was arrested at Spring City for u.c. and placed under bonds by Com. Jacob Johnson.

Mon. 11.—Wm. H. Brown died at Provo, Utah Co.

Sat. 16.—An excursion party, consisting of 85 members of the Kansas Editorial Association, arrived in Salt Lake City, on a visit.

Sun. 24.—The Granite Ward meeting house, Salt Lake Co., was dedicated.

—Wm. C. Winder and missionary companions, who had returned to Stanley County, South Carolina, were mobbed.

Mon. 25.—The corner stone of the joint city and county building was laid in Salt Lake City.

Tues. 26.—Sister Melissa N. Allred died at Lehi, Utah Co.

Sat. 30.—In the Fourth District Court, at Ogden, the cases of the following named persons, charged with polygamy, adultery, and u.c., were dismissed, on motion of U. S. Marshall Eli H. Parsons, who reported that it was impossible to secure evidence sufficient to justify a conviction: Lot Darney, James Kearl, John Burt, Edmond Clark, Joseph Gibbons, Milton D. Hammond, Milvin M. Hammond, Thos. R. Leavitt, John Wonlf, Samuel Simmons, Orson Eggleston, Gideon Olsen, Hans Hansen, A. D. Child, Ludvig Erickson, Moroni Brown, Arthur P. Welchman, James Haslem, Wm. Hurd,

Moroni Coleman, Wm. Bunderson, John J. Murphy, John I. Hart, and Hans J. Nielsen.

—A bill for the admission of Utah into the Union was introduced into the U. S. House of Representatives by Delegate John T. Caine.

Sun. 31.—The corner stone of St. Mark's hospital, near the Warm Springs, Salt Lake City, was laid.

August.—Samuel Tarwater, an old Missouri mobocrat, who was badly wounded by "Mormons" in the Crooked River battle, Oct. 25, 1838, died in Missouri.

Thurs. 4.—John Ball was drowned in the Jordan river, near Salt Lake City.

Sat. 6.—Lincoln Beach, ten miles northwest of Payson, Utah Co., was opened as a pleasure resort.

Sun. 7.—Prof. Francis Parker, of the Cook County school, Chicago, Ill., lectured in the Tabernacle, Salt Lake City.

Sat. 13.—Dilworth Grimshaw, of Beaver, was discharged from imprisonment in the Penitentiary, where he had been confined since Oct. 14, 1891, for u.c.

Sun. 14.—The Star Valley Stake of Zion was organized by Pres. Joseph F. Smith and Apostle Francis M. Lyman; Geo. Osmond, president; Wm. W. Burton and Anson V. Call, counselors; a high council was also organized.

—The South Lewisville branch, Fremont Co., Idaho, was organized as Grant Ward; Alfred K. Dabell, Bishop. The East Willow Creek branch was organized as Shelton Ward; John Shelton Howard, Bishop.

Mon. 15.—Judge Orlando W. Powers resigned his position as chairman of the Liberal city committee in Salt Lake City.

Fri. 19.—Wm. Douglass, an old citizen, died at Payson, Utah Co.

Sat. 20.—John Baird was discharged from the Penitentiary.

Mon. 22.—Elder John L. Dalton, who had been called to open a mission in California, arrived in San Francisco.

Sat. 27.—Wm. Pugsley, of Salt Lake City, was accidentally drowned in the Weber river, near its source.

Mon. 29.—The Latter-day Saints academy of the Weber Stake was dedicated at Ogden.

—The Tooele Stake academy building was dedicated at Grantsville, Tooele Co.

Wed. 31.—Elder Otto Lyman Chipman, of American Fork, Utah Co., died at Huntley, Waikato, New Zealand, where he had labored as a missionary. His remains were shipped home in charge of Thos. C. Stanford and Lewis J. Hawkes, returning missionaries.

September. *Thurs. 1.*—The Agricultural College at Logan, Cache Co., was reopened; many changes and improvements having been made for the convenience of students.

Fri. 2.—The Church cases came up before the Territorial Supreme Court. Arguments were made also on the next day.

Sat. 10.—Elder Wm. McGregor died in Salt Lake City.

—Wm. H. Dopp and Thos. W. Obray were discharged from the Penitentiary.

Sun. 11.—Elder Brigham Smoot baptized Alibate, near Mua, Tongatabu, the first convert to "Mormonism" in Tonga (Friendly Islands).

Tues. 13.—John R. Howard was discharged from the Penitentiary.

Wed. 14.—In the Second District Court, at Beaver, Charles Walker and Daniel Golding were fined six cents each by Judge Thos. J. Anderson, for infraction of the Edmunds law.

Thurs. 15.—The Utah Commission addressed an untruthful report on Utah affairs to John W. Noble, Secretary of the Interior.

Mon. 19.—In the First District Court, Provo, Lars J. Augustson was sentenced to two months' imprisonment, Thos. Bingham to three months, Ed. Thomas to three months, and P. M. Peterson to two months, all for u. c.

—In the Second District Court, Beaver, Gilbert Webb was sentenced to six months' imprisonment for "adultery."

Tues. 20.—In the Third District Court, Salt Lake City, Frank P. Hadlock was sentenced to six months' imprisonment, for u. c.

Wed. 21.—In the Second District Court, Beaver, A. Johnson was sentenced to four months' imprisonment, for "adultery."

Fri. 23.—Elder James W. Burbidge died in Salt Lake City.

Sun. 25.—A meeting house in the Dry Creek branch, of the Draper Ward, Salt Lake Co., was dedicated.

Wed. 28.—The sugar factory at Lehi, Utah Co., commenced its run for the season.

Fri. 30.—Charles W. Penrose retired from the editorship of the *Deseret News*, after serving in that capacity for fifteen years. He took an editorial position on the Salt Lake *Herald*.

October.—Elder John L. Dalton organized a branch of the Church in San Francisco, Cal.; Joseph Mattress, president.

Sat. 1.—The *Deseret News* Publishing Company, having leased the *Deseret News*, with all its properties, from the *Deseret News* Company, assumed control. The company consisted of Abraham H. Cannon, John Q. Cannon and others.

Mon. 3.—In the Fourth District Court, at Ogden, Levi J. Taylor was sentenced by Judge Miner to three months' imprisonment, for u.c.

—Geo. E. Cosier, who had been pardoned by President Harrison, was released from the Penitentiary.

—Elder Adolph Haag, of Payson, Utah, died at Haifa, Palestine, where he labored as a missionary.

Wed. 5.—Sister Lucy M. Smith, a widow of Geo. A. Smith, died in Salt Lake City.

Thurs. 6.—The semi-annual conference of the Church convened in Salt Lake City, continuing till the 9th.

Sat. 8.—In the Third District Court, Salt Lake City, Gilbert A. Marchant was sentenced to three months' imprisonment, for u.c.

Wed. 12.—Articles of incorporation of the National Woman's Relief Societies were filed with the county clerk, in Salt Lake City; Zina D. H. Young, president; Jane S. Richards, Bathsheba W. Smith and Sarah M. Kimball, vice-presidents; Emmeline B.

Wells, secretary; M. Isabella Horne, treasurer.

—N. C. Mortensen, of Huntsville, was discharged from the Penitentiary.

Sat. 15.—Thomas J. Anderson resigned his position of associate justice of Utah.

Mon. 17.—In the Fourth District Court, at Ogden, George Godfrey was sentenced by Judge James A. Miner to one year's imprisonment, for "adultery."

—Frank Meldrum was discharged from the Penitentiary.

—Elder David Hoagland Cannon, of Salt Lake County, Utah, died at Sorau, Germany, where he labored as a missionary. His remains were brought home.

Tues. 18.—The shares of gas stock owned by Salt Lake City were sold by the city council for $105,000.

Wed. 19.—Mrs. Lucy Whalen, niece of the Prophet Joseph Smith, died at Burlington, Iowa.

Thurs. 20.—Dr. W. R. Pike died at Provo, Utah Co.

Fri. 21.—The World's Fair was formally opened in Chicago, Ill., it being the four-hundredth anniversary of the discovery of America by Columbus. The day was observed by the people of Utah as a holiday, and a grand parade was had in Salt Lake City.

Sat. 22.—In the Third District Court, Provo, Lewis Smith was sentenced to one month's imprisonment, for "adultery."

Mon. 24.—Respectable and leading citizens, who were disgusted with the record of the Liberal party in municipal affairs, held a meeting in Salt Lake City and formulated a municipal ticket.

Tues. 25.—Bishop Hans Funk died at Newton, Cache Co.

—Henry Tuckett was discharged from the Penitentiary.

Thurs. 27.—The Indian Chief White Horse, who had taken an active part against the whites in southern Utah, during the famous Black-Hawk war, died near Greenwich, Piute Co., Utah.

Fri. 28.—Bishop Wm. Brown died at South Bountiful, Davis Co.

November.—Cedars branch, Fremont Co., Idaho, was organized as the Rudy Ward, by Apostle John Henry Smith; Jesse T. Clark, Bishop.

Sun. 6.—Elder James Barnes died at West Weber, Weber Co.

Mon. 7.—In the First District Court, Provo, John Oberg was sentenced to six months' imprisonment, August Svendsen to one year, and Anton Nelson to three months, all for "adultery;" and Bendt Larsen was sentenced to one month. Germand Ellsworth to one month, Jacob P. Albertson to two months, James Anderson to one month and John G. Jørgensen to two months, all for u.c.

Tues. 8.—At the general election in Utah, Joseph L. Rawlins (Democrat) was elected delegate to Congress, against Frank J. Cannon (Republican) and C. E. Allen (Liberal). The Liberals carried Salt Lake County.

—Grover Cleveland (Democrat) was re-elected president of the United States, against Benjamin Harrison (Republican).

Fri. 11.—Bishop Henry Giles died at Blue Valley, Wayne Co.

Sat. 12.—At a session of the Territorial Supreme Court, held in Salt Lake City, Chief Justice Charles S. Zane delivered an opinion in the case of the United States *versus* the Church of Jesus Christ of Latter day Saints, confirming a decision of the lower court, and authorizing the use of the personal property of the Church under the direction of a trustee, for the building and repairing of houses of worship and the support of the poor. The court appointed Bishop Leonard G. Hardy trustee, and fixed his bonds at $500,000.

Sun. 13.—Memorial services were held in the Tabernacle, Salt Lake City, in honor of Elders who had died while laboring as missionaries abroad. The speakers were Presidents Wilford Woodruff and Joseph F. Smith and Apostle Franklin D. Richards.

Wed. 16.—Bishop Robert R. Daines died at Hyde Park, Cache Co.

Sat. 19.—The Utah Sugar Factory at Lehi, Utah Co., completed its second annual run. It had been in operation about forty days, and during that time employed an average of one hundred men and manufactured 1¾ million pounds of sugar.

—Lars J. Augustsen and P. M. Petersen were discharged from the Penitentiary.

Sun. 20.—Susan Snively Young, a widow of Pres. Brigham Young, died in Salt Lake City; and Sister Almira Green died at West Weber, Weber Co.

Mon. 21.—The Street car line on Centre Street, Salt Lake City, was opened.

Tues. 22.—Lewis Smith was discharged from the Penitentiary.

Thurs. 24.—Elizabeth Carter Whitmore died in Salt Lake City.

Sun. 27.—Elder John L. Dalton organized a branch of the Church in Sacramento, Cal.; Aaron Garlic, president.

December. *Thurs. 1.*—A motor line from Five Points, north of Ogden, Weber Co., to the Warm Springs, was opened for traffic.

—I. A. Benton succeeded Eli H. Parsons as U. S. marshal for Utah.

—James Bywater was released from the Penitentiary, his sentence having been commuted by Pres. Harrison to one actual year of imprisonment from date of sentence, upon payment of costs.

Sun. 4.—The Saints, who had settled in Ogden valley, north of Eden, Weber Co., were organized as the Liberty Ward; Joshua B. Judkins, Bishop.

—Ed. Thomas was discharged from the Penitentiary.

Mon. 5.—Thos. Bingham was discharged from the Penitentiary.

Wed. 7.—Bendt Larsen and Germand Ellsworth were discharged from the Penitentiary.

Thurs. 8.—Charles L. Flake was shot and killed by a desperado, at Snowflake, Ariz.

Sun. 11.—The Treasureton branch of Clifton Ward, Oneida Co., Idaho, was organized as a Ward; Benjamin Hymas Bishop.

—The Saints who had settled on the Chama river, Rio Arriba Co., New Mexico, were organized as a Ward; Asael L. Fuller, Bishop.

Mon. 12.—A fire destroyed the most valuable business corner in Beaver, Beaver Co.

Sun. 18.—Levi J. Taylor was discharged from the Penitentiary.

Mon. 19.—Elder Wm. H. Shearman died in Salt Lake City.

Tues. 20.—In the First District Court, Provo, Eli A. Day was sentenced to one month's imprisonment, for "adultery."

Fri. 23.—Gilbert J. Marchant was discharged from the Penitentiary.

Sun. 25.—The Fifth Ward meeting house, at Logan, Cache Co., was dedicated.

—Sister Elizabeth Haven Barlow, an old and faithful member of the Church, died at Bountiful, Davis Co.

1893.

This year the Temple in Salt Lake City was dedicated and opened for ordinance work; Saltair was built in the Great Salt Lake; About seven thousand people from Utah visited the World's Fair in Chicago, Ill.

January. *Sun. 1.*—A. Johnson was discharged from the Penitentiary.

—Elder Joseph Lee Robinson died at Uintah, Weber Co.

Tues. 3.—Lucy S. Grant, wife of Apostle Heber J. Grant, died in Salt Lake City.

—In the Third District Court, Salt Lake City, Hiram S. Wright was sentenced to Judge Zane to six months' imprisonment, for u. c.

Wed. 4.—Pres. Benjamin Harrison issued a proclamation of amnesty to polygamists, for past offences, but recommended vigorous prosecution against future infractions of the Edmunds law.

Fri. 6.—Elder Thomas Day died at Circleville, Piute Co.

—James Anderson was discharged from the Penitentiary.

Sat. 7.—Jacob P. Altertson and John G. Jørgensen were discharged from the Penitentiary.

Sun. 8.—Andrew Bigler suicided at Mendon, Cache Co.

Wed. 11.—The Old Folks of Salt Lake City were treated to a free entertainment in the Salt Lake Theatre.

Fri. 20.—Benjamin Lewis was killed by an explosion of giant powder at Richmond, Cache Co.

—Eli A. Day was discharged from the Penitentiary.

Sun. 22.—Anton Nelson was discharged from the Penitentiary.

Sat. 28.—The Beehive house, formerly the property of Pres. Brigham Young, was sold at public auction in Salt Lake City.

Mon. 30.—A wind storm did considerable damage at Heber, Wasatch Co.

Tues. 31.—In the Fourth District Court, at Ogden, the cases against the following named individuals, for transgression of the Edmunds law, were dismissed on recommendation of U. S. Attorney Charles S. Varian, who gave as a reason that the evidence in these cases was insuffcient to put the defendants on trial: Levi W. Smith, Thos. Magram, W. E. Richardson, Charles

O'Connor, Wm. O'Connor, Caroline Phillips, Frank J. Sadler, Frank Sadler, Joseph Porter, Frank E. McWilliams, Albert Murdock, James Taylor, Sarah Nelson, Henry Hughes, W. S. Popperton, Orson Smith, Thos. Obray, John Archibald, Wm. Willey, Andrew J. Kershaw, Moroni Marriott, Wilmer H. Branson, Peter C. Geertsen, Wm. R. R. Stowell, Joseph Parry, Daniel F. Thomas, John Stoddard, Søren L. Petersen, B. C. Critchlow, Mark Lindsey, Christopher O. Folkman, Louis Howells, Chas. O. Card, Arthur Farrell, Thos. Leavitt, Peter Hansen, F. W. Christensen, Samuel Watkins, Christina Nielson, S. H. Putnam, Elisha Campbell, John. J. Johnson, Mary Williams, Christian Schneider, Elizabeth Manor, Wm. H. Dopp, Wm. J. Orchard, Mary A. Wheeler, Lars Johnson, Thos. Stirland, Wm. Blair, Peter Christensen, A. F. Randall.

February. *Sun. 5.*—John H. Rumel, jun., died suddenly in Salt Lake City.

Thurs. 9.—The name of South Iona Ward, Bingham Co., Idaho, was changed to Ammon.

Mon. 13.—In the U. S. Congress, Senator Wm. M. Stewart, of Nevada, introduced a bill providing for the refunding, to Geo. Q. Cannon, of $25,000, forfeited on an enormous bond imposed upon him by the Third District Court in 1886, when he was placed under arrest for u.c.

Tues. 14.—The gas and electric light companies of Salt Lake and Ogden consolidated by the incorporation of the Salt Lake & Ogden Gas and Electric Light Company.

Sun. 19.—Gilbert Webb was discharged from the Penitentiary.

Mon. 20.—Thos. H. Bullock was discharged from his third term of imprisonment in the Penitentiary for infraction of the Edmunds law. Frank P. Hadlock was also discharged.

Wed. 22.—Apostle Brigham Young sailed from Liverpool, England, for Utah, leaving Elder Alfred Solomon in charge of the European mission.

Sat. 25.—The Seventies residing in Mexico were organized by Brigham H. Roberts as the 99th quorum of Seventy; Helaman Pratt, John C. Harper, Anson B. Call, Geo. W. Hardy, Dennison E. Harris, Wm. W. Galbraith and Sullivan C. Richardson, presidents. This quorum had previously existed in the St. George Stake.

Mon. 27.—The first consignment of Utah exhibits for the World's Fair was shipped from Salt Lake City.

Tues. 28.—Elder Jens C. A. Weibye died at Manti, Sanpete Co.

March. *Mon. 6.*—In the Fourth District Court at Ogden, Nelson Arave was sentenced by Judge Miner to 60 days' imprisonment, for u. c.

Tues. 7.—In the First District Court, Provo, Josiah Gough was sentenced to six months' imprisonment for "adultery"; he was incarcerated in the Penitentiary April 10th following.

—In the Second District Court, Beaver, Wm. Bullam was sentenced to six months' imprisonment, for u. c. He commenced his term in the Penitentiary on the 11th.

Wed. 8.—In the Fourth District Court,

at Ogden, Wm. H. Watson, of Farmington, was sentenced by Judge Miner to four months' imprisonment in the Penitentiary, for u. c.

Fri. 10.—In the Fourth District Court, at Ogden, the cases against Sidney Stevens, David Eccles and Wm. Lishman, for u. c., were dismissed.

Sun. 26.—Elder Moses Martin died at North Jordan, Salt Lake Co.

—Nicholas H. Groesbeck was discharged from the Penitentiary.

Mon.27.—The corner stone of a new meeting house was laid at Sandy, Salt Lake Co.

Thurs. 30.—Miss Blanche B. Cox, of London, England, a captain of the Salvation Army, lectured in the Tabernacle, Salt Lake City, on the "Mission of the Army."

April. *Sat. 1.*—Nils C. Erickson was discharged from the Penitentiary.

—The Deseret Paper Mill, at the mouth of Big Cottonwood Canyon, Salt Lake Co., was destroyed by fire.

Tues. 4.—The sixty-third annual conference of the Church convened in Salt Lake City, continuing three days.

Thurs. 6. The Salt Lake Temple was dedicated, the prayer being offered by Pres. Wilford Woodruff. The dedicatory services were repeated almost daily till April 24th. Thirty-one meetings were held, which were attended by a total of nearly 75,000 people.

Fri. 7.—John Oberg was discharged from the Penitentiary.

—Caleb W. West was appointed governor of Utah, to succeed Arthur L. Thomas.

Thurs. 20.—Elders Joseph Wood and Reese Morris Harper, Mormon missionaries, laboring in the Indian Territory, were held up by a highwayman and robbed of their watches at Millan Bridge.

Tues. 25.—The Trans-Mississippi Congress convened at Ogden, Weber Co. Delegates from twenty States and Territories were present.

May. *Wed. 3.*—In the Second District Court, Beaver, Charles Harris was sentenced to three months' imprisonment, for u.c.

—Geo. Godfrey, having been pardoned by Pres. Cleveland, was discharged from the Penitentiary.

Thurs. 4.—A public reception was tendered Caleb W. West, the newly appointed governor for Utah, in the Salt Lake Theater, where the oath of office was administered to him by Chief-Justice Charles S. Zane.

Fri. 5.—Bishop Oscar Dunn, of College Ward, Cache Co., was arrested for u.c. and placed under $1,000 bonds.

—Nelson Arave was discharged from the Penitentiary.

Sat. 6.—Joseph L. Rawlins resigned his position as Utah's delegate to Congress and left Washington, D. C., for home. Later, however, he resumed his duties at the Capitol.

—Charles C. Richards, of Ogden, was appointed Territorial secretary for Utah. He entered upon the duties of his office on the 15th. :

Mon. 8.—Castle Gate branch, Emery Co., was organized by Apostle Francis M.

Lyman·· as Castle Gate ·Ward; Wm. T. Lamph, Bishop.

—Nat. M. Brigham was appointed U. S. Marshal for Utah, and Harvey W. Smith, associate justice.

Fri. 19.—Elder John S. Lewis died in Salt Lake City.

Tues. 23.—The Salt Lake Temple was opened for ordinance work, under the immediate direction of the First Presidency —Wilford Woodruff, George Q. Cannon and Joseph F. Smith. The following were the officers: Lorenzo Snow, president; John R. Winder, first assistant; Adolph Madson, second assistant; John Nicholson, chief recorder; Joseph H. Dean, janitor; William H. Salmon, doorkeeper, Zina D. H. Young, president of sisters' department, with Bathsheba W. Smith and Minnie J. Snow, her assistants.

Wed. 24.—Wm. H. Jennings, a prominent business man, committed suicide in Salt Lake City.

Thurs. 25.—In the Fourth District Court, at Ogden, Henry Stander was sentenced by Judge Miner to four months' imprisonment for "adultery".

Sat. 27.—The Wayne Stake of Zion was organized by Apostles Francis M. Lyman and Marriner W. Merrill, with Willis E. Robison as president. The new Stake comprised all of Wayne County, Utah, and that portion of Garfield County lying north and east of Potatoe Valley, known as the Boulder Plateau.

—The Bear River canal system, in Box Elder County, and all the lands lying under it, were sold to Geo. L. Walker, an eastern capitalist.

Wed. 31.—Articles of incorporation of the Mt. Pleasant (Sanpete Co.) Light Company were filed.

June—Apostle Anthon H. Lund succeeded Apostle Brigham Young as president of the European mission. Elder Alfred Solomon had presided temporarily since Apostle Young's departure for America.

Thurs. 1.—Saltair, the new bathing resort, built in the Great Salt Lake, about eighteen miles west of Salt Lake City, was opened to the public.

Sat. 3.—In the Fourth District Court, at Ogden, Henry Whetstone was sentenced by Judge Miner to ninety days' imprisonment in the Penitentiary, for inducing Geo. Craig (a witness in an adultery and u. c. case against John Hopkin) to leave Utah in February, 1893, and not appear before the grand jury.

—Hiram S. Wright was discharged from the Penitentiary.

Sun. 11.—Jesse W. Crosby, a Church veteran, died at Panguitch, Garfield Co.

—August Svendsen, of Spanish Fork, having been pardoned by Pres. Cleveland, was released from the Penitentiary.

Thurs. 15.—The Eureka branch, Juab Co. was organized as a Ward; Peter Loutensock, Bishop.

Sun. 18.—Wm. H. Watson was discharged from the Penitentiary.

Mon. 19.—Patriarch Milo Andrus, a veteran in the Church, died at Oxford, Idaho.

Sun. 25.—The Seventies residing at Salina, Redmond, Aurora and Vermillion were organized by Christian D. Fjeldsted, Brigham H. Roberts and J. Golden Kimball as the 107th quorum of Seventy; Thos. G. Humphries, Hans Jensen, Christian Meyer, Henry N. Hayes, Niels L. Christensen, Wm. E. Mason and Christian J. Mortensen, presidents.

Thurs. 29.—John Broom, owner of the Broom hotel, at Ogden, Weber Co., died.

July. Tues. 4.—Joseph Hancock, who had been a member of the Church since 1830, died at Payson, Utah Co.

Sat. 8.—Geo. A. Mears, an old resident of Salt Lake City, and a friend of the "Mormons", suicided by shooting himself in the head.

Sun. 9.—Eureka, Juab Co., was partly destroyed by fire.

Sat. 15.—After two trials in the Fourth District Court, at Ogden, the case against Wm. Butler, for infractions of the Edmunds law, was dismissed.

Mon. 17.—The Utah Commission, in accordance with Pres. Harrison's amnesty proclamation, ruled that former polygamists, who, since Nov.1, 1890, had not broken the Edmunds law, were entitled to vote at elections.

Tues. 18.—Susan E. Angell, widow of Truman O. Angell, died in Salt Lake City.

—The Utah Commission adopted a resolution advising that amnestied polygamists be allowed to vote.

—Charles Harris was discharged from the Penitentiary.

Mon. 24.—The Raymond Ward, Bingham Co., Idaho, was organized; David R. Sinclair, Bishop.

Tues. 25.—Mrs. Ruth Townsend was accidentally shot and killed, at Wasatch, Salt Lake Co.

Fri. 28.—Patriarch Lemuel Mallory died at Logan, Cache Co.

Sun. 30.—A branch of the Church was organized at South Park, near Marysvale, Wyoming, by Apostle Brigham Young.

August. Mon. 7.—Wm. Bullam and Josiah Gough were discharged from the Penitentiary.

☐ *Thurs. 10.*—Bolivar H. Roberts, Ex-Territorial treasurer, died in Salt Lake City.

Mon. 28.—Pehr A. Bjørklund, of Provo, Utah, died at Helsingborg, Sweden, where he labored as a missionary.

Tues. 29.—The Tabernacle choir and a number of friends (about four-hundred souls altogether) left Salt Lake City on a special train, for Chicago, Ill., whither the choir went to compete in a singing contest at the World's Fair. Presidents Wilford Woodruff, Geo. Q. Cannon and Joseph F. Smith were with the party.

Wed. 30.—Elder John M. Chidester, a member of Zion's Camp, died at Washington, Washington Co.

Thurs. 31.—The Supreme Court of Utah handed down a decision in the Church suits, to the effect that the government, under the escheat clause of the Edmunds-Tucker law of 1887, was entitled to confiscate the Gardo House, the coal lands and the Church farm; but that the Historians' office and the Tithing yard were excluded and legally the

property of the Church. The case was appealed to the U. S. Supreme Court.

September. Fri. 1.—Elder Lyman O. Littlefield, a member of Zion's Camp, died at Smithfield, Cache Co.

—The Tabernacle choir visited the Temple lot at Independence, Jackson Co., Mo.; and in the evening gave a concert in the Auditorium, Kansas City.

Sat. 2.—The Tabernacle choir gave a concert in the Music Hall of the Exposition Buildings, at St. Louis, Mo.

Mon. 4.—The Chamber of Commerce special train left Salt Lake City for the World's Fair.

Tues. 5.—Henry Stander was discharged from the Penitentiary.

—Gov. Caleb W. West and company left Salt Lake City, for the World's Fair, to be present on Utah day, (Sept. 9th.)

—The Sanpete Valley railway was completed to Ephraim, Sanpete Co.

Thurs. 7.—In the Second District Court, Beaver, Wm. E. Jones, of Paragoonah, Iron Co., was sentenced to five months' imprisonment, for "adultery".

Fri. 8.—The Tabernacle choir won the second prize ($1000) at the singing contest at the World's Fair, Chicago, Ill.

—This was Utah day at the World's Fair, Chicago. At Festival Hall, Presidents Wilford Woodruff and Geo. Q. Cannon and Governer Caleb W. West, of Utah, delivered short speeches.

Sat. 9.—The Tabernacle choir gave a concert at the Music Hall in Chicago, and then started for home.

Sun. 10.—The Tabernacle choir, on their homeward journey, sang at Omaha, Neb.

Mon. 11.—In the Second District Court, Beaver, Joseph P. Barton and Stephen S. Barton, both of Paragoonah, Iron Co., were each sentenced to five months' imprisonment, for alleged adultery. They were incarcerated in the Penitentiary Sept. 19th.

—The World's Parliament of Religions, at which the Latter day Saints were denied representation, commenced at Chicago, Ill.

Wed. 13.—The Tabernacle choir returned to Salt Lake City from their visit to Chicago, Ill.

—Elder Newman Bulkley, a member of the Mormon Battalion, died at Springville, Utah Co.

Fri. 15.—Sister Mercy R. Thompson, a veteran Church member, died in the Sixteenth Ward, Salt Lake City.

Mon. 18.—In the Second District Court, Beaver, Fred. W. Cook was sentenced to six months' imprisonment, for "fornication," and Robert B. Dalley to 18 months' for "adultery". Both were incarcerated in the Penitentiary the following day.

Wed. 20.—In the Fourth District Court, at Ogden, Bishop Benjamin M. Lewis, of Logan, was sentenced to six months' imprisonment, for "adultery".

Fri. 22.—Miss Augusta Anderson, a witness in the Oluf Hogan adultery case, was imprisoned in the Penitentiary.

Mon. 25.—On this and the following day, Elder Andrew Jenson, (who was on a special mission in Missouri and other States), copied the old Church record, written by the first Church Historian, John Whitmer.

The old record, after passing through several hands, was now found in the possesion of Geo. Schweich, at Richmond, Ray Co., Mo.

October. Mon. 2.—Augusta Anderson was discharged from the Penitentiary.

Thurs. 5.—A bill providing for the restoration of Church property to the rightful owner was passed in the U. S. House of Representatives. Delegate Joseph L. Rawlins championed the bill in an able manner.

Fri. 6.—The general semi-annual conference of the Church convened in Salt Lake City, continuing three days.

Sat. 7.—Elder John Rowley died at Colonia Pacheco, Chihuahua, Mexico.

Sat. 14.—In the First District Court, Provo, Hans Christensen was sentenced to two months' imprisonment, for u. c.

Mon. 16.—The Twin Groves branch of the Church, Bannock Stake of Zion, Idaho, was organized; Wm. D. Williams, presiding Elder.

Sat. 21.—The U. S. Senate passed a bill, providing for the restoration of Church property, with certain amendments.

Mon. 23.—The U. S. House of Representatives concurred in the Senate amendments to the bill providing for the restoration of Church property.

November.—Discoveries of rich gold bearing ore in the Camp Floyd mining district attracted general attention in Utah.

Tues. 7.—The general election in Utah resulted in the election of 5 Democrats, 5 Republicans and 2 Liberals to the legislative Council, and 8 Democrats, 10 Republicans and 6 Liberals to the House. In Salt Lake City the Independent-Citizens candidates were successful for all the municipal offices except treasurer for which a Liberal was elected. The Independent-Citizens elected ten councilmen and the Liberals five. Robert N. Baskin, Independent Citizens' candidate for mayor, was elected.

Thurs. 9.—The Salt Lake *Tribune* advised the Liberals to disband and divide on national party lines; leading Liberals favored the proposition.

Mon. 13.—In the Fourth District Court, at Ogden, John Hopkin was sentenced by Judge Miner to three months' imprisonment. for u. c.

—Wm. Smith, the last surviving brother of the Prophet Joseph, and once a member of the Council of Twelve Apostles, died at Osterdock, Clayton Co., Iowa.

Thurs. 16.—Bishop Wm. L. N. Allen, of the 21st Ward, Salt Lake City, died.

Wed. 22.—Sister Elizabeth Richards died at Union, Salt Lake Co.

Fri. 24.—In the Fourth District Court, at Ogden, Peter Svendsen was sentenced by Judge Miner to three months' imprisonment in the Penitentiary, for u. c.

—In the First District Court, Provo, Wm. A. Stewart was sentenced to three months' imprisonment, for u. c.

Sun. 26.—Richard Slater, a Church veteran, died at Slaterville, Weber Co. The settlement of Slaterville was originally named in his honor.

Mon. 27.—The Pioneer Electric Power Company was organized, with Geo. Q. Cannon as president.

Wed. 29.—In the Fourth District Court, at Ogden, Wm. Tyril was sentenced by

Judge Miner to three months' imprisonment, for "adultery."

Thurs. 30.—Bishop Levi W. Reed died at North Point, Salt Lake Co.

December. Tues. 5.—In the First District Court, Provo, Joseph F. Parker was sentenced to four months' imprisonment, for u. c.

Wed. 6.—Charles A. Allen was arrested at Beaver, for u. c.

Mon. 11.—Martha Seed Thornley, one of the first converts to "Mormonism" in England, died at Layton, Davis Co.

—In the Fourth District Court, Ogden, Wm. J. Orchard was sentenced to three months' imprisonment, for u. c.

Tues. 12.—Mrs. Lucy Pearson, a native of Sweden, died at Richfield, Sevier Co., 99 years old.

Thurs. 14.—In the Second District Court, at Beaver, Charles A. Allen. of Beaver, was sentenced to four months' imprisonment, for u. c.

—Hans Christensen was discharged from the Penitentiary.

Sun. 17.—The Saints who had settled on the St. Mary's river and tributaries, southeast of Cardston, Alberta. Canada, were organized as the Ætna Ward; Richard Pilling, Bishop.

Mon. 18.—At a convention of the Liberal party, held in the Theatre, Salt Lake City, it was resolved that the party disband.

Tues. 19.—In the First District Court, Provo, Jens L. Bruun, of Richfield, was sentenced by Judge Blackburn to 30 days' imprisonment, for u. c.

Wed. 20.—M. McMillian, of St. Louis, Mo., and E. B. Bronson, of El Paso, Texas, discovered the remains of five prehistoric towns below Eddy, New Mexico.

—In the Fourth District Court, Ogden, John Lutz was sentenced by Judge Miner to six months' imprisonment, for "adultery."

Sun. 24.—The Saints, who had settled on Fish Creek, Alberta, Canada, were organized as Mountain View Ward; Vincent I. Stewart, Bishop.

Mon. 25.—Joseph P. Barton, Stephen S. Barton and Wm. E. Jones were discharged from the Penitentiary.

Tues. 26.—Col. Jesse Carter Little, a Pioneer of 1847, died in Salt Lake City.

Wed. 27.—Martin Allred, of Fairview, Sanpete Co., was arrested on the charge of adultery.

Fri. 29.—Edmund Ellsworth, one of the Utah Pioneers of 1847, died at Showlow, Apache Co., Ariz. He led the first handcart company into Great Salt Lake Valley, in 1856.

Sun. 31.—The new Assembly Hall of the 22nd Ward, Salt Lake City, was dedicated.

1894.

The first settlement of the Saints in Sonora, Mexico, was organized as a Ward. The first Maori Saints, from New Zealand, arrived in Utah. Pres. Cleveland pardoned all polygamists, and restored them to their civil rights.

January. *Tues.* 2.—Don Maguire was selected as Utah's representative at the Midwinter Fair, San Francisco, Cal.

Fri. 5.—Ex Judge John W. Blackburn died at Provo, Utah Co.

Mon. 8.—The thirty-first session of the legislative assembly of Utah met in Salt Lake City and organized by the election of M. A. Breeden as president of the Council and A. B. Emery as speaker of the House.

Tues. 9.—Col. S. A. Merritt was appointed chief justice of Utah; he qualified on the 17th.

Wed. 10.—Wm. Ashworth was arrested at Provo, Utah Co., for u. c., and placed under $300 bonds.

—On report of special Master Bache the Utah Supreme Court ordered certain confiscated Church property valued at $438,174 to be turned over to the First Presidency.

Tues. 16.—Elder Wm. R. Smith, president of the Davis Stake of Zion, died at Centerville, Davis Co.

Wed. 17.—A bill was introduced in the Utah legislature to abolish the Utah Commission; also to create the county of Carbon out of a portion of Emery County.

—*Thurs.* 18.—Jens L. Brunn was discharged from the Penitentiary.

Sat. 20.—Annie K. Smoot, president of the Utah Stake Primary associations, died at Provo, Utah Co.

Sun. 28.—John Hopkin was discharged from the Penitentiary.

February. *Thurs.* 1.—The Saints who had settled on Snake river, near Riverside, Bingham Co., Idaho, were organized as the Grover branch of the Church; W. D. Grover, presiding Elder.

—Elder Thomas Emmet died at Ogden, Weber Co.

Tues. 6.—The legislative Council passed the eight-hour law; it was signed by the governor, Feb. 20th.

Thurs. 8.—Peter Svendsen and Wm. A. Stewart were discharged from the Penitentiary.

Sun. 18.—Fred. W. Cook was discharged from the Penitentiary.

—Elder Walter Herbert ¦ Barton, of Kaysville, Davis Co., died at McComb, Pike Co., Miss., where he labored as a missionary.

Mon. 19.—The House branch of the Utah legislature passed a bill to abolish the Utah Commission.

Tues. 20.—Wm. J. Orchard was discharged from the Penitentiary.

Sat. 24.—In the First District Court, Provo, Parley Young, of Fairview, Sanpete Co., was sentenced to 60 days' imprisonment, for u. c.

—Elder Charles I. Robson, president of the Maricopa Stake of Zion, died at Mesa, Maricopa Co., Ariz.

Mon. 26.—In the First District Court, Provo, Wm. P. Sampson was sentenced to three months' imprisonment and Wm. Ashworth, of Provo, to 50 days', both for u. c.

Tues. 27.—In the First District Court, Provo, Niels Peter Thomson was sentenced to one year's imprisonment, for polygamy.

—Gov. Caleb W. West appointed John T. Caine Territorial auditor and J. N. Whitehead Territorial treasurer.

Wed. 28.—In the First District Court, Frank Greenwell was sentenced to 90 days' imprisonment, for alleged adultery.

March.—Benjamin F. Grouard, once an active Elder in the Church, and one of the first missionaries sent to the Society Islands, died at Santa Ana, Los Angeles Co., Cal.

—Elders John Vetterli and Julius Billeter, jun., were banished from Prussia, where they labored as Latter-day Saint missionaries.

Thurs. 1.—John M. Allen was arrested at Clifton, Garfield Co., for u. c.

Fri. 2.—Elder Isaac Harrison, a member of the Mormon Battalion, died at Sandy, Salt Lake Co.

—Bishop Benjamin M. Lewis was discharged from the Penitentiary.

—The Utah legislature passed bills for bounties on silk and sugar beets.

Sun. 4.—Bishop Carl C. N. Dorius died at Ephraim, Sanpete Co.

Fri. 9.—The Utah legislature passed the bill for a bounty on canaigre root; also the mechanics' lien bill and free library bill. The governor vetoed the free library bill on the 10th.

Sun. 11.—The Saints who had settled on the Bavispe river, Sonora, Mexico, were organized by Apostles Brigham Young, John Henry Smith and George Teasdale as the Oaxaca Ward; Franklin Scott, Bishop.

Mon. 12.—Gov. West vetoed all the bounty bills, and the Utah legislature adjourned.

Wed. 14.—Charles A. Allen was discharged from the Penitentiary.

Thurs. 15.—Nabbie Young Clawson, daughter of Pres. Brigham Young and wife of Spencer Clawson, died in Salt Lake City.

Fri. 16.—Joseph F. Parker was discharged from the Penitentiary.

Fri. 30.—The Salt Lake City council authorized the issue of $800,000 in municipal bonds.

—A two days' discussion between Elder Willard W. Bean and a Campbellite minister was commenced at Sparta, White Co., Tenn. It resulted in victory to "Mormonism."

April. *Sun.* 1.—Elder Jesse Williams Fox, surveyor, one of Utah's early Pioneers and a prominent citizen, died at Bountiful, Davis Co.

Fri. 6.—The 64th annual conference of the Church convened in Salt Lake City, continuing three days.

Sat. 7.—Gov. West ordered out the Utah militia to head off General Kelley's commonwealth army, coming from California.

Sun. 8.—Kelley's commonwealers reached Ogden, 1200 strong, and were met and guarded by the militia. A squad of Salt Lake City police was sent to Ogden to help drive the "army" back. The municipality of Ogden fed the "wanderers."

Mon. 9.—Thos. C. Sharp, one of the main instigators of the murder of Joseph and Hyrum Smith, died at Carthage, Ill.

Wed. 11.—The "Industrial Army" of Kelley's commonwealers marched out of Ogden, boarded a train and were taken eastward.

Tues. 17.—Wm. Ashworth was discharged from the Penitentiary.

Wed. 18.—The Utah "Industrial" army was organized with H. E. Carter as general.

Sat. 21.—John H. Lutz, who had been pardoned by Pres. Cleveland, was released from the Penitentiary.

Wed. 25.—Parley Young was discharged from the Penitentiary.

Fri. 27.—The new Utah Commission organized with Geo. W. Thatcher as president. The other members of the commission consisted of A. G. Norrell, J. R. Letcher, Hoyt Sherman, jun., and E. W. Tatlock.

—The Utah Sugar Company issued bonds to the amount of $400,000.

Sat. 28.—Elder Ransom M. Stevens, president of the Samoan mission, died at Fagalii, Upolu, Samoa.

May.—The first election for the new county of Carbon resulted in Republican success. Price won the county seat.

Mon. 7.—The Utah Commission was permanently organized, with J. R. Letcher as chairman.

Tues. 8.—Robert B. Dalley was discharged from the Penitentiary.

Fri. 11.—Elder Edson Whipple, one of Utah's Pioneers of 1847, died at Colonia Juarez, Chihuahua, Mexico.

—Wm. P. Sampson was discharged from the Penitentiary.

Sat. 12.—General Carter's "Industrials" captured a Union Pacific train at Lehi and proceeded as far as Provo, where the engine was ditched. Gov. West called out the militia, and deputy marshals arrested 27 of the "Industrials," including General Carter, and took them to the Penitentiary.

Sun. 13.—Frank Greenwell was discharged from the Penitentiary.

—The Utah militia returned to Salt Lake City from Provo, and the "Industrial army" broke up.

Thurs. 17.—The Hot Springs' Railroad was completed to Centerville, Davis Co.

Fri. 18.—General Carter and nineteen of his "Industrials" were sent to the Penitentiary for contempt of court, in stealing a Union Pacific railway train.

Sat. 19.—John H. Rumel, an old Pioneer of Utah, died at Farmers Ward, Salt Lake Co.

Mon. 21.—Edward W. Tullidge, one of Utah's literary men, died in Salt Lake City.

—One hundred "Industrials" took possession of a freight train at Thistle Station, Utah Co. Subsequently sixteen of the leaders were arrested.

Wed. 23.—In the Second District Court, Beaver, John M. Allen, of Clifton, Garfield Co., and James A. Smith were each sentenced by Judge Geo. W. Bartch to 60 days' imprisonment, for u. c.

Thurs. 24.—Davis County applied for an injunction to prevent "General" Smith's "Industrial army" from marching through the county.

Fri. 25.—A squad of Salt Lake City police went to Davis County to aid in stopping the "Industrial army." The "army" was halted at the county line.

Sat. 26.—Judge Smith, at Provo, Utah

Co., sentenced 23 "Industrialists" to the Penitentiary.

Tues. 29.—Judge Merritt dissolved the injunction against the "Industrials" crossing the Davis County line.

Thurs. 31.—Elder Samuel F. Lee, one of the Pioneers of Tooele Co., died at Tooele, Tooele Co.

June. *Sat. 1.* — Smith's "Industrial" army marched into Salt Lake City.

Sat. 9.—Elder Francis A. Brown died at Ogden, Weber Co.

Sat. 16—Hirini Whaanga, Mere Whaanga, Apikara Whaanga and four children sailed from Auckland, New Zealand, bound for Utah. These were the first Maori Saints who gathered to Zion. They emigrated in charge of Elders William Douglas, Wesley Gibson and Lars Christian-Rasmussen, returning missionaries.

Fri. 22.—The workers in the Salt Lake Temple and a few of their friends left Salt Lake City on an excursion to Brigham City, Mantua and Willard, Box Elder Co.

July. *Sun.1.*—Salt Lake City railroad employees held a meeting and decided to join in the Pullman strike; the places of strikers were filled with non-union men; all trains were tied up at Ogden.

Mon. 2.—A complete tie-up of all trains by the strike existed; a stage line was established between Salt Lake City and Ogden.

Tues. 3.—A thousand strikers stopped a Union Pacific train at Ogden.

Wed. 4.—Strikers at Ogden overcame the United States marshall and deputies and prevented the running of trains.

Thurs. 5.—No railroad trains entered or left Salt Lake City.

Fri. 6.—Elder George M. Brown died at Colonia Diaz, Chihuahua, Mexico.

—Federal officers in Utah sent a telegram to Attorney General Olney, asking that troops be called out to subdue the strikers.

Sun. 8.—Incendiaries attempted to burn the city of Ogden, Utah. Seven fires were started in a little over an hour and property to the value of $135,000 was destroyed.

—John M. Allen and James A. Smith were discharged from the Penitentiary.

—The Sixteenth Infantry, stationed at Fort Douglas, was ordered out to protect Union Pacific and Southern Pacific trains.

Mon. 9.—The strike in Salt Lake City was broken, and train service was resumed.

Tues. 10.—The Old Folks of Salt Lake County had their annual excursion, this time going to Saltair.

Tues. 17.—The Riverside branch, Bingham Co., Idaho, was organized as the Riverside Ward; Charles Erastus Liljenquist, Bishop.

—The first train from San Francisco, Cal., since the strike was inaugurated, arrived in Salt Lake City.

—President Cleveland signed the Enabling act or Utah Statehood bill.

Wed. 18.—A company was organized to build a railroad from Fairfield station, Utah Co., to Mercur, a mining camp.

Mon. 23.—In the First District Court held at Manti, Sanpete Co., Eliott Hudson was sentenced to 30 days' imprisonment, for "fornication."

August. *Wed. 1.*—Acting - Governor Charles C. Richards issued a proclamation. ordering an election of delegates to the Constitutional Convention, under the Enabling Act.

Thurs. 2.—In the First District Court, Wm. A. Kirkwood was sentenced to 60 days' imprisonment, for "fornication."

Fri. 3.—In the Fourth District Court, at Ogden, John Welch was sentenced by Judge Miner to pay a fine of $25, for u. c.

Mon. 6.—Hon. Harvey W. Smith succeeded Judge James A. Miner on the bench of the Fourth District Court, at Ogden.

Sat. 11.—Utah exhibits at the Midwinter Fair, at San Francisco, Cal., carried off fourteen rewards.

Tues. 14.—John Morgan, one of the first Seven Presidents of the Seventies, died at Preston, Idaho.

Wed. 22.—Elder Peter C. Geertsen died at Huntsville, Weber County.

—Elliott Hudson was discharged from the Penitentiary.

Tues. 28.—The Cannonville Ward, Garfield Co., was divided by Apostle Francis M. Lyman into three Wards, namely Cannonville, Georgetown and Tropic. Wesley W. Willis was appointed Bishop of Cannonville and Geo. W. Johnson Bishop of Georgetown.

Thurs. 30.—Bishop Henry Clegg died at Heber City, Wasatch Co.

Fri. 31.—The Utah Supreme Court appointed John R. Winder Receiver of Church property, in place of Henry W. Lawrence;the new Receiver gave bonds in the sum of $100,000.

—Prof. Theodore B. Lewis succeeded Judge Jacob S. Boreman as Territorial School Commissioner.

September. *Sun. 9.*—Charles David Barnum, one of Utah's oldest Pioneers, died in Salt Lake City.

Tues. 11.—The Republican Territorial convention, at Provo, nominated Frank J. Cannon for Congress.

Thurs. 13.—In the Second District Court, Beaver, James A. Stratton was sentenced to 18 months' imprisonment,for"adultery."

Sat. 15.—The Democratic convention, held in Salt Lake City, nominated Joseph L. Rawlins for Congress.

Tues. 18.—Benjamin Goddard left Auckland, New Zealand, on a special missionary tour to Australia and Tasmania.

—A new oath was framed by the Utah Commission for polygamists.

Thurs. 20.—In the First District Court, Provo, Richard Crowther was sentenced to three months' imprisonment, for "adultery."

Thurs. 27.—Pres. Grover Cleveland issued a proclamation granting pardon and restoring civil rights to all persons who were disfranchised by the anti-polygamy laws, excepting those who had not complied with Pres. Harrison's proclamation of Jan. 4, 1893.

Sat. 29.—A new meeting house, erected by the Elders laboring in the Indian Territory mission, was dedicated in the Massy settlement, Choctaw Nation, Ind. Ter.

October. *Thurs. 4.*—Wm. A. Kirkwood was discharged from the Penitentiary.

—The Territorial Exposition was opened in Salt Lake City, with a grand military display.

Fri. 5.—The general semi-annual conference of the Church commenced in Salt Lake City. It was continued daily till the 7th. In voting for the general authorities of the Church, on the 7th, Edward Stevenson was sustained as one of the First Seven Presidents of Seventies, to fill the vacancy caused by the death of John Morgan.

Sun. 7.—Elder Hyrum Judd, a member of the Mormon Battalion, died at Colonia Juarez, Chihuahua, Mexico.

Tues. 9.—Edward Stevenson was set apart as one of the First Seven Presidents of Seventies.

—In· the First District Court, Provo, Thomas Ogden was sentenced to 100 days' imprisonment, for u. c.

Thurs. 11.—Elder Cyrus H. Wheelock, a Church veteran, died at Mt. Pleasant, Sanpete Co.

—In the First District Court, Provo, Poul Poulson was sentenced to 30 days' imprisonment, for u. c.

Sat. 13.—In the Fourth District Court, Provo, Hyrum G. White was sentenced by Judge Wm. H. King to six months' imprisonment, and John McKellar to a longer term, both for "adultery."

Mon. 22.—Elder Hyrum Carter, of Porterville, Morgan Co., Utah, died in South Carolina, where he labored as a missionary.

Fri. 26.—Elder James Bevan, a member of the Mormon Battalion, died at Tooele, Tooele Co.

November. *Mon. 5.*—Lewis Barney, one of Utah's Pioneers of 1847, died at Mancos, Colo.

Tues. 6.—At the general election in Utah the Republicans elected Frank J. Cannon delegate toCongress. TheRepublicans also elected 60 of the 107 delegates to the constitutional convention.

Fri. 9.—Elder Wm. W. Casto, senior president of the 61st quorum of Seventy and once a member of the Mormon Battalion, died at Big Cottonwood, Salt Lake Co.

Sat. 10.—Poul Poulson was discharged from the Penitentiary.

Wed. 21.—In the First District Court, Provo, David Bigelow, of Wallsburg, was sentenced to 50 days imprisonment, for u. c.

Thurs. 22.—In the First District Court, Provo, Zeb. Barkdull was sentenced to three months' imprisonment, for "fornication."

Tues. 27.—Southern Ute Indians from Colorado invaded southeastern Utah. Gov. Wells asked the Washington authorities to send them back.

Wed. 28.—James A. Stratton was discharged from the Penitentiary.

December. *Mon. 3.*—A delegation of settlers from San Juan County arrived in Salt Lake City, and appealed to the governor for protection against the Utes.

Tues. 4.—In the First District Court, Provo, Magnus Erickson was sentenced to three months' imprisonment, for "adultery;" he was incarcerated in the Penitentiary on the 9th.

Wed. 5.—Richard Crowther was discharged from the Penitentiary.

—Gov. West sent arms and ammunition to the San Juan settlers.

Thurs. 13.—General William Booth, of the Salvation Army, spoke in the Tabernacle, Salt Lake City.

Fri. 14.—As a result of a conference between Gov. West, Col. Tatlock, Colorado officials and the Utes, held at Monticello, Utah, the Indians agreed to return to their reservation.

Fri. 28.—The new City and County building in Salt Lake City was dedicated.

Mon. 31.—Thomas Ogden was discharged from the Penitentiary.

1895.

A State constitution was made and adopted by the constitutional convention, held in Salt Lake City, and every preparation made for Utah's admission into the Union as a State.

January. *Fri. 4.*—A delegation of settlers waited upon Governer West and presented affidavits to the effect that the Ute Indians were committing depredations in San Juan County.

Sat. 5.—Gov. West ordered Captains John Q. Cannon and Geo. W. Gibbs to proceed to the San Juan country and investigate the Indian troubles, caused by the presence of Colorado Utes in the county.

Thurs. 10.—The Board of Education inaugurated compulsory education in Salt Lake City.

—David Bigelow was discharged from the Penitentiary.

Sun. 20.—Elder John W. Turner, ex-sheriff of Utah County, died at Provo, Utah Co.

Fri. 25.—The first direct shipment of Utah flour to the Orient was forwarded from Salt Lake City.

Sat 26.—Niels Peter Thomson, who had been imprisoned since Feb. 27, 1894, serving a sentence for polygamy, was discharged from the Penitentiary.

—Major John H. Gilbert, who, as an employee in the printing office of Egbert Grandon, set the first edition of the Book of Mormon in type, in 1829–1830, died at Palmyra, N. Y.

—Captains Cannon and Gibbs returned to Salt Lake City from the San Juan country and reported on the Ute situation.

Thurs. 31.—The Utah militia organized and elected Henry Page colonel.

February. *Thurs. 7.*—Zeb. Barkdull was discharged from the Penitentiary.

Fri. 8.—Elder John A. Clark, of Farmington, Utah, died at Haifa, Palestine, where he labored as a missionary.

Sun. 10.—The Shelley branch, Bingham Co., Idaho, was organized as the Shelley Ward; John F. Shelley, Bishop.

Wed. 13.—The snow-fall in Sanpete Co. beat the record for twenty years.

Sun. 17.—Magnus Erickson was discharged from the Penitentiary.

Fri. 22.—West Layton Ward, Davis Co., was organized with David E. Layton as Bishop.

Sun. 24.—The Saints, who had settled on an island near Rexburg, Fremont Co., Idaho, were organized as the Island branch of the Church; Geo. Hibbard, presiding Elder.

Mon. 25.—In the First District Court, Ogden, Lorenzo Huish was sentenced by Judge Wm. H. King to 30 days' imprisonment, for u. c.

Wed. 27.—Richard W. Young was appointed brigadier-general of the Utah militia.

Thurs. 28—In the Third District Court, Salt Lake City, Edward Martin was sentenced by Judge Geo. W. Bartch to five months' imprisonment, for "adultery".

March. *Mon. 4.*—Utah's seventh constitutional convention convened in Salt Lake City.

Wed. 6.—Abraham O. Smoot, president of the Utah Stake, died at Provo, Utah Co.

Thurs. 7.—The laying of natural gas pipes was completed to Main Street, Salt Lake City. The next day (8th) the natural gas was turned on and lighted.

Fri. 8.—Prince Namah Imad Namey, of India, visited Salt Lake City.

Wed. 13.—Hyrum G. White was discharged from the Penitentiary.

Fri. 15.—Elder David Mustard died at Treasureton, Bannock Co., Idaho.

Mon. 18.—Womans uffragists appeared in the constitutional convention in Salt Lake City and presented memorials.

Wed. 20.—General Philip St. George Cook, who had charge of the Mormon Battalion during part of its march to California, in 1846-1847, died at Detroit, Mich.

Wed. 27.—Lorenzo Huish was discharged from the Penitentiary.

April. *Wed. 3*—The constitutional convention adopted the preamble and declaration of rights.

Fri. 5.—The sixty-fifth annual conference of the Church convened in Salt Lake City, continuing three days.

—The constitutional convention, after a heated debate of several days, adopted the woman suffrage clause.

Sat. 6.—The Natural History Society of Utah was organized. Its purpose is to institute original researches on the subjects of geology, mineralogy, archæology and biology in all their branches.

Tues. 9.—Bishop Richard S. Gibby died at Provo, Utah Co.

—The first carload of Utah guano was placed on the market.

Wed. 10.—Taxpayers held a mass-meeting in Salt Lake City and recommended the issuance of $300,000 5-per cent ten-year bonds.

Sat. 13.—Several county schools in Utah were closed for lack of funds.

Sun. 14.—The Saints, who had settled between Hyrum and Wellsville, Cache Co., were organized as the Mt. Sterling Ward; Wm. John Hill, Bishop.

Wed. 24.—The constitutional convention voted down the prohibition clause after an exciting debate.

Fri. 26.—Dr. Wm. H. Groves died in Salt Lake City. He left all his real estate, valued at $75,000 or more, for the founding of the Dr. W. H. Groves Latter-day Saints' hospital.

Sun. 28.—The Seventies residing in the

northern part of the Oneida Stake of Zion, Idaho, were organized by Seymour B. Young. Christian D. Fjeldsted and J. Golden Kimball, as the 108th quorum of Seventy. Wm. Thos. Higginson, Jonathan H. Hale and George Michael Smith were set apart as presidents.

May. *Sat. 4.*—John McKellar was discharged from the Penitentiary.

Mon. 6.—The constitutional convention adopted the constitution as a whole. The delegates were banqueted in the evening.

Wed. 8.—Delegates to the constitutional convention signed the constitution, and the convention adjourned *sine die*. The convention had been in session 66 days.

Sat. 11.—Elder Andrew Jenson left Salt Lake City, on a special mission to the different Latter-day Saint missionary fields throughout the world, in the interest of Church history.

Mon. 13.—Prince Francis Joseph, of Battenberg, visited Salt Lake City.

—The Intermountain Woman Suffrage convention convened in Salt Lake City; Susan B. Anthony presided.

Tues. 14. — Marysville Ward, in the Bannock Stake of Zion, Idaho, was organized by Apostle Franklin D. Richards and the Bannock Stake Presidency, with James H. Wilson as Bishop.

Wed. 15.—The great Western silver conference met in the Tabernacle, Salt Lake City; Hon. Thos. G. Merrill, of Montana, chairman.

Fri. 17.—The silver convention effected a permanent organisation under the name of the Bimetalic Union.

Fri. 24.—In the Fourth District Court, Ogden, Ole Sonne was sentenced to three months' imprisonment, for "fornication."

—Sister Ella Adella Moody, who, with her husband, labored as a missionary in Samoa, died at Fagalii, Upolu, Samoa.

June. *Fri. 7.*—Elder Philo Dibble, an aged Church veteran, died at Springville, Utah Co.

Sun. 9. — At a conference, held at Iona, Bingham Co., Idaho, the Bannock Stake of Zion was divided and its western part organized as the Bingham Stake; James E. Steele, president, Robert L. Bybee and Joseph S. Mulliner, counselors.

—The Saints comprising the three Bishops' Wards (Cardston, Ætna and Mountain View) in Alberta, Canada, were organized as the Alberta Stake of Zion; Charles O. Card, president; John A. Woolf and Sterling Williams, counselors.

—The Island branch, Fremont Co., Ida., was organized as a Ward; Geo. Hibbard, Bishop.

Tues. 11.—Elder J. Høglund baptized J. M. Lindeløf and wife (a Swedish family), in the river Neva, St. Petersburg, Russia. This is believed to have been the first baptism performed by divine authority in that country.

Thurs. 20.—The Saints who had settled at Bedford, Uinta Co., Wyo., were organized as a branch of the Church; John B. Thatcher, presiding Elder.

Tues. 25.—Commander in chief General T. G. Lawler arrived in Salt Lake City and was tendered a reception by the local G. A. R. members.

July. *Wed. 3.*—Edward Martin was discharged from the Penitentiary.

Thurs. 11.—The Old Folks of Salt Lake County, on their annual excursion. spent a pleasant day at Pleasant Grove, Utah Co.

Wed. 24.—Pioneer day was celebrated in grand style at Saltair, Salt Lake Co.

Wed. 31.—Elder Eli Bell died at Logan, Cache Co.

August. *Sat. 3.*—Elder Charles Scott Hall, of West Portage, Box Elder Co., died near Mineota, Wood Co., Texas, where he labored as a missionary. His remains were brought home.

Sun. 4.—Elder Miles Hudson Jones, a Church veteran died at Ogden, Weber Co.

Fri. 9.—Elder Peter O. Hansen, the last survivor of the first four Latter-day Saint Elders who introduced the gospel in Scandinavia in 1850, died at Manti, Sanpete Co.

—Ole Sonne was discharged from the Penitentiary.

Sat. 10.—In the Fourth District Court at Ogden, Judge Harvey W. Smith decided that women had a right to vote on the State constitution.

—The school building for the deaf and dumb in Salt Lake City sustained a severe loss by fire.

Sun. 11.—Elder Swen M. Løvendahl died at South Cottonwood, Salt Lake Co.

Mon. 19.—Forty-five buildings were burned at Bingham, Salt Lake Co., involving a loss of $200,000. Many people were rendered homeless.

Wed. 21.—Veterans from the Black Hawk Indian war had a re-union at Spanish Fork, Utah Co.

Thurs. 22.—Bishop John Carson died at Fairfield, Utah Co.

Sun. 25.—The Saints who had settled north of Salem, Fremont Co., Idaho, were organized as the North Salem branch; Heber C. Roylance, presiding Elder.

Tues. 27.—By order of the war department, and in accordance with the enactment of Congress that a star should be added to the national flag for each State admitted to the Union, a new star was added for Utah. This increased the number of the stars in the national emblem to 45.

—A fire in Cedar City, Iron Co., destroyed several buildings; damage, $4,000.

Wed. 28.—A Republican State convention was held in Salt Lake City.

Sat. 31.—The Utah Supreme Court decided that women were not entitled to vote at the November election.

September. *Thurs. 5.*—The Democratic State convention was held at Ogden.

Fri. 6.—Congressman Wm. J. Bryan, of Nebraska, lectured in Salt Lake City, on the silver question.

Sun. 8.—Darby Ward was organized in Fremont County, Idaho (Bannock Stake of Zion), with Emanuel Bagley as Bishop. Leigh Ward, in the same Stake, was organized, with Edwin S. Little as Bishop.

Sat. 14.—A Populist State convention was held in Salt Lake City.

—In the Fourth District Court, Ogden, Samuel K. Obray was sentenced to two years' imprisonment, and Mira Griffith Obray to one month's, both for "adultery";

Charles Bauer was sentenced to four months' imprisonment, for "fornication."

Tues. 17.—Republican women held a monster mass meeting at the Grand opera house, Salt Lake City.

Wed. 18.—Patriarch Robert Wilson died at Oakley, Cassia Co., Idaho.

—In the First District Court. Provo, James Stevenson was sentenced to seven months' imprisonment, for "adultery."

Mon. 30.—Patriarch Geo. W. Brimhall died at Spanish Fork, Utah Co.

October. *Wed. 2.*—The Denver choir, one of the best musical organizations in the West, gave a concert in the Tabernacle, Salt Lake City.

Thurs. 3.—The great Eisteddfod was opened in the Tabernacle, Salt Lake City, continuing three days.

Fri. 4.—The general semi-annual conference of the Church commenced in Salt Lake City, continuing three days.

Sat. 5.—The Republicans in Salt Lake City had the greatest political demonstration ever seen in Utah.

Tues. 8.—Zion's Maori Association, consisting of returned missionaries from New Zealand, Australia and Tasmania, was organized in Salt Lake City; Wm. Paxman, president; Benjamin Goddard, vice-president; Clarence W. Taylor, secretary.

Thurs. 10.—The court house at Ogden, Weber Co., was destroyed by fire.

Mon. 14.—Mira Griffith Obray was discharged from the Penitentiary.

Tues. 15.—Sir Michael Meyendorff, who had been an exile in Siberia, for taking part in the Polish attempt to obtain freedom from Russia, lectured in Salt Lake City, on his personal experience as an exile.

Sun. 27.—Palisade Ward, Bingham Co., Idaho, was organized by James E. Steele and Robert S Bybee, of the Bingham Stake presidency. Robert Oakden was ordained Bishop by Apostle Heber J. Grant, Dec. 14, 1895.

November.—Elder Daniel Jones Stewart, of Adamsville, Beaver Co., died in the Southern States, where he labored as a missionary.

—Elder Samuel E. Woolley succeeded Elder Matthew Noall as president of the Hawaiian mission.

This interesting mission was founded in December, 1850, and its first president was Hiram Clark. who was succeeded by the following Elders: Philip B. Lewis, Aug. 9, 1851; Silas Smith, July, 1855; Henry W. Bigler, *pro tem*, 1851; native Elders, 1858; Walter M. Gibson (without proper appointment), 1861; Ezra T. Benson and Lorenzo Snow (in temporary charge for reorganization purposes), April, 1864; Joseph F. Smith, April, 1864; Alma L. Smith, Oct., 1864; Geo. Nebeker, July, 1865; Fred. A. H. F. Mitchell, 1873; Alma L. Smith, (second term), Feb. 2, 1875; Ward E. Pack, June 20, 1876; Simpson M. Molen, March 20, 1878; Harvey H. Cluff, July 8, 1879; Edward Partridge, July 31, 1882; Enoch Farr, March 14, 1885; Wm. King, May 11, 1887; Ward E. Pack (second term), May 9, 1890; and Matthew Noall, Jan. 5, 1892.

Sat. 2.—Elder Lauritz Larsen died at Spring City, Sanpete Co.

Mon. 4.—Elder Geo. B. Bailey died at Mill Creek, Salt Lake Co.

Tues. 5.—At the general election in Utah, the Republicans elected Congressman Clarence E. Allen, a majority of the legislature, and the entire State ticket. Republicans also elected James Glendinning mayor of Salt Lake City.

Tues. 12.—At the instance and prearrangement of Fish and Game Commissioner A. Milton Musser, the generous fishermen of Utah and Sevier river lakes seined about six thousand pounds of the common fishes (including carp) from those waters; and the railroads forwarded them to Salt Lake City, free of charge, where they were distributed among the poor, through the Bishops, ministers and others, without distinction of class or color, under the supervision of Presiding Bishop Wm. B. Preston.

—Christopher B. Heaton was shot and killed while attempting to capture thieves, near Colonia Pacheco, Chihuahua, Mexico.

Wed. 13.—In the Third District Court, Salt Lake City, John Beck was fined $300 by Judge Wm. H. King, for u. c.

Fri. 15.—Elder Theodore Petersen who had just returned from a mission to Scandinavia, died at Logan, Cache Co.

Mon. 18.—Peter Rauck, one of Utah's early pioneers, died at East Mill Creek, Salt Lake City.

Tues. 19.—Bedford Branch, Uinta Co., Wyoming, was organized as Bedford Ward by Apostle John Henry Smith and others; John B. Thatcher, Bishop.

Thurs. 21..—Patriarch Lorenzo D. Young died in Salt Lake City. He was the last surviving brother of the late President Brigham Young.

Sat. 23.—Judge Harvey W. Smith, of the Fourth Judicial District Court, died at Ogden. Henry H. Rolapp was subsequently appointed his successor in office.

December. *Sun. 1.*—A part of South Hooper Ward, Davis County, was organized as Syracuse Ward; David Cook, Bishop.

Mon. 9.—At a special conference held at Colonia Juarez, Chihuahua, Mexico, the settlements of the Saints in Mexico were organized as the Juarez Stake of Zion by Apostles Francis M. Lyman and George Teasdale; Anthony W. Ivins, president; Henry Eyring and Helaman Pratt, counselors.

—Hiatt Ward, in the Bannock Stake of Zion, Idaho, was organized; Hyrum J. Lucas, Bishop.

Wed. 11.—In the First District Court, Provo, Benjamin Ralphs was sentenced by Judge Wm. H. King to five days' imprisonment for "adultery."

Sat. 14.—Sister Mary Loretta P. Teasdale, wife of Apostle George Teasdale, died at Colonia Juarez, Mexico.

—Elder Joseph M. Watson died in Salt Lake City.

Sun. 15.—East Jordan Ward, Salt Lake Co., was organized by Apostle Abraham H. Cannon and the Salt Lake Stake presidency, with Hyrum Goff as Bishop. The Saints thus organized had formerly belonged to West Jordan Ward.

Fri. 20.—Elder Henry Talbot, one of the first converts to "Mormonism" in South Africa, died at Layton, Davis Co.

Sat. 21.—Bishop George Knight died at Croyden, Morgan Co.

Sun. 22.—A branch of the Church was organized at Lima, Beaverhead Co., Montana; Daniel Clark, presiding Elder.

1896.

Utah was admitted into the Union as a State. A number of new settlements inhabited by Saints in Idaho were organized as Wards.

January. *Wed. 1.*—Elder Joseph Lawson died at Ogden, Weber Co.

—Charles Bauer was discharged from the Penitentiary.

Fri. 3.—Elder Hanmer Magleby died at Monroe, Sevier Co.

Sat. 4.—Pres. Grover Cleveland signed the proclamation which admitted Utah into the sisterhood of States. The occasion was honored by grand celebrations in Salt Lake City and other places in the new State. Geo. M. Cannon was chosen president of the State Senate and Presley Denny speaker of the lower house.

Mon. 6.—The State officers were installed. Great crowds gathered in Salt Lake City to witness the procession and attend the ceremonies. The State legislature convened.

Fri. 17.—Elder Elijah Mayhew died at Pleasant Grove, Utah Co.

Sun. 19.—Elder John Telford died at Richmond, Cache Co.

Tues.21.—Frank J. Cannon and Arthur Brown were elected United States senators from Utah, by the State legislature.

Wed. 22.—The Old Folks of Salt Lake City were entertained at the Theatre.

Fri.24.—James Stevenson was released from the Penitentiary, having been pardoned by Pres. Cleveland.

Mon. 27.—Senators Cannon and Brown were sworn in as Utah's first senators in the U. S. Congress.

Fri. 31.—Sarah Thompson Phelps, relict of Patriarch Morris Phelps, died at Mesa, Ariz.

February. *Fri. 9.*—The Stake Tabernacle at Brigham City, Box Elder Co., was destroyed by fire.

Wed. 12.—Elder Geo. Wm. Ingram died at Mesa, Ariz.

Fri. 14.—Bishop Henry Tingey died at Brigham City, Box Elder Co.

Wed. 19.—Bishop Edwin Lucius Whiting died at Mapleton, Utah Co.

Thurs. 27.—In Judge Higgins' court, at Beaver, the long pending indictment against John M. Higbee, for alleged participation in the Mountain Meadow massacre, was dismissed.

March. *Wed. 4.*—Almera Smith Barton, a widow of the Prophet Joseph Smith, died at Parowan, Iron Co.

Mon. 16.—Benjamin Ralphs was discharged from the Penitentiary.

Sun. 22.— Crescent branch (formerly called Dry Creek), of the Draper Ward,

Salt Lake Co., was organized as Crescent Ward; James P. Jensen, Bishop.

Mon. 23.—The Saints who had settled on Little Wood river, Blain Co., Idaho, were organized as a Ward by Apostle Francis M. Lyman; Geo. S. Harris, Bishop.

—Moreland Ward, Bingham Co., Idaho, was organized by Apostle John H. Smith and the Bannock Stake presidency, with Hans Peter Christiansen as Bishop. On the same occasion the Saints residing at Blackfoot, Bingham Co., Idaho, were organized as Blackfoot Ward; Edwin Watson. Bishop.

Tues. 24.—Patriarch Jacob Weiler, one of the Utah Pioneers of 1847, died in Salt Lake City.

Fri. 27.—Jane Wells Cooper Hanks, relict of Ebenezer Hanks, and an attache of the Mormon Battalion, died at Parowan, Iron Co.

April. *Fri. 3.*—A reunion of Australasian missionaries and other Saints was held in Salt Lake City by Zion's Maori Association.

Sat. 4.—The sixty-sixth annual conference of the Church convened in Salt Lake City; it was continued for three days. In voting for the general Church authorities, on the 6th, Charles W. Penrose was sustained as an assistant Church historian; Moses Thatcher, was not upheld as one of the Twelve, because of his refusal to sign a manifesto issued by the general authorities of the Church to the Saints, in which the leading men of the Church were requested to seek counsel before accepting political offices which would interfere with their ecclesiastical duties.

Mon. 6.—Edward Dalton, a member of the Mormon Battalion, died at Parowan, Iron Co.

Mon. 13.—The Tabernacle choir left Salt Lake City on a pleasure trip to California, having been invited to sing in San Francisco, and other cities of the Golden Gate.

—Patriarch Wm. Derby Johnson died at Colonia Diaz, Mexico.

Tues. 14.—The Tabernacle choir gave an evening concert at Oakland, Cal., and the next night the programme was repeated in San Francisco.

Sun. 19.—The Tabernacle choir gave a sacred concert in San Francisco, Cal.

Mon. 20.—The Tabernacle choir gave a concert at San Jose, Cal., and on Tuesday evening they gave their last concert in California, in Sacramento.

Thurs. 23.—The Tabernacle choir returned to Salt Lake City from their visit to California.

Sun. 26.—Bishop Elmer Taylor died at Juab, Juab Co.

Tues. 28.—Susan A. Stringam died in Salt Lake City.

May. *Wed. 20.*—The dead body of a woman was found in the basement of the Scandinavian Methodist church, Salt Lake City, which subsequently led to the discovery of at least two murders, alleged to have been committed by Rev. Francis Herman, the pastor of the Church, who, however, had disappeared.

—The Rio Grande Western Ry. was completed to Richfield, Sevier Co.

Tues. 26.—Geo. Ramsden, a gentleman long and favorably known in connection with Latter-day Saint emigration from Europe, died at Liverpool, England.

Fri. 29.—The Saints residing in the so-called Basin, Davis Co., were organized as Clinton Ward; Orlando Hadlock, Bishop.

Sat. 30.—Israel Evans, who had served in the Mormon Battalion, died at Lehi, Utah Co.

Sun. 31.—The Cannon Ward, Salt Lake Co., was organized by Geo. Q. Cannon, Apostle Abraham H. Cannon, and the Stake presidency; Lewis M. Cannon, Bishop.

June.—Fish and Game Commissioner A. Milton Musser was succeeded in office by Warden John Sharp. During the long period Com. Musser served in that capacity he introduced and planted in the public waters of Utah, practically without cost to the Territory, over eleven millions of choice fishes, which were brought from the Potomac, Delaware, Missouri, Mississippi and Illinois rivers, and from Lakes Michigan and Erie. They consisted of white fish, black bass, sunfish, shad, eel, perch, brook trout, crappie, rainbow trout, lake trout, scale, mirror and leather carp, catfish, and gold and silver fish.

Mon. 1.—The first number of *De Ster* (The Star), a monthly periodical, was published in Rotterdam, Holland, as the missionary organ of the Church, in the Dutch language.

Thurs. 4.—A branch of the Church was organized in Chicago, Ill., with Lars F. Søderlund as president. This was the first branch of the Church ever organized in that city.

Fri. 5.—A grand reunion of Pacific Islands or Polynesian missionaries was held at Calder's Park, near Salt Lake City.

Sat. 6.—The Saints who had settled a few miles west of Cardston, Alberta, Canada, were organized as the Leavitt branch.

Sun. 7.—Warren Ward, Weber Co., was organized by the Weber Stake presidency; Wm. L. Stewart, Bishop.

Tues. 9.—Patriarch Ephraim K. Hanks, a Church veteran, and a member of the Mormon Battalion, died at his home, on Pleasant Creek, Wayne Co.

Mon. 22.—The board of county commissioners divided Salt Lake City into 52 voting precincts, and the county outside of the city into 35 voting precincts—87 in all.

—Wm. Carter, one of the Utah Pioneers of 1847, died at St. George, Washington Co.

—Frank Allen, a prominent young man of Taylor, Ariz., was murdered by white men, on the Navajo Indian reservation, Colo. Parts of his body were recovered by friends, Aug. 2nd.

July.—Heavy floods did great damage in Utah this month.

Thurs. 2.—Immense crowds gathered in Salt Lake City to witness a midsummer carnival, which was kept up three days.

Mon. 6.—Elder Andrew Jenson, on his special mission around the world, arrived at Jerusalem, Palestine.

Thurs. 16.—The Old Folks of Salt Lake County enjoyed a pleasant excursion to Ogden, where they were royally treated by the citizens.

Sun. 19.—Apostle Abraham Hoagland Cannon died in Salt Lake City.

Thurs. 23.—Elder Rulon S. Wells, with Joseph W. McMurrin and Edwin F. Parry as counselors, succeeded Apostle Anthon H. Lund in the presidency of the European mission.

Fri. 24.—Elder George Mayer, a Church veteran, died at Spanish Fork, Utah Co.

—Dr. J. M. Benedict died in Salt Lake City.

Sun. 26.—Morgan Henry Merrill, counselor in the St. Joseph Stake presidency, died at Thatcher, Graham Co., Ariz.

August. *Wed. 5.*—Sister Margaret M. Foutz, a survivor of the Haun's Mill massacre, died at Pleasant Grove, Utah Co.

Sat. 8.—Elder Wilford E. Cragun died at North Ogden, Weber Co.

Sun. 9.—Gray Ward, Bingham County, Idaho, was organized by Robert S. Bybee, of the Bingham Stake presidency. Geo. H. Muir was ordained Bishop by Apostle John H. Smith, Sept. 11, 1897.

Tues. 11.—The Arcadia branch of the Church, in the Bannock Stake of Zion, Idaho, was organized; M. Joseph Kerr, president.

Thurs. 13.—Presidents Wilford Woodruff and Geo. Q. Cannon, with their wives, left Salt Lake City on a visit to Oregon and California. They returned Sept. 16th.

Sun. 16.—Twin Groves branch, Fremont County, Idaho, was organized as a Ward; Wm. D. Williams, Bishop.

Wed. 19.—Elder Andrew Bjørkmand, of Salt Lake City, Utah, died at Solfvarbo, Kopparberg's, Læn, Sweden, where he labored as a missionary.

Sun. 23.—The Sugar House Ward, Salt Lake Co., was divided, and a new Ward called Forest Dale was organized out of its southwestern part; James Jensen, Bishop.

Tues. 25.—Sister Ellen Spencer Clawson, wife of Bishop Hiram B. Clawson, died in Salt Lake City.

Fri. 28.—Patriarch Hiram Mace, a Church veteran, died at Fillmore, Millard Co.

Mon. 31.—Members of the Tabernacle choir, Knights of Pythias band and friends (about four hundred persons altogether) left Salt Lake City on a special train for Denver, Colo., to participate in the Great Western Eisteddfod; they arrived in Denver the next day.

September.—Elder John J. Tanner, a member of Zion's Camp, died at South Cottonwood, Salt Lake Co.

—Elder Ezra F. Richards succeeded Elder Wm. Gardner as president of the Australasian Mission:

This mission, which included Australia, New Zealand, Tasmania and some smaller islands, was opened in 1851, and John Murdock was the first president. He was succeeded in the presidency by the following Elders: Charles W. Wandell, June 2, 1852; Augustus Farnham, April, 1853; Absalom P. Dowdle, May, 1856; Andrew J. Stewart June 7, 1857; Thomas Ford, May 30, 1858; Wm. Broadbent, 1863; Robert Beauchamp 1867; Wm. Geddes, 1874: Job Welling, October, 1875; Isaac Groo, July 29, 1876

Fred J. May and Thos. A. Shreeve, August, 1878; Elijah F. Pearce, Dec. 25, 1878; George Batt, 1880; Wm. M. Bromley, Jan. 20, 1881; Wm. T. Stewart, July 17, 1883; Wm. Paxman, May 25, 1886; Angus F. Wright, Aug. 12, 1889; John S. Bingham, Oct. 6, 1890; Wm. T. Stewart (second term), Sept. 13. 1891, and William Gardner, Dec. 30, 1893.

Tues. 1.—Fred. H. Auerbach, a prominent merchant of Salt Lake City, died suddenly in New York.

—The Great Western Eisteddfod commenced at Denver, Colo. The Tabernacle choir, under the direction of Prof. Evan Stephens, and the Knights of Pythias band, under the leadership of Prof. Anton Pedersen, all of Salt Lake City, Utah, competed very successfully for the prizes awarded the best performers. The Eisteddfod continued its sessions four days.

Sun. 6.—The Tabernacle choir and their friends returned to Salt Lake City from their visit to Denver.

Wed. 9.—Elder Oscar O. Stoddard, a Church veteran, died at West Porterville, Morgan Co.

Sat. 12.—Elder Thos. Rowberry died at Rexburg, Idaho.

Mon. 14.—Eleanor Snow, wife of Apostle Lorenzo Snow, died at Brigham City, Box Elder Co.

—Elder Daniel F. Miller succeeded Elder Frank Cutler as president of the Society Islands mission.

This mission, which includes the Society, the Tuamotu and the Austral Islands, and is the oldest Latter-day Saint mission in Polynesia, was opened in 1844. Noah Rogers was the first president. He was succeeded by Addison Pratt in July, 1845, and he in turn by Benjamin F. Grouard, in March, 1847. Addison Pratt, on his return from America, in 1850, presided a second time. After the banishment of the American Elders by the French, in 1852, native Elders kept up more or less missionary work for forty years. The mission was reopened by two Elders from Zion (Joseph W. Damron, and Wm. A. Seegmiller), in January, 1892, and Joseph W. Damron, presided. He was succeeded by James L. Brown, in June, 1892, who was succeeded by Elder Damron, July 1, 1893. Frank Cutler succeeded Elder Damron as president, May 11, 1895.

Mon. 21.—Elder Warren S. Snow died at Manti, Sanpete Co.

Wed. 23.—Miguel Ahumada, governor, and Joaquin Cortezar, secretary, of the State of Chihuahua, Mexico, arrived at Colonia Diaz, accompanied by other leading officials of the State, and attended the opening of the Third Annual Exposition of Colonia Diaz.

October. *Fri. 2.*—Elder Samuel W. Richards and other Utah Elders visited the hill Cumorah, State of New York.

Sun. 4.—The general semi-annual conference of the Church was commenced in Salt Lake City, continuing till Oct. 6th.

Thurs. 8.—The Sixteenth Infantry, U.S. army, which had been stationed at Fort Douglas for some time, left for Fort Sherman.

Mon. 12.—Bishop Robert Dansie died at Herriman, Salt Lake Co.

Thurs. 15.—The first company of the Twenty-fourth U. S. Infantry (colored troops) arrived at Fort Douglas. They were ordered to take the place of the Sixteenth, which had left. The bulk of the troops arrived on the 22nd and 23d.

Sun. 18.—Patriarch John Stock died at Fish Haven, Bear Lake Co. Idaho.

November. *Tues. 3.*—At the general election in Utah, the Democrats elected most of their candidates. In the national election Wm. McKinley, Republican, was elected President of the United States.

Wed. 4.—Patriarch John Brown, one of the Pioneers of 1847, died at Pleasant Grove, Utah Co.

Sat. 14.—Lodi branch of the Church, Bannock Stake of Zion, Idaho, was organized with Hyrum Cunningham as presiding Elder.

Sun. 15.—Sister Helen Mar Whitney, relict of Pioneer Horace K. Whitney, died in Salt Lake City.

Wed. 18.—Eli H. Murray, ex-governor of Utah, died at Bowling Green, Kentucky.

Thurs. 19.—At a council of the Apostles, held in Salt Lake City, Moses Thatcher was dropped from the council of Twelve Apostles.

Mon. 23.—The Leavitt branch, in Alberta, Canada, was organized as a Ward; Frank Leavitt, Bishop.

Tues. 24.—Elder Henry Howell died at Fish Haven, Bear Lake Co., Idaho.

Fri. 27.—Elder Wm. S. Muir died at West Bountiful, Davis Co.

December. *Tues. 1.* — Elder Edward Phillips died at Kaysville, Davis Co.

Wed. 2.—Geo. Pierce Billings, a Pioneer of 1847, died at Manti, Sanpete Co.

Fri. 11.—Gov. Drake, of Iowa, arrived in Salt Lake City on a visit.

Mon. 14.—Tilden Ward was organized in Bingham County, Idaho, by Apostle John H. Smith and the Bingham Stake presidency; Geo. Y. Pugmire, Bishop.

Fri. 25.—Edward J. Wood succeeded Orlando Barrus, as president of the Samoan mission. This mission was founded in 1888 by Elder Joseph H. Dean, who was its first president. He was succeeded by the following Elders: Wm. O. Lee, August 16., 1890; Geo. E. Browning, Feb. 4., 1892; Ransom M. Stevens, Nov. 8., 1893; Thomas H. Hilton, May 17., 1894; John W. Beck, March 27., 1895; Orlando Barrus, April 22., 1896.

Mon. 28.—The mission house at Fagalii, near Apia, Samoa, was attacked by rebel natives, who destroyed considerable missionary property.

1897.

Utah celebrated the 50th anniversary of the arrival of the Pioneers in Great Salt Lake Valley.

January. *Fri. 1.*—Elder Peter Loutensock succeeded Elder Geo. C. Naegle as president of the Swiss and German mission.

This mission, which originally was known as the Swiss and Italian mission, was opened by Apostle Lorenzo Snow and fellow-laborers in 1850. After him the following Elders presided over the mission: Thos. B. H. Stenhouse from 1851; Daniel Tyler, Oct. 1., 1854; John L. Smith, Jan., 1856; Jabez Woodard, Oct., 1857;John L. Smith (second term) Jan. 24, 1861; Paul A. Schettler pro *tem.* Jan., 1864; Wm. W. Riter, 1864; W. P. Nebeker, 1865; Joseph S. Horne, May, 1867; Karl G. Maeser,June, 1868; Edward Schoenfeld, July, 1870; John Huber, June, 1872; John W. Stucki, June, 1874; Joseph S. Horne (second term) June, 1876; Henry Flamm, Oct., 1877; Serge L. Ballif, May, 1879; John Alder, May, 1881; Peter F. Goss, April 4, 1882; John Q. Cannon, Aug. 21., 1883; Fred W. Schoenfeld, May 16, 1884;John U.Stucki (second term), May 19., 1888; Theodore Brandley, Sept. 1., 1890; John Jacob Scharer, Sept. 15.,1891 ; J. H. Stoker, Feb. 7.,1894; and Geo. C.Naegle, April 28., 1894.

Sun. 3.—A branch of the Church was organized in Denver, Colo., where the headquarters of the Colorado mission, recently opened, were located.

Tues. 5.—Thomas Woolsey, a Pioneer of 1847, died at Kanosh, Willard Co.

Suu. 10.—Elder John P. Chidester died at St. George, Washington Co.

Mon. 11.—The first session of the Utah State legislature convened in Salt Lake City and organized by electing Aquilla Nebeker president of the State Senate, and John N. Perkins speaker of the House.

—The Seventies residing in the 22nd and 23rd Wards, Salt Lake City, and the adjoining Centre Ward, were organized as the 109th quorum of Seventy; Andrew Kimball, Matthew Noall, Henry Gardner, James T. Flashman, James F. Smith and Frederick Beesley, presidents. Later, Joseph Anderson was chosen as the seventh president.

Tues. 12.—Governor Wells' message was read to the State legislature.

Sat. 16.—At the close of a conference, Andrew Kimball and other Elders were assaulted and mobbed in Clay Co., Arkansas.

Tues. 19.—The first ballot for United States senator in the Utah legislature resulted in a draw. The chief candidates were Joseph L. Rawlins, Moses Thatcher and Henry P. Henderson.

Fri. 22.—A branch of the Church was organized by Apostle John W. Taylor at Pueblo, Colo.; John I. Hart, president.

Tues. 26.—The Seventies residing in the 4th, 5th, 6th and 7th Wards, Salt Lake City, and the adjoining Cannon Ward, were organized as the 110th quorum of Seventy; James Il. Anderson and Alexander Burt, presidents. Later, Archibald Freebairn, Carl August Ek, Hugh Watson, Robert Sherwood and Hugh J. Cannon were chosen as presidents.

Wed. 27.—Elder Edward Stevenson, one of the First Seven Presidents of Seventies; died in Salt Lake City.

Thurs. 28.—Sister Celia M. Hunt, relict of Capt. Jefferson Hunt, died at San Bernardino, Cal.

Sat. 30.—Bishop Jonah Evans died at Samaria, Idaho.

—The first Latter-day Saint Mutual Improvement Association in Tasmania was organized at Launceston.

February. *Wed. 3.*—After much balloting in the Utah legislature, Jos. L.

Rawlins was elected U. S. senator from Utah.

Mon. 8.—Elder John T. Rich died at Brigham City, Box Elder Co.

Mon. 15.—Elder Stephen B. Rose, a Church veteran, died at Pleasant Grove, Utah Co.

Wed. 17.—The First Presidency of the Church addressed an epistle to the Maori Saints in New Zealand.

—At a reception given at the home of Senator Jos. L. Rawlins, Gov. Heber M. Wells proposed to the legislature to place a statue of Pres. Brigham Young in the capitol, Washington, D. C.

Sun. 21.—The Seventies residing at Scipio, Holden, and Oak City, Millard Co., were organized as the 111th quorum of Seventy; Thomas Memmott, Henry Roper, Frederick Wasden, Sidney Teeples, John Peter Olsen, Andrew Stephenson, and John C. Poulson, presidents.

Wed. 24.—Bishop Wm. E. Jones died at Paragoonah, Iron Co.

Fri. 26.—Orlando Fish Mead, a member of the Mormon Battalion, died at Price, Carbon Co.

March. *Mon 1.*—The ninetieth anniversary of Pres. Wilford Woodruff's birthday was celebrated with impressive and interesting services in the Tabernacle, Salt Lake City, and was generally observed throughout the Church.

—Patriarch Charles N. Smith died at Monroe, Sevier Co.

Thurs. 4.—The inauguration of Wm. McKinley, as president of the United States, was celebrated by Republicans in Utah.

Sat. 6.—Brigham Young, jun., was appointed director-general of the Pioneer jubilee.

Thurs. 11. — Patriarch Martin Heiner died at Morgan City, Morgan Co.

Sun. 21.—Sister Elizabeth D. L. Noall, recently returned with her husband from a mission to Hawaii, died in Salt Lake City. She was the wife of Elder Matthew Noall.

Mon. 22.—The new Tabernacle at Brigham City, Box Elder Co., was dedicated.

April. *Sat. 3.*—Elder James T. Snarr died in Salt Lake City, Utah.

—Prof. James E. Talmage resigned his position as president of the Utah University; and Prof. Joseph T. Kingsbury was appointed his successor.

Sun. 4.—The 67th annual conference of the Church convened in Salt Lake City. It continued till the 6th.

Mon. 5.—Elder Samuel Keele died at Panaca, Lincoln Co., Nevada.

Tues. 6.—Madam Mountford, a native of Jerusalem, Palestine, lectured in the Tabernacle, Salt Lake City, on Village Life in Palestine. The next night she lectured at the same place on The Beduins of the Desert, and on Thursday night on The Life of Jacob. Her lectures were interesting and instructive.

Wed. 7.—Elder Wm. L. Webster died at Franklin, Oneida Co., Idaho.

Fri. 9.—Elder Nathan T. Porter, a Church veteran, died at Centerville, Davis Co.

Tues. 13.—Elder Samuel Wagstaff died at American Fork, Utah Co.

Wed. 14.—Samuel K. Obray, who was serving a two years' sentence in the Penitentiary, was released, having been pardoned by Pres. Cleveland.

Tues. 20.—Elder Israel Ivins died at St. George, Washington Co.

Tues. 27.—Patriarch Joseph Horne, a prominent churchman, died in Salt Lake City.

May. Sun. 16.—A branch of the Church was organized at Diamondville, Uinta Co., Wyo.; Samuel Kiddy, presiding Elder.

Sun. 23.—Mammoth branch, Tintic Valley, Juab Co., was organized as Mammoth Ward by Presidents Joseph F. Smith and Wm. Paxman; Geo. Hales, Bishop.

Sun. 30.—At the Wayne Stake quarterly conference, held at Loa, Wayne Co., the 112th quorum of Seventy was organized by Apostle Francis M. Lyman and Elder J. Golden Kimball; Walter H. Jeffery, Joseph Eckersley, John H. Petersen, James P. Anderson, Moroni Lazenby and Urban Van Stewart, presidents. Sidney A. Hanks was subsequently set apart as the seventh president.

June. Fri. 4.—Elder Andrew Jenson returned to Salt Lake City from his special mission, after two years' absence, during which time he had circumnavigated the globe, traveled about 60,000 miles, and visited British Columbia, Hawaii, Fiji, Samoa, Tonga, New Zealand, the Society Islands, the Tuamotu group, Australia, Ceylon, Egypt, Syria, Palestine, Italy, France, Great Britain, Denmark, Norway, Sweden, Germany, Switzerland, Holland, etc., in the interest of Church history.

Sun. 6.—A branch of the Church was organized at Independence, Jackson Co.,Mo., by Elders Bines W. Dixon and Brigham Fielding Duffin, with Richard Preator as president and Sunday school superintendent. This was the first branch established at Independence since the expulsion of the Saints from Jackson County in 1833.

Tues. 15.—Elder Erick Peterson died at Levan, Juab Co.

Tues. 22.—The Old Folks of Salt Lake County and visitors from the north and south were royally entertained in Salt Lake City. A visit was made to Fort Douglas, where Col. Kent addressed the veterans.

Mon. 28.—Elder Jens Hansen died from the effects of an accident at Spanish Fork, Utah Co.

July. Thurs. 1.—Wm. Jennings Bryan, the great American silver champion, arrived in Salt Lake City on a visit. He addressed an immense crowd in the Theatre in the evening.

—The corner stone of the BrighamYoung Pioneer monument, in Salt Lake City, was laid with appropriate ceremonies.

Fri.9.—Elder Theodore McKean died in Salt Lake City.

Wed. 14.—The ninth session of theTrans-Mississippi Congress was opened in the Assembly Hall, Salt Lake City. It continued its meetings for four days, with Wm. J. Bryan as president. Considerable business of importance was transacted.

Thurs. 15.—The first announcement of rich gold strikes in Klondike, Alaska, caused great excitement in Salt Lake City and throughout the country.

Mon. 19.—The second annual reunion of Polynesian missionaries was held at the Lagoon, at Farmington, Davis Co.

Tues. 20.—The Pioneer jubilee festivities were commenced in Salt Lake City. After a grand parade the Pioneer monument, surmounted by a bronze statue of Brigham Young, was dedicated by Pres. Wilford Woodruff, and a reception was tendered surviving Pioneers in the Tabernacle, where they were decorated with golden badges.

Wed. 21.—The Pioneer festivities were continued by a magnificent parade, illustrating Utah's advancement in fifty years.

Thurs. 22.—In the continuation of the Pioneer celebration in Salt Lake City, the Sunday School children parade was the predominant feature of the day. In the evening the gorgeous illuminated parade of "Great Salt Lake, Real and Fanciful," took place. Main Street was a solid mass of moving light, while the electrical decorations were magnificent. The night crowd was considered the greatest ever witnessed in Salt Lake City.

Fri. 23.—The Parade of the Counties was the distinguishing feature of the Pioneer jubilee this day. All the counties of Utah were represented by floats, showing their resources. A children's concert was given in the evening.

Sat. 24.—The 50th anniversary of the entrance of the Pioneers into Great Salt Lake Valley was commemorated in Salt Lake City by the greatest parade ever seen in western America. The parade included all the features of the four previous parades, besides the Pioneers in line, United States troops and the entire National Guard of Utah. At 8 p. m. a great display of fireworks on Capitol Hill brought the grand celebration to a close.

Sun. 25.—Memorial services in honor of the deceased Pioneers were held in the Tabernacle, Salt Lake City.

Mon. 26.—At the Oneida Stake quarterly conference, held at Marsh Centre Ward, Elders Lewis S. Pond, Thos. Preston, Denmark Jenson, George Z. Lamb, Gaston L. Braby and James R. Smurthwaite were called to open up a mission in the States of Oregon, Washington and Idaho. Elders Pond and Preston were sent to Boise City, Idaho; Elders Jenson and Lamb to Baker City, Oregon; and Elders Braby and Smurthwaite to Walla Walla, Washington. The mission was named "The Northwestern States Mission," and, agreeable to instructions from the First Presidency, it was placed under the direction of the Oneida Stake presidency.

August. Fri. 13.—After a long investigation before the High Council of the Salt Lake Stake of Zion, Moses Thatcher submitted to the decision of the council, and thus retained his standing in the Church.

Mon. 16.—Chapin Ward (Bannock Stake of Zion), Fremont County, Idaho, was organized; Ebenezer Beesley, Bishop.

Thurs. 26.—Elder Parley P. Pratt, son of Apostle Parley P. Pratt, died in Salt Lake City.

Sun. 29.—Centerfield Ward, formerly constituting a part of the Gunnison Ward,

Sanpete County, was organized by Apostle Anthon H. Lund and the Sanpete Stake presidency; Andrew Christian Fjeldsted, Bishop; Sylvester Whiting and Charles Henry Embley, counselors.

September. *Sun. 5.*—Freedom Ward, which formerly constituted a part of Moroni Ward, Sanpete Co., was organized by Apostle Anthon H. Lund and the Sanpete Stake presidency; Martin V. Taylor, Bishop; James W. Lowry and Stephen S. Ballinger, counselors.

—While two Latter-day Saint Elders were holding a meeting at the house of W. R. Moreland, on Dry Fork of Little Sinking river, Ky., Mr. Moreland was shot and severely wounded by Cal. James, a mobber, who came to disturb the meeting.

Sat. 11.—Methodist ministers, in conference assembled, declared that Statehood had been a detriment to Utah and that polygamy was still practiced by the "Mormons."

Sun. 12.—Bishop Moroni F. Brown, of Ogden, Weber Co., died at San Diego, Cal.

Sun. 19.—At a meeting held at Rexburg, Fremont Co., Idaho, the 113th quorum of Seventy was organized by Seymour B. Young and Christian D. Fieldsted, with Judson L. Stoddard as senior president. The next day, at a meeting held at Parker, Joshua Homer and Henry A. Grover were set apart as presidents.

Wed. 22.—Elder Janne M. Sjødahl had an audience with King Oscar of Sweden, at Stockholm; and his majesty was presented with a copy of the Book of Mormon in an onyx box, as a present from Scandinavians in Utah.

October. *Mon. 4.* — The 68th annual conference of the Church convened in Salt Lake City. It was continued three days. On the 5th, when the general authorities of the Church were submitted to the vote of the conference, Mathias F. Cowley and Abraham O. Woodruff were sustained as members of the council of Twelve Apostles, to fill vacancies caused by the death of Abraham H. Cannon and the rejection of Moses Thatcher. Joseph W. McMurrin was sustained as one of the First Seven Presidents of Seventies.

Thurs. 7.—Patriarch John Druce, an old and faithful member of the Church, died in Salt Lake City.

Wed. 13.—Pres. Wm. Paxman, of Nephi, Juab Co., died at American Fork, Utah Co., as the result of an accident.

Thurs. 21.—Apostles Francis M. Lyman and Matthias F. Cowley left Salt Lake City, on a special preaching mission to the Southern States.

Wed. 27.—Elder Ambrose Greenwell died at Ogden, Weber Co.

Thurs. 28.—The First Presidency, by letter, ordered the branches of the Church in Australia separated from those in New Zealand, and appointed Elder Andrew Smith, jun., to preside over the Australian mission, embracing Australia and Tasmania. Elder Ezra F. Richards was continued as president of the New Zealand mission.

Sun. 31.—Elder Lewis Jacob Bushman, of Escalante, Garfield Co., died of typhoid fever in Kentucky, where he labored as a missionary.

November.—Alfred L. Farrell succeeded Fred Pieper in the presidency of the Netherland (Holland) mission. This mission was founded in 1861, and Elder Paul A. Schettler was the first president. He was succeeded by Joseph M. Weiler, in 1864; Francis A. Brown, May 4, 1867; Marcus Holling, October, 1867; Jan F. Krumperman *pro tem*, in 1871; Sybren Van Dyk, Dec. 16, 1871; local Elders *pro tem*, 1874; Dirk Bockholt, Oct. 8, 1874; Peter J. Lammers, Oct. 9, 1875; Jan Hansink *pro tem*, June 23, 1877; Bernhard H. Schettler, Sept. 20, 1877; Peters, a local Elder, *pro tem*, June, 1878; Sybren Van Dyk (second term), May 19, 1880; Zwier Willem Koldewyn *pro tem*, June 17, 1882; Peter J. Lammers (second term), Nov. 7, 1882; Zwier W. Koldewyn *pro tem*, Dec., 1884; John W. F. Volker, Nov. 11, 1885; Francis A. Brown (second term), March, 1889; Timothy Metz, Jan. 3, 1891; Alfred L. Farrell, 1892; Edwin Bennion, May, 1893; Asa W. Judd, March, 1895; Geo. S. Spencer, March 20, 1896; and Fred. Pieper, Dec. 1, 1896.

Tues. 2.—The municipal election in Salt Lake City resulted in the election of a mixed ticket, of which John Clark, the mayor, was a non-partisan. He and most of the members elect of the council (mainly Democrats) were "Mormons."

Sat. 20.—Elder Truman Leonard died at Farmington, Davis Co.

Sun. 28.—Senator Frank J. Cannon lectured in the Tabernacle, Salt Lake City, on The Manners and Customs of the Japanese and Chinese.

December. *Wed. 1.*—James W. Huish, a Pioneer of Payson, Utah Co., died at that place.

Sat. 11.—Elder James Wadsworth died at Draper, Salt Lake Co.

Mon. 13.—At a meeting held at Georgetown, Bear Lake Co., Idaho, the Seventies residing at Georgetown, Bennington, Nounan and Soda Springs were organized by Seymour B. Young as the 114th quorum of Seventy; Herbert Horsley, sen., president.

Wed. 22.—Sister Lillis B. Barney, relict of Edson Barney, died at Provo, Utah Co. She had been a member of the Church since May 18, 1831.

Thurs. 30.—Elder Wm. Wright died at Ogden.

—Apostle Anthon H. Lund and Elder Ferdinand F. Hintze left Salt Lake City on a special mission to Turkey, Syria and Palestine.

1898.

President Wilford Woodruff died, and the First Presidency of the Church was reorganized; Lorenzo Snow, President. Three new Stakes of Zion were organized.

January. *Sat. 1.*—The Swiss and German Mission was divided into two, namely: the Swiss Mission, with H. E. Bowman as president, and headquarters in Berne, Switzerland; and the German Mission, under the presidency of Peter Loutensock with headquarters at Hamburg.

Mon. 3.—John Clark assumed the mayorship of Salt Lake City.

—A contract was closed at Los Angeles, Cal., for the erection of a beet sugar factory at Ogden, Utah, to be completed in time to handle the beet crop of 1898.

Tues. 4.—Elder Geo. Alfred Alder died in the Second Ward, Salt Lake City.

Wed. 5.—Ex-Gov. Arthur L. Thomas was appointed postmaster of Salt Lake City, and Geo. A. Smith receiver of the land office.

Sat. 8.—Elder Joseph Crook died at Payson, Utah Co.

—A convention of the presidency and conference presidents of the British mission was commenced at Birmingham, England. It was continued four days. Several matters of interest in connection with missionary labors were considered, and measures were adopted to bring about a greater uniformity of method in conducting the spiritual and financial affairs of the mission.

Sun. 9.—Wm. Smith, an old and faithful Elder in the Church, died at Providence, Cache Co.

—A branch of the Church was organized at Omaha, Neb.; L. S. Mecham, president.

—Congressman William H. King, of Utah, arrived in Tampa, Fla., from his trip of investigation in Cuba. He found the condition of the reconcentradoes most terrible, many of them naked and emaciated and dying in the streets.

—Madam Mountford, on her way from California to her home in Jerusalem, Palestine, addressed the congregation in the Tabernacle, Salt Lake City.

Mon. 10.—Elder John Edwards, one of Utah's early settlers, died at Sugar House Ward, Salt Lake Co.

Fri. 14.—At an Elders' council meeting, held at Anaconda, Mont., Pres. F. S. Bramwell presiding, the Montana mission, recently established, was divided into four conferences, named, respectively, Anaconda, Butte, Missoula and Sheridan.

Sat. 15.—Col. Miguel Ahumada, governor of Chihuahua, and other prominent officials, visited Colonia Juarez, Mexico.

Sun. 16.—Dr. J. H. Reiner, a prominent Roman Catholic minister, addressed the congregation in the Tabernacle, Salt Lake City. He was followed by Elder Chas. W. Penrose and Pres. Wilford Woodruff.

Wed. 19.—Elder Geo. A. Wadsworth died at Panaca, Nev.

Fri. 21.—General Nathan Kimball died at Ogden, Weber Co.

Mon. 24.—A grand celebration, in honor of the discovery of gold in California, fifty years before, was held in San Francisco, Cal. Among the specially invited guests, in attendance, were Elders Jas. S. Brown, of Salt Lake City, Henry W. Bigler, of St. George, Azariah Smith, of Manti, and Wm. Johnston, who, as members of the Mormon Battalion, were all present when Mr. Marshall first discovered the precious metal at Sutter's Mill, in 1848.

Tues. 25.—Ann Dilworth Bringhurst, a Utah pioneer woman, died at Springville, Utah Co.

Wed. 26.—A remarkably cold wave prevailed throughout Utah. At St. George, the coldest weather ever known there was experienced.

Thurs. 27.—The 115th quorum of Seventy was organized at North Jordan, Salt Lake Co., Utah, by Seymour B. Young; Hyrum Bennion, Geo. M. Spencer, Wm. O. Newbold, Henry Harker and Louis Bringhurst, presidents.

Fri. 28.—Jarvis Johnson, a member of the Mormon Battalion, died at Beaver Dams, Box Elder Co., Utah.

Sat. 29.—Andrew Kimball succeeded Christopher Layton as president of the St. Joseph Stake of Zion, Ariz.

Sun. 30.—Elder Goudy Hogan died at Richmond, Cache Co.

February.—Wm. R. Kingsford, one of Ogden's early settlers, died at Ogden, Weber Co.

Thurs. 3.—Zacharias W. Derrick, a president of the second quorum of Seventy, died in the Twelfth Ward, Salt Lake City.

Sat. 5.—On this and the following day the first general conference of the Eastern States mission (since the reopening of the mission) was held in Brooklyn, N. Y. Apostles Francis M. Lyman and Matthias F. Cowley were present. Elder Alonzo P. Kesler, president of the Eastern States mission, presided.

—The First Presidency published in the *Deseret Evening News* a letter vindicating the course of Col. Isaac Trumbo.

Sun. 6.—At the conference of the Eastern States mission, Apostle Francis M. Lyman and Congressman Wm. H. King addressed the congregation.

Mon. 7.—Caleb Robinson Barratt, formerly postmaster of Salt Lake City, died here.

—Elder Robert R. Anderson was appointed State bank examiner for Utah.

Sat. 12.—The Salt Lake *Tribune* published a statement, showing the bonded indebtedness of the State of Utah to be $900,000; that of Salt Lake County, $470,000; Salt Lake City, $2,548,000; Board of Education, Salt Lake City, $825,000; total, $4,743,000, over 70 per cent. of which was owing by Salt Lake City and its Board of Education. When the Liberal Party took possession of the city in 1890 the municipality had about $500,000 on hand, mostly in cash, besides other available means.

Tues. 15.—The news of the destruction of the battleship *Maine* in Havana harbor, Cuba, this day, caused great excitement in Salt Lake City and the State. The vessel was entirely destroyed and about 260 of her officers and crew were killed. The explosion shook the whole city of Havana.

Fri. 18.—The Public Library in the Joint City and County Building, Salt Lake City, was formally opened and dedicated.

Mon. 21.—Patriarch John L. Smith, an aged Church veteran, and a cousin of the Prophet Joseph Smith, died at St. George, Washington Co.

Wed. 23.—Agnes Macdonald, wife of Alexander F. Macdonald, was murdered by Mexicans at Colonia Garcia, Chihuahua, Mexico.

Sun. 27.—A new Latter-day Saint meeting house was dedicated in the Golansville branch, Caroline Co., Va.

Mon. 28.—James T. Little, president of the Deseret Savings Bank, died in Salt Lake City.

—The U. S. Supreme Court handed

down a decision, affirming the constitutionality of Utah's eight-hour law.

March.—The name of the Indian Territory mission was changed by the First Presidency to the Southwestern States mission, and was to include the States of Kansas, Arkansas and Texas.

Wed. 2.—Elder John Borrowman, a member of the Mormon Battalion, died at Nephi, Juab Co.

Fri. 4.—David Jenkins, the first surveyor of Ogden and a Weber County pioneer, died at Ogden, Weber Co.

Sun. 6.—The Arcadia branch, Fremont Co., Idaho, was organized as the Ora Ward; M. Joseph Kerr, Bishop.

—Elder Charles Hayes, an early convert to "Mormonism" from the "United Brethren," in Herefordshire, England, died at Bountiful, Davis Co.

Mon. 7.—Zaccheus Cheney, a member of the Mormon Battalion and one of the pioneers of California, died at Centerville, Davis Co.

Tues. 8.—Several Elders, including Hirani Whaanga, the Maori chief (70 years old), who had been a resident of Utah since 1894, left Salt Lake City, on missions to New Zealand; Elder Ezra T. Stevenson in charge of the company.

—Elder Joseph Hyrum Jenson, of Union, Salt Lake Co., Utah, died at Gothenburg, Sweden, where he labored as a missionary.

Thurs. 17.—Bishop Elias Morris died in Salt Lake City, from the effects of an accident, sustained by him the previous Monday (March 14th).

Wed. 23.—Elder George Lake, one of the first Latter-day Saint settlers in Mexico, and a Church veteran, died at Colonia Dublan, Chihuahua, Mexico.

Sun. 27.—Henry W. Brizzee, a member of the Mormon Battalion, died at Mesa, Ariz. Elder Walter Henry Hulsh died at Payson, Utah Co.

April. Sun. 3.—The Fifteenth Ward, Salt Lake City, was divided, and all that part of it lying west of Sixth West Street was organized as the Twenty-fourth Ward; Edward T. Ashton, Bishop.

Wed. 6.—The sixty-eight annual conference of the Church was commenced in Salt Lake City, continuing four days. When the general authorities were voted for, on the 10th, Andrew Jenson was sustained as an assistant Church Historian.

Thurs. 7.—Zion's Maori association was reorganized in consequence of the death of Wm. Paxman, the former president. Benjamin Goddard was chosen president; Wm. Gardner vice-president, and Heber S. Cutler secretary of the new organization.

—Samuel Allen Wilcox, sen., an aged Church veteran, died at Cedar Fork, Utah Co.

—Elders Brigham F. Duffin and Thos. H. Chambers arrived at Kingston, Caldwell Co., Mo., to open a mission in Caldwell and Daviess Counties. The next day (April 8.) they held their first meeting at Kingston in the Josephite meeting house. This is believed to be the first public meeting held in that part of the State by any Elders in the Church since the Saints were expelled from Missouri in 1838.

Sat. 9.—The foundation of the sugar

factory, near Ogden, Weber Co., was completed.

Sun. 10.—At the annual conference meeting of the Deseret Sunday School Union, held in the Tabernacle, Salt Lake City, Elder Geo. Goddard, assistant general Sunday School superintendent, was tendered an ovation, in appreciation of his long and faithful services in the Sunday School cause.

—Elder Thomas Alfred Jeffery died at Loa, Wayne Co.

Sun. 17.—Elders Brigham F. Duffin and Thos. H. Chambers held a meeting in a school house, near Lock Springs, Daviess Co., Mo.

—The new Utah Stake tabernacle at Provo, Utah Co., was dedicated, Pres. Geo. Q. Cannon offering the dedicatory prayer.

Wed. 20.—The 24th Infantry (colored troops, who had been stationed at Fort Douglas) left Salt Lake City for Cuba, to participate in the war with Spain.

Thurs. 21.—Sisters Lucy Jane Brimhall and Inez Knight, the two first Latter-day Saint lady missionaries sent from Zion to Great Britain, arrived in Liverpool, England.

—Fri. 22.—Elder Thomas Wm. Brewerton died at Willard City, Box Elder Co.

Sat. 23.—The Sixteenth U. S. Infantry passed through Salt Lake City en route for Cuba, and was accorded a rousing reception.

Sun. 24.—Sermons on the war were delivered in the Tabernacle and in all the churches in Salt Lake City.

Tues. 26.—In response to the call of the Federal government, Gov. Heber M. Wells issued a proclamation, calling for volunteers to serve in the army of the United States. Five hundred men were called for from Utah.

Wed. 27.—Elder Wm. Robinson died at Fayette, Sanpete Co.

Thurs. 28.—The First Presidency of the Church, in a letter addressed to Gov. Heber M. Wells, encouraged the young men of the Church to respond to the call for volunteers for the army.

May.—Elder LeRoy C. Snow was arrested and imprisoned at Munich, Bavaria, for preaching the gospel. After spending some time in prison, he was banished from the country.

Sun. 1.—Governor Heber M. Wells telegraphed the War Department that Utah's quota of volunteers was filled, and that the men would be at Fort Douglas, ready to be mustered into service, on May 5th.

Mon. 2.—The Utah volunteers pitched camp at Fort Douglas.

Wed. 4.—Governor Wells appointed Richard W. Young, grandson of President Brigham Young, and Frank A. Grant captains of Companies A and B, respectively, Utah (volunteer) Light Artillery.

Sat. 7.—The news of the destruction of the Spanish fleet at Manila, Philippine Islands, by the American fleet under Commodore George Dewey, May 1st, having reached Salt Lake City, an enthusiastic celebration in honor of the event was held.

Sun. 8.—Governor Wells named Joseph

E. Caine for captain of the troop of cavalry included in Utah's quota of volunteers. Other officers were also appointed.

Mon. 9.—The two batteries (A and B) of Utah's volunteer artillery were mustered into service at Fort Douglas.

—The first baptisms by divine authority in this dispensation at Jerusalem, Palestine, took place in Mary's Well, where Elder Ferdinand F. Hintze baptized Geo. Vezerian and Geo. Nadgarian, two Armenians from Asia Minor. They were both confirmed the same day, the first·named by Apostle Anthon H. Lund and the latter by Elder Hintze.

Wed. 11.—Mary E. Fenton Young, wife of Apostle Brigham Young, died in Salt Lake City.

Sun. 15.—A troop of volunteer cavalry, subsequently known as Troop I, of the Second United States Cavalry (Torrey's Rough Riders),was organized in Salt Lake City, and left for Cheyenne, Wyo.

Mon. 16.—George Gwilliam Bywater, a prominent and talented Elder in the Church, died suddenly from apoplexy in Salt Lake City.

Tues. 17.—John Q. Cannon was elected captain of Rough Riders, with J. Wash Young and Andrew J. Burt first and second lieutenants respectively.

Wed. 18.—Elder Theodore Nyström arrived in Paris, France, as a Latter·day Saint missionary, having been called by Pres. Bowman, of the Swiss mission, to introduce the gospel in the French capital.

Fri. 20.—Batteries A and B, Utah volunteers, under Captains Richard W. Young and Frank A. Grant, left Salt Lake City for San Francisco, Cal., on their way to the Philippine Islands.

Sat. 21.—Charles Shumway, one of the Utah Pioneers of 1847, died at Shumway, near Snowflake, Ariz.

Tues. 24.—Joseph Egbert, a Pioneer of 1847, died at Ogden, and Wm. Bond died at Henefer, Summit Co.

—The Utah volunteer cavalry left Salt Lake City for San Francisco.

Mon. 30.—Ole Christian Jensen, of Mayfield, Sanpete Co., Utah, died at Randers, Denmark, where he labored as a missionary.

Tues. 31.—Willard Young, son of Pres. Brigham Young, was nominated, by Pres. Wm. McKinley, colonel of the Second regiment of U. S. volunteer engineers.

June. *Wed. 1.*—Hon. Wm. H. King delivered an eloquent address in the Tabernacle, Salt Lake City, on Cuba and the War.

Fri. 3.—Elder Hyrum Maughan, of Weston, Oneida Co., Idaho, died at Anderson, Madison Co., Ind., where he labored as a misssionary.

Sun. 5.—At a conference held on this and the following day at Almy, Wyo., Woodruff Stake of Zion was organized by Apostles John Henry Smith, Heber J. Grant, Matthias F. Cowley and Abraham O. Woodruff; John M. Baxter, president; Byron Sessions and Charles Kingston counselors. The new Stake included the Wards of Evanston, Almy, Rock Springs and Bridger, which had formerly belonged to the Summit Stake, and Randolph, Woodruff, Argyle and Diamondville, which

formerly constituted a part of Bear Lake Stake.

—Geo. P. Canova, a local Elder and president of the Sanderson branch of the Church, was assassinated at Juncture, Florida; Brother T. Hill, his companion, escaped.

Mon. 6.—The International Mining Congress was opened in the Arsenal Hall, Salt Lake City, continuing several days.

Tues. 14.—James Ballard, alias "Schooner Jim," died in Salt Lake City.

Wed. 15.—The second Manila expedition, consisting of four large transports, carrying nearly 3,500 soldiers, sailed from San Francisco, Cal., for the Philippine Islands. Battery A, of the Utah Artillery (120 men), together with two companies of the regular U. S. army, sailed on the steamer *Colon*; one·half of Battery B, of Utah volunteers, sailed on the steamer *China*, and the other half on the steamer *Zealandia*.

Sun. 19.—Park City, Summit Co., was partly destroyed by fire. Nearly all the principal stores and many private residences were reduced to ashes. The loss was estimated at about $1,000,000. Among the buildings consumed was a Latter·day Saint meeting house, which has just been completed at a cost of about $5,000. This was considered the most disastrous fire that ever happened in Utah.

Mon. 20.—The enlistment of volunteer engineers for U. S. service was commenced in Utah.

Tues. 21.—Horace Burr Owens, a Church veteran, died at Woodruff, Navajo Co., Ariz.

—Bishop Samuel Carter died at Porterville, Morgan Co.

—Elder James Wareham, a Church veteran and an early settler of Manti, Sanpete Co., died there.

Thurs.23.—A terrific storm did considerable damage to property at Bunkerville and Mesquit, Lincoln Co., Nev.

Sat. 25.—Elder Andrew Hendriksen died at Levan, Juab Co.

July.—The fulness of the gospel was first introduced in North Dakota by Elders David J. Hammon, Charles A. Haacke, Elias Nielsen and Lorenzo Day.

—Elder James E. Talmage delivered his illustrated lectures on Utah and its People in some of the principal cities of Great Britain.

Fri. 1.—Elder Ben E. Rich succeeded Elder Elias S. Kimball in the presidency of the Southern States mission. Elder Kimball had been appointed chaplain in the Second regiment of U. S. volunteer engineers.

Sun. 3.—News reached Utah that the Spanish Cape de Verde fleet, under command of Admiral Cervera, had been entirely destroyed by the American squadron, off the harbor of Santiago de Cuba. News of the battle of San Juan hill, before Santiago de Cuba, brought grief to the soldiers' families at Camp Douglas, as many of the Twenty·fourth infantry were killed in the battle.

Mon. 4.—Elder Thos. Cox, sen., died at Castle Dale, Emery Co.

Wed. 6.—The Old Folks of Salt Lake County, in being treated to their regular annual excursion under the direction of the Old Folks Committee, spent a pleasant day at the Lagoon, Farmington, Davis Co.

The first of these popular Old Folks excursions took place May 14, 1875, through the special kindness of John W. Young, who arranged a free ride to the Great Salt Lake for the old people of Salt Lake County. The original committee of arrangements consisted of Bishop Edward Hunter, George Goddard and Charles R. Savage. In 1879, Wm. Eddington, Wm. Naylor, John Kirkman and Wm. L. Binder were added to the committee, which was further augmented in 1883 by the addition of Andrew Jenson, in 1885 by Nelson A. Empey, and in 1896 by Brigham S. Young. After the death of Bishop Edward Hunter, in 1883, Presiding Bishop Wm. B. Preston has acted as chairman of the committee.

—The first International Mining Congress was opened in Salt Lake City.

Thurs. 7.—Gov. Wells announced the appointment of Frank W. Jennings as captain of Battery C, Utah volunteer artillery.

☐*Sun. 10.*—The Utah U. S. volunteer engineers left Salt Lake City for San Francisco.

[*Mon. 11.*—Hadley D. Johnson, a prominent Utah politician and editor, died in Salt Lake City.

☐ *Wed. 13.*—Sister Melissa Lott Smith Willis, a widow of the Prophet Joseph Smith, died at Lehi, Utah Co.

☐—The troop of Utah cavalry volunteers, which had been stationed at San Francisco, were relieved from duty with the Philippine expedition forces and ordered to perform home duty.

Thurs. 14.—Battery C (Utah volunteers) were sworn into U. S. service.

Sun. 17.—The second Philippine expedition, which included the Utah batteries, arrived at Cavite, near Manila, Philippine Islands.

Tues. 19.— Four young ladies, Lucy, Emma and Susie Keele, of Payson, Utah Co., and Miss Bauer, of Homansville, Juab Co., were accidentally drowned in the Utah lake, near Benjamin, Utah Co.

Thurs. 21.—Elder August L. Hedberg, a late resident of Utah, died at Los Angeles, Cal., where he acted as a counselor in the presidency of the branch.

—In a council of the First Presidency and Apostles, held in Salt Lake City, it was decided to change the name of Bannock Stake, Idaho, to Fremont.

Sat. 23.—Elder Brigham F. Duffin and Leonidus S. Mecham, arrived at Watertown, South Dakota, having been called by Louis A. Kelsch, pres. of the Northern States mission, to open a missionary field in that State. On the night of July 27th, they held their first open air meeting, near the postoffice at Watertown.

Sun. 24.—Memorial services were held in the different settlements of the Saints and collections taken up for a monument, to be raised in honor of the American sailors who lost their lives, Feb. 15, 1898, by the explosion of the *Maine*, in the harbor of Havana, Cuba.

—Pioneer Square, Salt Lake City, was dedicated and set apart as a public park (Pioneer Park). Pres. Geo. Q. Cannon offered the dedicatory prayer; and addresses were made by Mayor John Clark, Pres. Wilford Woodruff, Congressman Wm. H. King and others.

—At a quarterly conference of the Oneida Stake, held in Gentile Valley, Idaho, the settlements of the Saints in that valley and neighborhood were detached from Oneida Stake and organized as the Bannock Stake of Zion, by Apostles Heber J. Grant, Marriner W. Merrill and Matthias F. Cowley; Lewis S. Pond, president; Denmark Jenson and Clarence Eldredge, counselors.

Mon. 25.—Wm. Tunbridge, a prominent citizen of Levan, Juab Co., was shot and killed by Andrew Hendriksen, who was supposed to be insane.

Wed. 27.—Elder Alexander Hood Hill died at Mill Creek, Salt Lake Co.

Sun. 31.—Elisha Hildebrand Davis, a prominent Elder and Church veteran, died at Lehi, Utah Co.

—The Utah artillery took a very active and brave part in the defence of the American position before Manila, Philippine Islands.

—Battery C, of the Utah volunteer artillery (about one hundred men), under command of Capt. Frank W. Jennings, left Salt Lake City, for California. This battery was Utah's contribution under the second government call for troops.

August. *Sat. 6.*—Lyman Curtis, a member of Zion's Camp and a Utah Pioneer of 1847, died at Salem, Utah Co.

Sun. 7.—A number of settlements, formerly belonging to the Oneida and Malad Stakes, were organized by Apostles Heber J. Grant and Matthias F. Cowley, as the Pocatello Stake of Zion. Wm. C. Parkinson (Bishop of Preston, Idaho) was appointed president of the new Stake.

—Patriarch Christopher Layton, late president of the St. Joseph Stake, Ariz., and a prominent Elder in the Church, died at Kaysville, Davis Co.

—Elder Theodore Nystrøm, who had been appointed to re-open a mission in France, held his first and only meeting in Paris. Soon afterwards he left the city, without making any converts.

Fri. 12.—Elder Christian Jensen, father of Historian Andrew Jenson, died at Richfield, Sevier Co.

—The American flag was raised over Hawaii, at Honolulu.

—The peace protocol, terminating the war between the United States and Spain, was signed at Washington, D. C.

Sat. 13.—Presidents Wilford Woodruff and Geo. Q. Cannon left Salt Lake City on a visit to California.

—Elder Cadwallader Owens died at Iona, Bingham Co., Idaho.

—The Utah cavalry, which had been stationed at San Francisco, Cal., left that city for Yosemite and Sequoia Parks.

—In the capture of Manila, the capital of the Philippine Islands, by the American troops, the Utah volunteers rendered effectual service.

Mon. 15.—Trooper Albert W. Luff Naisbitt died at San Francisco, Cal.

Tues. 16.—A contract between the Oregon Short Line Railroad and the promoters of a railroad from Milford to the State line was signed in Salt Lake City. The signers were officials of the Oregon Short Line, on one side, and A.W. McCune, David Eccles, Charles W. Nibley and others, on the other side.

Fri. 19.—Patriarch David M. Stewart, a prominent Elder in the Church, and, in his younger days, a successful missionary, died at Ogden, Weber Co.

Fri. 26.—In an altercation between natives and United States soldiers at Cavite, near Manila, Philippine Islands, Geo. H. Hudson, of Baker City, Ore., was killed and Wm. Q. Anderson, of Logan, Utah, severely wounded. Both men belonged to Battery B, Utah volunteers.

Sat. 27.—President McKinley promoted Captains Richard W. Young and Frank A. Grant to be brevet-majors of volunteers.

Tues. 30.—The sessions of the Utah Presbytery of the Presbyterian Church closed at Manti, Sanpete Co. Before adjourning, resolutions were passed, replete with "garbled statements and absolute falsehoods concerning the 'Mormon' Church."

September. *Fri. 2.*—Pres. Wilford Woodruff died at the house of Col. Isaac Trumbo, San Francisco, Cal., after an illness of only a few hours.

Mon. 4.—The train bearing the remains of Pres. Wilford Woodruff arrived in Salt Lake City, over the Rio Grande Western Ry.

Thurs. 8.—The funeral services over the remains of Pres. Wilford Woodruff were held in Salt Lake City. All of the Twelve Apostles were present and addresses were made by Joseph F. Smith, Lorenzo Snow, George Q. Cannon and Franklin D. Richards.

Fri. 9.—The Republican State convention nominated Alma Eldredge for Congress and Charles S. Zane for Supreme Judge in Utah.

Sat. 10.—Stephen H. Goddard, one of the Utah Pioneers of 1847, died at San Bernardino, Cal.

Tues. 13.—At a special meeting of the Apostles held in Salt Lake City, at which Lorenzo Snow, Franklin D. Richards, Geo. Q. Cannon, Joseph F. Smith, Brigham Young, Francis M. Lyman, John H. Smith, Geo. Teasdale, Heber J. Grant, John W. Taylor, Marriner W. Merrill, Anthon H. Lund, Matthias F. Cowley and Abraham O. Woodruff were present, Lorenzo Snow was nominated and sustained as President of the Church. President Snow then selected, with the approval of the council, Geo. Q. Cannon as his first and Joseph F. Smith as his second Counselor. Pres. Snow was also sustained as Trustee-in-Trust for the Church, and Franklin D. Richards as President of the Twelve Apostles. All the proceedings were unanimous.

Wed. 14.—The State Democratic convention held in Salt Lake City nominated Brigham H. Roberts for Congress and Robert N. Baskin for Supreme Judge.

Sat. 17.—Elder Andreas Peterson, of Logan, Cache Co., Utah, succeeded Elder George Christensen as president of the Scandinavian Mission.

This mission was founded in 1850 by Apostle Erastus Snow, who was its first president. He was succeeded by the following Elders: John E. Forsgren, March 4, 1852; Willard Snow, Dec. 20, 1852; John Van Cott, Aug., 1853; Hector C. Haight, Jan. 1, 1856; Carl Widerborg, Feb. 1, 1858; John Van Cott (second term), Jan. 1, 1860; Jesse N. Smith, May, 1862; Samuel L. Sprague *pro tem*, April 13, 1864; Carl Widerborg (second term), Aug. 1, 1864; Jesse N. Smith (second term), Sept., 1868; William W. Cluff, July 15 1870; Canute Peterson, June 23, 1871; Christen G. Larsen, June 27, 1873; Nils C. Flygare, June 25, 1875; Ola N. Liljonquist, June 22, 1876; August W. Carlson *pro tem*, Nov., 1877; Nils C. Flygare (second term), Jan., 1878; Niels Wilhelmsen, Aug. 30, 1879; Andrew Jenson *pro tem*, Aug. 1 1881; Christian D. Fjeldsted, Sept. 3, 1881; Anthon H. Lund, April 4, 1884; Nils C. Flygare (third term) Oct. 19, 1885; Christian D. Fjeldsted, (second term) October, 1888; Edward H. Anderson, September 29, 1890; Joseph Christiansen, September, 1892; Carl A. Carlquist, May, 1893; Peter Sundwall, April, 1894; Christian N. Lund, June 11, 1896; and George Christensen, May 19, 1898.

Sun. 25.—The hotel and buildings at Beck's Hot Springs, near Salt Lake City, were destroyed by fire.

—The first Latter-day Saint Sunday School in Providence, Rhode Island, was organized by Elder John M. Whitaker; Peter C. Cornia, supt.

Mon. 26.—Elder Joseph T. Ellis died at Spring City, Sanpete Co.

Fri. 30.—The Twenty-fourth Infantry returned to Fort Douglas, from their expedition to Cuba, having done gallant service at the battle of Santiago.

October.—The sugar factory, near Ogden, commenced running.

Sun. 2. — Elder Wallace Damron died at Thatcher, Graham Co., Ariz.

Tues. 4.—Elder Albert Spencer died at Taylorsville, Salt Lake Co.

Wed. 5.—Elder James C. Olsen died at Salina, Sevier Co.

Thurs. 6.—The 69th semi-annual conference of the Church convened in Salt Lake City, continuing four days.

Sun. 9.—At the afternoon session of the general conference of the Church, Lorenzo Snow was sustained as Prophet, Seer, and Revelator, and President of the Church, and Geo. Q. Cannon as his first and Joseph F. Smith as his second Counselor. Rudger Clawson was chosen to fill the vacancy which had occurred in the Council of the Twelve Apostles by the reorganization of the First Presidency.

Mon. 10.—Rudger Clawson was ordained an Apostle, in Salt Lake City, by Pres. Lorenzo Snow.

Fri. 14.—The new Stake Tabernacle, which was nearing completion, at Richfield, Sevier Co., was destroyed by an incendiary fire.; loss, about $30,000.

Sat. 15.—Joseph Cordon Kingsbury, an old and faithful Church veteran, died in Salt Lake City.

Mon. 17.—The Richfield *Advocate* office was burned to the ground.

—The Presbyterian synod of Utah, at its closing session in Ogden, passed resolutions declaring that polygamy was still practiced by the "Mormons" in Utah.

—William Andrew Parker (a native of Utah), of Troop H, Torrey's Rough Riders, died near Jacksonville, Florida.

Tues. 18.—Presidents Lorenzo Snow and Joseph F. Smith, Apostle Franklin D. Richards, Gov. Heber M. Wells and others left Salt Lake City, for Omaha, Neb., to visit the Trans-Mississippi Exposition.

—Elder Martin Lenzi, a Church veteran, died in Salt Lake City.

—The American flag was raised over San Juan, and the island of Porto Rico was formally ceded to the United States.

Thurs. 20.—Elder David M. Muir died of pneumonia, at Lochgelly, Scotland, where he labored as a missionary.

—This was Utah day at the Trans-Mississippi Exposition at Omaha, Neb. A speech of welcome was made by Wattles, president of the Exposition, and responses were made by Gov. Heber M. Wells and Presidents Lorenzo Snow, Geo. Q. Cannon and Joseph F. Smith.

Sun. 23.—Troop I (Utah's Rough Riders) were mustered out of service at Camp Cuba Libre, Panama Park, Jacksonville, Florida.

Wed. 26.—Shadrach Ford Driggs, an early settler of Pleasant Grove, Utah Co., died there.

Sun. 30.—Elders B. F. Duffin and Chas. A. Haacke were taken out of the Methodist Episcopal church at Henry, Codding-ton Co., S. D. (where they were sleeping during the night),by a mob of five men, led by Quin McMullen. The Elders were followed out of town, threatened with tar and feathers and otherwise abused. The night was a bitterly cold one, and the Elders nearly perished through exposure.

November. *Tues. 8.*—At the general election in Utah, Brigham H. Roberts (Democrat) was elected as Utah's representative to Congress, and Robert N. Baskin was elected to the Utah Supreme bench.

—Elder Richard Ballantyne, a Church veteran, organizer of the first Sabbath School and a faithful Sunday School worker, died at Ogden, Weber Co.

Sun. 20.—Elder Richard Henry Thorne died at Springville, Utah Co.

—The southeast part of Chesterfield Ward, Bannock Co., Idaho, was organized as Hatch Ward by Pres. Lewis S. Pond; Peter J. Williams, Bishop.

Mon. 28.—An important Latter-day Saint Sunday School convention was commenced in Salt Lake City. It was continued three days.

December. ・ *Thurs. 1.*—Sister Sarah M. Kimball, an old and respected member of the Church, and a faithful Relief Society worker, died in Salt Lake City.

Sat. 3.—The first number of the *Latter-day Saints' Southern Star*, a weekly periodical published in the interest of the Church in the Southern States, was issued at Chattanooga, Tenn.

Tues. 6.—Twenty-four "ministers of the gospel," mostly residents of Salt Lake City,met and adopted an address, prepared

by a committee of the so-called ministerial union, in which they "most earnestly" called upon the people of the United States to join them in a strong protest to Congress against the seating of Brigham H. Roberts, member elect from Utah.

Thurs. 8.—A terrific wind storm swept over the northern part of Utah, doing considerable damage in Weber and Davis counties. In Salt Lake City the greatest velocity the wind reached was 48 miles an hour.

—Presidents Rulon S. Wells and Joseph W. McMurrin sailed from Liverpool, England, homeward bound, leaving Elder Platte D. Lyman, with Henry W. Naisbitt as second counselor, in charge of the European mission.

Sat. 10.—The last number (No. 26, Vol. 57) of the *Deseret Weekly* was issued.

—Col. Willard Young, of Utah, commanding the battalion of engineers at Marinoa, Cuba, unfurled the stars and stripes over the city hall at that place.

Thurs. 15. — Pres. Lorenzo Snow, as Trustee-in-Trust for the Church, announced in the *Deseret Evening News* that the Church would issue bonds to the amount of $500,000, running for a period of eleven years, and bearing interest at the rate of 6 per cent per annum. This method of raising means was resorted to in order to lighten the burthen of the Church indebtedness.

Sat. 17.—Pres. Lorenzo Snow, as Trustee-in-Trust, announced in the *Deseret Evening News*, that that paper, with all its proper-ties and appurtenances, had reverted to the Church, and that on and after Jan. 1, 1889, a complete change in the management would be inaugurated, with Charles W. Penrose as editor and Horace G. Whitney as business manager.

Sun. 18.—Certificate of election (dated Dec. 10, 1898) was given to Brigham H. Roberts.

Wed. 21.—Battery C, Utah volunteers, were mustered out of U. S. service.

Thurs. 22.—Lydia Snow Pierce, wife of Elder Eli H. Pierce and daughter of Pres. Lorenzo Snow, died in Salt Lake City.

Fri. 23.—The ninety-third anniversary of the birth of the Prophet Joseph Smith was celebrated in the Sixteenth Ward meeting house, Salt Lake City.

—Troop A, Utah cavalry, was mustered out of service at the Presidio, San Francisco, Cal.

Sat. 24.—The new B. Y. College building at Logan, Cache Co., was dedicated.

Sun. 25.—Elder John Ritter, a member of the Mormon Battalion, died at Eden, Weber Co.

Wed. 28.—Mary Adaline Snow, wife of Pres. Lorenzo Snow, died at Brigham City.

Thurs. 29.—Pres. Lorenzo Snow, in a telegraphic communication to the New York *World*, declared officially that polygamous or plural marriages ceased in Utah with the issuance of the manifesto by the late Pres. Wilford Woodruff in 1890, and that the election of Brigham H. Roberts to Congress was an entirely secular affair, with which the Church had nothing to do.

Fri. 30.—Elder Albert Peterson, of Murray, Salt Lake Co., died at Upsala, Sweden, where he labored as a missionary.

, INDEX.

16